THE ROYAL NAVY'S AIR SERVICE
IN THE GREAT WAR

THE
ROYAL NAVY'S
AIR SERVICE
IN THE GREAT WAR

DAVID HOBBS

Seaforth
PUBLISHING

Frontispiece: Commander R Bell-Davies VC RN landing a Sopwith 1½ Strutter on HMS *Argus* during her flying trials in the Firth of Forth, October 1918.

First published in Great Britain in 2017 by
Seaforth Publishing,
Pen & Sword Books Ltd,
47 Church Street,
Barnsley S70 2AS

www.seaforthpublishing.com

British Library Cataloguing in Publication Data
A catalogue record for this book is available from the British Library

ISBN 978 1 84832 348 3 (Hardback)
ISBN 978 1 84832 349 0 (Kindle)
ISBN 978 1 84832 350 6 (ePub)

Typeset and designed by M.A.T.S., Leigh-on-Sea, Essex
Printed and bound in Great Britain by CPI Group (UK) Ltd, Croydon, CR0 4YY

Contents

Appendices:

Foreword

In 2013 David Stevens, then the Director of Strategic and Historical Studies at the Sea Power Centre – Australia, asked me to give a talk on the Royal Naval Air Service as part of the King-Hall Naval Historic Conference in Canberra which had as its theme The War at Sea 1914–18. It was a subject that had always interested me and, fortunately, I had gathered a considerable amount of research material on it over the years but had never found the time to put it to good use. Planning for the talk had the effect of focusing my attention and the more I read about the RNAS the more fascinated I became and so I determined to write a book about it as soon as I could fit it into my schedule for Seaforth Publishing. This is the result.

Fortunately my friend David Brown, when he was Head of the Naval Historical Branch, had shown me an unpublished 1919 Admiralty manuscript which contained material on naval aviation which had originally been intended for inclusion in the history of Great War naval operations. He allowed me to photocopy it and this proved to be doubly fortunate since the manuscript contained valuable material gathered from primary sources in the Admiralty archive and the original appears to have been lost when the Branch moved from Great Scotland Yard in London to its present location in Portsmouth Naval Base. As is so often the case, the more I found out about the subject the more I found that there was to know and a book that covered every aspect of the RNAS and its operational, technical and political history would be a very large one indeed. I decided, therefore, to compromise and produce a book that will, I hope, give the reader a good idea of what the RNAS did and how and why it did it, together with information about the ships, aircraft and weapons that it used. I have, as always, tried to make the story readable with plenty of human interest, a task made easier by the fact that from its very beginning the RNAS seems to have attracted some remarkable characters into its ranks. The last of them died years ago but many left their impressions in autobiographical books which I have used to give colour to events. Some of them left accounts that were so detailed that I almost feel I know the individuals concerned and certainly have a good impression on their thoughts and opinions.

Studying the RNAS in detail made me aware of just how great an influence it continued to have on naval aviation after its demise, not just in the RN but especially in the United States and the rest of the world. Captain G W Steele USN was tasked in 1918 with studying the part played by aviation in the Grand Fleet's operations and his subsequent report to the General Board stated that so many ideas had been gained from the British that any discussion of the subject must consider their methods. The RNAS achieved what it did against considerable antagonism, not just from the enemy, as one might expect, but also from British politicians, despite the fact that some of those who criticised it openly admitted to having no very clear idea of what the service actually did. Fortunately, more rational counsel prevailed in the United States and the USN managed to retain control of its air arm and carry forward the work from the point where the RNAS was forced to leave it.

It is a sobering thought that had Edwin Dunning not shown that deck landing was possible when he did and had *Argus* been completed as a *Campania*-like seaplane carrier, naval aviation might well have atrophied quickly after 1919 as the bomber lobby within the RAF claimed to have rendered all types of warship vulnerable and obsolete. Thankfully, the RNAS did enough in its short existence to show how fundamentally important aviation had become to every aspect of naval operations by 1918 and its legacy formed the basis of fact on which the Admiralty placed its long struggle through the years of joint control to regain full control of the aircraft that operated from ships that culminated with the Inskip Award of 1937. This book can therefore be considered as a prequel to my earlier books on the British Pacific Fleet and the post-1945 British Carrier Strike Fleet. As the editing work on this book begins I have already started work on my next book for Seaforth Publishing which is to describe the complicated progress of the Royal Navy's air component in the interwar years between 1919 and 1940.

David Hobbs MBE
Commander Royal Navy (Retired)
Crail
February 2017

Acknowledgements

As always, my efforts have been encouraged and helped by my wife Jandy and both my son Andrew and his wife Lucyelle. Over a number of years several people have helped me to broaden my knowledge of the RNAS and, both directly and indirectly, to write this book. Prominent among these is my friend the late David Brown, for many years Head of the Naval Historical Branch, who not only encouraged me to write but made me aware of several unpublished manuscripts in the Branch. Fortunately, before his untimely death in 2001 he insisted that I photocopy a number of them for use as future research material. His successors Christopher Page and Stephen Prince, together with Jenny Wraight, the Admiralty librarian, have also became friends and always proved supportive and helpful when I discussed projects and sought specific documents. Andrew Choong and Jeremy Michel of the Historic Photograph and Ship Plans Department of the National Maritime Museum at the Brass Foundry in Woolwich have also helped with research material and a visit to look at their archive material is always a pleasure to be keenly anticipated. I have learnt a great deal about the Grand Fleet and its operation from the events in Orkney which have been organised by Moya McDonald over the past decade and I am grateful both to her and John Leith for their enthusiasm and kindness. There is always so much more to learn about the Royal Navy and its air arm in the islands that surround Scapa Flow.

David Stevens is a friend of long standing and I have thoroughly enjoyed speaking at the King-Hall Historical Conferences he organised in Canberra, while he was the Director of Strategic and Historical Studies at the Sea Power Centre – Australia, from 2001 onwards. I have valued his incisive thoughts on both the RN and RAN together with his comments about the imperial nature of the RNAS. John Perryman, who took over from him as Director, has also been a valued source of information and illustrations, as was Terrence Hetherington of the Australian Fleet Air Arm Museum at RANAS Nowra. Commander David Goble RAN was kind enough to allow me to use photographs from the Goble Family collection and both Guy Warner and Phillip Jarrett helpfully allowed me to use photographs from their extensive photographic archives. This publication contains

Public Sector information licensed under the Open Government Licence v 1.0 in the UK. Apart from these sources, I was able to illustrate the book from my own photographic archive, a collection that I have built up over decades of research into the history of naval aviation. I am grateful to Anthony Cowland who painted the cover illustration and to Peter Wilkinson who drew the maps that appear throughout the book.

Over the years I have had the benefit of conversations with several friends who expressed views on naval operations in the Great War that have stimulated my own thought processes and encouraged me to look at events from different angles. These include Norman Friedman in the USA, the leading naval analyst of our generation, together with Joe Straczek and James Goldrick in Australia. Any errors and omissions in the text, however, are of course entirely my own. I am, as always, particularly grateful to my friend Rob Gardiner for his support. This is my sixth book for Seaforth Publishing and our successful partnership has now lasted for a decade. I have already started work on our next book.

David Hobbs

Abbreviations

AA	anti-aircraft
AAC	Anti-Aircraft Corps [of the RNAS]
ACA	Admiral Commanding Aircraft [Grand Fleet]
ACNS	Assistant Chief of the Naval Staff
ADNC	Assistant Director of Naval Construction
AFC	Air Force Cross
AFO	Admiralty Fleet Order
ANZAC	Australian & New Zealand Army Corps
ASI	Airspeed Indicator
ASW	Anti-Submarine Warfare
Avgas	Aviation gasoline
BEF	British Expeditionary Force
BCS	Battlecruiser Squadron
BS	Battle Squadron
CB	Companion of the Order of the Bath
CBE	Commander of the Order of the British Empire
CFS	Central Flying School
CID	Committee of Imperial Defence
C-in-C	Commander-in-Chief
CMB	Coastal Motor Boat
CO	Commanding Officer
CPO	Chief Petty Officer
CS	Cruiser Squadron
CW	Continuous Wave
DAD	Director of the Air Department
DAS	Director of Air Services
DCNS	Deputy Chief of the Naval Staff
DNC	Director of Naval Construction
DNI	Director of Naval Intelligence
DNO	Directorate of Naval Ordnance
DSC	Distinguished Service Cross
DSO	Distinguished Service Order

EI & ESS	East Indies and Egypt Seaplane Squadron
ERA	Engine-Room Artificer
FO	Flag Officer
ft	foot/feet
GCB	Knight of the Grand Cross of the Order of the Bath
GF	Grand Fleet
GOP	General Operations Plot
HA	high angle [gun]
HF	high frequency
HMAS	His Majesty's Australian Ship
HMCS	His Majesty's Canadian Ship
HMS	His Majesty's Ship
HSF	High Sea Fleet [of the German Navy]
hp	horsepower
IJN	Imperial Japanese Navy
in	inch
KBE	Knight Commander of the Order of the British Empire
KCB	Knight Commander of the Order of the Bath
knot	A speed of 1nm (*qv*) per hour
KT	Knight of the Thistle
lb	pound (imperial weight)
LA	low angle [gun]
LCS	Light Cruiser Squadron
MBE	Member of the Order of the British Empire
MF	Medium Frequency
mph	miles per hour
MVO	Member of the Royal Victorian Order
NHB	Naval Historical Branch
nm	nautical mile
NPL	National Physical Laboratory
OBE	Officer of the Order of the British Empire
PO	Petty Officer
pdr	pounder
QF	quick-firing [gun]
RAA	Rear Admiral Aircraft (Grand Fleet)
RAF	Royal Aircraft Factory/Royal Air Force
RAN	Royal Australian Navy
RCN	Royal Canadian Navy
RFC	Royal Flying Corps

RMA	Royal Marine Artillery
RMLI	Royal Marine Light Infantry
RN	Royal Navy
RNAS	Royal Naval Air Service/Royal Naval Air Station
RND	Royal Naval Division
RNH	Royal Naval Hospital
RNR	Royal Naval Reserve
RNVR	Royal Naval Volunteer Reserve
ROP	Report of Proceedings
SAP	semi-armour piercing
SHP	shaft horsepower
SIGINT	Signals Intelligence
SL	Sea Lord, written as 1SL, 2SL, 3SL, 4SL, 5SL as appropriate
SNO	Senior Naval Officer
SS	Submarine Scout [airship]/Steam-Ship
UK	United Kingdom
USA	United States of America
USN	United States Navy
USS	United States Ship
VC	Victoria Cross
WOD	Wind Over the Deck
W/T	Wireless Telegraphy

1 Origins

By the first decade of the twentieth century the Royal Navy had undergone a half-century of change like no other before it. Iron and then steel-hulled warships, steam propulsion, torpedoes, small warships in the torpedo-boat and torpedo-boat destroyer categories, submarines and the all-big-gun battleship *Dreadnought* had followed each other in quick succession and some visionary officers were involved in several important projects chronologically. Among them was Captain R H S Bacon RN, the Director of Naval Ordnance (DNO), head of the Admiralty Directorate responsible for the procurement of new weapons and systems. He had joined the RN in 1877 and specialised as a torpedo officer. By 1896 he was a commander and led a torpedo boat flotilla with conspicuous success in the annual manoeuvres that year. In 1899 he served under Admiral Fisher in the Mediterranean and was drawn into the 'Fish-Pond', a circle of young officers who enthusiastically supported Fisher's reforms. He was promoted to captain in 1900 and appointed as the first RN Inspecting Captain of Submarines, tasked with their introduction and development, making them into an effective weapons system and raising the fleet's awareness of their capabilities together with its own potential for countering enemy submarines. When Fisher became First Sea Lord in 1904 he chose Bacon to be his Naval Assistant and included him on the Committee of Designs that led to the rapid construction of *Dreadnought*, a warship so revolutionary that all subsequent battleships in every navy became known, generically, as Dreadnoughts. In 1906 he became the ship's first captain and carried out an extensive trials programme before she became operational. In 1907 he succeeded Jellicoe as DNO, one of the key appointments for a captain who was destined for flag rank.[1] Fisher and Bacon undoubtedly had a close working relationship and after studying the *Dreadnought* covers Norman Friedman described Bacon as both 'Fisher's protégé and advisor'.[2] When the Fisher/Beresford Scandal appeared to limit his future career prospects, Bacon resigned from the Navy in 1909 to become the managing director of the new Coventry Ordnance Works. He returned to the RN in 1914 and was appointed Admiral Commanding the Dover Patrol.

Over a century later, we look back at early aviation development with the full knowledge of what was to follow but in 1908 heavier-than-air flight was seen as the preserve of a few amiable eccentrics,[3] a source of wonder and delight to those stood on the ground watching but offering little obvious naval or military potential. It is widely known that the first manned flight in a powered heavier-than-air aircraft was achieved by the Wright Brothers at Kitty Hawk, North Carolina, on 17 December 1903 in an aeroplane of their own design named the 'Flyer'. Less well known is the fact that the engine was arguably a greater technological achievement than the airframe.[4] It weighed only 180lbs and produced 12hp and 90lbs of thrust. There was a strong wind of about 25mph at 10.30 on that day but the brothers were keen to prove that their machine worked before they packed up for the winter. Orville and Wilbur carried out two flights each with Orville flying the first.[5] Orville flew under control at about the height of a man's head for a distance of just over 150ft. The fourth and last flight that day lasted for 59 seconds and covered a distance of 852ft. The first controlled, powered flight in the United Kingdom was carried out by A V Roe at the Brooklands motor track on 8 June 1908 in an aeroplane he had designed but which was powered by a French Antoinette engine which delivered 24hp. He flew for about 180ft just over 2ft off the ground. The contemporary view of aeroplane development is placed into sharp focus by the reaction to a letter written by Roe to the *Times*; it was published but the newspaper added a footnote written by its engineering editor which warned readers that 'all attempts at artificial flight as described by Mr Roe were not only dangerous to human life but foredoomed to failure from an engineering standpoint'.[6] Roe's activities led to his being given notice to quit by the management of Brooklands and he moved to Lea Marshes on the outskirts of London where he worked on a tractor triplane powered by a 9hp JAP motorcycle engine which he eventually flew in June 1909. It was both the first all-British aircraft to fly and the lowest powered. The authorities attempted to prevent him from flying over a public place and at one stage police proceedings against him were threatened but when Louis Blériot flew the English Channel on 25 July 1909 a wave of aviation enthusiasm swept the country and the charges were quietly dropped. Roe moved to Wembley Park and then returned to Brooklands which was, by then, being run by a more progressive management.

After the Wright Brothers' early achievements, the French became the driving force in the design of both aircraft and engines and aviators enthusiastically compared their designs and sought new records. The first international gathering was held at Reims in August 1909 with thirty-eight aircraft present but of these only twenty-three succeeded in getting airborne.[7] Among these, Henri Farman succeeded in staying airborne for over three hours and travelled over 100km carrying two passengers. By 1905 the Wright Brothers had developed a practical aeroplane that had flown for 24 miles and remained airborne for 38 minutes before it ran out of fuel. However, their attempts to sell their patents to the US Government proved less successful. In 1907 Charles Flint, the Wright's European Agent, authorised Lady Jane Taylor to act on his behalf and offer Lord Tweedmouth, the First Lord of the Admiralty, a package including fifty aircraft capable of carrying two aircrew over a radius of action of 30 nautical miles from their airfield.[8] These aircraft were priced at £2000 each but Flint subsequently offered improved aircraft at £4000 each, hoping that the higher unit price would encourage the Admiralty to take the offer more seriously. The idea did not work and in his reply on 7 March 1907 Lord Tweedmouth informed Lady Jane that 'with regard to your suggestions as to the employment of aeroplanes . . . after the careful consideration of my Board, the Admiralty . . . are of opinion that they would not be of any practical use to the Naval Service'. At that moment in time, his view was undoubtedly correct and the Admiralty was right to stand back and monitor the further development of machines that had little but a few flights of short duration over land to commend them. Ballooning had a significantly longer history but only offered a controlled drifting where the wind took the pilot. A manned hydrogen-filled balloon flew across the English Channel in 1785, giving the press the opportunity to make alarmist statements about the potential for airborne attacks on Great Britain, but military balloons subsequently only found limited use in the localised observation of enemy activity. By 1907 Count Zeppelin in Germany had designed and flown the first practical powered rigid dirigible airship and such machines had obvious merit, both as a reconnaissance platform and for carrying out offensive action, even though they were clearly vulnerable to adverse weather and high winds. By 1914 the Zeppelin Company had produced nineteen airships but eleven of these had been destroyed in accidents. The German Navy ordered its first Zeppelin in 1908.

The catalyst that brought aviation into sharper focus within the RN was a letter from Bacon to the First Sea Lord dated 21 July 1908[9] which proposed that a new post of Naval Air Assistant should be created within the Naval Staff and also that the War Office should be asked to allow its Superintendent of Ballooning at Farnborough to be consulted[10] on air matters by the Naval Staff. The third proposal that was the most far-reaching, however, that the RN should fund the construction of a large rigid airship to evaluate the use of aircraft with the fleet. At the time Vickers had an exclusive contract with the Admiralty for the design and construction of submarines; Bacon had worked closely with this firm, both as Inspecting Captain of Submarines and as DNO, and he recommended that development could be hastened if Vickers were awarded a contract for the airship as well as bearing some of the development risk. A provisional cost of £35,000 for the airship was quoted from the outset, the same as an 'A' class submarine, making it likely that Bacon had already secretly discussed the project with his contacts at Vickers. It is also likely that Bacon's letter represented the opening move in a plan prepared carefully beforehand since only two days later, on 23 July 1908, Admiral Fisher wrote formally to the Prime Minister, Herbert Asquith, proposing the construction of a developmental rigid airship and Treasury approval, in principle, for the project was given on 4 August 1908. On 14 August 1908 Vickers was requested to forward a tender to the Admiralty as soon as it had calculated sufficient design data and it naturally hoped to gain another exclusive contract with the Admiralty similar to the one already in place for submarines. By July 1908 it was clear that airships had become a practical proposition for the RN. On 5 October 1907 the Army airship *Nulli Secundus*, piloted by Colonel Capper with Lieutenant Waterlow and Mr Cody as passengers, had flown from the Royal Aircraft Factory at Farnborough to London. High winds forced it to land at Crystal Palace on its return journey but by then it had established a world record with a flight of three hours and twenty-five minutes. This record was broken by the Zeppelin *LZ 4* on 4 August 1908 which remained airborne for twelve hours before being destroyed by a storm,[11] a disaster which nearly led to bankruptcy for the Zeppelin Company. However, press coverage led to an outpouring of public support from across Germany which secured enough finance to cover the cost of a new airship, *LZ 5*, which was intended to fly non-stop from Lake Constance to Berlin.

A Committee of Imperial Defence (CID) had been established by the then Prime Minister, Arthur Balfour, in 1902 after the Second Boer War. It had a political focus and reported directly to the Prime Minister about the material requirements of the RN, Army and Civil Service and their ability to meet Government policies and issues of strategy. The Admiralty and the War Department were both Offices of State in their own right with control over their own budgets which could be argued by their political heads in cabinet but since the CID reported directly to the Prime Minister, its views carried considerable weight and it would be difficult to proceed with projects that it opposed. Typically, it set up working subcommittees to investigate and evaluate specific topics and recommend ways forward and this was exactly what happened when aviation was considered. The German enthusiasm for rigid airships was a cause for concern at a time when the German Navy was undergoing considerable expansion, the only possible outcome of which was to challenge the power of the RN. On 23 October 1908, therefore, Asquith instructed the CID to set up a subcommittee under Lord Esher[12] to investigate what was known at the time as 'aerial navigation' and make recommendations. The subcommittee, within which Bacon was the RN representative, was tasked to study the recent successes achieved by aerial experiments in France, Germany and the USA and make recommendations. Its terms of reference[13] noted that Great Britain had, hitherto, been justified in spending less on aviation than the other powers but required comment on:

a) The dangers to which we would be exposed on sea or on land by any development in aerial navigation reasonably probable in the near future.
b) The naval or military advantages that we might expect to derive from the use of airships or aeroplanes.
c) The amount that should be allocated to expenditure on aerial experiments and the Department which should receive it.

The report, dated 28 January 1909,[14] contained an accurate summary of the state of aircraft development and the potential for various types to be used for naval and military operations. Under the heading 'Aeroplanes', the subcommittee noted that 'although great progress has been made towards the successful employment of aeroplanes within the last year, they can scarcely yet be considered to have emerged from the experimental stage'. Further, it noted that 'it has yet to be shown whether aeroplanes are sufficiently reliable to be used under unfavourable weather conditions'. On the other hand, the subcommittee attached great importance to the construction of dirigible[15] airships as naval scouts and noted that 'it is not unlikely also that they might also be of advantage for the purpose of attacking foreign warships, dockyards and canal gates'.[16] The subcommittee agreed, unanimously, that a rigid airship should be procured for naval experiments and unsurprisingly, given Bacon's membership, recommended the sum of £35,000 for its construction. This sum was compared favourably with £80,000 for the construction of a contemporary destroyer and £400,000 for a light cruiser. For fleet reconnaissance work it was pointed out that a lookout on the bridge of a warship could expect to see an enemy vessel at about 18nm in clear conditions whereas an observer in the car of an airship at 1500ft would expect to see the enemy at 80nm in the same conditions. Airships could remain airborne for protracted patrols and carry a large-enough crew to operate in watches; they could support a blockading force by using a wireless transmitter to tell the fleet commander what the enemy was doing in harbour and potentially even warn of torpedo boat and submarine attacks being generated against a blockading squadron. The full CID met on 25 February 1909 and accepted the subcommittee's recommendation without further comment. Two days earlier, on 23 February 1909, the Treasury had approved the inclusion of £35,000 in the 1909/1910 Naval Estimates for the construction of a rigid airship by Vickers.

The subcommittee took a less positive view about aeroplanes, however. Despite being relatively cheap and simple to construct in large numbers for less than £1000 each, they felt that it was 'not yet clear that under existing conditions the aeroplane would be of much value in naval operations. Until complete reliability and independence of meteorological conditions has been demonstrated it would be dangerous to utilize them for scouting purposes in the open sea.' The sub-committee's support for the construction of a naval dirigible airship was, thus, contrasted with its view that there was no necessity for the Government to experiment with aeroplanes provided that advantage was taken of private enterprise in this form of aviation. One can also detect the input from Bacon in the statement that 'it is understood that the Admiralty would not construct the dirigible themselves but would invite some firm of standing to contract for the work, including all necessary experiments. The design would be worked out jointly by a representative of the Admiralty and of the contractor. The advantage of this arrangement is that all the resources of a great firm would be available for the experiments necessary at every stage of the work, while the Admiralty representative should be in a position to consult all the scientific and expert opinion in the country. This mode of procedure was adopted in the case of submarines, and the subcommittee strongly recommend that it should be employed as combining the maximum efficiency with the minimum of cost . . .'

His Majesty's Rigid Airship Number 1

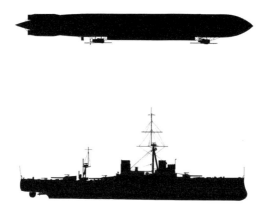

R 1 drawn to the same scale as HMS *Dreadnought* to
give an idea of her size. (Author's collection)

After receiving Treasury and CID approval, the Admiralty offered Vickers £30,000 for its share of the work to construct an airship. Vickers replied in April that it could construct the rigid structure, excluding the gasbags and outer covering, for £28,000, and offered to erect a suitable hangar within which the airship could be constructed, at no cost to the Crown. It also asked for a ten-year monopoly on airship construction for the RN under contractual terms similar to those already in place for submarines.[17] On 7 May 1909 the Admiralty accepted these terms and signed a contract with Vickers for the construction of *HM Rigid Airship Number 1*, officially designated *R 1*. It was stipulated that Vickers was responsible for the strength of the framework and the Admiralty was responsible for the gasbags, the outer covering and the size and positioning of fins and control surfaces.[18] The Admiralty was thus both the customer and a member of the design and construction consortium in rather the same way that the Ministry of Defence (MOD), acted as both customer and a member of the Aircraft Carrier Alliance that contracted to build HMS *Queen Elizabeth* a century later. This distribution of responsibility was to assume critical importance in 1911 after *R 1* was completed. The Admiralty specification required *R 1*:

a) To fulfil the duties of an aerial scout.
b) To maintain 40 knots for, if possible, 24 hours.
c) To moor by the nose to a post on water (or possibly on land also). Floating on water she was to be able to swing head into wind and, hopefully, remain out in all weathers and be independent of her shed except for docking, as in the case of surface ships.
d) To carry wireless telegraphy equipment.
e) To have facilities that allowed the crew to live on board without suffering hardship.
f) To ascend to a height of 1500ft or more.
g) To be used for experimental purposes and to be constructed as cheaply as possible.

Since structural weight increased as the square of mass but disposable lift increased as the cube of gas volume, it was obviously an advantage to design a large airship. Vickers had originally assumed an aluminium framework but found that wood was significantly stronger. Bacon insisted, however, that since wood was incapable of improvement and 'there was a certainty of better metal alloys being produced',[19] the experimental nature of the airship would be largely negated if it was constructed of wood and subsequent craft made of a metal alloy. At the same time plans were drawn up to refit the cruiser *Hermione* as an airship support vessel with a plant for producing hydrogen, accommodation for airship crews and a mooring mast to secure the ship while she was being replenished. A contemporary view of the *R 1* project can be gained from the 1910 edition of *Brassey's Naval Annual* in which Commander C N Robinson RN stated that in the construction of airships 'we have an invention at once reliable, capable of a large range of actions and of very good speed even in practically all types of weather'.

The Admiralty representatives on the design team were Bacon, who was promoted to Rear Admiral in 1909, Captain Murray Sueter, the newly-appointed Inspecting Captain of Airships,[20] and several other officers. Sueter had worked with both Bacon and Vickers on submarine development before this appointment. The group from Vickers was led by Sir James McKechnie, managing director of the firm's shipyard at Barrow-in-Furness, with Charles Robertson, the chief submarine engineer, B Comyn the manager of the Cavendish Dock, J Watson the works manager and S W Hunt the chief draughtsman. When the team started work in 1908 no Zeppelins had been ordered for the German Navy and *R 1* was the largest military aircraft project the world had yet seen. They drew heavily on their experience of submarine design along with what little information could be obtained about Zeppelins. *R 1* was 512ft long, only 14ft shorter than the battleship *Dreadnought*, and had a parallel-sided hull with a bow curve of twice the curvature of the hull and a stern of nine times the curvature. For ease of construction the hull was twelve-sided rather than cylindrical and material was ordered in May 1909. Work on its shed started at the same time in Cavendish Dock with one edge resting on the dockside and the other built onto piles driven into the dock bottom. These caused considerably more trouble than anticipated, however, and the shed's projected completion date had to be put back from August 1909 to June 1910; work on *R 1* could not start until it was ready. Once the shed was complete, a removable wooden 'deck' was built over the water, above which a cradle was erected on which the airship framework was assembled.

While they waited for the shed's completion, the design team considered the choice of structural material; Vickers preferred wood but Bacon continued to insist on metal. A trial section 37.5ft long was built in the shipyard workshops with one end made of hollow wooden spars, a central section made of wood and aluminium in equal proportions and the other end of aluminium. Wood proved by far the strongest and bracing wires made of extruded aluminium proved to be useless. However, in November 1909 Vickers' metallurgists learnt of an alloy made in Germany known as duralumin. It seemed to be perfect for this application and the firm bought the right to manufacture and use the alloy throughout the British Empire. Comprising 94 per cent aluminium and 4 per cent copper with the remainder made up with manganese, silicon and iron, it was found to have nearly the strength of iron with the weight of aluminium. In practical terms the new alloy made *R 1*'s structure twice as strong as wood but a ton lighter. The Admiralty approved the use of duralumin in 1910 and *R 1* became the first aircraft in the world to be constructed from it. The first duralumin Zeppelin did not appear until December 1914 and fixed-wing aircraft continued to be made of wood until after the First World War.

The Admiralty's selection of fabric for the seventeen gasbags proved difficult and considerable unforeseen research had to be carried out before suitable materials were identified. Although balloon flight was commonplace in 1909, nothing on this scale had been attempted before and previous gasbags had been fabricated with what was known as gold beater's skin, made from the intestines of oxen which were dried, glued to a cloth backing and varnished, but it was known to become brittle and had a short life. The Admiralty decided, therefore, to replace it with the Continental Rubber Company's number 21 fabric, which was made up with alternating layers of Egyptian cotton and rubber glued together, for fifteen of the seventeen gasbags which were then made by Short Brothers under an Admiralty contract. The other two bags were made with different fabrics for comparison; number 1 was made by the North British Rubber Company with its own material and number 17 was made by the Dunlop Rubber Company; both were donated to the Admiralty in the hope of gaining more airship work. Every bag had a valve at the top for venting gas; the design limit was for *R 1* to climb at up to 3000ft per minute venting gas at up to 4800ft³ per minute to prevent the bags being ripped open by gas expansion as it did so. The outer cover also presented considerable challenges and had to cover an unprecedented 66,000ft² whilst remaining as light as possible. It must not absorb rain water and heat absorption from sunlight had to be minimised. Silk was thought, at first, to be a good option but it degraded badly when rubberised and chemists found that a substance with the trade name 'Ioco' offered the best way of water-proofing silk without making it difficult to handle. It could not be sewn, however, and sheets of 'Ioco'ed silk had to be glued together, a process that took both time and skill to perfect. The material intended for the bottom of the airship was dyed yellow to make it more visible and, at first, the material intended for the top was painted with aluminium dust to reflect the sun's rays and prevent heat absorption. Unfortunately, this was found to weaken the silk as much as 'Ioco' strengthened it and a further process had to be devised in which the fabric was dusted with aluminium powder after being 'Ioco'ed. The area of outer skin aft of the engines was made of a fireproof material and the control surfaces were covered with two layers of Hart-processed silk stuck together, a process pioneered by Short brothers.

The control cars had to be waterproof and bear some of the airship's weight while they rested on the water, acting in effect as small boats. They were made of copper-sawn Honduras mahogany and were built by Saunders Roe of Cowes in the Isle of Wight. The forward car contained the control bridge and both cars contained a single Wolseley engine[21] with its radiator and control systems. *R 1* was originally to have carried 2000lbs of petrol and 2000lbs of water ballast but the design was re-cast in 1910 to use petrol for both purposes to give an extended endurance of up to 30 hours at full power. The control surfaces were originally based on those in submarines but in 1911 a Short Brothers' box rudder design was adopted after it was commented on favourably by the National Physical Laboratory. Once all the design problems had been overcome, construction from mid-1910 was straightforward. Frames were placed on a round wooden table and longitudinals added, onto which a second frame was fitted. The completed section was then carried to the shed and placed in the cradle where bracing wires were fitted and all frames joined together. Eventually the completed framework was suspended from the ceiling of the shed by 3in belly bands under alternate frames. It was raised into place by 300 sailors and marines using block-and-tackle technology that would have been familiar to Sir Francis Drake's seamen and in January 1911 the cradle was removed so that the keel could be installed together with the cars, fins and rudders.

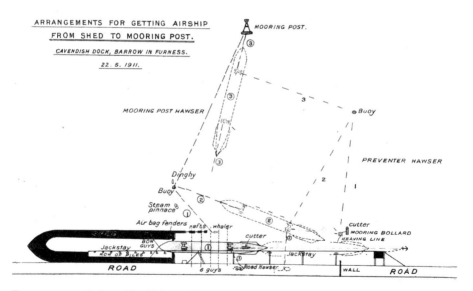

The arrangements for getting *R 1* out of her construction shed for the first time on 22 May 1911 were worked out in considerable detail and included this diagram which was used to brief all those who took part. It was subsequently included in the airship's handbook published by the Admiralty. (Author's collection).

On 13 February 1911, *R 1* began shed trials during which the engines were run and the control surfaces moved. Captain Sueter took charge but considered the weather unsuitable for basin trials in Cavendish Dock so the gasbags were not inflated at this stage and defects found during these trials were rectified. The seventeen gasbags were eventually inflated in May 1911. Nothing on this scale had ever been attempted in the UK before and 1050 cylinders of hydrogen had to be imported from Dutch firms, giving rise to questions in Parliament about the advisability of relying on foreign sources of supply. The remainder came from the Knowles Oxygen Company in Wolverhampton, Castnor Kellner Company in Runcorn and a few cylinders from the Royal Aircraft Factory at Farnborough. Special goods trains had to be run to carry the cylinders to Barrow and *R 1* took over 24 hours to fill with more than 700,000ft^3 of hydrogen. Some of the gas was unfortunately lost when Able Seaman Palmer slipped, fell through number 6 bag and ripped it, so there was a slight delay while the necessary repairs were carried out. Numerous gas cylinders were initially connected through a labyrinth of pipes and hoses and new lessons were learned. The high pressure led to sparking on the pipework and lower pressure had to be accepted, slowing the rate of inflation.

The two Wolseley engines were eight-cylinder water-cooled units with vertical piston movement, each designed to develop 180hp. In the original design the forward engine drove two propellers through bevel gearing at 500rpm; both were a fraction under 12ft in diameter and expected to give 606lbs of thrust. The after engine was to drive a single 15ft propeller at engine speed giving 1212lbs of thrust but when this was found to be impractical a number of modifications were made to propeller size and gearbox arrangements. The propellers were all made of laminated wood. *R 1* was the first aircraft to have a telephone exchange, a light-weight facility that connected the forward gondola, cabin, observation position on top of the rigid structure and the after gondola through a main terminal box in the cabin. The wireless telegraphy installation was designed specifically for *R 1* by HMS *Vernon*, the RN torpedo school, which was responsible for all naval electrical matters at the time. It was powered by an alternator driven by the after engine and was expected to have a range of about 600nm. The transmitter used spark gap technology but was 'quenched' to reduce the risk of igniting any trace of hydrogen that might be present in the cabin and it was surrounded by light metal screens intended to eliminate the risk completely. The receiver used a five-strand copper wire aerial 1000ft long which was to be lowered beneath *R 1* in flight and there was a facility that allowed it to be jettisoned immediately in the event of a sudden nearby electrical disturbance in the atmosphere.

Two crews were selected for the airship's trials and they underwent a compre-hensive training programme. They assembled on 25 January 1910 and in February they began their instruction Short Brothers' works at Battersea, focusing on the techniques of working with rubberised fabrics including the manufacture of joints, fabric pipes, model gasbags and sticking channel fabrics onto gasbags. In March they moved to Vickers' yard at Barrow-in-Furness where they were instructed on petrol engine technology using a 15hp Wolseley motor car engine. In April they were taught signals, aeronautics and meteorology and in May they returned to work with fabric. When the support ship *Hermione* arrived at Barrow in late September 1910 they joined her and carried out all the fabrication work on the gasbags and the outer cover, fulfilling the Admiralty's side of the construction agreement. In late 1910 when their training was deemed to be complete the Admiralty introduced flying pay by Order-in-Council and the personnel appointed to fly *R 1* as part of their naval duties were the first British service personnel to receive it. It was approved on 28 November 1910[22] and the formal request by their Lordships had stated:

R 1 being moved towards her mooring mast in Cavendish Dock on 22 May 1911. The shed in which she was built can be seen in the background to the left of the picture. (Philip Jarrett Collection).

Whereas we are of opinion that the Officers and Men of Your Majesty's Navy who may be selected for service in naval aircraft should receive some pecuniary advantage in recognition of the exceptional nature of their duties. We beg leave humbly to recommend that Your Majesty may be graciously pleased by Your Order-in-Council to sanction the following scale of allowances for Officers and Men employed in naval aircraft, Viz:

Officers, each	6 shillings per day
Chief Petty Officers, each	2 shillings and sixpence per day
Petty Officers, each	ditto
Leading Seamen, each	ditto
Able Seamen, each	2 shillings per day

R 1's first inflation was completed on 22 May 1911, the wooden decking in its shed was removed and the gondolas were lowered onto the water so that she could begin basin trials. Boats were secured on either side of the gondolas and padding was fitted to the shed doors which, surprisingly in view of the fact that Vickers had built it specifically for the construction of *R 1* and subsequent airships which could well be larger, were only just big enough for the completed airship to pass through them. An elaborate plan for the extraction was prepared and the ship, which lay with her tail near the door, was walked aft by 300 sailors and marines pulling on ropes until the nose was clear of the door. Orders were passed by a Royal Marine bugler who accompanied Captain Sueter wherever he moved and a launch towed *R 1* to the centre of Cavendish Dock where a special fitting in her nose was attached to a mooring tower designed to withstand a pull-force of up to 8000lbs. The wind was measured at 17 knots when she was attached and a pull-force of only 530lbs was recorded. A crew of nine remained on board *R 1* all the time she was moored to the mast, carrying out a number of acceptance tests although engine runs were cut short by problems with their radiators. On 23 May she successfully rode out a gale with winds estimated at up to 45 knots with no apparent mooring problems. Searchlights were played on the airship during the three nights she was out of her shed to check that all was well and during this time she was found to be buoyant but too heavy to begin the programme of flying trials. The gasbags were found to leak at the rate of about 1 per cent per day and cylinders of replacement hydrogen had to be brought out the airship in one of *Hermione*'s cutters. Getting *R 1* back into her shed on 25 May proved to be more difficult than her extraction because of a slight wind across the door. The evolution took over an hour, one side of the ship rubbed against the shed door and two sailors holding guide ropes were pulled into the dock, fortunately without being harmed. *R 1* was widely described as looking

Captain Sueter with his Royal Marine signallers supervising *R 1*'s first extraction from its shed. The green flag has been raised rather hesitantly and all three men have their attention fixed on what is happening. (Author's collection)

beautiful with her silver-grey and yellow hull but she was already over-budget at £41,000.

Back in her shed *R 1* floated 3ft above the water without crew, tools, the W/T set, hawsers, petrol or ballast. Sueter refused to accept her and insisted on the airship being lightened to allow it undertake the planned flying trials. She was hoisted back to her suspension points in the shed roof, the outer skin was peeled off and the gasbags deflated and removed. The keel, cabin and any equipment not needed in flight including an anchor, cable and a collapsible sea-boat, were removed and the heavier gondola moved from aft to forward. The control car was lightened and moved aft to replace it. By July *R 1* still lacked sufficient lift and advice was sought from the Advisory Committee on Aeronautics which recommended the insertion of an extra bay amidships containing a further 40,000ft³ of gas. However, the Admiralty decided not to adopt this measure because it would have meant waiting for the shed to be enlarged and it hoped that the weight-reduction programme

R 1's second extraction from its shed on 24 September 1911. Note that there are now two propellers on the after car and the keel structure between the two cars has been removed. The Royal Marine on the extreme right has a green flag raised which gives an idea of the breeze blowing across the shed entrance. (Author's collection)

already in hand would allow a limited trials programme to start before the end of 1911. After three years' work it wanted results. A further inflation on 17 August 1911 revealed that *R 1* was still too heavy and a further 1195lbs of equipment was removed after a further deflation. The forward propeller was reduced to 10ft in diameter and holes were drilled in the engine control levers to lighten them; tool boxes were replaced by canvas bags and the crew designed, made and installed a canvas water-ballast trimming system.

On 22 September 1911 *R 1* was inflated for what proved to be the last time using 1762 cylinders of hydrogen in just over ten hours, demonstrating that many of the earlier problems had been overcome. But by then the gasbags were over a year old and the rate of leakage increased significantly. Under pressure from the Admiralty Solicitor, Sueter accepted *R 1* for the Navy 'pending the completion of satisfactory air trials'. Her crew manned her on 24 September for the second extraction from her shed with Sueter in command. With him was Lieutenant Usborne, the commanding officer designate, to superintend the working of the valves and two other lieutenants, one of whom operated the rudders. A petty officer worked the diving rudder, a contemporary submarine term for the planes used to keep the airship horizontal in flight, and a second petty officer stood ready to work the W/T or replace his colleague on the planes. An engine room artificer (ERA) worked the engine in the forward car. In the after car the First Lieutenant of *Hermione* was in general charge assisted by a lieutenant who looked out for signals and discharged ballast if it proved necessary. A Chief ERA ran the after engine and an engineering lieutenant supervised the operation of both engines and the airship's systems. On this occasion *R 1* was pulled backwards out of the shed by electric winches but things went wrong as her nose was pivoted towards the centre of the dock. Witnesses heard cracking sounds amidships and she broke in two with only the outer fabric holding the two sections together. Some witnesses thought she had rolled onto her side when caught by a crosswind and it is possible that steadying ropes put an uneven strain on the hull which caused it to fail. Whatever the initial cause, considerably more damage was done cramming the damaged airship back into her shed. Sueter recommended that the airship should be repaired, at the very least for use as a training ship. Her crew clearly did not regard her as a write-off and the damage may have looked much worse than it really was. The estimated construction cost now exceeded £70,000 and there was certainly an argument for getting the most out of the investment but her fate was to be decided by a Board of Enquiry. Much had changed at the Admiralty while *R 1* was under construction. The radical Admiral Fisher had retired in 1910, replaced by the conservative Admiral Wilson and in 1911 Winston Churchill became First Lord. He was known to favour the development of heavier-than-air aircraft over airships, leaving Sueter as the airship's only advocate.

This photograph was taken only minutes after *R 1* began to break up after emerging from her shed in September 1911. The frames have been numbered to show exactly where the break occurred and a copy of this image may well have been used by the Board of Enquiry. The break appears to be at frame 24. (Author's collection)

The Board of Enquiry was convened at Barrow in *Hermione* on 18 October 1911 under Rear Admiral Sturdee who had opposed the Fisher reforms. Its importance can be deduced from the fact that both the First Lord and the Secretary for War attended on the first day. Three Army airship pilots were called as expert witnesses, together with Sueter and members of *R 1*'s crew and handling parties. The Board decided that the project should be terminated and the remains of *R 1* scrapped but Churchill refused to allow the full findings to be made public. The Board did, however, state that the damage was caused by the breaking of a longeron 'under less pressure than the designers thought it would stand'. The Admiralty instructed Commander Schwann RN, Sueter's deputy, to inform *R 1*'s crew that 'no blame was attachable to their actions'. The Board minutes have unfortunately been lost and so we will probably never know for certain why *R 1* broke as it did but it is interesting to reflect that in 1911 the Admiralty had refused to endorse the exclusive airship construction agreement with Vickers and was also trying to extract itself from the exclusive submarine construction agreement. Relations between the Admiralty and the firm were, therefore, somewhat strained and the alleged failure of an element of *R 1*'s design for which Vickers had been entirely responsible was an eminently convenient reason to give for her loss.

Had she flown successfully, *R 1*'s projected trials programme, contained in the Airship Handbook produced by the Admiralty, gives insight into the role envisaged for naval aviation in its earliest years. After tests to determine the flight envelope she was to be used to evaluate the usefulness of aircraft in locating minefields and submarines. She would also have been used in experiments to tow small vessels and see how best she could be moored to both ships and buoys. In due course she was to be used to determine how best to watch ports and spot ships entering and leaving them and to run along potentially hostile coasts taking photographs. Further trials were to evaluate the defence of airships against hostile aircraft armed with guns, what amount of petrol could be sacrificed for a gun armament and whether guns and/or bombs could be carried to attack ships or targets on the ground such as lock gates and docks. Not least, she was to have evaluated the logistic support requirements for deployed airships and *Hermione*'s worth as a support ship. After *R 1*'s loss the Admiralty Airship Department was disbanded in 1912 but it was re-formed a year later when Zeppelins began to show their value and the need for airships in operational service was accepted as being urgent. *R 1* was the largest and most technically complex aircraft of its day and the project was certainly not the ill-considered and poorly-executed failure that some critics have labelled it. Much was learned from it and in this context it is unfortunate that it was known, unofficially as the 'Mayfly'.

Development of Heavier-than-Air Aircraft

Far from being averse to the procurement of aircraft for naval purposes, the Admiralty did foresee uses for them but was following the CID's advice. Public funds had been invested in the design and construction of *R 1* but the recommendation that development of heavier-than-air craft could safely be left in individual hands for the time being was also heeded. Despite this, the Admiralty maintained a benevolent interest in the work of several naval officers who designed or purchased aeroplanes. One of the first was Lieutenant John C Porte RN,[23] who commanded one of the first operational submarines in 1908 based at HMS *Dolphin*, Gosport. Together with a colleague, Lieutenant W B Pirie RN, he designed and built a biplane glider[24] and planned to fit a 35hp JAP engine to the machine to allow powered take-off once he had proved its ability to glide. With the help of sailors from his submarine and a few interested friends he had the aircraft hauled to the top of Portsdown Hill, north of Portsmouth on 17 August 1909 on a four-wheeled trolley. It had a skid undercarriage and was placed, unsecured, on top of the same trolley for the take-off run in which it was literally pushed down the steep hillside along a wooden track constructed and laid for the purpose of giving a smoother ride than the surrounding grass tussocks. The aircraft's control arrangements replicated those of a submarine with two coxswains, Porte and Pirie,

Lieutenants Porte and Pirie RN sitting in their glider on its crude launch trolley at the top of Portsdown Hill in 1909. The quality of the image is unfortunately not good but it does capture a sense of what was happening and shows the mixture of sailors and civilians holding onto the brakeless trolley waiting for the two pilots to give the order to push it down the sloping trackway. (Author's collection)

who sat side-by-side with one controlling heading while the other controlled attitude and altitude. The aircraft did reach flying speed as the cart hurtled down the hill but the coxswains failed to achieve controlled flight and it was wrecked as it hit the ground. Porte subsequently abandoned this design and moved on but he did subsequently seek Admiralty funding to help with his experiments. It was refused because the aircraft had not achieved powered flight but by twenty-first century standards of human resource allocation, the unstinted use of twenty or more sailors for a considerable period had been a significant investment.

By June 1910 Porte was experimenting with a Santos Dumont monoplane fitted with a 35hp Duthiel-Chalmers engine with which he set out to teach himself to fly.[25] He modified the airframe with small wheels that projected outboard of the main wheels on the end of what he called stunsail booms to prevent it turning over sideways and a bowsprit projecting forward under the propeller to prevent it pitching onto its nose. He made a series of increasingly fast runs across the Hampshire aeroplane grounds at Fort Grange, Gosport[26] but unfortunately ran into what he described as a deep undulation which caused him to be brought up standing. The left wing was badly damaged and, again, Porte moved on. He was not one of the officers selected for the first official RN fixed-wing flying course in 1911 but by July of that year he had been awarded the Aero Club de France's Pilot Certificate number 548. He took part in the round-Britain air race in a Blackburn Mercury later in July but, unfortunately, he was invalided out of the RN in late 1911 suffering from pulmonary tuberculosis but secured a position as technical director and designer of the British Deperdussin Company at Gosport. He entered

Schwann at the controls of the Avro seaplane beginning to taxi across Cavendish Dock. (Author's collection)

Photographs of Schwann's pioneering activities at Barrow-in-Furness are extremely rare and, unfortunately, this example was folded in a pocket book for many years causing some crease damage. It does, however, show the Avro floating in Cavendish Dock after an unsuccessful run with Schwann swimming to the left of the aircraft and a boat being pushed out to help him recover it safely. Note the letters A V R O painted on the underside of the lower wing. Sponsorship perhaps? (Author's collection)

and flew one of their machines in the first War Office aircraft trials at Larkhill on Salisbury Plain in August 1912 but the entry of S F Cody was eventually selected as the winner. When the company went into receivership he went to the USA to assist Glen Curtiss in designing the Curtiss H1 America flying boat. On the outbreak of war in 1914 he left the USA immediately to join the RNAS with the rank of Squadron Commander.[27]

Another innovator was Commander Oliver Schwann RN[28] who stood by *R 1* at Barrow-in-Furness as Sueter's deputy and executive officer of *Hermione*. He used his own funds and raised more from friends and their wives to buy a 35hp Avro biplane which he had mechanics from *R 1*'s crew fit with floats which he designed himself and, like Porte, he taught himself the rudiments of piloting skill.[29] His seaplane was hangared in the airship shed and he taxied it at ever-increasing speeds around Cavendish Dock whenever the weather was suitable. Unfortunately, inefficient float designs caused it to nose under on several occasions and on one of these he is reputed to have shouted 'Save the damned aeroplane, I can look after myself' to the boat crew that rowed towards him after one particularly

Another photograph unfortunately damaged by folding but it shows *R 1*'s shed clearly in the background as Schwann carried out a successful high-speed run in Cavendish Dock. (Author's collection)

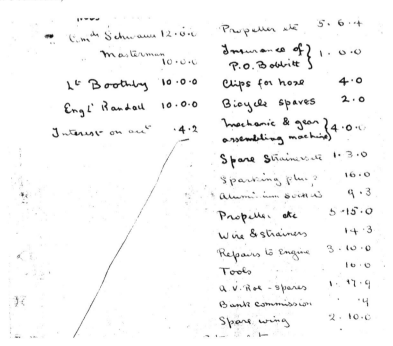

A page from Schwann's notebook from February 1912 showing the income and expenditure incurred by the Seaplane Club at Barrow-in-Furness. (Author's collection)

comprehensive ducking. The aircraft, and more importantly its engine, were salvaged and repaired for further tests and on 18 November 1911 Schwann took off during a high-speed run. Despite having no formal training and no pilot's certificate he was, thus, the first British aviator to take-off from water but his lack of experience let him down and the subsequent crash cannot be considered the first water landing even though both pilot and aircraft survived to fly again. Some idea of the cost of these early experiments can be gathered from the accounts of the 'Seaplane Club', hand-written in Schwann's notebook.[30] Income includes £10 each from Captain Sueter, Commander Masterman, Lieutenant Boothby and Engineer Lieutenant Randall. Mrs Sueter contributed £5. Outgoings included £1 12s 5d for aluminium, 16s for spark plugs, £3 10s for engine repairs and £2 10s for a spare wing. A pound was paid to insure Petty Officer Bobbitt for work on the Avro seaplane that was outside his normal RN duties.

Official Training

The Royal Navy's first official course to train heavier-than-air pilots began at Eastchurch in March 1911. Its early implementation was made possible by the generosity of Francis McClean, a wealthy businessman and enthusiastic aviator who had sponsored the Royal Aero Club facilities at Eastchurch on the Isle of Sheppey in Kent, near Sheerness Dockyard. He had been impressed by the number of RN officers and ratings who had visited the airfield from Sheerness wishing to see what was going on[31] and when he departed on a Government-sponsored expedition to witness a solar eclipse in Tonga in the first half of 1911, he gave instructions that two of his aircraft, Shorts S.26[32] and S.28, were to be made available to the Admiralty. He also arranged for flying tuition to be provided free of charge by Mr George Cockburn who had obtained British pilot's certificate number 5 and had already donated his services to teach Army officers to fly on Salisbury Plain. The Admiralty agreed to pay the aircraft's running expenses, to make good any damage and paid Horace Short, also based at Eastchurch, the sum of £20 for each pilot to give instruction in a wide range of technical matters. When the Admiralty called for volunteers over 200 officers applied but only four were chosen. These were Lieutenants C R Samson, R Gregory and A M Longmore of the Royal Navy together with G V Wildman-Lushington of the Royal Marine Light Infantry (RMLI). Before the course began, however, Wildman-Lushington was taken ill and he was replaced at short notice by Captain E L Gerard RMLI who was serving in *Hermione*, standing by *R 1*. The four officers were briefed, confidentially, by Admiral Drury that they were expected to become instructors, hence the longer than usual period of training. They were to 'keep in view the adaptability of aeroplanes for work at sea'[33] but they were not to give Short Brothers inside

Samson at the controls of Short S.27, Naval Aeroplane number 2, at Eastchurch in 1911.
Despite being seated in front of the petrol tank, he is smoking a pipe. (Philip Jarrett Collection).

information that would give them a commercial advantage. They were to make at least three dual flights before flying solo and were instructed not to fly on Sundays.

The first course lasted six months, much longer than the six weeks usually allowed at the time to obtain a pilot's certificate. Samson and Longmore obtained their certificates at the end of April, the other two slightly later. All four were given technical instruction at Short Brother's aircraft factory and at various French firms, most notably the Gnome aero-engine works. They also attended the French Military Aviation Trials at Reims before their course formally ended in September 1911, by which time they were considered to be expert in most aspects of aviation and well able to give advice to the Admiralty on developmental matters. They had put in as many hours flying as possible and on 19 August 1911 Samson had achieved a British record for the duration of a sortie.[34] Charles Rumney Samson was born in Manchester in 1883, joined the RN in 1898 and was described in his obituary in the *Times* on 6 February 1931 as 'a man full of the very spirit of adventure'. He served in the cruiser *Pomone* on the west coast of Africa and in the Persian Gulf and was promoted to lieutenant in 1904, after which he commanded Torpedo Boat 81 at Devonport. In 1909 he was First Lieutenant of the cruiser *Philomel* which suppressed gun runners in the Persian Gulf and on one occasion captured 20,000 rounds of ammunition in a vessel he intercepted in the cruiser's pinnace. He was promoted to commander on completion of flying training in 1911. He and the other three pilots began to establish aviation within the RN on a firm footing and, with the decision not to reconstruct *R 1* after the damage caused extracting it from its shed in September 1911, Eastchurch became the focal point for development and heavier-than-air aircraft were the centre of attention. Samson persuaded the Admiralty to purchase the aircraft lent by Frank McClean together with several new ones made to order by Shorts and formal training courses were

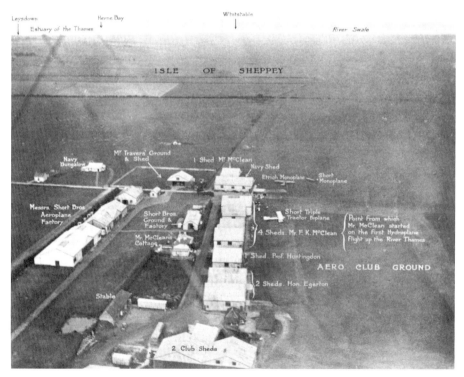

Eastchurch airfield in 1912 showing how small the complex was at the time. It grew rapidly as the RNAS training establishment expanded. (Philip Jarrett Collection).

established for new pilots and mechanics. The latter were drawn from the RN's pool of specialised carpenters and sailmakers together with a few engine fitters, giving a good idea of how aircraft were constructed in 1911. New ideas had to come quickly if aircraft were to work successfully at sea and specialists in torpedoes, gunnery, communications and other disciplines were appointed to Eastchurch. They were borne on the books of HMS *Actaeon,* the Torpedo School at the nearby naval base at Sheerness.[35] At the time the Torpedo Branch was responsible for all electrical systems, including W/T, and thus had much to offer the technical progress of aviation systems. Its commanding officer, Captain Godfrey M Paine MVO RN, became closely involved in the administration of air matters and was to become the first commandant of the Central Flying School established at Upavon by the embryo Royal Flying Corps in 1912 and subsequently held several senior appointments in the RNAS.

2 Practical Progress

Practical interest in aviation was not confined to the Royal Navy[1] and significant progress was made in France, the USA and Japan. Frenchman Henri Fabre was the first pilot to take off from and alight on the water in a single sortie, a feat considered at the time to be a key enabler in the development of what were referred to as 'hydro-aeroplanes'. It was thought at the time that they would be ideal for naval use since the sea surface would act as an airfield and aviation support ships were regarded more as floating hangars than as operating bases. The French modified the torpedo-boat depot ship *Foudre* to support hydro-aeroplanes in 1911. The Imperial Japanese Navy modified the mercantile *Wakamiya Maru* to support two Farman floatplanes for tactical exercises in 1913 but it was the United States Navy that made the most significant early demonstrations.

USN Progress
In the summer of 1910 Captain Washington I Chambers USN obtained funding from the Navy Department to equip a warship for flying trials. He invited Wilbur Wright to fly one of his aircraft off a wooden deck built over the forecastle of a light cruiser but he declined. Chambers then approached another aviation pioneer, Glen Curtiss, who accepted and offered his 50hp Model D pusher biplane and a Curtiss Company pilot named Eugene Ely to fly it. A temporary wooden flight deck was erected on the USS *Birmingham* in Norfolk Navy Yard during October 1910; it was 83ft long, 22ft wide and sloped downwards at an angle of 5 degrees from a point just forward of the bridge to the ship's bow. With the aircraft secured at its aftermost point it gave a take-off run of just over 50ft. The aircraft had no brakes and a hold-back prevented it from moving forward when the engine was started; it was embarked by crane and secured in place by rope lashings while the ship was still alongside. *Birmingham* sailed on 14 November 1910 to carry out the first aircraft launch from the deck of a warship in history. Ely recognised that there was a considerable element of risk and he wrapped inflated bicycle inner tubes around his shoulders to add buoyancy if he ended up in the water. He also wore a padded football helmet and goggles. The original intention was for the ship to

cruise in Chesapeake Bay at about 10 knots to give a wind over the deck that would assist take-off but rain squalls were encountered and she anchored in Hampton Roads to wait for them to pass. At about 15.00 the weather cleared and *Birmingham* began to weigh anchor while the aircraft lashings were removed but Ely was impatient to be off and started his engine. The noise just forward of the bridge and the hot oil blown aft by the aircraft's propeller thrust caused some confusion and the ship was still anchored when Ely waved his arm, the signal to his mechanic to release the hold-back and the aircraft began to move. Despite the sloping deck and the propeller thrust, the aircraft failed to accelerate to the 30 knots it needed to become airborne and literally fell off the forward extremity of the deck. Ely pushed the control column forward to trade what little height he had for as much extra speed as he could get and reached flying speed as his propeller tips touched the water, causing them to splinter. He was able to climb away but the vibration caused by the damaged propeller was a concern and he landed at Willoughby Spit about

Eugene Ely leaving the take-off deck of uss *Birmingham* on 14 November 1910. The aircraft has a downward trajectory and is already below deck level. Note also that the anchor cable is not straight up and down as it would have been if the anchor had broken free of the bottom; the ship was, therefore, still at anchor when he took off. The ship in the background is one of a number of supporting destroyers. (Author's collection)

three miles from the ship. The flight had demonstrated that the operation of a wheeled aircraft from a specially-prepared deck on a ship was feasible but it also highlighted the need for a naval pilot who understood what was going on around him. Glen Curtiss offered to train a naval officer at his own expense and the offer was accepted by the USN, pre-dating by several weeks Francis McClean's offer to the Admiralty in the UK.

Captain Chambers followed Ely's first success by persuading the Navy Department to fund another temporary deck on a cruiser, this time to demonstrate the feasibility of landing on, and the USS *Pennsylvania*, an armoured cruiser based in San Francisco, was selected. A wooden deck 120ft long and 32ft wide was fitted over the ship's after turret and quarterdeck; it sloped gently upwards from the stern where a pronounced ramp filled the space between the aftermost 'lip' of the deck and the quarterdeck underneath it. 'Arrester wires' comprising twenty-two ropes stretched athwartships across the deck with sandbags at their extremities were positioned to stop the aircraft by engaging hooks on its undercarriage when it hit the deck, replicating a method commonly used to stop contemporary drag-racing cars after their high-speed runs. The idea was possibly suggested by Lieutenant Ellyson USN, who became the first USN pilot. Ely was again the pilot and he carried out the first deck landing in history on 18 January 1911. Having demonstrated both a take-off and landing with a wheeled aeroplanes from modified warships, the USN turned its attention to hydro-aeroplanes. In order to justify the cost of procuring its own aircraft, the USN had to demonstrate to George Meyer, the sceptical Secretary of the Navy, that an aeroplane could be launched and retrieved from a warship without impairing its fighting efficiency.[2] On 17 February 1911 Glen Curtiss took off from San Francisco Bay in his C-III tractor-engined hydro-aeroplane and alighted on the water near *Pennsylvania*. He taxied alongside and the aircraft was hoisted inboard by a derrick and placed on the boat deck amidships. While Curtiss went to tea in the wardroom, mechanics inspected the aircraft and when he returned the engine was started and he was hoisted onto the water for take-off. These three successful demonstrations proved that aircraft, even at their present immature stage of development, could operate from warships but their usefulness depended on their ability to perform scouting and reconnaissance functions in adverse as well as clear weather and to carry weapons. From this point onwards it was the RN that made the most significant progress toward operational capability.

In photographs, the Short-designed aircraft flown by naval pilots at this time look like mobile birdcages and to begin to understand the skills required to fly them it must be borne in mind that their Gnome rotary engines were either 'on', running flat out, or 'off', depending on the position of the ignition switch selected by the pilot. There was no throttle as such and progress when approaching to land

Ely landing on the USS *Pennsylvania* in San Francisco Bay on 18 January 1911. The wind, as indicated by the American flag at the gaff on the main mast forward of the landing deck, is blowing from astern. This was not ideal and would have had the effect of increasing the aircraft's speed relative to the deck. Ely has clearly flown a very low, flat approach and his wheels are only inches above the round-down. Note the sailors crowded onto every possible vantage point. (Author's collection)

or taxi-ing was achieved by dextrous use of this switch.[3] Naval Aeroplane number 2, used by Commander Samson for his ship take-off demonstrations, had only three instruments for the pilot to monitor; a sight glass which, hopefully, gave evidence of engine oil pressure; an airspeed indicator comprising a flat plate pushed back by the airflow which was fitted to an outer strut; and a piece of string, about 18in long, tied to the elevator. If it moved sideways or up and down it showed that the aircraft was no longer in straight and level flight and corrective action needed to be taken. If it pointed towards the pilot all was well and, although crude, it was incapable of malfunction and was thus considered reliable. The aircraft had no system of dual control and the pupil sat behind the pilot as best he could and studied his actions. When both had gained confidence after a series of fast hops across the airfield, it said in the training manual[4] that the pupil could 'learn the movement of the lever by reaching over the instructor's shoulder and grasping it lightly, following the movements of the pilot'. There could be no conversation over the noise of the engine so the instructor would knock his pupil's arm out of the way if he wanted him to release his grip. After a series of straight flights about 30ft above the ground, gentle turns were demonstrated and then the pilot would be sent solo. If he survived this experience, practice was built up before taking the test to obtain a pilot's certificate. In 1911 this required potential pilots to make two flights, in each of which they had to fly a figure-of-eight pattern around two posts spaced 500m apart, attain an altitude of at least 50m and make two landings with the engine stopped which must not result in damage to the aircraft. After each of these, the machine was to come to rest within 50m of a designated point on the airfield which had been briefed before take-off.[5] Certificates were awarded under the authority of the Federation Aeronautique Internationale by the aero club of the nation concerned; in the case of the British Empire this was the Royal Aero Club. The certificate contained a section which read 'the civil, naval and military authorities, including the police, are respectfully requested to aid and assist the holder of this certificate' in English, French, Spanish, Italian, German and Russian; a polite request which reflected the expectation that many sorties would be curtailed by engine failure. Samson was awarded British pilot's certificate number 71 and Longmore number 72, both on 24 April 1911. As well as Commander Samson and his growing team of instructor pilots, there were twenty-three RN ratings at

HMS *Hibernia* getting under way in Weymouth Bay early on the morning of 2 May 1912 with RN Aeroplane number 2 on the take-off trackway. A long derrick has been rigged forward of the fore mast to lift the aircraft into position; it was subsequently removed together with the take-off track. (Author's collection)

Eastchurch. All were referred to as mechanics but their specific RN trades included thirteen sailmakers responsible for the aircraft fabric, six carpenters responsible for the wooden airframe and four blacksmiths responsible for the engines.

The American achievements would have been followed avidly by the groups at Barrow-in-Furness and Eastchurch and, once he was qualified, Samson sought Admiralty approval and funding to carry out take-off trials from a British warship. It was given in December 1911 showing continued Admiralty enthusiasm for aviation despite the recent termination of the *R 1* project. By then Samson's total flying hours would have amounted to tens rather than hundreds of hours in the air, making his ability to carry out a series of innovative flying trials in an unreliable aircraft all the more remarkable. The vessel selected for the first take-off was the battleship HMS *Africa* which was in partially-manned reserve in the nearby Sheerness Dockyard. She was fitted with two downward-sloping parallel wooden troughs and a lattice-work of supports over her forward turret and forecastle. She was also fitted with a long derrick on the foremast to lift aircraft from a lighter alongside onto the troughs. Samson flew Short S.27, constructor's number 38 and by then RN airframe number 2, fitted with a 50hp Gnome rotary engine, from Eastchurch to Sheerness where it was manhandled over a beach onto a lighter, taken out to *Africa* which was moored to a buoy and hoisted onto the troughs. On

Samson photographed seconds after getting airborne at the mid-point of the take-off track on 2 May 1912. Portland is just visible in the background showing that *Hibernia* had remained in the sheltered water close inshore near Weymouth Bay. (Author's collection)

Samson walking away from number 2 having landed at Lodmore Marsh. He is wearing civilian clothes, plus-fours and a heavy pullover and carrying a cloth cap. These were considered more suitable than uniform since they would inevitably get covered in oil and, with flights limited to low level and short duration, there was no great need for warmth. (Author's collection)

10 January 1912 he took off with a slight tail-wind, using just over 100ft of the available deck and flew back to Eastchurch. He was the first naval pilot and only the second man in history to take off from the deck of a warship. The next logical step was to take off from the deck of a warship that was under way and this was achieved by Samson on 2 May 1912, again in number 2, although by then it had been re-engined with a 70hp Gnome. For this demonstration a similar wooden structure was fitted to *Africa*'s sister-ship *Hibernia* which was steaming at 10.5 knots into a westerly wind in Weymouth Bay. With wind over the deck Samson got airborne in only 45ft, flew safely towards the coast and landed at Lodmore Marsh where a temporary airfield with tented accommodation had been set up. A third launch was made from the older battleship *London* by Samson in the same aircraft during July 1912.

All three launches had been successful but there were obvious concerns about pilot safety since Aeroplane number 2 was not fitted with floats. On 1 December 1911 Longmore had tested a set of flexible flotation bags fitted to number 2 by landing the aircraft on sheltered water in the River Medway near Sheerness Dockyard. Two bags were secured to the framework of the undercarriage and a third to the tailskid aft. They were essentially a safety measure to prepare for Samson's subsequent embarked operations and although the aircraft could land on sheltered water with them, it lacked the power or structural strength to take off from the water in the way that Schwann had done. RN Aeroplane number 2 was built by Short Brothers at Eastchurch with their construction number S.38. It replaced S.28 owned by Frank McClean which was damaged beyond repair during naval training and the customer appears in Short's order book as 'F. McClean (Navy)'. After its purchase by the Admiralty for £600[6] it was sequentially identified as Naval Biplane number 2, then B2, then T2 and finally number 2. Work started on it in May 1911 and it was first tested on 23 May 1911 by Samson.[7] It was 42ft 1in long and had a wingspan of 46ft 5in. The maximum take-off weight was 1540lbs and at first it was powered by a Gnome seven-cylinder air-cooled radial engine of 50hp, later replaced by a similar unit developing 70hp. It could operate with one or two pilots and had a wing loading of only 3lbs/ft², making it as light as a kite and difficult to handle on the ground or on deck in anything but the lightest breeze. Apart from the take-offs from battleship decks described above, Lieutenant W Parke RN made one of the earliest night flights in it in September 1912. It was damaged on a number of occasions, including when it was hoisted onto *London* for a take-off demonstration, and was the first airframe to be rebuilt by naval ratings rather than under contract by Shorts. Samson made his first night flight in it with Assistant Paymaster E B Parker RN as co-pilot in September 1913, after which it was fitted with dual controls for use by the naval flying school at Eastchurch. The First Lord of the Admiralty, Winston Churchill, flew in it with Lieutenant G V Wildman-Lushington RMLI as pilot on 29 November 1913 to better understand the way flying training was carried out. It continued in use with the school's 'C' Flight after the outbreak of war but Flight Sub Lieutenant A G Shepherd RNAS crashed it on 3 November 1914. Surveyed in February 1915, it was found to be beyond repair and written off.[8]

The Army had also been evaluating the use of aircraft and Colonel S F Cody won a War Office competition intended to identify the best machine for military use. The role that attracted Army attention at first was reconnaissance and it gave little thought to the use of aircraft intended to attack the enemy directly. From the outset the RN and Army used aircraft from different manufacturers and this proved to be a sound approach which broadened the industrial base that underpinned the new technology and encouraged the progress that was needed to overtake the lead that France and Germany had built up. The Government feared wasteful duplication, however, and in November 1911 the Prime Minister re-convened the standing subcommittee of the CID under the chairmanship of Lord Haldane[9] 'to consider future development of aerial navigation for naval and military purposes and the measures which might be taken to secure this country an efficient aerial service'.[10] The solution they devised was based on no very clear knowledge of what aircraft could achieve or indeed how developed aircraft would integrate with the fighting capabilities of the two Services which were both undergoing considerable modernisation and modification at the time. The subcommittee assumed, despite a complete lack of supporting evidence, that the employment of aircraft would differ so completely from conventional operations at sea and on land that it justified the creation of a new British aeronautical service to be known as the Royal Flying Corps (RFC). It was to consist of a Naval Wing, a Military Wing and a Central Flying School (CFS) and it was assumed by politicians that the primary roles of all military aircraft would be reconnaissance and spotting the fall of shot for artillery on land and the guns of battleships at sea. The RFC, with its three Wings, was constituted by Royal Warrant and came into existence on 13 April 1912.

The Army manoeuvres of 1912 had demonstrated that the deployment of aircraft with the British Expeditionary Force (BEF), was a practical proposition for the newly-formed Military Wing. Aircraft could operate from a flat field close to a divisional or corps headquarters and open out to look for an enemy field army that was unlikely to be moving faster than 4mph on foot (even cavalry moved slowly for most of the time in order to conserve the strength of its horses). Thus a pilot that spotted the enemy had time to fly back to his forward base and relay his information verbally to the commanding general in good time for suitable action to be taken. Naval reconnaissance had no such luxury as enemy warships moved quickly and were, thus, time-sensitive. Returning from a reconnaissance out to 100nm would take an hour during which a located enemy ship could move 20nm or more, a distance greater than the visibility range from a battleship's bridge, even on a clear day. Since the aircraft could not land on the flagship it would have to be recovered after alighting on the sea, and more time would be needed before the pilot could be debriefed to obtain his vital information. The 1913 manoeuvres showed clearly that W/T installations in aircraft were essential to relay the position, course and speed of a located enemy as soon as it was sighted and, since many sorties would end with engine failure, it was also needed to send a distress message so that the crew could be rescued. Army pilots could fix their position over land with a map but naval air operations had further complications since even if a well-flown reconnaissance aircraft found the enemy and reported it by W/T, both it and the fleet with which it was working would be using navigational techniques on the featureless sea that differed little from those of Nelson's Navy. Errors of position introduced by the effects of wind and sea currents were amplified by the higher speeds at which both ships and aircraft now moved with the result that the potential for accurate position reporting without the fleet flagship and the aircraft knowing the other's precise position on a common tactical plot was, therefore, not good. The Navy also wanted its aircraft to take direct action against the enemy wherever possible and this meant the development of weapon systems that were of little immediate interest to the Army. To justify its existence the Naval Wing had to become an effective element of naval operations by overcoming all the early hurdles and developing a way of operating with the fleet at sea, navigating with precision, and designing and producing weapons to take the fight to the enemy in all three dimensions. Most important of all, it had to be able to communicate with the fleet commander with secure transmissions and little or no delay.

Fortunately, the Royal Navy of 1912 was among the most technically complex organisations in the world and there were a number of gifted young men who were only too keen to help develop the necessary equipment and techniques. The Admiralty dealt with a complex spectrum of manufacturers and moved with relative ease into the competitive world of airframe, engine, weapon and what would later be known as avionics development. Critics subsequently claimed that the Admiralty had little enthusiasm for the concept of a unified RFC but it would be fairer to say that the Naval and Military Wings had disparate operational requirements and moved apart as they sought to achieve them. Such unity as there had been was mostly in the minds of politicians but elementary flying training was a practical area for co-operation and the first CFS commandant was Captain Godfrey Paine MVO RN, the former commanding officer of *Actaeon* and Longmore was one of the first instructors.[11] The RN also provided CFS with a number of mechanics. The Naval Flying School at Eastchurch could probably not have coped alone with the expansion that took place between 1912 and 1914 and CFS filled an important function as more and more pilots were enlisted. From the outset the two operational wings were administered differently, the Naval Wing by the Admiralty and the Military Wing by the War Office.

In 1913 the Military Wing began to enlist and train NCOs as pilots and it also enlisted and trained a cadre of reserve officer pilots to allow for wartime expansion should it be needed. In November 1913 Longmore was tasked to prepare a draft scheme for recruiting personnel into the expanding naval air organisation[12] and training them. On 8 January 1914 a meeting was held at the Admiralty chaired by the Fourth Sea Lord, Rear Admiral Sir Cecil Lambert. Also present were Captain Paine of the CFS, Captain Sueter now Director the of the Air Department, Commander Schwann his deputy, Commander Scarlett the Inspecting Captain of Aircraft, Commander Masterman in charge of the revived airship element, Commander Samson, Lieutenants Longmore, Gregory, Spenser Grey and Major Gordon.[13] 4SL began by observing that there was a need to define the role of naval aviation more precisely and the meeting is notable for the fact that the operational organisation was referred to for the first time as the 'Naval Air Service' rather than the Naval Wing. It was agreed that some pilots must continue to be trained by the

CFS but Eastchurch would function separately as the leading naval training facility. Moreover the orders for all naval aircraft and equipment would continue to be placed by the Admiralty.

Experience

In September 1912 Longmore took part in the Army autumn manoeuvres with Major Trenchard[14] as his observer, flying a number of different aircraft types that supported the Northern Army. They operated from a field at Thetford, near Peterborough, and a similar number of aircraft supported the Southern Army. The weather was good and on the first morning, at dawn, Longmore and Trenchard found the enemy's de-training centre and direction of advance.[15] After landing, Trenchard took the information to the army commander who valued it but was at a loss to know how to communicate it to his cavalry commander, General Allenby, who was some miles down the Thetford-Newmarket road. Longmore and Trenchard volunteered to fly their information to him and set off down the road at low level looking for staff officers on horseback. These were eventually located and Longmore landed near them in a field; the information was passed on but the aircraft's propeller had hit a tree stump on landing and needed repair. At the time it was common for long-distance flights to be followed by a support team in a motor car and in this instance Longmore was followed by his own Daimler driven by Parker, his driver, with ERA O'Connor, a spare propeller, tools and a carefully-selected range of spares including spark plugs. They were quickly able to change the propeller and both aircraft and car returned to base. The 1912 manoeuvres can fairly be said to have made the Army aware of the value of air reconnaissance.

The US, French and Royal Navies all used aircraft in their 1913 fleet exercises but the RN achieved the most practical value. The USN deployed an aviation detachment to its base at Guantanamo Bay in Cuba and the French operated seaplanes from *Foudre* to carry out coastal patrols near Toulon. The RN adapted the cruiser *Hermes* into a seaplane carrier by removing the forecastle gun and replacing it with a sloping take-off deck forward of a canvas hangar. A second canvas hangar was rigged on the quarterdeck with a derrick attached to the mainmast to lift seaplanes off the deck and onto the water. Both were capable of providing rudimentary protection for a single aircraft. Workshops and storerooms were also provided and she commissioned in her new role on 7 May 1913 to act as a headquarters ship for the naval air service, commanded by Captain G W Vivian RN whose terms of reference required him to administer all air personnel including those in the new coastal air stations. The exercise scenario matched the Blue Fleet against the Red with a total of 351 warships, many of which were brought out of reserve, and the two forces reflected the difference in size between the RN and the

Imperial German Navy. *Hermes* was attached to the Red or enemy fleet and tasked with evaluating the possibility of operating aircraft with a fleet at sea under operational conditions. Her secondary task was the replicate, as far as possible, the capability of an airship in the reconnaissance role. For this she was allowed to proceed to any point within 300nm of Great Yarmouth before launching an aircraft to complete a reconnaissance out to 400nm. She had to be back in Great Yarmouth within 48 hours of sailing.[16] Two aircraft were embarked; number 48, an 80hp Borel monoplane in the forward hangar, and number 81, the 160hp Short Folder, aft. The Borel was completely wrecked in its hangar by wind and waves when *Hermes* encountered extremely bad weather on 22 July and it was replaced by number 55, a Caudron G.III. Exercise war was declared on 24 July 1913. Bad weather precluded flying at first but on 28 July the Caudron took off successfully from the forward deck flown by Lieutenant F Bowhill RN. The Folder was flown by Samson with Lieutenant R Fitzmaurice RN as his observer and they flew six sorties during the exercise including one which ended with an engine failure about 60nm from *Hermes*. Fitzmaurice had been transmitting frequent reports and sent a distress message as the aircraft came down on the sea but it was garbled and unreadable when taken in by *Hermes*' W/T operators. However, they deduced from the lack of follow-up reports that the aircraft had come down and estimated by time where it was likely to be. *Hermes* with the destroyer *Mermaid* set off to locate the aircraft

HMS *Hermes* in Scapa Flow during October 1913, after the fleet exercises held in the summer. The image is not of good quality but does show number 81, the original Short Folder, taxiing towards the ship for recovery after alighting on the water. The aircraft derrick fitted to the fore mast has been turned out to port with the recovery pendant lowered ready for the aircraft to manoeuvre underneath it. When secured, it would be lifted onto the forecastle for stowage in the canvas hangar. (Author's collection)

which had come down only 2nm from the estimated position and found that both it and its crew had been picked up a German merchant ship. They were transferred to *Hermes* when she came up and the aircraft repaired for further sorties. After the exercise, *Hermes* and her Short Folder continued to operate, achieving more than thirty sorties by the end of October; the longest sustained period of embarked flying operations by any navy in the world at the time. The importance of W/T equipment both to report contacts and for the crew to send distress messages if necessary had been emphasised but it was also becoming clear that seaplanes were fragile and liable to damage when attempting to take-off or land on choppy water; naval aircraft needed to be designed for their purpose.

The Short Folder, RN Aeroplane number 81, was the first aircraft designed with folding wings to minimise the space needed to stow it in a ship's hangar. The work of Horace Short in consultation with Samson and Longmore, it had two-bay wings and was delivered to Eastchurch on 16 July 1913, just in time for embarkation in *Hermes*. Folding the wings back reduced the aircraft's width from a little over 56ft to 12ft with no increase in its 40ft length. It had a single 160hp Gnome engine just powerful enough to lift pilot, observer, a full tank of petrol and a Rouzet wireless transmitter into the air from a calm sea. The transmitter weighed 70lbs and there was insufficient lift for a receiver so the observer had no means of knowing whether his reports were being received or not.

The Development of Air Weapons and Equipment
The Admiralty took the seamanlike approach of evaluating what aircraft could actually achieve, rather than just accepting the untested claims of theorists.[17] It was clear, however, that aircraft had the latent potential to attack as well as locate the enemy. In January 1912 Lieutenant H A Williamson RN, a submarine specialist who had subsequently become a pilot, recommended the use of aeroplanes to locate submarines.[18] He also proposed the use of bombs fuzed to detonate 20ft below the surface to attack them, effectively predicting the use of depth charges, although their hydrostatic fuses would take some years to develop. Experiments near Harwich in June 1912 and Rosyth in September were carried out to ascertain whether a dived submarine could be seen from the air. It proved impossible to detect a dived submarine in the opaque waters off the UK's east coast but tests did show that in average conditions the crew of a seaplane could sight a submarine on the surface in diving trim and attack it before it could submerge. An experimental seaplane station was established at Calshot Spit near the entrance to Southampton water in January 1914 with Longmore in command. Such was the importance placed on anti-submarine operations that Churchill flew a trial sortie with Longmore to discover for himself the range at which a submarine could be

Winston Churchill, the First Lord of the Admiralty, being helped into a Maurice Farman seaplane in Portsmouth Harbour during April 1913. The pilot waiting for him in the cockpit is Lieutenant A M Longmore RN and this may well have been the submarine-detection sortie described in the text. Churchill also flew at Eastchurch with Lieutenant Gilbert Wildman-Lushington RMA who allowed him to take the controls making him the first cabinet minister in the British Empire to take control of an aircraft. (Author's collection)

detected. He signalled RNAS Calshot to say that he wanted a seaplane alongside the Admiralty yacht *Enchantress*, moored in Portsmouth Harbour, at 10.00 the next day and a Maurice Farman was duly flown across, landing with some difficulty in the crowded harbour. They made a timed rendezvous with a submarine off the Nab Light Vessel and the boat proceeded to dive and operate at pre-briefed depths for the First Lord to judge for himself the difficulty of detection.[19]

Experiments were made at Eastchurch using light bombs and grenades that could be thrown from their cockpits by pilots. Accurate weapon delivery with this method was uncertain, however, since the speed and height of the aircraft could not be accurately measured and nor could the wind that affected the bomb in flight, so the Air Department commissioned a series of academic studies into the flight of bombs in air as well as the ideal shape to lessen wind resistance and allow them to follow a common flight path. The Navy's own experts, among them Warrant Officer Scarff, a former ERA who was to have an outstanding career as a practical aircraft engineer with the RNAS, developed a practical means of fixing bombs to aircraft and releasing them. A gunnery officer, Lieutenant R H Clark-Hall RN, was appointed to Eastchurch first to qualify as a pilot and then to use his expertise in the development of air weapons including guns and bombs suitable for a growing list of tasks.[20] In these formative years the Military Wing of the RFC concentrated on reconnaissance work and paid significantly less attention to armament issues. Samson was involved in many of the early bombing experiments and in 1912 he dropped a dummy 100lb bomb, the equivalent of a 6in shell, from a Short pusher biplane. There were early concerns that blast as bombs exploded might damage the aircraft that dropped them and these were addressed in a series of tests during December 1913; low attacks were favoured because the short time of flight reduced the number of variables that might affect bombs' trajectories as they fell. No heavy bombs were available but floats containing explosive charges varying from 2.25lbs to 40lbs were moored off Eastchurch and fired electrically from a destroyer while seaplanes flew directly over them at a variety of heights. The effect on the aircraft was less than anticipated and it was calculated that an aircraft at 350ft or higher could safely drop a 100lb bomb containing 40lbs of explosive without danger.

On 26 October 1913 Churchill circulated a note on the Admiralty's air policy for the immediate future.[21] In it, he explained that both aeroplanes and seaplanes would be required for operations around the UK and on overseas stations. He recommended three new types of aircraft; first a fighting seaplane able to operate from a ship as its base, second a reconnaissance seaplane capable of working with the fleet at sea and third a fighting aeroplane for home service that could operate from land bases 'to repel enemy aircraft' that might attack vulnerable points in the UK such as dockyards and the fleet's ammunition storage depots. The First Lord went into considerable detail and described how he imagined the fighting aeroplane would attack a Zeppelin by 'descending on it obliquely from above and discharging a series of small bombs or fireballs at rapid intervals so that a string of them more than a hundred yards in length would be drawn like a whiplash across the gasbag'.[22] The feedback from Eastchurch about successful weapons trials encouraged the Admiralty to add direct attack on the enemy to its growing list of tasks for naval aircraft but a proviso was added that 'it is not a function on which the Board lay great stress, although undoubtedly many attempts in the way of aerial attacks on magazines, arsenals, dockyards etc will be made in time of war'.[23]

Concerns about the German use of Zeppelins for fleet reconnaissance and attacks on the UK mainland led to the evaluation of air-to-air weapons. One test involved an aircraft from Eastchurch towing an explosive grapnel intended to hit the outer envelope of an airship and ignite the gasbags inside it. It was clearly impractical to destroy an actual airship to prove this concept but simpler methods were subsequently tested.[24] These included dropping light bombs as suggested by Churchill and Hales grenades fired from rifles. Both would have to be fuzed sensitively to detonate on contact with the outer airship fabric and initial experiments were carried out at the Cotton Powder Company's works at Faversham in October 1913. Two sheets of fabric were stitched onto frames to resemble, as nearly as possible, the two skins of a rigid airship. When hit by a rifle grenade with a 4-ounce charge, the outer skin was blown to shreds and the rear skin had a hole about 6in in diameter blown in it. Subsequent experiments were carried out at the Royal Aircraft Factory at Farnborough using specially-prepared test sections of a rigid airship that included gasbags filled with hydrogen and these proved entirely successful. The gas was ignited and a full-sized Zeppelin would have been destroyed. These trials were followed by a series of tests by aircraft at Eastchurch which unfortunately revealed that the laboratory conditions at Faversham and Farnborough could not be replicated under operational conditions. Floating targets and small balloons released from aircraft were fired at but single rounds from rifles left no trace in flight to show whether they were hitting and it proved impossible, therefore, to correct shots onto the target. This problem was eventually overcome by the development of tracer ammunition which could be seen in flight but in 1914 the only anti-Zeppelin weapon that was considered effective was the Hales rifle grenade, some 200 of which had been made for the RNAS but many had been used up in experiments. Those that were left were hastily distributed among RN air stations by Clark-Hall himself.

Machine guns represented an obvious choice of armament because they delivered a high volume of fire with manageable recoil and at first it was thought that a fixture that would allow a gunner to train a weapon through wide arcs of bearing and elevation represented the best option. It soon became apparent, however, that aiming from a moving aircraft even against a static target was not easy and against a moving target such as another aircraft extremely difficult. Fixing the gun to the aircraft structure had advantages and appeared to favour pusher aircraft types but they lacked the higher speed of the tractor types that were emerging. No machine gun had been designed specifically for air application and experiments were made with Vickers and Lewis guns, both of which were capable of rates of fire between 500 and 600 rounds per minute depending on conditions. The former weighed 30lbs and a hardpoint to attach it to the airframe at least another 10lbs. Ammunition came in the form of a pre-loaded belt with 250 rounds which was nine yards long,[25] weighing 20lbs stowed in a container to the right of the gun which gave about 30 seconds of fire. The whole package, therefore, added about 70lbs to aircraft weight. In its ground application the barrel was cooled by a water-filled jacket connected by a hose to a can in which the steam generated once the water boiled could condense. It took about 1000 rounds, or four belts fired, to boil the water. Water-cooling was not practical in an aircraft and the airflow over the jacket was expected to provide sufficient cooling when the gun was fired in short bursts. The Lewis gun was slightly lighter at 26lbs but this figure included the ammunition which came in pre-loaded 47-round drum magazines known as 'pans' or 'trays'. Once these had been fired out, the pilot or gunner had to replace them in flight with further drums which had been stowed in the cockpit. Putting these figures into perspective the BE 2a, a type used by both the RNAS and RFC from 1912, had an empty weight of 1274lbs and a maximum take-off weight of 1600lbs which meant that 326lbs was available for the pilot, fuel and armament. Pilot weight obviously varied but a reasonable allowance for a man in warm flying kit with a pistol and maps would be about 200lbs. Ten gallons of avgas weighed roughly 80lbs leaving just enough weight for a Vickers with a reduced ammunition supply or a Lewis and several drums of ammunition.

Other guns were mounted for trials in addition to machine guns; these included a 1.5pdr Vickers semi-automatic gun which was mounted in the specially-designed Short S.81 pusher seaplane given the naval number 126 when it was delivered in 1913. It was flown by Clark-Hall who found that when the gun was fired, its recoil shook the aircraft badly and almost stalled it, a dive being necessary to regain flying speed.[26] Number 126 continued to give valuable service after the outbreak of war and was fitted with a dynamo and searchlight for hunting submarines on the surface at night in early 1915. Later it was fitted with a 6pdr recoilless gun for further experiments by Clark-Hall but this heavy weapon was found to be beyond the practical limit of the airframe. Number 126 was written off charge in late 1915.

The ultimate goal was to produce a weapon that could give aircraft a genuine ship-killing capability like that possessed by the new destroyers and submarines with torpedoes. A lightweight 14in diameter torpedo had been designed for use by picket boats deployed from larger warships to attack shipping in harbour or littoral waters unsuitable for regular torpedo craft to manoeuvre in. It weighed 900lbs and would obviously need a very powerful aircraft to get it into the air. Experiments were carried out at Calshot in 1914 using a development of the Short Folder which had larger, three-bay wings and a 160hp Gnome engine. Number 121 was part of a 1913 contract for four aircraft which were built at Eastchurch in early 1914 and it took part in the Royal Review of the Fleet flypast on 18 July 1914. It had experimental torpedo dropping gear fitted at Calshot between 23 and 25 July. Longmore, by then a Squadron Commander RNAS, noted in his autobiography that Churchill had visited Calshot after the Review and wanted these torpedo experiments speeded up.[27] By then number 120 had flown with a 14in torpedo lashed to its floats to prove that the aircraft could at least get airborne with such a weapon[28] but this was hardly a demonstration of operational capability. Once number 121 was fitted with the release mechanism, tests were carried out and on 28 July 1914 Longmore succeeded in getting airborne with a torpedo. He had no observer, fuel for only about 30 minutes flight and climbed to only a few feet above the water but succeeded in dropping the torpedo which then ran perfectly, the first occasion on which a British aircraft and pilot had done so. However, Longmore was quick to point out that this was a stunt; the aircraft was heavily overloaded and more development was needed before operational capability was achieved. It did, however, encourage Hyde-Thomson who had worked so hard to design the torpedo-carrying mechanism and modify the torpedo for air release.

Renewed Interest in Airships

In February 1912 the technical subcommittee of the CID had followed the loss of *R 1* by recommending against the further development of airships but the full CID instructed the subcommittee to investigate the matter further,[29] drawing their attention to a joint despatch from the naval and military attaches in Berlin dated 11 December 1911 and other reports about the success of military airships in Europe. Captain Sueter and Mr O'Gorman, Superintendent of the Royal Aircraft Factory, both members of the technical subcommittee, were sent on a fact-finding mission and their report made it clear that striking progress had been made, especially in Germany. They claimed that 'except in foggy or stormy weather, it is probable that no British war vessel or torpedo craft will be able to approach within many miles of the German coast without their presence being discovered and reported . . .'. It was, they said, 'difficult to exaggerate the value of this advantage to Germany'. The subcommittee therefore reversed its earlier view and laid stress on the fact that airships were demonstrably superior to aeroplanes 'for certain purposes, particularly prolonged operations across the sea'. The result of this re-appraisal was a recommendation, accepted by the full CID, that efforts should be concentrated towards the provision of airships for naval use and the training of crews to fly and support them. Since the Military Wing had more practical experience, it was instructed after 1912 to train and assist the Naval Wing until it could take over the task. In order to expedite matters, a new airship of the 'Gamma' type was to be built for the Navy at the Royal Aircraft Factory and a 'Willows' type airship which happened to be on the market was to be purchased immediately.

There was considerable discussion about the relative merits of rigid and non-rigid airship types and, notwithstanding the conspicuous failure of *R 1*'s structure, it was decided that both types should be developed. The impressive results achieved by German Zeppelin and Schütte-Lanz type airships led to Vickers being given a new contract to design and build a rigid airship, designated *R 9*, in June 1913.[30] The re-cast design took some time to develop, however: it did not fly until 27 November 1916 and was not delivered to the RNAS until April 1917 by which time it was obsolescent and used mainly for training. In November 1913 the Naval Wing formally took over responsibility for all British lighter-than-air flight and the RFC's remaining airships and experimental work on all airships was moved from

Farnborough to the new naval air station at Kingsnorth, under the direction of its
commanding officer, Wing Commander N F Usborne RNAS. At the outbreak of
war in 1914 the RNAS had seven non-rigid airships but only two of these, numbers
3 and 4, were considered fit for operational use.[31]

A Growing Number of Naval Air Stations
Aircraft were not yet able to operate practically from ships but they could carry out
patrols of limited duration over the North Sea from air stations on the eastern coast
of the UK. In the event of hostilities with Germany they were to search for
submarines on the surface, minelayers and Zeppelins approaching the coast; once
the enemy was located they were to report his presence and then intercept and attack
with whatever weapons were available. Aircraft were also to act in concert with local
flotillas wherever possible. Eastchurch was the first naval air station and from March
1911 it was planned that the Naval Flying School based there would form a War
Flight capable of operations. Next came Isle of Grain in December 1912, Calshot
in March 1913, Felixstowe and Yarmouth in April 1913 and Kingsnorth in April
1914. By then it was decided that accommodation at naval air stations should be
more permanent in nature with improved facilities for launching and recovering
seaplanes and flying-boats. Wherever possible, existing Coastguard facilities were
to be used or even taken over completely and it was hoped that coastal air patrols
could assume part of the duties carried out by that organisation. Forward plans in
1914 included the selection and construction of naval air stations at Scapa Flow in
the Orkney Islands, Peterhead, Newcastle and the Humber estuary.

In addition to air stations intended to be permanent, several temporary ones
had been established for the 1913 manoeuvres. Among these were Cromarty on the
south shore of Cromarty Firth. In May 1913 it had existed only in name[32] and
Longmore was sent north to find a suitable site from which seaplanes could be
operated. He found an area of flat ground on which fishermen dried their nets near
the Coastguard station but encountered difficulty in identifying its owner. Both
General Ross of Cromarty and the fishermen had some claim but honour was
satisfied when Longmore asked them both for their permission and both agreed.
Portable Bessonneau hangars were purchased in France, loaded into lighters at
Sheerness Dockyard and towed up the east coast to Cromarty. These comprised a
wooden framework which was bolted together and covered by waterproof canvas;
they were reckoned to be capable of sheltering about five aircraft and could also be
used to accommodate personnel. The aircraft arrived in June and were assembled
in the hangars by manufacturers' working parties assisted by about twenty sailors,
half from Eastchurch and others who had never seen an aeroplane before but had
been detailed off as handling parties. In addition to Longmore there were two other

pilots, Lieutenants Oliver and Ross RN, and their aircraft included a Maurice Farman Short-horn with a 100hp Renault air-cooled engine, a Sopwith seaplane with a 100hp Anzani air-cooled engine and a Borel monoplane with an 80hp Gnome rotary engine. Several distinguished visitors came to Cromarty to study their progress. Among them were Admiral Jellicoe who was flown around the fleet by Longmore in the Borel and Churchill who visited the Firth in the Admiralty Yacht *Enchantress* during his tour of naval establishments. He, too, was flown in the Borel by Longmore who was invited to dine on board *Enchantress* where he could talk to Churchill at length about aircraft and their capabilities. In the autumn of 1913 the air station was dismantled and the hangars moved to other locations.

The First Ship to Operate Aircraft
The Admiralty made a sum of £81,000 available in the 1914 estimates for the construction of a specialised aircraft-carrying ship[33] and set up a design team to consider its arrangements. It comprised J H Narbeth, a constructor who was also an aviation enthusiast and his assistant C J W Hopkins with Sueter and L'Estrange-Malone representing the RNAS. They agreed, after calculation, that a cruiser

HMS *Ark Royal* as completed. She is seen moored to a buoy and has seaplanes ranged on her forward deck with both steam cranes working. The hatch through which aircraft were raised from the hangar to the working deck was between the cranes and the bridge structure. This photograph clearly shows the flat deck area forward of the cranes which was intended to allow aircraft to take off from it but in practice the ship lacked the speed to enable them to do so safely and always lowered them onto the water for take-off. Throughout the Great War she invariable operated her seaplanes from a sheltered anchorage, not under way. (Author's collection)

conversion would not justify the cost of the necessary work or the loss of such a ship from other important duties. Narbeth listed what he considered to be the ideal properties of an aircraft carrier and he got it right in all the essential details. His list included aircraft stowage in an enclosed hangar below the upper deck, unobstructed deck space for handling aircraft and a flying-off deck. Seaplanes would need cranes to hoist them onto and off the water and the ship would need engine and airframe repair workshops together with ample space for the stowage of spare parts and aviation fuel. The latter, which was later known as avgas, a shortening of aviation gasoline, posed particular problems that were not fully understood in 1914 although it was appreciated that avgas vapour in confined spaces was potentially more volatile and dangerous than live ammunition or its cordite propellant. The group also looked to the future and insisted that a significant amount of space should be provided for aircraft weapons. The ship needed good sea-keeping qualities that would allow the transfer of aircraft, by crane, from the hangar to the deck but, above all, the team agreed that the ship in prospect must be a single-purpose vessel with no concessions to any other role than the operation of aircraft.

No conventional warship could meet these criteria and in the short time available, this meant accepting the machinery found in a typical merchant ship. To save time, the Admiralty bought a hull in frame on the stocks at the Blyth Shipbuilding Company that had been begun as a tramp steamer[34] in December 1913. The engine bearers were in the normal place amidships but they were moved aft as far as was possible. This allowed the incorporation of a hangar amidships on number 5 deck, the lowest continuous deck in the hull, that was 150ft long, 45ft wide and 15ft high and capable of containing up to ten seaplanes. A well-equipped airframe and engine workshop was installed above the hangar on number 2 deck and avgas was embarked in two-gallon cans, originally manufactured for the motor trade, which were bulk-stowed in a compartment forward of the workshop on number 2 deck. Protection for, and from, the dangerous liquid and its vapour was provided on all four sides and beneath by compartments filled with water and the only access was though a hatch in the flying-off deck. Aircraft were lifted out of the hangar, and returned to it, by one of two steam cranes sighted to port and starboard of the hatch, forward of which was a flat deck 130ft long intended to allow the take-off of wheeled aircraft or seaplanes with their floats on wheeled trolleys. Unfortunately the ship's single coal-fired triple expansion engine delivered a low maximum speed of only 11 knots, typical for a contemporary tramp but insufficient for operations with the fleet and also too low to allow aircraft to take off from the short deck; it was, however, a convenient space on which to tune aircraft and prepare them for flight. There was space on deck aft of the hatch, under the bridge, for aircraft to

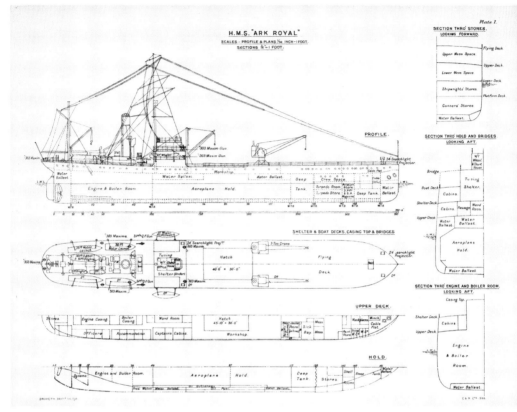

HMS *Ark Royal*. (Author's collection)

carry out ground runs. Named *Ark Royal*, she was the first ship designed to operate as a seaplane carrier and was completed in December 1914. She typified the early concept that aircraft-carrying ships were floating sheds intended to support their aircraft in operations from the sea. Lack of speed was her greatest shortcoming but another was soon found in the method chosen to get aircraft from the hangar up to the deck. Seaplane operations from *Hermes* had revealed the tendency of aircraft to swing against the ship's side when being lowered or recovered. In *Ark Royal* they had to be hoisted by crane through a fairly constricted hatch which gave rise to an even greater risk of bumping and damage in any but the calmest of conditions.[35] *Ark Royal* displaced 7450 tons at deep load, was 366ft long and had a beam of 50ft 6in. She had three single-ended tank boilers and a single-shaft triple-expansion reciprocating steam plant that developed 3000hp, giving her a maximum speed of about 11 knots, the exact speed depending on the quality of the coal in her bunkers and the number and skill of her stokers. She had a ship's company of 180 and could carry about ten aircraft depending on type.

Flying Ranks and Status
The requirement for potential service pilots to obtain a Royal Aero Club pilot's certificate before being accepted for flying duties was a yardstick against which ability could be judged but as aircraft and their tactical employment grew in complexity after 1915 it became less relevant. The early pilots were concerned that their skills were so specialised that senior officers with no flying knowledge might order a pilot to do something dangerous or unsound. To counter this, officers serving in the RFC after 1912 continued to use their naval and military ranks but their flying status was indicated by a new grading structure. Thus newly-qualified pilots were rated as RFC Flying Officers, those with more experience as Flight Commanders and those most experience as Squadron Commanders. Beyond that normal ranks applied but senior officers were not expected to order a pilot to do something without the concurrence of his squadron commander.

Official Recognition of the Royal Naval Air Service
The so-called Naval Wing of the RFC had gradually moved away from its military counterpart to operate as an integral part of the Naval Service like the Royal Marines or, more recently, the Submarine Service. Its exact status and name were officially confirmed in Admiralty Circular Letter CW.13964/14 dated 1 July 1914 entitled 'Royal Naval Air Service – Organisation'[36] in which it was stated that 'the Royal Naval Air Service will form part of the Military Branch of the Royal Navy and the various ranks will be added to the list of officers of the Military Branch in Article 169 of King's Regulations'. The document went on to make it clear that RNAS officers would not be able to command a ship unless they held existing rank in the Military Branch and were expressly authorised to do so by the Admiralty.

From 1 July 1914 the RNAS was administered by the Admiralty as, de facto, the Naval Wing had been and it was to comprise all naval aircraft and personnel either for active or reserve service. Its initial organisation included the Air Department at the Admiralty, the RN Flying School at Eastchurch and the new RN air stations together with 'all seaplanes, aeroplanes, airships, seaplane ships, balloons, kites and any other type of aircraft that may from time to time be employed for naval purposes'. Officers of the RN and RM who wished to fly could volunteer through normal channels in the same way that application could be made for any other branch and they would be expected to serve with the RNAS for at least four years after initial qualification. A certain number, however, were to be selected to go on to fill the higher-ranking positions in the RNAS. There was also an opening for

Flight Commander W G Moore DSC RNAS wearing the blue uniform approved for the RNAS in 1914. Note the eagle instead of a foul anchor in the cap badge and on the brass buttons. The eagle over the left cuff lace shows that he is a pilot and the star above it shows that he is a flight commander. (Author's collection)

civilians to enter the RNAS on direct entry after award of their Royal Aero Club certificate and this method expanded dramatically after August 1914. Both serving officers and direct entries would have the sum of £75, the standard Royal Aero Club tuition fee, refunded after full service qualification as a pilot was achieved. Officers of the RNAS were graded in a unique rank structure from July 1914. Those on the RN active list used their RNAS grade whilst appointed to flying duties but reverted to their RN rank, which could be higher or lower, on returning to general service. Direct-entry officers retained their RNAS rank throughout their service. The RNAS ranks were:

Wing Captain RNAS	equivalent to Captain RN
Wing Commander RNAS	equivalent to Commander RN
Squadron Commander RNAS	equivalent to Lieutenant Commander RN
Flight Commander RNAS	equivalent to a senior Lieutenant RN and senior to all Flight Lieutenants when appointed in command of a flight
Flight Lieutenant RNAS	equivalent to a Lieutenant RN
Flight Sub Lieutenant RNAS	equivalent to a Sub Lieutenant RN

Naval officers on the active list wore their standard uniform but if graded in a higher RNAS rank they could change their sleeve lace appropriately; on appointment back to general service they would have to revert to their RN rank lace. If they held a higher RN rank, they could continue to wear it on their uniform but their status in the RNAS would be based on their grading in the RNAS List. Flight and squadron commanders indicated their status over other lieutenants by wearing one or two stars over the rank lace on their left sleeve. All pilots wore an RNAS eagle badge above the rank lace on their left sleeve or above the left breast pocket when wearing khaki service dress on duties ashore.

In his autobiography, Vice Admiral Richard Bell-Davies, who was Samson's First Lieutenant at Eastchurch in 1914, explained how several senior RN pilots were invited to the Admiralty to discuss with the First Lord what uniform direct-entry pilots should wear.[37] They were told by Rear Admiral Lambert, Naval Secretary to the First Lord, that the choice lay between the non-executive uniform which lacked the executive curl on the sleeve rank lace or an executive uniform, complete with the executive curl, but the foul anchor device on cap badge and buttons replaced by RNAS eagles. Effectively, they were being asked their view on whether the RNAS really was to be part of the Military Branch of the RN or whether it was to have lower status as an auxiliary force. The Admiralty decided, wisely, that RN and RM officers on flying duties with the RNAS would continue to wear their normal uniform with the addition of a pilot's eagle badge where appropriate. Direct entry officers would wear an executive officer's uniform with straight sleeve lace and executive curls but with eagles substituted for foul anchors in the cap badges and buttons. Bell-Davies felt that Commodore Sueter had a lot to do with the decision which reflected much good sense.

3 The Outbreak of War

The British Empire declared war on Germany on 4 August 1914 after its unprovoked invasion of Belgium, a country it had been bound by international treaty to defend. By then the RNAS had grown to 130 officers, of which about 100 were qualified as pilots, together with about 700 petty officers and men. It had thirty-nine aeroplanes and fifty-two seaplanes, roughly half of which were assembled and available for immediate use, none of which represented any sort of standardised airframe or engine design. There were also seven airships of which three, the Parseval, Astra Torres and Beta, were capable of practical use for reconnaissance work. There was no formalised unit structure but aircraft were concentrated in naval air stations at Eastchurch, Isle of Grain, Felixstowe, Yarmouth, Killingholme, Calshot and the new airship station at Kingsnorth. Smaller operating bases, effectively satellites supporting Eastchurch, were situated at Westgate and Clacton-on-Sea.[1] Whilst this represented a considerable expansion since the procurement of the first heavier-than-air aircraft only three years earlier, progress had been largely experimental and the embryonic RNAS was far from being organised or equipped to make a significant impact on naval operations. Its capability as a reconnaissance force had not yet been tested under realistic conditions, there was no standardised tactical doctrine and only two aircraft and a single airship were fitted with machine guns.[2] The remainder had to use rifles and pistols as air-to-air weapons together with four Hales hand grenades each, distributed to Isle of Grain and a new air defence flight at Hendon but the balance of 150 hand grenades and 42 rifle grenades were concentrated at Eastchurch where the aircraft not immediately involved in training were grouped into an operational wing under Samson with Bell-Davies as his executive officer and First Lieutenant.

Surprisingly, considering that reconnaissance had been recognised from the beginning as the primary role for aircraft, no formalised air observer training had been carried out, largely because it was assumed that any naval officer capable of keeping a bridge watch on a ship would be perfectly capable of spotting and identifying ships from the air as well as accurately reporting their position, course and speed. Whilst this might have been a viable assumption in the early months of

RNAS seaplanes at Calshot for the Royal Review of the Fleet in July 1914. They include Short Type 74 numbers 74, 76 and 77 and the Sopwith Bat-Boat number 118. (Author's collection)

experimental flying, the reality of war operations soon exposed its weakness. The RNAS constituted only a tiny part of the Navy in 1914 and its rapid expansion meant that the number of pre-war regular officers was rapidly diluted by direct-entry pilots with no bridge watch-keeping experience. As important, it was found that the estimated aircraft position upon which pilots' reports were based might differ significantly from its true position within a few minutes of take-off due to inaccurately forecast winds. Sophisticated techniques had to be developed to give the enemy's position relative to a fixed geographical point or the fleet flagship and these took time to practise and perfect. Another factor was the limited power of aircraft engines in 1914 which meant that in those aircraft that had the power to lift off with an observer at all he had to be the lightest available. This led to the selection of observers by size rather than experience and midshipmen were a frequent choice. In the pages that follow you will read of RNVR officers, paymasters, surgeons and both Allied and British Army officers flying as observers. Whatever their background, efficient observers were soon found to be a priceless asset in a variety of operations and experienced pilots such as Samson insisted on flying with those who had proved their skill and ability.

In August 1914, the day-to-day administration of the RNAS was carried out by the Central Air Office at Sheerness under Captain F R Scarlett RN. Formerly the executive officer of *Hermes* with the title of Inspecting Captain of Aircraft, he was responsible both to Sueter, the Director of the Admiralty's Air Department (DAD), and to the Commander-in-Chief Grand Fleet for the provision of aircraft. During the crisis over the assassination of the Archduke Ferdinand that was to lead to the outbreak of war, most RNAS aircraft had been concentrated at Portsmouth, Weymouth and Calshot to participate in the Royal Review of the Fleet by His Majesty King George V between 18 and 22 July 1914. On 20 July a flight of seventeen seaplanes and two flights of aeroplanes flew over the fleet in formation led by Samson, one of the earliest recorded instances of close formation flying by a significant number of British aircraft and the result of several weeks of intense practice at Eastchurch. Notwithstanding the piloting skill required to achieve close formation with aircraft of widely differing power and flying characteristics, the feat was regarded at the time as a stunt rather than having any useful tactical application. When the review was over the seaplanes and airships returned to their bases and Samson led the aeroplanes on a pre-planned tour of Southern England, stopping first at Dorchester and then the CFS at Upavon. A few hours after they arrived at the latter, Samson received a telegram ordering him to concentrate his aircraft at Eastchurch to prepare for war operations and they arrived there on 27 July 1914. The seaplanes had already been instructed to prepare for coastal patrol work and these orders, together with those ordering the British fleet to remain concentrated and proceed to its war station at Scapa Flow, were among the very first British moves of the Great War.[3]

Opening Moves

The German auxiliary minelayer *Königen Louise* left Borkum on 4 August 1914 with orders to lay a minefield off the Suffolk coast. She was sighted on 5 August by the patrolling destroyers *Lance* an *Landrail*, supported by the cruiser *Amphion*, and a running fight ensued in which the German ship was sunk by gunfire and her survivors taken on board *Amphion*. Unfortunately, at 06.30 on 6 August, *Amphion* detonated two mines having unknowingly entered the newly-laid minefield and sank rapidly with the loss of one of her own officers, 150 men and many of the survivors from *Königen Louise*.[4] To counter the possibility of further raids a coastal air patrol was established by RNAS seaplanes between the Humber and the Thames Estuary from 8 August. Prior to their move to France some RFC aircraft also contributed to patrols north of the Humber and off the south coast. Pilots were briefed to look for hostile vessels, especially ships that appeared to be laying mines, but none were sighted. As soon as the BEF began to move to France a regular air patrol was established between Westgate and Ostend, intended to give early warning of German surface craft or submarines attempting to interfere with

HM Airship Number 4, the German-built Parseval, seen shortly before the outbreak of war in 1914. (Author's collection)

military shipping. A temporary seaplane base was established at Ostend under the command of Flight Lieutenant E T R Chambers RNAS to provide support and refuel aircraft prior to their return flights. Seaplanes flew the route at intervals of two hours but no enemy vessels were sighted. Although this tasking appears simple to later generations, these flights were some of the longest over-water missions ever undertaken and involved a significant degree of risk to the aircrew. The Admiralty's belief that airships would be better reconnaissance platforms with greater endurance than heavier-than-air aircraft soon proved to be justified and *HM Airship Number 4*, the German-built Parseval, patrolled the sea area between Harwich and the Thames throughout the night of 5/6 August 1914, remaining airborne for over nine hours. A regular airship patrol of the English Channel began on 10 August and continued for the rest of the month. *HM Airship Number 3*, the Astra Torres, flew a patrol line between the North Foreland and Flushing and *Number 4* covered the narrow Straits between Dover and Dunkirk. On a number of days, the airships flew for more than 12 hours searching for enemy activity at sea but none was found and the BEF together with its equipment were carried safely to France without interference from the enemy.

Specialised ships were obviously required from which aircraft could be launched to take part in fleet operations. *Ark Royal* was not yet completed and so the Admiralty requisitioned three fast Channel steamers, *Empress, Engadine* and *Riviera*[5] from the South-Eastern & Chatham Railway Company. They were taken in hand by Chatham Dockyard where the latter two were fitted with canvas hangars, pigeon lofts, derricks and workshops to allow them to operate up to four

HMS *Riviera* shortly after her initial conversion to a seaplane carrier in 1914. She has canvas hangars fore and aft and long derricks fitted to both masts to lift aircraft from the deck onto the water and to hoist them in. They were sufficiently long to keep aircraft clear of the ship's side if they swung. This photograph shows the ship at a buoy off Chatham Dockyard; she is flying the White Ensign but has not yet been painted grey and appears to have no guns in place. (Author's collection)

seaplanes each. *Empress* was initially only fitted as an aircraft ferry but was brought up to the standard of the other two in October. All three were considered too small for work with the Grand Fleet, however, and in September 1914 the former Cunard liner *Campania* was purchased for conversion to a seaplane carrier.[6] She had won the Blue Riband for the fastest crossing of the Atlantic in 1894, but by 1914 she was worn out and had actually been sold to T W Ward & Co for scrap. Demolition had not yet begun and she was considered for use as an armed merchant cruiser but rejected. However, on Sueter's recommendation her machinery was overhauled and she was converted into a seaplane carrier by Cammell Laird in Birkenhead, eventually emerging to join the Grand Fleet in May 1915.

Although the RN had no specific war plan for its air service in 1914, a number of disparate operations were initiated that required a range of capabilities and disciplines. German minelaying and submarine activity off the east coast of the UK had shown the need for coastal patrols and when the cruiser *Pathfinder* was sunk by torpedoes from *U 21* off May Island in the Firth of Forth on 5 September 1914[7] there were immediate calls for aerial patrols to be extended as far north as Scapa Flow. Although the RNAS could establish airfields relatively quickly, it had insufficient aircraft to carry out all the patrol work now found to be necessary. By the end of August embryonic seaplane bases had been established at Dundee, Fort George and Scapa Flow and airfields for wheeled aircraft were established at Dover and Newcastle. However, concerns about German raids by sea were matched by anxiety over the threat of Zeppelin attacks on London as well as the Dockyards

Short Admiralty Type 74 seaplane number 75. It took part in the Royal Review flypast in July 1914 and operated from the advanced bases at Clacton and Westgate on coastal patrol work after the outbreak of war. Unfortunately, it suffered an engine failure while being flown by Flight Commander C F Kilner RNAS off Ostend later in August and once down on the water was damaged by a tug. After repairs it operated from Dundee but side-slipped whilst turning on 24 February 1915 and crashed. It was subsequently written off. (Author's collection)

and naval magazines in the south-east of England. The RFC had been fully committed to operations with the BEF in France and had nothing left to defend the UK against air attack. Lord Kitchener, the Secretary of State for War, suggested, therefore, that the Admiralty should assume responsibility for the task and Churchill agreed. One can imagine his enthusiasm for taking absolute control over the evolution of equipment and tactics to fight a new form of warfare in which there were no hidebound theories or experienced senior officers to oppose any measures he proposed. The Admiralty assumed formal responsibility for the air defence of the UK from 3 September 1914.[8]

Air Defence
In 1914 air-to-air combat was obviously an unknown form of warfare but the RNAS had at least experimented with the use of a variety of potentially suitable weapons and, in practical terms, was better prepared than the RFC. With no means

of detecting Zeppelins until they were seen crossing the coast, their interception by placing the few aircraft available into the same piece of sky was impractical. Zeppelins had the advantages that they could jettison ballast and out-climb any aircraft and operate at greater altitude if aircraft were seen trying to intercept them. Moreover, there were simply not enough aircraft to carry out standing patrols over potential targets and they lacked the armament to guarantee the destruction of a Zeppelin even if an intercepting pilot was fortunate enough to see it and get close to it. There was no means of directing aircraft towards a Zeppelin from a controlling ground station and night flying was still both dangerous and far from being a routine operation. In 1914, therefore, aircraft were not the best anti-Zeppelin measure but their further development continued with considerable urgency.

Aware that patrolling aircraft would have difficulty locating Zeppelins and getting into a position to engage them, the Admiralty decided to set up a system of gun defences through which the enemy would have to fly to reach likely targets. To achieve this an Anti-Aircraft Corps (AAC) was established as part of the RNAS under the overall direction of the Air Department as quickly as possible[9] and the first element came into existence on 9 October 1914. It was manned by volunteers from the Metropolitan Police Force Special Constabulary augmented by gunnery and searchlight specialists from the RN and RNVR. Initial equipment included three searchlights; one each at Charing Cross, Hyde Park and Lambeth. By then the Admiralty was already fitting 3in high-angle (HA) guns to ships[10] and had taken delivery of seventeen with another forty-two on order. The Army had far fewer anti-aircraft weapons available at the time and by December 1914 RNAS AAC units had been established in Dover and Sheffield with mobile sections equipped with guns and searchlights mounted on lorries available by February 1915 for deployment in London, the Home Counties and an area centred around Newmarket. Foreign Service elements were formed from December 1914 onwards and used to defend naval air stations established in France, the Dardanelles and East Africa.

Once established, the London detachment of the AAC comprised a series of elements known as sub-controls acting under the authority of a central control situated on the roof of Admiralty Arch and connected to them by telephone. Each sub-control comprised one or more gun positions and one or more searchlight positions sited to be able to act in co-operation.[11] A duty central control officer responsible for the air defence of London was situated in the Air Department Anti-Aircraft Office, Room 10, Block IV within the Admiralty at all times. Captain L S Stansfeld RN was appointed as the Inspecting Captain of the AAC, assisted by Commander F C Halahan MVO RN who dealt with all administrative matters including the question of black-out precautions in cities. Commander G G Grey

Commodore Sueter inspecting men of the RNAS Anti-Aircraft Corps. The men are not dressed as seamen in square-rig but wear fore-and-aft rig with jacket, tie and peaked cap in common with all RNAS ratings. (Author's collection)

RN commanded the London Division. Lieutenant Commander Hincks RN and Lieutenants Pink and Sinclair RN acted as watch-keeping officers in the central control position.

Sueter was able to report to the First Lord by the second week in October 1914 that there were twenty gun and searchlight positions in central London with work on more sites started.[12] In his semi-autobiographical work *Airmen or Noahs* published in 1928, Sueter explained that the creation of an air defence organisation was 'a big nut for the Air Department to crack' and could not have been achieved in the short time available without unstinted help from the Admiralty Works Department, London County Council and Scotland Yard. Their engineers had, he felt, given the impression that they had been installing gun and searchlight positions together with their communications systems all their lives. Fortunately the first raid on London by a Zeppelin did not take place until the night of 31 May 1915 when about 100 small explosive and incendiary bombs were dropped by Zeppelins *L 11*,

L 13, *L 14*, *L 15* and *L 16*, killing five civilians and wounding a further fourteen. Many people came out onto the streets to watch anti-aircraft guns fire at Zeppelins illuminated by searchlights. Sueter watched from the central control position on Admiralty Arch and described the event as a 'fine spectacle' which resembled a firework display. Despite their slow movement, no Zeppelins were brought down but Sueter quoted an account published in the *Morning Post* by *Kapitänleutnant* Breithaupt, who had commanded *L 15* during the raid, entitled 'How we bombed London'. In it Breithaupt describes flying over the City with shrapnel bursting all round, his own bombs bursting below, flashes from the anti-aircraft guns and on either side of *L 15*, the other airships caught in the rays of the searchlights and clearly recognisable.

Forward Deployment

Aircraft of Samson's Eastchurch Squadron at Dunkirk in 1914. *HM Airship Number 3*, the Astra-Torres, can be seen in the background and from left to right in the foreground are Henri-Farman F.20, Samson's BE 2a number 50, a Sopwith tractor biplane and Short number 42. The latter suffered an engine failure on take-off from Morbecque being flown by Samson on 28 September 1914, hit a tree on landing and was damaged beyond repair. (Bruce/Leslie Collection via Guy Warner).

Churchill's active imagination soon came up with another means of countering the Zeppelin threat; a vigorous attack on the enemy's air sheds and aircraft at source before they could even take off to attack the UK. As early as 25 August Samson was ordered to deploy the Eastchurch Wing to Ostend as quickly as possible to carry out operations against Zeppelins in their bases, the earliest example in history of aircraft being used to attack an enemy threat at source. They were to act in concert with a Royal Marine brigade which had been deployed to defend the Channel ports on the western flank of the German advance. Samson's Wing had been formed out of the Eastchurch Naval Flying School and many of its men had been together since 1912. It nominally comprised three squadrons, each of twelve aircraft, but it actually comprised only three BE biplanes, three Sopwith biplanes, two Blériot monoplanes, one Henri Farman biplane, one Bristol biplane and a converted seaplane fitted with a wheeled undercarriage in place of its floats; between them they had three different types of engine. Deploying across the English Channel was still far from routine but a delay of 24 hours waiting for the Royal Marines to be deployed around Ostend led Samson and his men to worry that the war would be over before they could get into action.[13] There was no form of survival equipment available for issue and, like the American Eugene Ely, the pilots wrapped semi-inflated bicycle inner-tubes around their shoulders to provide some buoyancy in case they came down in the sea. Each pilot also carried a Webley .455in automatic pistol in case they came down near the enemy. The Webley automatic pistol was adopted as a standard sidearm by the RNAS in 1912 and offered a number of advantages, especially for pilots, over the Webley Mark 6 revolver that was the standard issue in the British Army at the time.[14] The automatic weighed only 2.5lbs fully loaded and could be drawn from its holster and used easily in flight, it did not need to be re-cocked between each shot, the magazine contained seven rounds rather than the revolver's six and it was easier to re-load

The Webley and Scott 1912 pattern automatic pistol adopted by the RNAS as its standard sidearm. (Author's collection)

Samson in his favourite aircraft, BE 2a number 50, about to fly a sortie from Dunkirk. The engine is running and chocks are in place because the aircraft had no brakes. Note the lanyard running from the port chock to the sailor on the port wing-tip. Once Samson waved away the chocks they will be pulled clear but the sailor will continue to hold onto the wing-tip to help the pilot turn the aircraft into wind for take-off. Note also the red and white roundel under the port wing. (Author's collection)

with a fresh magazine fitting neatly into the grip after the empty one was removed. In the revolver rounds had to be loaded individually into the chamber after the gun was broken open.

Surprisingly, the Wing eventually took off with no very clear idea where it was to land. Samson went first in his favourite aircraft, BE 2c number 50 which he described in *Fights and Flights* as an old BE biplane. It was actually delivered from the Royal Aircraft Factory to Eastchurch on 12 February 1914 and he had flown it in the Royal Review. The flight across the Channel was rather unpleasant, with low cloud and thunderstorms, but Samson said that it would have taken something pretty bad to stop them. They made the French coast at Calais and flew on past Dunkirk to Ostend, arriving after 90 minutes in the air. The only suitable landing ground that Samson could find was the Leopold racecourse but it was rather narrow and he had to land with a considerable crosswind. He was fired at by two Marines as he landed, both 'aching to let off their rifles at the first opportunity'; they were disappointed to find that he was a British naval officer. Until October 1914 RNAS aircraft bore no national insignia to distinguish them from enemy aircraft but on 26 October the Admiralty instructed all commanding officers of air units that it had 'decided that in future all aeroplanes and seaplanes of the RNAS shall carry a distinguishing mark in the shape of a union flag painted on the lower surface of each of the lower planes'. The size of this flag was to be as large as possible – up to 7ft by 5ft – and it was said that 'the colouring of the flag should be bright and it should be placed half way between the fuselage and the wing tip'. This method of distinguishing aircraft was found to be unsatisfactory and was replaced in early 1915 by circular roundels with red outer and white inner placed at the extremities of the upper and lower wings near the tips. A union flag was to be painted as conspicuously as possible on the tailplane or rudder. The individual aircraft number was painted in black on the after fuselage or rudder as most appropriate.

A Bristol Scout Type C, number 1250. The type was used extensively by the RNAS and this example clearly shows the early national markings with red and white roundels on the wings and a large union flag on the fuselage sides. (Philip Jarrett Collection).

A Rolls-Royce armoured car delivered in December 1914. A White Ensign is fitted to the mast attached to the machine-gun turret and there is a stout cable aft which could be used to tow another armoured car in difficulty. The letters 'RNAS' are prominently displayed, together with the car's squadron, flight and individual letter on the rear surface. The sailor is wearing standard blue RNAS uniform with puttees and an Admiralty-pattern leather belt with a bayonet attached. (Author's collection)

Samson's pilots included Bell-Davies, his second-in-command, Osmond, Courtney and Briggs, an engineer who always flew with a complete outfit of tools and 'a regular store of things'. His colleagues always wondered how his aircraft flew with the weight of material it was loaded with. Captain Barnby RMLI was camp commandant and Staff Surgeon H V Wells was wing doctor; both were also qualified pilots. Samson was careful, at first, to differentiate between these regular officers and Flight Lieutenants Sippe, Dalrymple-Clark, Beevor, Rainey and Lord Edward Grosvenor who were direct-entry RNAS officers but the distinction soon faded as these men proved themselves in operations. Mr Brownridge, a commissioned carpenter RN, was the aircraft repair officer who soon showed himself to be a capable and resourceful specialist in a variety of disciplines. Two of Samson's brothers, Lieutenants W L and F R Samson, were granted temporary commissions in the RNVR to act as observers, transport and intelligence officers, together with Sub Lieutenants Nalder, Glass, Huggins and

Isaac RNVR. The Wing deployed with about seventy air mechanics, all regulars from Eastchurch.

To support the aircraft, the Wing had ten motor touring cars, two 5-ton Mercedes lorries and eight London General omnibuses which were still painted red and carried advertisements on their sides. F R Samson recruited twenty specially-enlisted transport drivers to operate them, the majority of which had been motor mechanics and testers in the Rolls-Royce, Wolseley and Talbot motor-car companies. They were 'first class men who always kept the transport in first-class running order'. The motor cars were fitted locally with boiler plate and machine guns for use as armoured cars and were augmented eventually by armoured cars designed and built for the purpose in the UK. The incorporation of motor cars into an aviation unit may seem surprising to 21st-century readers but it must be understood that they had formed an important element of air station equipment in the UK prior to the war, driving out to support aircraft that had made forced landings away from the airfield with mechanics and spare parts. In the open warfare of 1914 it seemed entirely logical to use armoured cars both to search for aircraft that had come down away from their base and to set up temporary airfields whenever necessary. It was soon found that they had a number of other valuable uses, screening their bases against incursions by enemy cavalry patrols and for carrying out reconnaissance work both in concert with aircraft and in their own right. Once armed with machine guns they were well equipped to break up enemy patrols found in flat, open country.

After a few days at Ostend alongside the Royal Marines, the Admiralty ordered the Wing to return to the UK but on hearing this the British vice-consul at Dunkirk, Mr Sarel and the general officer commanding French troops in the Dunkirk area asked for the unit to remain in support of Allied operations. The Admiralty changed its mind, therefore, and ordered Samson's unit to remain in France based at Dunkirk. A telegram from the Admiralty to the French Ministry of Marine explained the intended policy for the Wing and is worth quoting.

The Admiralty considers it extremely important to deny the use of territory within a hundred miles of Dunkirk to German Zeppelins and to attack with aeroplanes all airships found replenishing there. With your permission the Admiralty wish to take all necessary measures to maintain aerial command of this region. The Admiralty proposes, therefore, to place 30 or 40 naval aeroplanes at Dunkirk or other convenient coast points. In order that these may have a good radius of action they must be able to establish temporary bases 40 to 50 miles inland. The Admiralty further desires to reinforce the officer commanding the aeroplanes with 50 to 60 armed motor cars and 200 to 300 men. This small force will operate in conformity with the wishes of the French military authorities but we hope it may be accorded a free initiative. <u>The immunity of Portsmouth, Chatham and London from aerial attack is clearly involved</u>.[15]

One can imagine that Churchill had a hand in drafting this letter even if he did not dictate the whole thing; achievement of the stated aim was clearly an impossible task for the wing's primitive aircraft but at least the telegram demonstrated that the Admiralty had a firm grasp of the potential uses to which aircraft could be put.

Samson's first action against German forces with his armoured cars took place on 4 September 1914. Some German motor cars had been reported passing through Armentières and Samson took two of his own cars to attempt an interception at a bend in the road two miles from Cassel. A German car got to the corner first and the small RNAS party opened fire on it with a car-mounted Vickers machine gun and rifles, wounding two Germans. Unfortunately, after about forty rounds the firing pin of the Vickers broke, putting the weapon out of action. The Germans made off in their damaged car but the postmaster in Bailleul, a recently-cultivated RNAS intelligence contact, telephoned to say that blood was seen dripping from the car when it arrived back in the town. Samson recorded that this fight gave the RNAS considerable prestige in the villages around Dunkirk and, for a time, stopped the Germans from pressing forward their reconnaissance of the area. Many more spirited actions were to follow. A day earlier Dalrymple Clark had carried out the first air attack on the enemy whilst on a reconnaissance flight towards Douai. He saw a number of German soldiers near a wood and dived down to low level to drop a 16lb bomb on them. Climbing away he observed that there were two or three casualties. After his return from Cassel on 4 September, Samson flew a reconnaissance flight in number 50 looking for Germans between Armentières and Bailleul and sighted three motor cars with about fifty troops halted on the road near the site of his earlier skirmish. He dropped two small bombs from a height of 2000ft but unfortunately missed with both. The two actions show the close interaction that had evolved between armoured car and aircraft operations. His mobile force was strengthened by the modification of one of the lorries to carry a 3pdr gun and armour plate to protect the engine, driver and gun's crew. It carried ninety-six rounds of 3pdr ammunition; four tins of petrol, a Lewis gun in case a close-quarters fight developed, a ladder to allow trees, posts or buildings to be climbed for fire to be observed, a spare-part box for the gun, ropes to pull the lorry out of a muddy ditch if necessary, and a supply of tinned food. In addition to aircraft, RNAS armoured car units and naval armoured trains were to play a significant part in the open war of movement in the autumn of 1914.

Training New Pilots

Within days of the outbreak of war, the Admiralty was inundated with applications from civilians who wished to join the RNAS.[16] There was therefore an urgent need to train pilots in greater numbers than the Eastchurch Naval Flying School and CFS could cope with and by 17 August 1914 the Air Department had made arrangements for officers to be trained at civilian schools including the Bristol School at Brooklands, the Grahame-White School at Hendon and the Eastbourne Aviation School. An additional training flight was also set up within the naval air station at Hendon. At the civilian schools students were instructed up to the standard required to obtain the Royal Aero Club's certificate after which they were appointed to Eastchurch or the CFS to finish their training before being sent to Calshot for training on seaplanes. All direct entrants from civilian life were commissioned as Probationary Acting Flight Sub Lieutenants RNAS; specialist RN officers were not required to qualify as pilots before training at Eastchurch or CFS. Large numbers of men with a technical background were recruited for training as air mechanics. many of whom passed through the RN training depot at Crystal Palace.

Sea Patrol Work

RNAS Great Yarmouth was typical of the air stations commissioned before the outbreak of war. On 4 August 1914 it was commanded by Squadron Commander R Gregory RNAS under whom there were seven officers, two warrant officers and about forty men, many of whom lived under canvas until more permanent accommodation was completed. This took the form of cottages vacated by Coast Guard families as they moved out. One of the two warrant officers, Mr H C Bobbett, the boatswain gunner, was the first warrant officer to qualify as a pilot. The air station had eight aircraft at first; one Maurice Farman biplane, one Short biplane, one Henri Farman seaplane, one Short seaplane and four Sopwith seaplanes listed as gun machines and bomb droppers although none was so fitted at first. On 5 September the station's daily report noted that Sopwith number 880 had a hole cut in its fuselage to allow a rifle to be fired from it by a passenger. A few days later dummy bombs were dropped from another machine but it was some weeks before all the machines were fitted with mechanisms to drop live bombs.

The first war patrols were flown on 9 August and there was some excitement when a pilot reported seeing a German seaplane which he followed along the coast but it turned out to be naval aeroplane number 154, a German DFW purchased for evaluation in March 1914, operating from another naval air station. As a precaution, it was promptly grounded to avoid a possible 'blue-on-blue' incident. From 14 August a system of dawn, midday and sunset patrols was instigated which were to continue until the end of the war. The importance of accurate navigation and the need to fly precise compass headings was soon appreciated but an unnamed pilot was quoted in Snowden Gamble's *The Story of a North Sea Air Station* as commenting that a lot of patrols ended up in a country field with the tail in the air. He went on to say that 'the skilful pilot of those days was one who was capable of landing near or on the lawn of some mansion so that he could be near a telephone. The collecting party, arriving later in lorries, were also agreeably surprised at the pilot's skill in selecting a suitable landing area as it usually meant a good feed.'

At the end of October 1914 Gregory reported to the Inspecting Captain of Aircraft that since the start of hostilities, aircraft from Great Yarmouth had flown 122 hours on war coastal patrols despite five aircraft having been detached to establish the air station at Scapa Flow. The shortage of spare parts had meant that, on average, only two aircraft were available for operational flights at any one time but, on a more positive note, much a had been achieved. Four pilots had been trained to fly seaplanes; a number of new recruits had been trained in the care and maintenance of aircraft; engines had been overhauled; aircraft had been rebuilt after forced landings and all hands had been busy with 'the fitting out of the air station which had been greatly delayed by the Review at Spithead in July'. From these modest beginnings a great deal was to grow very quickly in 1915.

4 The First Strikes by Aircraft

The Admiralty clearly believed in the future strike potential of aircraft but the policy of 'denying the use of territory within a hundred miles of Dunkirk to German Zeppelins' and attacking all those found replenishing within that radius was no simple task. The known Zeppelin bases and the factory where they were made were all beyond the radius of action of the aircraft based at Dunkirk and the effect of the tiny bombs they could carry had yet to be tested against real targets. In October 1914 the Eastchurch Wing was operating on the exposed seaward flank of the German Army that had thrust through Belgium and northern France. The aircraft could have moved north-east to operate from temporary airfields but the mobile squadrons of armoured cars and the 3rd Marine Brigade guarding Ostend and Dunkirk provided no real defence against a German move in strength towards the coast and, if deployed forward, the aircraft and their valuable pilots could be lost within hours. The Germans had brought up heavy howitzers to bombard Antwerp and the Belgian government had concluded that it must evacuate. The BEF had only six divisions and was unable to help but the newly-formed Royal Naval Division (RND), was available and could be deployed at short notice.

Operations with the Royal Naval Division
The RND had not existed before August 1914 but Churchill calculated that on mobilisation there would be up to 30,000 naval reservists for whom there was no immediate employment at sea.[1] He mentioned the fact at a meeting of the CID and obtained its agreement to form them into a division, to include a brigade of Royal Marines, for emergency deployment. The division came together in August and September 1914 around cadres of officers and men recalled to RN and RM service with some former Army officers. There were also a number of civilian volunteers including 600 miners from the north-east of England who had reputedly been waiting in a line of men intending to join the Durham Light Infantry or Northumberland Fusiliers when it started raining heavily. If the story is to be believed, they moved out of the rain into a spacious and dry naval recruiting hall and subsequently found themselves in the RND. The division was administered by

an Admiralty committee chaired by Churchill who thoroughly enjoyed having another novel organisation like the RNAS under his control with no prior doctrine or senior experts to argue against his ideas. Training was initially hampered by a lack of equipment but continued with gathering momentum through September. Unlike an Army division it consisted mainly of infantry with no artillery, engineer or logistical support and many sailors only received their rifles in the last week of September. They continued to wear their blue uniforms complete with bell-bottomed trousers, blue jean collars and brown leather Admiralty-pattern belts and ammunition pouches. By 1 October 1914 the RND comprised a Royal Marines Brigade made up of 50 per cent regulars from the depots at Chatham, Deal, Portsmouth and Plymouth and 50 per cent fleet reservists recalled to service; it had four battalions numbered 9, 10, 11 and 12 and this was the force that deployed to Ostend with the Eastchurch Wing. The two RN Brigades were made up almost entirely from fleet reservists recalled to service and civilian volunteers, concentrated in new camps at Betteshangar in Kent and Blandford in Dorset. Each brigade had

A convoy of motor omnibuses and cars preparing to move elements of the RNAS and RND forward to Antwerp in October 1914. The former London buses are still in their civilian livery complete with advertisements on the side but the motor car in the foreground has had RND painted on its bonnet. French or Belgian troops can be seen in marching order together with a number of interested civilians with their bicycles. (Author's collection)

four battalions of about 18 officers and 700 men. Churchill's committee made an inspired decision over the battalion identities and they were given names rather than numbers. The 1st Naval Brigade comprised the Benbow, Collingwood, Drake and Hawke Battalions, while the 2nd Naval Brigade comprised the Anson, Howe, Hood and Nelson Battalions.

The developing crisis at Antwerp was discussed at a meeting between Churchill, Kitchener, Prince Louis of Battenburg the First Sea Lord and Sir Edward Grey the Foreign Secretary in London on 1 October 1914 at which it was decided that the Belgian authorities must be urged not to withdraw. There was little that the BEF could do to help but at Churchill's instigation it was decided to deploy the RND to Antwerp to stiffen Belgian resolve and help in the defence of the port.[2] The RM Brigade with 2600 marines under General Aston was already in France together with the Eastchurch Wing, its new armoured car squadrons and a small team of twenty Royal Engineers. When General Aston was taken ill he was replaced by General Paris who was appointed to command the RND when it deployed. Paris' brigade and the RNAS were ordered to give the Germans the impression that they formed part of a considerably larger mobile force capable of threatening the German's western flank, cutting railway lines and generally interfering with

Sailors of the RND moving into defensive positions near Antwerp on 6 October 1914. Their bayonets are fixed ready for immediate action and they appear to be digging in as a protection against artillery fire outside the main fortifications of the city. (Author's collection)

their plans. The RM Brigade arrived in the vicinity of Antwerp on 3 October. The two naval brigades arrived on 6 October and were cheered by the civilian population with girls pinning silk flags on their blue uniforms and bringing the men jugs of beer. Ominously, however, they passed large numbers of ambulances and groups of dispirited Belgian troops moving in the opposite direction. Without artillery and with much of its infantry only partially trained, the RND stood little chance of halting the German offensive but Churchill had travelled to Antwerp and shocked his Cabinet colleagues by telegraphing Asquith on 5 October with a proposal that he resign his position as First Lord immediately in order take a commission and command of the defence of Antwerp. For an instant his love of action had overcome his political acumen but the proposal was bluntly refused and he was ordered back to London. Violet Asquith, the Prime Minister's wife, subsequently wrote of her 'amazement and shock' at Churchill's lack of a sense of proportion. Samson, on the other hand, described Churchill as being 'full of cheery optimism regarding the situation'.[3] The situation was certainly critical but from the RNAS' viewpoint Antwerp was the only base from which there was a realistic chance of striking at targets in Germany and returning.

The First Strike Operations in Detail

Flight Lieutenant R L G Marix RNAS had returned to Eastchurch in late August from Scapa Flow where he had been flying reconnaissance sorties for the Grand Fleet when Squadron Commander D A Spenser Grey RNAS telephoned him on 8 September 1914 and told him to drive up to the Admiralty immediately for a meeting with Churchill and the First Sea Lord. Spenser Grey was one of the officers who had given Churchill flying lessons before the war and the First Lord knew both officers from his visits to Eastchurch. The subsequent discussion is another example, if one were needed, of Churchill's love of detailed involvement in operations, especially those that involved the RNAS and RND. He wanted a strike operation to be mounted by aircraft operating from Antwerp against Zeppelins in their known bases at Dusseldorf and Cologne. There were no aircraft in service that were entirely suitable but Churchill had heard of two fast Sopwith aircraft that had been evaluated by the RFC at Farnborough and rejected because they were considered unsafe.[4] They were Schneider Trophy seaplanes, known as Tabloids, that had been modified with wheels rather than floats, with a wingspan of 25ft 6in and a length of 20ft 4in. The empty weight was 730lbs and fully-loaded weight 1120lbs. They were both powered by 80hp Gnome engines which gave an impressive maximum speed of 92mph at ground level and an initial rate of climb of 1200ft per minute. Endurance was 3.5 hours.[5] Churchill offered the two pilots the chance to try them and, if they thought them suitable, they would immediately

An early production Sopwith Schneider with a wheeled undercarriage that has not yet had its airframe number or national markings applied. 167 and 168 would have been very similar. (Author's collection)

be transferred to the RNAS. The two officers travelled to Farnborough a day later and agreed that if they were satisfied they would wave to each other after a few circuits and fly directly to Eastchurch. After dire warnings about the aircraft's instability at high speed they flew them and found both aircraft were very light on the controls but they considered that to be more of an advantage than otherwise. They duly waved and took the aircraft to Eastchurch where they were allocated the naval numbers 167 and 168.[6] These opinions about the two aircraft are interesting and reveal that the RFC was clearly used to accepting the products of the Royal Aircraft Factory with little question and wanted stable aircraft in which the pilot could concentrate foremost on his reconnaissance or artillery-spotting mission.

A 'bomb-dropping' unit, designated Number 2 Squadron of the Eastchurch Wing, was formed and prepared for deployment to Antwerp under the command of Squadron Commander E L Gerrard[7] RNAS. Spenser Grey and Marix were appointed to it on 1 September 1914 taking their new Tabloids with them. Other equipment included two BEs and two older Sopwiths and pilots included Flight Lieutenants C H Collett, Newton Clare and S V Sippe RNAS. The squadron began to assemble at an airfield near the shore at Ostend in early September and three aircraft were pegged down under the lee of some sand dunes on 12 September when they were hit by a violent squall. The pegs were torn out of the ground and the aircraft, fortunately not the new Tabloids, were blown across the sands turning cartwheels and were completely wrecked.[8] A week later two of the three Eastchurch Wing squadrons moved forward to Wilryck, an aerodrome just outside Antwerp to prepare for strike operations against the Zeppelin bases; the third operated in support of the Army at Morbecque about three miles south of Hazebrouck. The Tabloids had been modified with a rack under the fuselage capable of holding two 20lb Hale bombs. A lug on each bomb fitted between brackets with holes drilled through and a pin held the bomb in place. Wires were attached to each pin leading to toggles in the cockpit; when the pilot pulled the toggle the pin was extracted and the bomb fell free. There was no bomb-sight and the pilot had to judge his release point by eye. The 80hp Gnome engine had no throttle in the modern sense: it was either switched on or off although there was a mixture control lever which had to be adjusted frequently to give the optimum fuel/air ratio. If the pilot dived with the engine switched on, its revolutions would increase and this could lead to damage or complete failure; the usual technique was to switch the engine magnetos off and glide[9] down. The propeller would continue to rotate but there was always the nagging doubt that when the magnetos were switched on the engine might not re-start; it would in any case take some seconds to run up to full power slowing the time taken to get away from a bomb run. At Wilryck the officers were billeted in a mansion close to the airfield and the mechanics in houses nearby. Such intelligence as could be gathered about the Zeppelin bases was gathered and plans were made but in the meantime reconnaissance sorties were flown for the Belgian Army.

The Tabloid had a radius of action estimated at 100 miles but Dusseldorf was about 110 miles away and Cologne about 120 miles so it was clearly not possible to return to Wilryck after the attack without refuelling. The Belgian armoured car squadron in Antwerp was approached and its commanding officer, Baron de Caters, agreed to help. After discussion with the RNAS planners he agreed to take his vehicles to a carefully-selected field marked on maps about 50 miles east of Antwerp with cans of petrol and oil, together with a team of RNAS mechanics. Once in position they were to set out ground signals to show that they had arrived with no enemy forces nearby. The first strike took place on 22 September 1914 with a total of four aircraft, two for each target. Marix was briefed to attack Cologne and Collett Dusseldorf; all went well until the River Meuse, beyond which fog and low cloud were seen to extend some miles east of the Rhine. Only Collett succeeded in locating his target through a gap in the murk. He glided down towards Dussel-dorf from a height of 6000ft,[10] and entered a layer of mist at 1500ft. He identified the Zeppelin shed about a quarter of a mile from him when he was down to only about 400ft. His first bomb fell short and exploded but the second, which might have hit the shed, failed to explode probably because it was dropped so low that there was insufficient time for the arming device on the bomb to turn enough times to activate the fuze. All four aircraft found de Cater's armoured cars at the designated landing site and refuelled safely despite the presence of German cavalry patrols in the vicinity. They were safely back at Wilryck by early afternoon.

Another attack on the Zeppelin sheds was required but for the next few days the weather was too bad and the military situation around Antwerp deteriorated. The Germans closed in around the defences and it would no longer be possible for de Cater and his armoured cars to set up a refuelling site to the east. Spenser Grey and Marix solved the problem by designing an extra fuel tank which could be manufactured by Belgian engineers and fitted by RNAS mechanics to the two Sopwith Tabloids. It was not possible to modify the other aircraft so the next attack would be by these aircraft alone, one for each target. By early October the aircraft were ready but Antwerp was on the verge of collapse and Churchill had arrived with the RND to take personal charge. The British headquarters was in the Hotel St Antoine and Spenser Grey went there on the morning of 8 October to seek permission to carry out the strike. By then Churchill had lost some of his earlier optimism and said that it was now too late and orders had been given for Antwerp to be evacuated at once. The Germans, he believed, could be in the city that night and he told Spenser Grey that the RNAS was to leave Wilryck as quickly as possible. The next few minutes proved to be the stuff of legend. Apparently Churchill left the room to go to the toilet but he was followed by Spenser Grey who continued to argue his case through the locked door,[11] emphasising that the two aircraft could still return in time to evacuate Wilryck before nightfall. Churchill was either convinced by his argument which seemed to be the one positive note in a headquarters full of desperate talk of retreat or, more likely, consented in order to get rid of him. Whatever the true reason, Spenser Grey returned to the airfield and both aircraft took off in the early afternoon, Spenser Grey in number 167 heading for Cologne and Marix in number 168 heading for Dusseldorf. Spenser Grey was unable to locate the Zeppelin shed which was not where their intelligence sources had marked it on his map. With little fuel to spare he dropped his two bombs successfully on the city's main railway station, which appeared to be full of traffic, and returned safely to Wilryck.

Marix was altogether more successful. He too found that the Zeppelin shed was not where it had been marked on his map but he flew around at 3000ft looking for it, gradually attracting a significant amount of machine-gun and small-arms fire from the ground. He eventually found the shed and dived towards it with his Gnome engine still on. This strained the engine but he wanted to make a fast getaway as soon as his bombs were released. His engine stood up well and he dropped his two bombs sequentially at about 500ft with his eyes fixed firmly on the enormous shed. In his peripheral vision he saw the flashes as a number of anti-aircraft guns fired at him and as he pulled out of the dive he looked over his shoulder and saw what he subsequently described as 'a magnificent sight', enormous sheets of flame pouring out of the shed which clearly had an inflated Zeppelin inside it. To his momentary consternation, however, he found that the rudder bar was locked solid but he managed to turn slowly onto a course towards Antwerp.[12] As it began to get dark he worked out that the wind had shifted and he was a few miles north of his intended track; the search for his target had used up fuel and it was becoming clear that he did not have enough to get back to Wilryck. The prospect of a forced landing in the dark in open country with no rudder control had little appeal so he decided to land at the next suitable field while he could still see it. Once on the ground he was lucky enough to find some Belgian gendarmes who confirmed that he was some miles north of Antwerp. Helpfully, they told him that a railway engine would pass through a nearby station shortly with the intention of getting into Antwerp to bring out a trainload of refugees, and that he could travel on the footplate. While he waited Marix examined 168 and found that a bullet had cut through the port wire that connected the rudder bar to the rudder and that the starboard wire had been jammed onto one of its guides by a bullet strike. One of his two wing-warping control wires had also been cut through by a bullet; he had been lucky to fly as far as he had and to land safely. He also found that his uniform cap, which hung against his back suspended by a string around his neck so that he could wear it immediately after landing, had a bullet hole through the peak. In all, there were about thirty bullet holes in the wings and fuselage.

Marix arranged for the gendarmes to mount guard on the aircraft and told them, optimistically, that a party would come to recover it in the morning but his adventures were still far from over. The engine duly arrived and took him to within five miles of Antwerp but he then had to dismount. Some sources say that he 'borrowed' a bicycle from a Belgian; in his own account Marix said that he 'commandeered' it but either way he had little chance of returning it to its rightful owner. He pedalled off towards the city but found his way obstructed by a bridge that was 'strongly blocked with barbed wire', which he got round with the help of a sentry by hanging the bicycle on his back and clambering along the outside supports of the bridge. The centre of Antwerp was deserted with houses on fire and the Hotel St Antoine, the British headquarters only hours earlier, was empty except for an elderly caretaker who produced a bottle of wine and some food. Suitably refreshed, Marix set off once more, found some Belgian soldiers with a motor car and persuaded them to take him to Wilryck where they went to a house next to the officers' quarters. The few serviceable aircraft had flown off to Dunkirk but Sippe and some mechanics were in a darkened room about to leave when they heard the two Belgians with Marix speaking in Flemish. Assuming them to be

German they were about to shoot when fortunately Marix said something in English and they held their fire. He eventually got away in a lorry with the last road party, making their way through roads to the west that were crowded with refugees carrying everything they could on small carts and wheelbarrows. They eventually reached Ostend where they rejoined the Eastchurch Wing. Number 168 was abandoned and struck off charge on 14 October 1914.

There had indeed been an airship in the Dusseldorf shed on 8 October, the new German Army Zeppelin Z IX, construction number *LZ 25*, which had only recently been inflated. There were concerns in Berlin that the British had timed the attack to catch the airship in its shed and these led to accusations that British agents were working as clerks in the American Embassy and a number were questioned. Marix became a celebrity and was awarded the DSO on 21 October 1914 and promoted to Squadron Commander RNAS on 31 October.

The Friedrichshafen Strike

The Allied withdrawal from Antwerp ended any chance of launching air strikes against the Zeppelin sheds at Cologne and Dusseldorf in the immediate future but Sueter was already considering an imaginative plan to strike at the factory where they were built. This was at Friedrichshafen on the northern shore of Lake Constance and by mid-October the Air Department had gathered intelligence material about it from a Canadian, Colonel Grant Morden. There was no British airfield from which any RNAS aircraft would have the radius of action to reach the target and return but there was a French airship base at Belfort close to the point at which the French, German and Swiss frontiers met to the west of the lake. For some reason Sueter wanted to 'relieve the naval pilots from anxiety'[13] and, rather than instructing a senior RNAS officer to plan the operation, he entrusted the work to a maverick adventurer and inventor called Noel Pemberton Billing. In 1913 he had learned to fly and obtained his Royal Aero Club pilot's certificate within 24 hours to win a bet, set up an aircraft factory near Southampton and designed a series of aeroplanes, none of which, at the time, had been ordered for the RNAS[14] or RFC. He came to Sueter's notice after, of all things, recovering a steam yacht from Monte Carlo for a Southampton shipbuilder that had been chartered by a German officer but not paid for. Sueter later described how the task had required ingenuity, daring and bravado to pull off and Pemberton Billing was sent to France with instructions to liaise with the French authorities and, if this proved successful, to arrange the clandestine transport of suitable aircraft from the UK to Belfort. To give him some authority for his discussions with the French, Sueter arranged for him to be commissioned as a Lieutenant RNVR on 14 October and he sailed for France a week later, driving to Belfort in his own touring car.

The French authorities agreed to allow a detachment of RNAS aircraft to be moved to Belfort but gave the RNAS only thirty days to carry out the operation; after that they intended to carry out an attack themselves. Pemberton Billing added more detail to the known intelligence material on the factory and drew up a chart with a proposed route to and from the target. He returned to the UK on 28 October and travelled to Manchester to organise the details of moving the aircraft selected to carry out the attack to the French airfield. The aircraft selected was the Avro 504 which had flown first in April 1913 and was already serving in limited numbers with the RFC in France. A batch of 504s was ordered by the Admiralty under contract CP.46635/14, the first of which was given the naval number 179. Under the system used by the Admiralty at the time the type was, therefore, known officially as the Avro Type 179. Three other 504s were prepared specially for the Friedrich-hafen strike and allocated numbers 873, 874 and 875. They had a wingspan of 36ft and a length of 29ft 5in. Empty weight was 924lbs and fully-loaded weight was 1574lbs. They were powered by 80hp Gnome engines which gave a maximum speed of 82mph at ground level and allowed them to climb to 3500ft in seven minutes. Fuel capacity was 21 gallons in a main pressurised tank with a further 4.5 gallons in a gravity tank giving an endurance of 4.5 hours. Oil capacity was 6 gallons.[15]

For planning purposes the four aircraft were known as the Avro Flight and Pemberton Billing worked out their transit arrangements with the manufacturer in considerable detail. They were carried to Southampton in a dismantled state by rail, arriving in time to be loaded on board ss *Manchester Importer* which sailed for France on 10 November 1914.[16] After disembarkation they were taken by road to Belfort at night and moved into the airship shed in their crates. The pilots and mechanics were accommodated inside the shed so that they would not be seen by spies. The Avro Flight was commanded by Squadron Commander P Shepherd and

A fascinating image which is, unfortunately, of poor quality. It is, however, good enough to show Avro 504s number 873, 875 and 874 lined up at Belfort ready to start up for the attack on Friedrichshafen on 21 November 1914. A head count shows that a number of French personnel must have helped the eleven RNAS mechanics to arm the aircraft and prepare them for flight. (Author's collection)

he had four other pilots with him. These were Squadron Commander E F Briggs, Flight Commander J T Babbington, Flight Lieutenant S V Sippe and Flight Sub Lieutenant R P Cannon RNAS,[17] supported by eleven air mechanics. The aircraft arrived on the night of 13 November and work began immediately to assemble them. Unfortunately Shepherd was taken ill and the weather deteriorated with a constant strong easterly wind that would prevent the aircraft from reaching the target and returning. No problems were found assembling the aircraft and Sueter subsequently thanked Avro for their supervision of the aircraft's construction and the quality of their workmanship. There was no standardised bomb-carrying rack at the time but Avro mechanics designed and fitted racks to these aircraft which worked well enough. On 21 November the weather improved sufficiently for the strike to take place and at 09.30 the aircraft were brought out of the shed and lined up on the western side of the airfield where their engines were run up and bomb-release mechanisms tested. These were completed successfully and the aircraft armed, after which they took off at intervals of five minutes. Briggs was first in 873, followed by Babbington in 875 and Sippe in 874. Cannon had difficulty taking off and his aircraft suffered a broken tailskid which caused him to abort the mission.

The three aircraft followed each other along the Rhine valley at a height of about 5000ft. For much of the time they were able to see each other in the clear air and they arrived over the western tip of Lake Constance where they let down to only about 10ft above the water so that there was less chance of them being seen from the German shore. When they estimated they were about five miles from the target they climbed to 1200ft. Sippe subsequently described how he saw anti-aircraft shells bursting around 873 ahead of him as it neared the target. At half a mile from the target he positively identified the airship sheds and dived to 700ft, noting several hundred men lined up to the right of the shed. He dropped his first bomb early, hoping to put the gunners around the enclosure off their aim and then two more into the airship shed. The fourth failed to release. During all this time he was under heavy fire from anti-aircraft guns, machine guns and rifles. He continued his dive and evaded the gunfire flying north at low level and then turned back to try and release his hung-up bomb on the waterside shed. It would still not release and so he turned to the west at low level over the lake and began his flight back to Belfort where he landed at 13.50. An independent account of the strike was given by a Swiss engineer who watched it from his hotel window near the Zeppelin factory. He described how he saw bombs fall on the sheds which badly damaged one airship and destroyed the gasworks which exploded, sending huge flames into the sky. He counted nine bombs which fell within an area of 700 yards around the centre of the factory. The three British aircraft were said by several onlookers to have manoeuvred at such speed that there appeared to be a larger number of them in the

Avro 504 number 873 in closer detail. The four 20lb bombs can just be seen on their rack near the trailing edge of the lower wing. The men to the right appear to be in French Army working dress. (Author's collection)

strike force but the defenders were not completely taken by surprise. A machine-gun section succeeded in shooting down Squadron Commander Briggs in number 874 but he managed to carry out a successful forced landing. On clambering out of the aircraft, however, he was attacked by a civilian mob that beat him unconscious. German soldiers soon arrived and took him prisoner, however, and he was taken to Weingarten Hospital where he was treated with respect and care, if not a little admiration for his exploit.

After their return to Belfort the surviving aircraft were dismantled and returned to the UK for further service with other units. Briggs' aircraft, 874, was reportedly patched up and exhibited in Germany. After the strike the Admiralty issued the following communiqué which was quoted by Sueter in *Airmen or Noahs*:

On Saturday 21 November a flight of aeroplanes under the command of Squadron Commander E F Briggs RNAS with Flight Commander Babbington and Flight Lieutenant S V Sippe as pilots flew from French territory to the Zeppelin airship factory at Friedrichshafen. All three pilots in succession flew down to close range under heavy fire from guns, machine guns and rifles and launched their bombs according to instructions. Commander Briggs is reported to have been shot down wounded and taken to hospital as a prisoner. Both the other officers have returned safely to French territory though their machines were damaged by gunfire. They reported positively that all their bombs reached their objective, and that serious damage was done to the Zeppelin factory. This flight of 250 miles, which penetrated 120 miles into Germany across mountainous country in difficult weather conditions constitutes, with the attack, a fine feat of arms.

On 25 November Sueter passed on a message from the new First Sea Lord, Admiral Fisher, who asked Sueter 'to express to all concerned his high appreciation of the service rendered both by the officers who carried out the recent daring raid on Lake Constance and also by the officers of the Air Service in general'.

Strike from the Sea

After the fall of Antwerp the Eastchurch Wing was concentrated at Dunkirk and flew reconnaissance sorties for the Army in what became known as the First Battle of Ypres. By then Churchill was already pressing for the three recently-converted seaplane carriers to be used to launch a strike from the sea against the airship base believed to be near Cuxhaven. The Admiralty's original intention for these vessels had been for them to operate with the Grand Fleet based at Scapa Flow to provide an aerial scouting force but after their modification they were allocated to the Harwich Force under the command of Commodore Tyrwhitt to support his cruisers and destroyers during their frequent operations in the southern North Sea. Tyrwhitt had been summoned to the Admiralty for a planning session with Churchill and Prince Louis of Battenburg on 22 October. Vice Admiral Sir Doveton Sturdee, the Chief of Staff, was also present but Sueter was not.[18] The plan that emerged was based on an earlier, unsuccessful, surface operation by the Harwich Force with the addition of the three seaplane carriers and one can deduce Churchill's enthusiasm from the fact that it was to be acted upon almost immediately. The Force sailed at 05.00 on 24 October to arrive at the planned launch position at dawn on 25 October.[19] The weather, which had been good at first, deteriorated through the night and by dawn the force encountered fog and torrential rain that made it impossible for the seaplanes to take off and the strike was aborted.

Tyrwhitt had spoken enthusiastically about the operation in conversation with Churchill but he was bitterly disappointed with its cancellation, unfairly blaming 'those idiots' of the air service and declaring himself 'sick to death of everything connected with aviation'.[20] He was not the first to imagine in those early days that aircraft could easily carry out every task that was envisaged for them but practicality returned during a further meeting with Churchill on 27 October in which the failure and potential future naval air operations were discussed at length. Churchill's own flying lessons had given him practical knowledge to add to his burning enthusiasm and Tyrwhitt left him eager to have another attempt at what he now called the 'aerial game'. As autumn replaced summer it became obvious that the number of occasions on which North Sea weather conditions would allow seaplanes to take off would be limited and Churchill was among the first to realise that wheeled aircraft launched from platforms on ships would stand a better chance of getting airborne. On 26 October he minuted Sueter advocating immediate action to procure long barges from which aircraft could be launched by an accelerating windlass. On completion of their mission the aircraft would return and ditch alongside the warship towing the barge for the aircrew to be rescued. Whilst this idea could be said to contain the genesis of the flush-deck aircraft carrier, development was needed and the idea was of little use in the short-term imperative to strike at the Zeppelin sheds. There were further delays as the Harwich Force was involved in a series of operations and then, on 28 October 1914, Prince Louis of Battenburg resigned as First Sea Lord after an unjust campaign against him in the press because of his German ancestry. He was replaced by Lord Fisher who focused his attention on other matters after the battle of Coronel and the subsequent dispatch of two battlecruisers under Sturdee to hunt down and destroy Von Spee's Asiatic Squadron. When attention did return to the proposed strike against the Cuxhaven Zeppelins, another element was added to it by Admiralty planners who saw a chance of drawing the High Sea Fleet into action. The air attack was still part of the scheme but had become secondary to the overall plan which now involved the Grand and Battlecruiser Fleets sailing in support of the Harwich Force, albeit at a considerable distance, to destroy any German force lured out by the activities of the seaplane carriers and their aircraft. Admiral Jellicoe was told of the plan on 20 November and his ships sailed at dusk on 22 November to rendezvous in the North Sea. The Harwich Force sailed on the morning of 23 November but that evening the Admiralty cancelled the air element of the operation for no very clear reason. Jellicoe subsequently wrote that 'it was thought that the enemy had a force present in the Bight which would be too strong for our detached vessels.'[21] On the other hand, Churchill said that 'in the weather prevailing the seaplanes could hardly get off the water'.[22] Neither comment appears to make any sense; Jellicoe described the weather on the morning of 24 November when the strike would have been launched as 'fine and bright with high visibility' and Tyrwhitt described it as 'lovely, calm and clear'. Surely the presence of an enemy force was exactly what the Admiralty planners wanted, a chance for the Grand Fleet to bring enemy surface forces to action and destroy them. Why else was it there if not to support the 'detached vessels' in a surface action? German seaplanes had no difficulty taking off from their base at Heligoland after the smoke from British warships was seen and they attacked the light cruiser *Liverpool*, albeit without success. This was the first time in history that a British warship had been attacked by aircraft.

The scheme that was eventually carried out was known as Plan Y and involved the Harwich Force under Commodore Tyrwhitt with two light cruisers and eight destroyers of the Third Flotilla escorting *Engadine, Riviera* and *Empress* each of which had three seaplanes embarked. Commodore Keyes' submarine force was deployed to intercept any German ships that tried to interfere and to rescue aircrew who came down in the sea, making this the first use of a significant combat search and rescue capability in support of a strike operation. Like its predecessor, this plan brought together a number of objectives and, although the destruction of the airships in their sheds remained primary, importance was also given to reconnaissance of enemy ships in harbour and the possibility of bringing part of the High Sea Fleet to action if it sortied. To achieve the latter aim the Grand and Battlecruiser Fleets sailed to give support but in practical terms but they were too far away to give immediate assistance to Commodore Tyrwhitt's force if it was needed.

The Harwich Force sailed at 05.00 on Thursday 24 December 1914 and arrived at the launch position at 06.00 on Christmas Day, 25 December. The weather conditions were good with a clear sky and calm sea but it was bitterly cold. The seaplanes were run up and hoisted onto the water by 07.00. Seven of the nine aircraft got airborne but two failed to overcome the suction effect of the sea surface on their floats and failed to get airborne.[23] They were hoisted back onto their ships.

The three Folders were part of a batch of four which had been delivered in May 1914 and which had taken part in the Royal Review in July. They were basically improved versions of the original Folder that had operated from *Hermes* in 1913 with a wingspan of 67ft and a 160hp Gnome rotary engine which gave a speed of

Short Folder number 119 which was flown on the Cuxhaven strike by Flight Commander R P Ross RNAS. (Author's collection)

Aircraft embarked for the Cuxhaven strike

119	Short Folder	*Engadine*	Flight Commander R P Ross RNAS – pilot
120	Short Folder	*Engadine*	Flight Lieutenant A J Miley RNAS – pilot
122	Short Folder	*Engadine*	Flight Commander A B Gaskell RNAS – pilot
135	Short 135	*Riviera*	Flight Commander F E T Hewlett RNAS – pilot
136	Short 135	*Riviera*	Flight Commander C F Kilner RNAS – pilot
			Lieutenant R Erskine-Childers RNVR – observer
811	Short 74	*Riviera*	Flight Lieutenant C H K Edmonds RNAS
812	Short 74	*Empress*	Flight Lieutenant R J Bone RNAS – pilot
			Air Mechanic Waters – observer
814	Short 74	*Empress*	Flight Sub Lieutenant V G Blackburn RNAS – pilot
			Chief Petty Officer J Bell – observer
815	Short 74	*Empress*	Flight Commander D A Oliver RNAS – pilot
			Chief Petty Officer Budds – observer

78mph at the maximum all-up weight of 3040lbs. They were designed to carry a 14in torpedo on crutches between the floats but had been modified to carry three 20lb Hale bombs instead. As in other contemporary RNAS aircraft, the bombs were released from their carrier by extracting pins at the end of cables which led to toggles in the cockpit. Numbers 135 and 136 were a batch of two aircraft derived from the Folder with a slightly smaller wingspan at 54ft 6in but a greater maximum all-up weight of 3700lbs. Number 135 had a 135hp single-row Canton-Unne rotary engine but 136 had an impressive 200hp double-row Canton-Unne engine, making it arguably the best naval aircraft at the time.[24] The four Type 74s came from a batch of eight and were only delivered to the RNAS a few days before the strike. Their exact dimensions have been lost over the years but they had 100hp Gnome

Short Folder number 120 being manhandled into the water from a slipway at the RNAS Felixstowe. (Author's collection)

rotary engines and could carry the same bombload as the Folders. When not embarked, the aircraft operated from the RN air station at Felixstowe on the opposite side of the estuary of the River Orwell from Harwich.

The aircraft and personnel that took part in the strike had not been formed into a single unit, they were brought together for the operation and represented the state-of-the-art in December 1914. Both aircraft and aircrew came together because they were available, taking priority over the expansion of coastal patrol organisations at naval air stations. Squadron Commander Cecil L'Estrange Malone RNAS was only 24 years old in 1914 but was appointed in command of the aircraft, the men who were to fly and maintain them and the seaplane carrier *Engadine*. He was also the senior officer in tactical command of the three seaplane carriers and was given the task of planning the air element of the Cuxhaven strike, a task he fulfilled with thoroughness and efficiency. The other seaplane carriers

were also commanded by qualified pilots, Flight Lieutenant E D M Robertson RNAS in *Riviera* and Flight Lieutenant F W Bowhill RNAS in *Empress*.[25] Malone was helped during the planning stage by Lieutenant Erskine Childers RNVR, author of *The Riddle of the Sands*, who was able to use his unique knowledge of the German coast to good effect. He prepared the charts that were used by the pilots to navigate their way to the estimated position of the Zeppelin base they had been given by British intelligence sources.

Dawn on that Christmas Day was bitterly cold and the mechanics had great difficulty in starting the aircrafts' engines. Edmonds' number 811 was idling while it lay on the water after being started by CPO Mechanic Wright and Air Mechanic

Flight Commander R P Ross RNAS photographed later in the Great War after he had been promoted to Wing Commander. (Author's collection)

Kent but the engine stopped after they were taken off the aircraft's floats by boat. Both men bravely dived into the freezing water and swam back to the aircraft in order to swing the propeller and get the engine started again. At 06.54 Malone judged the light to be sufficient for take-off and ordered the preparatory signal, two black balls, to be hoisted on *Engadine*'s foremast indicating that the launch was to start in five minutes. The less-powerful Folders were to take off first, followed after a further five minutes by the others. The lower black ball was hauled down as the signal for the Folders to take off but all three had difficulty, probably because their engines were not yet sufficiently warmed up. Gaskell's number 122 failed to get airborne, either because his engine was not developing full power or because his floats would not break free of the surface suction. Malone decided to delay a further five minutes before hoisting down the second ball to give the remaining engines time to warm up but 135, 814 and 815 actually took off before it was lowered, followed by the others except for 812 which suffered a complete engine failure. At 07.22 Malone ordered the 'negative' to be hoisted to end the take-off and both aircraft that had failed to get airborne were hoisted back into their carriers. Far from being helpful, the light wind and calm sea had actually made the take-off more difficult for the heavily-loaded seaplanes forcing some of them to run at full power for over four minutes to get airborne and using up a great deal of fuel.

Individual aircraft took different times to get off the water and they flew at differing speeds so they soon lost sight of each other and it took them about an hour to reach the German coast. Some saw Zeppelin *L 6* to the west and others thought they saw *L 5* further to the west as well, an indication that the airships were not at their base, but as the aircraft went 'feet dry' over the coast they all encountered a thick ground fog that obscured everything except the land immediately beneath them. Most pilots descended in an attempt to make out features that might lead them to the supposed Cuxhaven airship base. Hewlett in number 135 encountered fog earlier than most and came down to 200ft over the sea where he saw the masts of cruisers that opened fire on him. Turning inland he found nothing and, after losing sight of the ground at 200ft turned back out to sea. He saw an airship emerge from cloud 1500ft above him at about 08.40 but had no way of attacking it and so, with no target for his bombs, he set off for the Harwich Force at its briefed recovery position to the west of Heligoland. Ross in number 119 found the mouth of the Elbe at 07.40 and saw ships that fired at him before the fog closed in. He descended to 150ft and cruised about over sand dunes finding no trace of the target but discovered that his fuel pressure system was leaking so badly that none was being transferred from the aircraft's main to its gravity tank. This gave him less than 15 minutes endurance and so he turned out sea and saw what he thought was a submarine diving and dropped a bomb on it which failed to explode.

He then alighted on the water and worked on the pump which he managed to repair sufficiently to feed fuel into the gravity tank, after which he took off and headed for the rendezvous with the carriers. Miley in 120 found a railway line after crossing the coast and searched for the target without success before turning to carry out the alternate reconnaissance of Wilhelmshaven. The fog prevented him from finding it but he did fly over the Jade, Weser and Schillig Roads, coming under fire from moored ships as he did so. Oliver in 815 also found the railway line and spent 30 minutes searching for the airship base without success. Turning towards the sea he flew over the Weser and saw two cruisers and a number of destroyers which opened fire on him and he eventually released his bombs over a row of sheds on Langeoog Island without observing the result. There were no military targets on the island so his target was probably a line of fishermen's cottages which took on a more sinister aspect in the poor visibility.

The only pilot to bomb an important target was Edmonds in 811. Like others he found the railway line and followed it south for a few miles but not far enough; the

Flight Commander D A Oliver RNAS who flew Short 74 number 815 on the Cuxhaven strike wearing his warm flying jacket and boots. (Author's collection)

airship base was actually at Nordholz about eight miles, or six minutes flying time, south of Cuxhaven. Turning west for the coast he saw the two cruisers in the Weser estuary, now known to be the *Stralsund* and *Graudenz,* and attacked them in a shallow dive releasing his three bombs at an estimated 800ft. The Germans fired at him with quick-firing cannon, machine guns and rifles. The nearest bomb detonated about 200 yards on the beam of *Graudenz* and the others fell unseen by Edmonds or the Germans. On his way to the recovery position he flew over the Schillig Roads and observed three battlecruisers, several other warships and an armoured cruiser he correctly identified as the *Roon*. Blackburn in 814 also sighted the railway line and searched for his target in the fog without finding it. Like several other pilots he believed that he was under 'extremely hot anti-aircraft fire', especially, in his case, on the outskirts of Wilhelmshaven. He dropped two bombs on what he took to be a battery that had him under fire and his third on the centre of the city. Kilner, with Erskine Childers as his observer, descended to 200ft in the fog and searched for the target without success but suffered from a misfiring engine with revolutions dropping to as few as 800 rather than the normal 1300. Prudently they turned for the coast and the misfiring stopped as they cleared the fog. They flew over the Schillig Roads where the engine began to misfire again but they made their way through the lines of anchored ships at 1500ft under intense and accurate anti-aircraft fire 'with excellent fusing which caused frequent bursts which caused damage to an undercarriage strut and severed two rigging wires'. Notwithstanding this Childers was able to identify the battlecruisers *Seydlitz, Moltke* and *Von der Tann* and the armoured cruiser *Roon*, together with numerous other warships, some of which he miss-identified as battleships of the *Deutschland* and *Braunschweig* classes which were actually not there on that day. Surprisingly, they decided not to bomb any of these ships as they felt that a hit would be unlikely and their weapons might be better employed against a submarine base they thought to be on the island of Wangeroog.

The fog that had hampered the British pilots so effectively also prevented the Germans from building a coherent picture of what was happening. Nordholz airship base had been clear of fog at dawn but it closed in shortly after Zeppelin *L 5* was launched. An aeroplane engine was heard at 08.20 and during a momentary clear patch 10 minutes later a seaplane was seen at an altitude of about 1000ft which appeared to head for the airship shed and men on the ground opened fire on it with machine guns and rifles. It then appeared to change direction and head for the gas plant that manufactured and stored the base's hydrogen supply and dropped two bombs that fell into a nearby wooded area before disappearing back into a fog bank. The subsequent official German naval history therefore correctly identified Nordholz as the target of this strike and described this aircraft as deliberately attacking the base's gas plant. No British pilot had claimed to locate or drop bombs on the base and only ten bombs had been dropped on specific targets. Malone's briefing had included permission to jettison bombs over the land at the pilot's discretion if the primary target was not located in order to reduce weight and, therefore, save fuel to increase endurance for the return flight. No pilot reported doing so in his report but possibly they considered that jettisoning unused bombs was too trivial to mention. It would be reasonable to assume, therefore, that the bombs which the Germans believed to have been deliberately aimed at the hydrogen plant in order to limit Zeppelin operations from Nordholz for the immediate future were in fact dropped at random by a pilot who failed to see the base, perhaps either Ross or Miley. After more than a century since the operation we will never know for certain but it is interesting to reflect that although the strike must be regarded as a failure, it came much closer to success than anyone in the RNAS realised at the time.

After the aircraft had been launched, the Harwich Force steamed west to pass about 10 miles north of Heligoland and then turned south to be in a position about 20 miles north of the island of Norderney for the recovery after 10.00. The ships adopted a cruising formation ordered by Tyrwhitt with his own cruiser *Arethusa* at the centre of a line of eight destroyers, four on each beam. *Engadine* took station 3 cables astern of *Arethusa* with *Empress* on her port beam at 5 cables and *Riviera* a similar distance to starboard. The cruiser *Undaunted* took up a position 1.5 cables astern of *Engadine*.[26] This tight formation was intended to facilitate control of the force by flag signals and give visual warning of enemy surface forces ahead of the line of advance. Tyrwhitt ordered 20 knots but *Empress* struggled to maintain it due, Lieutenant Bowhill her commanding officer believed, to having coal of inferior quality in her bunkers. RNAS mechanics were used to back up the hard-pressed stokers shovelling coal into the furnaces but she gradually dropped astern of the force. From about 07.30 a number of German airships and seaplanes located the force and attacked it. Zeppelin *L 6* shadowed the force but thought that the seaplane carriers might be minelayers; a location report was prepared but the radio broke down at this critical point and no report was ever transmitted. A succession of seaplanes had no difficulty in finding the force after taking off from their base at Heligoland and carried out bombing attacks but failed to score any hits. The ships all carried out zig-zag manoeuvres to spoil the pilots' aim, probably the first time that warships had done so to counter an air attack. *L 6* attacked *Empress,* which was by then fairly isolated from the rest of the formation, at about 09.30 but failed to score a hit. Bowhill continued to zig-zag while his ship's 12pdr guns and a number of men with rifles engaged the airship without causing any significant damage, while *Undaunted* dropped back to support her. Several of the cruiser's shells burst close to *L 6* which jettisoned the remainder of its bombs to reduce weight and climbed into the cloud cover. They found that as the airship flew overhead to aim its bombs, its rudders were plainly visible and Bowhill was quick to turn to port when he saw the airship begin to turn to starboard and vice versa, an effective way of spoiling its aim. Still unable to transmit an enemy report it flew back to Schillig Roads and dropped a written report of the British force's position course and speed onto the cruiser *Roon*. It played no further part in the action.

Although the activities on that day are generally referred to as the Cuxhaven Raid, they could fairly be described as a battle since opposing forces exchanged fire. Surprisingly, considering that a lightly-armed British force had cruised close to the main bases of the German High Sea Fleet for over six hours, enemy surface forces played no part in the action at all. This was just as well as the Grand Fleet was over 100 miles away and the Battlecruiser Fleet about 60 miles; too far away to intervene in time if a surface action had developed. However, German naval airships and seaplanes had located and attacked the Harwich Force and one enemy seaplane had remained airborne for over five hours, still a remarkable achievement in 1914 and another attacked what it believed to be a British submarine at periscope depth. German U-boats had also been involved; between 10.45 and 12.15 *U 22*, *U 30* and *U 32* had all attempted gain firing solutions but were frustrated by the frequent British alterations of course, high speed and the dense funnel smoke issuing from their hard-worked boilers. Only *U 20* got within effective range but scored no hits.

The aircraft recovery had been carefully planned but nothing like it had ever been attempted before. The aircraft were to go 'feet wet' at the Schillig Roads and fly west to seaward of the island chain off the German coast until they reached Norderney and then turn north to find the carriers 20 miles out to sea.[27] The aircraft embarked in *Riviera* had been fuelled for four hours' flight but those in the other ships had been fuelled for only three to save a significant amount of weight but this proved to be insufficient for them to get back to their ships. Kilner and Childers in 136 continued to suffer engine problems but located *Riviera* and landed close to her. Edmonds arrived about five minutes later in 811 and the ship only had to heave-to for 10 minutes to hoist in both aircraft at about 10.15. Ross in 119 was desperately short of fuel as he turned north from Norderney but saw Keyes' destroyers *Lurcher* and *Firedrake* 10 miles to the north of the island; he landed near the former and she towed the aircraft north to intercept *Engadine*, arriving close to her at about 10.30. These were the only three aircraft to be recovered.

The submarine *E11*, commanded by Lieutenant Commander M E Nasmith RN, was submerged about six miles north of Norderney when he saw a seaplane through the periscope. It says something for the new RNAS markings that even though the aircraft was at 1200ft he was able to identify it as British and he surfaced. The aircraft was Miley's 120 and he too was almost out of fuel. British submarines were marked with red and white bands around the conning tower at this time so that Miley was in turn able to identify the boat as British and he alighted alongside it. Miley clambered into the submarine which began to tow his aircraft towards the Harwich Force at about 09.50. However, shortly afterwards lookouts spotted an airship closing from the east and a submarine on the surface approaching bows-on so that it could not easily be identified. To add to Nasmith's problems two further British seaplanes closed him. The first of these was Blackburn in 814 who had flown past some minutes earlier but turned back to seek help when he failed to sight the Harwich Force to the north. He landed near the submarine but his damaged strut collapsed as he taxied closer, leaving the aircraft with its engine underwater and its tail in the air. Oliver in 815 landed soon afterwards having also failed to locate the Harwich Force and nearly run out of fuel. At this point the submarine was seen to dive, an action that had to be interpreted as hostile although it was in fact the British *D6* commanded by Lieutenant Commander R C Halahan RN, who was one of several submariners who had also qualified as a pilot, further demonstrating the synergy between the two branches and their new forms of warfare. He had been on his way to assist *E11* but dived as saw the airship getting closer.

The airship was *L 5* which had seen the submarine and was closing to attack it. Faced with imminent attacks, as he saw it, from above and below the surface Nasmith cast off 120's tow, manoeuvred sufficiently close to 815 for the crew to jump onto the casing and ordered Blackburn and Bell to swim for it quickly. Once the aircrew were on board he opened fire on the seaplane's floats with a machine gun brought up for the purpose from below and Oliver joined in with his pistol. Hoping to have left the aircraft in a sinking condition he then dived. *L 5* dropped two bombs which shook both submarines but damaged neither. According to his subsequent report, Nasmith took his boat down to rest on the seabed and the five aircrew joined the submariners' Christmas lunch complete with turkey and plum pudding.

At 12.15 the Harwich Force withdrew at its best speed to the west, leaving Keyes and his submarines to cover them for a few more hours. The fate of Hewlett's 135 was still unknown, however, and he was feared lost. By 09.25 he had been uncertain of his position over the sea when his engine began to misfire badly but, fortunately, he saw a small fishing boat flying the Dutch flag and alighted near it. He punched holes in the floats and left the aircraft sinking after he was taken off but the vessel, the *Maria van Hattem*, spent a further week at sea fishing before returning to Ijmuiden on 31 December where he made contact with the British vice consul. His return to the UK was soon agreed by the neutral Dutch authorities who accepted that he was a shipwrecked mariner who had been rescued on the high seas.

Although the strike failed to achieve the destruction of the airship sheds, it pointed towards the future of naval warfare. A small British task force had operated in three dimensions and fought the enemy above and below the surface of the sea, a form of warfare that that was to become all too familiar after 1939 but was so novel in 1914 that its full implications were not yet understood. The RNAS had shown, however, that it was already capable of playing a limited part in naval operations that spread sea power across enemy-controlled waters and inland.

5 Technology and Technique

The BE 2a aeroplane number 50 that Wing Commander Samson flew to Dunkirk in August 1914 was one of two examples built by Hewlett & Blondeau Ltd at their Omnia Works in Clapham during 1913.[1] It was transferred from the RFC to the embryonic RNAS in February 1914 and it effectively became Samson's personal machine from then until the end of the Dardanelles campaign when, considered unfit to transport, it was broken up when 3 Wing prepared to return to the UK.[2] It had a 70hp Renault air-cooled, in-line upright 90-degree V-8 engine which proved reliable in service although the rich fuel/air mixture used to assist cooling meant that it was less efficient than newer engines.[3] The Renault aero-engine concern was actually British, although the parent company was French, and the engines were designed and manufactured by Renault Ltd at their West Brompton factory. The BE 2a could be flown as either a two-seater or a single-seater with an extra fuel tank and the disposable load was determined by the difference between the empty weight of 1274lbs and the maximum take-off weight of 1600lbs. BE 2s had no standardised armament and pilots and observers carried rifles and pistols for use against other aircraft. Samson and his squadron initially pioneered the use of bombs up to 110lbs for strike operations, some of which were 6in shells fitted with stabilising fins. The type had a maximum speed of 70mph and could climb to 7000ft in 35 minutes; service ceiling was 10,000ft.

1914 was a year of dynamic progress, even before the stimulus of war, and aircraft of increased power and performance were delivered from a number of manufacturers. In September 1914 Short delivered number 136 to the RNAS which was used in the strike against Cuxhaven described in the previous chapter. It was the latest in the Short 'Folder' series and had a 200hp engine designed by the Frenchman Henri Salmson for the Swiss engineers George Canton and Pierre Unne. The version fitted in number 136 was a 2M7 14-cylinder, two-row, water-cooled radial engine giving 200hp at 1300rpm, manufactured under licence in the UK, one of 300 made by the Dudbridge Iron works Ltd at Stroud in Gloucester-shire.[4] This powerful engine gave number 136 a maximum take-off weight of 3700lbs; more than double that of the BE 2a. It survived operations in the North

Sea and was allocated to the seaplane carrier *Ark Royal* at Sheerness in February 1915 for use in the Dardanelles campaign. At the time it was considered 'quite the best' aircraft in that ship and was the only one capable of operating in marginal weather.[5] Even this increase in performance was not considered good enough now that the Admiralty had seen the value of aircraft for strike and long-range patrol operations and in December 1914 the Admiralty issued an imaginative staff requirement for a twin-engined, land-based aircraft with a crew of two pilots and capable of carrying six 112lb bombs over a significant radius of action. It was to have a speed in excess of 72mph.

Commodore Sueter's 'Bloody Paralyser' of an Aeroplane

In 1913 the *Daily Mail* offered a prize of £10,000 to be won by the first pilot to fly across the Atlantic. Frederick Handley Page designed a large aeroplane, the L/200, for the project but the war stopped work on it. However, the design gave Handley Page the confidence to design large aircraft for long-range applications[6] and a sketch design was shown to Sueter. He saw the merit of the design but believed that the original specification, advanced as it had seemed, could be further improved to produce 'a bloody paralyser' of an aeroplane. The Air Department ordered a prototype and an initial twelve production examples of the new aircraft, designated the Handley Page 0/100. It was to have been powered by two Sunbeam

Squadron Commander Spenser-Grey DSO RNAS arriving at RNAS Coudekerque in Handley Page 0/100 number 3116 on 2 April 1917. It was the first of the type to arrive at this airfield where it was allocated to 7(N) Squadron and given the individual code B3. (Author's collection)

water-cooled engines, each of 150hp, but while the prototype was under construction in 1915, Rolls-Royce produced a new engine, later named the Eagle. It
was a 12-cylinder, liquid-cooled, 60-degree V-12 engine[7] capable of delivering 225hp
at 1600rpm. One hundred and four Eagle 1 engines were built to an Admiralty
contract, produced in both left-hand and right-hand turning versions to counteract
torque when fitted in the 0/100. They were fitted in armoured nacelles placed
between the biplane wings and supported by struts with radiators at the front and
fuel tanks at the rear. The engine first ran in February 1915 and, although the first
example did not fly until December 1915, their specification shows the pace of
development forced on manufacturers by the Admiralty as the war entered its
second year and that the part that aircraft could play in naval warfare was
appreciated. The 0/100 was to have an empty weight of just over 8000lbs and a
maximum take-off weight slightly in excess of 14,000lbs when it entered service
and was to carry up to sixteen 112lb bombs.

An Advanced Seaplane Armed with a Torpedo

Impressive as the Handley Page 0/100 was to become, it could not be operated from
a ship at sea and the Admiralty regarded the need to acquire a seaplane capable of
being armed with a torpedo as an urgent priority. Longmore had demonstrated
that a torpedo could be carried and released from a modified Short Folder in July
1914 but a more powerful aircraft would be needed to use such a weapon
operationally. The Short 166 was designed and produced in small numbers,
effectively a development of number 135. Although fitted with torpedo release gear,
none ever used the weapon operationally although several were embarked in *Ark
Royal* during the Dardanelles campaign. Sueter sent for Horace Short in late 1914
and explained that a larger, more powerful and robust aircraft would be required
and the result was a new aircraft designated by the Admiralty as the Type 184.[8]
Less advanced in concept than the 0/100, it was a biplane powered by a single
Sunbeam Gurkha engine rated at 225hp at 2000rpm. It was a 12-cylinder, liquid-
cooled V-12 engine with a prominent radiator on top of the fuselage just forward
of the cockpit where it partially obscured the pilot's view ahead. Engine production
took place at Sunbeam's works at Wolverhampton where seventy-four engines of
this type were made for use by the RNAS in the Short 184, before production
shifted to more advanced types, like the Gurkha all named after tribes. Early Type
184s had an empty weight of 3798lbs and a maximum take-off weight of 5100lbs.
A two-seater, it could carry a single 14in torpedo between the floats held in place
a quick-release mechanism. Alternatively, it could carry a single 500lb bomb or
four 112lb bombs and there was a fitting in the observer's cockpit for a Lewis gun
with several 47-round trays of ammunition.

Short 184 number N1622 being lowered onto the River Dart from HMS *Riviera*. It is armed with what appear to be three 100lb light case bombs fitted to the weapons carrier under the fuselage and is evidently about to carry out an anti-submarine patrol. This particular aircraft was manufactured by S E Saunders, a sub-contractor at East Cowes on the Isle of Wight, under Admiralty contract A.S. 1247/1 and delivered to Calshot in 1917. After embarkation in *Riviera* it served for a while at RNAS Newlyn and was finally written off charge in 1919. (Philip Jarrett collection)

Progress with Lighter-than-Air Craft

Throughout the autumn of 1914 German U-boats became an increasing threat in British coastal waters, sinking the cruiser *Pathfinder* in September and the battleship *Formidable* at the beginning of January 1915. At the end of January 1915 *U 21*, which had sunk *Pathfinder*, surfaced off Barrow-in-Furness and audaciously shelled the Vickers airship shed with its deck gun, fortunately causing little damage. The Admiralty's renewed interest in rigid airships had led to further contracts but these were unlikely to produce hardware in the short term. Realising that a critical situation could develop, Fisher called a meeting at the Admiralty on 28 February 1915 attended by Wing Commander Masterman RNAS, an airship expert, and other senior RNAS officers together with representatives of Airships Ltd and Armstrong Whitworth. The First Sea Lord said that a new type of airship was urgently required to search coastal waters for submarines; the basic requirement was for a small airship with a speed of between 40 and 50mph, able to carry a crew of two with stowage for bombs up to a total weight of 160lbs, W/T equipment and fuel for eight hours' flight. A maximum ceiling of about 5000ft was desirable but above all else, the design was to be simple and robust, both to

An early production SS airship. Note the BE 2c fuselage used as the control car, retaining the same 70hp Renault engine as the aeroplane. The object that looks like a tube sloping upwards just aft of the propeller took some of the thrust to keep the envelope inflated at low pressure to maintain its shape. The hydrogen gas used to give lift was contained in a number of gasbags secured inside the envelope. (Author's collection)

hasten production and allow aircrew to be trained as quickly as possible.[9] The new airships were to be designated as Submarine Scouts (SS), and were to be ready as soon as practically possible, weeks rather than months. The two firms were instructed to put forward tenders and the RNAS representatives were told to put forward their own proposals.

Ernest Willows of Airships Ltd designed a contender which the firm built by the end of March, designated *SS 2* but the car contained a single engine that drove two swivelling propellers through three gearboxes which would have been expensive,

Wing Commander N F Usborne RNAS, the commanding officer of RNAS Kingsnorth, photographed when he was a Lieutenant Commander RN. (Guy Warner collection)

slow and complicated to manufacture and it was not taken forward. Armstrong Whitworth produced a prototype, designated *SS 27*, that was considered viable for longer-term development but which did not meet Fisher's requirement for extreme urgency. It is a measure of the quality of those serving in the RNAS that the Service was able to put forward its own, successful contender, designated *SS 1*. Wing Commander N F Usborne, the commanding officer of RNAS Kingsnorth, Flight Lieutenant Cave-Brown-Cave and F M Green of the Royal Aircraft Factory joined to put forward a solution that was simple, effective and which made use of existing materials to minimise the amount of design work required. The spare 35,000ft^3 envelope of *Airship Number 2*, the Willows, had been used for training, was removed from Farnborough and taken to RNAS Kingsnorth where it was attached to the fuselage of a BE 2c aeroplane fitted with a 70hp Renault engine. The BE's wings were removed and by early March *SS 1* was ready for flight testing. One or two minor snags were found – for instance the nose was driven in by air pressure at speed – but these were easily corrected.[10] On 18 March 1915 Flight Lieutenant W Hicks RNAS carried out a final trial and, less than three weeks after the requirement briefing, *SS 1* was declared ready for operational service. Fisher is said to have noted that the RNAS had done what he had asked of it but now he wanted forty more airships like it! Production SS airships differed in having slightly larger envelopes containing two ballonets with a total capacity of 60,000ft^3 of hydrogen. They were 143ft long and had a diameter of 28ft. Short Brothers subsequently offered another design, designated *SS 3* but it was not taken forward. *SS 4* to *SS 26* were built to much the same design as *SS 1*. *SS 28* to *SS 39* were built to a revised design by the Airship Company using a Maurice Farman aeroplane fuselage. The Armstrong Whitworth design, *SS 27*, had slightly better endurance than *SS 1* and several repeat examples, numbered *SS 39A* to *SS 49* were constructed, the last two examples being sold to France.

Another remarkable invention was the airship-plane designed by Squadron Commander N F Usborne RNAS in 1915. It was already apparent that by dumping its ballast a Zeppelin could out-climb any fighter in British service to evade interception. and Usborne devised the simple but brilliant expedient of suspending an armed BE 2c under an airship envelope similar to that adopted for the SS series. The idea was that it could patrol the skies near London as an airship then, when a Zeppelin was seen, it could dump its own ballast to climb quickly above it. The aircraft would already have its engine running and once in position it could be slipped to carry out an interception, opening the gas-bag valves as it departed so that the envelope would eventually fall to earth. Usborne wrote to Admiral Fisher[11] that 'the idea is to substitute a complete aeroplane for the car normally carried by a small airship. This aeroplane will be attached in such a way

AP-1 photographed at RNAS Kingsnorth in 1915. (Guy Warnert collection)

as it can slip itself from the envelope once it has established itself above the Zeppelin.' Designated the *AP-1*, the concept was greeted with some enthusiasm within the Admiralty and the first example was flown without separation by Flight Commander W C Hicks RNAS in August 1915. The first separation with no crew in the BE 2c was carried out successfully on 19 February 1916 and permission was given for a manned separation trial.

This flight, using BE 2c number 989 as the aircraft component of the *AP-1* assembly, took place on 21 February 1916 with Usborne and Squadron Commander W P de Courcy Ireland, the commanding officer of Yarmouth RN air station at the controls. They took off from Kingsnorth and climbed in a series of circles to 4000ft watched by a group of officers on the ground. Unfortunately *AP-1* apparently exceeded its equilibrium height and gas was vented off, causing instability which resulted in the premature detachment of the forward suspension cables. The nose of the aircraft dropped, overstressing the remaining two wires which subsequently failed. It is thought that Ireland had unstrapped so that he could climb along the fuselage to release the rear cables but when they failed the aircraft was seen to sideslip and then turn over, throwing Ireland out who fell into the River Medway and was drowned. The BE's controls were probably damaged as the cables parted and although Usborne remained with the aircraft, he failed to recover the situation and crashed into Stroud railway station goods yard. He died on impact and the Admiralty immediately banned any further work on the project. There was inevitably a Board of Enquiry and although its findings have been lost, a supplementary note has survived. It was unsigned but said that 'I cannot speak too highly of Commander Usborne's and Lieutenant Commander Ireland's sacrifices. They were trying to evolve a machine that could compete with Zeppelins and they gave their lives in this endeavour.'

Flying Boats

John C Porte last appeared in Chapter 1 when he was invalided out of the RN and went to work for the Curtiss company in the USA. By 1914 he was a company test pilot and was preparing for an attempt to fly the Atlantic in the Curtiss H 1 'America' when war broke out. He joined the RNAS as a Squadron Commander and was appointed to the naval air station at Felixstowe, persuading the Admiralty as soon as he arrived to purchase two Curtiss H 4 flying boats, allocated numbers 950 and 951, which were delivered in October 1914. They were used mainly for development work by Porte at Felixstowe but 951 did carry out operational patrols against enemy aircraft and submarines in 1915. They were followed by sixty-two production aircraft which were subsequently named the 'Small America' after procurement of the Curtiss H 12 which was known as the 'Large America'. H 4s were powered by a variety of engine types including two Curtiss OX-5s rated at 90hp each; two Anzani rated at 100hp each or two Clerget rated at 110hp each. Wingspan was 72ft with an empty weight of 2992lbs and a maximum take-off weight of 4983lbs. They had a crew of four comprising two pilots and two gunners or engineers. The H 4s were augmented from 1917 by a total of seventy-one H 12 Large Americas which were originally fitted with two 160hp Curtiss engines but these proved inadequate and they were replaced in RNAS service by two Rolls-Royce Eagle 1 engines, each developing 275hp. The engines were constantly updated, however, as more powerful versions became available, the last examples being fitted with 375hp Eagle VIIIs. The H 12 was armed with four Lewis guns on flexible mountings throughout the fuselage with a plentiful supply of ammunition in pre-loaded 47-round trays. Up to four 100lb bombs or two 230lb bombs could be carried on racks fitted under the wings.

Porte was a pioneering advocate of flying boats as offensive weapons[12] and he took an intense interest in the development of techniques and tactics as well as devoting a great deal of time and effort to airframe design. He was appointed to command Felixstowe in 1915 and when he flew the Curtiss boats operationally, he found them to have a weak hull that limited their seaworthiness and, thus,

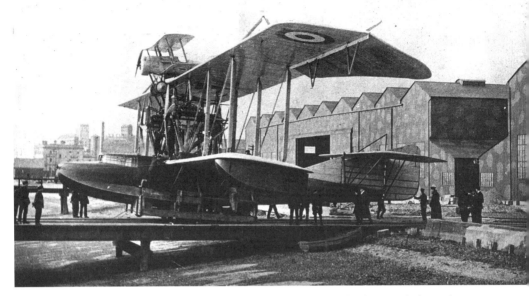

An example of Wing Commander J C Porte RNAS' imaginative design, this photograph shows the composite experiment with Bristol Scout number 3028 mounted on the upper wing of a prototype Porte Baby flying boat at Felixstowe. On 17 May 1916 a trial separation was made in flight at 1000ft over Felixstowe with Flight Lieutenant M J Day RNAS flying the Scout and Porte flying the Baby. The separation was controlled by Day and proved completely successful. The concept behind the experiment was to get the Scout into a position in the eastern North Sea where it could be launched to intercept a Zeppelin if it was encountered. The flying boat could then, in theory, land to rescue the pilot if he came down in the sea. Whilst it had been proved possible, the concept was not taken forward because it was regarded as too cumbersome and dangerous. (Goble Family collection)

operational capability. Assisted by his senior engineer officer, Lieutenant J D Rennie RN, he set about re-designing the hull of the Curtiss H 4 using a succession of aircraft which were rebuilt by the staff at Felixstowe to have a more pronounced vee-shaped bottom with a step near the centre of gravity which helped the aircraft break free of the surface suction on lift-off. Porte's fifth development aircraft, number 3580, had a hull that differed completely from the H 4 both in construction and appearance although it retained the wings and tailplane of the original Curtiss. Since it represented a radical change the boat was at first called the Porte 1 and then officially named the Felixstowe F 1.[13] Its hull was a cross-braced wooden box girder with a vee planing bottom with three steps and longitudinal fins. It proved itself in trials to be superior to its predecessors in every way and the new bow design was found to be especially good at keeping water away from the open cockpit. Unlike the H 4, production Felixstowe F 1s were fitted with 150hp water-cooled Hispano-Suiza engines. Following this success, Porte designed a series of flying boats of more than twice the size of the F 1.

The Evolving Technique of Operating Aircraft at Sea

By the end of 1914 aviation in the RNAS was evolving into three complementary but distinct forms with wheeled fixed-wing aircraft and lighter-than-air craft operating from air stations ashore and seaplanes fitted with floats operating from ships. Flight from ships at sea was proving the most difficult to advance because of the technical problems that had to be overcome but the embarkation of aircraft in *Hermes* during 1913 had shown that it was possible. Operations in the winter of 1914/15 exposed the weakness of the concept of operating seaplanes from the surface of the open sea. Floats added weight to airframes but no commensurate increase in engine power was possible; when the wheeled Sopwith Tabloid was transformed into the float-fitted Schneider, for instance, the three floats and local strengthening added 200lbs to the empty weight of the airframe but the same 100hp Gnome engine was retained. Added weight without added power meant an increase in the distance needed to achieve flying speed and the time taken to reach it and floats had a bigger area, or footprint, in contact with the surface than wheels and thus more drag. This effect could be lessened by using vee-shaped floats like those pioneered by Schwann and his mechanics at Barrow-in-Furness with which the footprint decreased as the aircraft began to lift and a step reduced the float's water contact still further as it lifted. The slab-sided, flat-bottomed floats fitted to most Short, Sopwith and, later, Fairey aircraft in 1915 proved not to be a good design and placed more, not less, of the lower surface in contact with the water as the aircraft nose was raised for take-off. The result, with engine power that was only marginally sufficient to get airborne at all, was that small waves were required to break the contact between the float and the water. In calm conditions with neither wind nor wave to help, such as those found during the strike on Cuxhaven, failures to get airborne at all were common. The size of the waves had to be just right,

HMS *Campania* as she appeared in 1915 after her initial conversion to a seaplane carrier. Note the short, almost level flying-off deck built over the forecastle, the two large derricks just forward of the bridge for lifting aircraft onto and off the water and the guns mounted at intervals along the ship's side. (Author's collection)

however, and increasing amplitude brought further problems. Spray thrown up by the floats could hit the propeller, reducing engine revolutions and thus transmitted power and sometimes causing physical damage. Rotary engines were generally enclosed in cowlings, named after their appearance as 'bull-nosed' or 'horse-collar' types. Both were cut away at the bottom to improve engine cooling in flight and allow access for maintenance but the opening could allow significant quantities of spray or even actual water to hit the engine, flooding magnetos and the ignition system and potentially causing the engine to stop. Early seaplanes had no shock-absorbers and the impact of waves on the rigid float attachment points had a jarring effect on aircrew, airframe and the undercarriage structure with the result that the latter often failed. One pilot described take-off in a choppy sea as 'like being on the end of a stick pulled along park railings'.

The operation of seaplanes from the sea surface was obviously far more difficult than had been anticipated and Admiral Jellicoe began to doubt that such aircraft would be of any value to the Grand Fleet. He wrote that aircraft could not be relied upon to spot for his ships' guns or to deny similar information to the enemy 'unless it be by the use of aeroplanes [by which he meant aircraft with wheels, not floats] rising from the deck of *Campania* . . . able to land on the water and be supported sufficiently long by airbags to allow the rescue of pilots'.[14] Although he did not stress the urgent need to overcome the technical difficulties which prevented the operation of wheeled aircraft from ships, Jellicoe had, perhaps unwittingly but nevertheless accurately, described the next step towards a solution. *Campania* was larger than the previous seaplane conversions, and work on her was undertaken by Cammell Laird in Birkenhead and completed in April 1915. She emerged with a hangar aft of the forward funnel capable of stowing up to ten seaplanes depending on their size, with workshops and fuel stowage similar in capability to those in *Ark Royal*. The most significant improvement, however, was a take-off deck 120ft long by 30ft at its widest point fitted over the forecastle intended to allow seaplanes to take off with wheeled trolleys under the aircraft's floats which fell clear into the sea after they were released by the pilot. Her refitted machinery allowed speeds up to 21 knots for short periods depending on the quality of the coal in use and the number of stokers working each boiler. Despite these improvements, *Campania*'s trials proved to be disappointing. Her sheer size was one unexpected limitation and difficulty was found hoisting aircraft from the deck onto the water and back. Her greater beam meant that derricks needed greater reach than those in the smaller conversions and with the ship moving in a swell aircraft suspended from the derrick had a pronounced tendency to swing. Seaplanes continued to receive minor damage even when fended off by poles with soft padded tips. Disappointing trials continued through June and July and on 6 July 1915 Flight Lieutenant W L Welsh RNAS

Sopwith Schneider number 3736 being hoisted back onto HMS *Brocklesby*. This seaplane fighter was constructed by Sopwith at its Kingston factory and assembled at Woolston. It was embarked in *Brocklesby* for anti-Zeppelin patrols off the UK east coast and was actually launched against *L 33* on 2 August 1916 flown by Flight Sub Lieutenant H B Smith RNAS. Unfortunately it failed to get close enough to the enemy airship to engage it. (Philip Jarrett collection)

successfully took off in a Sopwith Schneider from the deck on *Campania*; the event was described[15] by her commanding officer Wing Captain Oliver Schwann RNAS who we last met in Barrow-in-Furness carrying out seaplane experiments while standing by airship *R 1*.

The Schneider was a development of the Tabloid with an airframe that weighed 1060lbs with only eight gallons of fuel in a 25-gallon tank to minimise weight, the pilot weighed a further 160lbs and the wheeled trolley fitted under the floats 18lbs giving a combined take-off weight of 1268lbs, significantly less than the maximum allowable take-off weight of 1715lbs. The ship steamed at 17 knots into a 13-knot wind and the aircraft was positioned as far aft as possible on the deck with its tail against the bridge supports where the wheels were measured to be 152ft from the bow. Neither trolley nor aircraft had brakes but a wire strop held it back until the order to release was given by the pilot; it was positioned in a tail-down rather than a flying attitude. After the bridge gave permission for the launch to go ahead, Welsh ran his engine up to the full 1050rpm and, when he was happy, signalled for the strop to be released. The 100hp Gnome spluttered a little as the aircraft accelerated and it took 30ft for the tail to come up into the flying attitude, Welsh kept it straight with rudder and pulled the nose up when he felt he had reached flying speed. The aircraft was observed to leave the deck 39ft from the bow and 32ft from the point

Wing Captain Oliver Schwann RNAS photographed when he was in command of HMS *Campania*. (Author's collection)

at which the deck became too narrow for the wheel-track. The whole take-off took six seconds and, once safely airborne, Welsh released the wheeled trolley which fell close to one of the ship's motor boats which recovered it for further use. Although the launch had shown the concept to be achievable, it could only be considered a partial success since the aircraft was only a lightly-loaded fighter; a fully-fuelled and armed seaplane could not have got airborne and, in the light of this experience, no attempt was made to launch heavier Short Folders and their derivates, Type 184s. Some thought was given to disposing of the ship after these disappointing results but Schwann argued that alterations to increase the size of the deck and other improvements shown to be necessary by experience would improve matters. He was supported by both Jellicoe and the Air Department so the ship was taken in hand for further modifications.

Another ship taken up from trade for use as a seaplane carrier in 1915 was more successful. She was the *Vindex*, larger than the three early conversions but smaller than *Campania*. She was fitted with a hangar aft capable of taking four Short 184s and a Sopwith Baby fighter and the usual outfit of workshops and stowage for avgas in two-gallon cans. The new feature was a small take-off deck 64ft long by 25ft wide fitted forward over a small hangar capable of taking two Sopwith Babies with their wings removed. It was appreciated from the *Campania* trials that this deck was too small to launch the Babies on wheeled trolleys but lowering them into the water by derrick hardly seemed the best way of launching fighters to intercept Zeppelins when they were encountered or indeed of making the best use of the ship's potential. In October 1915 the ship's officers obtained permission from the Air Department to evaluate launching a wheeled fighter from the forward deck and Bristol Scout C number 1255 with an 80hp Gnome engine was allocated for the task. The only modification it required was an anchor point for the hold-back strop and this was quickly fitted. This aircraft had been delivered in early 1915 and used operationally at the RN air stations at Dover and St Pol. It had a maximum take-off weight of 1198lbs. On 3 November 1915 *Vindex* steamed at 12 knots into a 15-knot wind giving a wind over the deck of 27 knots from right ahead[16] with Flight Lieutenant B F Fowler RNAS strapped into the cockpit of number 1255.[17] When approval to launch was given, the strop was released and the aircraft accelerated along the deck. It, too, had started in the three-point attitude with the tail down and it took 20ft to reach a level attitude with the tail skid off the deck. Even so, it was airborne with a run of only 42ft in 2.5 seconds, showing that the lighter Bristol had a much greater rate of acceleration than the Sopwith Baby seaplane. Its wheels had been covered with chalk which showed that they had left the deck 18ft from the bow. Further launches demonstrated that the minimum acceptable wind over the deck for a Bristol Scout was only 22 knots. These successes were further pointers showing that wheeled aircraft launched from a flight deck

Flight Lieutenant R J J Hope-Vere RNAS' Deperdussin number 1378 on the take-off deck fitted over the forecastle deck of HMS *Aurora* in 1915. (Author's collection)

were far more effective than seaplanes and they formed an important step in development. A day after the first take-off from *Vindex*, on 4 November 1915, Flight Lieutenant R J J Hope-Vere RNAS took off in Deperdussin monoplane number 1378 from a deck fixed over the forecastle of the cruiser *Aurora*. This was intended to demonstrate an operational capability to counter Zeppelin reconnaissance of the Grand Fleet. Three other cruisers were fitted with similar decks but no operational launches were made from them.

Experiments continued ashore at RNAS Isle of Grain, the experimental centre, and soon found an improved technique which brought significant benefits. The aircraft's tailskid was placed onto a small wooden trestle, raising the aircraft into the flying attitude before the hold-back was released. This reduced the take-off run considerably and the minimum wind over the deck was reduced to 19 knots, less than the maximum speed of *Vindex,* making it possible to launch a Bristol with no natural wind. The launches showed that the operation of high-performance aircraft from the deck of a ship was a practical proposition under operational conditions and the technique was analysed so that it could be fully understood and applied to a wide range of ships. The only drawback, of course, was that there was still no means of landing the aircraft back on the ship. If it was out of range of land, the pilot had to ditch nearby and if he survived his arrival in the water he had to stay afloat long enough for a sea-boat to reach him. Pilots began to wear inflatable life-saving waistcoats, examples of which could be bought from Gieves' naval outfitters. The technique evolved for an ideal ditching was to fly low over a destroyer to get the captain's attention and then ditch about 500 yards ahead of the ship so that by the time the ship came up the sea-boat would be swung out ready and could pick the pilot up after a minimal time in the water. The waterlogged wreckage of the aircraft was seldom recovered but if there was time the engine and guns were cut free and salvaged.

In 1914 the Admiralty was an independent purchasing department with enormous technical expertise and wide contacts among industry. Many firms were encouraged to produce cutting-edge designs and materials which could then be manufactured in the UK faster than anywhere else in the industrialised world. It is not surprising, therefore, that the Admiralty was able to initiate such rapid advances in design so soon after the outbreak of war as aircraft began to show their worth. The design skills of Porte, Usborne and many others were complemented by the ability of their uniformed personnel to construct innovative designs based on practical experience. Looking back at the RNAS' achievements in the first year of its existence with the full knowledge of events in the century after its formation, it still shows a dynamism in both technical progress and operational capability that can only be described as remarkable.

6 A Widening War

In the first months of the Great War RN air operations had been directed towards coastal patrols intended to locate enemy warships, especially minelayers, close to the British coast and strike operations against enemy airship bases. Following the almost complete German occupation of Belgium, however, and the establishment there of submarine bases, the extension of anti-submarine operations became an increasingly powerful influence on naval air policy.[1] As 1915 progressed the RNAS became involved in operations in the eastern Mediterranean, Middle East and East Africa as well as those in the UK, North Sea and Western Europe.

Operations in Home Waters

HMS *Empress* in 1915. By then she had been more extensively modified as a seaplane carrier with a hangar capable of taking four aircraft aft and a small working deck on which her aircraft could be prepared for flight before being lowered onto the water by crane. (Author's collection)

The menace of German U-boats based in the Flanders ports of Zeebrugge and Ostend to ships in the English Channel was emphasised on 1 January 1915 when the battleship *Formidable* was torpedoed by *U 24* off the Isle of Wight[2] in bad weather and sank with the loss of 547 men out of a ship's company of 780. With only limited potential for operations by surface forces against Zeebrugge because ships were being sent to the eastern Mediterranean to prepare for the attempt to force the Dardanelles, the possibility of using aircraft to strike at the new German bases was considered. *U 21*'s bombardment of Barrow-in-Furness on 29 January 1915 showed that U-boats could reach the west coast of the UK through the Irish Sea and on 4 February the German government announced that as from 18 February 1915 the waters surrounding the UK would be regarded as a war zone in which all British ships would be sunk and neutrals would navigate at their peril. The Admiralty took prompt steps to concentrate an air bombing force for operations against the Belgian bases and aircraft were drawn from naval air stations at Eastchurch, Hendon and the seaplane carrier *Empress* to reinforce those already at Dover and Dunkirk. Two Curtiss flying boats from Felixstowe were also ordered

Sopwith Type 807 Folder number 818 operated from HMS *Engadine* for strikes against targets at Zeebrugge and Ostend in February 1915. It had been delivered from the manufacturer in December 1914 and was eventually withdrawn from service in August 1915; aircraft of this era had very short active lives. (Author's collection)

to take part. A series of attacks was planned, timed to begin on 11 February with the aim of limiting the number of U-boats that would be at sea a week later. Unfortunately, flying conditions on 11 February proved to be bad with both snow and fog preventing all but one of the aircraft finding a target; it managed to drop three 20lb bombs each on harbour installations at both Ostend and Zeebrugge. Two other pilots failed to find the primary targets but sighted and bombed alternatives including enemy gun positions along the coast. The two flying boats from Felixstowe also failed to find the briefed targets but succeeded in returning safely to Felixstowe after a round trip of 150 miles in adverse conditions.

A further attack on 12 February proved more successful with twelve aeroplanes and a single seaplane finding the target area and claiming hits on harbour installations and docks at Ostend together with others on the mole at Zeebrugge and a power station. On 16 February seventeen aeroplanes and seven seaplanes hit harbour installations and the railway marshalling yard at Ostend with thirty-seven 20lb bombs and two further 20lb bombs hit the mole and dock area at Zeebrugge, killing seven men of the German Marine Artillery Corps. Three seaplanes and one aeroplane failed to return from this strike; one seaplane pilot

Squadron Commander Ivor T Courtney RNAS who led the attack on Hoboken shipyard. He is wearing the uniform of a captain in the RMLI, his parent service, with his RNAS 'wings' worn over the left breast pocket. (Author's collection)

was interned in Holland but the fate of the others was unknown. This strike was supported by eight French aircraft which attacked the German airfield at Ghistelles to prevent fighters getting airborne. In view of the limited capability of the aircraft available at the time and the tiny bombs they carried, these early strikes were little more than a demonstration of latent capability but they did show the potential for more advanced aircraft to contribute to wider naval operations in due course. At the end of February Samson's unit, the original RNAS unit at Dunkirk now designated Number 2 Wing, was withdrawn to Dover and from there to the eastern Mediterranean. It was replaced in France by the new Number 1 Wing under Longmore.

The Flanders U-boat bases developed rapidly and a new type of boat intended especially for operations in confined waters, known as the UB class, was assembled in Antwerp from component kits supplied from German shipyards. It was followed by another class intended primarily for minelaying duties designated the UC class and both types were allocated to a Flanders U-boat Flotilla formed on 29 March 1915. Once the Admiralty became aware of the construction work at Antwerp, 1 Wing was ordered to bomb the assembly slipways at Hoboken and an attack was carried out on 24 March which was described by Flight Lieutenant Harold Rosher RNAS in a collection of his war letters published in 1916.

Yesterday morning we were to have gone but the weather was not good enough and last night we slept at the aerodrome so as to get off at the crack of dawn. This morning we got up at about 03.30 (thank goodness the weather was warm) and breakfast followed. It's mighty hard to get down eggs and bread and butter at that hour. We cut for the order of starting but decided to keep as near one another as possible. I went off last but one at 05.30 and streaked out straight across the sea. We were pretty heavily loaded and my bus wouldn't climb much. I saw one machine ahead of me but lost it almost immediately in the clouds which were very low (2500ft), and it was also very misty. Our course was right up the coast past Zeebrugge and then cut in across the land. At the mouth of the Scheldt I got clear of some of the clouds and saw Squadron Commander I T Courtney RNAS behind and 2000ft above me, my machine being about 5000ft only. He rapidly overtook me (we were all on Avro 504s but his was faster) and from then on I followed him over the clouds. Unfortunately, over Antwerp there were no clouds. Courtney was about 5 or 6 minutes in front of me and I saw him volplane out of sight. I had to go on some little way before I spotted the yards myself. I next saw Courtney very low down flying away to the coast with shrapnel bursting round him. He came down to under 500ft and, being first there, dropped his bombs before he was fired on. As the wind was dead against me I decided to come round in a semi-circle to cross the yards with the wind so as to attain a greater speed. I was only 5500ft up and they opened fire on me with shrapnel as soon as I got within range. It began getting a bit hot so before I got quite round I shut off my petrol and came down with a steep volplane until I was 2500ft when I turned my petrol on again and continued my descent at a rate of well over 100mph. I passed over the yards at about 1000ft only and loosed all my bombs over the place. The whole way down I was under fire, 2 anti-aircraft in the yard, guns from the forts on either side, rifle fire, mitrailleuse or machine guns and, most weird of all, great bunches (15 to 20) of what looked like green rockets but I think they were flaming bullets. The excitement of the moment was terrific. I have never travelled so fast before in my life. My chief impressions were the great speed, the flaming bullets streaking by, the incessant rattle of the machine gun and rifle fire, and one or two shells bursting close by knocking my machine all sideways and pretty nearly deafening me . . . I found myself across the yards and felt a mild sort of surprise. My eyes must have been sticking out of my head like a shrimp's! I know I was gasping for breath and crouching down in the fuselage. I was, however, by no means clear for shrapnel was still bursting around me. I jammed the rudder first one way and then the other. I banked first on to one wing tip and then on to the other, now slipping outwards and now up and now down. I was literally hedged in by forts and only 1000ft up and had to run the gauntlet before getting away. My return journey was trying. Most of the time I had to fly at under 500ft as I ran into thick clouds and mist. I pottered gaily right over Flushing and within a few hundred yards of a Dutch cruiser and 2 torpedo boats. I got back home about a quarter of an hour after Courtney having been nearly 4 hours in the air and having covered, I suppose, getting on for 250 miles . . . on return I found my machine was only hit twice – rather wonderful; one bullet hole through the tail and a piece of shrapnel buried in the main spar of one wing. I have now got it out.[3]

After his return, Rosher had a second breakfast, a very hot bath and wrote out his report. A day later, on 25 March 1915, the Secretary of the Admiralty issued the following communication from Longmore.

I have to report that a successful air attack was carried out this morning by 5 machines of the Dunkirk Squadron on the German submarines being constructed at Hoboken near Antwerp. Two of the pilots had to return because of thick weather. But Squadron Commander Ivor T Courtney and Flight Lieutenant H Rosher of the RNAS reached their objective and after planing down to 1000ft dropped 4 bombs each on the submarines. It is believed that considerable damage has been done to both the works and to submarines. In all 5 submarines were observed on the slip. Flight Lieutenant B Crossley-Meates RNAS was obliged by engine trouble to descend in Holland. Owing to the mist the 2 pilots experienced considerable difficulty in finding their way and were subjected to a heavy gunfire while delivering their attack.

A second strike took place on 1 April by a single aircraft flown by Flight Sub Lieutenant F G Andreae RNAS. He dropped four 20lb bombs across the shipyard but subsequent analysis of the two attacks by the Admiralty led to the conclusion that sporadic attacks at long range with the lightweight bombs available were unlikely to produce decisive results and strikes against Antwerp were given up for the time being so that bombing could be concentrated on closer targets at Bruges, Ostend and Zeebrugge that were of greater short-term significance. One can sense the feeling of frustration in the Admiralty; it knew what it wanted aircraft to

RNAS Luce Bay from the air, clearly showing its large shed and the windbreaks at either end of it to protect airships as they were manoeuvred in and out of it. The neatly laid-out workshop and accommodation area is visible beyond the shed and a ground-handling party is moving an SS airship to the right of the picture. (Guy Warner Collection).

achieve and the RNAS pilots had done all that was asked of them but their flimsy aircraft and light bombs were not yet up to achieving the effect that was needed.

Towards the end of April the Germans began to use a heavy-calibre gun to shell Dunkirk and during its third bombardment on 30 April, six naval aircraft were sent up with instructions to note the big gun's flashes from the arc of a circle that had Dunkirk at its centre. Before taking off, each observer had synchronised his watch with the airfield clock and over the enemy lines noted the exact time of every gun flash. After landing, these times were compared with the exact time that shells had fallen on the town and after allowance was made for the time of flight of each shell, the gun's location was fixed at Clercken, south-east of Dixmunde,[4] by Flight Lieutenant D C S Evill RNAS. Now that the gun had been located, action could be taken against it and RNAS aircraft both bombed it and corrected the fire of French heavy artillery batteries against it. The enemy gun was finally put of action by two French naval guns on 9 August.

At sea the new SS airships were used to patrol the Dover Straits and the entrances to the Irish Sea as they came into service with the first base intended for their use opened at Capel near Folkestone on 8 May 1915 and the second at Polegate near Eastbourne on 6 July. A portable airship shed was also set up at Marquise in France by the end of June which was subsequently donated to the French Navy for the operation of the two SS airships it had purchased. By the end of 1915 Capel had five airships with 4 more under construction and Polegate had three. A further base opened at Luce Bay on 15 July from which airships patrolled the north channel into the Irish Sea and by the end of the year it had three. A portable shed for emergency landings was erected on the Irish coast at Larne which faced Luce Bay and a further base was completed on Anglesey in mid-September which had four airships in operation at the end of the year.

The Zeppelin Threat

At the same time as the U-boat offensive, the threat from German Zeppelins became a reality and, following several reconnaissance sorties close to the English east coast, two enemy airships dropped bombs on King's Lynn, Yarmouth and Sheringham on the night of 19/20 January 1915.[5] They were believed to be naval Zeppelins operating from the north German sheds and so plans were prepared for another strike from the sea against them. On 20 March *Empress*, escorted by the Harwich Force of cruisers and destroyers, sailed to launch an attack against the German wireless station at Norddeich from which it was believed that both Zeppelins and U-boats obtained navigational bearings. The pilots were also briefed to carry out a reconnaissance of Norden in order to locate the exact position of the airship sheds. The attempt to launch the seaplanes proved unsuccessful, however,

HMS *Engadine* after her full conversion into a seaplane carrier. The aircraft on the working deck right aft is a Short 184. Note the two cranes on the after bulkhead of the hangar which were used to lower aircraft onto the water, the port crane could already be attached to the seaplane. (Author's collection)

because of a rough sea and strong, gusty winds. A further attempt on was made on 23 March in which the cruisers *Arethusa* and *Aurora* also embarked seaplanes to augment those in *Empress*. This too proved to be unsuccessful, this time because of thick fog near the enemy coast. After further Zeppelin raids against East Anglia during April, another attempt to strike at Norddeich with seaplanes was carried out on 3 May, this time with three carriers, *Engadine, Riviera* and the newly-commissioned *Ben-my-Chree*,[6] a larger vessel than *Engadine* with a hangar aft for four seaplanes and a small take-off deck, 63ft long by 12ft wide, forward. Once again a rough sea made it impossible to launch the seaplanes and the sortie was a failure. On 6 May another attempt was made; this time the sea was calmer but the strike had to be aborted because of coastal fog.

Undaunted by this series of failures, the Harwich Force sailed again on 11 May 1915 and as it approached the German coast a Zeppelin was sighted in the distance. By now the difficulty of getting aircraft off the water was fully appreciated and so an attempt was made to launch a Sopwith Schneider from the forward deck of *Ben-my-Chree*[7] with a jettisonable wheeled trolley positioned under its floats. The pilot warmed up his Gnome rotary engine after it was started but, while he was doing so, it backfired so violently that the aircraft fell off its launch trolley and was sufficiently badly damaged to cause the launch to be aborted. Three seaplanes were lowered from *Engadine* and succeeded in taking off but their pilots soon flew into

Flight Commander A W Bigsworth RNAS standing in front of Avro 504 number 1009 in which he damaged Zeppelin *LZ 39* on 17 May 1915. (Author's collection)

thick fog and had to turn back. One of them alighted safely and was hoisted in; a second crashed on alighting and the pilot was rescued although the aircraft was lost. No trace was ever found of the third who presumably became disorientated and spun into the sea whilst turning back.

Intelligence had reached the Admiralty that the Germans were building Zeppelin sheds in Belgium at Evere and Berchem St Agathe and in early 1915 these had been used on an occasional basis by naval Zeppelins but from late April they housed the new Army airships *LZ 37*, *LZ 38* and *LZ 39*. Offensive action against these bases became a priority for the RNAS unit based at Dunkirk and an opportunity came early in the morning of 17 May when the three Zeppelins set out for a raiding patrol along the French and British Channel coasts. At 03.15 *LZ 39* was seen off Dunkirk and nine aircraft took off to intercept it but only one, an Avro 504 flown by Flight Commander A W Bigsworth RNAS, succeeded in getting close to it. His aircraft was not fitted with a machine gun and without tracer or exploding ammunition it is doubtful if it would have been effective if he had but he did have four 20lb bombs. He took time to climb above *LZ 39* and then dived along its length dropping his bombs at short intervals. They detonated but the damage they did was not great; *LZ 39* lost gas but was able to return to Evere where it made a heavy landing.

On 7 June 1915 the three Army airships left their bases again to take part in a combined naval and military raid on the UK; *LZ 38* had engine trouble and returned to Evere where it was put back into its shed. Coincidentally four naval aircraft of 1 Squadron had taken off from Dunkirk in the early hours of the same day to attack the airship sheds and the two forces were airborne at the same time.

The two remaining Zeppelins had encountered fog, abandoned the raid and were returning to their bases when at 01.00 Flight Sub Lieutenant R A J Warneford RNAS, who was on his way to bomb Berchem St Agathe in Morane-Saulnier Type L monoplane number 3253, saw *LZ 37* some distance away emerging from the fog near Ostend. He turned towards the enemy, climbed to get above it and was nearly in an attacking position at 01.50 over Bruges when machine-gun fire from the airship forced him to turn away and attempt to gain more height. The airship commander turned after him and kept him under fire for some time but Warneford gradually out-climbed his adversary until he was well above it at 11,000ft. He switched off his engine[8] and dived along the length of the airship dropping his six 20lb bombs as he did so, passing about 150ft above the enemy. As he released the last bomb, a terrific explosion tore *LZ 37* apart and tossed 3253 upwards and onto its back. Warneford regained control after a steep dive and observed that the airship wreckage was already burning on the ground. In his book *Airshipwreck*,[9] Len Deighton described how some of the airship crew jumped to their deaths from the blazing wreck but the helmsman lay on the floor of the control car which fell clear of its mountings and crashed through the roof of a convent. He was thrown clear onto a bed; the only

Flight Sub Lieutenant R A J Warneford VC RNAS. (Author's collection)

man to survive the crash. Two nuns on the floor below were killed but the helmsman allegedly survived to fly again with the Army airship service.

When Warneford regained control of his aircraft he found that a petrol feed pipe had broken and he was unable to re-start the engine. By then visibility was good in clear moonlight and he identified a suitable field behind the German lines and landed. There was no sign of the enemy and he spent 35 minutes repairing the pipe after which he swung the propeller in an attempt to re-start the engine. At first he was unsuccessful but after several attempts it started and the aircraft, which had no brakes, began to move forward and he had to scramble to get into the cockpit but succeeded and took off. He was uncertain of his exact position and low on fuel but he identified Cape Griz-Nez and landed on the Allied side of the lines to refuel. When he finally returned to Dunkirk and reported his achievement he was awarded the Victoria Cross. It was only the second to be awarded to a pilot but was the first to be communicated by telegram and quickest to be confirmed, the King's private secretary having written to the First Lord, Balfour, proposing the honour on 8 June.

On 8 June 1915 Warneford dictated the following action report, slowly, to the Squadron Writer. It conveys a vivid impression of the man and the scene that afternoon in the squadron office as Warneford and his colleagues took in the scale of his achievement.

> Number 1 Aeroplane Squadron
> 8 June 1915

Sir,

I have the honour to report as follows:

I left Furnes at 1.00 am, on 7 June on Morane 3253 under orders to proceed to look for Zeppelins and attack Berchem St Agathe airship shed with six 20lb bombs.

On arriving at Dixmunde at 1.5 am, I observed a Zeppelin apparently over Ostend and proceeded in chase of the same.

I arrived at close quarters a few miles past Bruges at 1.50 am and the airship opened heavy Maxim fire, so I retreated to gain height and the airship turned and followed me.

At 2.15 am he seemed to stop firing and at 2.25 am I came behind, but well above the Zeppelin; height then 11,000ft, and switched off my engine to descend on top of him.

When close above him (at 7,000ft altitude) I dropped my bombs, and, whilst releasing the last, there was an explosion which lifted my machine and turned it over. The aeroplane was out of control for a short period, but went into a nose dive and then control was regained.

I then saw that the Zeppelin was on the ground in flames and also that there were pieces of something burning in the air all the way down.

The joint on my petrol pipe and pump from the back tank was broken, and at about 2.40 am I was forced to land and repair my pump.

I landed at the back of a forest close to a farm house; the district is unknown on account of the fog and the continuous changing of course.

I made preparations to set the machine on fire, but apparently, was not observed, so was enabled to effect a repair, and continued at 3.15 am in a south-westerly direction after considerable difficulty in starting my engine single-handed.

I tried several times to find my whereabouts by descending through the clouds, but was unable to do so. So eventually I landed and found out that I was at Cape Gris-Nez, and took in some petrol. When the weather cleared I was able to proceed and arrived at the aerodrome about 10.30 am.

As far as could be seen the colour of the airship was green on top and yellow below and there was no machine-gun or platform on top.

I have the honour to be, Sir,
Your obedient Servant
R A J Warneford
Flt Sub Lieutenant[10]

Sadly, Warneford was killed in a flying accident only days later on 17 June 1915. He had visited Paris, staying at the Ritz Hotel, and had been asked by Longmore to fly

Warneford's Morane Saulnier MS-3 Type L monoplane number 3253 at St Pol. It had only been delivered to 1 Wing by the manufacturer on 30 April 1915 and after Warneford's death it remained in service with the same unit until 1916 when it was withdrawn from service because of what was described as fair wear and tear. It was subsequently preserved for exhibition at Hendon until March 1918 but its ultimate fate is unknown. What a treasure it would have been for the National Museum of the Royal Navy if it had survived. (Author's collection)

St Pol airfield was used a major base and aircraft depot by both the RNAS and the French air services. This aerial view gives an idea of its size and extensive hangarage. (Philip Jarrett collection)

back to Dunkirk in a new Henri Farman biplane that had been allocated to the squadron but first he was to give it an acceptance test flight at Buc airfield just outside Paris. Longmore had warned him that the new machine was not capable of the aerobatic manoeuvres he had performed in his Morane but otherwise the acceptance flight was quite straightforward. The French authorities asked him to fly an American journalist named Henry Needham over Paris and Warneford agreed. After giving some friends a demonstration flight he drove to the RNAS Office in the Avenue Montaigne, picked up Needham and drove to Buc.[11] Whatever went wrong in the subsequent flight, observers saw the aircraft '. . . go into a spin. It dived steeply, then pulled out and appeared to fling up its tail which, with a crack that was heard on the ground, snapped off and caught the propeller, shearing part of it away. The machine started to roll and, at about 700ft, it turned upside down. To the horror of the watchers both occupants, neither apparently strapped in, fell one after the other to the ground . . .' Both were killed; Needham instantly and Warneford on his way to hospital. After an initial plan to bury Warneford in the hospital grounds it was decided to give him a public funeral in the UK. His body was taken from France to the UK, arriving at Victoria Station in London on 21 June where crowds had already lined the streets an hour before his train arrived but only his mother and two of his sisters were allowed onto the platform. Eight Leading Seamen from the RND placed the coffin onto a gun carriage which was pulled by twenty-two sailors on its slow journey to Brompton Cemetery where it lay overnight in the annexe to the cemetery chapel. The funeral took place on 22 June attended by officers representing the Admiralty, the RNAS, the RFC and the Armoured Car Section of the RNAS and two chaplains from the RND conducted the service. A funeral firing party of fifty men was fallen in by the grave side and men from the armoured car squadrons and RND with reversed arms lined the route from the chapel to the grave. Police and servicemen had to hold back the huge crowd and after the burial thousands passed by the grave to see the coffin before it was covered.

While Warneford was in action with *LZ 37*, the other pilot who had been briefed to attack Berchem St Agathe was forced to land in the darkness at Cassel and crashed but Flight Lieutenant J P Wilson and Flight Sub Lieutenant J S Mills RNAS in Henri Farman biplanes flew through the mist on compass courses to attack the other airship base at Evere. Wilson arrived first, just after 02.00 while it was still dark, and a searchlight on the ground flashed a signal at him. He replied promptly with short flashes from his pocket lamp and this seemed to satisfy those on the ground and earn him immunity from anti-aircraft fire for the 15 minutes he circled the airship base waiting for the first light of dawn. At 02.20 the shed was visible from 2000ft and he released three 65lb bombs which appeared to hit the centre of the target from which dark smoke but no flame appeared. At 02.30 Mills arrived and was met by accurate fire which forced him to turn away and gain height. He returned at 5000ft and released his four 20lb bombs which also appeared to hit. Suddenly the whole countryside was lit by a flash as the hydrogen in *LZ 38* exploded and both it and its shed went up in flames. It had been the first Zeppelin to bomb London a week earlier on 31 May 1915. Despite drifting fog, both pilots made their way successfully back to the front line after which Wilson landed in a field near Montreuil and Mills, after coming down low over the sea, landed on the beach between Calais and Dunkirk.

Having lost two Army Zeppelins in a single night, the Germans withdrew *LZ 39* to the Eastern Front where it was destroyed by fire in a shed near Kovno in November 1915. The German Army decided that it was too dangerous to operate airships from these forward bases and they were abandoned except for use as emergency landing grounds. The Admiralty policy of aggressive defence which had led to the stationing of RNAS units at airfields around Dunkirk had been justified by its successful results.

Defending UK Airspace
Offensive action against enemy airships at source had proved successful but the Admiralty accepted that some were still likely to get through to the UK and it was

therefore necessary to strengthen the defences around likely targets, especially London. During 1915 guns and searchlights were regarded as providing the best defence, with aircraft used to patrol the coast at dawn and dusk to provide early warning of airships' approach. Aeroplanes were also flown on night patrols from air stations in areas that attacking Zeppelins might pass over but none of these met with any success. After an attack on the Tyne area in June 1915, the Admiralty took steps to strengthen the defences of north-eastern England by establishing a group of air stations along the coast at Whitley Bay, Redcar, Scarborough and Hornsea. Later in the year night landing grounds were established at Narborough, Bacton, Holt, Sedgeford, Aldeborough, Covehithe, Goldhanger and Rochford from which aircraft could take off to intercept Zeppelins making landfall along the coast between the Wash and the Thames Estuary. Aeroplanes were distributed to these before dark and their pilots kept at immediate readiness throughout the night. However, the Admiralty placed greater emphasis on aircraft operations in Flanders and the Dardanelles and the only pilots immediately available for this task were newly qualified with little experience of night flying. Even those who became proficient had nothing to guide them towards the enemy on dark nights unless the Zeppelins were illuminated by searchlights or the explosion of bombs on the ground gave their position away. Zeppelins appear to be large objects in daylight when seen at close quarters but with no moonlight they were relatively small objects in a very large sky. By September 1915 naval aircraft had carried out eighty-nine night flights in attempts to intercept enemy airships over the UK that met with no success. Twenty aircraft were wrecked or damaged attempting to land at night resulting in the death of three pilots and serious injury to eight more.

Night interception techniques did not become a practical proposition until the advent of radar and VHF radio telephony in the late 1930s made it possible to build up an 'air picture' of the battle-space and control fighters into a position from which they could engage the enemy. The Admiralty must be given credit, however, for trying everything that was available to it with the technology available in 1915. The RN was the first to develop a plotting table which allowed the fleet commander to see the moving position of his fleet and that of the enemy in nearly real time. Similar techniques began to be used ashore so that pilots could be briefed before take-off on the likely positions of enemy aircraft. Unfortunately, without radio ground control of the interception was not possible and the pilot had to carry out a visual search of the limitless sky to seek a chance encounter with the enemy. The Air Department calculated that it might prove possible to intercept Zeppelins in daylight before they made landfall at dusk if aircraft could operate at about 50 miles off the coast. Trawlers had often reported sighting enemy airships at about this distance in broad daylight and so, from May 1915, a number of seaplane fighters were embarked in steam trawlers from Yarmouth and taken out to sea and lowered onto the water to carry out anti-Zeppelin patrols in daylight. None of these ever succeeded in sighting the enemy, however. A step further was taken in November when the Admiral commanding the Patrol Service recommended the use of large paddle minesweepers to carry up to six aircraft each on offshore patrols. This idea was not taken up but in March 1916 the Admiralty did requisition two paddle ferries named *Killingholme* and *Brocklesby* which were both equipped to embark three Sopwith Schneider seaplane fighters. The aircraft were provided by the air stations at Killingholme and Yarmouth but, like the trawler detachments, they met with no success and the experiment was not continued.

Further Strikes from the Sea

German naval Zeppelins sometimes joined their Army contemporaries in attacks on the UK but their main threat was believed to be from their perceived ability to carry out long-range reconnaissance missions over the North Sea. Admiral Jellicoe felt that this gave the High Sea Fleet a distinct advantage over the Grand Fleet and he pressed the Admiralty to take countermeasures. A further strike by seaplane carriers with the Harwich Force was therefore planned for the beginning of July 1915 with the double object of drawing Zeppelins into an action in which they might be damaged or destroyed and a reconnaissance of the Ems River and the neighbourhood of Borkum where transport ships were reported to have been collected. The force arrived off Ameland at dawn on 4 July 1915 where *Engadine* and *Riviera* stopped to lower their seaplanes onto the water and destroyers circled them to provide protection against U-boats. The four seaplanes from *Riviera* were away by 02.50 but the single Short from *Engadine* crossed the wash of a destroyer, the rough water split its propeller and it had to be recovered. Of the others, two suffered engine problems before they reached the island of Borkum and turned back. The third searched the water around the islands of Juist and Borkum but ran into cloud on its way back to the force and failed to find it; eventually it ran out of fuel at 07.00 and the pilot alighted alongside a Dutch trawler[12] which ran down and destroyed the seaplane at the pilot's request and then took him back to Holland, from where he was soon repatriated as a shipwrecked mariner. The fourth seaplane, flown by Flight Lieutenant H Stewart RNAS, made a careful recon-naissance of the islands and the Ems River and was able to say with certainty that there were no transports in the area. He dropped two bombs on a coastal gun battery and two more on destroyers anchored in the Randzel Gat, after which he flew back towards the Harwich Force followed part of the way by an enemy seaplane which did not attack him. German intelligence had warned of a strike at about this time and an extensive search by Zeppelins had been ordered; four found the force and loitered overhead, ironically helping to guide Stewart back to *Engadine*. This was just the sort of situation the Air Department had hoped for and three Sopwith Schneiders had been embarked in *Engadine* with the object of intercepting enemy airships. An air/sea battle did not develop, however, because the floats of all three fighters broke up as they attempted to take off. Two of the aircraft sank, the third was salvaged but all three pilots were rescued. Fortuitously, the Zeppelins contented themselves with reporting the British force and failed to take any offensive action, thus for both sides events proved disappointing and the Admiralty lost interest in offensive seaplane operations off the enemy coast for a while. No further strikes were attempted until January 1916.

The Success of Observation Balloons
Captive balloons were recognised as a viable alternative to seaplanes as a source of reconnaissance information. Their use had been recommended to the Admiralty as early as December 1914 and drawings of the French 'Drachen' type of balloon were requested so that manufacture could be carried out in the UK. Two balloons were purchased from the French government and a training establishment for their operation was set up at Roehampton on the outskirts of London and balloon sections were commissioned as equipment became available. Their first use was in the Dardanelles campaign where warships found difficulty in locating concealed Turkish gun batteries and the concept of operating a kite balloon tethered to a ship was worked out. The small tramp steamer *Manica* was taken up from trade and equipped for this purpose. A vessel of 4120 tons completed in 1900, she was acquired from Ellerman & Bucknall in the early months of 1915 and fitted out for duty as a kite balloon vessel by Grayson in Liverpool. She was the first kite balloon vessel in RN service and equipment fitted for her new role included plant for the manufacture and storage of hydrogen, means for inflating, deflating, working and protecting the balloon, storage for silicol, soda and workshops for the repair of equipment and accommodation for the officers and men required to work the balloon. The Type 'A' hydrogen plant was fitted aft on the starboard side with storage cylinders fitted in wooden securing chocks on the port side. Once made, the gas was passed into a 'nurse balloon' which acted as a low-pressure reservoir and a suction was taken from this to the compressor plant from which it fed to the storage cylinders at 1800psi. Arrangements were also made for the gas to be taken direct to the balloon at low pressure without having to use the storage cylinders. Current for driving the compressor was taken from a steam dynamo of 105 volts and 500 amps fitted for the purpose. The balloon itself was carried forward and considerable alterations had to be made to the ship to provide the necessary space. The foremast was removed, all

HMS *Manica* operating her kite balloon. (Author's collection)

fittings between the bridge and forecastle cleared and a wooden platform built over the long forward well deck just below the hatch coamings. For hauling down the balloon a special portable kite winch was installed at the after end of this platform. When preparing the ship it was considered that the kite balloon section might be required to operate on land and with this view in mind a number of suitable vehicles were stowed in the after holds and on the after deck.

The results obtained from *Manica*'s early work in the Dardanelles campaign were sufficiently encouraging to warrant other ships being fitted out for similar tasks and *Hector* and *Menelaus* were taken up from trade. Unlike the earlier two ships, *Menelaus* was able to carry her balloon fully inflated and she was commissioned for service with the Dover Patrol in July 1915 to spot for bombardments of German batteries on the Belgian coast. It was soon realised, however, that at useful observation ranges the ship was too large a target to survive long against counter-fire and so experiments were made in August 1915 to see if the fully-inflated balloon, complete with its observers, could be passed to the trawler *Peary* for work close inshore. These proved successful, with the balloon being passed from one ship to the other and then back again on several occasions with no damage. The practicability of housing a kite balloon in a parent ship or base ashore and transferring it, inflated, to another vessel for towing purposes at sea having thus been proved, the development of kite balloons by the RNAS for both fleet and anti-submarine operations subsequently developed along these lines. It was encouraged by Admiral Beatty who wrote to the Admiralty in August and September 1915 stressing the need for a balloon ship capable of scouting work with the Battlecruiser Fleet in the early stages of a fleet action. 'Balloons could', he said 'often be sent up in weather when it would not be possible to launch a seaplane and, probably, in weather that would be prohibitive for Zeppelins.'[13] The Admiralty responded by placing Number 9 Kite Balloon Section at his disposal for experimental work, based at Rosyth. Trials followed on 17 and 19 October using *Engadine* which had, by then, been attached to Beatty's Fleet. She worked up to a speed of 22 knots in heavy seas with a balloon flying at the end of its cable and found that it rode quite smoothly despite the ship's violent pitching and rolling motion and followed each change of course, however drastic, without undue strain being placed on the cable. The trial had been arranged under the supervision of Rear Admiral Hood, flag officer 3rd Battlecruiser Squadron, and in his report he stated that it had exceeded expectations and urged that a balloon ship with the speed to accompany the Fleet should be fitted out with the minimum delay. In forwarding Hood's report, Beatty added that 'the advantage that the enemy has hitherto possessed by the aid of his Zeppelins in obtaining early information of the position, disposition, course and speed of our Fleet will, by the use of kite balloons, be in a great measure nullified'. He advocated the use of balloons in *Campania* in place of some of her seaplanes and his suggestion was approved by the Admiralty and plans for the reconstruction of *Campania* were modified to enable her to carry an inflated balloon in a well deck aft. In the discussions which preceded this decision Rear Admiral F C T Tudor, Third Sea Lord, made the interesting suggestion that some of the existing balloon ships, whose speed was insufficient to allow them to work with the fleet, might be used as sheds from which balloons could be transferred to light cruisers. The practicality of such a scheme had already been demonstrated off the Belgian coast but for some reason, the idea was not adopted widely until mid-1916.

In April 1915 the Army appealed for balloon support on the Western Front where the rapidly-expanding requirement for artillery observation was beyond the resources of the RFC. Despite its own urgent needs, the Admiralty responded positively to the appeal and Number 2 RNAS Kite Balloon Section was deployed to France on 8 May. At the end of the month Field Marshal Sir John French, C-in-C of the BEF, asked for another section to be deployed as quickly as possible and Number 4 Section was deployed to France. A further section, Number 6, was deployed in August, after which the War Office assumed responsibility for the formation of balloon sections for Army operations although the Admiralty continued to provide balloons and other equipment until 1916.

Re-organisation of the RNAS
Handing over kite balloon observation work ashore to the Army was only one of a number of changes in RNAS organisation that followed the departure of Churchill. On 15 May 1915 Lord Fisher had resigned following a disagreement

with Churchill over the Dardanelles campaign. Two days later Asquith was forced to form a coalition government after widespread criticism of the conduct of the war thus far. Churchill resigned on 27 May and was replaced by Arthur Balfour with Admiral Sir Henry Jackson as 1SL. Both were aware that under Churchill a number of elements had been created within the RNAS that had drawn its focus away from core naval activities. These included development work on what was to become the tank, the deployment of fifteen armoured car squadrons on land-based operations, three armoured trains operating in Flanders, the kite balloon sections working with the Army and the AAC numbering over 1500 officers and men for ground-based defence of the UK against enemy air raids. These now were regarded as 'side-shows' and because development was now so rapid, attention had to be focused on naval aviation if it was to deliver the results which were becoming possible. One of Balfour's first acts on becoming First Lord was, therefore, to discuss matters with Kitchener and it was agreed that all these shore-based organisations should be handed over to War Office control.

Further re-organisation followed. The Admiralty had already decided that the rapid expansion of the RNAS meant that it could no longer be administered effectively by the Nore Command and so the Central Air Office at Sheerness was closed and the Air Department assumed responsibility for all air operational and administrative matters. Balfour did not like this arrangement and, after wide-ranging discussion with the Board and the C-in-C Grand Fleet, he took the view that air stations should come under the command of the Senior Naval Officers (SNOs), in the same way as destroyers and submarines, within the areas in which their aircraft worked. Admiral Jellicoe fully agreed with the change and, in a memorandum dated 4 June 1915, listed the important functions that the naval air service should fulfil.[14] These were, he wrote, observation duties from the coast generally and from naval bases in particular and the attacks on enemy aircraft wherever they were encountered. Next in importance came the aerial defence of all naval centres, such as dockyards and magazines 'since the Army who, properly speaking, should carry out this work have apparently turned it over to the Navy'. Last in importance he put scouting for enemy submarines and enemy minelayers which properly comes under the heading of reconnaissance work. It is interesting to note that he appeared to place no emphasis on the strike operations upon which so much importance had been placed by the previous regime and which had so nearly led to a surface action off Heligoland. Nor did he appear to place much emphasis on the use of aircraft or kite balloons in either a fleet action or spotting for shore bombardment. There can be little doubt that Jellicoe, whilst fixated by the supposed advantage that Zeppelins gave the High Sea Fleet, had too little concept of the advantages that the RNAS could offer him if the operation of aircraft from ships at sea were to be given the priority it deserved. It must also be concluded that he lacked sufficient naval air input from his staff to help him appreciate the full potential of his own air service.

The change was accepted by the Board and appeared in revised regulations for the RNAS issued on 1 August 1915. The immediate gain was that liaison between air and surface craft became much closer. To improve matters still further, an experienced RNAS officer was appointed to the staff of each SNO as an advisor on air technical matters. Inland air stations such as Hendon, Chingford, Wormwood Scrubs and Roehampton where there was no appropriate SNO were placed under the direct control of the Admiralty. As soon as the question of naval air stations was settled, the board looked at the structure of the Air Department itself and decided that an officer of flag rank should be placed in charge of air matters. Rear Admiral C L Vaughan-Lee was, therefore, appointed as the new Director of Air Services (DAS) and took up his duties on 8 September 1915. Sueter was re-appointed to the new post of Superintendent of Aircraft Construction, a position that should have appealed to him after his constant complaints that new aircraft types were not being delivered as quickly as he wished but, perhaps understandably, he resented the loss of authority and viewed the changes made to the RNAS with growing dislike. An officer who had previously served as captain of *Hermes*, Wing Commander C L Lambe RNAS, was appointed in operational command of the Wings at Dover and Dunkirk together with the SS airship stations at Capel and Polegate with the acting higher rank of Wing Captain, reporting to Vice Admiral R H Bacon who we last encountered in the earliest days of naval aviation and was now in command of the Dover Patrol.

Other changes followed under which the RNAS became more closely integrated as part of the wider naval service in much the same way as the Royal Marines. The Air Department was divided into two elements, Administration and Construction, each of which undertook a wide range of activities with a total of eight sections, each controlled by a responsible officer. Of these eight only two, Squadron Commander Clark-Hall RNAS, responsible for aeroplane and seaplane design, and Squadron Commander W Briggs RNAS, responsible for engines, were early members of the air service. The new administrative officers had an RN background with little previous knowledge of air operations but they were chosen for their power of organization, strict sense of discipline, untiring energy and sense of pride in their Service.[15] The swashbuckling ethos of some of the early aviation pioneers had been reigned in and a more disciplined outlook was to prevail; this was not universally popular but it was essential to make the necessary progress if aviation was to form an integral part of fleet operations.

Home Operations in the Autumn of 1915

The first German submarine offensive continued with the sinking of the unarmed White Star liner *Arabic,* torpedoed without warning on 19 August 1915. The sinking of the *Lusitania* off the south coast of Ireland on 7 May had already strained relations between the USA and Germany and the *Arabic* episode caused further loss of American lives which brought the two countries to the brink of war. In consequence the Kaiser issued an order on 27 August that U-boat commanders were not to sink passenger steamers in the prohibited zone without warning and before the removal of passengers and crew had been achieved. Under these conditions submarine warfare in British waters became untenable and so, on 1 September U-boats were ordered to withdraw from the Channel and the west coast of the UK. Some were ordered to the Mediterranean but the Flanders boats continued to operate off the east coast of the UK where fishing boats suffered especially heavy losses. Admiral Bacon had formulated a plan for bombarding the Belgian submarine bases and ordered the construction of a range on the Thames Estuary that exactly replicated the features of the enemy-held coast around Zeebrugge. It was used for a rehearsal using seaplanes from *Riviera* to spot the fall of shot from the guns of monitors. The Dover/Dunkirk group of air stations were now part of Bacon's Dover command and from 5 August Lambe became air staff officer on Bacon's staff. From this time onwards his air units grew in both size and importance.

On 1 August Number 2 Wing, commanded by Wing Commander E L Gerrard, replaced Number 1 Wing at Dunkirk and was soon in action. It was able to participate in the destruction of a Zeppelin on 9 August when five German naval airships carried out a raid on British east coast towns from their north German bases. One of them, *L 12*, arrived over Westgate and Ramsgate in misty conditions and flew on to Dover where it dropped a few bombs but was hit by an anti-aircraft shell. It turned at once for Belgium but lost gas rapidly and came down in the sea a few miles short of the enemy-held coast. It was located and bombed by Number 2 Wing aircraft but the enemy managed to tow the wreck to a quayside at Ostend. Bombing attacks on the wreck continued and so the Germans gave up any attempt to salvage it and broke it up *in situ*. Number 2 Wing spent only a short time at Dunkirk before being withdrawn on 15 August for service in the Dardanelles. It was replaced by Number 1 Wing.

On 23 August 1915 Bacon's first bombardment of the Belgian coast was carried out with aircraft from 1 Wing providing protective air patrols over the assembled shipping. The target was the system of locks and caissons that connected Zeebrugge with Bruges. *Riviera* lowered three seaplanes onto the water which managed to get airborne despite a heavy sea. They climbed to 2500ft but from that height cloud obscured the target area and the bombarding ships were forced to rely on spotting corrections from observers on what were called 'portable islands', in reality small camouflaged barges that were towed close to the coast for the purpose. Agents ashore gave optimistic reports of extensive damage caused by the bombardment but air reconnaissance two days later revealed that no damage had been done to the lock gates and only slight damage to the Solway Works power station. Ostend was chosen for the next attack which took place on 7 September. Again *Riviera* launched three Short seaplanes which were over the monitors at dawn ready to observe the fire but mist began to form between the ships and the shore making it necessary to postpone the shoot. One spotting aircraft and two fighters operating from Dunkirk flew over the force to give it protection until their fuel state compelled them to return and a diversionary air strike on enemy storage hangars was carried out with some success by seventeen French and six British aircraft according to the original plan. The bombardment force was still off Ostend at 12.45 when three German aircraft attacked it from about 8000ft. One bomb hit the cruiser *Attentive*, killing two men and wounding others as well as putting a gun out of action. Bacon ordered his ships to open out but later in the afternoon they concentrated again to begin the shoot and *Riviera*'s three Shorts were launched successfully and got into position. Fire was opened at 18,000 yards but almost immediately German heavy shore batteries replied and soon found the range. Bacon turned at once to open the range but enemy shells continued to straddle their targets and the monitor *Lord Clive* was damaged. Bacon had to accept that his monitors were outranged and he broke off the action. One of *Riviera*'s seaplanes had, however, pinpointed the exact location of the four enemy 28cm guns, known to the enemy as the 'Tirpitz' Battery, that had been the problem. They had an effective range of 35,000 yards and it would need monitors armed with 15in guns to stand a chance of destroying them.

After the bombardment the Dunkirk aircraft continued to fly offensive sorties along the Belgian coast during which they sighted and attacked several U-boats. On 26 August Bigsworth was on the outbound leg of a sortie to attack Zeebrugge in a Henri Farman when he surprised a U-boat on the surface off Ostend. He dived to 500ft and released two 65lb bombs which he thought were direct hits. The aircraft was thrown out of control for a few seconds by the blast but when he was able to look at the target again it appeared to be disappearing under the water stern-first, obviously not under control. Two more U-boats were attacked in September. On 26 September a further coastal bombardment was carried out in conjunction with the Battle of Loos. Flight Sub Lieutenant G H Beard RNAS saw a surfaced U-boat off Ostend and attacked it unsuccessfully but then flew back to the vicinity of the monitor *Sir John Moore* and used his pocket handkerchief to signal by waving it in the Morse code. The monitor took in the word 'submarine' but could not read the rest of his message but that was enough and the ships increased to full speed. After Beard returned to Dunkirk and explained what had happened, five further aircraft were sent off to search for the U-boat. Two of them found it still on the surface but it submerged after further bombing attacks without being hit. During October and November there were other attacks on Flanders U-boats and although none of them were sunk, the post-war German naval history did note that air attacks became more aggressive after September and that *UB 6* and *UC 1* had been damaged.

There were few RNAS encounters with German aircraft off the Belgian coast during 1915 but two decisive combats were recorded. On 28 November one of four German seaplanes escorting a destroyer was shot down into the sea by a flying boat from Felixstowe. The second encounter followed the stranding of a merchant ship on sandbanks near the Whistle Buoy on 12 December. Bad weather prevented it being towed off and on 14 December enemy aircraft made several attempts to bomb it. A continuous air patrol was therefore mounted over it and a Nieuport two-seater piloted by Flight Sub Lieutenant Graham RNAS with Flight Sub Lieutenant A S Ince RNAS as observer and gunner spotted a large enemy seaplane directly over the vessel. After a short combat the enemy was shot down into the sea in flames and its bombs detonated on impact. The Nieuport had not emerged unscathed, however, and suffered a bullet hole through its petrol tank which rapidly emptied, forcing it to ditch. The aircraft turned over on hitting the water and dragged Graham under but he managed to free himself with the aid of Ince and they were subsequently rescued by a minesweeper. Ince was awarded the DSC.[16]

The Dardanelles Campaign

On 2 August 1914 a secret agreement was signed in Constantinople between the German government and the leaders of the Turkish Committee of Union and Progress in which the latter undertook to do all they could to bring the Ottoman Empire into line with the Central Powers. On 10 August when the German warships *Goeben* and *Breslau* passed through the Dardanelles to reach Constantinople they were nominally purchased by the Ottoman government and in October large Turkish forces began to assemble in Palestine where they posed an immediate threat to British interests including the Suez Canal and Egypt. On 27 October a Turkish fleet steamed into the Black Sea with the object of bombarding Russian ports and so a British naval force was concentrated at the island of Tenedos and on 30 October an ultimatum from the British and French governments to the Ottoman government was presented at Constantinople and on the following day both governments commenced hostilities against Turkey. On 3 November the Tenedos

HMS *Ark Royal* anchored at Kephalo in August 1915 with one of its seaplanes overhead. (Author's collection)

force carried out a 10-minute bombardment of the outer forts guarding the Dardanelles, partly as a demonstration and partially to test the effective range of the enemy guns. The Turkish commander of the batteries said subsequently that this action caused more damage than any later naval bombardment but whether this was true or not it did have the unfortunate effect of encouraging the Turkish Army to strengthen the defences that covered the approaches to the narrows. No further operations against the forts were undertaken in 1914.[17]

On 2 January 1915 the Russian government asked the Western Allies make a demonstration against the Turks to relieve the pressure on its own forces in the Caucasus. The British War Council discussed various options and decided on 13 January to adopt a scheme put forward by Churchill to use elderly battleships which had little value in the North Sea to force a passage through the Dardanelles to reach Constantinople. The new battleship *Queen Elizabeth* was, however, added to the force since she had to carry out extensive test firings of her new 15in guns which, it was thought, might as well be done in anger against Turkish forts. The seaplane carrier *Ark Royal* was also included to the task force which was to be commanded by Admiral de Robeck because it was believed that her seaplanes could spot the fall of shot and order corrections that would allow ships to engage the forts from long range with greater accuracy. She sailed at midnight on 1 February with one Short and two Wight seaplanes, each fitted with 200hp Canton Unne engines, plus three Sopwith seaplanes with 100hp engines and two Sopwith Tabloid aeroplanes with 80hp Gnome engines for operation ashore. *Ark Royal* arrived at Tenedos on 17 February 1915 and launched a seaplane which examined the forts of the outer defences and the coast for four miles into the narrows. On 19 February she hoisted out the Short seaplane to carry out a reconnaissance of the coast from Besika Bay 8 miles south of the entrance to Gaba Tepe 12 miles north of it; she then moved to a new anchorage near Mavro Island at 09.00. The seaplane returned at 09.15 and the observer was able to give the exact position of the barracks and fort at Helles and confirm that the guns at Cape Tekke could not fire north of north-west and could not, therefore, engage the position chosen for the battleship *Triumph*

A view of *Ark Royal*'s hangar hatch, steam cranes and working deck looking forward from the bridge at Kephalo in 1915. The nearest aircraft is either 162 or 163; both were Short Type Cs, later designated as Type 166. They were shipped out to the Aegean from the UK in May 1915 and assembled on *Ark Royal*. This photograph may show them both being erected for the first time. (Author's collection)

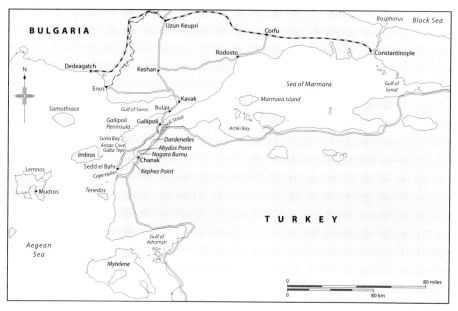

The Dardenelles. Theatre of Operations.

to bombard the Helles fort. At 11.00 a Wight seaplane was lowered and took off
to spot for the battleship *Cornwallis* against the fort at Orkanie but before it could
get into position the ship ceased fire and the pilot was ordered by searchlight to
examine the damage done by the morning's bombardment. The pilot reported that
the guns at Orkanie, Kum Kale and Sedd el Bahr were still intact. In the afternoon
ships were ordered to close the coast and overwhelm the forts with a short-range
bombardment. While this was being carried out, two seaplanes over Helles
attempted to spot for the battlecruiser *Inflexible* against the fort but both had
problems with their W/T equipment. They were fitted with the only two Sterling
W/T sets brought out in *Ark Royal* but both were still hardly out of the
experimental stage and the this was their first operational use. In one case the aerial
became snagged and in the other the transmitter short-circuited. So many ships
were firing different-calibre weapons at the same target, however, that any attempt
at spotting an individual ship's fall of shot would not have been practical. At 17.30
the bombarding force withdrew and at 19.05 *Ark Royal* hoisted in her seaplanes and
moved away to anchor back at Tenedos. The first day of the major bombardment
had not been a success. Worryingly, little thought had been given to the practicality
of using the aircraft to best advantage.

Later that evening the weather broke and was not suitable for a further
bombardment until 25 February when *Queen Elizabeth* and *Agamemnon* succeeded

in putting the only four long-range Turkish guns out of action. A number of attempts were made to get seaplanes airborne but the sea proved to be too choppy and none were successful; spotting had to be carried out from other vessels. On 26 February it was observed that the Turks had abandoned the outer forts and demolition parties were landed on both sides of the straits. An observer in the Short seaplane who had reconnoitred the area earlier in the day had reported that three guns at Sedd el Bahr, three at Kum Kale and one at Helles appeared to be in place but all the other guns in these forts, as well as those at Orkanie, appeared to be out of place, although not necessarily destroyed. The demolition parties rapidly destroyed the guns at Sedd el Bahr and Orkanie but had no time to deal with Kum Kale before dusk set in. The following day a further party was landed at Sedd el Bahr and destroyed six modern 6in howitzers on the cliffs to the east of the fort and on 1 March a party reached Kum Kale. Here the demolition party found that only one of the nine guns had been rendered unserviceable and they had to destroy the rest. Six 12pdr guns and four Nordenfeldt guns, together with a searchlight on a motor lorry, were also blown up.

Bombardment of the inner defences began on 5 March 1915 with *Queen Elizabeth* expected to play a leading part by firing over the Gallipoli peninsula into the rear of the forts. The targets would not be visible from the ship and so complete reliance was placed on spotting by seaplanes and from other ships inside the straits. At 10.00 *Ark Royal* closed *Queen Elizabeth* off Gaba Tepe and got a Sopwith away just over an hour later manned by Flight Lieutenant W H S Garnett RNAS as pilot and Flight Lieutenant H A Williamson RNAS, another pilot acting as observer, in time for the shoot to commence. The weather was perfect but as the aircraft climbed through 3000ft the propeller disintegrated and the aircraft crashed into the sea out of control. Both aircrew were rescued by the destroyer *Usk*; they were badly shaken and Williamson suffered injuries that kept him in hospital for several weeks.[18] A replacement Sopwith was sent off at once but as it was flying over the peninsula at 3000ft the pilot was hit in the leg by a rifle bullet and the sortie had to be aborted. Another pilot took over the same aircraft and it arrived on task in time to make some corrections before bad light forced *Queen Elizabeth* to cease fire. Reconnaissance the next morning revealed that, although a number of rounds had hit the forts, no guns had actually been damaged. Another shoot was arranged for the next day but the sea was too rough for seaplanes to get airborne and the Turks succeeded in partially jamming wireless signals from spotters on ships. Indirect fire having failed, an attempt was made to use *Queen Elizabeth* inside the straits on 8 March and a seaplane got airborne to spot for her. Unfortunately the targets were obscured by low cloud and squalls which also hampered the spotters in ships and this attack also ended in disappointment.

Ark Royal subsequently spent three days off Xeros Island and seaplanes flew across the isthmus of Bulair to reconnoitre the fortifications. She returned to Tenedos on 12 March and her seaplanes flew a number of sorties marking gun emplacements on both shores together with information on enemy camps but particular importance was placed on looking for mines in the straits, even though there could be no certainty that minefields would actually be visible from the air. Between 13 and 17 March seaplanes flew searches for mines on every day and reported fields between the narrows and Kephez Bay. Again, however, the planners had given too much warning of their intentions to the enemy and on the night of 17 March the Turkish minelayer *Nusret* laid a new field parallel to the shore in Eren Keui Bay in an area that had already been swept and which had, until the night of 17 March, been clear. Mines now proved to be the all-important factor and on 18 March a force of Allied battleships was to enter the narrows in an attempt to suppress the gun defences so as to allow civilian-manned minesweepers to clear a passage. The observation of the ships' fire was left entirely to *Ark Royal*'s seaplanes and one was to be sent up every hour.

At 11.30 on 18 March the ships were in position and opened fire. An hour later a Wight seaplane reported that four of the forts at the narrows were manned and firing rapidly but that one, Chemenlik, was not occupied. Three of the forts were being hit repeatedly but, owing to the amount of smoke and dust, no accurate damage assessment was possible. Forts at Mount Dardanos and Kephez Point were also seen to be unmanned but a number of mobile batteries were in action. A Sopwith relieved the Wight on station and reported that only Hamadieh, south of Chanak, was now firing with any determination. All its guns were firing but shells from the ships were exploding in the centre of the fort and doing little or no damage to the guns. The fort was firing at the battleship *Irresistible* which struck a mine and had to be abandoned in a sinking condition. Worse was to follow, *Inflexible* struck a mine shortly after 16.00 but managed to get back to Tenedos where repairs sufficient for her to return to Malta Dockyard were carried out. At 18.05 the battleship *Ocean* struck a mine as she was turning to withdraw and sank, the French battleship *Bouvet* struck yet another mine and sank rapidly with the loss of over 600 lives. The French battleships *Gaulois* and *Suffren* were badly damaged by mines.

Clearly there was little to be gained from operating battleships in waters that had not been efficiently swept and the attack was broken off. The seaplanes had reported that the ships' fire appeared to be effective and that Turkish fire had slackened but the Turks subsequently claimed that very little permanent damage had been done to the forts although they had been forced to cease fire on several lengthy occassions to clear dirt and grit from the guns due to hits on the parapets around them. The events of 18 March were a serious setback for the Allies; bombarding ships could not operate in the narrows until the mines were cleared, the minesweepers could not clear them until the forts and mobile batteries on shore were silenced and ships could not close to effective range for bombardment until the mines were cleared. The whole plan of action needed to be re-considered and it was realised that the object of the campaign could only be achieved if troops were landed in strength to neutralise the guns. Whereas parties of sailors and marines had landed virtually unopposed in February, the Turks had realised the peninsula's vulnerability and were making considerable efforts to strengthen defences on the ground and bring in reinforcements. A decision to build up British military forces in the Eastern Mediterranean had been taken on 16 February but they would not be ready to land until late April; again Allied intentions had been revealed to the Turks in good time for defensive preparations to be made. Major General Sir Ian Hamilton was appointed in command of the Middle East Expeditionary Force on 11 March.

The RN contribution to the force included the RN Division and Samson's unit, now designated 3 Squadron RNAS, which had been withdrawn from Dunkirk. It arrived at Tenedos and its aircraft were brought ashore after a gale on 26 February. The unit had eighteen aircraft of six different types including eight Henri Farmans, two BE 2c, two BE 2, two Sopwith Tabloids, one Breguet and three Maurice Farmans. There were eleven pilots, three observers, four technical officers and 100 men. Nigger, a German cavalry horse captured from a patrol of Uhlans in Belgium, was brought as Samson's personal mount. His arrival was described by Bell-Davies in *Sailor in the Air*.

Getting Nigger ashore when we reached Tenedos was another piece of combined equestrian and nautical expertise. By a combination of towing by the ship's cutter and swimming by Nigger, he reached the beach safely, where he galloped furiously inland dragging the tow rope after him. One of our old Eastchurch hands, Able Seaman Elsden, gallantly clung to it through a maze of thorn bushes until he was able to catch a turn with the rope round the branch of a stunted oak tree, bringing the runaway up all standing.[19]

Admiral de Robeck decided to use the newly-arrived aeroplanes for reconnaissance over the Gallipoli peninsula and the straits. *Ark Royal* was to use her mobility to operate her seaplanes further afield in places the shore-based aircraft could not reach. The first operational sortie by 3 Squadron was carried out on 28 March and aircraft subsequently flew over the peninsula on every day that the changeable weather allowed. Aeroplanes with wheeled undercarriages were found to be more effective and easier to operate than seaplanes. The aircrew systematically built up an accurate plot of enemy positions, controlled ships' fire against mobile batteries, especially those in the rugged country on the Asiatic shore, and photographed the projected landing beaches. They also wrote descriptions of the beaches, their landward approaches, apparent defences and corrected the outdated maps with which the expeditionary force had been issued. Samson insisted that bombs were carried on every sortie and dropped on enemy positions but reconnaissance was the more important task as there was no other way of gathering information about enemy positions and movements. Aerial photography was in its infancy but one officer, Flight Lieutenant C H Butler RNAS, emerged as a driving force in its application. He used a small folding Goertz Anschutz camera at first but 'borrowed' a better camera from a French Army air unit that arrived in May. The camera was fixed outside the cockpit nacelle of his aircraft and used extensively until he was badly wounded in late June; by then he had taken over 700 photographs, many of which could be pieced together into what became known as mosaics to form maps of important areas which were of vital use to the command. On 15 April a reconnaissance sortie located a Turkish airfield at Chanak and a

A rare glimpse into *Ark Royal*'s hangar deck in 1915 showing disassembled Sopwith Schneider seaplane fighters and the mechanics working on them. The airframe number can be seen; this was a Schneider shipped to Imbros in September 1915 and allocated to the ship. Apart from a brief period embarked in the cruiser *Lowestoft* this aircraft operated from *Ark Royal* between October 1915 and May 1916 when it was wrecked sideslipping into the sea, injuring Flight Lieutenant C W H Pulford RNAS. (Author's collection)

strike against it was organised on 18 April which dropped six 100lb bombs.

Ark Royal's movements allowed her seaplanes to appear in different places where their operations were intended to make the Turks suspect that landings might take place in a number of different locations. On 31 March she joined an Allied task force off Mitylene from where she operated her seaplanes to search the northern coast of the Gulf Adramyti, then returned to Mudros to refuel and embark a new Wight seaplane. Next she proceeded to the Gulf of Smyrna where two sorties were flown on 4 April to map the defences. On 6 April *Ark Royal* moved to the Gulf of Enos to launch a seaplane which carried out a reconnaissance of the town of Enos as part of a feint landing on 7 April. A day later she returned to Mudros where she embarked two Sopwith Schneiders and then sailed for the Gulf of Xeros, arriving on 12 April when her aircraft spotted for a bombardment by *Lord Nelson*. On 16 April her aircraft spotted for a further bombardment which destroyed an enemy magazine at Taifur Keui. On the same day, two Sopwiths searched the Gallipoli peninsula and bombed the Turkish battleship *Turgud Reis* which was anchored nearby. A day later *Ark Royal* returned to Mudros and no further flying was carried out by her seaplanes until after the Allied landings on 25 April. A further augmentation for the RNAS units in this theatre arrived at Mudros on 9 April. *Manica* had left the UK on 27 March and had its balloon ready for operations on 15 April. It spotted for its first shoot, by the cruiser *Bacchante*, on 19 April and was immediately found to have a number of advantages over aircraft. Firstly, it did not rely on an engine with its limited fuel supply and could thus remain aloft on its mooring wire throughout the hours of daylight. Secondly, and almost as important, the observer was in direct telephone communication with *Manica* and so his instructions could be passed to the firing ship much more reliably than they could be from the primitive wireless transmitters fitted in seaplanes at the time.

Sir Ian Hamilton elected to land his forces at the southern end of the Gallipoli peninsula with the aim of capturing Kilid Bahr and neutralising the forts that covered the narrows so that the naval attempt to force a passage could be resumed. The places chosen were a group of four small beaches about Cape Helles, a broken cliff some three miles up the coast and a beach north of Gaba Tepe, later known as ANZAC Cove, from where it was hoped that the force might cut the enemy's communications at their most vulnerable point. For the greater part, the landings were to be made using open boats towed by steam picket boats, all of them provided from the fleet. The one exception was at Sedd el Bahr where strong Turkish defences were known to surround the beach; here the modified collier *River Clyde* was to be run aground and the infantry were to make their way ashore across a bridge of lighters. To give them covering fire as they did so, eleven Vickers guns in armoured casemates were mounted on the ship's forecastle and manned by men from Numbers 3 and 4 Armoured Car Squadrons and Number 10 Motorcycle Machine Gun Squadron of the RNAS, all of which had been deployed with the expeditionary force at Churchill's instigation to improve the Army's firepower in what was expected to be a brief, mobile campaign by planners who had no very real idea of the rugged terrain. The *River Clyde* beached at the right place but the beach gradient was found to be shallower than anticipated, great difficulty was experienced getting the lighters into position and they were not ready until 08.00. Turkish fire was concentrated on them and attempts to get men ashore ended with heavy casualties. Supporting battleships could do little to suppress enemy fire and the bulk of the men could not be landed until nightfall. Throughout the day the RNAS machine-gunners kept their guns in action despite the fact that in all eleven casemates every man was wounded. At ANZAC Cove the landing began at 04.00 in the twilight before dawn but the men never quite reached the dominating high ground that was their aim. Unfortunately, as it transpired, five of 3 Squadron's aircraft had bombed a concentration of enemy troops at Maidos on 23 April and caused a considerable number of casualties. The unforeseen consequence was that the Turks dispersed them and thus two reserve infantry battalions were moved to a camp some miles nearer to the ANZAC landing and it proved possible to bring these into action much more rapidly than would otherwise have been the case.

Number 3 Squadron supported the landings at Helles while *Ark Royal* and *Manica* supported the more distant ANZAC landing. The weather was perfect for flying and aircraft were maintained all day over the Helles area and the Asiatic coast where a French force had landed. The first were over the coast at dawn briefed to spot for ships covering the landing and urgent wireless signals were sent from them as soon as Turkish batteries were seen to come into action. Once the Army got its own artillery ashore, the naval aircrew were briefed to communicate sighting corrections to them by Verey light signals as the Army gunners were unable to receive wireless transmissions. The aircraft also bombed Turkish gun positions and troops on the ground, took photographs of the enemy defensive positions seen to be in action and reconnoitred the whole peninsula as far as the isthmus of Bulair and the Asiatic shore. Their reports gave Sir Ian Hamilton and his headquarters afloat very detailed information about the rapid movements being made by the enemy to oppose him. The seaplanes and the balloon watched ANZAC Cove but were hampered by the broken nature of the ground although, frustratingly, they could actually see the narrows in the distance beyond the peninsula. The balloon ascended at 05.21 and 14 minutes later the observer saw the Turkish battleship *Turgud Reis* in the narrows. Its position was passed to the battleship *Triumph* which opened fire and the Turkish ship withdrew. Soon after 09.00 the Turkish ship returned and began to bombard the ANZAC transport ships which had to move

Wing Commander C R Samson RNAS about to take off from Imbros in a Henri-Farman biplane with the first 500lb bomb ever used on a strike mission. The engine is already running but the chocks have not yet been pulled away. There appears to be great interest among the ground crew and Samson's face shows what can only be described as a grin. His enthusiasm for the sortie is obvious. (Author's collection)

away out of range and stop unloading. *Triumph* engaged it again using spotting information from the balloon and *Turgud Reis* moved away once more, allowing the transports to resume unloading. At 14.00 the balloon was hauled down to relieve the observer who had worked ceaselessly for nine hours. In contrast, the seaplanes had great difficulty in locating the Turkish mobile gun batteries which were well concealed in scrub, especially since the gunners tended to hold their fire when an aircraft was near them. Once he was aware of this, General Birdwood, who commanded the ANZAC force, asked that a seaplane be kept as close as possible to the front line, especially while troop movements were taking place. In this way the aircraft were able to take some of the enemy pressure off the infantry.

Manica's balloon made seven ascents on 26 April to spot for *Triumph* and *Queen Elizabeth* and its observers did well. Spotting for the latter, an observer directed the ship's fire so successfully that a shell scored a direct hit on a magazine at Kojadere. On 27 April the balloon observer saw Turkish transport ships below Nagara and directed *Queen Elizabeth*'s fire onto them. His correction for the first shot was 50 yards short and the second 50 yards over. The third shot scored a direct hit on the ss *Scutari*[20] at a range of 14,000 yards and sank her. Unfortunately, this was the only ship that had no troops embarked but the others were diverted to Ak Bashi Liman where the ships were screened from the balloon observer by a line of hills but there were only limited landing facilities. The balloon crews more than justified the faith that had been placed in this form of aerial observation.

The RND, together with units from the Commonwealth and France, suffered heavy losses during the continued attempts to break out of the Helles and ANZAC bridgeheads. Overall they met with little success but nor did Turkish attempts to dislodge the invaders. On the morning of 17 May 1915 Flight Lieutenant R L G Marix RNAS, now serving in 3 Squadron, was patrolling above the peninsula looking out for enemy aircraft when he saw unusual activity in the port of Ak Bashi Liman and a large camp just inland from it already filled with troops. This pointed to the arrival of a new Turkish division, in fact the 2nd Division which had just been brought from Constantinople, and so Samson planned a strike against it on that afternoon. Marix flew in a Breguet armed with a single 100lb and fourteen 20lb bombs with Samson in the observer's seat. This was the first air strike against the port and it caused widespread panic among the dock workers and killed fifty-seven soldiers. Marix and Samson then carried out a detailed reconnaissance of the forces on the ground and passed the information to GHQ which concluded that an attack on the ANZAC positions was likely. The warning was received in the trenches at 22.00 on 18 May and when the enemy attack came at dawn the next day it was robbed of surprise and driven back with heavy loss of life. An airstrip was cleared within the Helles bridgehead in May so that aeroplanes could land for their observers to pass urgent information to Corps Headquarters with the minimum delay but it was under direct observation from Turkish positions on Achi Baba and was heavily shelled whenever an aircraft landed on it. It remained a useful relief landing ground when a renewed attempt to break out of Helles towards Krithia was made in early June. On 4 June the armoured cars of 3 and 4 Squadrons RNAS were used for the first time in this theatre but it was found that the rough nature of the roads and tracks meant that there was little they could do to support the infantry and they were withdrawn after a few hours' fighting. However, ten dismounted machine guns from Number 10 Motorcycle Squadron did good work in the forward edge of the assault.

During another assault later in June aircraft directed artillery fire onto enemy reinforcements and ammunition columns and dropped bombs on enemy troops on the ground. On 28 June aeroplane observers saw considerable movements of enemy troops towards ANZAC and were again able to give sufficient warning to rob the planned enemy attack of surprise and ensure its failure. By then the situation at sea had been made worse by the arrival of a German U-boat, *U 21*, which torpedoed and sank *Triumph* off Ari Burnu on 25 May and *Majestic* off

Sedd el Bahr two days later. Other U-boats joined her from the Adriatic and the threat they posed was considered so severe that several large support ships were withdrawn from the immediate area. *Ark Royal* was considered to be too slow to operate in unprotected waters and she remained at Kephalo Bay in the island of Imbros for a considerable period as a static depot ship for aircraft. Her seaplanes operated from a base established in Aliki Bay on Imbros until the end of October 1915 when the ship was ordered to re-embark them and move. She used them to carry out a reconnaissance of Smyrna and then left the Dardanelles area to take part in the Salonika Campaign.

Ben-my-Chree arrived at Mitylene on 12 June but by then the Admiralty was concerned that the provision of aircraft now needed to reflect the fact that it had become a land campaign and it sought advice from Colonel F H Sykes who had been responsible for the configuration and effectiveness of the RFC squadrons deployed to France and had actually commanded the force for a short period but lacked the rank to continue to do so as it expanded. In early 1915 there had been arguments within the BEF over whether air units should be controlled centrally or by corps or divisional commanders. Sykes' centralist views had proved unpopular and his services had been placed at the disposal of the Admiralty.[21] His report was delivered on 9 July 1915 and recommended the concentration of all flying units at Kephalo on Imbros and the supply of aeroplanes of a standard type for the shore-based squadrons as well as new photographic equipment, machine guns, wireless equipment, signalling lamps and an additional kite balloon section. In practical terms he was recommending an end to the period of making do with what could be made available and asking for equipment and tactics like those on the Western Front. He recommended the deployment of eight SS airships for anti-submarine work and additional seaplanes for spotting, patrol and strike operations. The recommendations were accepted by the Admiralty and Sykes was appointed in command of the RNAS units in the eastern Mediterranean with the dual ranks of Colonel Royal Marines and Wing Captain RNAS. Opinions about his appointment varied but Samson took a neutral line in *Fights and Flights*, writing that 'Colonel Sykes and his staff didn't worry me at all, but left me to go on in my own routine as usual, the only thing being that we had to send in reports to him as well as to all the usual people. In fact, as far as my Wing was concerned they might not have been there at all.'[22] Samson cannot have been an easy man to deal with and Sykes appears to have concentrated on administrative and logistic matters rather than risk a clash over operational plans. Samson also wrote that 'his staff started to try to build up an aeroplane repair section but no one ever saw any result, although they had quite a large party who were reported to be carrying out mystic rites over a Voisin they had in a hangar'. He was clearly not impressed.

In fact a second kite balloon section had already arrived aboard *Hector* on the day that Sykes' report was completed. The new airfield on the east side of Kephalo Harbour proved not to be a great success and Greek working parties augmented by Turkish prisoners guarded by Australians were used to clear a new landing ground at Kephalo Point. Imbros was closer to Suvla Bay where Sir Ian Hamilton intended to carry out a new amphibious landing on 6 August using reinforcements sent out from the UK. A number of reconnaissance sorties were flown over the area before this which had to be planned in such a way that they did not arouse Turkish suspicions. Aircraft flew at high altitude and only remained over the target area for brief periods during which the existing trenches and gun emplacements were carefully noted and sketch maps prepared for use by GHQ. Most of the gun emplacements were seen to be unoccupied and on 6 August the only enemy troop movements seen were actually moving away from the coast. During the night of 6/7 August 20,000 British troops were landed quietly at Suvla and, as predicted by air reconnaissance, they encountered no opposition. Unfortunately those in command failed to take advantage of the situation and their men waited on the beach while stores and water were landed. On 8 August aircraft reported that Turkish troops in large numbers were advancing from camps around Bulair and that some had already reached villages facing the British landing force. When the assault was resumed on 9 August no progress could be made and the Suvla landing, for all its potential promise, ended in another stalemate. Tragically a simultaneous assault from ANZAC also failed to make progress despite being pressed with the greatest determination.

RNAS reinforcements arrived in August comprising Number 2 Wing with twenty-two aircraft, sixteen pilots and 200 ground personnel. The aircraft were still not of a single standardised type, however; there were six Morane Parasol two-seater monoplanes, six BE 2c biplanes, six Caudron biplanes and four Bristol Scout biplane fighters. The kite balloon ship *Canning* arrived on 2 October to replace *Manica* which was to return to the UK for a refit. *Canning* was a major advance over her predecessors in that she could carry her balloon inflated in a large hold space forward of the bridge. The reinforcements increased the amount of support given to the Army on the ground and the number of bombing sorties flown against enemy supply lines. The German general who commanded Turkish forces in Gallipoli, Liman von Sanders, regarded the supply lines to his Fifth Army on the peninsula as being extremely vulnerable.[23] From Constantinople they travelled by sea or by the Thracian Railway to Uzun Keupri and thence by road through Keshan and Bulair. From there columns of camels, pack animals and Turkish ox carts carried supplies to the front line. Thus the Fifth Army had to rely to a large extent on water transport for some if not all its supplies; British and French submarines had passed through the narrows and attempted to cut off these supplies but had never quite succeeded in doing so.

Aircraft could add to the weight of attack but torpedoes had still not quite been developed into a true ship-killing weapon. However, *Ben-my-Chree* had brought 14in torpedoes and Short Type 184 aircraft equipped to carry them with her to the Mediterranean. Their chance came on 12 August when a Short armed with a torpedo and piloted by Flight Commander C H K Edmonds RNAS was lowered from the seaplane carrier in the Gulf of Xeros. It took off and flew across the isthmus where it was to attack shipping. Off Injeh Burnu Edmonds saw a large steamer and glided down to within 15ft of the surface to attack it, releasing his torpedo at a range of 300 yards. It detonated abreast the main mast and he believed that he saw the steamer settle slightly in shallow water. In fact, the vessel had already been shelled by a British submarine on the surface and had been left partially beached but the weapon's usefulness had been proved. On 17 August Edmonds flew another sortie against shipping bringing troops and supplies from the Asiatic coast into Ak Bashi Liman and this time his torpedo hit one of three steamers under way and set it on fire; it was badly damaged but did not sink and was eventually towed to Constantinople for repair. A second Short was launched at about the same time, piloted by Flight Lieutenant G B Dacre RNAS, but he suffered engine problems and was forced to alight in the straights near Galata. He saw a ship in False Bay and, taxi-ing towards it, saw it to be a large steam tug; he released his torpedo which hit and the tug gave a violent lurch and then sank. Dacre turned out of the bay under fire and, after a run of nearly two miles, succeeded in getting airborne and flew back to *Ben-my-Chree*. He was landing nearby when his engine failed completely but he was near enough to be recovered. During this period other aircraft, mainly armed with bombs, succeeded in wrecking a lighter and six dhows.

When Bulgaria entered the war in October, the railway that ran through it to Turkey assumed strategic significance and the RNAS considered making bombing strikes against it. Before it could do so, however, the Bulgarians overran Serbia, opening the Berlin-Constantinople railway to carry munitions directly from Germany to Turkey. The line was known to have a vulnerable point, however, which was within range of aircraft based on Imbros. This was a point south of Kuleli Burgas where a bridge carried the track across the River Maritza. On 5 November the Admiralty authorised an attack on the bridge which, it was now realised, would also cut the line to Salonika which branched off near its western end. On 8 November the first strike was carried out by an aeroplane from Imbros and two of *Ben-my-Chree*'s Short seaplanes. For the aeroplane this meant a total flight of 200 miles of which 60 were over the sea and 120 miles for the seaplanes of which,

Wing Commander
R Bell-Davies VC
RNAS. Note that
despite his extensive
RN background his
cap has an RNAS
Badge. (Author's
collection)

paradoxically, only 10 were over the sea. The aeroplane carried two 112lb bombs which were released over the target at 800ft. They missed but detonated together about five yards from the south side of the bridge and caused enough strain on one of the piers to delay traffic for two days while repairs were made. The seaplane's bombs missed the bridge but did some damage to the track at one end of it. Other strikes were carried out on 10, 13, 16, 18 and 24 November, the attack on the 13th being carried out at night by moonlight. No direct hits were scored but some damage was done to embankments, track and Uzun Keupri station.

Ferrejik Junction, where a branch left the main line towards Dedeagatch. was bombed by groups of up to six aircraft on 13, 16, 18 and 19 November and on 1 December. In all seventeen 112lb and twenty-four 20lb bombs were dropped on it and destroyed the main buildings, rolling stock and various sections of track. In the attack on 19 November Bell-Davies became the second RNAS pilot to be awarded the VC. He described the incident in some detail in *Sailor in the Air*:

The Henri Farman that Flight Sub Lieutenant G F Smyllie RNAS was flying was hit in the engine and forced down into the marshes on the far side of the Maritza River in Bulgarian territory. These marshes were very wide, cut up in winter and spring by a large number of water courses. In November, after a long dry summer, most of the water courses were dry, the beds being baked mud and gravel. In one of these Smyllie had safely landed and I decided to go down to pick him up. It never occured to me that we were likely to be interfered with by enemy troops. The marshes were wide and rough with tall banks of reeds and scrub. What did worry me was the possibility of finding 2 men to rescue, for I knew that some of our military observers had been detailed to take part in the operation as bomb-aimers. An experienced gunner officer was much more valuable than a newly-trained sub. RNAS. I could only carry one passenger but I could not imagine Edwards, Jopp, Walser or Knatchbull-Hugesson agreeing to come away and leave the pilot. As I circled down I could see the Farman burning. I flew low round it looking for Smyllie and received an almighty shock when the plane suddenly blew up. I had had no idea there was a bomb still on board and, in case there were any more, I hastily climbed away. Then I saw Smyllie emerge from a little hollow in which he had been lying and wave. I learned later that Smyllie had seen a party of Bulgarian troops approaching. He had therefore fired the plane and set off to cross into Turkish territory, preferring to be taken prisoner by Turks rather than Bulgars. On seeing me coming down to rescue him, he had realized the danger if the bomb exploded after I had landed, so he took cover in the hollow, fired at the bomb with his pistol and succeeded in exploding it with his third shot. To my great relief I found that Smyllie was alone. All the same, it was no easy matter to accommodate him in my plane as there was no passenger seat, a cowl now covering the space where one had originally been. He had to climb over me, slide under the cowl and crouch on all fours between the rudder bar and the engine bearers with his head bumping on the oil tank. He managed somehow to stow himself away looking most uncomfortable. By this time enemy troops were coming close so I lost no time in taking off.[24]

On 1 January 1916 the *London Gazette* announced that:

The King has been graciously pleased to approve the grant of the Victoria Cross to squadron Commander Richard Bell-Davies DSO RN and of the Distinguished Service Cross to Flight Sub Lieutenant G F Smyllie RNAS in recognition of their behaviour in the following circumstances. On 19 November 1915 these two officers carried out an attack on Ferrijik Junction. Flight Sub

Lieutenant Smyllie's machine was received by very heavy fire and brought down. The pilot planed down over the station, releasing all his bombs except one, which failed to drop, simultaneously at the station from a very low altitude. Thence he continued his descent into the marsh. On alighting he saw the one unexploded bomb, and set fire to his machine, knowing that the bomb would ensure its destruction. He then proceeded towards Turkish territory. At this moment he perceived Squadron Commander Bell-Davies descending and, fearing that he would come down near the burning machine and thus risk destruction from the bomb, Flight Sub Lieutenant Smyllie ran back and from a short distance exploded the bomb by means of a pistol bullet. Squadron Commander Bell-Davies descended at a safe distance from the burning machine, took up Sub

An SS airship landing at Mudros after an anti-submarine patrol with the handling party in position to grab the mooring rope and 'walk' the airship into its shed. The tube aft of the propeller that maintained air pressure inside the envelope is clearly visible, as is the BE 2 origin of the control car. (Author's collection)

Lieutenant Smyllie, in spite of the near approach of a party of the enemy, and returned to the aerodrome, a feat of airmanship that can seldom have been equalled for skill and gallantry.[25]

Another weak point was Bodoma Junction but this was within range of ships' guns and *Ben-my-Chree*'s seaplanes were used to spot for several shoots against it. Aircraft attacks against Turkish troops after they had landed on the peninsula also grew in intensity, especially the principal landing points at Maidos, Ak Bashi Liman, Kilia Liman and Gallipoli. Ships' guns were also spotted onto Ak Bashi Liman with success, for instance on 30 August when the monitor *M 15* lying off ANZAC cove opened fire on ships off the east coast of the peninsula under the

This well-known image shows Wing Commander C R Samson RNAS when he was in command of 3 Wing during the Dardanelles campaign stood in front of a Nieuport Scout in July 1915. Note the Lewis gun mounted to fire upwards through a gap in the upper wing. Samson is carrying a Webley & Scott automatic in his right hand and, notwithstanding the fact that he is standing next to an aircraft with a full tank of avgas, he is smoking a cigarette. (Author's collection)

control of an airborne observer; it sank one ship and set another on fire at a range of 18,000 yards with hills up to 1000ft high between the monitor and the targets.

There was a flour mill in Gallipoli which supplied most of the Turkish Fifth Army's needs; it was bombed frequently but, situated in a crowded, built-up area it was a difficult target to hit. One 122lb bomb hit a flour storage building, completely destroying it and killing two soldiers. Airborne observers also spotted for ships firing at the mill and, although it was never put completely out of action, it seldom reached its full output because of continual damage to buildings and machinery. Aircraft also carried out bombing attacks against Turkish camps, especially in the reserve area at Soghanli Dere. Strafing attacks with machine guns against troops moving across open ground behind the front line were developed and these had the effect of forcing the Turks to split columns of men into small sections moving a mile apart with instructions to halt and take cover whenever an aircraft was seen. Anti-submarine patrols by both seaplanes and aeroplanes continued throughout the latter part of the campaign augmented from mid-September by an SS airship. Three had been deployed to the theatre in response to Sykes' recommendation but it was found that only one was needed to cover the danger area and, since they was found to be difficult both to handle and house, the remaining two were not inflated. On 21 October the SS unit moved from Imbros to Mudros where conditions were considered more suitable. Considering the urgent need for these airships in UK waters, Sykes' request for eight SS airships seems to have been rather out of touch with reality. His idea of centralising all shore-based air assets at Kephalo on Imbros also seems questionable given the number that subsequently moved to locations better suited to their operations.

The Dardanelles campaign proved not to be the decisive stroke envisaged by Churchill. Whatever strategic brilliance the idea might have had in concept, it had resulted in another costly stalemate and on 27 October 1915 General Sir Charles Monro relieved Sir Ian Hamilton. He soon recommended evacuation and it was decided on 7 December to withdraw from Suvla and ANZAC, something Hamilton had recommended against because he feared heavy losses. In fact the operation was completed on 20 December without the loss of a single man. Three days after Christmas Monro was ordered to evacuate the Helles area as well and by 9 January 1916 the last men had left the peninsula, again without a single casualty. The evacuation, under extremely difficult circumstances in the face of a determined enemy, had proved to be the most brilliantly planned and executed feature of the whole campaign. By then the Turkish Air Service had been reinforced by three Fokker monoplane fighters. These immediately made their presence felt but RNAS Bristol Scouts fitted with Lewis guns were able to oppose them effectively. Between 6 and 12 January three British aircraft were shot down in air combat with four aircrew killed and one wounded and taken prisoner. Despite these late losses, enemy reconnaissance failed to detect the imminent departure of the Allied forces.

Operations against the Cruiser *Königsberg* in the Rufigi Delta

The German cruiser *Königsberg* had sailed from Dar-es-Salaam when war broke out for a raiding cruise against Allied shipping in the Indian Ocean. She sank the British cruiser *Pegasus* off Zanzibar on 20 September 1914 and then took refuge in one of the channels that formed the Rufigi River delta. The cruiser *Chatham* arrived off the coast with orders to destroy her and two colliers were sunk in the main channel to block her exit but from the sea it was not possible to see exactly where she was lying. By chance a civilian pilot, Mr H D Cutler, was giving public exhibition flights with two 90hp Curtiss flying boats from a beach near Durban. One of these aircraft was requisitioned by the Admiralty and Cutler was given a temporary commission in the RNAS to fly it operationally. The flying boat was found to be in poor condition but after repairs it was taken to Niororo Island about 18 miles off the Rufigi coast and Cutler flew his first reconnaissance mission on 22 November 1914. Before even reaching the coast, however, he flew into a tropical storm and became uncertain of his position. Flying at the limit of his ability in torrential rain he was forced to land on the beach of an uninhabited island where, fortunately, he was found and taken back to Niororo with the aircraft. Further repairs were carried out and he tried again on 24 November in better weather and succeeded in finding *Königsberg* some 12 miles inland close to the bank and well hidden by trees and foliage. Although it was still tidal, such was the shallowness of the channel she was found in that some doubt was expressed about the accuracy of his information and two RN officers were flown over the delta in early December to confirm Cutler's original report.[26] The second of these discovered that *Königsberg* had shifted her berth and so on 10 December Cutler was sent on a further sortie briefed to try and ascertain whether she was trying to work her way out to the open sea. Unfortunately his engine failed while he was over the delta; he came down in the river and was taken prisoner by a party of Germans. The flying boat, however, was not allowed to fall into enemy hands. It had been beached on a mud bank and was recovered by a British motor boat under the cover of machine-gun fire from an armed tug. It moved in quickly, attached a line to the aircraft and towed it back to the base on Niororo Island. It was considered that *Königsberg* was not intending to break into the open sea but where she lay she was beyond the range of *Chatham*'s guns; only shallow-draft monitors could bombard her and the ships allocated for the task by the Admiralty, *Severn* and *Mersey*, could not arrive for some months.

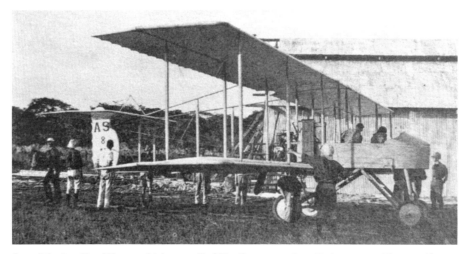

One of the two Henri-Farman biplanes with 80hp Gnome engines that were used in operations against the German cruiser *Königsberg* in 1915. It is seen here being prepared for flight at the airstrip on Mafia Island. The building partially visible behind the aircraft is the corrugated-iron hangar that was constructed especially for them. (Author's collection)

Cutler's improvised unit was replaced by a detachment under Flight Lieutenant J T Cull RNAS which arrived on Niororo Island on 21 February 1915 equipped with two Sopwith 100hp seaplanes which had been assembled in Bombay after a voyage in crates from the UK. They were found to be unsuited for work in the tropical conditions and proved to be of little or no use. At the beginning of April two Short seaplanes arrived which were better suited to the conditions and a reconnaissance by one of these on 25 April 1915 found the *Königsberg* again and took photographs but it was unable to climb above 600ft and was shot down by rifle fire on the return flight. The pilot managed to carry out a safe water landing, however, and the aircraft. with its important photographs, was towed back to Niororo. The two monitors arrived in June and on 18 June a larger RNAS force arrived commanded by Squadron Commander R Gordon RNAS. It comprised two Henri Farmans with Canton Unne engines and two Caudrons with 80hp Gnome engines which were landed on the beach at Mafia Island and then towed along a jungle track to an airfield that had been cleared especially for them in the centre of the island. Unfortunately, during the practice shoots which preceded the bombardment of *Königsberg* one Henri Farman and one Caudron were wrecked.

Just after dawn on 6 July 1915 the two monitors entered the northern channel of the delta and opened fire on *Königsberg* at a range of 10,000 yards with an aeroplane spotting the fall of shot. The enemy returned the fire with salvoes which were sufficiently accurate to damage *Mersey* and force her to open the range and carry out repairs. *Severn* continued in action and achieved a number of hits on her target which tried to move in order to confuse the British gunners' aim. At 16.00 the monitors withdrew to seaward but aircraft observers reported that, while *Königsberg* appeared to have been damaged, she remained capable of action and the shoot would have to be repeated. During the day the two aircraft had flown for over 15 hours between them and one of the observers had been airborne for a total of nine hours. At about midday on 11 July *Severn* and *Mersey* re-entered the shallows and Flight Lieutenant Cull RNAS with Sub Lieutenant H J Arnold RNVR as his observer took up a position where they could see the enemy cruiser. They had been briefed that only *Severn*'s fall of shot would be corrected and that *Mersey* would move continually in an attempt to divert the enemy's fire. The first five salvoes from *Severn* were unobserved but the sixth was seen to fall in the forest behind the enemy and to the right. Two corrections from the observer produced hits on *Königsberg*'s forecastle at 12.42 but at that very moment the aircraft was hit in the engine by anti-aircraft fire and the pilot was forced to glide down and ditch the aircraft but as he did so, Arnold was able to transmit a message that they were hit, coming down and needed a rescue boat. Coolly, he also transmitted the vital information that the last shells had hit the enemy forecastle and that *Severn* should fire for effect. This brought a small alteration of deflection and *Severn*'s subsequent salvoes produced a big explosion which tore *Königsberg* apart, followed by fire and a thick column of smoke. The aeroplane ditched and turned over about 500 yards from the *Mersey* and the observer was thrown clear but the pilot became entangled with the wreckage and had difficulty getting clear. He eventually got to the surface and both men were rescued by a motor boat. Ranging was now achieved by cross-reference on the column of smoke from the burning cruiser and further salvoes brought explosion after explosion. When the second aircraft arrived on task the observer was able to report that *Königsberg* was little more than a burning wreck and the action was terminated at 14.20.

After the completion of these operations the RNAS unit moved at first to Zanzibar and then to Mombassa where it was reinforced by two Caudron aeroplanes and three Short seaplanes. Before they left the theatre, however, Admiral King-Hall ordered a party to return to Mafia Island with one of the Caudrons to fly a reconnaissance sortie that could assess the damage to *Königsberg*. One has to wonder why this was not done in July with the one remaining aircraft but the new sortie was flown in August and the observer took photographs which confirmed that the ship would never move again. Worryingly, however, they also revealed that the Germans were unshipping her guns for use ashore. On 12 August 1915 Gordon with the three Short seaplanes left Mombassa for service in Mesopotamia and on 8 September the remainder under the recently-promoted Flight Commander Cull moved inland to Maktau for co-operation with the Army in the east African Campaign.

7 Armoured Cars, Trains, Tanks and Aircraft Procurement

From the earliest days of naval flying, motor cars formed an important element of an air organisation's equipment and after arriving in France Samson expected to use them for the location of aircraft that had been forced to land by mechanical failure, the establishment of temporary airfields and the carriage of mechanics and spare parts wherever they were needed. However, the RNAS soon found that vehicles had tactical uses which complemented aircraft and that motor cars could often operate when aircraft could not. Sailors had often proved adept at carrying out essential tasks ashore and ships had landed men in support of operations throughout the British Empire for a considerable time, most recently in the Boer War when naval brigades with their 4.7in guns mounted on improvised field carriages had fought alongside the Army with conspicuous success. Sailors were trained in infantry tactics at gunnery schools and companies of both sailors and Marines could be landed from deployed cruisers, potentially offering the only armed force available in the early stages of a crisis. Not only were naval officers and men trained and accustomed to think in terms of disembarked, mobile operations but it was expected of them and in *Fights and Flights* Samson described how, as early as 29 August 1914, General Aston who commanded the Royal Marine Brigade at Ostend sent for him and asked if it was feasible to carry out a motor-car reconnaissance as far as Thourout and Bruges.[1] Samson thought it 'an excellent idea' and, together with his brother Felix, selected two vehicles for the job, one of which was Felix's Mercedes fitted with a machine gun; the other had a large wagonette body capable of carrying several passengers. Samson set off with four other officers and four of 'the fiercest-looking Eastchurch men we had' and in Thourout the Mayor informed the RNAS party that German cyclists had reconnoitred the town only an hour earlier. In Bruges they were greeted by enthusiastic crowds who took them for the advance guard of a larger British force. Having gained information of value, the party returned to Ostend having 'enjoyed themselves immensely although some of the more bloodthirsty members were disappointed at not getting a fight'. Samson reflected that 'the trip made us consider the question of motor-car operations and ideas were discussed for armouring the cars'. The Wing's daily work at this stage consisted of flights over the area enclosed by Ypres, Lille, Douai, Cambrai and Valenciennes looking for German troop movements. At this stage it was a war of movement and neither side had a clear idea of where the opposing forces were. The work required long flights in slow, unreliable aircraft and because of the possibility of forced landings Samson began armed car patrols between Dunkirk, Cassel and Bailleul so that a breakdown party 'would be in attendance on an aeroplane as soon as possible in case of a forced landing'.[2] Road patrols also trained personnel in the possibilities for motor-car reconnaissance and Felix Samson worked hard at plans to improve the available cars.

Armoured Cars

Samson soon realised 'that this motor-car work was daily gaining in importance and that it would be more efficient if he could go out with a stronger force'.[3] He therefore wrote to the Admiralty asking for fifty Marines to be sent out to him for motor-car operations. Churchill took a keen interest at this stage, sent out a force of Marines and also ordered 'a considerable number of motor cars to be armoured'. He gave instructions that officers and men were to be enlisted directly into the RNAS for service in the rapidly-expanding armoured car force. Samson also commented on Sueter's enthusiasm for armoured cars but it is not clear whether this was the Director of the Air Department's own enthusiasm or whether he was motivated by Churchill's drive for new weapons. By the time the Eastchurch Wing moved to Morbecque it was capable of defending itself against enemy reconnaissance parties with two armoured lorries and an armoured car. They were all manned and kept ready for action throughout the night. Armour plates were fitted to the vehicles' chassis by the Forges et Chantiers de France in Dunkirk to a design prepared by the Samson brothers with the idea of providing protection for a force of infantry to accompany the cars. The only sheet metal available was boiler-plate which proved to be of little use against rifle or machine-gun fire at close range but was effective at longer ranges. Twelve Marines could be carried in each lorry and loopholes were cut in the armoured sides for them to shoot through. With the added weight of the armour, however, the lorries were too slow to keep up with the cars and Samson reverted to carrying riflemen in light touring cars. Of interest, the Wing also established a section of cyclists, twelve Marines commanded by Samson's other brother Bill. As they gained fitness they developed into a useful reconnaissance force, gathering information from a network of Boy Scouts who were 'each provided with a bicycle and one franc a day'. The Scouts knew the country well and were 'able to get into places which were occupied by Germans without fear of capture'.[4]

A new Rolls-Royce armoured car photographed before the application of its RNAS markings. Note the towing cable stowed neatly on the starboard running board. (Author's collection)

Shortly after the Wing arrived at Morbecque the new purpose-built armoured cars began to arrive in small batches from the UK. They had been designed without consulting Samson and proved unpopular at first because, although the chassis, engine and driver were well protected, the remainder of the crew were not, so that 'any man behind a hedge could pick them off with ease'. The chassis used were from Rolls-Royce, Talbot and Wolseley; of these the Rolls-Royce was by far the most reliable and suitable. Major Risk RM, who had served with the RNAS at Eastchurch before the war, arrived to command the first armoured car squadron. The second squadron commander was Lord Annesley who brought his own motor car which he had armoured himself in a local garage for the purpose. With him came his driver Ryan who later became Samson's coxswain. Annesley's design was good but his armour plate comprised soft iron of little value which was badly secured to the car with the result that bits kept dropping off. This caused some amusement and it was said, rather unkindly, that Annesley must have connections in the scrap-metal trade but he was considered a great fellow and was soon deemed indispensable. The armour was, however, soon removed and the car used for light despatch work.

On 1 October 1914 a new squadron of improved armoured cars arrived under the command of Lieutenant Commander Josiah Wedgewood MP RNVR, who soon proved himself to be a determined exponent of armoured car operations. By then he had the benefit of a 'Drill Book' on the subject prepared by Samson which brought a new level of professionalism to the expanding force based on experience. When the Wing moved forward to Antwerp Samson had under his command seventy motor-omnibuses carrying personnel escorted by eleven armoured cars, six of which were fitted with machine guns, and the two armoured lorries. The omnibuses had just arrived, having been taken directly off the streets of London. The drivers and conductors had all volunteered to come with them and had yet to be issued with uniforms. Samson observed that 'what they lacked in discipline and uniform they made up for in driving skill and cheerfulness'. The problem of escorting such a large road convoy was a difficult one but Samson solved it by sending ahead sections of armoured cars to cover portions of the route with orders to rejoin when the buses had passed their patrol area. The remainder of the cars were divided up with two sections in amongst the buses and the remainder as advanced and rear guards respectively. A total of 120 Marines were spread throughout the convoy with ten in every sixth bus so that whatever part of the long line might be attacked an escort of cars or Marines would be close at hand. 'The omnibuses kept splendid station and rumbled along at a steady 10mph; the clouds of dust they kicked up were appalling and the only comfortable position' was the

A Lanchester armoured car; number 4 of 'A' Flight 15 Armoured Car Squadron RNAS. All RNAS armoured cars flew the White Ensign in action from a small ensign staff fitted to the turret which helped to differentiate them from enemy vehicles. (Author's collection)

one Samson chose at the head of the procession.[5] After 20 miles he discovered that the bus drivers had not eaten since the day before and nothing had been organised for them. He therefore sent a car ahead to Ghistelles which returned loaded with bread and sausages to solve the problem. When the convoy arrived on the outskirts of Antwerp, Samson decided to make 'an impressive entry into the city to hearten up the inhabitants' so the armoured vehicles moved to the head of the procession looking 'extremely shipshape and warlike'. The streets were crowded with people who cheered the British force to the echo although Samson later admitted that 'the martial look of the procession was rather spoilt by the number of children and other civilians who scrambled onto the buses' but it still cheered up the inhabitants.

The number of different armoured car types at first made them difficult to support but their obvious usefulness was held to justify the production of large production batches of improved versions to Admiralty designs. The first was the short-lived stopgap that was criticised by Samson but the second which gave end, side and overhead protection for the whole crew together with a revolving turret which carried a machine gun was an altogether more successful design that was to remain in service with British armed forces for decades. The body could be mounted on chassis made by Rolls-Royce, Lanchester, Talbot and Delauney-Belleville but the first two were considered the best. By March 1915 totals of seventy-eight Rolls-Royce, thirty-six Lanchester and three Talbot armoured cars had been produced and the armoured car element of the RNAS had grown into a Division led by Commander E L Boothby RN. It was originally to comprise fifteen squadrons and a divisional headquarters. Each squadron comprised three sections, each of four cars. Command and control was assisted by a number of other vehicles including ordinary motor cars used by messengers, trucks, some of which contained mobile workshops, wireless-telegraphy vehicles and ambulances. Each armoured car was marked with the letters RNAS and an individual identity, for instance 15.A.4 was the fourth armoured car in A Section of 15 Squadron. In the event only ten of the squadrons were equipped with armoured cars and the remaining five received machine-gun equipped motorcycle combinations. By December 1914 there were sufficient squadrons to allow one to be based in the UK to guard the east coast against possible German raids and by January 1915 there were eight squadrons in commission, not all of which had their machine guns fitted because of the priority given to supplying the BEF in France. The problem was resolved, however, by removing guns from older warships. By March 1915 when Squadron Commander the Duke of Westminster led Number 2 Squadron to France each armoured car squadron had been further equipped with three Seabrook lorries, each fitted with a single Hotchkiss 3pdr gun and ammunition stowage. The spring of 1915 saw the end of tactical movement on the Western Front, however, with

Heavier firepower to support the armoured cars' machine guns could be provided by this Seabrook 5-ton heavy armoured car which was equipped with a 3pdr naval gun and up to four Vickers machine guns. Note the ensign staff fitted right aft and the 8mm armoured sides which have been lowered to give the guns clear arcs of fire. They could be raised quickly to protect the crew against small-arms fire at close quarters when necessary. In this view the crew is demonstrating how the port bow Vickers and the 3pdr would be brought into action. Ammunition for the latter was stowed right aft. (Author's collection)

lines of trenches behind thick belts of barbed wire limiting the usefulness of armoured cars.[6]

The lack of roads and the difficult terrain on the Gallipoli peninsula were not appreciated before the land campaign got underway and two Rolls-Royce squadrons, Numbers 3 and 4, were landed but their vehicles spent most of their time in deep dugouts to protect them from enemy artillery fire and, as mentioned earlier, their gunners played a gallant part in the *River Clyde* landing. Some armoured cars were fitted with winches, wire and grapnels with which they were able to pull away a section of Turkish barbed wire prior to an assault but overall they proved to have little value and were withdrawn to Egypt. Here the terrain was more suitable and they were used to defend the Suez Canal and for operations in the Western Desert against revolting tribesmen. Another Roll-Royce squadron was deployed to German South West Africa in 1915[7] and landed at Walfisch Bay where they found the deep soft sand in the coastal belt impossible and they had to be taken 50 miles inland by rail. Here the ground was firmer and, although there were no roads, the unit was involved in a number of successful actions against German colonial forces including ambushes by day and night. The armoured cars proved to be particularly suitable for night operations, using their headlights to illuminate targets for the gunners. On at least one occasion their speed and tactical mobility allowed them to break up an enemy attack and it would be fair to say that they played a significant part, with other Imperial forces, in bringing the campaign in South West Africa to a successful conclusion.

On the other side of Africa an RNAS armoured car squadron equipped with Lanchesters co-operated with mobile Army units in British East Africa in operations against German forces to the south which had attacked the Uganda railway. This was an important link that carried supplies and was being extended to facilitate future operations against the enemy. The terrain was, if anything, worse than South West Africa and cars had to cross areas of swamp and shifting sand before they could be brought into action. The Lanchesters were reinforced by a Rolls-Royce section from South West Africa and in one instance it took large gangs of native labourers all day to haul four armoured cars through a swamp that was only a few hundred yards wide. The armoured cars were given the task of patrolling the existing railway line and the new part that was still under construction. They managed to clear tracks through the bush and soon established complete control of their operational area. Heavy casualties had been inflicted on raiding parties which made no further attempt to damage the railway. One of the more noteworthy RNAS armoured car operations took place in the Western Desert of Egypt when shipwrecked survivors from the ss *Tara* were rescued. She was a small cargo ship that had been sunk off the north coast of Africa; those of the crew who got ashore were captured by Senussi tribesmen who took them to Bir Hakim about 100 miles inland. Once the British headquarters in Cairo heard about their fate, a force comprising nine Rolls-Royce armoured cars under Squadron Commander The Duke of Westminster RNAS was ordered to cross the desert and rescue them. In support the squadron had three unarmoured Ford cars fitted with Lewis guns and a further twenty-eight touring cars and ambulances. When the Senussi saw the armoured cars working their way into a position from which to attack they fled before fire could be opened, leaving their captives behind. The aim of the expedition was thus achieved without bloodshed. This was the first time that a group of motor vehicles had successfully crossed the featureless and unmapped Western Desert and the fact that they all returned safely was a great technical achievement.

As with the AAC based in the UK, the Admiralty had begun to question the operation of its land-based armoured car organisation and, as part of the more general reorganisation of the RNAS in August 1915, the division was disbanded with the exception of Number 1 Squadron which eventually deployed to Russia under Commander Locker-Lampson RN. The cars had been generally successful but had outgrown their usefulness in co-operation with the air squadrons and become part of wider land operations. The RNAS armoured cars and their support vehicles were handed over to the Army which formed them into what were known as Light Armoured Motor Batteries of the Motor Machine Gun Corps. Many of them served effectively in Egypt, Palestine, Syria, Mesopotamia and Persia and one former RNAS armoured car is worthy of mention. This was a Rolls-Royce Silver Ghost built in 1913 and requisitioned for the RNAS in 1914. It was subsequently handed over to the Army in 1915 and given the War Office number LC 305. As the campaign in Palestine expanded it was recognised that armoured cars were particularly useful and Colonel T E Lawrence, Lawrence of Arabia, made a number of references to LC 305 which acted in his support and which he referred to as 'Blue Mist'. It subsequently served with the 4th Armoured Car Company of the Tank Corps and was later transferred to the RAF in 1922. It eventual fate is, unfortunately, unrecorded but at the time of its transfer to the RAF it had over 100,000 miles recorded in its logbook and it was still described as being in excellent condition.

Number 1 Squadron remained in commission when the other RNAS armoured car units were disbanded and remained in Flanders until October 1915 when it returned to the UK to prepare for service in support of the Russian Army.[8] The Russians actually had the world's largest armoured car force at this time, with over 500 in service including many British-built Austins. Number 1 Squadron was mainly equipped with Lanchesters but had a single Rolls-Royce on strength. Records of its operations are scarce but it is known to have disembarked at Archangel in June 1916 and then travelled by train to Vladikavkas. From there the unit travelled across country in the absence of any paved roads to join in Russian operations against Kurdish forces in the region of Ezeroum. When these operations ended the squadron moved to Odessa and thence by sea to Romania where it became involved in the retreat from Dobrudja and encountered temperatures of –40 degrees Celsius in the harsh winter of 1916/17. The squadron later moved to Galicia where it took part in General Brussilov's failed offensive after which it returned to the UK and disbanded, the vehicles and equipment being handed over to the Army. The vehicle speedometers indicated that they had travelled an average of 53,000 miles during their deployment.

Technical characteristics
All RNAS armoured cars were rear-wheel drive with four wheels on the rear axle and two on the front. The engines were relatively simple side-valve units with an engine-driven pump to get fuel into the carburettor; a hand pump was fitted on the dashboard for starting. Magneto ignition was standard and the gearbox was a four-speed sliding pinion type with no synchro-mesh mechanism. The drivers required

considerable skill to apply a 'double-declutching' technique to avoid grating noises and possible damage when changing gear, especially on hills. The 1914 Rolls-Royce Admiralty pattern armoured car weighed 3.5 tons and was 16ft 9in long; 6ft 3in wide and 7ft 7in high. It was armed with a single Vickers .303in machine-gun in a revolving turret with 3000 rounds of belted ammunition. The chassis was a standard Silver Ghost pattern but the suspension springs were strengthened to take the extra weight of the armour and the engine consisted of two three-cylinder blocks mounted on an aluminium crank-case. It was always reliable and had dual ignition with one spark plug on the inlet valve cap and another in the centre of the head; it could achieve a maximum speed of 60mph and run economically at 8 to 10 miles per gallon on reasonable road surfaces but much less on rough terrain in constant low gear. In addition to the Vickers gun the three crew, driver, gunner and gunner's mate, would each have been armed with a Webley .455in automatic pistol, the standard-issue sidearm of the RNAS, although a few officers purchased their own Webley-Fosbery automatic revolvers instead.

Armoured Trains

The RNAS armoured car squadrons were not the only armoured units to come under RNAS control in 1914/15 and three armoured trains also merit a brief description. They were put into service in 1914 with Belgian rolling stock, locally modified with armour plate and equipped with RN guns and ammunition to be commissioned as His Majesty's Armoured Trains *Churchill*, *Deguise* and *Jellicoe.* The first and last flew the White Ensign,[9] and were manned by parties of volunteer RN officers and men drawn from the staffs of the home port gunnery schools; *Deguise* was named after a Belgian general, manned by the Belgian Army with a Belgian commanding officer but had seven RN gunlayers assisted by Belgian volunteers to man its main armament which was provided by the RN. According to the lists of men awarded the 1914 Star, HMT *Churchill* had a complement of forty and *Jellicoe* thirty, both with RN commanding officers. After a lot of help from the Belgian railway authorities together with Captain Servais, a retired artillery officer who commanded *Deguise*, and Commandant Lefevre, a Belgian engineer officer who had been largely instrumental in their design and modification, the armoured trains acted in support of the RND at Antwerp under RNAS operational control. Armoured trains were not new and an earlier example manned by sailors under Captain 'Jacky' Fisher RN equipped with a 40pdr Armstrong gun and two Gatling guns was used in the capture of Alexandria in 1882. A special 'Naval Armoured Train' badge was produced.

Lieutenant L F Robinson RN, an Australian serving in the RN as a gunnery specialist. commanded HMT *Jellicoe* and wrote a book about his experiences after the war entitled *Naval Guns in Flanders 1914-1915*. *Jellicoe* was armed with 6in and

4.7in guns and he described a number of actions around Antwerp with the engine sheltering in a junction during the night and moving out to pre-surveyed kilometre positions after dawn to engage the enemy.

> We went to a position behind Donk Wood beyond [position] K8 . . . in front of most of the field artillery which were barking away on both quarters and only a

Photographs of the RN armoured trains are extremely rare. This image shows a 4in naval gun in action from an armoured train halted near Antwerp. The gunlayer next to the breech is a sailor with a Admiralty-pattern pistol holster, attached to a leather belt, on his left hip. The man on his left is observing the fall of shot. Ammunition for the gun was stowed in the semi-covered area between the gun and the camera. (Author's collection)

mile from our Marines holding the line in front of us west of Lierre. Our first target was a double battery of field guns which a Belgian balloon observed to be in action in a position at Blijenhoek 2,000 yards to the south-west of Lierre. We opened fire with Lyddite and shrapnel and after half an hour we were informed that the enemy had ceased fire and were moving away. We were told to open fire on the pontoon bridges used in last night's attack so a slow bombardment was directed on this area. After about 20 minutes we must have been spotted by the balloons for a battery opened fire on us with shell of a medium calibre. Their first salvo straddled us – one shell landed and exploded 100 yards on one side and another as much on the other, whilst one landed, a 'dud', in the ditch alongside the train. We did not wait for more but went back to K7 and from there watched the continued shelling of our previous position.[10]

Similar tactics were used by the armoured trains during the First Battle of Ypres with such conspicuous success that German prisoners later informed the Allies that the Kaiser had offered a £1000 reward for any soldier who killed the commanding officer of an armoured train. The train comprised a steam engine at either end, ensuring that one would always provide motive power if the other were hit, wagons fitted out as offices, magazines and accommodation, and flat-bed trucks on which the guns were mounted.

The war on the Western Front became static and without Churchill's driving enthusiasm at the Admiralty there seemed to be even less point in retaining the armoured trains than there had been in keeping armoured car units as part of the RNAS. The trains were handed over to the Belgian authorities and the men were re-appointed to other gunnery duties throughout the fleet. Two other armoured trains were brought into temporary service by the RN in Russia during the Great War but neither had any connection with the RNAS. The first was used in Northern Russia on the Murmansk to Archangel railway line and was armed with 4in guns taken from RN warships. Another armoured train manned by Royal Marines was used against the Bolsheviks after the Russian Revolution. This travelled to Siberia and back in August 1918, a total distance of 24,000 miles, armed with a 6in gun and four 12pdrs taken from HMS *Norfolk* which remained at Vladivostok.

Tanks

Few projects illustrate Churchill's enthusiasm for absorbing peripheral activities into the RNAS and Sueter's acceptance that he must do so as well as the early development of the tank. In *Airmen or Noahs*, Sueter recounted that Churchill had followed a letter to the Prime Minister on the subject with a minute to the Air Department dated 18 January 1915 which proposed using steamrollers linked

Flight Commander Hetherington RNAS with Flight Lieutenants Stern and McGrath demonstrating the ability of the Killen-Strait caterpillar tractor to clear rough ground at RNAS Wormwood Scrubs in June 1915. Their work led directly into full-scale development of the tank. (Author's collection)

together to tow a roller which was to 'smash enemy trenches in'. The ultimate object was 'to run along a line of trenches, crushing them all flat and burying the people in them' and the matter was 'extremely urgent and should be pressed to the utmost'.[11] Sueter referred the matter to Lieutenant Barry RN, his motor-car expert, who explained that steamrollers would be absolutely useless for the task as they were intended for use on hard road surfaces and would become bogged down in any soft earth. He recommended the use of caterpillar-tracked vehicles and described the American Holt as 'the most efficient form of tractor in existence'.[12] Instead of a heavily-loaded machine, what was really needed to cross the broken ground in No Man's Land was the exact opposite, a lightly-loaded machine with caterpillar tracks. Tellingly, Sueter added that 'I was getting rather fed up and exasperated at Mr Churchill's policy of giving me all the hard nuts to crack, as anything new he wanted was always given to the Air Department, a compliment we did not, with so much air work in hand, always appreciate. Nevertheless, I was making every endeavour to get a useful weapon for trench warfare to keep this forceful man quiet.'[13] It is a measure of the Air Department's perceived isolation from the Admiralty Board at this time that Sueter felt unable to appeal to 1SL or any of his

Board colleagues and that naval resources continued to be devoted to this project at the civilian First Lord's insistence.

On 16 February 1915 Sueter briefed Churchill that he had solved the steamroller problem in another way and invited him to attend the demonstration of a Diplock caterpillar truck loaded with a heavy weight of stones on Horse Guards Parade. He agreed and subsequently 'pushed the caterpillar truck about Horse Guards Parade and was amazed at the ease with which this truck with a full load of stones could be moved'.[14] He added that Churchill had the sharpest brain for grasping new ideas that he had ever met and saw at once that a derivative of the turreted armoured car fitted with caterpillar tracks instead of wheels could be effective and gave his approval for eighteen so-called 'landships' to be constructed as soon as possible. With the First Lord's authority, Sueter involved the Director of Naval Construction, Mr Eustace Tennyson D'Eyncourt, in the landship scheme since his department was already providing the armour plate for armoured cars. Interestingly, at this stage the Fourth Sea Lord, Commodore C F Lambert RN ordered Sueter to concentrate on the Air Service and not to devote too much attention to armoured cars;[15] he therefore asked D'Eyncourt, despite his enormous responsibilities, to run the show and surprisingly he agreed. A Landship Committee was set up to take matters forward which resulted in a Killen-Strait caterpillar machine with Bullock caterpillar tracks being purchased in America and shipped to the UK for a demonstration. This took place at RNAS Wormwood Scrubs on 30 June 1915 when Squadron Commander Hetherington RNAS drove the machine over and through a number of specially-prepared obstacles and barbed wire in front of Lloyd George, Churchill and other VIPs. Administratively, Sueter wanted to operate tanks in the same way that the RNAS had operated armoured cars and 20 Squadron was actually formed with the intention of helping with their development but by then Churchill was no longer First Lord and the new Board had little enthusiasm for a weapon intended wholly for operations on land. Eventually the project was handed over to the War Office and the Royal Tank Regiment formed to operate them. Tanks were eventually to play an important part in the battles of movement that ended the stalemate on the Western Front but as part of the Army. Sueter could claim some part in the conception and early development of a number of weapons that came to prominence in the twentieth century including torpedo-armed aircraft, long-range bombers and armoured cars, but it seems to have been the tank that really caught his imagination. After his appointment in command of RNAS units in Italy, a long way from the administrative 'heart' of naval flying, his career effectively ended when he incurred the Admiralty Board's displeasure by writing to King George V suggesting that an honour would be appropriate in recognition of his work on the tank. He was relieved of command and given no further employment between 1918 and 1920 when he retired with the rank of rear admiral. His application to transfer to the RAF was also refused.[16]

Aircraft Procurement

The growing effectiveness of the RNAS in 1915 was recognised by enlarged orders for aircraft. Among these were 300 aeroplanes at £1750 each for a total cost of £525,000 and ninety-six seaplanes at £3000 each for a total of £288,000. Most of this work went to designated Admiralty contractors such as Short Brothers, Sopwith, Vickers and Beardmore in the same way that ships and their machinery were procured; these firms gave naval orders priority since they had a long-standing relationship with the Admiralty and its technical departments. Orders for foreign aircraft, mostly French and American, were placed through the Naval Attachés in Paris and Washington and orders for twenty-two specialist foreign aircraft such as Curtiss flying-boats and Nieuport scouts were valued at £150,000. Here, too, the Attachés gave the Admiralty something of an advantage since their military equivalents usually had little in the way of technical background and the War Office itself was unused to buying military equipment competitively and in bulk from contractors. The Army in general obtained its equipment from government-owned organisations such as the Royal Ordnance Factory and the Royal Gun Factory; the RFC relied heavily on the Royal Aircraft Factory at Farnborough for both aircraft and engines although these did not always represent the best that were available. Throughout the war the Admiralty maintained a policy of encouraging private design work and in the case of the RNAS this certainly produced the best results.[17] The prestige of winning naval contracts was an advantage among engineering concerns since it gave them priority for the production of war materials that they might not otherwise have enjoyed at this stage of the war.

After the outbreak of war the most important aspect of procurement for the RNAS had been to lay the foundations for a vast supply organisation which included not only aircraft, including aeroplanes, seaplanes, airships, but their engines, magnetos, instruments, weapons and every other kind of accessory.[18] The heading of weapons can be further broken down into a number of sub-categories including machine guns, mountings, sights, bombs of various sizes, bomb-release gear and flares. The shortage of engines was an early limitation on the supply of aircraft and had it not been for the help given by the French aero-engine industry the RNAS would have been severely constrained in 1915. Immediately after the outbreak of war the British Daimler Engine Company signed a licence agreement with the Société des Moteurs Gnome in Paris, makers of the Gnome engine, for their production in the UK. They produced their first 80hp Gnome engine on 30 September 1914, a remarkable achievement considering that 1100 drawings had to be copied and tools, jigs and gauges had to be manufactured before production could commence. Daimler also undertook the licence production of the Royal Aircraft Factory's 90hp air-cooled engine. Other firms that turned successfully to aero-engine production included Rolls-Royce, Sunbeam Motors, William Beardmore & Company and the Green Engine Company.

Besides engines there was a severe shortage of components since, before the war, roughly 300,000 magnetos had been imported into the UK annually, about 90 per cent of these from the German firm Bosch which was the undoubted leader in the field. There was only one British magneto maker, Thomson Bennett & Company of Birmingham, whose annual output had been about 1000. The RNAS had to subsist, together with the other armed forces, at first on refurbished Bosch magnetos that were available in the UK, those that could be purchased in America and those that became available as British production was ramped up. Spark plugs posed similar problems in 1914 since they were manufactured by only three British firms with a total annual output of about 5000. In October 1914 only 420 spark plugs were produced in the UK, far short of the number required. Despite all these problems, the number of aircraft gradually increased.

Later in the war some senior RFC officers complained that the RNAS had outbid the RFC for aircraft and equipment and had taken more than its fair share, thus leaving the Army's air component short at critical periods. To some extent Roskill supported this view in *Documents Relating to the Naval Air Service, Volume 1* but a detailed examination of the facts about procurement show that the Admiralty was actually remarkably generous in supporting the RFC when called upon to do so. The politics of the RFC's claim for total control of air matters will be covered in more detail in Chapter 14 but it is appropriate to point out several pertinent facts here. During early 1916 the Admiralty began to implement its plans to establish a new Number 3 Wing RNAS as a bomber force at Luxeuil-les-Bains with the object of striking at German industrial centres in the Saar valley. Captain W L Elder RN was appointed in command of the Wing and went to France to prepare for the arrival of the Wing's aircraft and equipment. It was to comprise fifteen Short Bombers and twenty Sopwith 1½ Strutters. However, before the Wing's aircraft could be delivered the Admiralty received an urgent request from General Trenchard who commanded the RFC in France asking for as many aircraft as possible to be released to enable the RFC to make up serious deficiencies in its order of battle before the Somme Offensive timed to begin on 1 July 1916. He stated that the RFC was twelve squadrons short of the numbers that had been planned.[19] Generously, the Admiralty immediately handed over a number of 1½ Strutters and Short Bombers to the RFC, seriously delaying the establishment of Number 3 Wing which consequently proved unable to begin operations until October.

In addition to handing over a large number of aircraft to the RFC, it could also be argued that Samson's Eastchurch Wing had directly helped the RFC in the manner originally envisaged for the Naval Wing to support the Military Wing if it were called upon to do so. After the Battle of the Somme had begun the RNAS was requested to provide fighter support for the RFC and formed a new squadron from Number 5 Wing at Dunkirk in order to do so. This was 8 (Naval) Squadron which was to earn fame on the Western Front operating under RFC control. Initially it had 1½ Strutters and Pups but the former were soon replaced and it became an all-Pup unit.[20] Another example of Admiralty even-handedness followed a request to the War Office by General Sir Douglas Haig, Commander-in-Chief of the BEF in France, in November 1916 for a further twenty fighting squadrons. This was amplified by a request from Trenchard for everything the RNAS could spare to be handed over to the RFC, especially 100 Rolls-Royce engines, fifty Hispano-Suiza engines and up to four complete fighter squadrons. The Admiralty responded by transferring sixty French Spad S.7s from its own contract for 120 to the RFC immediately.[21] At about the same time both the Admiralty and the War Office had placed contracts for the Sopwith Triplane. As with all Sopwith designs, the contract for RNAS machines was to be fulfilled by the parent company as it was an Admiralty contractor; those for the RFC were to be built by subcontractors and these amounted to about 266 machines. In February 1917 the Admiralty further agreed to hand over all 120 Spad S.7s to the RFC on completion in return for the balance of the Sopwith Triplanes. The offer was accepted with alacrity but in fact none of the 266 sub-contracted Triplanes was ever built and the RNAS only received Sopwith-built examples, the RNAS being the only service to use the type operationally. It was operated by 1, 8, 9 and 10 (Naval) Squadrons on the Western Front and earned an outstanding reputation for itself.

As technology improved, the adoption of any new type of aircraft or aero-engine became more of a gamble as their merits could not be assessed without test programmes of growing complexity. Because of this, orders had to be contracted and production started on any machine which showed promise before it had been proved ready or even effective.[22] As new roles for aircraft evolved, modifications had to be made to machines in service to cater for them and new types with a wider range of capability had to be designed but despite all these impediments, the number of aircraft produced continued to rise. By December 1915 the number of single-seaters produced for both the RNAS and RFC had increased from 30 a year before to 391, two-seaters from 107 to 2003 and seaplanes from 52 to 262. Engine output from all sources for the two flying Services in 1914 had totalled 138; by December 1915 it had reached 2632 of which 1721 were produced in the UK.

8 The RNAS at Sea and Ashore

In early 1916 the RNAS was relieved of two major tasks; in January the Gallipoli campaign ended and in February the War Office assumed responsibility for the air defence of the UK. A number of men and machines thus became available for re-tasking and offensive operations against German bases in Belgium were intensified. Plans were prepared for long-distance bombing raids against industrial targets in Germany itself. Some of the most notable advances, however, involved an expansion in the number and type of airships available for patrol duties.

Progress with Airships

Shortly after taking over from Churchill in 1915, the new First Lord, Balfour, called a conference at which it was decided to limit the number of SS airships produced to fifty and switch production to an improved and larger type known as the Coastal or 'C' type which was to be capable of more protracted patrols at longer ranges from their bases.[1] The prototype had been completed by RNAS technicians at Kingsnorth in the autumn of 1915 and tenders were issued for the remainder to be fabricated by industry. They were intended to patrol the sea areas off Pembroke, Land's End, Selsey Bill, off the mouths of the Rivers Humber and Forth, north of Aberdeen and off the coast of Norfolk. To achieve this, new RN air stations were to be established at Pembroke in January 1916, Pulham in February, Howden (north of the Humber) and Longside (north of Peterborough) in March, Mullion (near the Lizard) in June, East Fortune (on the south bank of the First of Forth) in August and Cranwell where a large training centre for aeroplanes and airships was being established. The prototype Coastal had used an Astra Torres envelope and a control car fabricated by joining two Avro 504 fuselages end to end after their tails had been cut off. Contractors who bid successfully for the contract to manufacture them assembled the airships at Kingsnorth with a total of twenty-seven being completed for the RNAS. Four more were supplied to the Russian Navy and one to the French.

At this time airships had only a limited ability to attack U-boats and the Coastals were intended to detect enemy submarines on the surface and force them to dive

Coastal airship *C 1* changing crews, with its control car hauled down onto the quarterdeck of the cruiser HMS *Canterbury* on 6 September 1916. (Author's collection)

rather than destroy them. Their whole value, therefore, rested on the ability of the observer to communicate news of a sighting to the local SNO who was responsible for the work of destroyers, sloops and auxiliary patrol vessels. It was essential that the SNO's organisation knew the exact location of a Coastal as soon as it reported sighting a U-boat so that warships could close it as quickly as possible. The problem with this was that airship pilots operating out of sight of land could not be relied upon to give an accurate position; the solution from August 1916 was an agreement between the Admiralty and the Marconi Company to establish a number of wireless direction-finding stations around the coast in conjunction with the airship bases. There were two kinds, those which could only receive and others which could also transmit up to a range of 150 miles. Instructions for airship commanders stated that, whilst on patrol, they should make their call-sign every hour to enable two or more stations to get regular cross-bearings in order that their progress could be tracked.

By the end of 1916 the fifty ships of the SS programme had been completed plus the four that were supplied to France and another four to Italy. An improved derivative of the SS, designated the SS-Zero, was developed under the orders of the Vice-Admiral Dover Patrol at RNAS Capel in June 1916, intended to be towed to the Belgian coast by a small warship, where it would be used to spot the fall of shot for monitors. The engine drove a pusher propeller at the rear of the control car and the car itself was strengthened to withstand the stresses imposed by a towing shackle at its forward end. Towing trials with the monitor *Sir John Moore* were carried out off Capel on 7 September 1916 and repeated off Dunkirk on 23 September and, although they were both successful, it was soon realised that that its low speed when released made the airship so vulnerable to attack by enemy aircraft and gunfire that its operational use in this role would be impractical.

SS-Zero class airship *SSZ 37* over sloop *PC-61* on coastal convoy work. (Guy Warner collection)

Nevertheless, the SS-Zero proved such an advance over the earlier SS class that it was adopted as a standard design for coastal patrol work around the UK. By July 1917 there were sixteen in service.

The SS-Zero towing trials were not the first of their kind since as early as November 1914 the Astra Torres, *Airship Number 3*, had been towed by the steamship *Princess Victoria* up to a speed of 21 knots under a variety of wind conditions. No further development along these lines seems to have been made until March 1916, however, when the question of increasing the effective range of airship patrols by refuelling them from ships at sea was considered. Preliminary trials off Kingsnorth proved satisfactory and on 12 May 1916 exercises were carried out in the harbour at Harwich with the light cruiser *Carysfort* which towed *C 1* with ease. Further experiments followed on 16 May with the towing pennant being passed between two ships and on 6 September the light cruiser *Canterbury* towed *C 1* at speeds up to 26 knots without undue strain. She then slowed to 12 knots and hauled the airship down to the quarterdeck where the crew was changed, after which the tow was let out to 100ft and the airship was refuelled though a hose, 60 gallons being transferred in eight minutes. From this height the crew was changed for a second time, being hauled up one at a time in a boatswain's chair. These experiments proved that non-rigid airships could be towed by warships with relative ease in fair weather but it was felt, however, that in average North Sea conditions little reliance could be placed on this technique and that only rigid airships would be capable of all-weather fleet reconnaissance work.

HM Rigid Airship *R 9* in flight shortly after its completion. (Author's collection)

In 1916, however, the RNAS did not have a rigid airship in service although the 1915 conference had agreed that work should resume on *R 9* which had been suspended earlier in the year and that three further rigid airships should be built. That number was later increased to four and the design, designated the 23 Class, was intended to follow the principal features of *R 9*; orders for the first three were placed in October 1915 and the fourth in January 1916. Vickers was contracted to build the lead-ship *R 23* and *R 26* at Barrow-in-Furness, William Beardmore was contracted to build *R 24* at Inchinnan, Renfrewshire and Armstrong Whitworth was contracted to build *R 25* at Barlow near Selby in Yorkshire. The first three eventually made their initial flights in September and October 1917 but *R 26* was not completed until March 1918. In February 1916 the construction of four more rigid airships was authorised. These were to be built to an improved 23X design with orders for two each being given to Beardmore and Armstrong Whitworth. Two rigid airships to a modified Schütte-Lanz design were ordered from Short Brothers' Cardington factory later in the year. In September 1916, however, the German naval Zeppelin *L 33* was forced to land north of Mersea Island and although it caught fire little damage was done to it and experts were able to analyse its construction. Consequently, it was decided to cancel two airships of the 23X Class and replace them with five airships based on the design of *L 33* to be known as the 33 Class. They were laid down before the end of 1916 but not completed until after the war had ended.[2] Infrastructure to support the big rigids was taken forward as a matter of urgency and large hangars were completed at RNAS

R 23. Note the size of the handling party these big rigid airships required. (Author's collection)

R 24 under construction by William Beardmore & Co at Inchinnan, Renfrewshire.
(Author's collection)

Howden in December 1916, Pulham in February 1917, Longside in March 1917, East Fortune in April 1917 and Cranwell in June 1917. *R 9* made her first flight on 27 November 1916 when it was found that its disposable lift was less than that specified in her contract and she was handed back to Vickers for modifications. These included the substitution of a single Maybach engine from *L 33* in place of the original two engines in her after car and the airship was eventually delivered to Howden in April 1917. Attempts to use *R 9* for operations did not prove successful, however, and she was therefore used almost entirely for training airship crews.

Seaplane Carriers

The seaplane carrier HMS *Vindex* in 1916. Note the tiny take-off deck built over the forecastle and the stowed derricks on the two foremasts that were used to lift aircraft onto it. The hangar aft could accommodate up to four seaplanes depending on type. They were lowered onto the water by one of two cranes; the port example is turned aft ready for use and the starboard is stowed athwartships out of sight. The small working deck aft of the hangar was used to prepare aircraft for flight by spreading their wings and warming up their engines. (Author's collection)

The operation of aircraft with the Grand Fleet will be described in detail in the next chapter but gradual progress with seaplane carriers was made during 1916. *Vindex* joined the fleet in September 1915 and, as explained above, her forward flight deck had demonstrated the potential for wheeled aircraft to take off in November 1915. *Campania* re-joined the fleet with an enlarged take-off deck and facilities for a kite balloon aft on 12 April 1916. Two strikes against German Zeppelin sheds known to be at Hage were attempted by *Vindex* in January 1916 but both had to be aborted, the first because of fog in the planned launch area and the second because enemy submarines were sighted during the approach to the German coast before the aircraft could be hoisted out; stopping to do was not, therefore, a good idea. In spite of these failures, a further strike against the Zeppelin base believed to be at Hoyer on the Schleswig coast was planned for 25 March 1916. The strike force in *Vindex* comprised three Short and two Sopwith Baby seaplanes and she was escorted by the Harwich Force with the Battlecruiser Fleet in support. Commodore Tyrwhitt led his force to sea at dawn on 24 March and the task force made its way across the North Sea through snow squalls to a position inside the Vyl Light Vessel at 04.30 on 25 March. *Vindex* proceeded further east to her briefed launch position and her aircraft succeeded in getting airborne by 05.30. At 07.00 the first two aircraft returned amid further snow showers and reported that there were no Zeppelin hangars at Hoyer. One pilot had, therefore, dropped his bombs on a target of opportunity he identified as a large factory but the other flew further inland and discovered that the airship base was at Tondern. He attempted to attack from low level but his bomb-carrier had become choked with ice and snow, the bombs failed to release and he was forced to bring them back. After waiting a reasonable time for the two Shorts and a Sopwith, *Vindex* returned to Harwich but a group of light cruisers and destroyers searched the area to the

HMS *Campania* seen in 1916 shortly before the completion of her second, more extensive, period of modification by Cammell Laird in Birkenhead. Two smaller funnels have been fitted forward, allowing the flying-off deck to be extended further aft between them. Note that the deck has a pronounced slope to help seaplanes resting on wheeled trolleys to accelerate and that a new compass platform is being fitted between the funnels. (Author's collection)

eastward for any sign of them without success. All had come down after suffering engine failures caused by defective magnetos; the three pilots and two observers had survived but were taken prisoner by the enemy.

One of the strike's aims had been to draw the German High Sea Fleet into action and this very nearly happened. The force searching for the lost seaplanes encountered two armed trawlers off Rom Island and sank both of them. While they were picking up survivors, two of the British destroyers collided and one of these was so badly damaged that she had to be taken in tow to the west. Shortly after the tow was established, German seaplanes located the force and dropped bombs, fortunately without causing any further damage. At about this stage the Admiralty believed the High Sea Fleet was leaving harbour and Tyrwhitt was ordered to withdraw as quickly as possible and warned that he might be intercepted by enemy destroyers during the night. Admiral Beatty deployed the Battlecruiser Fleet off the Horns Reefs to cover the withdrawal but after sunset the destroyer under tow was abandoned. During the hours of darkness the light cruiser *Cleopatra* saw enemy destroyers crossing her bow and, turning towards them, rammed one and cut her clean in two but the manoeuvre brought her into collision with the light cruiser *Undaunted* which was damaged to the extent that her speed was reduced to 6 knots. On learning about the danger this posed to the Harwich Force, the Admiralty ordered Admiral Jellicoe to sail the Grand Fleet and concentrate it in a position to give support. For some hours the two major fleets converged and an action seemed possible but the High Sea Fleet encountered heavy seas which were considered unsuitable for a fleet action and it returned to harbour before the Grand Fleet could make contact.

As this strike had appeared to show that the enemy could be induced to sail his main force by the threat of an air strike from a position close to the German coast, plans were made for a repeat operation but a diplomatic dispute between the USA and Germany caused a change in the way the German Navy planned to use the High Sea Fleet. On 24 March 1916 the British cross-Channel steamer *Sussex* had been torpedoed and sunk without warning by a U-boat with heavy loss of life. Many of the dead were American citizens and a strongly-worded note was sent from the US government to Berlin threatening to break off diplomatic relations if such attacks were not terminated. As a direct result the Germans ended their unrestricted submarine campaign on 24 April 1916 and Admiral Scheer withdrew all U-boats from British waters to participate in fleet operations which he was planning in the North Sea. On 25 April a group of German battlecruisers supported by a scouting force of four Zeppelins crossed the North Sea to bombard Lowestoft and Yarmouth. Seaplanes and aeroplanes took off from the air stations at Great Yarmouth and Felixstowe to attack the enemy ships with bombs but no hits were scored; one of the pilots was wounded and his aircraft damaged by anti-aircraft fire from the ships. Two other pilots chased one of the Zeppelins for 65 miles out to sea and attacked it with bombs and Ranken darts but without any success. (The Ranken dart was the first operational anti-airship weapon, designed by Engineer Lieutenant Francis Ranken RN. These were carried in canisters of twenty-four fitted under a fighter and dropped from above an airship. The weight of an individual dart caused it to rip through the outer fabric where vanes expanded on contact to grip it in place and initiate the detonation of a small explosive charge. The need to climb above the airship put seaplanes at a disadvantage since airships could easily out-climb them and no Zeppelin was ever brought down by this weapon.)

A week later, in early May, the plan for a renewed attack on the Zeppelin base at Tondern was implemented. It was on a far larger scale than its predecessor and involved the laying of a minefield across the High Sea Fleet's probable line of advance and the pre-positioning of the Grand Fleet off the Skagerrak. At 03.00 on 4 May 1916 *Vindex* and *Engadine* hoisted out their aircraft, a combined total of eleven Sopwith Baby seaplanes each fitted with two 65lb bombs, off the island of Sylt but their attempts to take off proved to be an almost complete failure. Eight of the eleven seaplanes suffered engine failure or broken propellers and failed even to lift off the water. Of the three that did get airborne, one snagged the wireless aerial of a destroyer and crashed into the sea; the pilot sank with the wreckage of

HMS *Campania* moored to a buoy during sea trials after her second reconstruction. The hangar can be seen under the after part of the flying-off deck and the area aft of the after funnel has been stripped down for the operation of a kite balloon. (Author's collection)

the aircraft and was lost. Another had to return after only a few minutes in the air with a rough-running engine and only one reached the target at Tondern. He found the airship sheds shrouded in mist and dropped his two bombs where he thought they were but failed to achieve hits on anything significant. The enemy fleet did not rise to the bait and leave its harbours but Zeppelin *L 7* did leave Tondern at 09.00 and closed the British force. It was sighted by the light cruisers *Galatea* and *Phaeton* which damaged it with anti-aircraft gunfire, forcing it to come down on the water where it was destroyed by the surfaced submarine *E31* with its deck gun. By 14.00 when there was still no sign of the enemy fleet, the various British fleets and forces turned to the west and returned to their bases.

Campania's modifications were found to be largely successful and a number of exercises with the Grand Fleet showed encouraging progress. The training of a number of senior communications ratings to act as observers in her Short 184 reconnaissance aircraft had improved their ability to transmit wireless messages to the battlefleet in Morse code. She was able to operate any of the wide range of seaplane types in service and had extensive workshops for both airframes and engines as well as a pit aft that was 100ft long by 45ft wide from which a kite balloon could be operated in almost any weather. Trials towing a new streamlined balloon had given successful results. There were also a number of detailed improvements including a quick-release slip gear on the slings of the aircraft derricks that allowed seaplanes to be lowered onto the water while the ship was still under way at up to 10 knots, thus saving a considerable amount of time and reducing the risk of torpedo attack. Under-way recoveries of seaplanes up to 4 knots was also possible but only for two-seater aircraft since the pilot was fully occupied keeping the aircraft in position alongside the ship while the observer attached the slings.[3] The most important improvement, however, was the flying deck which was lengthened by removing the navigating bridge and forward funnel. Two new athwartship funnels were installed 22ft apart with the new deck passing between them. They were connected by bracing near the top and a new navigating platform about 18ft above the rear extension of the steeply-sloping deck. The charthouse and wheelhouse were part of the supporting structure below the flying-off deck. It was 30ft wide over the wheelhouse and flared to its maximum width over the forecastle although it had originally followed the plan of the hull and narrowed to a point at the bow, it now had a platform added on each side that extended the useable width right forward to only 22ft from the bow. After only a year of shipborne aircraft operations, these changes significantly improved her ability to provide aircraft as an integral part of Grand Fleet operations. On 29 May 1916, the day before the Grand Fleet sailed for the Battle of Jutland, she launched five Sopwith Babies from the deck, using wheeled trollies under their floats,

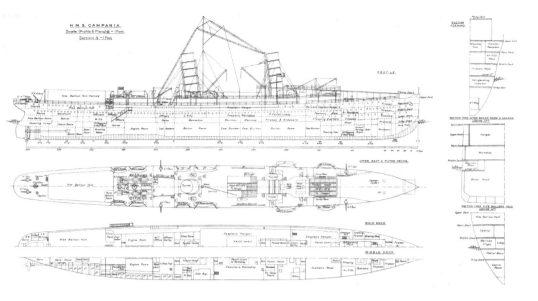

HMS *Campania* (Author's collection)

demonstrating that what had been considered a dangerous experiment only a few weeks earlier was now a matter of everyday routine.

The Battle of Jutland

Admiral Scheer's original plan had been to use his battlecruisers to bombard Sunderland, hoping to draw Admiral Beatty's Battlecruiser Fleet out of its base at Rosyth from where it would pass over a carefully deployed line of U-boats which were expected to cause heavy British casualties. Any British battlecruisers that survived were to be drawn towards the German battlefleet and destroyed by gunfire but the scheme relied on adequate Zeppelin reconnaissance of the Grand Fleet's movements to warn in good time if the High Sea Fleet itself was in danger of being intercepted by more powerful British forces. The U-boats were deployed in mid-May but the favourable weather the Zeppelins required was conspicuously absent from the North Sea in the second half of May 1916 and day after day the naval airship commander had to report that no air reconnaissance could be counted upon. By late May Scheer had to sail if he was to derive any benefit from his deployed U-boats which would have to return by 1 June at the latest. The scheme to bombard Sunderland was, therefore, dropped and an alternative plan for a sweep into the Skagerrak was ordered. The German fleet left the Jade on the morning of 31 May but the Admiralty had already learnt from wireless activity intercepted by the Admiralty's Room 40 that it was preparing for sea and both Jellicoe and Beatty had sailed on 30 May with orders to concentrate east of an area of the North Sea known as the Long Forties.

Unfortunately, *Campania* did not sail with the Grand Fleet. Seaplane carriers did not anchor close to the battlefleet off the north shore of the island of Flotta in

Scapa Flow but, instead, anchored at the northern edge of the Flow near the naval air stations at Scapa Bay, Smoogroo and Houton so that they were close to where their aircraft disembarked while the ships were in harbour. On 30 May *Campania* was off Scapa Bay, probably hoisting in the Sopwith Babies she had launched on the trials the day before. This meant that she could have been anchored as much as nine miles from the fleet signal station on Flotta and not much less from the flagship *Iron Duke*. Room 40 obtained a great deal of information about enemy

A Fairey Campania seaplane taking off from HMS *Campania* using wheeled trolleys under its floats which would fall into the sea after the aircraft became airborne. Although this photograph was taken in 1917, it illustrates the same technique that was used by her Sopwith Babies and Short 184s during 1916. (Author's collection)

fleet movements from its wireless transmissions in harbour and, so that a similar advantage was not given to the enemy, all British harbour signals were relayed visually by flags, flashing light or semaphore. *Campania* took in the preparatory signal for all ships to be in readiness to sail from Scapa Flow but her individual stationing signal sent out at 22.54 was not taken in. It was not until two and a half hours later when the King's Harbour Master asked somewhat tartly when she was going to sail so that he could close the boom defences that she realised that the rest of the fleet had sailed. She weighed anchor at once and worked up to maximum speed in an attempt to overtake the Grand Fleet but by the following forenoon when Jellicoe was informed that she was not with the fleet, she was still some miles astern without a close escort. Concerned that she might be vulnerable to submarine attack he ordered her to return to Scapa and therefore she played no part in the action that was to follow.

Flight Lieutenant F J Rutland
RNAS photographed before
Jutland. (Author's collection)

Engadine was attached to the Battlecruiser Fleet based at Rosyth in the Firth of
Forth and sailed as part of it with two Short Type 184s and two Sopwith Baby
seaplanes embarked. Her senior aviation officer was Flight Lieutenant F J Rutland
RNAS, subsequently known to many as 'Rutland of Jutland'. A detailed account
of the whole Battle of Jutland would be beyond the scope of this book but the part
played by *Engadine* and her aircraft was significant as the first occasion on which
an aircraft-carrying ship and one of its aircraft, Short 184 number 8359,[4] took part
in a major naval battle. Scouting cruisers from both fleets saw a stationary Danish
steamship at about 14.00 on 31 May 1916 and closed it to investigate. At 14.20 the
light cruiser *Galatea* made the signal 'Enemy in sight' and 12 minutes later the
Battlecruiser Fleet altered course to cut off the German force from Horns Reefs.
At 14.40 Beatty ordered *Engadine* to launch a seaplane to scout to the north-north-
east in which direction *Galatea* had reported a large amount of smoke. One of the

Shorts already had its engine warming up on the aft deck with Flight Lieutenant Graham Donald RNAS and his observer strapped into their cockpits[5] waiting for instructions with the lifting strop attached to the derrick ready to lower the seaplane onto the water. He estimated that they could have been away in a little over a minute but Rutland ordered them to get out and said that he had the Captain's sanction to fly the mission with his own observer, Assistant Paymaster G S Trewin RN.[6] Once they were strapped in, *Engadine* turned into wind and 8359 was lowered onto the water but the changeover had delayed things slightly. The aircraft was on the water at 15.07 and airborne at 15.08.

In his subsequent report,[7] Rutland described how he flew slightly east of north towards the last reported position of the enemy under a cloud ceiling at approximately 1000ft with patches down to 900ft. He remained below the overcast and sighted the enemy after about 10 minutes; at first he found it difficult to tell what the ships were and he closed to within a mile and a half to identify them, coming under heavy fire as he did so. His low altitude meant that the enemy could engage him with low-angle as well as anti-aircraft guns but he was not driven off and suffered no damage. Trewin identified the enemy ships as three cruisers and five destroyers; he counted them before encoding and transmitting his contact report while Rutland opened out to about three miles and kept the enemy force in sight. While Trewin was sending his report, the enemy reversed course and this fact was also transmitted. The reporting technique in use at this stage involved the observer encoding each enemy report and then transmitting it in Morse with the seaplane's low-powered Rouzet set to *Engadine*. The transmitter had a range of about 60 miles and inside that distance the seaplane carrier would take in the messages and re-transmit them to *Lion*, the flagship of the Battlecruiser Fleet, using her higher-powered transmitters. *Engadine* took in Trewin's carefully observed and concise contact reports and re-transmitted them but unfortunately they were not taken in by *Lion*. As the enemy turned, Rutland turned with them to maintain a position on their bow at about three miles. At this stage the weather cleared slightly, Rutland saw the Battlecruiser Fleet and judged by their course that Trewin's messages must have got through but for most of the time he was airborne it was not possible to climb high enough to see both fleets at once. Unfortunately, at 15.45 the petrol pipe leading to 8359's left carburettor broke, the engine revolutions dropped from 1000 to only 800 and Rutland was forced to alight on the water. RNAS pilots underwent sufficient technical training to understand how their frail machines worked and Rutland was able to make a repair by ripping the inflation tube from his life-jacket and using it to replace the broken pipe. He then got airborne again and reported to *Engadine* that he could go on but the ship ordered him to return alongside to be hoisted in. By then the Battlecruiser Fleet was in action with the enemy and Beatty gave no further orders for aircraft to be launched. By then it was estimated in *Engadine* that the visibility had reduced to the extent that aircraft would have to fly very close to the enemy to see them. The enemy had begun to jam Trewin's transmissions with their ships' much higher-powered radios when they had become aware of the aircraft's purpose and any subsequent sorties close enough to see the enemy would probably have achieved very little. British aircraft played no further part in the battle.

Rutland was born in 1886, joined the RN as a boy seaman in 1901 and was commissioned as a mate in 1913. When the war broke out, he was serving in the battleship *Audacious* and visited Kiel in her during June 1914. On mobilisation he was re-appointed to the old battleship *Goliath* at first and then Torpedo-Boat *Number 36*. He was appointed to RNAS Eastchurch for flying training in December 1914 and went solo for the first time after only two hours' instruction. Initial, advanced and operational training seem to have been achieved with only 10 hours in the air and he was appointed to *Engadine* in early 1915. By May 1916 he was a substantive Lieutenant RN graded Flight Lieutenant RNAS and senior flyng officer in the ship.

In May 1916 Rutland flew a French naval officer in Short 184 number 8359, the aircraft that was to fly during the Battle of Jutland. He is seen here climbing off the starboard float while Rutland on the extreme left and a party of sailors hold the aircraft steady. The engine, radiator and cockpit section visible here, without the wings or floats, are on display at the National Museum of the Royal Navy at Yeovilton. (Author's collection)

Air reconnaissance by Zeppelins did play a significant part in German plans for the sweep that resulted in the Battle of Jutland. Five airships were briefed to search ahead of the High Sea Fleet but bad visibility delayed their departure until 11.30 on 31 May and three of them never encountered visibility good enough to enable them to see the Grand Fleet; they actually saw and heard nothing of the battle.[8] The continuing uncertainty of the weather led to all five airships being recalled between 16.00 and 18.00 but before dawn on 1 June a further five Zeppelins which had been held in reserve were ordered to take off to locate and screen the High Sea Fleet. The information they transmitted to Admiral Scheer about the disposition of the Grand Fleet proved mostly to be inaccurate and misleading but since by then the German fleet had reached the shelter of the Horns Reef, their reports made no material difference to the situation.

Activities at Sea

After Jutland there was a lull in Zeppelin activity; the force was not required to carry out reconnaissance of the North Sea in the short term and the summer nights were not dark or long enough for air raids against the UK to be carried out with any degree of safety until August. On 29 July the Admiralty received intelligence that a new raid was imminent and *Vindex* was ordered to one hour's notice to sail and place her aircraft into a position where they could intercept and destroy returning Zeppelins. She was ordered to sail from Harwich on the afternoon of 2 August with the light cruiser *Conquest* and several destroyers as escort and at about 19.00 Flight Lieutenant C T Freeman RNAS flew off her small forward deck in a Bristol Scout to intercept a Zeppelin that had been seen some distance off. While it was still a long way off he sighted two other enemy airships, closed the nearest and attacked it with Ranken darts from a position about 500ft above the airship. He failed to achieve any hits in his first two passes but on his third pass some of the darts were seen to hit. He watched as the Zeppelin dropped by about 3000ft and turned towards the east, heading for its base. Freeman had no ammunition left and so he turned towards *Vindex* but unfortunately ran out fuel and had to ditch near the North Hinder Light Vessel. Air bags kept the Bristol afloat for a while but the weight of the engine gradually dragged the nose down, forcing him to climb onto the tailplane. It got dark after about another hour but about 30 minutes after that he saw a passing steamer on its way to Holland and managed to attract the attention of the officers on its bridge by burning letters and firing his revolver into the air. He was rescued and taken to Holland but was soon released as a shipwrecked mariner for return to the UK rather than being interned.

In August 1916 Admiral Scheer decided to carry out another sweep across the North Sea to bombard Sunderland in an attempt to cut off and destroy a part of the Grand Fleet. It was of paramount importance to him that he was not surprised and cut off as he so nearly had been on 31 May so he ordered his Zeppelin and U-boat forces to form two outpost lines calculated to protect the flanks of his advance. He had eight Zeppelins available and four were ordered to take up a patrol line between the coast of Norway and Peterhead; one was to watch the Flanders Bight and the remaining three were divided between patrol stations off the Firth of Forth, Sunderland and the Humber/Wash area. The High Sea Fleet left its harbours at 20.00 on 18 August but, again, the interception of German wireless traffic had given the Admiralty prior warning and the Grand Fleet was already at sea. The fatal flaw in the German plan had been the deployment of Zeppelins where they were expected to see the British fleet in daylight as it reacted to German movements. In fact the British intelligence advantage meant that it was already at sea when the German fleet sailed and it passed unseen in the darkness through the northern Zeppelin patrol. Later reports from his airships, particularly the *L 13* patrolling the Flanders Bight, so misled Admiral Scheer about the strength and disposition of British squadrons that after steaming into the middle of the North Sea he altered course to the south to engage what had been reported to him as a battle squadron. This was in fact the Harwich Force of cruisers and destroyers on patrol and, after a fruitless pursuit, Scheer abandoned his original plan and returned to base.

Meanwhile the Grand Fleet was steaming towards the southern part of the North Sea. *Engadine* was with the Battlecruiser Fleet again but *Campania* had developed machinery defects and had once more been left in Scapa Flow, this time deliberately. Her absence was particularly unfortunate since she had now demonstrated the ability to launch two-seater reconnaissance seaplanes as well as single-seat fighters from her deck using trolleys. She did not therefore have to stop to lower them into the water, although she would have to stop at some stage to recover them. Since Jutland two-seaters had flown off her deck successfully on a number of occassions, the first on 3 June. She had also received the first of the new 'M' type kite balloons which had a triple air-inflated tail and before the fleet left Scapa Flow this had been transferred to the battleship *Hercules* by drifter, together with a small number of officers and men capable of operating it. It was taken to sea and although for some reason no observers were sent aloft in it, it was kept airborne for 28 hours and did at least prove that the concept was entirely viable. At the end of that time it was hauled down because of fears that it might give away the fleet's position to the enemy. When a Zeppelin was seen at some distance, *Engadine* hoisted out a Sopwith Baby to intercept it but the sea was moderately rough and when it tried to take off its propeller was shattered by spray and it had to be recovered; proof, if more were needed, that the concept of operating seaplanes off open water was a failure. After receiving intelligence that the German fleet was returning to its bases, the Grand Fleet returned to its own bases in Scotland.

At about this time officers in the Harwich Force and Dover Patrol put forward the idea of using high-speed motor boats armed with torpedoes to attack the German Fleet at its anchorage in the Schillig Roads. The boats, known as coastal motor boats or CMBs were actually built[9] and the idea was that they should be carried across the North Sea aboard light cruisers and launched near their objective for a dawn attack at high tide across the Mellum flats. Preliminary air reconnaissance was needed to reveal the exact disposition of the enemy ships and to check whether any booms had been placed across the flats. A Curtiss H4 America flying boat was selected to carry out the reconnaissance and was to fly from Felixstowe to intercept a specially-fitted destroyer of the Harwich Force off the German coast. After refuelling from this at sea it was to carry out the reconnaissance, return to the destroyer to refuel again and then to return to Felixstowe. On 29 September 1916 the flying boat took off at 06.15 in doubtful weather; the pilot was Flight Lieutenant A Q Cooper RNAS with Erskine Childers as observer. After flying through patches of fog and low cloud, the crew arrived, accurately, at the rendezvous at 10.00 but were informed by flashing light that the weather was unsuitable for the reconnaissance and that they were to refuel and return to base. The sea was quite rough and, although the pilot landed successfully, the flying boat's wing hit the destroyer while the fuelling hose was being passed and was too badly broken to allow it take off again. Its crew was taken off and it was towed westwards but, just as the British coast came into sight, it suddenly collapsed and sank.

A Curtiss H4 America flying boat at RNAS Newlyn showing how maintenance could be carried out by beaching the aircraft at high tide. Note the ladders and platforms reaching from the beach to the port engine. (Goble Family collection)

A more successful attempt was made on 22 October. This time *Vindex* travelled to the launch position, supported by the Harwich Force, and lowered two Short seaplanes into the water. Both succeeded in taking off before dawn without a hitch and *Vindex* left the area to return to Harwich. Shortly after 09.00 the first seaplane returned to the Force, followed 15 minutes later by the second. Both were safely hoisted in by light cruisers and the force headed to the west but unfortunately fog over the entrance to Schillig Roads had denied them any chance of carrying out the briefed reconnaissance despite both pilots flying as low as 50ft looking for gaps. One of the pilots had landed off Heligoland and, after discussing options with his observer, they had elected to try again but with the exception of some trawler and destroyer movements, nothing could be seen of the fog-shrouded German fleet at anchor. The other aircraft, baulked of its primary objective, photographed the islands of Heligoland, Lanfeoog, Baltrum and Nordeney together with some enemy destroyers seen moving off Heligoland at high speed. No further reconnaissances of this nature were carried out and the projected CMB attack did not take place.

Although it was not appreciated at the time, the destroyer movement was significant. A new German U-boat offensive against shipping was soon to begin and to help the Flanders-based submarines get through the Dover Strait Admiral Scheer had detached two of his destroyer flotillas from Heligoland to Zeebrugge in order to carry out attacks on the net drifters guarding the passage. It was the preliminary movements of these vessels, which arrived at Zeebrugge on 24 October, that had been photographed on the 22nd. The Admiralty became aware that these destroyers had arrived almost at once and, despite bad weather, air patrols from Dunkirk detected and reported unusual activity along the Belgian coast and a number of armed barges moored in the canal between Ostend and Bruges on 26 October. The hostile destroyers made their sortie on the same night and sank six of the unarmed drifters that patrolled the net lines together with a destroyer and an empty transport ship. The enemy's success was not followed up, however, and bombing attacks on Zeebrugge by naval aircraft in November forced Scheer to send one of his flotillas back to Wilhelmshaven for their own safety.

Countering the new U-boat Offensive
The new German submarine offensive caused the Admiralty considerable anxiety. Attacks on shipping were spreading westwards through the English Channel and into the open waters of the Western Approaches. Already in September 1916 there had been losses off the Isle of Wight and Portland Bill where U-boat commanders found it easy to fix their position near points where shipping tended to concentrate.

On 16 September the C-in-C Portsmouth considered the position to be so disquieting that he asked for a new seaplane base to be established at Portland to supplement the one at Calshot. Before the Admiralty could decide on the issue an incident demonstrated the value of increasing the number of aircraft patrols; a seaplane was flying near the Casquet rocks when the pilot saw a U-boat on the surface about to sink the Norwegian steamer *Borgundi-i*. The crew had already taken to their boats and were pulling toward the submarine when its commander saw the aircraft heading towards him. He made ready to dive but kept the boats alongside to shelter his boat from a bombing attack. It was not until the U-boat had finally slipped below the surface that it became possible for the aircraft to attack it and by then it was too late for the small bombs to have any effect. The pilot then landed to see that the merchant ship's crew were all right and, after talking to the captain he took off to report the presence of a U-boat in the area, warning three nearby trawlers. The Norwegians re-boarded their vessel and resumed their interrupted voyage.

On 28 September the Admiralty approved the establishment of a Channel Patrol Flight of four seaplanes to be based at Portland and in November it was further decided to expand a base at Bembridge in the Isle of Wight which had originally been set up as a temporary facility. It too was to have four seaplanes which were to search the English Channel out to a radius of 60 miles. The new patrols soon demonstrated their effectiveness and in late November a U-boat was reported operating off the Casquets; the message was taken in at Portland and a Short seaplane was despatched to search the area. Thirty minutes later the pilot flew over a steamer which signalled by light a bearing on which the U-boat had last been seen. Flying along this bearing the pilot came up with what appeared to be a small tanker and another merchant ship flying the Norwegian flag. Half a mile north of these he saw an oil slick on the surface and, deducing correctly that it came from a dived U-boat,[10] followed it until he found the boat at periscope depth. Noting its position, he flew back to the ships and warned them by signal lamp of the U-boats' proximity; the boat surfaced at this point and the pilot went straight for it and dropped a 65lb bomb as it disappeared below the surface again, but unfortunately the boat was down by the time it detonated and it caused no damage. The tanker now revealed its true identity as a 'Q'-Ship, HMS *Q-7*, and instructed the pilot to land alongside and pass details of the U-boat's position. Unhappily the seaplane stalled on taking off and crashed into the sea; *Q-7* closed the wreck, rescued the crew and was about to hoist the wrecked aircraft inboard when the U-boat, now identified as *UB 19*, surfaced again and manned its deck gun. *Q-7* cleared its own guns for action and a short, sharp exchange of gunfire ensued during which the submarine was sunk at close range.

Air Defence of the UK Mainland

When the War Office resumed responsibility for the air defence of Great Britain in the spring of 1916, the RN reverted to its original role of intercepting and bringing to action hostile aircraft over the sea, both those approaching the UK and those returning to their bases in Germany. Anti-Zeppelin patrols were carried out from naval air stations on the east coast and from their satellite night-landing fields whenever intelligence reported that a raid was imminent. At first these found it extremely difficult to find Zeppelins in the night sky, a problem that was almost impossible to overcome in the pre-radar era, but after many disappointments success was eventually achieved on the early morning of 28 November 1916. Seven naval Zeppelins had attacked the north-eastern and Midland counties of England and *L 21* was intercepted off Lowestoft. As dawn was breaking three BE 2c aircraft piloted by Flight Lieutenant E Cadbury, Flight Sub Lieutenant R W G Fane and Flight Sub Lieutenant E L Pulling RNAS took off from Great Yarmouth and its satellite airfields at Burgh Castle and Bacton, having been briefed at the last moment that an airship had been seen over Dereham. Shortly after 06.30 Cadbury and Fane attacked the Zeppelin; the former got into a position behind and below the airship at about 200 yards and fired four trays of ammunition into its after part from his Lewis gun and was able to tell from the tracer rounds that his fire was hitting. Fane then closed to within 30 yards on the enemy's starboard side and saw his rounds hit before his gun jammed. Pulling watched the first two attacks and then approached the Zeppelin's port quarter and opened fire, closing to within 20 yards, but after a few rounds his gun also jammed but as he turned away hard to clear the target he saw fire break out in the airship's stern. The flames spread rapidly and within a minute *L 21* was falling towards the sea in a blazing mass. All three British pilots had come under fire from the airship's machine guns and noted that they continued to fire for a short time after it started burning. Another airship from this raid, *L 34*, had been shot down just before midnight over West Hartlepool by Lieutenant I V Pyott RFC.

The Dover/Dunkirk Command

Within days of taking over command of this organisation in August 1915 Wing Commander Lambe showed himself to be a dynamic force. His first step was to gain Admiralty approval for the amalgamation of the individual RNAS units stationed at Dover and Dunkirk into a single Wing comprising eight squadrons, six of which were to be at Dunkirk and two at Dover. Each squadron was intended to comprise six aircraft but it took some months to build the wing up to these numbers because of the importance placed, initially, on the Gallipoli campaign. By early November, however, it was clear that with the number of men under training in the UK and increased aircraft production, the new 1 Wing would be able to reach its established strength in early 1916;[11] Lambe went a stage further, therefore, and recommended to the Admiralty that aircraft should be used for a vigorous offensive against the enemy in the spring of 1916. He envisaged the use of specialised bombing wings which, to be effective, needed not only to attack in force but to sustain such attacks until their aim was achieved. Number 1 Wing based at St Pol would be fully occupied with the work of reconnaissance, photography and activities in support of naval operations off the coast of Belgium and so two new strike Wings would be required together with new airfields from which they could operate. Again the Admiralty agreed with his proposals and authorised work to commence at Coudekerque and Petite Synthe. Each new Wing was comprise four squadrons, each with six aircraft and to cope with their logistic and repair requirements the existing organisation was enlarged, re-equipped and given a separate identity as the RNAS Central Repair Depot. Shortly after this, the Admiralty agreed to change the nomenclature of operational RNAS units and from early 1916 a unit of six aircraft was known as a Flight; two or three Flights constituted a Squadron and Wings comprised a variable number of squadrons. These changes brought the RNAS more closely into line with the RFC structure.[12]

The first operations by 1 Wing in conjunction with ships of the Dover Patrol took place on 26 January 1916 when ships bombarded enemy gun positions near Westende in support of operations by the French Army. The shoot was technically interesting as the first use of a single airborne observer to register the guns of five different monitors firing systematically with all rounds marked. This was achieved by transmitting a buzz signal from the aircraft at the precise moment he saw every shell explode and then giving his spotting correction. The gunnery control officer in each monitor knew the exact time of flight of his shells and so, on receiving the buzz, he could identify his own shots and know at once that the spotting correction which followed referred to his gun. The shoot was a complete success but no further bombardments were carried out in the winter months. At about this time German aircraft began making raids on the coast of Kent from air bases in Belgium and Lambe made plans to use his new strike wings to attack them in order to neutralise, or at least reduce, the threat. Number 5 Wing formed at Dover under Squadron Commander D A Spenser Grey RNAS and moved to its new base at Coudekerque in early March 1916. Before it was completely established it was ordered to take part in an Allied air attack on the enemy airfield at Houttave, between Ostend and Bruges, and the seaplane base at Zeebrugge. The attack was carried out at dawn on 20 March 1916 by eight British, ten French and eleven Belgian bombers escorted by eighteen fighters and was co-ordinated with a strike on the enemy seaplane base by seven seaplanes launched from *Riviera* and *Vindex* off the coast and three more from Dunkirk. Aircraft of 5 Wing dropped twenty-five 65lb bombs on their target and the seaplanes a total of twenty-eight on theirs. The French and Belgian aircraft dropped a total of eighty-six bombs of various sizes. Aircrew reported a number of hits observed on both targets and the strike was judged to be a success. From now onwards the fighting in the Straits of Dover and along the Belgian littoral was a three-dimensional affair in which the Dover/ Dunkirk Command was to play an essential part. It had become the largest operational command in the RNAS.

In April 1916 extensive mining operations were carried out off the Belgian coast intended to limit the activities of the U-boats based in Flanders and the minelaying vessels needed to be protected against enemy air attack while they did their work. Thus the ability of the RNAS to achieve what would now be called air dominance played an important part in the campaign to limit the enemy submarine offensive. Number 5 Wing had by this time been fully equipped with Sopwith 1½ Strutter fighters and French-built Breguet and twin-engined Caudron bombers. It achieved the aim in two ways, by providing fighter patrols over the minelayers and by striking at the new airfield at Mariakerke where, intelligence sources claimed, the enemy aircraft that had attacked the ships of the Dover Patrol were based. Seaplanes from Dunkirk also carried out anti-submarine patrols in the area where the British ships were operating. The first strike against Mariakerke was carried out on 23 April by eight bombers of 5 Wing and on the following morning, while mines were actually being laid, twelve bombers from 4 and 5 Wings dropped a total of thirty-two 65lb and twenty-four 16lb bombs on the airfield. Later that day German seaplanes from Zeebrugge attempted to bomb the drifters that patrolled the anti-submarine nets laid across the Channel but were driven off by RNAS fighters; one enemy aircraft was shot down after a 15-minute combat with a Nieuport two-seater and was blown up by its own bombs as it hit the water. Mariakerke airfield was attacked again in the early hours of 5 May 1916 with nineteen bombers from the two wings dropping a total of fifty 65lb bombs. Ghistelles airfield was bombed on 19 May and Mariakerke was struck again on 21 May.

German retaliation soon followed and air attacks were carried out on the port of Dunkirk by day and night between 19 and 22 May. In all 372 bombs fell on the town which killed thirty-two people and wounded a further eighty-nine. On the afternoon of 21 May naval Nieuport fighters from St Pol intercepted a force of enemy bombers and shot down two of their number. Fighters were at last showing themselves to be capable of engaging and destroying enemy aircraft and air combat was recognised as becoming an increasingly important RNAS capability. Allied measures to protect Dunkirk were discussed and Lambe agreed to release two Flights from 1 Wing at St Pol, to be known as 'A' Flight, to operate alongside a

French fighter squadron at Furnes airfield. Their patrols had barely begun, however, when the French unit was ordered away to reinforce the Verdun sector and the RNAS had to assume sole responsibility for air defence in this region. 'A' Squadron remained at Furnes, where it had taken over the French accommodation and workshops, because it was 10 miles nearer the front line and was appreciably closer to the area of operations at sea off the Belgian coast. Aircraft could thus be launched quickly to protect ships of the Dover Patrol when they were attacked and with a better chance of intercepting enemy bombers when they were located in flight. They were also better placed to oppose German spotting aircraft operating in the Nieuport sector of the front line.

RNAS bombing policy changed after a decision by Admiral Bacon announced on 8 June that day bombing should be limited to participation in set-piece Allied strikes or attacks on enemy U-boats or surface warships at sea. Night bombing was to be restricted to attacks on enemy ships in harbour when they were gathered in sufficient numbers. All available aircraft were now to take part with other forces ashore and afloat in attempts to destroy the German 'Tirpitz' Battery with its four 28cm guns. A British naval 12in gun, known as the Dominion Battery, was mounted especially at Adinkerke 27,000 yards from the enemy battery and every precaution was taken to prevent the enemy locating this gun and its ammunition supply arrangements. It was elaborately camouflaged and naval fighters flew constant patrols to keep enemy aircraft away from it. The RNAS' ability to do this had been increased in June with the arrival in service of the Sopwith Pup, an agile fighter with an 80hp Le Rhône engine and a single synchronised Vickers machine-gun. The first Pup[13] arrived with 'A' Squadron at Furnes in late May 1916. In the middle of June the even more powerful Sopwith Triplane, powered by a 110hp Clerget engine and with the same armament, entered service with the squadron at Furnes. It could climb higher and faster as well as out-turn any enemy aircraft and the Triplane soon earned a formidable reputation in the hands of RNAS pilots who became famous. Everything was ready for the bombardment of the 'Tirpitz' Battery in early July but the visibility along the Belgian coast was poor and did not improve until 8 July. On that day a carefully-planned shoot was put into effect with the Dominion Battery and two French 9.2in railway-mounted guns on sidings near Coxyde. Seven spotting aircraft from Dunkirk at any one time operated over the enemy battery in relays at heights ranging from 11,000ft to 16,000ft from 14.00 to 20.00. They could all receive as well as transmit wireless signals and were informed by a buzz every time a gun was fired as part of a carefully-orchestrated timetable which insured that the appropriate correction was applied to the correct gun after every shot. The arrangements were described in the subsequent report as working perfectly.[14] Kite balloons were also deployed as backup but although the balloon

The barge *Arctic* with her kite balloon hauled down onto the deck and secured. (Philip Jarrett collection)

of 11 Section at Coxyde reported a few rounds, the smoke of bursting shells and haze obscured the target from the observer for most of the day. The balloon ship *City of Oxford* and the barge *Arctic* carrying a further balloon were stationed off the coast with the monitors in an attempt to give the enemy the impression that the heavy-calibre fire was coming from the sea. The aircraft over the 'Tirpitz' battery got the Dominion Battery gun onto the target at the seventh round fired which was the third round spotted and corrected. Continuous fighter patrols over a large area from Dover and Dunkirk protected the spotting aircraft and prevented the enemy from locating the British gun.

On 9 July the attack was repeated with relays of spotter aircraft on task from 10.50 to 19.00 and the clear weather allowed 11 Section's balloon to provide unbroken observation for nine hours. The British and French guns fired a total of 109 rounds, only eleven of which were not seen by the balloon crew. Both aircraft and balloon spotting was of such a high standard that the target was found with the third round fired but the photographs taken by aircraft twice on this day from 13,000ft showed that although the concrete gun emplacements had been hit, the four enemy guns themselves had apparently escaped permanent damage. Bad weather prevented further firing until 20 July and even then low cloud and variable winds meant that only eleven rounds were fired. The 'Tirpitz' Battery had by then found the range of the British gun but a smokescreen made its shooting ineffective. From 21 July the Germans also used smokescreens to mask their guns. Further photographs of the 'Tirpitz' Battery were taken on 19 and 20 July using a new camera designed and built by RNAS experts at Dunkirk. Its results were excellent and showed guns, mountings and shell holes with greater clarity than before and at twice the size. Further firing was attempted on 3 August but its effect was negated by the enemy smokescreen. It was decided, therefore, to end this phase of attacks on the enemy battery but to mount more guns on the coast which could be used in conjunction with a land offensive to clear the Germans from the area.

The important work carried out by aircraft of both sides spotting for artillery and on reconnaissance work led to the deployment of increasing numbers of fighters to defend them. From July 1916 German warships off the Belgian coast showed a growing inclination to attack patrolling seaplanes and even U-boats showed a willingness to remain on the surface and fight. On 24 July a seaplane from Dunkirk saw a U-boat on the surface 12 miles off Zeebrugge and prepared to attack it but was hit in the engine at a range of about a mile by one of its anti-aircraft shells and forced to alight on the water. The pilot still had sufficient engine power to taxi towards Holland but, whilst doing so, he was overtaken by a German torpedo boat and taken prisoner. Seaplanes from Zeebrugge also proved to be more aggressive and from August it was considered necessary to escort patrolling seaplanes with Sopwith Baby fighters.

On 2 August 1916 an organised bombing campaign was resumed in an attempt to take some of the pressure off the RFC which was suffering very heavy casualties during the prolonged Battle of the Somme. The first targets were a new enemy airfield at St Denis Westrem to the south-west of Ghent and a nearby ammunition dump at Meirelbeke. Ten twin-engined Caudrons and a Henri Farman of 4 and 5 Wings escorted by five Sopwith 1½ Strutters arrived over the airfield at 13.30 and observed eight enemy aircraft dispersed on the ground and a number of sheds and buildings. The eleven bombers had flown to the target in a wedge formation which had been adopted as the most effective way of keeping aircraft under control, maintaining an all-round lookout for enemy aircraft and providing the best combination of defensive firepower. Visual signals for the bombers to manoeuvre were given by the pilot of a Sopwith flying close to, but independent of, the bomber wedge. Just short of the target the bombers were instructed to form into line-astern and they bombed individually in succession, their forty 65lb bombs plus four smaller bombs were seen to fall among the parked aircraft and buildings. At Meirelbeke three Sopwith 1½ Strutters of 5 Wing dropped thirty-one Le Pecq bombs on the ammunition dump and associated railway sidings, scoring a number of direct hits. Twenty-eight single-seater fighters in four different formations patrolled the return route flown by the bombers to protect them but the only opposition came from anti-aircraft fire which hit and destroyed one fighter at 12,000ft. The Wings were also instructed to attack Hoboken shipyard and, now that airship raids on the UK had resumed, Zeppelin bases in Belgium. On 9 August

Flight Sub Lieutenant S J Goble RNAS
photographed at the end of his flying training
at RNAS Chingford. (Goble Family collection)

two Sopwith 1½ Strutters attacked the airship sheds at Berchem St Agathe and
Evere, one of them achieving eight hits on the latter. Four 1½ Strutters attacked an
ammunition dump at Lichtervelde on 18 August and left it on fire; two others flew
a round trip of 240 miles to attack Zeppelin sheds at Cognelee but failed to hit
them and one of the pilots was forced to land in Holland after a navigational error.

On 5 September three 1½ Strutters of 5 Wing attacked Hoboken shipyard in a
hailstorm which prevented them from observing the results of their attack and the
enemy airfield at Ghistelles was attacked on 3, 9 and 23 September. St Denis
Westrem was attacked on 7, 17 and 21 September and Handzaeme on 9 and 24
September but there was little enemy opposition in the air and it seemed that the
objective of forcing the enemy to withdraw fighters from the Somme front had not
succeeded. The Germans did carry out a weak attack on St Pol, Furnes, Petite
Synthe and Dunkirk, however, but failed to achieve any damage and on 24
September 1916 Flight Sub Lieutenant S J Goble RNAS flying a Sopwith Pup shot
down an LVG two-seater, having taken off only two minutes after the first bombs
fell near Dunkirk. On the other hand, enemy seaplanes showed increased activity
and from the end of September most air combats were with these machines. Of
the eight enemy aircraft shot down by RNAS pilots from Dunkirk between 24
September and 23 October, six were seaplanes which were no match for the Sopwith

Pups or Nieuport Scouts that were responsible for their destruction. Two enemy balloons observing for the 'Tirpitz' Battery were shot down in flames on 7 September and 20 October by Nieuports armed with Le Prieur rockets, both in the face of heavy anti-aircraft fire. Towards the end of October 1916 the RFC asked the RNAS Dunkirk Command to provide more direct support for air operations in the prolonged Somme offensive. Again, generously, the RNAS agreed and both aircraft and pilots were withdrawn from other units to form a squadron of eighteen aircraft to fight under RFC operational control on the Somme. The unit was designated as 8 (Naval) Squadron and placed under the command of Squadron Commander G R Bromet. It comprised three flights, one of Sopwith Pups, one of Sopwith 1½ Strutters and one of Nieuport fighters, and deployed to Vert Galand on 26 October. The Pups proved to be significantly superior to the other types and by the end of the year all three flights were equipped with them. By the end of 1916, 8 (Naval) Squadron had made a considerable name for itself, destroying twenty-four enemy aircraft for the loss of two pilots.

By the end of October, the enemy was known to have concentrated a number of destroyers at Zeebrugge for an attack on the Dover net barrage and so air strikes on the Belgian ports were resumed on 9 November 1916 by six Short 184 seaplanes sent out at intervals from 18.40 to attack Ostend and Zeebrugge. One of these failed to return and another suffered an engine failure which forced it to alight off Nieuport. It remained afloat for eight hours and, despite being strafed by an enemy seaplane, it was located by a French patrol boat and towed back to Dunkirk. The remaining four Shorts dropped one 500lb and nine 65lb bombs onto the dock area at Ostend and eighteen 65lb bombs around the Zeebrugge mole without achieving any significant measure of success. At dawn on 10 November the attack was continued by aircraft of 4 and 5 Wings which dropped seventy-five le Pecq bombs, thirty-nine 65lb and thirty-four 16lb bombs on Ostend. Further strikes were carried out on 12 and 15 November, on the latter date by two seaplanes from Dunkirk and twenty-two aircraft from 4 and 5 Wings which dropped eighty le Pecq, sixty-nine 65lb and fifty-nine 16lb bombs around the Ateliers de la Marine and the Slyken power station at Ostend. The bombers included two new Short bombers with 250hp Rolls-Royce engines which had been designed to carry up to 900lb of bombs each. On 17 November the strike was repeated by twenty bombers and hits were observed on the Ateliers de la Marine but not on the power station which continued in operation.

Two final attacks on 22 and 28 November concluded the RNAS bombing offensive in 1916; both carried out by Sopwith 1½ Strutters by day against Zeebrugge. Although the material effect of these strikes had not been great, nor could they have been with the aircraft and bombs available, the threat of an attack had a paralysing effect on the operations of enemy destroyers which were moved along the canal to Bruges where they were considered to be less vulnerable.

Operations in Eastern Waters

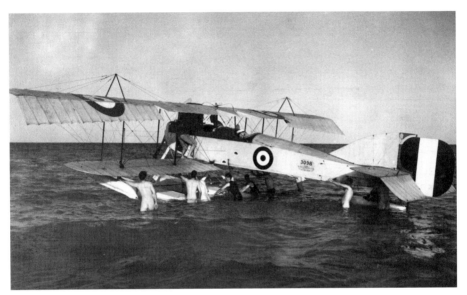

By 1916 RNAS aircraft were operating all over the world. This is Curtiss tractor seaplane number 3098, one of twenty seaplanes built in the USA to contract CP 102967/16. It was delivered to RNAS Isle of Grain in December 1915 as a presentation aircraft funded by public subscription and named 'Britons Overseas Number 6'. It was shipped to Mombassa at first and then used on the Cape Station and is seen here being launched in water sufficiently warm for the handlers to dispense with their wading trousers and, in some cases, everything else. Note that by 1916 the RNAS had adopted as standard the blue, white and red national marking. (Goble Family collection)

After the conclusion of operations on the Gallipoli Peninsula, a significant naval force was retained in the Eastern Mediterranean to enforce a blockade of the coasts of Turkey and Bulgaria and to protect Allied merchant shipping. The air element of the task force based at Imbros for this purpose comprised 2 Wing which was brought up to strength by the transfer of personnel and aircraft from 3 Wing which was disbanded, together with an airship base on Mudros, two seaplane carriers and two kite-balloon ships. Early in 1916 Captain F R Scarlett RN was appointed in command of RNAS units in the area and he pressed immediately for an additional Wing to be formed with the object of bombing railways and other infrastructure in enemy territory he considered to be vulnerable to air attack, together with an extra squadron for 2 Wing and at least one extra seaplane carrier.

Le Prieur rockets being test-fired from BE 2c number 8407. This aircraft was delivered to RNAS East Fortune in December 1916 and this photograph was probably taken there. (Author's collection)

After considering his request, the Admiralty did not feel able to provide a second wing but did agree to maintain 2 Wing at a strength of one two-seater fighter squadron, one reconnaissance squadron and two squadrons of bombers. Its headquarters was transferred to Mudros where the SS airship had been based. A conference of Allied admirals was held in Malta during March 1916 and at this it was agreed that the RN area of responsibility was to be extended to include the coast of Asia Minor as far south as Cape Alupo. To support this expansion the RNAS was tasked with keeping a suitable force of aircraft within striking distance of the whole enemy littoral within the limits of the expanded British area of responsibility, keeping the bombing squadrons mobile so that all or part of them could be concentrated when required. The RNAS logistic support organisation was moved to a position where it would be reasonably secure from enemy air attacks. Two new airfields were prepared, one at Port Kharos on Mudros and the other on the island of Thasos. From these some 200 miles of enemy road and railway track were accessible along which troops and supplies for the Turkish and Bulgarian Armies were moved in quantity. A small flight comprising three Henri Farmans, one Nieuport and two Bristol Scouts was detached from 2 Wing and moved to Thasos at the end of May. The French provided a number of Maurice Farmans and Nieuports which were to operate under RNAS orders and the composite unit was known as 'A' Flight.[15] It carried out its first operation on 1 June 1916 and subsequently made repeated strikes against bridges and other vulnerable points on the tracks as well as rolling stock, road traffic, troop encampments and ammunition dumps. During June and July crops in southern Bulgaria were targeted and laid bare by incendiary bombs, one fire-attack alone clearing an area 1.5 by 0.5 miles of any usable crops.

One of 'A' Flight's most important targets was a bridge which carried the railway line over the Nester River at Buk and on 15 October, three Henri Farmans escorted by two Bristol Scouts attacked it. One of the pilots glided down to 1200ft despite a great deal of rifle fire and scored a direct hit on the track over the bridge's second span with a 100lb bomb. His other two bombs fell within 15 yards of the target and probably caused shock damage to its structure. A reconnaissance flight on 23 October found that the second span had collapsed into the river and trains were backed up at junctions on either side. A lightweight trestle bridge had been constructed across the river on which a small number of wagons were being used to ferry stores from one train to another. More strikes were launched against rolling stock but no direct hits were observed. Attempts were then made to cut the railway line at inaccessible points on either side of Buk between which road transport could not easily be used as a replacement. The first point selected for attack was the bridge at Yeni Keui, 12 miles south-east of Buk. Three 100lb bombs were dropped on it from about 1000ft on 24 October but no direct hits were achieved. A day later another strike produced no better result and, as later generations of naval pilots were to discover in the Aegean and in Korea, bridge spans were not easy targets to demolish before the era of guided weapons. The bridge at Shrimshirli on the western side of Buk was the next target selected and on 30 October it was attacked by two aircraft. The first dropped three 112lb bombs from 1000ft, the first of which hit the third span from the Buk end and tore a large hole in the permanent way, the second hit the track west of the bridge and the third further west. After dropping his bombs the pilot descended to low level and strafed the bridge gunners with machine-gun fire, causing them to take cover while the second aircraft made its bomb run. These bombs also hit, causing the two centre spans of the bridge to collapse into the river. Photographic reconnaissance in early November showed that the damage had rendered the section of railway line between Buk and Drama useless but another on 20 November found that the bridge at Buk had been repaired and that a number of trains had been assembled ready to cross it. A strike was launched against it immediately but found that such strong anti-aircraft gun defences had been mounted around it that bombing from the heights necessary to ensure hits was no longer possible and the bridge remained undamaged. Further attacks in December fared no better.

During the second half of 1916 the enemy began to oppose air operations from Thasos more effectively; several aircraft were lost on strike missions after being intercepted by enemy fighters and there were occasional attacks against Thasos airfield. Enemy seaplanes were active as well, operating from a base at Gereviz on Lake Boru from which they attempted to attack Thasos but achieved few positive results. The RNAS retaliated strongly and launched strikes against airfields at Drama, Xanthi and Gereviz. On 29 November the latter was bombed by two Henri Farmans and a fire was seen to break out among outbuildings which was fanned by a strong easterly wind, spreading it to the remainder of the camp. A column of dense black smoke was visible from Thasos 35 miles away and subsequent reconnaissance showed that only one hangar had survived. In addition to 'A' Flight, there was another RNAS unit on Thasos; this was 'D' Squadron based at Stavros and it was tasked with spotting, reconnaissance and photography in support of British warships in the area and support for the Army's 80 Brigade fighting on the lower Struma. The latter task involved interdiction of enemy camps, supply dumps, troops and transport on the move in the area immediately behind the forward edge of the battle area. It also involved denying enemy aircraft the ability to search behind the British lines. An SS airship was operated on daily anti-submarine patrols in the Gulf of Salonika from a forward base at Kassandra from June onwards. While these units were operating over the lower Struma, 'B' Squadron at Mitylene and 'C' Squadron at Imbros carried out bombing, anti-submarine and recon-naissance operations in the Smyrna and Dardanelles areas.

In March 1916 a small force of Royal Marines, RNAS personnel and Greek irregulars was landed at Long Island in the Gulf of Smyrna to construct an advanced airfield, On being detected by the enemy, however, they came under fire from the Turkish mainland despite counter-battery fire from the monitor *M-30*. The enemy shelling increased in both accuracy and intensity and on 16 May *M-30* was set on fire and a Bessonneau hangar, together with the aircraft inside it, were destroyed. An evacuation was therefore carried out without delay, with the RNAS detachment retiring to Mitylene.

Air operations from Imbros were largely offensive and directed against shipping in the Dardanelles and the Sea of Marmara, the railway between Sofia and Constantinople together with the enemy forces and their stores dumps on the Gallipoli Peninsula. They also attacked Turkish coal mines, crops and herds of domestic animals in the area of European Turkey around Constantinople. On 15 April a bombing attack was carried out on Constantinople itself, two aircraft dropping incendiary bombs and propaganda leaflets during a round-trip of 360 miles. The weather had been fine at Imbros when they set out but rain and hailstorms were encountered over the Sea of Marmara. One pilot became so exhausted during the return flight that he ditched near Cape Xeros and was rescued by the crew of a trawler. Two other aircraft set out to attack Adrianople but one was forced to turn back because of bad weather. The other made it to the target and dropped bombs and leaflets as briefed during a round-trip of 230 miles. In June long-range reconnaissance flights were made over the Turkish railway system in the Ferejik, Malgara and Keshan districts and in July the information gathered was used to plan attacks on the railway junction at Ferejik and barracks on the Gallipoli Peninsula, setting the latter on fire on 20 July.

There was little enemy air activity over the Aegean until November 1916 when attacks were made on RN air stations at Mitylene, Imbros and Mudros. On 21 November an LVG and a seaplane attacked the airship shed on Mudros; one of four bombs dropped by the aeroplane exploded within 50 yards of the shed and splinters pierced the envelope of the airship inside it. The seaplane was engaged by anti-aircraft fire, dropped its bombs in the hills nowhere near the target and made off pursued by a Sopwith Schneider. The Schneider pilot soon caught up with the enemy aircraft and fired three trays of ammunition from his Lewis gun into it from close range, watching it make a forced landing. In mid-December a series of attacks were launched against the important railway bridge at Kuleli Burgas. During the first, on 13 December, four Henri Farmans dropped three 100lb and nine 65lb bombs near the target but none were direct hits. On 4 January 1917, however, a subsequent attack hit the centre of the bridge with a 100lb bomb and another made a direct hit on the permanent way across the western section of the bridge and three 65lb bombs fell close to a viaduct that carried the track across an island in the centre of the river. Another 65lb bomb hit the iron road bridge south of the railway bridge. In addition to these operations from shore bases, the seaplane carrier *Empress* had arrived at Kephalo on 2 May and took part in an attack on Bulgarian coastal targets the next day. She left for Port Laki in the Budrun area on 6 May and from there both reconnaissance and bombing sorties were flown over the coast of Asia Minor south of Smyrna. On 28 May she was placed under the orders of the SNO Port Iero to assist in further operations against railway bridges where the line ran close to the coast of the Gulf of Scala-Nuova. An observer in a Short 184 spotting for the cruiser *Grafton* and the monitor *Earl of Peterborough* on 3 June gave corrections that resulted in two direct hits on a railway bridge south of Ayasuluk at a range of 10 miles. After that *Empress* returned to Mudros for a maintenance period and then left for Milo where, as part of a 'gentle' blockade by Britain and France, she stood by in case diplomatic relations with Greece were broken off. The blockade ended on 22 June and she sailed for Port Laki again for operations in the Turkish littoral. In August she moved to support operations in the Lower Struma fighting and, from a position off Stavros, her seaplanes operated over the Orfano region and the Struma Estuary for the remainder of the year.

The entry of Romania into the war on the side of the Allies in August 1916 led to another task for the RNAS. The nation had no effective air arm and the

Germans took advantage of this to begin an unopposed bombing campaign against Bucharest and other cities. The Romanian government made an urgent appeal to the Allies for help and the Admiralty agreed to detach a flight from the eastern Mediterranean to Romania as quickly as possible. On 25 October three Nieuports and two Henri Farmans left Imbros for Bucharest. Only one pilot managed to fly the whole way in a single flight which took him over six hours; of the remainder, one landed 40 miles south-west of Bucharest following a navigational error after crossing the Danube, another landed near Bucharest and the last just short of the airfield. The first two completed their journey by road and the third flew in a day later. One aircraft did not arrive for several days. This was a Nieuport that encountered severe thunderstorms over the Balkan mountains, lost his bearings completely and ended up near Ismail in Russia after a flight of about 400 miles. He eventually arrived at Bucharest three days later after a journey that could genuinely be called exciting. On 21 November a further three Nieuports and a Henri Farman flew from Imbros to Bucharest without incident. The situation in Romania was still critical and the Admiralty agreed to send a squadron of 1½ Strutters and their supporting ground crew via Russia to help. Before they could deploy, however, German troops overran Romania and so the arrangements were cancelled. One other RNAS unit did come into action alongside Russian and Romanian forces in this theatre; 10 Squadron with its armoured cars under Squadron Commander R Gregory RNAS was involved in fighting in the neighbourhood of the Tchernavoda Bridge over the Danube during November and December.

HMS *Anne*. Note the folded seaplanes on deck and the derricks for handling them.
(Author's collection)

After the evacuation from Gallipoli, *Ben-my-Chree* had been placed under the orders of the C-in-C East Indies and based in Port Said. A small seaplane force already existed in the area with the former tramp steamers *Anne* and *Raven II*,[16] each operating two seaplanes flown by French pilots with British Army intelligence officers as observers. At the end of January 1916 they were all formed into a single squadron known as the East Indies and Egypt Seaplane Squadron (EI & ESS), which included *Empress* until May. When not embarked the aircraft operated from a seaplane base supported by an RNAS depot at Port Said. It has some claim to be considered as the first British aircraft carrier task force and certainly demonstrated the mobility and tactical flexibility that were to be expected from such formations in later years. In January 1916 seaplanes from *Ben-my-Chree* carried out reconnaissance sorties over the defences of Smyrna and the coastal waters of Palestine. In February she was off the coast of North Africa for reconnaissance sorties over Bardia and Sollum. In March photographic reconnaissance was carried out over Gaza and the new railway line that the Turks were constructing from Beersheba. The last part of May was spent off Jaffa where both strike and reconnaissance sorties were flown successfully by her seaplanes.[17]

On 2 June 1916 *Ben-my-Chree*, now commanded by Samson, left Port Said and deployed through the Suez Canal into the Red Sea. The Sultan of Lahej in the Yemen was a British ally and he had been attacked by Turkish forces under General Said Pasha; the Sultan sought refuge in the British Protectorate of Aden and left his territory under the control of Said Pasha's subordinate, Mahmed Soubhy Bey. However, the Arab uprising in Hejaz to the north of Yemen effectively cut off the Turkish force in the Yemen from its main body and made it difficult for it to obtain reinforcements, supplies and ammunition. It was forced to rely on local produce which made it heavily dependent on some measure of support from local sultans and it was imperative, therefore, that the Turks maintained a show of authority if they were not to be defeated. The British command at Aden ruled out the possibility of an assault by land forces on the Lahej Delta because of the extreme heat in summer and so air attack and bombardment were accepted as the only practical means of attacking the Turkish force. *Ben-my-Chree* arrived off Aden on 7 June and a Short 184 was flown off to reconnoitre the delta. This and subsequent reconnaissance sorties made it clear that the two best objectives for attack were the camps in the gardens north of Lahej and the large camp and depot at Subar. Darb, Waht and Fiyush were also seen to be defended by trench systems supported by artillery and there were camel and donkey camps at Malhalla and elsewhere.[18] For a further five days aerial photographs were taken of most important Turkish positions. An operational plan was prepared, intended to produce the maximum moral as well as material effect.[19] This was achieved by launching two strikes of seaplanes armed with bombs every day. Lahej was attacked by the first aircraft with 112lb bombs dropped from only 400ft on a gun redoubt, killing seven men. The second aircraft attacked Waht and similar strikes were launched every day until 12 June with the Turkish forces never knowing where or when they would be hit. The last strike in this series was against the encampment at Subar which was left on fire. On the evening of 12 June *Ben-my-Chree* left Aden and she arrived off Perim Island early on the following morning. Seaplanes carried out strikes against camps near Jebel Malu and Jebel Akran and the seaplane carrier even used her guns to bombard enemy positions ashore. That evening, having recovered her seaplanes, she sailed for Jidda where she joined a naval force tasked with supporting the Sherif of Mecca. After a day of shore bombardment and bombing by seaplanes, the Turkish garrison at Jidda surrendered and *Ben-my-Chree* returned to Port Said.

By the beginning of July *Ben-my-Chree* was off the coast of Syria where she relieved *Raven II* which had been operating its seaplanes off El Arish throughout June. *Raven II* then moved to Castelorizo Island of the south-west coast of Turkey to the east of Rhodes and from there her seaplanes were used to reconnoitre and bomb targets along the coast of Asia Minor in the Levisi district. Later she deployed through the Suez Canal to operate in the Gulf of Akaba at the head of the Red Sea. Meanwhile *Ben-my-Chree* was carrying out operations off El Arish and then moved north to Beirut where shipping in the harbour was bombed and a number of reconnaissance sorties flown inland. After a short spell in Port Said for maintenance, she launched further reconnaissance sorties around Nazareth and along the El Arish to Auja Road to watch the movement of troops and stores towards the Turkish Army operating in the Sinai Peninsula. At this time, despite the efforts of French patrol vessels, a considerable amount of war material was reaching the enemy in dhows and schooners running along the Syrian coast. *Ben-my-Chree*'s seaplanes were used to counter this traffic and one ship they were particularly briefed to destroy was a red-painted schooner which was supposed to be carrying ammunition. While *Ben-my-Chree* headed north at the end of July, she sighted three schooners heading south; as soon as they saw the British warship they made off but a seaplane was launched which prevented them from heading towards the shore and drove the leading vessel, which turned out to be the long sought-for red schooner, towards *Ben-my-Chree*. One of the vessels was run ashore but the red schooner was fired on by the French torpedo-boat destroyer which was acting as *Ben-my-Chree*'s escort and blew up with a large explosion, leaving no doubt about the nature of her cargo.

On 25 August 1916 *Ben-my-Chree, Raven II* and *Anne* concentrated in Haifa and, between them, launched ten seaplanes which flew in echelon up the Haifa-Afuleh valley looking for targets of opportunity. They found that the anti-aircraft

HMS *Raven II* photographed in Castelorizo Harbour during 1916. (Author's collection)

defences around Afuleh had been greatly strengthened since the last strike in the region and the aircraft came under fire from machine guns and quick-firing cannon. A train heading south was attacked; its last carriage was wrecked and a length permanent way destroyed. The line was damaged in several places and a steam engine, fourteen carriages and a large quantity of stores set on fire. On the return flight the ten seaplanes took different routes and carried out pre-briefed reconnaissances and all of them returned safely despite all having bullet holes from small-arms fire. That night the three ships separated and *Ben-my-Chree* proceeded south along the coast to Askalan where she hoisted out seven seaplanes to attack the camp known to be at Burier and the railway viaduct over the Wadi-el-Hesi. The bombs failed to destroy the viaduct but did cause damage to the adjacent line and embankment. Damage was also caused to the camp by strafing which caused tethered camels to break loose and stampede. *Anne* had gone to Iskanderuneh, 20 miles north of Jaffa where one seaplane was launched to bomb the railway station at Tulkeram and a second to bomb a large camp four miles north-west of Ramleh and dumps of stores near the station. *Raven II* had gone north-west the Gulf of Adalia in Asia Minor and on 27 August her seaplanes attacked a factory near Phineka. Two days later *Ben-my-Chree* was in Alexandretta Bay from where her seaplanes reconnoitred Adana and bombed the main railway station and bridge over the River Jeihan. From there she returned to Port Said. In all, five strikes had been carried out against the single railway line that linked Turkey with its forces in the Sinai Peninsula, cutting it successfully. The enemy had suffered surprise attacks on places as far apart as the coast of Asia Minor near Rhodes and the Egyptian frontier.

In September 1916 *Ben-my-Chree* returned to the area off El Arish and her seaplanes spotted for the fire of monitors which bombarded enemy camps and an airfield. After co-operating with a small French task force off Castelorizo Island in November, she returned to the coast of Palestine at the beginning of December where she joined *Raven II* in the Bay of Ayas in the Gulf of Alexandretta to launch an attack on the bridge at Chilkadere which carried the main Baghdad railway across the River Irmak about 18 miles east of Adana. The attack was carried out in three waves on 27 December, the first targeting the defences so that the following seaplanes could attack the bridge from low level to enhance their accuracy. A number of hits on the bridge were observed and on the embankments either side of it. Unfortunately, the 65lb and 16lb bombs dropped were not powerful enough to cause major damage and there was no cessation of rail traffic.

9 The Use of Aircraft in Fleet Operations

The need to overcome the technical difficulties that prevented aircraft from operating off ships with the battlefleet had been one of the principal reasons that caused the RNAS to move away from the land-oriented RFC to concentrate on its development but there can be little doubt that this early resolve was weakened after the outbreak of war as the Air Department's attention, and even that of early protagonists such as Samson, was drawn towards static anti-aircraft defences, armoured cars, tanks, armoured trains and aircraft operations that were oriented towards land warfare. Churchill's enthusiasm for novel weapons and peripheral campaigns also drew attention away from what should have been the overriding requirement to get aircraft to sea. If Sueter's claim that pressure was placed on him by the First Lord to produce armoured vehicles for the Western Front is taken at face value, Churchill cannot have given the development of carrier-borne aircraft the level of importance they required. Aircraft were expected to act as a means of reconnaissance, the role that had defined the requirement for *R 1*. That they could, one day, act offensively was widely believed but the amount of development that would have to underpin such a capability was not yet understood. Aircraft would not be able to carry, or even aim with any degree of accuracy, a true ship-killing weapon until more powerful engines and robust airframes became available from late 1917 onwards.

An observer in an aircraft in a clear air mass by day was expected to see ships at ranges considerably beyond those possible for officers on the bridges of even the largest warships. The ability to use this advantage to the benefit of a fleet or task force on a reliably regular basis, however, was limited by factors of preconception, technology and geography. With the benefit of hindsight it seems strange that the RNAS had the preconceived idea, without any systematic evaluation under average conditions, that any officer qualified to stand a bridge watch on a warship would be capable of carrying out the duties of an airborne observer. The principal necessity was the ability to identify any warship and transmit a sighting report in coded Morse groups by wireless telegraphy. Thus the early observers deemed to have such skills were not even members of the RNAS. Many were midshipmen chosen because of their relatively light weight or air mechanics who might be able to repair a minor defect that had forced a seaplane to alight before returning to its parent carrier. Most of the officers who volunteered to fly as observers did so because they hoped to become pilots; there was an official reluctance to stand in their way and this led to them moving on as soon as they showed a degree of competence. This simplistic approach failed to take into account the true complexity of the observer's task. Ships viewed from a high angle on a misty day in the North Sea might be more difficult to recognise, or even locate, than those at shorter ranges on the surface. Prior to 1916 there was not even a standardised enemy contact report since the need to transmit data in an easily-assimilated form had yet to be revealed in operations or realistic fleet exercises. In the days of sail it had been sufficient for a reconnaissance frigate's captain to signal his admiral the bearing on which the enemy fleet could be seen in order for him to train his telescope accordingly and judge the enemy's strength for himself. In 1914 an airborne observer was capable of locating an enemy force which might or might not be the whole German High Sea Fleet travelling at 20 knots about 50 nautical miles away from his flagship which might itself be travelling directly towards or away from the enemy at a similar speed. The information an observer could give in such a situation could be of critical value in creating an accurate plot that would give the admiral what is now known as situational awareness of the two fleets' composition and movement. In the shortest time possible he had to evaluate the enemy force's composition, position relative to the flagship, nearest point of land or an agreed datum point on the flag plot, course and speed. He also had to take into account that the enemy's movements in the short term after sighting may be due more to an anti-submarine zig-zag evasion measure than to the fleet's planned intended movement. Shadowing was, therefore, both an art and a skill that could only be acquired through practical experience.

To be fair the general idea was understood by 1916 but its practical implementation on an everyday basis was not sufficiently refined until Jutland exposed the shortcomings. The technology available between 1914 and 1918 did not allow the aircrew to fix their position with any degree of accuracy and they had to rely mainly on dead reckoning with the disadvantages inherent from winds of unknown strength and direction at varying heights. 'Never to be seen again' was the epitaph for a number of naval aviators who flew for long distances over the sea. One example is Flight Commander B D Kilner RNAS who took off from *Vindex* on 25 September 1917 to intercept a German airship and never returned.[1] Despite significant progress in engine and airframe development there was still no such thing as a safe flight or a totally reliable aircraft, even in 1918.[2] Weather was another important factor and although ship's communications with the Admiralty had improved by 1914, there was little in the way of an accurate forecast available to pilots as they were briefed for a sortie from a ship. Oceanic weather is more rapidly changeable than weather systems over land masses; storms are more frequent, fog more abundant and wind, temperature and atmospheric pressure more changeable. The aircrew in seaplanes had not only to contend with the state of the weather while they were airborne but the state of the sea surface when, or if, they managed to return to their parent vessel.

There were other problems in 1914 caused by rapidly-evolving naval technologies and these affected the way the whole Grand Fleet could be navigated, commanded and controlled as much as the need to assimilate aircraft, submarines, torpedoes and long-range gunnery into fleet operations. Despite its name, the German High Sea Fleet had been designed and intended to fight close to its own bases in the southern North Sea against British squadrons that the German Naval Staff had expected to attempt a close blockade off their bases. Thus Zeppelins would operate close to the coast and not at ranges where their navigational accuracy would deteriorate. The Admiralty's decision to adopt a distant blockade enforced by ships based at Scapa Flow meant that when the Grand Fleet reacted to intelligence information and sailed to intercept the enemy, it had to assume that it would encounter the High Sea Fleet in the open sea and would thus have a less certain sense of position[3] during the encounter phase before the battle. Air and submarine reports of the enemy could, therefore, include a considerable error factor but aircraft launched from ships within the fleet would stand the best chance of having a position that conformed to the flagship's plot.

The Admiralty had worked for some years prior to 1914 to create a system of controlling fleets at sea with information gained from signals intelligence (SIGINT) and 'enemy in sight' reports fused in its own War Room.[4] A relatively simple plot of known foreign warship movements was maintained in the War Room during peacetime but it was brought into full operation during large-scale naval manoeuvres. Even so, operational experience was limited and the division of control between the Admiralty and the C-in-C afloat was one area that had not been adequately defined when war broke out. Here too there were preconceptions that led to early misunderstandings and a lack of clarity in the early fused plots caused by a lack of synthetic training in the years before 1914. In the previous centuries battles at sea had been fought by compact groups of ships moving at a relatively slow pace and largely within the sight of their commanding admirals. The Grand Fleet with its associated Battlecruiser Fleet was four or five times larger than any previous British fleet and capable of operating at much higher speed.[5] The Harwich Force was expected to operate both in concert with the Grand Fleet, making a rendezvous in the open North Sea when ordered to do so, and also to operate under direct Admiralty control on sorties that were considerably displaced from any support the Grand Fleet could give. The battle space covered by the Grand Fleet had, by 1915, expanded to the point where an admiral on his flagship bridge could no longer see or even fully appreciate his own fleet's positions, courses and speeds, let alone the enemy's. Even on a clear day with extreme visibility, his vision would be compromised by smoke from funnel gases and gunfire,[6] another factor that had not been adequately foreseen in pre-war exercises carried out at lower speeds.

W/T had helped with the command and control of large fleets but there were still significant technical and tactical problems to overcome. Prior to 1914 the increased expenditure on new warship construction programmes limited the funding available to the Admiralty for realistic exercises and there had been severe limitations on the amount of fuel burnt and hence warship speed. Not only had Jellicoe and Beatty never commanded such large fleets before, they had never commanded fleets that fought at the high speeds used after August 1914 or engaged targets at the very edge of visibility. Both the Admiralty War Room and the C-in-C's plot in his flagship *Iron Duke* were devised to display fused data about the British and enemy fleets. These plots, therefore, had a critical part to play in the hours before contact with the enemy was made. The only way that data could be updated at a meaningful rate once the Grand Fleet had sailed from its bases was by W/T,[7] but this technology also had shortcomings. Wireless performance depended on power available as well as wavelength which, itself, depended on aerial size. Bigger ships, therefore, had longer range outfits which had to operate on different frequencies to those of smaller ships. Transmitters in smaller ships and aircraft were limited, with 60 miles being the accepted range for a destroyer and slightly less for a Short 184 reconnaissance aircraft in flight under good conditions. W/T installations were expensive and, because they had only recently been brought into service, there was a shortage of skilled ratings to man them with the consequence that even battleships lacked sufficient sets to cover all the frequencies in use within the Grand Fleet. The solution to this shortcoming was the strict implementation of a system in which nominated big ships guarded frequencies used by small ships, submarines and aircraft and relayed important messages from them to the flagship. The success of this system varied and, as explained in the last chapter, it failed at Jutland when Trewin's message was taken in and relayed onward by *Engadine* but never taken in by its intended recipient, Beatty's flagship *Lion*. Atmospheric anomalies could affect reception and low-powered transmissions could be jammed by higher-powered transmissions from enemy warships in close proximity. Congestion, in other words the sheer volume of W/T traffic to be taken in, decoded and distributed, was another problem, especially if the delayed messages referred to changes of course or disposition within the Grand Fleet or vital information about the enemy's movements. Timeliness could, however, be bought at the expense of security if it was deemed appropriate to transmit uncoded messages in clear English since even the simplest signals had usually to be encoded by hand before transmission and decoded at the other end after reception.

In 1914 the RN was the only navy that had come close to solving the problem of adequate situational awareness at sea following a suggestion by the Grand Fleet Gunnery Officer Captain Frederic Dreyer RN that a plot should be maintained to show Admiral Jellicoe the relative positions of his own and the enemy's forces. Effectively this was a wide-area chart fixed to a table on the flag bridge with the latest information drawn on it in pencil by a staff officer. It was supposed to allow the C-in-C to follow the relative movements of his own and the enemy fleet by constant reference to it as contact was made but, while this was a sound concept, it was far from perfect in the early years, largely because senior officers failed to realise the amount of practice that needed to be devoted to making it so. It was not something that could be activated the day before a battle and then put away until the next occasion of need. Given the state of technology at the time, it was not possible to relay this plot to other flagships and so it was not possible for individual squadrons to run plots that were co-ordinated, or fused, with that of the C-in-C. Jellicoe could not, therefore, easily devolve aspects of overall command to his subordinate admirals but he could order a specific squadron to a position where it might be needed relative to the flagship. The plot was an important asset that grew in effectiveness and importance as the war progressed and beyond[8] but it was a hostage to the quantity, quality and accuracy of the information provided to it by his own reconnaissance sensors. The need for a formalised enemy sighting report when receiving information from a remote sensor by W/T has already been mentioned and in *Fighting the Great War at Sea*, Norman Friedman notes that at Jutland, as the Battlecruiser Fleet ran to the north towards the Grand Fleet, Jellicoe's signalmen repeatedly asked for the enemy's course and speed to feed the plot. Beatty, who seemed not to have understood how important this might be, only signalled the direction of the enemy from his own flagship, which did not really help. It was into this sort of situation that air reconnaissance had to fit if it was to offer anything effective and even in 1916 insufficient practice had been carried out to perfect it into a reliable system or define its practical limitations. Had Jellicoe but known it, the same limitations applied to the German naval Zeppelin force.

The Zeppelin Threat

On the other side of the North Sea the Imperial German Navy found itself very deficient in the number of scouting cruisers it would need once it was realised that the British were not going to conduct an inshore offensive blockade[9] or even attempt to launch a Copenhagen-style attack against its new enemy. Tirpitz had created the High Sea Fleet on the assumption that the RN would operate close to the German coast where blockading squadrons could be defeated in detail, gradually whittling the Grand Fleet down to a size where it could be brought to action with a reasonable chance of defeating it. However, the British fleet literally disappeared after the 1914 Fleet Review[10] and the German Navy had no idea where it had gone or what it intended to do. Once it was realised that the British were implementing a distant blockade, the Germans had to accept that their opponent would need to be located in the open North Sea and Zeppelins offered a relatively immediate and inexpensive substitute for the cruiser force that was now known to be too small for its new tasks. As in the RN, however, the German Navy had devoted too little time before 1914 to analysing the complexity of air reconnaissance and there were not yet enough airships for them to make a difference. They did not accompany the Fleet to sea at all until 29 March 1915 after which they operated with the battlefleet on a more regular monthly basis. Admiral von Pohl, who had assumed command of the High Sea Fleet in February 1915, wrote a set of recommendations to the Naval Staff in Berlin which were to form the basis of airship deployment tactics in support of fleet operations for the remainder of the war. He emphasised the shortage of light cruisers in the High Sea Fleet and stated that airship reconnaissance was a prerequisite for all its operations, adding the valuable contribution they were expected to make in other fields such as antisubmarine operations and estimated that eighteen airships would be the minimum required in service. That figure was accepted and the airship service was expanded.

Fortunately for the RN, von Pohl's enthusiasm was not matched by an effective appreciation of how best to employ the new airships and his airmen's lack of fleet experience prevented them from compensating for this shortcoming. Here too, preconceived ideas were a factor and the presumption that airships could mount an effective bombing campaign against the UK mainland was a considerable distraction from their continuous development for fleet operations in the open sea where navigational difficulties would be as big a factor as the requirement to pass viable tactical data to the command. Von Pohl assumed that since airships took the place of scouting cruisers they must be allocated to the stations close to the battlefleet that such ships would have occupied; sometimes they were kept so close to the fleet that they were able to maintain contact by visual signalling methods. This meant that the airships were likely to be limited to chance encounters with the enemy in much the same way that the surface fleet would be, albeit at slightly greater range. Fortunately for the British, it does not seem to have occurred to von Pohl or the Naval Staff that airships could be used for long-range strategic scouting covering the distant part of the North Sea to find where the Grand Fleet actually was, rather than hoping for a chance encounter when the High Sea Fleet ventured out.

From the British perspective

Jellicoe had flown in a civilian Zeppelin, the *Schwaben*, on 15 November 1911 shortly after the demise of *R 1*, and been so impressed by its potential for reconnaissance over the sea that he argued in favour of reinstating a British rigid aircraft programme. His apprehension that whenever he took the Grand Fleet to sea it would be located and shadowed by airships never left him and it would be fair to say that he considerably overrated the capability of enemy airships to do so. As the number of Zeppelins grew, they were believed to pose a two-fold threat, aerial reconnaissance over the North Sea and bombing raids against the UK. At first there was only one practical solution to both problems, to attack airships in their sheds at their bases but after the advances by the German Army into most of Belgium in 1914 strikes against airship bases could only be achieved from the sea as they were now beyond the range of land-based aircraft, hence the seaplane operations described earlier. Dynamic officers such as Tyrwhitt soon saw that seaplane operations from ships in the Heligoland Bight might tempt the High Sea Fleet to sea and thus provoke a major fleet action on terms dictated by the British but this never happened. A succession of failed seaplane operations did show, however, that they were totally unsuited to operations in open water and that the technical difficulties of operating wheeled aircraft from the decks of warships would have to be overcome.

A growing number of defensive aviation measures were introduced after 1915 when even relatively small warships such as the 'Racecourse' class minesweepers were modified to embark two Sopwith Baby or Schneider seaplane fighters to intercept Zeppelins when they were sighted. Here again, seaplanes proved to be a failure since the enemy airships could see the ship stop to hoist them out and then climb to a safe height much faster than any seaplane could try to close them. This is why seaplane carriers began to be fitted with flying-off decks and Flight Lieutenant B F Fowler RNAS had demonstrated the ability of a wheeled Bristol Scout to take-off from *Vindex* in November 1915. In Germany, Admiral Scheer, who replaced von Pohl in early 1916, continued to believe that airships were an indispensible part of his fleet but he added the rider that its operations would therefore be limited to fine weather deemed suitable for Zeppelin flight. Thus the strategies of the two fleets were constrained by the perceived capability of Zeppelins: the Germans would only sail in fine weather conditions to optimise the ability of their airships to locate the Grand Fleet so that it could be evaded, while the British were intimidated by the perception that Zeppelins would give Scheer sufficient situational awareness to lead the Grand Fleet over a U-boat trap or minefield. Neither perception was valid with the technology available in 1915/16 and if the British had considered the capability they ascribed to Zeppelins carefully and logically, the command and control problems that needed to be overcome to allow Scheer to lead his own ships through such a trap without 'blue-on-blue' engagements or self-inflicted mine damage would have been recognised as immense.

Fleet fighters
It was not enough to rely on set-piece strikes against enemy airship bases, the fleet at sea had to be defended against Zeppelin reconnaissance and, potentially, bombing attacks. By 1916, therefore, most British warships were fitted with high-angle anti-aircraft guns. Even slow-moving airships proved difficult to hit, however, and only two airships were brought down by surface ships' gunfire during the entire war. It had become clear that fighter aircraft launched from the decks of warships would provide a better defence against both Zeppelins and enemy aircraft but Fowler's Bristol Scout had no designed armament and very little capacity to fit anything that weighed more than 100lb. Standard 0.303in ball ammunition fired by Lewis and Vickers machine guns had been found to have very little effect since it

Airborne photographs of RNAS aircraft are relatively rare and those firing their armament are even rarer. The quality of this photograph of a Sopwith Baby seaplane fighter firing Le Prieur rockets is not good but it does give a unique image of these weapons in use. (Author's collection)

did not ignite the hydrogen gas and so a new range of ammunition had to be developed before fleet fighters could become effective. The recoilless Davis gun had been tested in 1914 but had proved difficult to aim and was not considered to be of sufficient value to produce in quantity.

The next anti-airship weapon was designed by Lieutenant Yves Le Prieur, a French naval officer, in April 1916. It was a solid-fuelled, stick-stabilised incendiary rocket comprising a cardboard tube filled with 200 grams of black powder with a conical wooden head in which was fixed a triangular metal blade to rip open the airship fabric. The stick was of square section, usually made of pine and just short of 5ft long. They were not heavy and up to four rockets in their launch tubes could be fitted onto the interplane struts of most biplane fighters. They were mounted at a distinct upward angle compared with the aircraft's attitude in level flight and were launched in a steep dive along the line of the airship, preferably as nearly into wind as possible. Steeper dives were found to give greater accuracy but firing had to take place at fairly close range, about 125 yards, which meant that the pilot had to break away sharply after firing. They were fired electrically in sequence by depressing a switch in the cockpit but the interval between rockets could vary and the pilot had to continue to track the target until the last rocket had been discharged. The standard front gunsight was used to aim the rockets which proved to be fairly successful when used against static observation balloons on the Western Front, but no Zeppelin was ever brought down by them.

Explosive machine-gun bullets were recognised as having greater potential but technical difficulties had to be overcome with these, too, before they became effective. The standard ball rounds could puncture gasbags but it would take a lot of leakage to bring a Zeppelin down. Also, pilots were unable to see where ball rounds were going and, except at very close ranges, were unable to correct their fire onto the target. This problem had been identified by the RNAS before the outbreak of war and as early as 1914 James Buckingham provided a solution in the form of a tracer round. This had a hollow base filled with phosphorous which ignited on contact with the air, allowing the gunner to see where his rounds were going and correct his fire onto the target. Unfortunately the use of tracer rounds had been banned by the Geneva Convention but after the German use of poison gas in 1915 British resolve hardened and their use became widespread. Tracer rounds were initially referred to as Buckingham ammunition but by 1916 the term tracer was more widely used. They solved the problem of tracking bursts of fire onto a target but they did not ignite the hydrogen gas in an airship's gasbags. That was achieved by two different types of explosive 0.303in round introduced from 1915 onwards. The first was invented by Wing Commander F A Brock RNAS, a member of the family that had become famous for its production of fireworks. His Cartridge SA

Incendiary BIK .303in (VIIK) Mark 1 had a standard cartridge case but the cupronickel envelope and lead antimony core had a cavity into which a potassium chlorate composition was placed. The priming charge in the nose of the bullet comprised a mixture of potassium chlorate and mercury sulphocyanide. It protruded through the envelope and was covered by orange varnish. The result was an extremely volatile explosive round which detonated with a flash on impacting surfaces as thin as airship fabric.[11]

The second explosive round was invented by John Pomeroy from New Zealand who travelled to the UK in 1914 to offer his invention to the War Office which unfortunately showed little interest in it and he returned to his home country disappointed. In 1915, however, the Admiralty learnt of his invention and paid for him to return to the UK and develop it for anti-airship use by the RNAS. His round used a similar cupro-nickel case enclosing a lead-antimony core but in this application there was a copper warhead at the nose with a small hole at the front and it was sealed at the rear by a millboard disc. The tiny warhead was filled with a dough-like composition comprising 73 per cent nitroglycerine and 27 per cent kieselguhr. A small lead shot was placed at the base of the warhead to increase sensitivity on impact. In service this round was known officially as the Cartridge SA Ball .303in PSA (VIIAA) Mark II. However, at unit level the two types of ammunition were widely referred to as 'Brock' and 'Pomeroy' rounds. Thus for anti-Zeppelin sorties an aircraft would have bullets loaded into Lewis gun trays or Vickers' belts in the order ball, Buckingham/Tracer, Brock, Pomeroy and then ball again repeating the order. In service from 1916 this combination proved very effective and the rounds were adopted for use by the RFC as well as the RNAS. Reading Len Deighton's *Airshipwreck* and other airship sources it appears that prior to 1918 the Germans built 115 naval and military airships. Of these fifty-three were shot down or destroyed by attacks on their sheds. A further twenty-four were so badly damaged that, though salvaged, they were subsequently deemed to be beyond economical repair. These figures emphasise their vulnerability to the right combination of aircraft ammunition and light bombs.

Getting Fighter Aircraft to Sea
In retrospect it is difficult to understand exactly why it took so long to get wheeled high-performance fighters onto the decks of warships and, as is so often the case, there were a number of different reasons.[12] At first the need had not been recognised because seaplanes taking off from and alighting on the water were expected to carry out the roles of reconnaissance and fighter interception. Once experience showed this concept to be flawed, there was still some reluctance to operate aeroplanes with wheels over the sea because their unreliable engines were expected to

lead to excessive aircrew losses when they ditched. At least seaplanes gave some hope of rescue while they floated. Another reason was that aircraft could not carry out reconnaissance, fighter or strike missions in bad weather or at night. The fleet had therefore to operate without aircraft when conditions were unsuitable for their launch and there was a reluctance to remove warships from other tasks to provide partial and, at first, unproven capabilities. A 'chicken and egg' situation developed after 1915 in which aircraft could not prove what they could do until they had a big-deck carrier from which to operate and until they proved what they could do beyond doubt, warships could not be made available to be fitted with big decks. The requisitioned seaplane carriers were a partial, but not ideal, solution as they mostly lacked the speed to operate with the battlefleet and, even after aircraft could take off from a flight deck, the ship would still have to stop in order to recover the pilot after he had ditched since he could not land on the ship. The last and most important reason for the delay is the fact that it was not easy to land an aircraft on a ship. The only man to have done so prior to 1914 was Eugene Ely in January 1911. The fact that Samson did not seek the funds to build a wooden landing deck on *Africa* in 1912 probably indicates that he saw no need for it. Realisation only came after the failure of seaplane operations later in 1914 and 1915.

Hermes had demonstrated the practicability of operating aircraft at sea in the 1913 fleet manoeuvres and the Admiralty decided to augment the seaplane carriers requisitioned on the outbreak of war by fitting fixed, wooden forecastle take-off platforms, derived from the design of the temporary structure fitted to *Hermes*, onto four cruisers of the Harwich Force in May 1915. These were HMS *Arethusa, Aurora, Penelope* and *Undaunted*. *Penelope* embarked Deperdussin monoplane number 1378 and the other three embarked Sopwith Schneider seaplanes but all of these aircraft suffered damage from exposure to rough sea conditions and it unlikely that any of them ever took off from the platforms, all of which were removed by August 1915.[13] The improvements to *Campania* which brought her up to a useful standard in 1916 were described in the last chapter and although he did not join her as senior RNAS officer until the spring of 1917, Bell-Davies gave a vivid description of aircraft operations from her in *Sailor in the Air*.[14] The hatch down into the seaplane hangar was on the former boat deck aft of the take-off deck with the hangar itself beneath it in the area that had formerly contained first-class saloons when the ship was a Cunard liner. Below it, at main deck level, was the large and well-equipped workshop complex. On either side of the boat deck abreast the seaplane hatch were a mast and a steam-powered derrick. Seaplanes could be lifted out of the hangar by either derrick and placed on the take-off deck to be launched on a wheeled trolley or swung over the side for a water-borne take-off. The wings could be spread on the take-off deck or, if going into the water, the

A Fairey Campania being ranged ready for take-off on HMS *Campania*. The aircraft has had its wings spread and its handlers are pushing it aft to give it the longest possible take-off run. Its tail will eventually fit between the two fore-funnels. Note the wheeled trolley fitted under the floats to allow a deck launch. The compass platform fitted between the two funnels has a canvas screen to provide some protection against the elements; the fact that it is un-manned indicates that this move is a practice evolution being carried out in harbour. The two box-like structures projecting forward from the canvas screen, known as a 'dodger', are chart tables. (Author's collection)

seaplane could be lowered onto the boat deck for preparation before being lowered onto the water. For seaplane recovery there was a swinging boom about 50ft long hinged at upper deck level some distance forward of the derrick on either side. A long wire with a hemp 'tail' on its outboard end, known as the seaplane wire was rove through a block at the boom head. The inboard end of the wire was controlled by a steam winch on the upper deck.

At sea *Campania* was always accompanied by two destroyers and when a seaplane returned all three ships turned into wind and the destroyers steamed ahead at high speed to break up the seas and make a slick on which the aircraft could alight in relatively calm water. When it was ready the seaplane was ordered to land by a flag signal and the pilot aimed to touch down about a quarter of a mile ahead

HMS *Manxman* at anchor. The flying-off platform over the forecastle is clearly visible, as is the projecting gantry structure right aft which was intended to allow seaplanes to taxi up astern of the ship for recovery while it remained under way at about 5 knots. It worked reasonably well in calm weather but not in rougher conditions. (Author's collection)

of the carrier. As soon as it was down the ship was manoeuvred to bring one of the booms over it while the pilot used his engine and rudder to keep the seaplane head to sea. Two sailors clambered along the boom, one of them holding the hemp tail of the seaplane wire, the other a steadying line attached to the hook of the derrick purchase wire. When he had hauled in the end of the wire and attached it by means of a snap hook to a becket on the nose of the inboard float, the slack of the wire was hove in and the seaplane was in tow from the boom head. Meanwhile the pilot had climbed on to the top plane and the second boom-head sailor swung the derrick hook to him and he hooked it onto the aircraft's slings. It could then be hoisted in, the seaplane wire acting as a guy to hold it clear of the ship's side. Two men holding long bamboo poles with padded heads stood by on the upper deck to keep the aircraft clear of the ship's side if it swung. The whole evolution depended for its success on the team spirit of the RNAS handling party and Bell Davies believed that his efficient team could hardly be bettered. He timed recoveries at sea in moderately fresh wind conditions and the average, from breaking out the flag recovery signal to the ship's engine telegraphs being put ahead once the seaplane was on deck, was about 4 minutes 30 seconds. Of interest, the ship's thirteen old-fashioned cylindrical, through-tube boilers all had to maintain maximum steam pressure if the ship was to regain its position with the fleet after a recovery, Thus when the telegraphs were put to slow or stop every safety valve lifted simul-taneously and the roar of steam from the escape pipes close to the seaplane hatch was literally deafening. No verbal order could be heard and everything had to be done by signal or left to the initiative of the sailors concerned.

When she sailed belatedly on 31 May 1916 *Campania*'s air group comprised three Sopwith Babies, four Sopwith Schneiders and three Short 184s. The Sopwith Baby had a wingspan of 25ft 8in and a length of 22ft 10in. It was powered by a 110hp Clerget engine which gave it a maximum speed of 92mph at sea level; it took 35 minutes climb to 10,000ft and petrol tankage of 25 gallons gave it an endurance of 2.25 hours. Oil capacity was six gallons. It could be armed with a single Lewis gun mounted in an aperture in the centre section of the upper wing to fire at a shallow angle upwards to clear the airscrew. Two or three replacement 47-round trays of ammunition were carried in the cockpit. Alternatives, constrained by weight, included two 65lb bombs on racks under the fuselage, Le Prieur rockets or Ranken darts.

Whether he had heard of Williamson's proposal or not cannot now be known but in 1916 Flight Lieutenant Frederick J Rutland DSC AM RNAS, who had flown the Short 184 from *Engadine* at Jutland, had put forward similar proposals of his own, adding the need for an ideal top speed of 35 knots. In December 1916 he was appointed as the senior flying officer in the newly-converted seaplane carrier *Manxman* which was to be attached to the Battlecruiser Fleet. Her conversion had followed what was by then a standardised design with a hangar aft for four Short 184 seaplanes and a smaller hangar forward under a minimal take-off deck capable of taking four Sopwith Baby seaplanes with their wings removed. The deck was 86ft long by 28ft wide, just big enough for the Babies to take-off on wheeled trollies that were arrested at the end of the take-off run as the seaplane lifted off.[15] The 184s had to be craned onto the water for take-off and recovered by crane after alighting; both evolutions requiring the ship to be stopped. *Manxman*'s acceptance trials were carried out in the Firth of Forth in January 1917 during which Rutland found the Babies' marginal take-off performance to be unacceptable. He wrote a paper that outlined the advantages of using wheeled fighters such as the Sopwith Pup rather than seaplanes, pointing out that *Campania*'s pilots had found that it took at least 80ft for a Baby on a trolley to get airborne from a deck and that since its rate of climb fell off markedly above 6000ft it could never hope to intercept a Zeppelin. *Manxman*'s flight deck was marginal for seaplane fighter launches but as soon as she arrived in the Firth of Forth to join the Battlecruiser Fleet Rutland instigated a series of launches to evaluate the true potential of the ship and its aircraft. He made the first take-off himself with 20 knots of wind over the deck and flew away successfully but when one of his more junior pilots followed he pushed the stick too far forward, lowering the aircraft's nose and scraping the floats on the deck, causing it to lose speed. It failed to get airborne and trickled over the bow into the water. Fortunately the pilot was saved but the aircraft was lost and Rutland made the point that safe flying operations could only be carried out under ideal

Rutland carrying out the first take-off in a Sopwith Pup from HMS *Manxman* in the Firth of Forth. The aircraft is fitted with tubes for Le Prieur rockets on the interplane struts and has a Lewis gun fitted to fire upwards through the gap between the upper wings. (Author's collection)

conditions. Together with his commanding officer he sought Admiralty approval to re-equip his flight with Sopwith Pups. Approval was given but such was the demand for Pups in the Dover/Dunkirk Wings and with the RFC on the Western Front that they could not be provided until April 1917.[16]

While he was waiting for them, Rutland encountered opposition from a surprising quarter when his pilots expressed doubts about the wisdom of flying aircraft over the sea that were not fitted with floats. With engine failures still a frequent occurrence, they believed that their chances of being rescued after ditching a wheeled aircraft would not be good. In answer he instructed a seaplane pilot to alight close the *Manxman* off May Island at the entrance to the Firth of Forth in March 1917 and switch his engine off while a photographer and the other aircrew watched results from the ship. It was a windy day with a choppy sea and after a short time the seaplane's tail was driven under and it turned upside down with only a few inches of float showing above the surface. Further tests with a surplus wheeled aircraft fitted with airbags in the rear fuselage showed that aircraft so-fitted had the potential to float upright for a considerably longer period. These practical demonstrations won the argument and the Admiralty elected to replace Babies with Pups in *Manxman*, *Campania* and the new *Furious* when she completed in July. This was good but the carrier would still have to be in exactly the right place to launch a Pup against a Zeppelin and it would obviously be better if fighters could be carried in a number of other warships, preferably on the light cruisers that were likely to be the first ships to come into contact with the enemy. At first only about fifteen Pups were available in a pool at RNAS Smoogroo on the mainland of Orkney near the north shore of Scapa Flow and wider embarkation would mean more aircraft would be needed but as Sopwith Triplanes and later Camels began to replace Pups in the Dover Command and France, more Pups became available for fleet work in the second half of 1917.

Rutland's enthusiasm had led to him being appointed as technical advisor to the Battlecruiser Fleet Aircraft Committee chaired by Rear Admiral Phillimore, Flag Officer 1st Battlecruiser Squadron (1 BCS), who was soon to become Rear Admiral Aircraft (RAA), Grand Fleet. Earlier take-off platforms in warships had either masked the forward guns or required their removal and Admiral Beatty, who had replaced Jellicoe as C-in-C Grand Fleet, was reluctant to limit the firepower of battleships or battlecruisers to modify them for flying operations but he did agree to have light cruisers modified if the dimensions of the deck could be kept to a minimum. Argument within the committee, therefore, focused on exactly how long the take-off deck needed to be and what effect it would have on the forward gun of a light cruiser. It had been assumed at first that the 80ft required to launch a Sopwith Baby with wheels under its floats from *Campania* would still apply but Rutland challenged that. He said that he was curious to know just how long a run a Pup really needed with 20 knots of wind over the deck[17] and that by his calculations it would require less than 20ft. Again Rutland organised tests from *Manxman*, this time using a Sopwith Pup and the relatively less-experienced pilots from his flight. Chalk was rubbed into the aircraft tyres so that the exact length of each take-off run could subsequently be measured. The less-experienced pilots took off first and demonstrated a spread of runs ranging from 35ft to well over 40ft. Rutland then demonstrated that by easing gently back on the stick about two seconds after the aircraft's release he could be safely airborne in less than 20ft. His pilots were still reluctant to get airborne in less than 30ft, however, and so Rutland took the tests a stage further. With his captain's approval he had a 20ft platform 12in high built on top of the after part of the original deck. He chose the after part so that pilots who failed to get airborne in 20ft still had a 60ft safety margin before them. This time he went first to boost the others' confidence and take-off runs were all less than 18ft. With practice Rutland eventually took off with a 20-knot wind over the deck in only 15ft.

When the Battlecruiser Fleet Aviation Committee next met it was asked to consider a design for a flying-off deck which was 45ft long prepared by Lieutenant Commander C H B Gowan RN, the gunnery officer of the light cruiser *Yarmouth* at the instigation of Rear Admiral Phillimore and Wing Captain R M Groves RNAS. It allowed the forward 6in gun to remain in place but masked its arcs of fire; Gowan envisaged, therefore, that the platform would need to be partially dismantled after the aircraft had launched. After some discussion Rutland revealed that he was prepared to fly off a deck only 15ft long. Gowan, like many other gunnery officers, was slightly deaf and thought he had said 50ft and said that he was afraid that no more than 45ft would be possible. When Rutland corrected him the committee apparently fell silent as the possible implications were realised since, at long last, the fleet could now carry its own fighters with a realistic chance of intercepting Zeppelins. To emphasise his point, Rutland took committee members to sea in *Manxman* and consistently demonstrated take-off runs of 15ft with 20 knots of wind over the deck. It was agreed that *Yarmouth* would be fitted immediately in Rosyth Dockyard with a short take-off platform over the forecastle gun mounting. Before the new deck could be tested under ideal conditions in the Firth of Forth, however, the Grand Fleet staff decided to use *Manxman* with

HMS *Yarmouth*'s Sopwith Pup on its tiny take-off deck seen from the forecastle. The ship is weighing anchor (note the ERA at the control for the steam-driven capstan) and, judging from the amount of general activity, preparations are being made for the first take-off, hence the presence of a cameraman on board to record events. (Author's collection)

Sopwith Pups embarked to intercept a Zeppelin reconnaissance which was known to make a morning patrol of the Horns Reef every day. The plan, which was arguably over-confident, involved *Manxman*, escorted by a cruiser squadron led by Rear Admiral Sinclair flying his flag in *Galatea,* proceeding to a point about 100nm from the Horns Reef and launching a force of Pups to intercept and destroy the enemy airship. A German minefield prevented the ships getting any closer and Rutland had little confidence in the plan because it involved an outbound flight of an hour, out of sight of the fleet or land, an attempt to find an airship that might or might not be there visually in unknown weather conditions, winds that could not be accurately forecast and a return over the minefield of similar length. This would involve at least two hours' flying in an aircraft that had an endurance of only 2.5 hours and which had no navigational aids. Engine failure or the inability to locate the task force after the return flight would result in the certain loss of the aircraft and probably the pilot as well. He exposed the plan's shortcoming through the chain of command but, while Admiral Pakenham, commander of the Battlecruiser Fleet, was sympathetic and agreed that there was little chance of intercepting a Zeppelin that had not been sighted by the fleet, he felt that the Staff's instructions must be carried out.

Manxman sailed on 17 May 1917 and launched two Pups as dawn broke a day later. There was a strong wind from the west and a rough sea that caused the ship to pitch badly, conditions that caused Admiral Sinclair to signal 'What do you think of this?' Rutland's reply was 'Weather suitable for flying but unlikely that Zeppelins can fly today.'[18] The Admiral said later that had word 'definitely' rather than 'unlikely' been used in *Manxman*'s reply to his signal he would have felt justified in cancelling the operation but since the expert advice had left a chance that the enemy might be airborne he had little alternative but to order 'Proceed in execution of previous orders'. Two Pups took off flown by Rutland and a Canadian Flight Sub Lieutenant. The latter circled the ship and ditched near a destroyer, subsequently explaining that his engine was running hot, although Rutland believed that he had hardly been airborne long enough establish this for certain. Both he and his captain had been at pains not to mention their criticism of the plan because they had not wanted to undermine their pilots' confidence.

Rutland continued to the area of the Horns Reef alone, estimating his drift by looking back at the light cruisers which he asked to point towards the target area as he took departure. His feel for the wind at 1000ft had no accurate basis in analysis but it must have been about 45 knots, double the surface wind. As he flew on, the seas became heavier and the clouds lower and he eventually reached the Horns Reef at 800ft with a visibility of about two miles in heavy rain. Aware that no Zeppelin could be flying in such conditions he turned immediately onto a heading that he hoped would take him back to the task force but at this stage a crack developed in his compass and the alcohol ran out leaving the card tumbled and wedged without movement in the empty container. With no means of checking his heading he had to hope that the wind direction had remained unchanged from the west and he continued to fly into it. In fact it had backed about 45 degrees and was now coming from the south-west. When he estimated by dead-reckoning that he might be near the task force he came down to sea level and searched for about 15 minutes and then turned onto an easterly course with his engine running on the leanest possible mixture to get the greatest range out of his remaining fuel. He might well have become one of the pilots that were never seen again after take-off but by good fuel management and a degree of luck he found a coastline which he was able to identify as Danish and then flew two miles back out to sea and ditched. The aircraft sank almost immediately but he started to swim towards the shore; it was still only 06.00 but a small fishing boat rowed up and rescued him. Once ashore, he was met by a local doctor named Toft who offered assistance. A coast-watcher intervened and said that he had ditched only 3km off the shore, inside Danish territorial waters, but Rutland managed to convince Dr Toft that he had instruments in the cockpit that measured his exact distance offshore and that he had been just over 3nm from the beach. Thus informed, the coast-watcher admitted that he could have been wrong and Rutland was not interned but treated as a shipwrecked mariner who had been rescued from the high seas. Luckily the storm over the Horns Reef had not yet arrived and the fisherman who had rescued Rutland later informed him that had he ditched only an hour later they could not have launched their boat to rescue him.

To Rutland's astonishment he found that he had been blown to the far north of Denmark and after his status as a shipwrecked mariner was confirmed the British Embassy issued him with a diplomatic passport and he travelled by ferry to Sweden and then by train to Oslo in Norway, then known as Christiania. When he eventually returned to the UK he was awarded a bar to his DSC and a mention in dispatches for his brave attempt to carry out an impossible operation. He was also promoted immediately to Squadron Commander RNAS, ahead of many officers senior to him on the list. At his instigation, the Admiralty sent a silver inkstand to Dr Toft and a silver watch to each of the five fishermen who had rescued him. Each was inscribed with their name and the words 'Presented by the Lords of the Admiralty in appreciation of the services rendered to a British airman off the coast of Jutland'.

The Sopwith Pup had a wingspan of 26ft 6in and a length of 19ft 3in. It was powered by an 80hp Le Rhône rotary engine which gave a maximum speed of 112mph at sea level and took 14 minutes to 10,000ft. Nineteen gallons of petrol gave an endurance of 2.5 hours and the oil tank contained 5 gallons. It could be armed with a single 0.303in Lewis gun mounted on a tripod forward of the cockpit angled to fire forward and upwards at an angle of 30 degrees through an aperture in the centre section of the upper wing, thus missing the airscrew. The gun could be pulled back along a rack to have the 47-round ammunition tray changed or to fire vertically upwards. Two or three spare trays were carried in cockpit stowages. Pups operating ashore had an alternative fit of a single Vickers 0.303in machine gun mounted forward of the cockpit with an interrupter mechanism which allowed it to fire through the airscrew arc. As an alternative, a total of eight Le Prieur rockets could be carried on the interplane struts. RNAS Pups embarked for anti-Zeppelin duties had the upward-tilted Lewis gun fitted because their ammunition trays were loaded with tracer, Brock and Pomeroy explosive bullets as well as ball. Interrupter mechanisms were still not perfect and it was not unusual for the odd round to pass through a propeller blade; if this happened with a ball round the result was survivable but if it happened with an explosive round the result would be disastrous, hence the foolproof angling of the gun above the propeller arc. The angle also gave pilots the chance to engage airships from below without having to pull the nose up to fire with the consequent risk of stalling at high altitude. Embarked Pups were fitted with a flotation bag in the rear fuselage and a strong-point for a hold-back device to be attached to the undercarriage. The bag was fitted with a bung or stopper that was left out in normal flight to allow for pressure changes with altitude. It was essential therefore that the pilot remembered to insert it before ditching.

HMS *Yarmouth*

While Rutland had been making his way back from Denmark and Norway, *Yarmouth* was taken into Rosyth Dockyard and fitted with a flying deck 30ft long, the after part of which was bolted to the armoured conning tower and the forward part cantilevered out over the forecastle 6in gun mounting. It did not affect the gun's arc of fire or elevation and thus did not impair the cruiser's efficiency in a surface gun action.[19] The aircraft was secured at the after end of the deck with its tail skid on a trestle that both positioned it in a flying attitude and kept it straight during the first 2ft of movement when the hold-back was released. There was 16ft of deck between the wheels and the front of the deck and on 28 June 1917 Rutland took off with ease into a 25-knot wind over the deck to prove that the concept was viable. Chalk on his tyres showed that the actual take-off run had covered 14ft 9in of deck. Cruiser decks clearly represented a quick and efficient way of getting fighters to sea and Beatty immediately sought Admiralty approval to fit take-off decks with frame and canvas hangars to protect the aircraft in rough weather

Rutland taking off into a 20-knot wind from the cruiser HMS *Yarmouth* on 28 June 1917. His deck run was measured at exactly 14ft 9in and his wheels are seen in this photograph almost at the instant they left the deck. (Author's collection)

aboard five further light cruisers and the light battlecruisers *Courageous* and *Glorious*. Approval was soon given.

Yarmouth was declared operational with her new capability and issued with Sopwith Pup N6430. Her pilot was Flight Sub Lieutenant Bernard A Smart RNAS and he was supported by a rigger and a fitter, the former responsible for the airframe and the latter for the engine. On 8 August 1917 she was moored to H 4 buoy off Rosyth in the Firth of Forth taking on coal from the collier *Cedar Tree* which had arrived alongside at 06.40;[20] the process was completed shortly after noon when, having cleaned ship, the ship's company was given a 'make and mend'[21] for the afternoon. After sunset she slipped her moorings with other ships of the 1st Light Cruiser Squadron (1 LCS), and sailed to cover a minelaying operation off the German coast. On the morning of 21 August the force was east of the Dogger Bank in an area known to be patrolled by Zeppelins. Smart was a meticulous pilot who left nothing to chance; he had arranged to be called at 02.30 and, having dressed, he climbed up onto the aircraft which was securely lashed to the deck and helped his two mechanics to strip off the protective tarpaulins that had covered N6430's engine and cockpit overnight. Next he climbed into the cockpit and, after his fitter had turned the propeller to prime the cylinders, started the engine to warm

Flight Lieutenant B A Smart DSO
RNAS. (Author's collection)

it up and checked that he could achieve full power against the hold-back. Next he
checked the breech mechanism of the Lewis gun and correct fit of the 97-round
double ammunition tray with which it was fitted. When he was satisfied that the gun
was fully serviceable, he fired twelve rounds to confirm that it was ready for action.
By then it was getting light on a clear, sharp morning and Sharp noticed how
brightly the aircraft's blue, white and red national roundels stood out in the
sunlight. He ordered his mechanics to get a tin of 'pusser's grey' to cover the
markings to improve his chances of closing on a Zeppelin without being seen.
Having run the engine he checked the tank had been topped up to the full 19
gallons of petrol and that the two spare trays of Lewis gun ammunition were neatly
stowed in the cockpit. As always, he had checked the night before that every round
in the trays had been lightly oiled to avoid a gun-jam in action and he made sure
that his two lifebelts and a flask of brandy were in the cockpit to help him survive
the inevitable ditching if he was launched. When all these preparations were

complete *Yarmouth*'s commanding officer Captain H H Grace RN, leant over the front of the bridge and told Smart to get some rest until he was called for action.

Only 30 minutes later at 05.00 he was ordered to the bridge to be told that a destroyer on the task force screen had reported sighting a German seaplane which had been driven off by the fleet's gunfire. When this excitement was over he went below to his cabin again but was called back to the bridge at 05.30 when lookouts saw a Zeppelin to the south-west running on a course parallel to 1 LCS. Captain Grace ordered Smart to man his aircraft and stand by to be launched. By the time he was strapped in and ready to start up the Zeppelin was about 8nm away and matching the task force's movements. Wireless transmissions had been detected from it as it reported the British ships' course and speed. While Smart pulled on his leather helmet and goggles Captain Grace turned *Yarmouth* hard into wind; starting the warmed-up engine went well and Smart ran up to full revolutions as the ship steadied into the light breeze. N6430's rigging wires began to sing but nothing registered on the aircraft's airspeed indicator and Smart asked the captain for more speed to increase the wind over the deck. When he was happy he raised his arm to indicate to the bridge that he was ready to launch and the captain signalled the commander, his second-in-command, who lay underneath the aircraft with the quick-release lanyard attached to the hold-back. Despite his seniority he had undertaken the task himself to make absolutely sure that there were no mistakes. As soon as the commander pulled the lanyard, the hold-back released and N6430 rolled forward. It was airborne in 16ft and Smart climbed hard into a glorious morning that was still bright and sunny. He used such cloud cover as there was to mask his climb to 9000ft and took frequent compass bearings on the Zeppelin in gaps to ensure that he could still intercept it if it managed to use cloud to hide its position. Thus far his climb to height had taken him just over 12 minutes.

The Zeppelin, *L 23*, was 585ft long and 61ft in diameter powered by four Maybach engines which gave a nominal speed of about 50 knots, roughly half that of the Pup. The German crew saw *Yarmouth* turn into wind, guessed that she had launched a fighter and immediately sought cover in cloud. At about this time they sent what proved to be their last W/T message to their base at Tondern; it was intercepted by the fleet's wireless intercept specialists and read 'Am pursued by enemy forces'. Smart regained visual contact as he followed his compass bearing out of cloud and found that he had a considerable height advantage over the airship which by then was heading for Germany. He dived at about 100 knots and manoeuvred to keep the airship end-on so that the gunners in the gondolas would be unable to get a clean shot at him. On his first pass he cut under the stern at about 250 yards and opened fire but his tracer rounds showed that they and his incendiary rounds were missing high. On his second pass he pressed home his attack to within 100ft and saw his bullets striking home through the airship's fabric into the gasbags inside before he had to break away hard and descend to avoid a collision. He levelled out at 3000ft and saw *L 23* on fire aft; the flames spread rapidly and the stern began to drop so that it slid backwards into the sea with the nose pointing upwards at an angle of about 45 degrees and the engines still turning the propellers. It crashed into the sea and continued to burn for several minutes. There were no survivors and a subsequent search by German seaplanes found only a large oil slick and a charred wooden airship propeller at the place where *L 23* had been shot down.

After Smart had watched his target come down he looked around but could see no sign of the task force so he turned onto the reciprocal of the compass bearing that he had followed on the outbound flight but edged a few degrees to

Smart's Sopwith Pup N6430 after ditching with its tail held above water by its internal buoyancy bag. Smart is sitting in HMS *Prince*'s whaler and although a rope appears to have been attached to the aircraft, it was not salvaged and was subsequently written off charge. The 'pusser's grey' paint applied over the red, white and blue markings on the rudder to make
the aircraft less conspicuous in the clear, early morning light can just be made out.
(Author's collection)

port so that he would get a better view of the ships against the glare of the sun on the sea surface to starboard of the aircraft's nose. After 45 minutes there was still no sign of a British warship and he began to consider flying east to Denmark rather than ditch in an empty sea. Just then he saw the ships about seven miles away to port moving at high speed away from where he had expected them to be. They had seen the smoke from the burning *L 23*, thought it might be the German High Sea Fleet coming out and were clearing to the west quickly, leaving the pilot to take his chances. Smart set himself up to ditch alongside two destroyers that were nearer than 1 LCS. First he inserted the bung into the flotation bag in the rear fuselage, then he undid his straps and switched off the engine ignition having set up a gliding approach to a position ahead of the destroyers. When he estimated that his height was about 15ft he pulled back hard on the stick and stalled, wings level, into the water. The weight of the engine pulled the nose down but the tailplane stayed out of the water and Smart was able to cling onto it until a sea-boat from the destroyer *Prince* picked him up. Unfortunately N6430 was not salvaged. At 07.40 *Prince* signalled *Yarmouth* to say that the pilot had been recovered safely and that he had shot down the Zeppelin. Minutes later *Prince* received a signal from the Commodore 1 LCS in *Caledon* which said 'You have done most splendidly and I am sure your reward will be prompt'. At 01.50 on 22 August the Commodore sent a further signal which read 'Flight Sub Lieutenant Smart is to be returned to *Yarmouth* on anchoring. Commodore wishes to see him at 10.00 today Wednesday. Boat will be sent to *Yarmouth*.'

At 03.45 *Yarmouth* moored to H 4 buoy at Rosyth again and Smart re-joined her at 04.00. The collier *Agnes Duncan* came alongside at 07.05 and the ship's company began again the hard routine of preparing for another North Sea sweep. A replacement Pup was brought out by lighter from the Fleet Replacement Air Park at Turnhouse near Edinburgh[22] on 23 August and a new pilot, Flight Sub Lieutenant Williams RNAS, joined. Smart was appointed to the new *Furious* and on 14 September 1917 the *London Gazette* announced that he had been awarded the DSO for his action in shooting down *L 23*. It had required courage to sit in the open cockpit of a Sopwith Pup behind a not very reliable engine just after dawn feeling the ship's movement as it turned hard into wind and then taking off in such a short run. So too did the combat against a large opponent equipped with a number of machine guns and the calm way in which he carried out his search for 1 LCS which was nowhere near the position in which he had expected to find it. Smart was an outstanding pilot who had ably demonstrated what the RN's new air service could achieve at sea once it had the right equipment.

Turret platforms and rotatable take-off decks

Smart's success operating from *Yarmouth* led to the rapid implementation of a number of schemes to get both fighter and reconnaissance aircraft to sea with the Grand Fleet as quickly as possible. Lieutenant Commander Gowan continued to put forward imaginative ideas, noting that the need for cruisers to turn into wind to launch aircraft from a fixed platform could cause problems with task force co-ordination in a surface action. His solution was to fit platforms 45ft long onto the main-armament turret roofs of battleships and battlecruisers. These offered the advantage that the turret could be turned into the 'felt wind' resulting from a combination of the ship's motion and the natural wind. Thus, while the turret trained into the relative wind the ship could remain in its designated formation with other warships.[23] The first such platform was fitted to 'B' turret of the battlecruiser *Repulse* and a successful trial launch was carried out from it on 1 October 1917 by Rutland. In his subsequent report on this important event her temporary commanding officer, Captain J S Dumaresq CB MVO RN,[24] described the launch in detail. The ship was steaming four miles off Inchkeith Island in the Firth of Forth at 10.00 on an initial course of 145 degrees at 24 knots. The true surface wind was observed to be from 230 degrees at 17 knots and so he ordered two course adjustments totalling 45 degrees towards the true wind to bring the relative wind forward of the ship's beam. The turret was trained in local control using the left sighting hood from where the trainer could see a wind vane fixed to the left gun muzzle in line with his eye. Final small adjustments were made under Rutland's instructions using a flag held in front of the aircraft by a sailor as a sensor. With the turret now trained into a relative wind of just over 30 knots Dumaresq gave the order to launch and Rutland took off without any difficulty in Sopwith Pup N 6453, the same aircraft in which Squadron Commander Dunning had carried out the first deck landing during trials on *Furious* in 1917, an event which will be described in detail in Chapter 11.

As in *Yarmouth*, a tail-guide trestle and hold-back device were used, the former holding the aircraft's tail up in the flying attitude and providing directional stability until sufficient airspeed was achieved for the rudder to become effective and the latter allowing full power to be achieved before the take-off run started. One detail improvement in the trestle was a groove in the top surface into which a ball fitting at the bottom of the aircraft's tail skid was located to ensure that it remained in contact until the forward edge of the trestle was reached. The hold-back was a standard device like those used on cruisers comprising a slip hook attached to a cross-wire stretched between the undercarriage struts. From this hook a wire ran aft to an anchor point on an eye-bolt fixed to the deck of the turret platform. A lanyard with wooden toggles to allow cold, wet hands to ensure a firm grip was

The area of clear deck forward of HMAS *Australia*'s 'Q' turret from which Flight Lieutenant F Fox RNAS took off on 18 December 1917. The ship is anchored in the 'battlecruiser row' to the west of the Forth Railway Bridge which is visible in the background, together with other battlecruisers. The aircraft on the extended 'Q' turret platform is a Sopwith 1½ 'Ship' Strutter. (Author's collection)

attached to the slip hook. When the pilot indicated that he was ready by raising an arm and the bridge gave the executive order to launch, a firm pull on the lanyard released the hook and the aircraft flew off. Then, and still today, the decision to launch rested with the captain who takes full responsibility for everything that happens in his ship. As in *Yarmouth*, it is indicative of the importance placed on safe launch techniques that the commander or second-in-command of *Repulse* worked the quick-release lanyard.

The same platform was then dismantled and re-assembled on 'Y' turret aft from which Rutland took off successfully in the same aircraft on 9 October 1917. In this case the platform was rigged so that the aircraft took off over the rear of the turret as it was thought that this would reduce the amount of training necessary because the relative wind was often found to be forward of the beam. However, experience showed that this variation was unnecessary and only five battlecruisers, *Repulse, Renown, Lion, Tiger* and *Princess Royal*, were thus modified. In all other capital ships the platform was fitted to face toward the gun barrels on the after as well as the forward turrets.

Sopwith Pup N6453 in position on HMS *Repulse*'s 'Y' turret platform. This photograph was probably taken as the ship got under way for flying trials in the Firth of Forth. (Author's collection)

Having shown that relatively light, high-performance fighters could fly off a turret platform 45ft long, the next logical advance was to see if it would be possible to launch a two-seater reconnaissance aircraft from a battlecruiser. On 18 December 1917 Flight Lieutenant Frederick Fox RNAS took off from the unobstructed area of HMAS *Australia*'s upper deck forward of 'Q' turret without heading directly into wind.[25] It was, however, decided that this was not a practical proposition for routine launches and further work was carried out in the Second Battlecruiser Squadron to perfect a suitably lengthened turret platform. Two-seater aircraft would be needed to fly off capital ships tasked with locating the enemy and spotting their own ships' fall of shot at long ranges. The aircraft selected for this task was the Sopwith 1½ Strutter, subsequently known as the 'Ship' Strutter after modifications to fit a W/T set operated by the observer. The first attempt at extension was fabricated from canvas stretched over a steel wire net fitted on 'B' turret of *Repulse*.[26] On 4 March 1918 Flight Commander D G Donald RNAS

Flight Commander D G Donald RNAS taking off from HMAS *Australia*'s 'Q' turret platform in a Sopwith 'Ship' Strutter on 7 March 1918 in the Firth of Forth with a sea-boat close by in case of accident. Note that the aircraft is being flown solo without an observer in the rear seat. The ship in the background is HMS *New Zealand*. (Author's collection)

attempted to take off in 'Ship' Strutter 9744 but found that the weight of the aircraft caused the canvas to sag and the propeller hit the netting and shattered during the short take-off run. The aircraft ditched and Donald was lucky to escape with only minor bruises. He was rescued by a sea-boat from the destroyer *Rival*.

Admiral Leveson, who combined the tasks of Flag Officer 2 BCS and Senior Officer of the Australian Squadron, flew his flag in *Australia* and believed that this ship's echelon turrets offered better wind exposure and a safer take-off position than turrets at the bow or stern. He therefore designed a portable wooden extension that ran out over the gun barrels of 'Q' turret. It comprised 2in planks attached to angle-irons strapped to the gun barrels. The planks at the junction between the original turret platform and the extension over the barrels were quickly removable so that the guns could be elevated to their full extent and, given reasonable warning that action was imminent, the remainder of the extension could be dismantled quickly. It would, in any case, disintegrate when the guns were fired so there was no limitation on the use of the ships' main armament from these aircraft arrangements. On 7 March 1918 Donald took off successfully from this platform in 'Ship' Strutter N5644 into a relative wind of 20 knots. To save weight it had no observer, wireless or gun but the concept was successfully proved. Fox carried out the first fully-loaded take-off on 4 April and by the end of the month *Australia* had carried out several flights without difficulty, including one while the ship was at anchor. Phillimore was impressed and noted that this flight showed 'considerable possibilities in the way of carrying reconnaissance machines in battlecruisers or, if desired, in other capital ships'.[27] and the turret platform rapidly became an effective and reliable method of launching fleet fighter and reconnaissance aircraft; by late 1918 the Grand Fleet had over 100 aircraft embarked.

Aircraft launched from turret platforms and small take-off decks were still one-shot systems, but in the short term this was considered to be acceptable since there were sufficient reserves of aircraft to replace those that ditched. By mid-1918 there were not enough and French-built single-seat 1½ Strutters, which were being replaced in the bombing role, were purchased and modified to 'Ship' Strutter standard to meet the Grand Fleet's growing need. Light cruisers did not have power-operated turrets like those in capital ships and their gun mountings were relatively small; they could not, therefore, be fitted with turret platforms but here too Gowan's innovative mind came up with a solution and he designed a turntable modification to the type of deck fitted in *Yarmouth* that enabled the deck forward of the small aircraft shelter to be rotated into the relative wind provided that it was forward of the beam, still without interfering with the forward gun mounting. The first flight from this improved deck took place on 8 December 1917 when a Sopwith Pup was launched from HMAS *Sydney*. Further trials from *Sydney* were carried out in Scapa Flow by Flight Sub Lieutenant A C Sharwood RNAS, again in a Pup.

Rutland photographed in Sopwith Pup N6453 as he became airborne off HMS *Repulse*'s 'Y' turret platform on 9 October 1917. (Author's collection)

10 1917 – Expansion and Reorganisation

1917 was a year of unprecedented technical and tactical progress. It saw squadrons formed which comprised a single aircraft type with common engines and armament to improve tactical cohesion and simplify maintenance and support arrangements.

Anti-Submarine Warfare

An outstanding feature of air operations against submarines in home waters was the success of flying boats which, unaided by surface craft, attacked a number of U-boats located on the surface. These boat-hulled seaplanes were developed at Felixstowe by Wing Commander J C Porte RNAS and gave the RN an aircraft that was capable of extended patrols over the sea and highly manoeuvrable. This feature meant that they could quickly get into an attacking position when a U-boat was sighted and even engage Zeppelins and other enemy aircraft with a good chance of success. Flying boats proved capable of flying from air stations at Yarmouth, Felixstowe and Killingholme to surprise and engage Zeppelins in their own waters. During 1917 two hostile airships were shot down in flames and a third damaged in this way.[1] Airships came into their own after the introduction of the convoy system in 1917, demonstrating unique qualities of low speed and long endurance that were ideal for airborne escorts. Airship stations established in 1916 were, by then, able to provide escorts for the majority of coastal convoys as well as periodical searches of swept channels for newly-laid mines.

Important changes had been made in the composition of the Admiralty War Staff in November 1916 and these resulted in the creation of an Anti-Submarine Division to co-ordinate existing measures and devise new ones to counter the enemy attack on shipping. At the beginning of 1917 other changes took place in the administration of the RNAS in conjunction with the formation of the government's second Air Board. Among the most important was the appointment of the DAS to the Board of Admiralty as Fifth Sea Lord, a new post which was to be responsible all naval air matters, both within the Service and as a member of the Air Board. Rear Admiral C L Vaughan-Lee who had held the post of DAS until then was relieved by Commodore G M Paine RN who had been associated

Six Felixstowe F2A flying boats on one of the slipways at RNAS Felixstowe. A seaplane lighter can be seen at anchor just beyond the end of the slipway and another can be seen beyond the wind-sock on the walk-way to the right of the picture. (Author's collection)

with air matters since 1912 and had been the first Commandant of the CFS. The Government had decided that the design and procurement of aircraft should be handed over by the Admiralty and War Office to the Ministry of Munitions and the Admiralty staff who had formally dealt with this work were transferred to that Department.

The new Anti-Submarine Division allowed both heavier-than-air and lighter-than-air aircraft to be fully developed as part a comprehensive strategy and one of the Division's first acts was to prepare a scheme for the extension of air patrols into the western approaches to the English Channel. To support them new seaplane bases were established at Cattewater in Plymouth Sound and at Newlyn in Cornwall by early 1917. Facilities for mooring flying boats were provided at Port Mellon in the Scilly Islands and an additional seaplane base was established at Fishguard in Pembrokeshire during March 1917. An additional shed for a Coastal airship was erected at Mullion in February to enable patrols to operate in the area to the north-west of Cornwall and in April these air stations were grouped under a single command designated the South Western Group with its headquarters at Plymouth. At the same time the seaplane bases in the mid-Channel area were designated the Portsmouth Group. They comprised a main air station and school at Calshot with sub-stations at Bembridge and Portland. In May the opening of an air station at Newhaven added to the strength of this group and in July a further air station on the other side of the Channel at Cherbourg increased it still further.

RNAS Yarmouth. (Author's collection)

In addition to this expansion, definite areas of search for seaplanes operating from air stations on the east coast were laid down and an organised system of patrols was put into operation.

While this expanded patrol organisation was being built up, the Germans declared a state of unrestricted submarine warfare against the Allies in February 1917, changing U-boat tactics from surface attacks by gunfire to submerged attacks by torpedo without warning. This was the change of policy that finally brought the United States into the war on the side of the Allies and by April 1917 the German offensive had reached an unprecedented intensity with up to half the U-boat force believed to be at sea between 17 and 27 April. On the most disastrous day, 19 April 1917, eleven British merchant ships and eight fishing vessels were sunk by U-boats and a further two by mines. The daily loss for that month averaged over five ships compared with an average over the previous year of less than three. The daily average figures for 1915 and 1916 were less than one. This critical situation gave impetus to the development of every form of countermeasure among which aircraft began to form an important part.

It was found that German submarines consistently revealed their positions in the same way that Zeppelins did by the frequent use of W/T. These messages were detected by direction-finding stations set up by the Admiralty across the UK which were able to fix the positions of U-boats accurately at the time of the transmission. By this means it was found in the spring of 1917 that U-boats, particularly the small UB and UC classes, were in the habit of passing close to the North Hinder Light Vessel on their way to their hunting grounds in the waters close to the UK. Furthermore, because of their restricted radius of action on battery-powered electric motors when forced to dive, the majority of U-boats

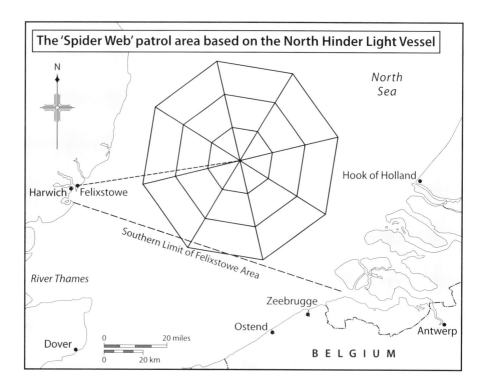

The 'Spider Web' patrol area based on the North Hinder Light Vessel

passed through this area on the surface. It was, therefore, decided to organise offensive operations against boats passing the North Hinder Light Vessel using flying boats based at Felixstowe. A method of search was devised, centred on the light vessel, which was to become known as the 'Spider Web'. It comprised an octagonal figure 60 miles in diameter with eight radiating arms, each 30 miles in length and three sets of circumferential lines joining the arms 10, 20 and 30 miles out from the centre. Eight sectors were thus provided for patrolling flying boats and a variety of different combinations could be worked out. The 'web' allowed for accurate searches to be carried out over 4000 square miles of sea that lay right across the path of U-boats headed for the UK. A boat 10 miles outside the 'web' on the surface entered a danger zone in which it stood a good chance of being seen from the air. At cruising speed it took 10 hours for a U-boat to cross the 'web'; if it dived it would be much slower and would use up valuable battery charge before even arriving in its operational area[2] and crew fatigue would be induced by the depletion of oxygen in the hull while it remained underwater. Under average conditions, a flying boat could search two sectors, a quarter of the whole 'web', in five hours or less. A chart was kept at Felixstowe and used to brief aircrew, showing the position, dates and times of day that U-boat positions were fixed by the direction-finding stations. From this the most profitable sectors for a patrol's search plan were determined.

The 'Spider Web' patrol came into operation on 13 April 1917 and although only five flying boats were available at first, twenty-seven patrols were flown in the first eighteen days. Eight enemy submarines were sighted and three of these were bombed while another patrol located and attacked four enemy destroyers. The success achieved by Curtiss Large America flying boat 8663 gives a good idea of how immediately successful the 'Spider Web' patrols became. Its crew sighted a U-boat on 22 April and another which dived on 26 April. A further U-boat sighted 22nm south of the light vessel was attacked with bombs on 19 May and on 20 May 8663 helped to sink *UC 36* after sighting it 10nm north-east of the light vessel. After seeing the U-boat on the surface the flying boat closed it and fired recognition signals. No reply was given and the submarine began to dive so the pilot turned sharply and dived along the length of the boat as it disappeared below the surface. Two bombs were released which hit the boat forward of the conning tower. A large patch of oil was seen on the surface but there was no sign of wreckage in the failing light and at 21.00 the flying boat set heading for Felixstowe. The crew on that occasion was Flight Sub Lieutenant D R Morrish DSC RNAS first pilot, Flight Sub Lieutenant H G Boswell RNAS, Air Mechanic W P Caston and Leading Mechanic A E Shorter. Unfortunately the aircraft, which had only been delivered in January, was completely wrecked on landing back at its base because of a heavy swell that had built up and it subsequently had to be written off.[3] This was the first time that an RNAS aircraft had sunk a U-boat.[4]

Enemy air attacks continued to pose a threat and on the night of 23/24 May 1917 several Zeppelins raided the eastern counties of the UK. Two Sopwith Baby seaplanes took off from the air station at Westgate at 03.40 in an attempt to engage them but one, piloted by Flight Sub Lieutenant H M Morris RNAS, returned at 06.45 having seen no sign of them. The other, flown by Flight Sub Lieutenant L G Maxton RNAS failed to return within its three hours' maximum endurance and so Morris, without hesitation, took off in a Short seaplane at 08.10 with G O Wright as telegraphist to search for it. Unknown to him, however, Maxton had suffered an engine failure, alighted on the water and been towed to the Isle of Grain air station. Morris spent several hours carrying out a fruitless search and had just decided to return to Westgate when he, too, suffered an engine failure and had to alight on the water some 30 miles off the coast inside a British declared minefield. There were no ships in sight and with a significant swell running the seaplane broke up quite quickly. Soon only a single float remained with both aircrew clinging to it. In accordance with standard operating procedures for the time, however, they had flown with two homing pigeons in the aircraft. The first of these was released with a message but was never seen again. The second landed in an exhausted condition on a trawler engaged in minesweeping operations. It appears that the crew did not see the note and certainly did not act on it but they fed the bird and in due course the revived bird was released. There is no record that any action was taken when it arrived, probably because three days had elapsed and the weather was so misty that it was felt that a further search would involve a great deal of risk with very little chance of success. Meanwhile the two aircrew clung to their float for five days and nights. For most of that time the wind had died away and there was a thick fog that obscured them. They had glimpsed British warships and aircraft in the distance but had not themselves been seen by them. They managed to survive on a few milk tablets which Morris happened to have had in a bottle in his pocket.

On 29 May the fog that had covered much of the North Sea began to lift and just after noon two flying boats took off from Felixstowe to carry out a 'Spider Web' patrol. Forty miles from the coast the fog closed in and one of them turned back but the other, piloted by Flight Sub Lieutenants J L Gordon and G R Hodgson RNAS pushed on until they were 23 miles beyond the North Hinder Light Vessel. By then the fog became so thick that they could no longer see the sea surface and they decided to return. Shortly after passing over the light vessel again to take an accurate departure for Felixstowe they saw something on the surface through a break in the fog and, spiralling down to 600ft they saw the two men on their upturned float. On making a low pass they observed that despite the fog there was a strong surface wind with a heavy sea running. They therefore took the prudent step of climbing to 1000ft to transmit their position to Felixstowe in case anything went wrong before landing close to the survivors. Waves burst in spray over the bows of the boat as it taxied up to the wreckage and the first attempt to recover the men failed. On the second attempt Gordon taxied right up to the float and his two mechanics stood on the fins each side of the bow, with waves washing up to their waists, ready to grab Morris and his observer. This time they succeeded and the two were dragged into the boat through the nose hatch in an exhausted condition. Gordon then made several attempts to take off in which the boat was damaged and so he elected instead to taxi back, navigating by dead-reckoning. Four hours later he cleared the fog and saw the Shipwash Light Vessel three miles away to the north which showed that he was only a mile off his intended course, a not inconsiderable feat of seamanship and navigation under the most adverse conditions. Morris and Wright were revived during the taxiing by being given sips of brandy and cocoa until, after firing Verey lights as distress signals, Gordon's boat was seen and taken in tow by the merchant ship *Orient of Leith* bound for Yarmouth. Half an hour later HMS *Maratina* came up and took over the tow and the two casualties were transferred to HMS *White Lilac*. Gordon remained with his

A Porte Baby flying boat being launched from one of the slipways at RNAS Felixstowe. (Author's collection)

boat to see it towed safely into harbour. Unbroken by their experience, both Morris and Wright returned to flying operations some months later.

The success of RNAS flying boat operations centred on the North Hinder Light Vessel forced the German Navy to take countermeasures and in early May 1917 it began sending seaplane fighters into the area to intercept them. Several combats ensued but none had a decisive outcome and the flying boats were subsequently armed with a number of Lewis guns. They adopted offensive tactics on patrol, searching for and attacking U-boats on the surface, Zeppelins and seaplanes in the air. Unable to drive the flying boats away from the patrol area, the Germans attacked the air station at Felixstowe. On 4 July 1917 a force of fourteen enemy aircraft attacked the Harwich area at 07.00 during which twelve bombs were dropped on the airfield's hangars. One Curtiss Large America flying boat was destroyed and another damaged; five ratings and three civilians were killed and a further nineteen ratings and one civilian wounded. Three other ratings were killed at the kite balloon base at Shotley. The bombing caused no interruption to the 'Spider Web' patrols, however, and on 24 July 1917 a flight of five flying boats from Felixstowe were patrolling in formation when a U-boat was sighted on the surface 5nm away, six miles to the south-south-west of the light vessel. The aircraft immediately altered course to attack and the first, Curtiss large America 8689,[5] dropped two 230lb bombs which appeared to explode 50ft in front of the periscope as the submarine dived. 8676 and N65 also dropped bombs a few seconds later and as the water subsided from the shallow explosions a large bubble of air, oil and wreckage rose to the surface. Later in the day patrolling seaplanes saw a small circular red buoy at the edge of the oil patch which marked the last resting place of *UC 1*.[6] 8689's crew on this occasion comprised Flight Lieutenant T H Newton

RNAS, Flight Sub Lieutenant T C Trumble RNAS, Air Mechanic W Blacklock and Leading Telegraphist T E Jacques.[7] Five days later on 29 July another Curtiss Large America, 8676, with 8662 in company sank *UB 20* when she was seen on the surface 7nm from the light vessel. When it received no answer to its recognition challenge, 8676 dropped four 100lb bombs which hit the stern of the U-boat and damaged it sufficiently to prevent it from diving. 8662 then dropped a further two 100lb bombs which sank the boat. It was later discovered that *UB 20* was a small, single-hulled boat based in Zeebrugge which had sailed for trimming trials at sea and had three Army officers and several nursing sisters on board as guests. There were no survivors.[8] The crew of 8676 comprised Flight Lieutenant W R Mackenzie DSC RNAS who was awarded a bar to his DSC for this action, Flight Sub Lieutenant G E Ball RNAS, Air Mechanic H L Curtiss who was awarded the DSM and Air Mechanic (W/T) W H Grey who was also awarded the DSM. 8662's crew comprised Flight Sub Lieutenant C L Young DSC RNAS, Flight Sub Lieutenant A T Barker RNAS, Air Mechanic W J Priest and Leading Telegraphist H T Wilks.[9]

The Curtiss Large America flying boat had a wingspan of 95ft and a length of 46ft 1.5in. It was powered by two 345hp Rolls-Royce Eagle VIII engines and had a maximum take-off weight of 10,670lbs. It usually flew with a crew of four comprising two pilots and two rating aircrew who could be mechanics, gunlayers or telegraphists, all cross-trained to carry out a variety of tasks. Armament included twin Lewis guns on ring mountings in the bow and amidships with provision for two further Lewis guns to fire through ports in the side of the hull. Bombs of various weights up to 230lbs could be carried on racks under the wings.

Anti-Air Warfare

By the middle of 1917 flying boats had demonstrated their value in anti-submarine work and also in offensive operations against enemy airships. Attempts by seaplane carriers to launch strikes against airship sheds in Germany had largely met with failure and both the seaplanes and their converted merchant ship carriers were now recognised as being unsuited to the task. The RNAS constantly sought other means to counter the Zeppelin threat at sea and in April 1917 it was decided to use Curtiss Large America flying boats from Felixstowe, Yarmouth and Killingholme to intercept and destroy enemy airships carrying out reconnaissance missions over the North Sea. The possibility of a chance encounter was remote and so a system had to be devised to provide the air stations with information about enemy airship movements and when wireless signals were intercepted by the Admiralty's listening stations that fixed an enemy airship within 150nm of the British coast, one or more flying boats were launched to intercept it. As further fixes were calculated, they enabled the enemy's position, course and speed, but not height, to be relayed to

Curtiss H.12 Large America number 8666 was delivered to RNAS Felixstowe for erection in February 1917 and moved to Yarmouth in May. It is seen here on the beaching trolley used when it was brought ashore with the tailplane supported by a trestle. Note the Lewis guns mounted in the bow, above the cockpit and further aft. They do not have trays of ammunition fitted but do have the canvas bags used to catch spent cartridge cases as they were ejected in order to prevent them from hitting the propellers and causing damage. This remarkable aircraft survived the war and was finally disposed of in 1919. (Author's collection)

the flying boats. Shortly after dawn on 14 May 1917 Curtiss Large America 8666, an aircraft that was to become famous for a number of spirited actions by its crews over the North Sea, was on patrol over a sea surface that was obscured by thick mist under lowering cloud. Its crew comprised Flight Lieutenant C J Galpin RNAS, Flight Sub Lieutenant R Leckie RNAS, Chief Petty Officer V F Whatling (W/T operator) and Air Mechanic J R Laycock. They had taken off from Yarmouth to hunt down a Zeppelin that had been reported airborne near the Terschelling Light Vessel and the aircraft was armed with three Lewis guns, two on a flexible mounting in the nose and one aft of the cockpit, bombs for use against opportunity targets on the surface and as much fuel as the aircraft could carry.

They headed straight for the light vessel and maintained radio silence, listening but not transmitting, so that the aircraft's position was not revealed to the enemy. At 04.48 the pilots saw a Zeppelin dead ahead some 10 to 15 miles away, moving slowly at about 3000ft. Its crew failed to notice the flying boat as Leckie, who was at the controls, used banks of mist and cloud to mask its approach. When the airship was sighted 8666 was at 5000ft and Leckie climbed to 6000ft while the others manned the guns. At this stage the airship appeared to reach the end of its patrol and turned first north and then north-east. Leckie continued to fly 8666 while Galpin manned the two nose Lewis guns which had trays loaded with the usual mixture of tracer, ball, Brock and Pomeroy ammunition. 8666 soon got into a position 850 yards astern of the airship and closed in on it rapidly, maintaining an airspeed of 90 knots. As he drew level Galpin opened fire with both guns at 50 yards range and saw his rounds hitting the envelope[10] but both guns jammed and he indicated to Leckie that he must turn away while he attempted to clear them. While they were turning the crew observed a glow developing rapidly inside the airship envelope and 15 seconds later its lower half was seen to be thoroughly alight. A few seconds later they watched the whole airship become a glowing mass which began to fall vertically by the tail. Less than a minute after Galpin opened fire the Zeppelin, subsequently identified as *L 22*,[11] was reduced to a bare skeleton as the envelope had burnt off and plunged into the sea leaving a mass of black ash on the surface from which a column of brown smoke rose to a height of about 1500ft. By then 8666 was about 18nm to the north-west of Texel island so heading was set for Yarmouth where it arrived at 07.50 after flying through a torrential rain storm for over two hours.

The next success came on 14 June 1917 when Curtiss Large America 8677 was carrying out an offensive air patrol off Vlieland. Its crew comprised Flight Sub Lieutenant B D Hobbs DSC RNAS, Flight Sub Lieutenant R F L Dickey, Air Mechanic H M Davis and Air Mechanic A W Goody.[12] They were flying at 500ft when they saw an airship, subsequently identified as *L 43*,[13] heading north 5nm away at about 1500ft. The crew went to action stations with Hobbs flying the aircraft, Dickey manning the bow Lewis guns, and the W/T operator Davis and the engineer Goody standing to the midship and stern Lewis guns. As they closed on the Zeppelin Hobbs dived for its tail at 100 knots and the midship gun opened fire with tracer ammunition as they passed diagonally across the airship. Dickey opened fire with tracer, ball, Brock and Pomeroy ammunition at close range and after two short bursts the Zeppelin was seen to be on fire. Hobbs turned hard to starboard to pass over the airship again but by then it was completely enveloped in flames and falling very fast. Three men were seen to jump clear as it fell and smoke was seen for some time rising from the point where the wreckage crashed into the sea.

It was appreciated that a Zeppelin which saw a flying boat approaching it that was still out of gun range could attempt to out-climb it by jettisoning ballast. Surprise was, therefore, the essential element of any attack but this was harder to achieve after the destruction of *L 22* and *L 43* because the Zeppelin crews were more vigilant and flew their patrols at much higher altitudes. This was nonetheless a tactical success for the British flying boats as Zeppelins were now less likely to spot surface contacts in the mist and cloud below them. Next, the RNAS tried methods of interception in which fighters capable of out-climbing Zeppelins could be brought into action against them. Two alternative methods were considered; one was to use an aeroplane with a greatly increased radius of action which would be capable of flying across the North Sea and back again from a base on the British east coast with a margin of fuel to allow a single combat before it returned. The second, which had the greater potential, was to carry aircraft on ships and launch them at the point where they were needed as part of a fleet operation. The successful launch of Smart's Sopwith Pup from the cruiser *Yarmouth* to intercept and destroy *L 23* using the latter method was described in the last chapter.

The shore-based long-range fighter option was tested in September 1917. Two de Havilland DH 4 aircraft were modified at Hendon, the RN air station where new aircraft were both erected and modified, with enlarged fuel tanks which gave them a remarkable endurance of up to 14 hours. They were also camouflaged with matt dope in sky blue and biscuit colours which made the aircraft very difficult to see from below. They had originally been intended to carry out a photographic reconnaissance of German naval bases west of the Kiel Canal but when this project was cancelled, they were made available for the long-range fighter project. Once work on them had been completed they were deployed to the night-landing ground at Bacton but it was soon decided that they would be better placed at the naval air station at Yarmouth itself, from where it had been decided to attempt a long-range interception to simplify close liaison with the flying boat crews.[14] When intelligence was received that a Zeppelin was patrolling near Terschelling, the plan was to launch one of the DH 4s in company with a Curtiss Large America flying boat. The two aircraft would operate together with the DH 4 keeping the flying boat in sight but flying at greater altitude. If a Zeppelin was encountered the flying boat was to carry out a feint attack forcing the airship to climb to a higher altitude where it would be engaged by the DH 4. Another important factor was that the flying boat would be close at hand to rescue the DH 4's crew if the single-engined aircraft was forced to come down in the sea because of an engine failure. The chance to put the scheme to the test came on 5 September 1917 when a DH 4[15] was launched with Flight Lieutenant A H H Gilligan RNAS as pilot and Flight Lieutenant G S Trewin DSC RNAS, Rutland's observer during the Battle of Jutland, as observer/gunner. The accompanying flying boat was the redoubtable 8666 piloted by Leckie, now a Flight Lieutenant, accompanied by Squadron Commander V Nicholl RNAS, who was to be in charge of the whole operation, and Air Mechanics Thompson and Walker were the W/T operator and engineer respectively. After take off Leckie carried out a cruise-climb intending to arrive over Terschelling at 12,000ft, the aircraft's practical ceiling. To his surprise, Nicholl sighted two Zeppelins, *L 44* and *L 46*, about 30 miles short of Terschelling. Both were at about the same height as 8666 and for about 10 minutes Leckie stalked them but when it became obvious that he was overhauling them rapidly the DH 4 was ordered by Aldis lamp to 'Climb as high as possible and attack the Zeppelins'. The reply by light was 'Where are the Zeppelins?' and Nicholl signalled that they were dead ahead and repeated his order to close and attack. The situation now became more complicated as Gilligan manoeuvred to get above the Zeppelins and attack because the British aircraft flew over German surface vessels which opened an accurate fire on them; Gilligan subsequently reported that they were two divisions of light cruisers with four destroyers off Ameland. Astern of them were a number of minesweepers and more light cruisers. Trewin took photographs of them but the negatives were subsequently lost for a reason that will soon become clear.

L 44 began to climb and 8666 tried to close on it as quickly as possible with Nicholl manning the nose Lewis guns. He opened fire as the airship dumped water ballast and climbed away from the flying boat which had reached its ceiling. Over the next hour Nicholl fired 400 rounds at the enemy whenever Leckie got him close enough to make it worthwhile; he saw his tracer hitting but saw no discernible effect from the explosive rounds. *L 44* for its part returned fire with its machine guns while *L 46* got away. Gilligan was still some distance away trying to climb above the Zeppelin but his engine was not pulling well and he signalled at 13.30 that he could climb no higher than 14,000ft. *L 44* dumped more water ballast and continued to climb, at one point even turning to fly over the fighter and drop bombs on it, but the DH 4 managed to open fire on the enemy from long range with both front guns and the twin Lewis guns on a flexible mounting in the rear cockpit. One of Trewin's guns jammed three times and one round of Brock exploded in the breech but Trewin managed to clear the gun, re-cock it and continue firing. At 14.00 Gilligan signalled that he now had a serious engine problem and, with no chance now of closing to decisive range on *L 44*, Nicholl signalled the DH 4 to follow 8666 as best it could back to Yarmouth. However, as soon as they cleared the enemy surface ships in Trewin's words 'our airscrew came to an untimely rest, the engine having seized up owing to lack of water, presumably the radiator having been punctured by an enemy bullet'. 8666 had been hit by shell fragments when she was engaged by the enemy surface ships but was able to fly normally and remained close to the DH 4 as it glided towards the sea surface. Surprisingly it had not been fitted with flotation bags and as it got lower both crew saw a heavily breaking sea below them. It took about 20 minutes to descend, enough time for them to argue about which way the wind was blowing. Gilligan subsequently described how, when he estimated

Unfortunately this photograph is of poor quality but it shows the four officers who survived the ordeal in 8666 after it came down in the North Sea. They have been rescued by HMS *Halcyon* but, in keeping with the standards of the time, Thompson and Walker, the two ratings who shared their experience, were not included. From left to right they are Flight Lieutenant G S Trewin, Squadron Commander V Nichol, Flight Lieutenant R Leckie and Flight Lieutenant H H Gilligan RNAS. Note that Trewin's uniform still has his paymaster's rank lace without an executive curl. The aircraft behind them is Flight Sub Lieutenant E A Bolton RNAS' Sopwith Schneider with its engine covers on. (Author's collection)

that the aircraft was about 10ft above the water, he pulled the nose up and 'pan-caked, a horrid crash and all I could see was blue water above'. He couldn't free himself from the cockpit at first but then remembered that his headphone attachment was still plugged in and as soon as he disconnected it he shot to the surface 'to find Trewin swimming towards the relics of the machine'.

By then 8666's port engine was giving trouble; the contact breaker of one of the two magnetos had broken so the engine was only running on one bank of cylinders, making the return flight to Yarmouth a difficult proposition at best. As soon as they saw Gilligan and Trewin ditch, however, they knew there was only one option open to them and they landed in the water and taxied up to the two men who were clinging desperately to the wreckage of the DH 4 but both tried to swim to the flying boat as it drew near. Both were weighted down by their thigh-length boots and heavy leather coats but Gilligan was the stronger swimmer and was dragged aboard the boat fairly quickly. Trewin nearly drowned but Leckie did a fine job keeping 8666 close to him and he was eventually dragged aboard. The wreckage of the DH 4 sank almost immediately afterwards but, by a curious chance, one of its wheels was washed up on a beach near the air station at Yarmouth some weeks later. The flying boat now had six men on board, a hole in the lower hull near the step caused by a shell splinter from a round fired by one of the German warships and a dud port engine. Leckie made several attempts to take off but failed because of the lack of engine power and the rough sea prevailing. The only option now was to try to taxi towards the British coast with a heavy following sea and insufficient petrol to complete the journey on the water. Constant bailing was necessary to prevent the boat from sinking and the ends of some empty petrol tins were knocked in to make rough-and-ready bailers. At first Leckie tried to taxi on a heading of 260 degrees but the waves lifted the tail and forced the bow under water, pouring yet more water into the hull. After some experimentation he found that a course of 300 degrees could be held which he thought might take them towards the war channel near Cromer although they had not enough fuel to reach it. He used the rudder to hold grimly on course with water up to his knees while the others all bailed as fast as they could. The W/T set had not survived the ingress of water after landing but 8666 did carry the standard flying-boat outfit of four carrier pigeons. Two of these were released by Nicholl at 16.00, each bearing a message which read 'H 12 N 8666 We have landed to pick up DH 4 crew about 50 E by N of Yarmouth. Sea too rough to get off. Will you please send for us as soon as possible as boat is leaking. We are taxiing W by S. V Nicholl.' One of these pigeons and its message was never seen again and the message from the other one did not reach the air station until 11.30 on 8 September 1917, the third day after the DH 4 had ditched.

At about 19.30 on 5 September both of 8666's engines stopped when the fuel ran out and the six men were faced with the task of keeping the flying boat afloat. They had no food but did have two gallons of fresh water in a former petrol tin. They made a sea-anchor out of five petrol tins and a length of rope but it did not prove very effective. Leckie and Nicholl took turns every hour holding the rudder straight as this was found to prevent the aircraft from yawing badly but during the night the wing-tip float of the damaged starboard wing was carried away so each man 'rested' from bailing by crawling out on to the other wing-tip for a two-hour stint to keep the damaged one out of the water. They remarked, subsequently, that 'it was a terrible job because one minute they would be 20ft up in the air clinging

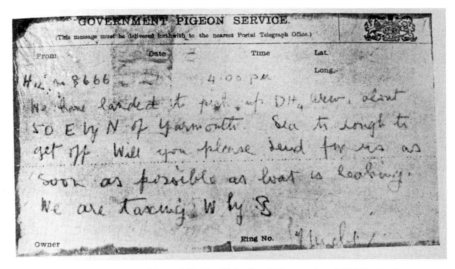

The pigeon message dispatched from 8666 by Nicholl on 5 September 1917. (Author's collection)

to the outer struts and the next 'the wing would come down with a hell of a crash and we'd be buried under water to be jerked out, spitting and gasping' to go through it all again. By the next day Leckie was desperately ill with sea-sickness which was causing him to retch blood but he still took his turns bailing and holding the rudder. Trewin was becoming weak but continued to stick to the task of bailing. At 07.00 on 6 September Nicholl released another pigeon with a note modified to say that they has probably drifted north overnight but this bird, too, was never seen again. At 15.00 on the afternoon of the same day he released the last pigeon with a message that read '3 pm. Very urgent. Seaplane 8666 to C.O. Air Station Great Yarmouth. We have sighted nothing. The wind has been drifting us west-north-west ever since we landed, so we may have missed Cromer. We are not far from the coast as we keep seeing small land birds. Sea is still rough. Machine intact still. We will fire Very's lights every 45 minutes tonight. V. Nicholl.' This message was received at the air station at 10.45 on the next day, 7 September.

Throughout the time they had been in the water large numbers of aircraft and ships had searched for 8666 but found nothing. One of them was *Halcyon*, a gunboat used for coastal patrol work that carried a Sopwith Schneider seaplane fighter which had sailed on 6 September to search eastwards towards the Terschelling Light Vessel. When no trace was found she returned to Lowestoft to take on stores and her captain. Lieutenant Commander B S Bannerman RN, went ashore to see if there was any news of 8666. When told of the pigeon message that had included the words 'may have missed Cromer' he obtained permission to continue the search, returned on board, sent for his Schneider pilot, Flight Sub Lieutenant E A Bolton RNAS, and set about working out where the ditched flying boat might be found. Taking into account the known position of the fight with the Zeppelin, the probability that it had been engine trouble that head brought the aircraft down and the amount of fuel it probably had to taxi, the wording of the text seemed to indicate that 8666 was north of Cromer. Allowing for the effect of wind and currents Bannerman calculated that the boat could be in one of three positions:

1. Inside the minefield off the Wash, an area not likely to have been searched by aircraft.
2. In an area north by east of Cromer.
3. Slightly north of a line between Cromer and Terschelling and about the middle of the North Sea.

Halcyon proceeded to the Haisborough Light Vessel and lay off it overnight ready to search areas 1 and 2 from dawn on 8 September; the intention was to use the Schneider to extend the search radius but the aircraft was found to be unserviceable because one of the turnbuckles that held the two fuselage sections together had torn away from its fastening. Attempts to make a repair, helped by the ship's carpenter, proved unavailing and the ship was limited to a visual search. However, about 30 minutes after dawn the Coastal Airship *C 26* was sighted and its pilot informed Bannerman that he had just searched area 1 thoroughly without result and so *Halcyon* proceeded to area 2, expecting to arrive at about 12.00. At 12.45 the First Lieutenant sighted 8666 about five miles ahead and as the ship drew near it 'we manned ship and gave them a heartening cheer, to which those aboard the flying boat tried to answer'.[16] A boat was sent across to collect the survivors and Bolton made arrangements to tow 8666 to safety. Eventually the six survivors were brought ashore and the flying boat brought back to the air station to be repaired for further operational service.

The safe rescue of the aircrew was not quite the end of the story, however, because shortly before they were seen from *Halcyon*, at 11.30 on Saturday 8 September, the message that Nicholl had sent by pigeon three days earlier at 16.00 on 5 September finally arrived at Yarmouth air station. The pigeon in question, NURP./17/F.16331, had fought its way to land against the strong prevailing wind but had died, apparently from exhaustion, on gaining the shore. Its dead body was found by a stroke of good fortune at Walcot, near Bacton, by Second Lieutenant D W Hughes of A Company, 4th Battalion, Monmouthshire Regiment, who picked it up at 11.00 on that morning and took the bird and its message to a military signaller who took them to the station officer of the War Signal Station at Bacton. From there the message was telephoned to the air station. 8666 was found only minutes later but when they learned about the pigeon that had given its life for them, the survivors were deeply moved and had its body stuffed and placed in a glass case in the air station's wardroom with a brass plate which bore the inscription 'A very gallant gentleman'.[17]

Kite Balloons

The number of kite balloons embarked in warships during 1917 increased significantly. It will be recalled that in the summer of 1916 successful trials had been carried out with the Type M balloon in *Campania* and *Hercules* and that *Chester* had been fitted with a winch to operate a balloon and carried out trials in the Firth of Forth. These had proved successful and an extensive programme of kite balloon procurement had followed so that a number of ships in the Grand Fleet could be equipped in 1917. Air stations to support kite balloon detachments were set up at Houton Bay on the north shore of Scapa Flow and at North Queensferry near Rosyth. Although they were intended at first primarily for gunnery spotting and observation, it soon became apparent that they had value in extending the range at which a U-boat on the surface could be seen from destroyers and 'P' class escort vessels, particularly after the introduction of the convoy system in April 1917. In this application, the balloons were inflated at air stations ashore and then taken by lighter to the towing vessel to be attached to its winch. Suitable

The cruiser HMS *Cardiff* operating a kite balloon in the Firth of Forth. (Author's collection)

air stations were established at Sheerness, Shotley, Lowestoft, Milford Haven, Merifield (Devonport), Tipnor (Portsmouth), Berehaven, Rathmullen (Lough Swilly) and Immingham by the end of 1917 and winches were fitted to a considerable number of escorts for patrol and convoy work.

On 12 July 1917 the perseverance of those who had worked hard to get kite balloons to sea was rewarded by the destruction of *U 69* with the aid of a balloon flown from HMS *Patriot* in the North Sea. The submarine was sighted from the balloon and the towing ship was guided towards it in time to sink it before it could carry out an attack of its own. This success gave still further impetus to balloon work including the deployment of captive balloons to ships of the Grand Fleet in the second half of 1917. Perhaps the most interesting experiments were those carried out in October with a balloon towed by a 'K' class submarine, a high-speed, steam turbine-powered design intended for operations with the surface fleet. These demonstrated that 'K' boats were quite capable of towing a balloon, both on the surface and when submerged, with no adverse effect on either the boat or the balloon. The weather in the vicinity of Scapa Flow was particularly severe in September 1917 but although some balloons broke away from their anchor points, most continued to be operated satisfactorily; for example one balloon being towed by *King George V* with observers in it rode out an 83-knot gale for 30 minutes. Before that a kite balloon had been towed by *Campania* for six days in a row without being hauled down.

The introduction of the convoy system for the protection of merchant shipping not only led to a considerable increase in the use of kite balloons attached to seagoing ships, but also created a pressing demand for airships to work with coastal convoys. Their qualities of long endurance, slow speed and the ability to keep station on the convoy made them superior to seaplanes for this work and many were brought into service as soon as they were completed. By early 1917 the larger air stations situated at Longside, East Fortune, Howden, Pulham, Mullion and Pembroke, which had been established during 1916, were by then equipped with an adequate number of Coastal airships able to carry out extended patrols. The various air stations had differing tasks to perform; for example, north-bound convoys from the Humber were escorted by Howden airships to the northernmost limit of their endurance where airships from East Fortune took over. Convoys that proceeded further north were escorted by airships from Longside. In this way merchant ships in convoy could be escorted by air from Spurn Head to the extreme north of Scotland. Cross-Channel shipping was escorted between Folkestone or Dover and the French ports by airships from Capel while the Larne and Stranraer steamers and convoys proceeding through the north-west passage of the Irish Sea were accompanied by airships from Luce Bay. Airships from the air station at

Mullion were responsible for escorting ships from the Atlantic beyond the Scilly Isles as far up-Channel as Plymouth and those from Pembroke escorted ships proceeding from the Atlantic into the Bristol Channel. Airship patrols were standardised with definite patrol areas being laid down for every air station. The SNO in each region was, thus, able to arrange for shipping channels to be systematically swept, for local bases to provide the appropriate surface escort forces and for adjoining air stations to co-ordinate their efforts so as to avoid any overlap or break in cover.

North Sea Airships
While the Coastal and SS airships were ideal for patrolling inshore waters, the growing need to operate protracted patrols further out to sea necessitated craft with greater capacity and endurance and so a new type was introduced in 1917 known as the North Sea, or NS, type. These were designed to carry out patrols of up to 20 hours using an envelope of 360,000ft^3, derived from the 'Astra', from which an enclosed control car made of wood with steel wire bracing was suspended. They were powered by two 250hp Rolls-Royce engines carried in a separate power unit structure. The first NS airship carried out trials in February 1917 and attained a speed of 44 knots and five more had been delivered by the end of the year.[18] *NS 1* was delivered to Pulham in April 1917 and subsequently carried out a notable flight

North Sea class airship *NS 4*. (Guy Warner Collection).

lasting no less than 49.5 hours and travelling 1500nm.[19] It was known that U-boats intending to operate in the northern waters of the UK made landfall on the Coquet Island lighthouse off the coast of Northumberland just south of Alnmouth and then followed a track running north-east. In July 1917, therefore, it was decided to station all NS airships at East Fortune for the double purpose of carrying out anti-submarine patrols along this track and reconnaissance for the Grand Fleet. *NS 1* was transferred from Pulham in September and joined *NS 3* in carrying out exercises with the Battlecruiser Fleet based in the Firth of Forth. The new airships encountered a considerable amount of technical trouble, however, and in December both *NS 1* and *NS 5* were wrecked following engine failure. The whole airship-building programme for the RNAS came under government scrutiny in the latter part of 1917 and it was decided that the ideal numbers for active service would be sixteen rigid airships of the *R 33* class, twelve NS airships, twenty Coastals and thirty-eight SS Zero class.

Enemy seaplane activity in the southern part of the North Sea led to some modification of the areas patrolled by coastal airships off the British east coast after *C 17*, operating from Pulham, strayed from its intended course in bad weather and drifted south to a point 15nm east of the North Foreland. It was attacked and shot down in flames on 21 April 1917 by German seaplanes from Zeebrugge with the loss of two officers and three ratings. After this loss airships on patrol were instructed to have their positions fixed by bearings taken from W/T transmissions every hour. This certainly helped navigation but the airships' transmissions revealed their positions to the enemy and the Zeebrugge seaplanes could potentially intercept them. On 11 December 1917 Coastal Airship *C 27* left Pulham and proceeded to its patrol area off the coast of Norfolk. For two hours wireless signals were exchanged but at 09.40 they ceased abruptly and, despite repeated attempts to communicate, nothing more was heard from the airship and it was assumed that it had met the same fate as *C 17* with the loss of all five crew. The next day its sister-craft *C 26*, patrolling in the same area, suffered an engine failure and drifted to the east, eventually coming down at Eesmess in Holland where the crew were interned. The proximity of these patrol areas to German seaplane bases and the consequent danger to the vulnerable airships led to sorties being terminated and the operations from Pulham were restricted to the big rigid airships. The first of these, *R 23*, had already arrived from Howden at the end of October 1917 and Pulham subsequently specialised in airship experimental and research work.

The Continuing Importance of Anti-Submarine Warfare

The primary task of both heavier and lighter-than-air aircraft in anti-submarine warfare was the destruction of U-boats with bombs but this remained a difficult

Squadron Commander S J Goble DSO
DSC RNAS who served in 'B' Flight of 8
(N) and went on to command 5 (Naval)
Squadron at RNAS Petite Synthe. He
ended the war with ten aerial victories.
(Author's collection)

objective to achieve. This was especially the case for airships because their slow
speed and relatively poor manoeuvrability gave submarine commanders sufficient
time, after seeing the airship, to dive and alter course before it could reach the
optimum weapons release point. The secondary task of keeping U-boats
submerged, however, could be achieved by their presence and there were many
instances of vessels being saved by the timely, albeit unsuccessful, attack by an
escorting airship. One such occurred on 9 August 1917 when the USS *Cleveland* with
a convoy carrying American troops to Europe was escorted through the English
Channel by RNAS aircraft. At 05.30 a Large America flying boat took off from the
Scilly Islands, made contact with the convoy and escorted it until relieved by a
Short seaplane from Newlyn. At about 09.00 two airships from Mullion, *C 2* and
SSZ 14, took over the airborne escort and took up stations on the port and
starboard bows of the convoy matching its speed of 8 knots. At about 10.00 both
airships saw, at the same moment, a submarine on the surface about 7nm south of
the convoy, steering north at high speed to intercept it. Both airships turned
towards the enemy and dropped two 100lb bombs into the wake left as the U-boat
dived. They were joined by a Short seaplane and the three aircraft continued to
search the vicinity but without success. *C 2* then flew towards the convoy and made
to *Victor*, one of the escorting destroyers, by lamp 'Submarine submerged under
us'.[20] Two British and two US destroyers were dispatched along the bearing to the

Minifie standing next to Sopwith Triplane N6303 in which he shot down an enemy Albatross D-V in flames south of Houthurst Forest on 8 August 1917. (Philip Jarrett collection)

datum point where the U-boat dived and they dropped depth charges from time to time but failed to gain contact. The important point, however, was that the airships' prompt action had forced the enemy to dive and the continued aggressive searching had held it down while the convoy proceeded safely on its passage. By keeping the

A line-up of 10 (Naval) Squadron's Sopwith F.1 Camels. The conspicuous stripes showed the aircraft's flight. In this case the black and white stripes denote 'A' Flight. 'B' Flight had pale blue and white stripes and 'C' flight had red and white. The designs on the wheels showed the identity of individual aircraft and used the same colours as the stripes. In the days before radio telephone contact between aircraft it was important to be able to pick out other aircraft and identify leaders in a formation. (Philip Jarrett collection)

U-boat down they had forced it to run on its slow battery-powered electric motors and it was outside the limiting lines of submerged approach within which it could have got into a torpedo firing position while dived. Denied the ability to surface and use its diesel engines, it was unable to attack and its air supply must have begun to become foul because the airships remained over the dive datum searching for several hours. Three aircraft joined them from Mullion but unfortunately nothing further was sighted.

Air patrols over the shipping routes in mid-Channel were mostly provided by seaplanes from the Portsmouth Group and to facilitate a cross-Channel patrol between Calshot and the French coast a seaplane sub-base was established at Cherbourg on 21 July 1917. It soon justified its existence when, on the afternoon of 18 August, the pilot of a Wight seaplane sighted a U-boat on the surface about 4nm distant, 25nm north-east of Cherbourg. He attacked immediately and three minutes after first sighting the enemy he dropped a 100lb bomb close to the periscope in the swirl of water where the submarine was diving. Turning hard to attack again, he dropped a second 100lb bomb which detonated 30 to 40ft along the track the U-boat had been steering as it dived and it detonated amid a large patch of oil which was already appearing on the surface. Nothing more was seen but the pilot was subsequently credited with having sunk *UB 32* with his first bomb.

Pilots of 1 (Naval) Squadron standing in front of their Sopwith Triplanes at Bailleul during July 1917. From left to right they are Kincaid, Foreman, Wallace, Spence, Everitt, Rowley, Luard, McGrath, Crundall, Sneath, Burton, McAfee, Rosevear, Minifie, Dallas, Ridley, de Wilde, White and Holden. (Goble Family collection)

In addition to the new seaplane base at Cherbourg there was an existing RNAS base in Dunkirk harbour which formed part of the Dover/Dunkirk Command. This was administered as a satellite to the main base at Dover with seaplanes and personnel moving freely between the two. The patrols carried out by seaplanes in enemy waters off the Belgian coast presented problems that differed fundamentally from those off the British coast since, apart from the very real prospect of an engine malfunction, they had to contend with anti-aircraft fire near the coast which kept the aircraft at high altitude and be prepared to meet attacks by enemy aircraft when near their bases. Every patrol, therefore, had to be escorted by two or more fighters. In May 1917 the menace of German fighters became so serious that fighters with wheeled undercarriages replaced seaplanes and in June the Admiralty decided that Dunkirk should give up its seaplanes and be re-equipped with wheeled aeroplanes fitted with internal flotation bags in case they ditched. However, this decision was not fully implemented until 1918. Meanwhile in July 1918 a Curtiss H12 Large America flying boat was based at Dunkirk for anti-submarine patrols. This always flew with an escort of two Sopwith Camel fighters. The limited fuel capacity of the latter tended to reduce the duration of the patrols, however, and care had to be taken arranging the position and timing of relief fighters to ensure that there was no gap. Some patrol time was inevitably lost whilst effecting the changeover but, despite this limitation these patrols did prove successful. During the early morning of 22 September 1917 the flying boat with its two Camel escorts sighted a U-boat moving slowly on the surface to the north of the West Hinder Light Vessel. The flying boat immediately dived to attack and dropped two 230lb bombs from 800ft on the submarine which was still on the surface; both struck the hull just aft of the conning tower and detonated. The U-boat, later identified as *UC 72*, heeled over and sank almost immediately, leaving wreckage and a quantity of oil on the surface. The success led the senior RNAS officer at Dunkirk to request that more flying boats could be deployed to the base but Admiral Bacon was strongly of the opinion that land-based aeroplanes would be more effective than flying boats or seaplanes and, in consequence, the Dunkirk seaplane base was closed down in early January 1918. To compensate, 17 Squadron RNAS was formed with de Havilland DH 4 aircraft at Bergues to carry out offensive patrol work in the Straits of Dover and Belgian coastal waters. These were not, however, the first land machines to be used on anti-submarine work. In April 1917 the alarming amount of shipping being lost in the English Channel and the Western Approaches led to four Sopwith 1½ Strutters each being sent to Pembroke, Plymouth (Prawle Point) and Mullion to replace seaplanes. Unfortunately, in August the demand for pilots to man RNAS fighter squadrons seconded to the RFC on the Western Front led to these units being disbanded, another example of the Admiralty generously giving up its own important tasks when asked to provide support for the hard-pressed RFC.

At the end of August 1917 the increased U-boat activity in the vicinity of the Tees and consequent merchant shipping losses led to calls for increased air patrols in this area. To try and meet them the Admiralty withdrew a flight of Handley Page 0/100 aircraft from Coudekerque on 3 September, complete with their pilots, observers and ground personnel, and moved them to Redcar. From there they began anti-submarine patrols off the north-east coast of England on 5 September, a creditable achievement given the complexity of the aircraft and the distance moved. They flew a total of forty-two flights over shipping lanes between Hawthorn Point and Filey Brig in a month but on 2 October 1917 the unit was ordered to move to Manston in Kent. Once there it was to be reconstituted as a bombing unit to be known as 'A' Squadron for bombing operations that were to be independent of the extant naval or military command structures against industrial targets in southern Germany. It was to form part of an organisation to be known as the 41st Independent Wing RFC. While at Redcar the 0/100s aircrews had sighted seven U-boats on the surface and attacked several with bombs but with no visible result.

The Felixstowe War Flight met with more success. At 07.20 on 28 September 1917 a flying boat left the air station to hunt down a U-boat whose wireless signals showed it to be operating close to the North Hinder Light Vessel. After an hour in the air the telegraphist picked up signals from a vessel he estimated to be within 10nm and 10 minutes later a U-boat was seen a mile ahead on the surface with its aerial mast rigged. The flying boat dived towards it and fired recognition signals which were not answered; it flew over the submarine and dropped a single 250lb bomb before turning to make a second attack. The U-boat opened fire with a deck gun and a shell exploded about 50ft in front of the aircraft and, almost at the same moment, the bomb burst on the boat's stern. Red flashes appeared in the haze ahead of the aircraft and the crew made out three other U-boats with three enemy destroyers close to them in line abreast. To make matters worse, they then made out two seaplanes over the enemy ships but these did not attack, presumably because of the gunfire being put up by the destroyers. Undeterred, the flying boat continued its attack and dropped a second bomb which exploded a few feet forward of the U-boat's bow and the cumulative damage caused it to sink immediately. The flying boat turned for home and sent an enemy contact report which resulted in three further flying boats being despatched to hunt for the remaining enemy ships and seaplanes. They were sighted but the barrage of fire that they put up prevented any effective attack being carried out. The submarine that had been sunk was subsequently found to have been *UC 6*, a minelayer based in Zeebrugge. More U-boats were sighted and their positions reported to surface craft during the remaining months of the year and several were attacked with bombs but no further U-boats were destroyed by this means alone.

Operations off the Belgian Coast
The major factors that influenced the scale of RNAS operations off the Belgian coast during 1917 were the campaign against U-boats, countering the enemy air raids on London and south-eastern England and support for the military operations in Flanders. The important enemy base at Bruges and the airfields used by German heavy bombing squadrons were all vulnerable to air attack and a series of strikes were carried out in a determined and systematic effort to make them untenable.[21] The effectiveness of any bombing attack depends on the type of aircraft and its weapons and so, although bombing attacks had been carried out from Dunkirk periodically by a variety of aircraft since the earliest days of the war, it had to be admitted that with a few exceptions the effect on the enemy was almost negligible. In the spring of 1917, however, new and considerably more effective aircraft became available and with these an intensive campaign of bombing operations became possible. The year had started with a period of exceptionally cold weather in January and when this was over photographic reconnaissance sorties were flown over Ostend, Zeebrugge and Bruges to see what the enemy had

done with his destroyers and U-boats in the winter months. Photographs showed that the harbour at Bruges was iced in and that nineteen destroyers and three U-boats were trapped. Accordingly, advantage was taken of the clear but extremely cold weather conditions to carry out a series of attacks by both seaplanes and aeroplanes which commenced on 3 February. They were continued by day and night until 16 February by which time over 5 tons of bombs had been dropped and subsequent aerial photographs showed that substantial damage had been caused and that the Germans were trying desperately to release their frozen vessels. A deterioration in the weather prevented further attacks during the last two weeks in February but 1 March proved to be a fine day and the attacks were resumed. Two photographic reconnaissance sorties from St Pol were flown in order to ascertain what had happened during the period of aerial inactivity, both flown by Sopwith 1½ Strutters. The first was briefed to take photographs of the coast and all important points between Wenduyne and Ostend but when it reached Breedene it was attacked by a German Halberstadt fighter which was eventually driven off by the observer's return fire from his Lewis gun. The enemy had, however, fired at least seventy rounds which had severed a longeron, smashed the engine oil pump and damaged the RPM gauge. Fortunately neither of the aircrew was hurt but the engine stopped shortly afterwards. The pilot had sufficient height to glide over the remaining photographic targets and ordered the observer to expose the rest of his glass plates before he turned back to Furnes where he was able to carry out a safe landing. Meanwhile the second 1½ Strutter was taking photographs over Bruges

Squadron Commander G R Bromet DSO RNAS who commanded 8 (Naval) Squadron on its formation to work alongside the RFC. (Author's collection)

Flight Sub Lieutenant C D Booker DSC RNAS served in 'C' Flight of 8(N) and achieved twenty-three aerial victories with the unit. He is seen here wearing the khaki service dress with riding breeches worn by the RND and RNAS during operations ashore. On 1 April 1918 he was transferred to the RAF and took command of 201 Squadron, the former 1 (Naval) but was killed in action on 13 August 1918. (Goble Family collection)

Sopwith Triplanes of 1 (Naval) Squadron lined up. N5454 side number 1 was delivered to the RNAS in February 1917 and deleted from charge in November. From August it was often flown by Flight Lieutenant R P Minifie DSC* RNAS, an Australian 'ace' who achieved seventeen victories in Triplanes and four more in Camels before being shot down and taken prisoner on 17 March 1918. (Philip Jarrett collection)

Number 5 (Naval) Squadron officers celebrating Christmas Night 1917 in the officers' mess at RNAS Petite Synthe. The commanding officer, Squadron Commander S J Goble DSO DSC RNAS, is seated in the centre in his blue uniform; the others are in various forms of khaki service dress and seated around him in various degrees of merriment. (Goble Family collection)

when it was attacked by a formation of five enemy fighters, one taking up a position astern, three diving on the port side and one making a head-on frontal attack. The hostile aircraft to the front and rear dived simultaneously, each firing about 100 rounds. The observer, Sub Lieutenant C K Chase RN, held his fire until the fighter diving on the tail was within a few yards and then fired a complete tray from his Lewis gun into the pilot's face; it was then seen to stall, sideslip and then go down in a spinning nosedive. At almost the same moment the pilot, Flight Lieutenant C R Edwards RNAS, opened fire with his front Vickers gun on the aircraft attacking from ahead and saw his rounds hitting home. It, too, was seen to go down out of control. Edwards had been shot through the shoulder and in both feet but he succeeded in breaking away and landing safely at St Pol. After being taken to La Panne Hospital he was visited by His Majesty the King of the Belgians who conferred upon him the Insignia of a Chevalier of the Order of Leopold. He was also awarded the DSC and the French Croix de Guerre.

Fighting with the RFC on the Western Front
As well as its important operations over the Belgian coast during 1917, the RNAS Dover/Dunkirk Command was also tasked with providing fighter squadrons to reinforce the RFC on the Western Front. At the end of October 1916 the acute shortage of both aircraft and pilots in the RFC had led to 8 (Naval) Squadron being deployed to Vert Galand where it operated as part of 22 Wing RFC. Towards the end of the Battle of the Somme it became apparent that the Germans had produced several new and improved types of fighter and intended to use them to make a strong bid for aerial supremacy. In order to meet this threat, more

fighter squadrons would be needed on the Western Front and the RFC felt that it could not provide them unaided. A further appeal was made to the Admiralty which quickly and unselfishly agreed to provide four more fighter squadrons for military operations to be organised from the Dunkirk command, to the detriment of its own air operations off the enemy coast and in the Channel. On 1 February 1917, 3 (Naval) Squadron under the command of Flight Commander R H Mulock RNAS relieved 8 (Naval) at Vert Galand. All the latter's aeroplanes and equipment were turned over to the new squadron and 8 (Naval)'s personnel returned to St Pol where they were split up to form the nuclei of two new squadrons, 8 (Naval) and 9 (Naval). Meanwhile 3 (Naval) was followed into action by 1 (Naval) equipped with Sopwith Triplanes under Flight Commander F K Haskins RNAS, which moved to Chipilly from Furnes on 15 February 1917. On 15 March 6 (Naval) under the command of Acting Squadron Commander J J Petre RNAS and equipped with single-seater Nieuports moved to La Bellevue. On 28 March 8 (Naval) under the command of Squadron Commander G R Bromet RNAS, which had been re-equipped with Sopwith Triplanes moved to an airfield at Auchel (Lozinghem). Thus, by the end of March 1917 the Admiralty had provided and equipped four fighter squadrons, Numbers 3, 1, 6 and 8 (Naval), to fight alongside the RFC and, having accepted this commitment in addition to its own operations, considerable difficulty was experienced in finding pilots of sufficient experience to man the new squadrons effectively. To make good this deficiency the Admiralty decided in April 1917 to disband 3 Wing, the specialised strike unit at Luxeuil les Bans and release its fifteen pilots for the pool at Dunkirk. This allowed the formation of 10 (Naval) Squadron under the command of Flight Commander B C Bell RNAS and equipped with Sopwith Triplanes which was deployed from Dunkirk to join II Brigade RFC on 15 May. On 15 June 9 (Naval) Squadron under Squadron Commander H Fawcett RNAS was commissioned, also with Sopwith Triplanes, to enable the units on loan to the RFC to be rotated in order to give the pilots rest periods out of the line. Thus 9 (Naval) relieved 3 (Naval) in the line and deployed to Flez, 12 miles west of St Quentin to operate as part of IV Brigade RFC. During the four and a half months that 3 (Naval) had been in action it had shot down eighty enemy aircraft for the loss of nine of its own, an outstanding performance. From August 1917 onwards the crisis passed and the RNAS fighter squadrons were gradually withdrawn to Dunkirk. By the end of the year only one squadron was attached to the RFC. It is interesting to note that, despite moving naval aviation away from the original RFC and forming its own air service, the Admiralty did not hesitate to come to the aid of its sister-service when asked for assistance, one of the aspirations that had led to the original RFC being set up as a joint force.

An aerial view of RNAS Coudekerque. (Philip Jarrett collection).

RNAS Operations from the Dunkirk Bases

After the detachment of the four fighter squadrons in April 1917, a reorganisation of the units based around Dunkirk was carried out. The headquarters of 4 Wing was moved to La Panne with its three fighter squadrons operating from Furnes and Bray Dunes. The bulk of the air fighting in the immediate area fell to these units and their tasking included offensive patrols, escorting photographic reconnaissance aircraft, aircraft spotting the fall of shot for bombardments and strike missions. They were also used to intercept enemy aircraft raiding the UK and Allied installations around Dunkirk and to protect RN warships in the narrow seas and off the Belgian coast. As can be imagined these commitments represented a major undertaking that required outstanding aircraft, well-trained pilots and leaders of above-average ability. Number 5 Wing comprised 5 and 7 (Naval) Squadrons based respectively at Petite Synthe and Coudekerque. It was tasked with carrying out both day and night bombing missions against targets in the Belgian littoral and further inland. 1 Wing at St Pol was tasked almost exclusively with spotting for the gunfire of monitors and siege guns manned by the Royal Marines onto coastal targets including enemy gun batteries and missions that would today be termed intelligence, surveillance and reconnaissance (ISR) of the enemy bases on the Belgian coastline.

Squadron Commander C P O Bartlett DSC RNAS about to take off with Colonel Dugdale, a guest of Squadron Commander Goble, in the rear seat of his de Havilland DH 4 for a look at the enemy lines during January 1918. (Goble Family collection)

Short bombers had been the best aircraft available but they were replaced by the far more effective Handley Page 0/100s as they became available from the spring of 1917. A few of the new aircraft had been in service with 3 Wing at Luxeuil les Bans since December 1916 and the first arrived at Coudekerque in March 1917. Whereas the older Short had been able to carry eight 65lb bombs with a pilot and gunlayer, the 0/100 could carry fourteen 112lb bombs with a pilot, observer (who could operate one of the Lewis guns if necessary) and a gunlayer. By the end of April five Handley Pages had been delivered to form 7 (Naval) Squadron and they were used at first to carry out daylight patrols along the coast as far as Zeebrugge. Their first success came on 25 April 1917 when a formation of four aircraft encountered four enemy destroyers at sea off Ostend and carried out an immediate attack with bombs. They sank one enemy vessel and damaged others. One of the 0/100s, however, ventured too far away from the fighter escort and was attacked by an enemy fighter which scored a number of hits. Among them, several rounds penetrated the petrol tanks of both engines. The pilot turned towards the coast and attempted to make Nieuport but both engines ran out of fuel and the aircraft ditched about 2nm off the coast. The wreck floated for a time and immediately came under heavy fire from enemy coastal batteries but two French three-seater flying boats had seen it come down and gallantly attempted to rescue the crew. The first one landed alongside the ditched aircraft amid a hail of shrapnel from bursting shells and managed to pick up the observer who had been wounded. Despite having a large hole in the top wing caused by a shell burst it managed to take off and flew safely back to Dunkirk. The second flying boat was less fortunate. It, too, landed near the wreck and managed to recover a crew member but damage from shellfire prevented it from taking off. Hostile motor boats soon came up from Ostend and the whole party, British and French, were taken prisoner. The incident had underlined just how dangerous air operations in the Belgian littoral were and it was decided to restrict the tasking of the 0/100s to night bombing of specific targets. At first these were only flown on moonlit nights from 9 May onwards but as experience was gained and the pilots became expert in night operations it was found to be possible to fly on every night that weather conditions permitted. Strikes were flown almost without a break during the autumn months of 1917 and no port in Belgium was outside the radius of action of these aircraft. Bombing raids were also carried out on the town of Duren, near Cologne, in Germany.

The de Havilland DH 4 made its appearance in operational service at about the same time as the Handley Page 0/100. The new type was powered by a single Rolls-Royce Eagle engine of 250hp and offered a big advance over the Sopwith One-and-a-half Strutter that it replaced. With a crew of two, pilot and observer/gunlayer, and fitted with a wireless transmitter/receiver as standard, it proved to be equally successful in a variety of roles including both photographic

DH 4s of 5 (Naval) Squadron being prepared for a strike sortie from RNAS Petite Synthe in 1917. Bombs can be seen loaded under the aircraft nearest the camera. (Author's collection)

and tactical reconnaissance work and day bombing. As these aircraft arrived from
the manufacturer they were taken into the aircraft depot at St Pol to be fitted with
photographic and wireless equipment and issued to 2 (Naval) Squadron for work
with the fleet. Not only was the DH 4 faster than the 1½ Strutter, it was capable
of climbing considerably higher to over 20,000ft compared with the earlier
aircraft's ceiling of about 15,000ft. Given the increasing quality and quantity of
anti-aircraft fire near the coast this feature was vitally important. As soon as the
new aircraft were ready they were used to create a photographic mosaic, with
images taken from 22,000ft, of the enemy-held Belgian coast up to about four
miles inland. As more DH 4s became available they replaced the 1½ Strutters of
5 (Naval) Squadron at Petite Synthe. From July 1917 the DH 4s took on all the day
bombing commitments while the Handley Pages operated at night. One of the
effects of the night bombing attacks on the enemy's coastal bases was to compel
his destroyers to put to sea and spend the night anchored off the Zeebrugge Mole.
Once this was appreciated, a combined strike was carried out against them by
high-speed coastal motor boats and bombers from Dunkirk. The bombers caused
the enemy to focus his attention upwards while the motor boats attacked with
torpedoes out of the darkness to seaward. They sank one destroyer and severely
damaged another.

In mid-1917 the German seaplane units at Ostend and Zeebrugge showed
increased activity and carried out attacks on the south-eastern coast of the UK, on
the Allied naval forces operating in the Straits of Dover and off the Belgian coast.
Enemy seaplanes began to use torpedoes rather than bombs as offensive weapons
and on the morning of 19 April an abortive attack by six seaplanes, three of which
were armed with torpedoes, was carried out on shipping anchored off Ramsgate
and the Downs. None of the torpedoes hit its target and one of them, presumably
intended for the nearby monitor *Marshal Ney*, was found to have ended its run in
the mud at the edge of the harbour. Two enemy seaplanes were more successful on
1 May, however, when they torpedoed and sank the merchant ship *Gena* off
Lowestoft.[22] It was armed and opened fire on its attackers, shooting one of them
down before it sank. The whole crew managed to abandon ship without loss and
both they and the German seaplane crew were subsequently rescued. Three weeks
later two German seaplanes carried out an attack on an Admiralty collier; both
torpedoes missed but they strafed the ship and hit it with about forty rounds but
no serious damage was caused. On 14 June two other vessels were attacked by
seaplanes armed with torpedoes, bombs and machine guns near the Shipwash Light
Vessel but neither was damaged. A day later, however, the merchant ship *Kankakee*
was attacked and sunk with the loss of three lives and on 9 July the *Haslingden* in
company with three other vessels was attacked by four seaplanes armed with

Sopwith F.1 Camels of 3 (Naval) Squadron lined up with their engines running about to take off together for a sortie. Note the handlers ready to pull the chocks clear when the pilots give the signal. The aircraft nearest the camera, B7275 side letter 'P', was one of a batch of 100 Camels built for the RNAS by Clayton and Shuttleworth at Lincoln. It has a distinctive RNAS eagle painted on the side of the fuselage. (Philip Jarrett collection)

torpedoes off Southwold. None was hit but *Haslingden* shot down one of the enemy aircraft with her 12pdr gun. Another seaplane landed to rescue the crew but was unable to take off again with the extra weight and had to surrender to the armed trawler *Iceland* when it came close. Several other vessels were attacked at about this time but there were no further losses until 10 September when ss *Storm* was attacked by seven seaplanes near the Sunk Light Vessel off Harwich. One torpedo missed but two others hit, one forward and one aft. They then attacked the ship with bombs, one of which hit the captain's cabin below the bridge, wrecking both bridge and steering gear. The ship sank in a minute and a half, before any boats could be lowered, with the loss of three out of a crew of eight. An attempted attack on destroyers of the Dover Patrol on 26 July by four torpedo-armed seaplanes was driven off by Sopwith Camels of 3 (Naval) Squadron which broke up their formation and chased them back to Ostend. One of the four was shot down 2nm short of the port and seen to crash into the sea.

In addition to the seaplane operations the German destroyer flotillas based in Flanders were also active and in April they attempted to bombard Ramsgate, Broadstairs and Dover. These destroyers were normally berthed at Bruges when not at sea, where the Germans thought them to be sufficiently far inland to be invulnerable to bombardment from monitors. The destruction of the lock gates at the seaward end of the canal that connected Bruges to the sea at Zeebrugge and thus making the canal tidal was, therefore, given a high priority. Detailed plans for a bombardment by monitors aimed at achieving this were prepared by the Vice Admiral Dover Patrol's staff and a task force had arrived in its firing position on three occassions only to have the shoot cancelled because of adverse weather. On the morning of 12 May 1917 the three monitors *Erebus, Terror* and *Marshal Soult* took up positions off Zeebrugge escorted by destroyers, minesweepers and motor launches to produce a smokescreen, some forty vessels in all. The smokescreen was laid as a defence against fire from enemy coastal batteries and fire was opened by the monitors at 04.45 at a range of 26,200 yards. Using air observers to spot the fall of shot and order corrections was a key element of the plan and the first aircraft left St Pol at 03.00 to be in a position to observe the fire by 04.00. For some time the visibility was bad and the aircraft and its fighter escort had to wait 45 minutes before the first shot was fired. The spotter aircraft, a Sopwith 1½ Strutter, was flying at 14,500ft and for the next 45 minutes it observed and reported the forty-five shots that were fired but the aircraft that was intended to replace it on task suffered an engine failure and came down in Holland. The first aircraft had to return to base after four hours in the air when its fuel reached a safe minimum and so the last 30 minutes of the bombardment had to be carried out without the benefit of air spotting but continued using the ranges previously registered. Subsequent aerial photography of the target area showed some slight damage to the lock gates and, encouragingly, mud banks which showed that the level of water in the canal had been lowered. Enemy aircraft had attempted to drive off the spotting aircraft and to range their own coastal batteries onto the ships beyond the smokescreen and a prolonged series of engagements with the escorting RNAS fighters took place. One

Bristol Scouts and other aircraft at RNAS Dover. (Goble Family collection)

particular formation of fifteen enemy aircraft was attacked and broken up with three hostile machines shot down and seen to crash into the sea.

Next the bombardment of the dockyard at Ostend was attempted. Adverse weather in May caused three projected attacks to be abandoned but the shoot eventually took place early in the morning of 5 June 1917. This time, however, the smokescreen was not as efficiently laid as the earlier one and the enemy coastal batteries got the range of the monitors and engaged them. After 40 minutes firing, smokescreens ashore obscured the target from the spotting aircraft after 115 rounds had been fired and the bombardment was discontinued. On this occasion the spotting aircraft were DH 4s; they took off at 02.30 and as soon as they were over the target at 16,000ft they signalled 'ready to observe' to the monitors and fire was commenced at 03.20. Fifteen minutes later the observer got the monitors' guns onto the target but smokescreens began to make spotting difficult and by 04.00 it became impossible. Fighters maintained patrols for the protection of the spotting aircraft and the fleet but no enemy aircraft attempted to interfere with this operation. One enemy kite balloon was, however, seen to ascend shortly after firing commenced and was promptly shot down by a Camel of 4 (Naval) Squadron. Photographs taken after the bombardment showed that the main object of damaging the workshops of the Atcliers de la Marine had been achieved and this would have the effect of handicapping the repair activity that kept U-boats serviceable.[23] Out of eight principal workshops, two were entirely demolished and a further three were seen to be severely damaged.[24] The lock gates at the Bassin de la Marine were damaged which allowed it to empty at low tide but the floating docks inside this basin, among the most important targets, remained untouched. A further operation was planned but the conditions of tide and weather prevented it being carried out until 22 September 1917 when the monitor *Terror* with air spotting got three direct hits on the dockyard, sinking one dry dock and damaging the other. Three enemy seaplanes attempted to register the powerful 'Tirpitz' Battery and others onto *Terror* but they were attacked by fighters of 4 (Naval) Squadron and shot down into the sea. The pilot of one, together with wreckage from his machine, was picked up by a British destroyer. After this bombardment the Germans began to reduce their use of Ostend.

In May 1917 the Germans began to use Gotha bombers to carry out daylight attacks on the south-eastern counties of England and in June they bombed London. As in the past, the RNAS Dunkirk Command was instructed to carry out counter-strikes against the airfields from which the enemy was launching these raids. While these were relatively straightforward to locate, they were difficult targets to neutralise and would require continuous, concentrated bombing before major damage could be achieved. Throughout the summer and autumn of 1917, therefore, frequent attacks around the clock were carried out by the RNAS bomber squadrons on German airfields in Belgium, principally Gontrode and St Denis Westrem where the Gotha bombers that attacked Britain were based. Fighters from Dunkirk were also used to intercept and attack the bombers themselves on their homeward journey, having been warned from Dover that they were airborne.[25] On 4 July 1917 a large formation of enemy bombers attacked the naval base at Harwich and the naval air station at Felixstowe. Once news of the raid reached Dunkirk, flights of Sopwith Camel fighters were launched which intercepted the formation of Gothas about 30nm north-west of Ostend flying at heights between 12,000ft and 15,000ft. Having gained position, the naval fighters dived into the middle of the formation and shot down two bombers immediately while a third came down near Ostend. After that the Germans launched fighters to meet the bombers during their return flight and escort them through the danger zone near Dunkirk. On the morning of 22 September 1917 two flights of Sopwith Camels took off to intercept enemy bombers but encountered about twenty-five enemy fighters between Ostend and Ghistelles. A large air engagement took place in which several enemy aircraft were shot down. No RNAS aircraft were lost and all managed to return to Dunkirk but several had taken hits and one was found to have 113 bullet holes in it when it landed, with several having gone through both petrol tanks.

Just prior to the military offensive that became known as the Third Battle of Ypres, or more commonly Passchendaele, which began on 31 July 1917 a vigorous air offensive was carried out by both the RFC and RNAS against enemy aircraft and their airfields. In this connection RNAS units in the Dunkirk area were tasked to carry out continuous bombing attacks on airfields by day and night and to seek out and destroy enemy aircraft working over the seaward flank of the BEF. The latter duty was undertaken by 4 Wing and the strikes against airfields by 5 Wing. Furthermore, in order to disrupt the transportation of German reserves, stores and ammunition to the Ypres sector, strikes were carried out against railway communications immediately in the rear of his front line. On the night of 16 August in conjunction with the British attack on Langemarck, the Dunkirk Command carried out one of its largest and most successful strike operations. The target was the railway junction and ammunition dump at Thourout and it was attacked by fourteen Handley Page 0/100s of 5 Wing. All of them succeeded in identifying the target and multiple hits were achieved on the railway tracks at the northern and southern junctions. A fire of unusual intensity, which could be seen plainly from the Allied side of the front line, broke out in the ammunition dump and was followed by a series of violent explosions for an hour and a half afterwards. In all 189 bombs ranging from 65lbs to 250lbs were dropped, a total weight of over 9 tons. On the night of 25 September a similar tonnage was dropped on the railway triangle around Thourout, Lichtervelde and Cortemarcke and many direct hits were obtained. Similar strikes were carried out at frequent intervals with the result that enemy rail traffic was completely suspended in the area attacked for several days while in others a number of trains had to be diverted onto undamaged lines. On the night of 29 September a long-distance attack of 250 miles was carried out by a Handley Page 0/100 on the bridge across the Meuse at Namur. Four 250lb and eight 65lb bombs were dropped and two of the 250lb were seen to hit the western end of the bridge from a height of 4400ft during the second pass over the target. The enemy's air and naval bases in Belgium were also the subject of a series of offensive operations. Two of the Handley Page squadrons at Coudekerque, 7 and 7A, flew every night that the weather permitted and the DH 4s of 5 (Naval) Squadron at Petite Synthe continued the offensive during daylight. The extent of the bombing attacks carried out during this period can be judged from the fact that between 2 and 5 September 1917 these squadrons dropped 18 tons of bombs between them on Bruges docks alone.

The enemy bombing attacks on London and the Home Counties intensified during September, culminating in a week of raiding at the end of the month. At the same time Dunkirk was subjected to attacks from the air, enemy gun batteries inland and the sea. The most intense of these caused considerable damage to the RNAS aircraft depot which had buildings damaged by explosions and fire which resulted in the loss of a number of replacement aircraft, engines, equipment and stores together with important records in offices. The depot was effectively put out of commission and it was decided to decentralise it with immediate effect. The reserve aircraft park was re-established at Furnes, a repair section was set up at Malo and a new aircraft acceptance park at Dover. The renewed raids on London were countered by a series of attacks on the Gotha bases and St Denis Westrem alone was hit by 8 tons of bombs between 27 September and 1 October. On the night of 30 September a direct hit was scored on a large shed on the south side of the airfield which caught fire and flames were seen to spread rapidly to other buildings. The resulting conflagration could be seen 30 miles away and afterwards the enemy moved the surviving bombers away to another airfield at Mariakerke to the west of Ghent. The remaining Gothas were moved from Gontrode to Oostacker, north of Ghent. In addition to these direct attacks, efforts were made continually to intercept airborne Gothas by night flying patrols. On 29 September a Handley Page especially fitted with five Lewis guns and eight 65lb bombs, flown by a pilot and four gunlayers, was tasked to patrol at 10,000ft to the north of Ostend in the hope of encountering enemy night bombers returning from attacks on the UK. In the course of its four-hour patrol, three Gothas were intercepted and two of them engaged. In one case a Gotha that passed between the Handley Page and the moon was fired at from only

50 yards range and after the gunlayers had emptied three trays of ammunition the enemy bomber was seen to go into a steep spiral dive and disappear. It was later discovered that that a Gotha had been forced to land in Holland on that night after being damaged and this was probably the one.

The Passchendaele offensive continued into November and the Dunkirk Command continued to provide support by continuing the attacks on the enemy's rail communications and airfields in Belgium. On the night of 28 October six Handley Page bombers flew to Antwerp and attacked the Cockerill Works at Hoboken together with the main railway sidings to the north of the town. While this attack was in progress another Handley Page which had taken off an hour later made its way through rain and mist towards Cologne. By the time it reached Duren the weather was too bad for it to continue and twelve 112lb bombs were dropped on a brilliantly-lit factory to the east of the town. The aircraft then turned for home but the conditions were so bad that no landmarks were visible and the pilot had to fly a compass course for two and a half hours. He crossed the front line at 2000ft under machine-gun fire and found the RFC airfield at Droglandt where, despite the lack of landing lights and the relatively small size of the field for such a large aircraft, it landed safely at 02.15 after seven and a half hours in the air. It was flown back to Coudekerque successfully the next day. During the remaining months of 1917 bad weather seriously interfered with naval air operations on the Belgian coast and bombing operations were only possible on a limited number of days. Early in December the German airfield at Oostacker was located and became an important target for strike missions when they were possible.

Eastern Waters

The work of the RNAS in the Eastern theatres of war during 1917 was extensive and varied, the main areas of activity being the Eastern Mediterranean, the Adriatic, the Red Sea, Palestine and East Africa. In the Eastern Mediterranean operations during the early part of the year were conducted by aeroplanes at Thasos, Stavros, Thermi, Imbros, and Mudros, by seaplanes at Suda Bay and by airships at Kassandra. The approximate RNAS strength in the region on 1 February 1917 was fifty-seven pilots, seventy-eight aeroplanes, twenty-nine seaplanes, five SS airships and Number 7 Kite Balloon Section. Operations from *Empress* and *Ark Royal*, the latter known as an RNAS depot ship, were closely integrated with those from the air stations ashore. 'A' Squadron at Thasos and 'D' Squadron at Stavros were used in the main for strikes and both tactical and photographic reconnaissance of targets in southern Bulgaria and on the front line at Struma and during the first half of the year repeated, successful attacks were carried out on the enemy's lines of communication, especially the Xanthi to Drama and Drama to Kavalla railway tracks. Frequent strikes were also carried out on Kavalla harbour, Pravi and enemy airfields at Drama and Gereviz. Anti-submarine patrols were flown and, whenever required, aircraft were provided as spotters for monitors' bombardment fire.

On 3 June 1917 'A' Squadron at Thasos was temporarily reinforced by 'F' Squadron, another bomber unit, in order to carry out concentrated attacks on the enemy's arable farming district of Nestos. When these were successfully completed 'F' Squadron returned to Mudros on 18 June. 'E' Squadron was attached to a RFC wing in Macedonia. A re-organisation of RNAS units based at Thasos and Stavros was carried out in August 1917 with spotting and reconnaissance aircraft concentrated at Stavros and Thasos becoming used mainly for anti-submarine and as an advanced base for aircraft from other air stations. 'Z' Squadron remained at Thasos. Naval air operations over the Dardanelles and Asia Minor were carried out from Imbros and Thermi during most of 1917. These included reconnaissance, spotting and ranging for monitors bombarding enemy gun emplacements and strikes against Turkish targets of opportunity which included crops as they ripened south of Aivali and the granaries intended to store the grain once it had been harvested. The surface infrastructure of coal mines at Soma were also attacked together with adjacent railway tracks and junctions. On 30 July the squadrons carrying out this work were reinforced temporarily by 'F' Squadron from Mudros for operations in the Smyrna area. 'F' commenced operations from Mitylene on 1 August with a strike on enemy railway workshops at Halka Bounan in which a number of bombs made direct hits and a large fire was started at one end of the building which spread rapidly to the whole structure. Offensive operations continued until 17 September when the bombers returned to Mudros, leaving the fighters at Mitylene. During one of the attacks on the Manissa railway the pilot of one of the bombers noticed that he had dropped astern of his intended position in the bomb-dropping formation and, in attempting to regain position, he put the nose down to gain speed but misjudged the manoeuvre and flew under the next aircraft ahead. As luck would have it, the other aircraft dropped its bombs at exactly that moment and one passed between the spars of the lower aircraft's upper right wing, cut through the internal bracing wires, severed the extra drift wire and passed through the leading edge of the lower wing just missing the front spar and grazing the aileron control wire. The aircraft immediately became right-wing heavy but by using full opposite aileron and flying at 13,000ft to avoid the worst turbulence its pilot managed to fly back to base.

On 9 October 1917 the air station at Thermi was moved to Kalloni on Mitylene and 'C' Squadron was moved to a new airfield at Gliki on Imbros from which a considerable number of strikes were flown against Adrianople, the Berlin to

Constantinople railway and warehouses on the Gallipoli peninsula during the last months of the year. During the early part of 1917 Mudros had been used as a stores depot as well as a base for seaplanes and airships but later in the year it became a major base for bombers[26] and the first successful attack on Constantinople was carried out from there. This attack was described by the Admiralty as 'undoubtedly the outstanding achievement of the RNAS in the eastern Mediterranean during 1917' and it was emphasised that the Handley Page 0/100 that had carried it out had flown all the way from the UK for the purpose, a journey of 2000 miles and a remarkable achievement in itself. It flew via Paris, Lyons, Frejus, Pisa, Rome, Naples, Otranto and Salonika in a total time airborne of 31 hours. Heavy rainstorms and high winds were encountered but the aircraft kept to its planned schedule and arrived safely at Mudros on 8 June 1917. Poor weather conditions delayed the attack until 9 July and the Handley Page took off at 20.45. It arrived over Constantinople at 23.45 and flew over Stenia Bay where the *Goeben* and *Breslau* were moored and the pilot flew around the bay three times in order to work out the direction of the surface wind as accurately as possible to ensure accuracy when releasing bombs. When he was satisfied he carried out a bombing run over the *Goeben* from the direction of the moon and dropped four 112lb bombs. Despite his careful preparation, the bombs missed the battlecruiser but detonated among the destroyers and submarines that were secured alongside it and a large explosion was followed by an extensive fire. A further run over *Goeben* was carried out and this time all four 112lb bombs were observed to hit her squarely in the centre of the deck a little forward of amidships. Bombs of this weight were unlikely to sink her but they were able to cause significant damage which would prevent her from going to sea in an operational condition. The pilot then flew to the upper waters of the Golden Horn and attacked ss *General* which was believed to house the German headquarters for operations in the Ottoman Empire and two bombs were dropped and both were observed to hit the upper part of the ship. The Turkish War Office was then located and attacked with the last two 112lb bombs, both of which were observed to hit the centre of the building and start fires. Very little anti-aircraft fire was encountered and the aircraft returned safely to Mudros at 03.40 after seven hours in the air. In addition to this attack, a number of strikes were carried out successfully by 'F' Squadron at Mudros against shipping in Chanak Bay and Galator airfield on the Gallipoli peninsula.

Towards the end of July 1917 a new unit designated 'G' Flight was formed at Marsh airfield on Mudros to carry out day and night anti-submarine patrols in the vicinity of Lemnos and to make night bombing attacks on targets of opportunity. It started flying operations on 4 August with an attack on the enemy barracks at Suvla and further attacks were made on shipping in the narrows; similar operations continued for the remainder of the year. Extensive anti-submarine operations in the theatre were carried out by SS airships from an air station at Kassandra and by seaplanes from Suda Bay. Late in the year an additional seaplane base was established at Syra and patrols from there commenced in December 1917. Another new unit, 6 Wing RNAS, was formed at Otranto which, together with a seaplane base in Malta, provided aerial reconnaissance against enemy submarines emerging from the Adriatic Sea. Patrols from these air stations commenced in June 1917 and continued throughout the remainder of the year; a number of submarines were sighted and attacked.

The presence of the *Goeben* and *Breslau* as a task force in being was a constant worry that led to a number a number of air operations intended to neutralise them that continued into 1918. At dawn on 20 January they were sighted five miles out to sea off Kusu having bombarded Kusu and Kephalo and sunk the monitors *Raglan* and *M-28* at anchor. They took up a southerly course shadowed by RNAS seaplanes which reported their position, course and speed by wireless but unfortunately the enemy managed to jam all their transmissions. Nevertheless a number of seaplanes from Imbros continued to harass the enemy ships, causing *Breslau* to steer a zig-zag course which took her into a minefield to the north of Rabbit Island where she hit a mine and sank rapidly. *Goeben* steered to the south for about 20 minutes under continuing attack from bomb-armed seaplanes which scored a number of hits. By now listing 15 degrees to port she altered course for the entrance to the Straits at 10 knots but aircraft continued to hit her with bombs and she ran aground at Nagara Burnu. For a further seven days RNAS bombers from Mudros and Imbros made repeated attacks on the stranded vessel but bad weather conditions prevented the use of torpedo-armed aircraft that would have finished her off and also limited the effectiveness of the bombers. In all 270 attacking sorties were flown and a total of over 15 tons of bombs were dropped but under cover of the bad weather the enemy succeeded in refloating *Goeben* and she was able to return to Stenia Bay.

The East Indies and Egypt Seaplane Squadron
RNAS operations in the East Indies, Egypt and the littoral waters of Palestine were largely carried out from the seaplane carriers of the East Indies and Egypt Seaplane Squadron (EI & ESS), based at Port Said. At first these had consisted mainly of attacks on enemy lines of communication in Palestine and Arabia but tasking grew to encompass ranging and correcting the fire from battleships and monitors bombarding the coastal towns of Palestine. Air operations in conjunction with the attack on Wejh on the Red Sea coast were carried out in January 1917 by seaplanes from *Anne* and when the town surrendered on the morning of 24 January this

HMS *Ben-my-Chree* on fire and sinking off Castelorizo Island in 1917. (Author's collection)

effectively marked the end of RNAS operations in this area. By February the EI &
ESS comprised twelve seaplanes, the seaplane carriers *Anne* and *Raven II*, Kite
Balloon Sections 13 in Aden and 14 in Mesopotamia, and twenty-one pilots.
Observers were drawn from a variety of sources outside the RNAS including the
British Army and the French Navy. *Ben-my-Chree*, commanded by Wing
Commander Samson, had formed part of the squadron but in January 1917 she
was sunk while at anchor off the island of Castelorizo, less than a mile from the
coast of Asia Minor, by Turkish artillery sited ashore. She was the only British
aviation vessel to be sunk during the First World War.

During the army's advance through Palestine in October and November 1917
seaplanes from *City of Oxford* carried out reconnaissance and target-ranging tasks
in support of the battleships and monitors bombarding Gaza. The railway station,
Dier-Sineid bridge, enemy trenches and gun emplacements west of El Nuzle were
all successfully ranged and gunfire was observed onto them. Bombing sorties were
also carried out by seaplanes against stores and docks at Beirut, the Jiljulie Bridge,
Haifa and various other targets in Palestine. On 19 March 1917 *Raven II* left Aden
in company with the French cruiser *Pothneau* to search for the German commerce
raider *Wolf* which was reported to be in the Indian Ocean. A number of flights
were carried out in the vicinity of the Chagos and Maldive Island groups but no
enemy vessel was sighted. *Raven II* and her escort returned to Port said on 9 June.

11 Deck Landing

Before 1917 the potential operation of aircraft with wheeled undercarriages from the decks of warships had become a circular argument. On the one hand the technical difficulty of landing on a deck was hard to overcome and so no ships were made available for conversion to fit big flight decks. On the other hand the lack of suitable big-deck ships meant that no ships were available for experimental landings to prove whether landing was feasible. 1917 could reasonably be considered as the turning point because the safe launch of wheeled fighters from take-off decks built over the bows of a variety of seaplane carriers had become sufficiently standardised to be considered routine. With no means of recovering the aircraft, however, this was a one-shot weapon and every sortie would end with a ditching if the aircraft had insufficient fuel to fly to a suitable landing place ashore. Since the majority of the Grand Fleet's operations took place in the eastern part of the North Sea, a long way from the UK mainland, ditching had become the normal end of every operational sortie.

Experiment and Evaluation

Lieutenant Williamson's proposal to the Admiralty had recommended that naval aviation would be most efficiently conducted by using wheeled aircraft operating from a ship fitted with a large, uninterrupted flight deck on a specially-constructed hull. He had also recommended 'the drastic measure of moving all upper deck essentials to one side of the ship' and made a rough model that gave three-dimensional expression to his idea by emphasising the flat upper deck and 'on the starboard side, a streamlined structure to contain the navigating bridge, searchlights etc, above which rose a mast and funnels'. He had effectively defined the aircraft carrier as we now understand it,[1] but unfortunately the importance placed on aircraft operations with the fleet was not yet felt to justify the cost of procuring such a vessel. His design concept had even included a system of retaining and arrester wires intended to hold the aircraft securely after landing and arrest its forward progress after touching down on the deck.[2] Both were to be stretched over a slightly inclined ramp. In late 1915 a wooden dummy flight deck was constructed at the Port Victoria Experimental Depot, Isle of Grain naval air station, and trials of Williamson's retaining/arresting system were carried out by a variety of aircraft types including Avro 504s. These continued into early 1916 and showed some promise but, since no ship was envisaged at the time with a deck big enough for aircraft to land on, they were not taken forward with any great urgency.

On 2 August 1916 Flight Lieutenant C T Freeman RNAS had been launched in Bristol Scout 8953 from the seaplane carrier *Vindex* to intercept Zeppelin *L 17* when it was spotted from the fleet. Armed with two containers of Ranken darts, he had eventually succeeded in climbing above the airship and had carried out three attacking runs on it but unfortunately none of them was successful. Unable to land back on his ship he had no option but to ditch and he was picked up by the Belgian steamer *Anvers*. However, his action came to the attention of the Third Sea Lord, Rear Admiral F C T Tudor, who asked the DAS to submit proposals for better armed fighters capable of destroying Zeppelins. In the same paper dated 9 August 1916 he recognised the potential for carrier-borne aeroplanes to provide the sort of air-defence capability that the fleet clearly needed and he instructed the RNAS experimental depot at Isle of Grain to resume deck-landing testing with greater

Sopwith Pup number 9922 fitted with an arrester hook and skid undercarriage carrying out deck-landing trials at RNAS Isle of Grain. It was one of a batch of fifty Pups built by Beardmore and was delivered to Grain for deck-landing trials in March 1917. It was flown modified to the standard seen here by Squadron Commander H R Busteed RNAS in July 1917. (Philip Jarrett collection)

urgency. The original dummy deck still existed and an arrangement of three arrester ropes were rigged athwartships across it with a 30lb sandbag at both ends of all three. Unlike modern arrester wire systems in which the aircraft's deck hook snatches a single wire, this embryonic system used a hook with a large bill which was intended to catch successive ropes in order to provide a gradually increasing force of retardation. The ropes were spaced 20ft apart and supported by wooden planks placed fore and aft which kept the ropes 6in above the deck. This height made it easier for the large hook to engage the wires but meant that aircraft had to be fitted with a propeller-guard to prevent damage. The first aircraft to simulate deck landings using this system was Avro 504 number 1485 on 19 September 1916 and the tests that followed were considered to be encouraging although flying was limited to days when the wind was aligned with the dummy deck. The experimental department believed that a bigger deck could be used on a larger number of occassions and requested that a wooden deck 200ft square should be constructed at an estimated cost of £800. Admiral Tudor accepted this but the DAS, Rear Admiral C L Vaughan-Lee, took the idea a stage further and suggested that the improved deck should be a circle 210ft in diameter so that it could be used in any wind direction and this is what was built.

The new deck was in use by February 1917 when Sopwith Pup 9497 was fitted with an arrester hook and joined 1485 in the trials programme. The revised deck used transverse arrester wires which were supported at heights between 6in and 2ft above the deck, the latter proving quite a challenge for the light frame fitted ahead of the undercarriage to protect the propeller. The hook itself was hinged onto the lower longerons to lay flush with the airframe in flight but was pulled down and held in place by a length of rubber bungee cord which had the secondary purpose of preventing hook bounce, effectively holding the hook down to scrape along the deck until the wires were taken. The fact that the need for such a device was uncovered by the trials shows their general success but, disappointingly, there were still concerns that the lightweight fighters of the era would be vulnerable to wind gusts on deck immediately after landing. It was not fully appreciated that the arrester wires would hold the aircraft firmly until a handling party had taken charge of it and further experiments were made with retaining wires fitted fore and aft which were intended to engage with hooks on the undercarriage axle to hold the aircraft on deck after landing. Number 9497 was one of eighteen Sopwith Pups used at the Isle of Grain Experimental Depot during the latter part of 1917 in experiments to develop embarked aviation techniques. In addition to deck-landing trials they were used on test of emergency flotation gear, hydro-vanes intended to keep aircraft from nosing underwater as they ditched and skids as replacements for wheeled undercarriages. When not engaged on trial work they were armed and used for air-defence sorties over littoral waters when required.[3] A number of pilots were attached to the Experimental Depot, among them Squadron Commanders H R Busteed and H M Cave-Brown-Cave RNAS and Flight Lieutenants C T Freeman and E H Dunning RNAS. Dunning was known to have carried out several landings in 9497 on the dummy deck during March 1917.

Flying on to the Deck

By 1917 primary flying controls, especially those of fighter aircraft, had evolved from the earlier wheel-type aileron control which moved fore and aft to operate the elevators into the 'joystick', a single control that carried out both functions. A system of wires and pulleys was attached to its base that caused elevator movement when it was moved fore and aft and aileron movement when it was moved laterally. The amount of displacement governed the amount of control movement and great care had be taken when rigging the aircraft to ensure that the controls were harmonised without one control surface feeling lighter than the other. Rudder control was achieved by a bar moved by the pilot's feet, rigged so that a displacement of the bar to the left caused the aircraft to turn left and vice versa. The linkage of wires followed the same basic principle as those fitted to the rudders of small ships with the difference that the aircraft fuselage tended to flex in flight, especially when turning hard in combat, and designers tended to opt for the wires to be kept under tension to prevent the slight lessening of control that would have followed if they became slack.[4] Although there were some variations, the 'joystick' was generally situated in the centre of the cockpit between the pilot's knees and moved by the right hand, leaving the left hand free for engine and armament control.

Engine control was as important as the primary flight controls and the majority of RNAS fighters had rotary engines which operated over a very narrow range of revolutions. All had a crankshaft fixed to the engine bulkhead about which both propeller and cylinders rotated, an arrangement that was deemed lighter than fixed cylinder blocks in which a rotating crankshaft turned the propeller. There was no throttle control for the engine as such but there were two other engine controls, both of which needed the pilot's constant attention. The first was a mixture control with which the optimal amount of fuel was allowed into the engine for the altitude and degree of manoeuvre being undertaken. The only instant control of the engine for diving at high speed or landing was an ignition thumb switch at the top of the 'joystick'.[5] Pressing this switch turned the engine magneto on or off to control speed, particularly on an approach to land, producing a characteristic 'blipping' sound which became synonymous with descriptions of the technique. Whilst 'blipping' the pilot would set the mixture control to what he considered the best position to ensure smooth engine running when he selected the ignition on. Usually the ignition was only kept off for a few seconds so the propeller continued to rotate and the engine would stay hot. If, for any reason, the propeller ceased to rotate there was no way of re-starting the engine as it had to be hand-swung before initial start-up[6] and if the if the ignition was left off long enough for the engine to cool down appreciably, that too might prevent it from re-starting in flight.

With the rotating mass of cylinders and the propeller, the torque effect of rotary engines on small fighters was significant.[7] Newton's Law states that 'to every action there is an equal and opposite reaction' so as the engine and propeller spun clockwise when seen by the pilot looking forward, the aircraft would, if left unchecked, tend to spin around its fore and aft axis in the opposite direction, anti-clockwise. Full right rudder had to be applied on the take-off run until the airflow over the built-in twist of the tail-fin became sufficient to counter the tendency to turn left. The considerable gyroscopic effect of the rotating engine mass combined with the torque of the propeller to create an effect on the fore and aft control of the aircraft that forced pilots think carefully about how best to execute a turn. Under combat conditions, for instance, it might well be quicker to add aileron and rudder to the combined gyroscopic and torque effects to 'pull' the aircraft round through 270 degrees to the left rather than oppose them with aileron and rudder and attempt to turn through 90 degrees to the right. In general flying conditions, however, a turn left would be under greater and potentially more accurate control. There were other factors to take into account. In a right-hand turn the gyroscopic effect would cause the aircraft's nose to drop but in a left-hand turn it would cause it to rise. Pilots tended, therefore, to make left-hand turns at low level before landing and the this practice subsequently become the rule. All military aircraft throughout the world fly left-hand patterns to land unless there is a particular local reason not to do so. The left-hand pattern evolved not only from the widespread use of rotary-engined warplanes in 1917 but the fact that the majority of pilots were, and still are, right-handed also had something to do with it in that it was found easier to displace the 'joystick' from right to left with the right arm when turning into a left-handed landing circuit than to pull it from left to right. From this combination of circumstances, the practice had developed by 1917 that pilots flew left-handed circuits to land at airfields ashore and this technique read across into deck landing.

Sopwith Pup N6453
Sopwith Pup N6453 was one of thirty aircraft ordered from the shipbuilding firm of Sir William Beardmore & Co on 16 February 1917 under contract A.S.19598/17 and constructed at Dalmuir. All were equipped with airbags for operation from ships and were fitted for alternative armaments of a single Lewis gun mounted

Sopwith Pup N6453, the aircraft in which Dunning made his historic first deck landing, at RNAS Smoogroo on the mainland island of Orkney. It has a Lewis gun fitted to fire upwards through a gap in the top wing but lacks the white paint mark on the outboard end of the starboard lower elevator in this image which was probably taken soon after *Furious'* arrival in Scapa Flow. (Guy Warner collection)

forward of the cockpit and angled upwards to fire clear of the propeller arc or Le Prieur rockets mounted on the interplane struts. The Lewis gun was preferred to the Vickers gun mounted on land-based Pups because it was easier to load with tracer, Brock and Pomeroy ammunition and it was angled to shoot clear of the propeller arc to avoid the danger of an explosive round hitting and shattering it. The lack of an interrupter mechanism also allowed a higher rate of fire. N6453 together with N6450, N6451, N6452 and N6454 were delivered immediately after their construction to *Furious* at Scapa Flow, arriving between 9 and 11 July 1917, only days after her completion at Sir W G Armstrong-Whitworth & Co's Walker Naval Yard on the Tyne on 4 July. Beardmore-built Pups could always be distinguished by their having red, white and blue stripes painted on the elevators as well as on the rudder. This batch of Pups were all fitted with 80hp Le Rhône rotary engines and had an airscrew diameter of 8ft 6in. Maximum weight with pilot, full fuel, gun and ammunition was 1225lbs. The fuselage had longerons made of ash and spacers made of spruce. The whole assembly was braced as a boxed girder with wire and behind the fireproof bulkhead there were diagonal struts of ash and fairings were fitted on each side of the fuselage behind the circular engine cowling.[8] A rounded top decking of ply was fitted along the full length of the fuselage and, apart from having an aluminium sheet behind the engine cowling and plywood around the cockpit, the fuselage was covered with doped fabric. The wings had spars made of spindled spruce, spruce ribs and birch riblets. Steel tubes were used for the wingtips and trailing edges. The ailerons were remarkably small and hardly seemed capable of making the Pup as manoeuvrable as it proved to be and they were hinged to the rear spars and inter-connected by wire cables. A balance cable ran inside the upper wing in front of the forward spar. The tailplane was of composite construction with a rear spar of steel tube but the remainder of wood with fabric covering. The elevator, fin and rudder were all made entirely of steel tubing. The undercarriage had two plain steel-tube vees and the split-axle wheel attachment used by Sopwith on most of their designs. Shock-absorption was achieved by rubber cords and the simple tail skid was attached to the stern post and also sprung by rubber cord.

The Grand Fleet Aircraft Committee
In January 1917 Admiral Beatty, who had succeeded Jellicoe as C-in-C Grand Fleet on 29 November 1916, set up a Grand Fleet Aircraft Committee[9] which was instructed to report on the Fleet's aviation requirements and make recommendations. At the same time, Commodore G M Paine RN was appointed to the

HMS *Furious* anchored in Orphir Bay, Scapa Flow. The Yorkshire breaks have been raised to protect the two Sopwith Pups secured on the after part of the take-off deck, over the hangar, and the two derricks are in the stowed position. (Guy Warner collection)

Hoisting a Sopwith Pup out of the hangar. Note how it had to be tipped nose-up to fit through the gap and how little clearance there was even then. Hoisting it out in a rough sea would have been difficult, if not impossible. The Yorkshire breaks are partially raised and the flat objects lying on the deck to starboard were fitted over the hatch to support the canvas that made it weather-tight. A seaplane trolley is visible at the forward end of the slot that kept it on deck when the aircraft became airborne. (Author's collection)

Admiralty as the DAS and Fifth Sea Lord. The Committee rendered its first report on 5 February 1917, the speed with which it did so indicating the growing importance of its subject matter. It recommended the deployment of Sopwith Pups aboard the largest possible number of suitable warships in addition to *Campania* and *Manxman*. Of even greater significance it recommended the completion of the light battlecruiser *Furious* with a flying-off deck forward to act as a fast fighter and seaplane carrier capable of operating with the Battlecruiser Fleet. The Committee's recommendations were forwarded to the Admiralty with Beatty's support after only two days, on 7 February 1917, another indication of the importance attached to embarked aircraft operations. By 18 March the Board had approved the plan to modify *Furious* and a sketch design had been prepared. The ship had originally been designed as a large light cruiser of 19,100 tons at deep load and capable of 31 knots on 90,000shp with four shafts. She was to have had a main armament of two single 18in guns fitted in single turrets, one forward and one aft. Only the after one was ever fitted: the forward barbette was plated over and a hangar 120ft long, 57ft wide and 18ft high built over it. A flight deck 228ft long was constructed over the forecastle, the after part of which formed the hangar roof. Aft of the deck was a hatch through which aircraft were hoisted from the hangar by topping lifts attached to two derricks, one to port and one to starboard.[10] Aircraft on deck near the hatch could, if necessary, be protected from wind blast by wooden palisades known as 'Yorkshire breaks' after similar structures used in the farming industry. These were timbers attached vertically to the outboard hangar bulkheads by metal brackets. In use they were slid vertically upwards and locked in position; gaps between them allowed some wind to pass through but at reduced strength; when not in use they were slid down until the tops were level with the flight deck and locked in position. The take-off run ahead of the hatch was 160ft long by 57ft wide at its rear end tapering to 36ft at the forward end of the hangar and to a point at the bow.

Furious was designed to embark a flight of Sopwith Pup fighters and a second flight of Short 184 seaplane reconnaissance aircraft. Both types could have could have taken off easily from the deck, the latter with their floats fitted onto four-wheeled trollies with runners that ran along a centreline slot which kept the aircraft straight and retained the trolley on deck for further use once the aircraft lifted off it. The Pups took off using their normal wheeled undercarriages. In some respects, however, the aviation arrangements were not as good as those in *Campania* and revealed the haste with which the ship's final design was sketched. Bell-Davies was the senior aviation officer in *Campania* and in conversation with his opposite number in *Furious,* he learnt that electric winches had replaced the reliable steam winches used in the older ship; these were found to have a tendency to trip the

A view forward from *Furious'* bridge over the take-off deck. The two Sopwith Pups give an idea of the space in which Dunning had to land forward of the armoured conning tower and bridge structure. Note how the deck narrows to little more than the width of the Pup's wingspan (26ft 6in) forward of the hangar. The stripes on the Pup's elevators show them to be Beardmore-built machines. (Author's collection)

overload switch at the slightest provocation and were considered harder to use. The flight-deck support structure right forward was relatively weak, preventing her from being driven hard into even moderate seas but the new ship provided a steadier deck and higher speed which allowed all the aircraft capable of embarking in her to take off from her deck even in calm conditions.

Furious joined the Grand Fleet at Scapa Flow on 6 July 1917 under the command of Captain Wilmot S Nicholson RN who was not a pilot but who wanted to see his ship perform well in its new role. The embarked aircraft initially comprised three Short 184s and the five Sopwith Pups recently delivered by Beardmore. Although she was only considered to be a stopgap that could be introduced to service quickly, her newly-appointed senior RNAS officer, Squadron Commander E H Dunning DSC RNAS, was impressed by both the size of the deck and the ship's speed. He was to earn a place in history as the first naval pilot in the world to land an operational aircraft on the deck of an operational warship under way at sea, showing at last how the technical difficulties could be overcome by a man with drive and initiative.

Edwin Harris Dunning was born on 17 July 1892 and began a conventional naval career at the Royal Naval Colleges Osborne and Dartmouth, passing out as a midshipman in January 1910. His first ship was the battleship *Hibernia* and his confidential report from this period signed by Captain Maclachan[11] describes him as being 'zealous and promising'. He was noted as speaking colloquial French but a subsequent report signed by Captain De Salis RN described him as 'zealous and capable but not always attentive'. His next appointment was to the battleship *Russell* in the Mediterranean Fleet and he was due to take it up in August 1910 but ill-health had become a problem and on 27 June he was admitted to the Royal Naval Hospital (RNH) Portland with suspected bronchitis. On 6 July he was transferred to RNH Haslar and, after treatment, granted pre-foreign service leave that amounted to fifty-three days at home.[12] In August 1910 he took passage in *Duncan* to join *Russell* but his lung condition deteriorated and he was diagnosed with suspected tuberculosis. On 24 April 1911 he was invalided back to the UK, travelling in the hospital ship *Maine*, and was admitted to RNH Plymouth. His father, Sir Edwin Dunning of Bradfield in Essex, asked permission to take his son home and the Admiralty agreed but stipulated that he must bear the cost of his son's treatment if he removed him from a naval hospital. He left RNH Plymouth on 6 June 1911 and was borne on the books of HMS *Victory* at Portsmouth while on sick leave; a medical board on 6 September found that he was still medically unfit and his sick leave was extended. Notes on his service record subsequently confirmed that a medical board on 5

Squadron Commander E H Dunning DSC RNAS in 1917. He has the RNAS eagle over his left sleeve lace but an RN officers' cap badge with its foul anchor. (Author's collection)

March 1912 found that he was still unfit after a total of 276 days' sick leave during which he had presumably undergone civilian treatment. A last note states that he was declared medically unfit for further service due to 'tubercle of lung' on 6 March 1912 and that officers' appointment list CW 9230/1912 had confirmed his medical discharge from the RN.

A second and far more successful career was to follow shortly after the outbreak of war in 1914, however. On 4 October 1914 Dunning joined the RNAS, his new service history[13] noting that he had served as a Midshipman RN between January 1910 and March 1912 and that he had been discharged with suspected tuberculosis but was now 'perfectly fit'. He obtained pilot's certificate number 949 at the naval flying school at Eastchurch on 24 October 1914 and was appointed as a Flight Lieutenant RNAS on 21 November 1914 with seniority back-dated to the day he joined the RNAS. Direct entries into the RNAS would normally have spent a period in an initial acting rank before being confirmed. Because of his prior RN service, Dunning's record stresses that his rank of Flight Lieutenant was 'continuous'. Like the majority of fixed-wing pilots of the period, he was trained to fly seaplanes and he would have got an early appreciation of their weakness on 8 January 1915 when he attempted to take off from Southampton Water in Sopwith Type 807 number 809 and the structure connecting the floats to the fuselage collapsed.[14]

On 7 May 1915 he was appointed to the seaplane carrier *Ark Royal* from which he flew a number of seaplane sorties during the Dardanelles campaign and earned a distinguished record. Williamson had been his flight commander and Dunning must have shared his poor opinion of seaplanes and recognised their limited value early on. On 16 March 1915 Dunning damaged a float on Short Type 807 number 807 while attempting to take off. The aircraft had already shown itself to be under-powered and unable to climb, even when flown without an observer, and it was subsequently dismantled and used for spares. Another of *Ark Royal*'s seaplanes was Short Folder number 136 which had taken part in the strike against Cuxhaven in 1914. On 27 April 1915 Dunning flew it on a mission with Lieutenant W Parke RN as observer to spot *Triumph*'s fall of shot when she engaged a Turkish battleship in the narrows. Number 136 was badly damaged by enemy rifle fire, however, a consequence of its inability to gain much height and it was forced to come down in rough sea conditions with the port chassis strut and the port lower wing shot through. It was recovered to *Ark Royal* and repaired but when Dunning next tried to take off on 2 May the chassis struts collapsed and the aircraft capsized; on this occasion his observer was Lieutenant A G Brown RNR. The aircraft was repaired again and Dunning flew it on 17 May but this time the floats broke up as he landed because, it was believed, they had struck wreckage just beneath the surface.

Trying to get the best from underpowered seaplanes must have been a daunting task but Dunning's determination was recognised by authority when he was mentioned in despatches for his efforts during the campaign. He subsequently operated from the air station at Mudros and got the opportunity to fly Nieuport Scouts, which were far more effective machines powered by 110hp Le Rhône engines with wheeled undercarriages. He was awarded the DSC after a sortie on 20 June 1916 in a Nieuport from Mudros to Port Lagos during which he encountered and attacked two enemy seaplanes which he put to flight, one of which was damaged.[15] Communiqué number 14 from Mudros dated 19 July 1916 stated that 'Flight Lieutenant Dunning was wounded in the leg and his observer, Sub Lieutenant C B Oxley RN, had to take over the controls while a tourniquet was being applied'. After the award of the DSC, the Admiralty expressed their Lordships' appreciation for Dunning's services 'in the engagement with enemy aircraft on 20 June in which they considered great credit was due for his presence of mind and gallant conduct, although wounded in the leg'. Probably as a direct result of this wound, Dunning was appointed back to the UK on 30 June 1916 and promoted to Flight Commander.

After a period of convalescence he was appointed to the Eastchurch War Flight on 14 September 1916 and, among other flying duties, he is known to have flown a hostile aircraft patrol in a Bristol Scout Type D against enemy aircraft that had been sighted near the coast on 22 October 1916. On 12 December 1916 he was appointed to the Admiralty for 'B' Section of the Air Department which was looking into ways of operating wheeled aircraft from ships and in the early weeks of 1917 he is known to have carried out deck landings on the dummy deck at Isle of Grain in Sopwith Pup 9497, no doubt keeping abreast of the development work that was being carried out there. When the Admiralty endorsed the Grand Fleet Aircraft Committee's recommendation to complete *Furious* as a fighter carrier with Sopwith Pups embarked, with his background, experience and enthusiasm he was clearly the ideal candidate for the task of senior aviation officer. On 15 June 1917 he was appointed to Armstrong Whitworth's Walker Naval Yard at Newcastle on the Tyne to stand by *Furious* in the last stages of her conversion and take charge of her air department. He was promoted to Squadron Commander on 30 June 1917.

The First Deck Landing on a Warship Under Way
Furious was completed on 4 July 1917 and sailed to join the Grand Fleet in Scapa Flow, arriving on 6 July. Her five new Sopwith Pups were delivered to the small air station at Smoogroo on the north shore of the Flow on the island of Mainland. Like the other aircraft-carrying ships of the Grand Fleet, *Furious* anchored close to the airfield and her aircraft disembarked to maintain flying practice; in *Furious'*

A Sopwith Pup being brought out to *Furious* from Smoogroo on a locally-constructed raft made from seaplane floats and timber, towed by one of the ship's steam picket boats. (Author's collection)

Preparing to hoist a Sopwith Pup onto *Furious* from its raft. The sailor's white uniforms were working dress in 1917, easier to wash than blue serge. (Author's collection)

case this was in Orphir Bay a mile and half west of the airfield. Having now seen the ship at sea and realised the implications of its high speed and large deck, Dunning grasped the potential for Sopwith Pups to land on her while she was under way. The Pup's landing speed was about 45 knots; the stalling speed at which the wings would no longer give lift and the nose would drop was somewhat less, the exact speed depending on the aircraft's weight at the time and a light aircraft with minimal fuel, no gun and no ammunition would stall at a lower airspeed than a fully-loaded, heavy one. Given sufficient ship's speed into an adequate head wind, the aircraft's speed of approach relative to the deck could be very slow indeed. Dunning calculated, as an illustrative example, that if the ship steamed at 25 knots into a 20-knot headwind a pilot of reasonable ability should be able to move his aircraft over the deck and literally hover over the most suitable spot. The most significant moment of danger would actually come after landing, since the aircraft wings would remain close to or even above the minimum flying speed and a sudden gust of wind or reduction in aircraft weight, such as the pilot climbing out of the cockpit, could easily cause it to lift off the deck. An aircraft approach speed, relative to the deck, of about 10 knots greater than the wind over the deck was expected to give a reasonable margin of safety.

Dunning took every opportunity to fly one of the Pups from Smoogroo the short distance along the coast to Orphir Bay and while the ship lay with its head to the strong prevailing south-westerly wind he practised flying low-level left-hand circuits on *Furious'* port side to perfect his approach and landing technique. He would have briefed Captain Nicholson what he was doing and received his full support. As he gained confidence he ended each circuit by flying close up the port side of the ship until he was clear forward of the bridge and the armoured conning tower. The aircraft's elevators would have given precise attitude control, even at low air speed, and 'blipping' the engine ignition on and off would have allowed him to control his forward movement relative to the deck. The ideal landing spot was on the widest part of the flight deck on top of the hangar, just forward of the access hatch, and to make sure that he could aim accurately at the right point a white 'eye line' was painted across the deck. By keeping himself immediately over this line he knew he was in the right place fore and aft, he had only to position himself over the centre of the deck by glancing forward to the point of the bow. He may have evaluated different techniques for positioning the Pup over the deck; one option was a flat or 'S' turn using rudder but another option was to 'sideslip', canting the nose off the centreline with rudder while bank was applied with opposite aileron, giving a better view of the deck but more rapid loss of height. After positioning himself, Dunning needed to get the aircraft into a 'three-point' attitude in which the wheels and tail-skid would touch the deck together. Whichever technique he used, there would

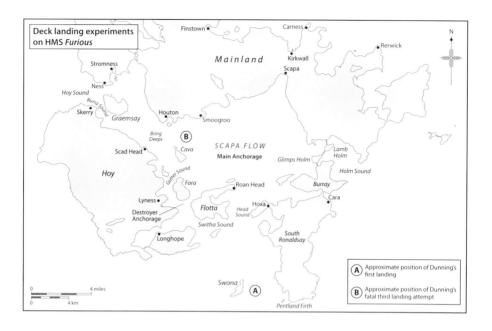

Deck landing experiments on HMS *Furious*

have been some wind turbulence, known as 'cliff-edge' effect.[16] On at least one occasion Dunning touched his wheels on the deck during one of his practice approaches and then 'blipped' his engine ignition on to fly away. The probability is that Captain Nicholson witnessed these touch-and-go approaches because when Dunning asked for permission to carry out a full-stop landing when the ship was under way, Nicholson not only gave it unreservedly but invited a number of senior officers to come aboard to witness the event.

The next suitable occasion proved to be on 2 August 1917 when *Furious* was scheduled to carry out rangefinder exercises for her gunnery systems in the Pentland Firth to the west of Swona Island between 09.30 and 10.55. Anchor was weighed in Orphir Bay at 08.33 and *Furious* passed through the Hoxa Boom, the main entrance into and out of Scapa Flow for big ships, at 09.14. Dunning was waiting and as soon as the rangefinder exercise was completed, *Furious* hoisted the 'affirmative' flag and he joined the landing circuit. The ship steamed at 20 knots into a stiff but constant wind estimated at 26 knots to give a felt wind over the deck of 46 knots from directly ahead. This was slightly greater than the ideal and meant that Dunning had to overtake the landing area on his final approach; it also meant that the aircraft would touch down at a speed slightly greater than its stalling speed making it unstable on deck. It would have to be grabbed immediately by a handling party and held firmly while the pilot climbed out and the ship slowed down and turned its bow away from the wind.

Dunning's first deck landing on 2 August 1917. The handling party of officers and ratings can be seen running to grab N6453 which is slightly to the left of the deck centreline and has drifted a few feet forward of the white eye line painted on the deck. The positions of the controls show that the aircraft is still moving slightly to starboard. Note the triangle of white paint at the right rear of the starboard lower elevator which is slightly raised. For this landing, the aircraft did not have a Lewis gun fitted, although its pyramid-shaped mount can be seen just forward of the cockpit, and 'grab handles' had not been fitted to help the handling party. The idea for them only came after the experience of this landing had been discussed and analysed. (Author's collection)

Dunning made his approach in N6453 exactly as he had practised. The aircraft had no gun or ammunition to minimise weight and fuel in the main tank was the minimum necessary to get back to Smoogroo if for any reason the landing-on had to be cancelled. He entered smoother air as he passed over the deck edge at an eye height of about 10ft leaving good clearance between the wheels beneath him and the deck edge. Any higher than this and the deck would have been partially obscured by the aircraft fuselage underneath him, making it more difficult to judge his landing point; any lower and he would have risked catching the deck edge with his wheels or tail skid. As the photograph shows, Dunning judged things perfectly; he was on top of the eye line as he moved over the deck but, having had to overtake the deck, he still had some forward motion relative to it as he 'blipped' the ignition off and he moved slightly forward before touching down; a historic event that *Furious'* log records as having happened at 11.00.[17] He would not have wanted to move any further forward as the deck can be seen not only to narrow significantly but also to slope downwards in order to help Short 184s accelerate on take-off.

With N6453 held firmly on deck by willing hands, Dunning climbs out of the cockpit on 2 August 1917. The island of Swona, which had been used by *Furious'* gunlayers for ranging exercises before the landing, can just be made out on the horizon to the left of the picture. (Author's collection)

The photograph of this historic first landing shows the handling party running up to grab the aircraft. N6453 can be recognised by the triangle of white paint on the outboard rear corner of the lower starboard aileron which covered a previous repair. It should also be noted that for this first landing the aircraft was not fitted with leather grab handles on the trailing edges and there is no Lewis gun on the triangular mounting forward of the cockpit. Five and half years after Eugene Ely had landed on an American cruiser, a British operational fighter flown by an RN pilot had landed on an operational warship under way at sea. The solution to the technical difficulties that had dogged embarked flying had been demonstrated and Dunning had shown that a high-performance aircraft could both take-off and land on an aircraft carrier at sea with a sufficiently large flight deck. Dunning's pilots were delighted because taking off from the deck had already become an everyday event and now landing-on was a practical proposition. The ability to re-use fighters would also have the effect of making *Furious'* air group more effective because aircraft would no longer have to ditch at the end of every sortie. August 2nd had proved to be a most successful day and at 11.42 *Furious* passed back through the Hoxa boom to anchor in the main fleet anchorage north of Flotta island at 12.10 so that the senior officers could be transferred by boat back to their own ships. On 6 August she carried out sub-calibre firing practices against towed targets in the forenoon and was back in Orphir Bay by noon. Of interest, at 19.45, she picked up

Dunning's second landing at 13.54 on 7 August 1917. The aircraft is N6453 again and it still has the triangle of white paint on the starboard lower aileron but for this landing a Lewis gun with its tray of ammunition has been fitted forward of the cockpit and the riggers have sewn 'grab handles' onto the lower aileron trailing edges and under the fuselage to help the handling party secure the aircraft. Dunning is applying left rudder and aileron to stop his movement over the deck nicely on the centreline but the aircraft is slightly aft of the ideal position indicated by the eye line. (Author's collection)

a floating corpse from the battleship *Vanguard* which had blown up at her anchorage in Scapa Flow on 9 July 1917. It was sent to the mortuary at the small hospital used by the RN in Kirkwall.[18]

Unfortunately, Dunning's later demonstrations were not as successful. On 7 August *Furious* weighed anchor from Orphir Bay specifically for flying operations with courses and speeds set to the south of the bay as necessary. Dunning intended to carry out one further landing himself and then to allow other pilots, starting with his second-in-command Flight Commander W G Moore RNAS, to make a series of landings to show that they were not stunts but something that could be repeated regularly by a variety of pilots. He used the same Pup, N6453, but this time it was at operational weight with a Lewis gun fitted forward of the cockpit and several trays of ammunition. Leather strops had been sewn by the riggers onto the training edge of the lower wing and the underside of the fuselage to help the handling party get hold of the aircraft and keep it firmly on deck in the moments after landing. He took off at 13.40 and landed-on at 13.54 but the handling party were somewhat over-enthusiastic on this approach and actually pulled the aircraft down onto the deck. The wind conditions were more gusty than they had been on 2 August despite the ship maintaining a steady 20 knots and the handlers were unable to prevent the aircraft being blown backwards into the hatch-coming as Dunning 'blipped' the engine ignition off. This caused some damage to the elevators and, on stepping out of the cockpit, Dunning briefed the handling party that they were to wait until the aircraft's wheels were actually on the deck before grabbing it in future landings. N6453 needed to be repaired before it could fly again so Dunning walked across to N6452 which Moore was about to fly and said 'Come out of that Moore, I'm not satisfied with that run and I'm going again'.[19] After strapping in, he took off for the second time that day at 14.40 but was not happy with his first approach. His second was no better and he went round again to set up for the third approach to the deck which was to prove fatal. This time he was too high as he moved over the deck and he continued to move well forward of the eye line. Over the narrower part of the deck the cliff-edge effect would have been a significant factor, especially in the gusty conditions encountered at the time. Later

Dunning's third and fatal attempt to land on *Furious* at 14.51 on 7 August 1917. This time the aircraft is N6452; there is no triangle of white paint, it has no Lewis gun fitted but it does have 'grab handles' sewn in place for Moore's programmed first landing. The aircraft was already well forward of the eye line when the photograph was taken and is to starboard of the centreline. The right wing has dropped and Dunning is applying left aileron and full left rudder in an attempt to level the wings. The aircraft is still moving forward and the handling party is having to run in a desperate bid to help as things begin to go very wrong. (Author's collection)

Now out of control, Dunning goes over the side with his controls centralised. The handling party is still running towards him but they are powerless to help. The cameraman in the foreground is raising his camera and moving to the starboard side of the deck but is probably too shocked to capture the impact as the aircraft hit the water. (Author's collection)

in the day the wind was described in the ship's log as being south-easterly Force 3 and calm but it had obviously reduced in strength during the afternoon. Accounts differ as to what precisely happened next. The handling party tried to grab the Pup but Dunning waved them away; at the same time he 'blipped' the engine ignition on but instead of cutting in it choked and lost power. The aircraft stalled and photographs show N6452 well forward over the deck with its port wing lifting slightly and both ailerons and rudder deflected to the left as if trying to counter a roll and swing to starboard, but with the wheels still astride the centreline. It came down heavily onto the starboard wheel and cartwheeled over the side, beyond any hope of the handlers restraining it. The most probable cause of the aircraft's departure from controlled flight, other than the obvious problem with the choked engine, was a gust from fine on the port bow, causing cliff-edge effect to raise the port wing and literally blow the aircraft, stalled, over the starboard side of the ship. Without the engine, Dunning stood no chance of recovering the situation and ditching was inevitable.

Surprisingly, there was no plane-guard launch or trawler in attendance and *Furious* itself had no sea-boat at immediate readiness, perhaps because the consequences of an uncontrolled ditching had not been fully appreciated. The ship's log states that at 14.51 'Squadron Commander E H Dunning, whilst attempting to land on flying deck in Pup fell into sea and was drowned. Aeroplane wrecked'.[20] It took *Furious* 20 minutes to slow and turn back to N6452 which was kept afloat by the airbag in the rear fuselage; unfortunately the weight of the engine dragged the nose under and it floated with the cockpit under water. As the ship stopped close to the wreck the sea-boat's crew were sent away but they found Dunning still strapped into the cockpit underwater. It was believed that he must have been knocked unconscious when the aircraft hit the water and subsequently drowned before rescuers could reach him. At 15.25 the wrecked aircraft was hoisted back onto the deck and Dunning's body removed, *Furious* then returned to Orphir Bay where she let go the starboard anchor at short stay in 19 fathoms at 16.07. At 17.00 she weighed and proceeded to anchor in the main fleet anchorage, letting go the port anchor at 17.35; the move was probably ordered to bring her into closer proximity to Grand Fleet flagships where senior officers would want to be briefed on what had happened. At 19.35 Dunning's body was taken ashore to the mortuary in the Kirkwall Hospital. In his subsequent report, Captain Nicholson wrote that 'I shall never cease to admire him. He was so keen and full of enthusiasm and such an excellent, capable fellow in every way. Both

N6452 floating with its tail out of the water but the nose dragged under by the weight of the engine. Dunning was probably knocked unconscious as the aircraft hit the water and was drowned as the cockpit sank. (Author's collection)

One of *Furious'* sea-boats, a 32ft cutter, stands by N6452 as it is hoisted out of the water by one of the ship's derricks. Dunning's body was still strapped into the cockpit at this stage. (Author's collection)

officers and men serving under him deeply feel the loss of so fine an officer and gentleman.'[21] He was only 25 when he died.

Dunning was buried in St Lawrence's churchyard near the family home at Bradfield in Essex beside the grave of his mother. Inside the church itself there is a memorial on which is inscribed:

Sacred to the memory of Squadron Commander Edwin Harris Dunning DSC RNAS of HMS *Furious*. Born on 17 July 1892, second son of Sir Edwin Harris Dunning, Knight, of Jacques Hall in this Parish. Wounded on 20 June 1916 while bombing enemy territory in a fight with enemy seaplanes and was awarded the Distinguished Service Cross for gallantry on this and other occasions. Killed 7 August 1917 and buried in Bradfield Churchyard beside his mother.

Nearby there is a copy of a letter from the Admiralty to Sir Edwin Dunning which stated that:

N6452 about to be lowered onto *Furious*' deck. It was written off charge on 20 August 1917.
(Author's collection)

The Admiralty wish you to know what great service he performed. It was in fact a demonstration of landing an aeroplane on the deck of a man-of-war whilst the latter was under way. This had never been done before and the data obtained was of the utmost value. It will make aeroplanes indispensable to the fleet and possibly revolutionise naval warfare. The risk taken by Squadron Commander Dunning needed much courage. He had already made two successful landings but expressed a wish to land again himself before other pilots did so and in this last run he was killed. My Lords desire to place on record their sense of loss to the Naval Service of this gallant officer.

At last the 'technical difficulties' had been overcome by an officer with the drive and enthusiasm to see the way forward. As a carrier pilot myself, with over 800 deck landings in my logbook, I have to say that I was deeply moved as I uncovered the details of Dunning's achievement. He deserves his place in history and it is fair to say that every carrier landing by every naval pilot in the world owes something to him.

What Happened Next
After Dunning's loss no further full-stop landings were authorised on *Furious*' deck but Flight Lieutenant F M Fox RNAS and Flight Sub Lieutenant W D Jackson

RNAS both carried out a number of experimental approaches during October. Squadron Commander F J Rutland DSC* RNAS was eventually appointed to succeed Dunning after a few weeks in which Flight Commander Moore OBE DSC RNAS had led the air group. Although respected for his skill and competence as a pilot, Rutland was not popular and the fact that he declared himself not to be in favour of the technique tried by Dunning did not help. In his view the aircraft was still at flying speed when it touched down and would be unmanageable unless some means were in place to hold it firmly onto the deck but, possibly because he could not explain his own opinion to pilots who had watched Dunning land without demonstrating that he understood what had been achieved, he tried out Dunning's landing technique for himself. He reported that he 'came in [with his wheels] about four feet above the deck and my wing tip within two feet of the conning tower. Blipping my engine, I landed only a couple of fuselage lengths from it and sat there for perhaps ten seconds with the tail up, literally flying the plane with my wheels on the deck. Then I flew off and landed ashore at Smoogroo.'[22] He added that 'with training any good pilot can land on *Furious*' flying-off deck' but estimated that 'the life of a pilot will be approximately ten flights'. This view was accepted by Captain Nicholson, who had little alternative. Rutland's opinion was somewhat negative, perhaps because the landing had not been his own idea, and it was also a great disappointment to the other Pup pilots who would all have loyally followed Dunning anywhere. In the short term he was undoubtedly wrong since he made no comparison between his approximation of ten flights culminating in deck landings and one-shot launches after which the inevitable ditching could easily lead to the loss of the pilot, probably significantly less than a one in ten chance. He was nearly lost himself after just such a ditching and a deck on which landing was demonstrably possible would surely have been a better option.

For the short term then, Rutland's advice led to *Furious* remaining a one-shot carrier but the positive outcome of Dunning's work was the acceptance by the Admiralty that wheeled aeroplanes could be landed on aircraft-carrying ships with suitably large flight decks. A more extensive modification than that applied to *Furious* had already been approved; this was the cruiser *Cavendish,* the name ship of a new class. She was originally designed with nine 7.5in guns in single mountings on a 9800-ton hull which was 605ft long and capable of 30.5 knots.[23] Her modification into an aircraft carrier entailed the suppression of five guns, only the extreme fore and aft and two beam mountings being retained. A hangar was erected forward of the bridge in place of 'B' mounting with space for six folded aircraft, over which a flying-off deck 106ft long was constructed. Abaft the two funnels a landing-on deck 193ft long by 57ft wide was constructed on a raised platform. This deck was the first to be based on the experimental work carried

HMS *Vindictive* steaming at high speed in Scapa Flow in 1918. Note the raised Yorkshire breaks and the derricks at the after part of the take-off deck and the lack of a hangar under the landing deck aft. (Author's collection)

out at the Isle of Grain and she was the first warship in the world designed both to launch and recover wheeled aircraft rather than seaplanes. In 1918 she was renamed *Vindictive* to keep the name of the ship made famous in the attack on Zeebrugge in the active fleet. There was initially some enthusiasm in the Admiralty that this design might lead to a new hybrid type of warship in which the speed and much of the gun-power of a large cruiser could be combined with the ability to operate fighters and reconnaissance aircraft in reasonable numbers. In practice, however, it soon became apparent that such a ship could excel in neither role and would not be an attractive proposition.

The Grand Fleet Aircraft Committee discussed the implications of Dunning's work at its meeting on 18 September 1917 and recommended that, as soon as possible, a landing deck should be added aft of *Furious*' funnel in place of the remaining 18in gun turret. It was to be similar to the deck already designed for *Vindictive* and was to be stressed for the recovery of Pups and 'Ship' Strutters and, since the drawings for the latter ship had already been prepared, extra design work was minimal and Admiralty approval for the work was given before the end of October. *Furious* left Rosyth for the Tyne on 14 November 1917 to have the work carried out by her original builder but enthusiasm for the scheme on board was muted. Captain Nicholson wanted to retain the big gun but was overruled by the Admiralty's Gunnery Department which stated that a single gun was of little value in a ship-to-ship action. Briefed by the majority of his pilots, he also expressed the view that light aircraft such as the Pup would be unable to land safely in the turbulence and funnel exhaust aft of the superstructure which was to remain in its original position amidships. Opinion in the Construction Department was that the superstructure was minimal and could easily be streamlined. Actual experience soon proved the captain and his pilots to be right and left the RN with concerns about the airflow over aircraft carrier flight decks that were to remain throughout the twentieth century. While the ship was back in the builder's hands, the opportunity was taken to introduce a number of detail improvements including the construction of a second hangar under the after landing deck. This was 116ft long by 33ft wide and 15ft 6in high and was to be capable of containing six folded aircraft, increasing the total number that could be embarked and struck down into the hangars to fourteen. A lift 48ft long by 18ft wide replaced the forward hatch to move aircraft between the forward hangar and the take-off deck with a similar one built into the after hangar. Both were designed by Waygood Otis and, as in all subsequent British aircraft carriers, they formed part of the flight deck when locked in the up position, leaving a well in the hangar deck. For comparison the forward lift was hydraulically powered and the after one electric. The former was found to be better in operation. Both were capable of lifting 6000lbs and moved at a rate of 40ft per minute. The derricks were retained to recover seaplanes from the water if necessary but could be un-shipped when not needed.

The lifts were found to speed up the process of ranging and striking down aircraft significantly and to facilitate movements in rough weather since there were no more concerns about aircraft hanging from a derrick being eased through a small hatch. Aircraft could be lashed to the lift platform and held firm by the handling party when moved off it. Two trackways linked the decks, each 11ft wide and 170ft long, which would have been difficult to use in rough weather. The landing deck itself was 284ft long and 70ft wide, scaled up from the *Vindictive* design and built over the after hangar. The deck itself was 26ft above the former upper deck, built as superstructure with space between the hangar roof and the underside of the flight deck that allowed air to pass under as well as over the deck. It was hoped that this would have the effect of lessening turbulence but in practice it was found to make no difference. The after hangar also opened aft onto the former quarterdeck so that seaplanes, when carried, could be moved onto and off the water from this lower level, avoiding the problem of swing that had plagued the high-sided *Campania*.

Further Work at the Isle of Grain Experimental Establishment
While work on *Furious* and *Vindictive* progressed, work had continued on the dummy deck at the Isle of Grain under its commanding officer Squadron Commander H R Busteed RNAS. The idea of using transverse wires with sandbags at their ends had been improved upon by the engineering firm of Armstrong Whitworth which retained the transverse wires but achieved deceleration by paying

out the wire from drums under the deck controlled by an electric motor. This had two advantages in that the aircraft was held steady by the tension in the wire until the hook was lifted clear when the handling party took charge of it; almost as important the wires were easily reset from a single control position rather than having to be carried back and re-set by parties of sailors. However, Busteed, like Rutland, was concerned about the instability of light aircraft in the period immediately after landing when the aircraft might flutter like a kite until the wind over the deck could be reduced. He favoured an alternative scheme in which a number of parallel fore-and-aft retaining wires were anchored and held taught at each end by strong points in wooden ramps which held the wires some inches above the deck. They covered a rectangular area forward of the ideal touchdown point and were to be engaged by hooks fixed rigidly to the spreader bar between the aircraft wheels. After landing the pilot technique was to steer the aircraft, which had no brakes, into the retaining wires where the hooks would be engaged to hold the aircraft firmly on deck. The wires were not intended to arrest the aircraft's forward movement but to hold it firmly on deck until handlers were able to move it. The wires were held up off the deck by boards which were knocked flat as the

A Sopwith Pup embedded in *Furious*' crash barrier. Note the planks used to raise the retaining wires off the deck, several of which have been knocked flat by the aircraft's forward motion as it landed. (Author's collection)

aircraft passed them. Initially, these retaining wires were referred to as the 'Busteed gear' and it was fitted to the dummy deck together with arrester wires to form a complex grid which was difficult to walk across.[24] It was found to be capable of both arresting and retaining aircraft after landing but it was extremely difficult to extricate aircraft from it and reset the wires and it acquired a number of less polite epithets as handling parties struggled to disentangle them. Torpedo-carrying aircraft could not use the retaining wires since they carried their weapons between the wheels and therefore had no spreader bar to which the retaining wire hooks could be fitted.

Busteed also came up with the idea of replacing the Pup's wheels with skids after making a number of approaches to the dummy deck. He believed that skids came 'as near to perfection for deck landings as one was likely to get' because they gave the necessary retardation and braking effect coupled with good lateral stability that helped the pilot to steer into the parallel retaining wires. More to the point Busteed observed that they were more likely to engage freely with longitudinal wires than conventional wheels. Skids were not sprung or fitted with any form of shock

A skid-fitted Sopwith Pup drops its left wing in turbulence as it enters the retaining wires trying to land on *Furious*. Wisely the cameraman stood behind the barrier and several of its vertical rope strands are visible in the foreground. (Author's collection)

absorber initially and tended to break if they hit the deck hard. Despite Busteed's enthusiasm they were not a success although it was found in ditching trials that they offered less water resistance than wheels and thus gave the aircraft less of a tendency to pitch nose-down. Apart from a tendency to collapse on hitting the deck, skid undercarriages were found to have inadequate directional stability on take-off and they did not prove popular with pilots. On Busteed's recommendation the Admiralty decided to fit *Furious*' landing deck with both fore-and-aft retaining wires and athwartship Armstrong Whitworth arresting wires while she underwent modification. As a last-ditch safety measure she was also fitted with a rope barrier strung across the forward end of the landing deck in a structure like football goalposts to prevent aircraft that failed to stop from crashing into the funnel.

While *Furious* was back in shipyard hands, Flight Commander Moore spent some time at the Isle of Grain experimental establishment and took part in several trials. These included launches out of wind by a 'Ship' Strutter fitted with skids and ditching experiments intended to improve the chances of aircrew that came down in the water; Dunning's death was a catalyst that led to a number of ideas that were intended to keep ditched aircraft afloat on an even keel after hitting the water so that the pilot and observer stood the best chance of getting out. The crosswind take-off experiment involved fitting vertical planks onto the take-off deck of *Vindex* so that the aircraft's skids were held firmly into what was effectively a slotted groove along the deck which prevented it from being blown sideways by an off-centre wind over the deck. At the end of the groove it would yaw sharply into wind but the concept meant that the ship would not have to turn into wind, possibly away from other ships in the task force. Moore took off from *Vindex* to test the concept 'with a nice breeze blowing bang across' the deck in the Thames Estuary.[25] All went well 'although it felt pretty awful and unnatural', so it could be fairly said that the idea worked. However, it was soon appreciated that the slotted groove would have to accommodate every dimension of skid and this was impractical for the variety of aircraft that were already operated from carriers and the idea was quietly dropped.

One of Busteed's ideas was an improved approach to ditching and flotation gear. These included a hydroplane between the wheels of aircraft such as the Pup to prevent them from nosing over when they hit the water. Another, rather better, idea was a set of airbags along each side of the forward fuselage inflated when the aircraft hit the water by compressed-air cylinders. When inflated, these kept the aircraft level on the surface which was a positive advantage. Their only disadvantage was the extra weight they added to the airframe and the consequent slight loss of performance. What was becoming apparent in the trials at Grain was that naval aircraft were evolving along their own path of development. It was no longer good enough to put an aircraft that did well ashore onto a ship and hope that it would work; it had to be designed from the outset to work from an aircraft carrier if it was to do well.

The Modified *Furious*

Furious re-commissioned with her landing deck on 15 March 1918 and began flying trials 10 days later.[26] The first four attempts to land-on showed immediately that there was a problem and that Captain Nicholson and his pilots had been right to anticipate problems with turbulence over the deck. The 'Busteed' retaining gear proved ineffective because of the complicated air flow astern of the bridge and funnel. Several Pups were wrecked as they 'dropped on to the deck like shot partridges' when they stalled in the fluctuating air flow and another went into the barrier at 30 knots in spite of a relative wind measured on the bridge at 30 knots from right ahead. During the fourth attempted landing the wind over the deck appeared to be blowing from dead astern despite the ship steaming at 22 knots into a 10-knot wind from ahead. Turbulence just astern of the deck was so bad that the pilot was lucky to maintain control of his aircraft long enough to overshoot to port. On the other hand, the turbulence caused by funnel gases appeared to flow 20 to 30ft above the deck but was more predictable. The most serious turbulence was found to be over the protruding quarterdeck, caused by the interplay between the two air streams along the sides of the hull and the blunt after end of the landing deck. The disturbed air extended 30ft either side of the hull and for about 300ft

HMS *Furious* in 1918 after she was modified with a landing deck aft. The rope barrier fitted at the forward end of the deck to protect the funnel can be seen clearly, as can the disruptive pattern paint scheme adopted at this time. (Author's collection)

astern of it. Before trials were resumed on 27 March, an attempt was made to reduce it by stretching canvas between the after lip of the flight deck and the stern but this had no discernible effect. In discussion after the first landing attempts, pilots decided that they had failed because they had approached just above stalling speed and had then found the aircraft to be barely controllable as they encountered the turbulent air just aft of the deck.

Turbulence had actually been predicted by wind-tunnel tests with ship models in 1916 but its severity in the real world came as a surprise. It may be that those who ran these tests were not made aware of the actual flight paths that pilots would follow and thus failed to appreciate the impact airflow would have on their landing approach. Rutland made two unsuccessful landing attempts before finally landing-on in a manner that could still hardly be called successful. With the ship steaming at 28 knots and virtually no natural wind he crossed the after end of the deck just above stalling speed, just above deck level. The aircraft began to wallow in severe turbulence which he later admitted to underestimating and he thumped into the deck breaking the skid undercarriage. In one of his failed landings he tried approaching the deck in a nose-high attitude with a high rate of descent from the starboard side, hoping to avoid the turbulence at the after end of the deck and pass through the funnel smoke with minimal forward travel. Relative to the deck, therefore, the aircraft had a considerable rate of descent and significant crossing momentum from starboard to port. The aircraft bounced on impacting the deck, broke the skids and continued to port without engaging the retaining wires and came to rest with one wing over the side. On a split-second impulse, Rutland jumped clear and fell 50ft into the water. The aircraft remained caught on a torpedo tube two decks below the flight deck and hung there. Rutland kept himself afloat with the aid of a cushion and was rescued by a sea-boat after 20 minutes in the water.

Variations were tried and some landings met with success. Transverse arrester wires were rigged across the retaining wires; the complicated result was time-consuming to rig but it did allow faster, better-controlled landings with a hook down. Two Pups landed safely using this technique on 19 April 1918, watched by the First Lord and senior officers. In both cases the ship was steaming at low speed, lessening the problem of funnel smoke and reducing the wind over the deck to between 21 and 26 knots. One successful landing was carried out with only 10 knots of wind over the deck and almost no turbulence. The aircraft was then manhandled to the forward deck, took off and landed successfully for the second time in succession. *Furious*' officers made a number of suggestions about how to improve the system of retaining and arrester wires[27] but by then the flush-decked *Argus* was nearing completion and none was felt worthy of implementation in *Furious*. Neither the 'Busteed' gear nor the arrester wires were popular; the latter often

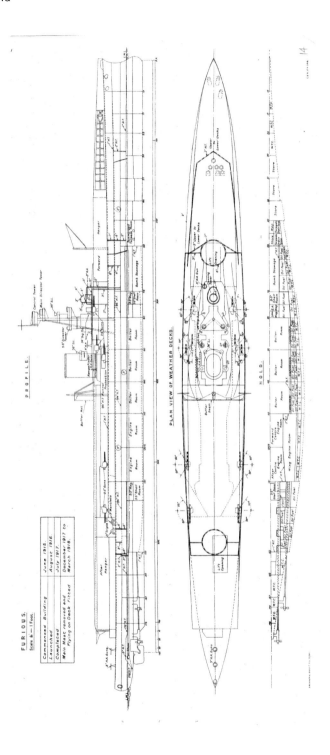

HMS *Furious*. (Author's collection)

became caught up in the former and the resulting tangled mess often took some minutes to unravel and reset. Interestingly, one of the Pup pilots, Squadron Commander Gallehawk RNAS, continued his landing approach despite being given a negative signal by the ship which was still turning into wind and encountered no turbulence at all. He was stopped successfully in 65ft by the combined efforts of the two types of wire. By then, however, the consensus opinion among the pilots was that attempting to land on the after deck was more dangerous than the experimental landings on the take-off deck forward had been. Squadron Commander Busteed tried to land-on in a Pup with the appropriate name of 'Excuse Me' painted on the fuselage while the ship was at anchor; he hit the rope barrier hard and was lucky to get away with only cuts and bruises. The landing trials were abandoned and no further attempt was made to use *Furious* as a true carrier but she did continue to operate as a one-shot ship, however, and was able to carry a usefully large air group. *Furious* formed an important link between the earlier seaplane-carrying conversions and the first true aircraft carrier *Argus*. Her various landing trials had highlighted, through practical experience, the underestimation of the effect of turbulence on aircraft on the final approach to the deck and their failure led directly to the re-design of the superstructure intended for *Argus, Hermes* and *Eagle*. From 1918 aircraft carrier models were studied in the wind tunnel at the National Physical Laboratory with greater realism and areas that needed to be addressed recognised. The abrupt, flat lip at the after end of *Furious*' landing deck was found to generate much of the turbulence and by rounding the after end of the flight deck and narrowing the deck sides, it was eventually eliminated although these cures were found to bring their own problems.

Vindictive was not completed until three days after *Argus* in September 1918 and by then the problems of trying to land lightweight fighters onto a ship with centreline superstructure were well understood. She joined the Grand Fleet's Flying Squadron but saw no active service before the end of the war. Interestingly, however, a single Pup was flown onto her deck by W W Wakefield on 1 November 1918. Apparently the pilot encountered no turbulence and the landing was completely successful.[28]

12 Training and Experience

When war broke out in 1914 the RNAS had 130 officers on its books, roughly 100 of whom had qualified as pilots since 1911, and about 700 senior and junior ratings, the majority of whom were technicians who had undergone 'cross-over' training to modify their skills as mechanics and carpenters and enable them to erect, repair and maintain aircraft. The air service had expanded rapidly and the number of pre-war regulars was diluted by direct-entry officers and men with no previous naval experience. By 1918 the RNAS had grown to 55,000 men and, given the number of casualties that had been suffered during four years of war, a number significantly greater than that had been trained.[1] Out of the latter total, only 397 officers, 217 ratings and 604 boys, a total of 1018 men, were permanent members of the RN but many of the experienced and skilful people who had served on a temporary basis during the war may well have wished to remain in the peacetime service after the end of hostilities. By any standard, the enormous expansion of the RNAS in such a short time whilst steadily improving both standards and capability was a remarkable achievement

Training Pilots

At first candidates were required to demonstrate their piloting skill by paying for a course of instruction at a civilian flying school. Bell-Davies was a typical example; he had been 'tremendously impressed'[2] while serving in the battleship *Dominion* during 1910 when he saw Grahame-White fly over the fleet at Sheerness. He promptly joined the Royal Aero Club to find out more about aviation and obtain his own copies of *Flight* magazine[3] but, since his ship was short of officers, he felt it unlikely that he could be selected early for flying training at Eastchurch. However, in the pages of *Flight* he saw an advertisement for Grahame-White's flying school at Hendon and decided that his best chance of learning to fly would be to apply for a course during his Easter leave. Prior to that he called on Grahame-White in his office in Clifford Street and told him what he wanted. 'He was very business-like, telling me that it would cost me £50 with a further £25 deposit against damage, which he would return if I did not smash anything, and that there would be no

Flight Sub Lieutenant Riggall RNAS photographed at the controls of a Grahame-White School Bristol Box-Kite. His left hand is on the engine ignition switch, his right is on the control column. The cable running from the column connects the 'blip' switch to the ignition system. Note how the pilot was completely exposed to the elements in a tiny seat with only a lap-strap to hold him in place. (Author's collection)

charge for petrol. Fearing that most of the male population of the country would be wanting to learn to fly that spring, I closed with the offer and insisted on paying cash there and then to make sure of a place in the class though Grahame-White assured me it was unnecessary.' Bell-Davies added the comment that 'flying was regarded as such a lunatic occupation in 1911 that I kept quiet about it. On my first day off after the *Dominion* returned to Sheerness I travelled to Hendon where Grahame-White employed one pilot and two mechanics. The pilot, who acted as instructor, was Clement Greswell and his job cannot have been easy. He was expected to instruct pupils as well as take up joy-riders at a guinea a time. Of course he could not do both at once. The engine mechanic was Carr and the rigger Bill Hoare. There were two aeroplanes, both original Farman box-kites.'

Flying, early in 1911, could only take place in a flat calm. The weather through-out that spring was generally bright and sunny but a fresh wind usually started in the late forenoon and continued until not long before sunset. There was, therefore, a great deal of standing around waiting for the wind to drop. Bell-Davies explained that 'during the first morning I kept the machine on the ground, running it up and down the aerodrome, but by the second day I felt confident I could get it into the air . . . I experimented and lifted her about 10ft off the ground. Nobody had told me anything about landing but I concluded that if I cut the engine the machine was bound to return to earth. It worked well and from about 10ft the resulting "Pancake" was comparatively gentle.' An American pilot named Martin, who was teaching his English wife to fly, suggested that a better technique was to land firmly with the engine at full power and Bell-Davies adopted this method. He went on carrying out longer and higher hops and was convinced that he could pass the test for his Royal Aero Club certificate. This involved flying two groups of five figures-of-eight, landing within 50 yards of a given spot and reaching a height of 300ft. He had 'got as far as making circuits of the aerodrome with assurance but had not yet experimented with a right-hand turn. The pusher box-kite with the rotary Gnome engine tended to turn to the left owing to torque so a right-hand turn was considered more difficult.' Before he could try the weather deteriorated and limited the time he had available. He eventually found Grahame-White and told him that 'if I could not have an aeroplane now to try for my certificate it would mean a postponement until August. He gave me the use of his exhibition machine. This was the newer of the two Farmans which he kept for his own use and no pupil had been allowed to fly it before.' That afternoon was spent practising right-hand turns while Grahame-White arranged for the necessary observers to watch and certify the test the next morning. One was Barber who had designed the Valkyrie monoplane; the other was a pilot named Ridley-Prentice. 'I made an early start, put in some more practice before they arrived and then passed the test without difficulty. Rather surprisingly they made no comment on my method of landing. My certificate was British Empire Number 90.' Having achieved this qualification, he returned to his naval duties in *Dominion*.

Bell-Davies was eventually appointed to the Naval Wing of the RFC and arrived at the Eastchurch naval flying school in February 1913.[4] Commander Samson was in command with Lieutenant Gregory as First Lieutenant and other officers included Major Gordon RMLI, who was senior instructor, and Lieutenants Wildman-Lushington and Courtney RMLI, Lieutenant Sheppard RN, Sub Lieutenant J L Travers RNVR and Byrne the paymaster. The surgeon was Hardy-Wells and E F Briggs was engineer officer as well as being a pilot. Bell-Davies was 'tacked on to them'. His first flight at Eastchurch was in Naval Aeroplane number 1, one of the original machines lent by McClean to the Admiralty and subsequently purchased. 'The Admiralty was in the habit of buying aeroplanes of nearly every type produced in the early days. No doubt it was sound policy at a time when ideas as to how aircraft were to be used in naval war were entirely nebulous.' Bell-Davies found that the two years that had passed since the award of his 'ticket' had not made much difference. In 1913 'the qualification for the grade of Flying Officer

RFC was not strictly laid down. It depended on the recommendation of the commanding officer, but it normally involved 100 hours as pilot and making at least two cross-country flights satisfactorily. It was the second half of April by the time I had qualified and was graded Flying Officer.'

Direct entries were still expected to have undergone experience that demonstrated an aptitude for flying but not necessarily to have obtained a pilot's certificate. Harold Rosher had suffered from acute asthma and bronchitis at school and an open-air life was considered essential for him, so he became a student at the South Eastern Agricultural College at Wye. One the day war was declared he volunteered for a commission in the RNAS.[5] In order to save time he went immediately as a civilian pupil to Brooklands where, several months previously, he had once been taken up in the air as a passenger. In the few days which elapsed before the War Office commandeered the Brooklands aerodrome and ejected every civilian, Harold progressed rapidly in the craft of flying. He was gazetted a Probationary Flight Sub Lieutenant in the RNAS on 18 August and reported himself at Hendon. He remained there about six weeks, obtaining his pilot's certificate. Rosher wrote to his father from the 'The Blue Bird', Brooklands on 11 August saying that the Bristol & Colonial Aeroplane Company's instructor, Mr Stutt, 'sits immediately behind you [in the school box-kite], controls the engine switch and covers your hand on the stick. He took me straight up two or three hundred feet and then volplaned down. He always does this with new pupils to see how they take it. I think I managed to pass the ordeal all right.' Later in the same letter he described having 'two more lessons this morning, of about 15 minutes each, and took both right and left-hand turns, part of the time steering by myself'. Ominously, however, he described an accident involving another student. 'One of the Blériot people was taxiing in a machine without wings. He got too much speed on and the machine went head over heels and was utterly wrecked – man unhurt. With the Blériot machine you first have to learn to steer on the ground as it is much harder than ours.' On 11 September he wrote to his father again to say that 'yesterday I did five straight flights alone and managed quite well, having excellent control of the machine, and making good landings except for the first straights in the morning when it was rather windy and in consequence the machine was all over the place'. Candidly he also described an accident that he thought might have been reported in the papers. 'Lieutenant G— went up in the Henri Farman and on coming down made a bad landing – internal injuries – machine absolutely piled up.' The accident was expected to have rather a bad effect on the morale of the pupils but, he told his father, 'personally it doesn't affect me and anyhow I didn't see G— at all'. Early in October he was appointed from Hendon to the new RN air station at Fort Grange, Gosport. Although qualified as a pilot he was not yet graded as a 'flying officer' when he carried out his first cross-country flight. During it he suffered three engine failures and had to make three forced landings from heights of about 4000ft, all of which he managed to carry out without damaging the aeroplane. The engine was subsequently found to be faulty and Rosher commented on his new commanding officer's pleasure that he had made such a good beginning to his flying career.

It must be remembered that the Royal Navy in 1914 was an imperial force that spanned the globe. The Royal Australian Navy had only taken over the tasks formerly carried out by the RN's Australia Station in 1913; there was a New Zealand Division of the RN rather than a Royal New Zealand Navy and the defence of Canada was still largely vested in the North America Station of the RN despite the existence of a small Royal Canadian Navy. It was hardly surprising, therefore, that many young men from Australia, Canada and New Zealand sought to join the RN and its embryonic air service on the outbreak of war. One of the Canadian volunteers was Raymond Collishaw who went on to become the RNAS' top scoring fighter pilot with sixty confirmed aerial victories to his credit, the highest-scoring Canadian fighter pilot of all time. In *Air Command* he described how he was a Merchant Navy officer in 1914 and 'applied for a more active sort of sea duty but nothing came of it. Then early in 1915 I heard that the RNAS was recruiting pilots in Canada.'[6] On learning this he decided that he would 'have a try'

Squadron Commander R Collishaw DSO DSC RNAS photographed in the cockpit of a Sopwith F.1 Camel. Note how close the gun breeches are to his face so that he can easily reach the cocking levers in flight. The tubular object visible above the guns is the Aldis sight. (Author's collection)

and as soon as his shipboard duties allowed he put in an application. Some months later he was asked to appear for an interview with the SNO at Esquimalt in British Columbia, on successful completion of which he appeared before a final interview with Admiral Charles Kingsmill, the head of the Canadian naval service. Kingsmill told Collishaw that reports on his previous service were good, his interview had been satisfactory and that he had been accepted as a Temporary Probationary Flight Sub Lieutenant RNAS. 'There was, though, one hurdle to clear before I could actually be sworn in and appointed to a commission. Entirely at my own expense I had to seek out a suitable private flying school, make arrangements for admission, pay the tuition fee and qualify for a pilot certificate as issued under the regulations of Federation Aeronautique Internationale.' This proviso was not peculiar to his own case; all those accepted in Canada at this time by the RNAS or RFC had to hold certificates and had to pay their own tuition fees. Technically, at this stage, he was an RNAS Candidate. He went on to point out that all Canadians who flew against the enemy in the First World War did so as members of the British air services but at the end of 1915 there was only one proper flying school in Canada, the Curtiss Aviation School in Toronto. Collishaw was concerned that with a lot of candidates in the queue ahead of him it might be a long time before he achieved his qualification.

The situation improved after Captain W L Elder RN was sent out by the Admiralty to expedite matters and also with the manufacture of Curtiss aeroplanes in Canada to expand the size of the school and pass more RNAS recruits through it. They still had to pay $400 but they received 400 minutes of instruction on Curtiss F-type flying boats and wheeled JN-3s. Collishaw described it as 'about as good a school as could be found anywhere on this side of the water and in the two years that it operated no-one was killed or seriously hurt. Most of the instructors came up from the United States and they were very good.' Many of Canada's most famous pilots received their initial training in the school which operated in the flying seasons of 1915 and 1916, among them Bob Leckie and Wilf Curtis. In retrospect, Collishaw commented in *Air Command* that he had never been able to understand the tremendous importance that both the RFC and RNAS placed on the prior possession of a pilot's certificate. At the time he was accepted as an RNAS Candidate fairly substantial numbers of young men from the Canadian Expeditionary Force overseas were beginning to go into the flying services, particularly the RFC, and in their cases they were either rejected or accepted and, if the latter, they were fed into the normal training scheme 'without any nonsense about having to go off and arrange for instruction on their own at private schools'. He believed that it 'had little value as a means of screening out potentially good pilots from the duds' and he never heard of anyone being 'washed out' from the Toronto

Curtiss School except for those who just ended up dead broke and had to drop out. 'Pretty well everyone who started at one of the private schools ended up getting his certificate . . . if his money and the school held out long enough.' Both the RNAS and the RFC dropped the requirement for a certificate during the latter half of 1916 for recruits from Canada. Collishaw and many others were surprised that it took so long to do so.

Once he arrived in the UK, Collishaw was appointed to Redcar for his formal flying training in February 1916. His first flights were in Caudron G3s, two-seater tractor biplanes which depended on wing-warping rather than ailerons to make a banked turn. Training was plagued by bad weather at first and then by engines that shed their exhaust valves with great regularity with the result that he did not fly solo until June. He had not flown at all between 12 February and 21 April and those who did had suffered a number of engine failures that led to forced landings. His confidence improved after going solo which was just as well because 'on one occasion . . . I was flying an Avro 504c and was at 5,600ft when I tried to switch off the engine but found that neither the on/off switch nor the "blipping" switch had any effect. Finally I turned off the petrol switch and glided down to the aerodrome. The trouble was reported and repairs were made. The next day I took the same machine up and was only 150ft off the ground when the engine cut out completely. I was able to land in a field bearing a crop of oats and was just rolling to a stop when the wretched engine took it into its head to start again full out. The off switch had no effect and before I knew it I had run into a steep bank bordering the field, smashing the undercarriage. The engine then dutifully stopped.' He went on to explain that 'at this time the RNAS had an odd idea that pilots under training would benefit greatly from being given the opportunity to fly a number of machines of widely differing types and characteristics. In theory, perhaps, the idea was a good one but in practice it meant that just as you were learning how to handle a particular type properly you were yanked off it and given a completely different sort of machine to take up. The result was that most of us finished our training at Redcar as rather mediocre masters of a number of different sorts of aircraft without ever having had the chance to learn what we should have done about any of them. While I was at Redcar I flew the Caudron, Avro 504c, Grahame-White Type XV and the Curtiss JN-4. At Eastchurch where I went after finishing at Redcar, I flew seven additional types including the Curtiss JN-3 and the Maurice Farman Shorthorn. However most of us survived the training period so perhaps the system had some merit to it.'[7] On the subject of accommodation he explained that 'Redcar at that time was a small station and there were no quarters and no mess available on the aerodrome for officers under instruction. We had to arrange for our own accommodation in the village, about half a mile away from the field and we had our meals there, too. This meant walking the route four times a day and we logged a much larger amount of time on Shank's ponies than we did in the air.' Collishaw remained at Redcar until July 1916 and then moved to the Gunnery School at Eastchurch by which time he had logged 33 hours in the air, 20 of which were solo. Most of the flying from then on comprised what would now be called operational flying training and involved aerial gunnery and bomb-dropping practice in JN-3s and Shorthorns. One of his instructors was Flight Sub Lieutenant John Alcock RNAS who he described as being 'an exceedingly competent pilot'. On the successful completion of this course Collishaw was confirmed in the rank of Flight Sub Lieutenant and in August 1916 he joined 3 Wing at Manston.

Australian R A Little, known to his family in Melbourne as Alec, had a slightly different experience before gaining a commission in the RNAS. His younger brother had simply gone to the nearest recruiting depot and joined the Australian Army but Alec was determined to become a pilot. The chances of joining the diminutive Australian Flying Corps were not good so he determined to travel to the UK, obtain a pilot's certificate and join the RNAS. His father is said to have advanced him the money for both[8] and he joined the P&O steamer *Malwa* at Melbourne on 27 July 1915. Once in the UK he made his way to Hendon where he could choose between five different civilian flying schools to get his licence. He selected the London & Provincial School where he met Leonard 'Titch' Rochford who was also keen to get his 'ticket' as a means of gaining entry into the RNAS. In his own memoirs, Rochford explained that London & Provincial's fees were higher at £100 rather than the other schools' £75 but it was 'the only one that did not use dual control, its method being to put the pupil into the machine alone and get him into the air by stages, giving him verbal instructions on the ground at each stage. Experience had shown that that this system was just as successful as the dual control one; pupils learned just as quickly and the likelihood of a crash was no greater.'[9] He was also sure that it inspired more confidence in the pupil and this was probably a view that Alec Little shared. Both Little and Rochford stayed in a guest house named Hatherley run by Mr and Mrs Michael; Rochford stayed in touch with the Michaels after the war and their daughter Isabel eventually left him the establishment's guest book signed by every student pilot that stayed there. It became one of his most treasured possessions. At the end of the course Little took the same Royal Aero Club test as his contemporaries, passed and was awarded British Empire certificate number 1958 on 27 October 1915. Rochford had obtained certificate number 1840.

On 14 January 1916, aged 20, Little was commissioned as a Temporary Probationary Flight Sub Lieutenant RNAS and appointed to the Eastchurch naval flying school. Fortunately his logbooks and notebooks survived and were valued by his family after his death. In an undated notebook he wrote about engines and sketched carburettors besides describing lectures on the theory of flight. It also contained the addresses of a number of Australians and Canadians and, of all things, a six-page summary of the first book of Samuel from the Old Testament, his only known reference to religion. His flying logbook records his first flight in a naval aircraft on 23 January 1916, a Caudron trainer, with an instructor. Later in the same day he flew the aircraft solo. On 1 February while flying a Maurice Farman Shorthorn he noted 'switch got caught in sleeve and engine stopped, made a good landing in a field, got a soldier to start my prop and got away all right'. On another flight later that day the engine stopped without any known cause and he side-slipped on turning towards the airfield in a glide and had to land in a field. His own comment was 'made good landing, there was no wind when I left and on

Flight Commander
R A Little DSO DSC RNAS.
(Author's collection)

coming down there was a wind blowing 25mph; this no doubt put me out in my judgement'. He instructor's verdict written underneath, 'Bad judgement', was blunter. One of several further forced landings took place on 19 February when a gudgeon pin broke and a connecting rod 'smashed cylinder walls and crank case'. He made a good landing just outside the airfield. Although these incidents were largely not his fault, his commanding officer noted on 6 March 1916 that 'As a pilot he is variable, usually flying well and plucky, but occasionally is very erratic. Has a trick of landing outside the aerodrome. Has done about 19 hours . . . as an officer is not very good. Generally fairly satisfactory; not good at theoretical work. Recommended for seaplanes.'[10] He was appointed to Felixstowe a day later and was taught to fly the Curtiss Large America; his first patrol as second pilot of an America followed on 21 March 1916. This was a 3 hour 10 minute patrol to the Kentish Knock off the Kent and Essex coast. On 7 April he flew an America solo and noted in his logbook that he 'got along alright'. Reputedly, however, he made it clear to everyone who would listen that he had no great enthusiasm for flying boats. His bad luck continued, for on 9 April he was on patrol in an America when the port engine began to misfire. He saw some trawlers and landed alongside them but 'on landing the starboard engine moved in its bed and the prop hit the side of the boat and broke, hitting the port engine and then going through the top plane'. He fired a red Verey flare to indicate distress and a trawler took the aircraft in tow. Soon a motor launch came up and towed the aircraft to isle of Grain from where the crew returned to Felixstowe by train.

Little's next mishap was medical; he caught measles and spent 10 days in RNH Shotley. While he was there his commanding officer wrote of him that 'as an officer he is quite hopeless and likely to remain so. As a pilot he displays considerable courage and keenness, although somewhat lacking in skill. Apparently he would prefer to fly land machines. I think he could be made use of as an aeroplane pilot at Dunkirk or some other front. I do not think it would be of any advantage to this station for him to remain here.' The view of the Naval Secretary's Department in the Admiralty was expressed in a letter on 5 May 1916 which stated that 'this officer has been reported on unfavourably and he must be informed that if a further adverse report is received, his commission will be terminated'. His new commanding officer was to report on his progress and ability by 8 June 1916. On 9 May Little was appointed to the naval air station at Dover where he was to fly land-based fighters on Channel reconnaissance and intercept German bombers. Not only did he take immediately to flying fighters, he got the message and a further confidential report stated that he 'has conducted himself satisfactorily. Has an amount of pluck and is extremely hardworking. As soon as he learns to be less irresponsible and, when flying, to use his head to better advantage, I shall feel confident that he will do exceptionally well on active service.' He did. On 30 June he was appointed to 1 Wing operating from Dunkirk with 119 hours and 20 minutes flying time in his logbook. He was to earn fame as a fighter pilot with forty-seven aerial victories to his credit and was awarded the DSO and bar, DSC and bar and the French Croix de Guerre. He was not a brilliant pilot as such but he was an outstanding marksman and utterly fearless in taking the fight to the enemy.

In 1916 it was finally accepted that the award of a pilot's certificate at a civilian school was no longer of any great value and both the Admiralty and the War Office looked for alternatives. The Crystal Palace at Sydenham in South London had been taken over by the RN in early September 1914 and commissioned as HMS *Victory VI* to act as the depot for the RND. It also became the initial training establishment for all RNVR personnel. RNAS technical ratings were trained there and, from 1 April 1916, all newly-entered RNAS officers were sent to Crystal Palace for basic disciplinary and technical training after which they were sent directly to their flying training establishments. Caudron 8947 was used as an instructional airframe for some time and over 125,000 men passed through Crystal Palace between 1914 and 1918. Jack McCleery from Belfast in Northern Ireland volunteered for the RNAS when he was 18 and arrived at the Admiralty for an interview on 18 October 1916.[11] He had heard others describe the interview as consisting of random questions about the candidate's ability to ride a horse, sail a boat or ride a motorbike but he must have done well as he was instructed to attend a medical which he passed. He was informed that he was now a Probationary Flight Officer and was to stand by to be called up for training. When this happened he would 'go to Crystal Palace for a month or two and then on to an aerodrome and later possibly Windermere' where flying training on seaplanes had been carried out by the RNAS since 1915. He had been the only candidate to get through the medical test which had involved climbing a rope naked, hopping around a room on one foot and a colour-blindness test sorting various beads.

After arriving McCleery wrote home on 12 November 1916 to say 'here I am at Crystal Palace. There seems to be no end to it so far! I sleep in a house called Ashurst in a room with three other chaps. I paid 5 shillings for servants' wages in the house. I am writing this at the club which is situated in the CP itself and is very nice and comfy. I think the distance record for not having to salute must be 4.5ft here! We were told that we would be here for 5 weeks and then be sent to our air station, presumably to learn to fly.' Two days later he wrote that 'life is very strenuous here if one really wants to get on, there is little time for letters . . . we get our first drill at 07.30 and its work from that until 19.30' when they had dinner. He did not tell his parents but found out at about this time that his roommate had served in France from 1914 but had been invalided out of the Army with 'shell-

shock and broken nerves'. Hopefully he had fully recovered if he was now about
to be taught to fly. Further letters contained more details such as 'have been drilling
a squad, learning musketry and revolvers and later the Lewis Gun. At present it is
nearly all military drill except for a class in seamanship – tying knots. Also Swedish
physical drill.' Food was good and on 19 November he told his mother that
'breakfast . . . consists of good porridge, toast and bacon or fish (or both) and then
tea or coffee, that's all right!! Lunch is . . . soup, meat or pie or fish, potatoes,
vegetables and usually stewed fruit or tart after. Cheese and if one wishes coffee can
be got at the club (you can get stronger things too). Tea is at 16.45, bread butter,
tea or coffee, jam, marmalade or honey. Dinner is . . . entree (all sorts of weird
things), soup, meat of some sort, good rolls, potatoes and vegetables and tea or
coffee and the King's health in water.'[12] He also described technical subjects in
some detail, 'we did revolver shooting last week – a huge, long Mark VI Webley. I
did all right and pretty well in the miniature rifle shooting. I passed my test in the
Lewis Gun all OK and was being instructed in the Webley Scott automatic pistol
yesterday. You can strip them in under 6 seconds! I did it in 12 which was the best
of our squad. We are having lectures on aero engines and theory of flight in the
evenings. It is very interesting but there are a lot of notes!'

Towards the end of his time at Crystal Palace, McCleery thought that he might
be sent to the new RNAS training depot at Vendôme to the west of Orleans in
France. It had been set up because of the bad weather in the UK during the winter
of 1915/16 which had severely curtailed flying training and Vendôme had been
chosen with French help because it could reasonably expect better weather. It was
commanded by Wing Commander H D Briggs RNAS and by the beginning of
1917 had fifty training aircraft on strength, the majority of them Caudrons with
some Curtiss JN 4s and even a small number of Maurice Farman Longhorns, most
of which were held in reserve. In the event, however, McCleery went to Eastchurch
in December 1916. It was 'home' to various new squadrons as they formed, and
also comprised the RN flying school, the air gunnery school, the observers' school,
a test flight, a spotting flight and a war flight. It was commanded by Wing
Commander A Longmore who noted that 'it had grown considerably since I had
last seen it and the aerodrome had been extended to the north-east with new
hangars. Total strength was 90 officers and 900 men.' It also had over 100 aircraft,
not all of which were serviceable at any one time. They included BE 2Cs, Bristol
Scouts, JN4s, Short bombers and the ever-faithful Maurice Farman Longhorns.
As usual, McCleery was quick to tell his parents about his new surroundings. 'If
the weather is good we have to fly on Sundays as this is a war station. It's about the
biggest aerodrome in the country, miles from anywhere decent. This place is a sea
of mud literally. No drinking water as the huts are new and it's not all laid out yet.

Caudron G-IIIs lined up at RNAS Vendôme ready for the day's instructional sorties to begin. (Philip Jarrett Collection).

So I drink lime juice and soda and most of the others, things more manly.' He also warned them that 'you will probably get a note from Gieves, [naval] tailors, saying I have opened an account, the reason is that we were advised to when we left CP as this place is so far away . . . I bought a . . . helmet (black and fur-lined) for 37 shillings; goggles (triplex unbreakable glass, fur-lined) for 16 shillings and sixpence; gloves (tanned leather gauntlets, rabbit fur inside) for 18 shillings and sixpence and [signed for a further] 9 shillings and sixpence as I was short of cash.' It is interesting to note that even at this stage of the war, officers were still expected to buy their own flying clothing from naval tailors. A Gieves advertisement in the 1918 edition of the *Aviation Pocket Book* describes the firm as being 'Royal Naval Outfitters and specialists in flying kit to the RNAS' and as 'inventors and patentees of the Gieve life-saving waistcoat'.[13] It had branches in London, Edinburgh, Paris and at all principal naval ports in the UK. Despite everything Gieves had to offer, McCleery still asked his mother for a few things which he described in some detail;

I would like a good thick cardigan and a blue knitted muffler, both worn for flying. Any mittens will be very useful. On account of the mud I would also like a pair of plain black rubber (leather heeled) knee boots. These are what is usually called gum boots but not thigh boots . . . if you're sending a parcel, would you mind putting in some Oxo or Bovril cubes as we are going to cook in our room in the mornings before early parade? I'm afraid this letter is nothing but please send me etc so far [but] I'd like two pieces of Pears soap and two one shilling tubes of toothpaste! We were told today to get flying kit that we hadn't got yet – boots and coat – so if father would send me £11.11.0, I would buy them here. The boots are black knee boots lined with fur and the coat is black chrome leather with fleece lining. I will have to get them sometime and they last for nearly ever, I might as well get them now.

Although he wrote with the optimism of youth, one can imagine his parents willingly sending him the money if they thought that the garments might really spend a long time in his possession.

When he started flying McCleery could hardly contain his excitement, writing to a friend that 'I managed to get my belt fastened around me. The engine was warmed up – they tick over very nicely with pilot jets, then accelerated and with a roar we bounded forwards.' But 'there was a yell and one of the mechanics pointed to something at the engine. Some stud was gone, so we had to get out and I didn't go . . . I was the only one in our lot not to go up.'[14] A day later, however, he had better news for his parents:

I've some great news to tell you and you can easily guess what it is. Yes I've been up! Absolutely grand, ripping, gorgeous etc. I was up for about 10 minutes this morning in a Maurice Farman Longhorn and up to about 1,200ft. I could have yelled for joy. First of all you are strapped in, then you hare along the ground at about 50 and then almost without any warning you find you're up in the air. People and sheds get smaller and smaller as you go up and you gradually lose all sense of speed as you rise till you nearly crawl, even though you're doing 55 to 70mph. Then she turns and you feel the wind. Banking is great fun; you look almost sheer over the side, right down clear to the ground. You see roads and trees . . . as you come down the pace seems to get quicker as you near the ground. You don't feel her land at all if well done – I didn't and then we taxied back. It's simply fine. I'll dream about it tonight!

As the course continued he too flew different types of aircraft. On 8 February 1917 he flew a Curtiss JN-4 'up to about 5,000ft (some view) then spiralled down. Stayed up 80 minutes and had a ripping time. Drifted several miles coming down. When I landed, instructor said you seem to know all about them now so I'll put you on Avros.' On 16 February he was told that he was moving to the new RNAS central training establishment at Cranwell.

Being based on a ship at Scapa Flow could be a fascinating and enjoyable experience. Two pilots are seen here having a picnic on the shore. (Guy Warner collection)

The Admiralty had established a number of training airfields at which pilots and more recently observers were taught to fly aeroplanes, seaplanes, airships and kite balloons. Several had developed their own variations and there was no standardised curriculum, so the Admiralty decided to set up a central training establishment to develop common curricula and raise the level of tuition across a number of disciplines to the highest standard. There is an apocryphal story that the site at Cranwell was chosen because, like Eastchurch, it was a long way from centres of population and thus there would be few distractions for the students undergoing training. Another, probably equally apocryphal, story would have it that a naval pilot was ordered to fly round the area until he found land that was likely to be large enough and flat enough for the purpose. Whatever truth there might be in these stories, the site was undoubtedly chosen because it offered a large expanse of cheap, flat land free of dykes and ditches but served by good road and rail links. It was suitable for expansion in any direction, fairly central but sufficiently close to the growing number of airfields in south-east England to support them. It was also intended to be a war station for airships and was close enough to the coast to use existing and planned firing and bombing ranges. Cranwell Lodge Farm was requisitioned for the Admiralty from Mr Usher Banks by Chief Petty Officer Whitlock on 23 November 1915 and was commissioned as HMS *Daedalus* on 10

December 1915.[15] The first ship's company had a day's journey from London in a lorry with an officer, a CPO, thirteen men and their baggage in pouring rain. All were soaked to the skin and were not amused when they found their accommodation was in a barn that was still full of corn and inhabited by rats. The original lodge was used as the commandant's office and wardroom until early 1916 when new hutted accommodation was completed.[16] At first it was commanded by the redoubtable Commodore Paine who had obtained pilot's certificate number 217 in 1912 and had been the first commandant of the CFS at Upavon.

By the time McCleery arrived at Cranwell it had over 100 aircraft including Bristol Scouts, BE2Cs, Avro 504s, Nieuports, some Sopwith Pups and the inevitable Maurice Farmans. By 1 March he was flying Avro 504s with the advanced flying school and 'put in about 2.5 hours'. There were, however, 'an awful lot of crashes which wound up by a chap called Daglish coming down upside down from 10,000ft and killing himself'.[17] McCleery didn't see it, he told his parents, but 'it fairly put the wind up everyone. There were either 8 or 10 crashes, one being a collision.' The funeral was on Sunday, 4 March and he described it as 'rather touching. Fearfully cold day. No flying at all.' Towards the end of the course in April there were written examinations in meteorology, navigation, theory of flight, engines, aircraft construction, armament and signals as well as the flying tests, all of which McCleery passed. After passing through an armament training course at Freiston and an introduction to seaplane operations at Calshot he was appointed to *Furious,* joining Squadron Commander Dunning's unit in the ship at Newcastle at 18.00 on 30 June. He had done very well and one his last confidential reports under training described him as a keen and capable officer and pilot.

Lighter-than-Air Pilot Training

What was probably the first controlled flight by a British dirigible airship took place in 1905; it was designed and built by Ernest Willows, the son of a Cardiff dentist and remained airborne for just over an hour.[18] In 1907 Colonel Capper became head of the Army Balloon Factory at Farnborough and supervised the construction of the first military airship, the *Nulli Secundus,* and for the next seven years all aspects of airship flight were the responsibility of the Army although towards the end of that period some RN pilots were trained including Wing Commander N F Usborne RNAS. On 1 January 1914 all the Army airships were transferred to the Navy and the aircrew who did not elect to fly heavier-than-air aircraft were allowed to transfer to the RNAS. At the time the airship section, which subsequently became known as the Airship Service within the overall RNAS structure, comprised only 198 men of all ranks under Wing Commander E A D Masterman RNAS. Specific airship crew training was carried out at the air stations at Kingsnorth and Wormwood Scrubs at

Flight Sub Lieutenant T P Yorke-Moore RNAS in the centre cockpit about to begin an instructional sortie in SS 23 from RNAS Luce Bay. (Donnie Nelson collection via Guy Warner)

first but with the rapid expansion of the airship element after 1915 training spread to other establishments including Cranwell.

Airship pilots were taught the theory of flight from a viewpoint that differed from that of their heavier-than-air colleagues. The non-rigid airships of the SS and subsequent classes were simple and reliable and did not therefore require a great deal of instruction. They comprised a fabric envelope with several internal gasbags to provide lift. The envelope retained its aerodynamic shape because air was continually blown into it from the propeller thrust. A control car, often referred to as a gondola, was suspended beneath the envelope by suspension lines which distributed its weight evenly; it contained the crew, controls, engine, armament, equipment and the necessary ballast. All RNAS airships used hydrogen to provide the necessary lift.[19] This had the advantage of being the lightest gas and was far more efficient than coal gas but also the enormous disadvantage that it was highly flammable and, when mixed with air, explosive. Helium would have been a better alternative, despite being slightly heavier, since it was inert but in the early twentieth century it was too rare and expensive to be a realistic alternative. Hydrogen was easy to produce and could be readily stored in cylinders. It weighs approximately 5lbs for every 1000ft³ of gas compared with air which weighs about 76lbs for the same volume at sea level. The amount of lift provided by an airship's hydrogen bags depends on the amount of air displaced minus the weight of the gas displacing and the craft's structure. In rough terms, every 32,000ft^2 of hydrogen would give a disposable lift of one ton.

Airship pilots had to be trained to take into account the fact that as they climbed the outside air pressure would decrease, allowing the gas inside the bags to expand. When further expansion would be dangerous, 'pressure height' is said to have been reached and the hydrogen is vented through automatic valves. Venting gas lowered the gas pressure so that there would be a new pressure height that differed from the first. Another factor had also to be taken into account; hydrogen reacts to ambient conditions more quickly than air and so direct sunlight on the envelope could cause what was known as super-heating when the gas reached a higher temperature than the air around it. This caused a phenomenon of false lift which could be helpful or dangerous depending on circumstances. If the gas cooled below the ambient air temperature in a patch of warmer air, the opposite effect might be encountered, with a rapid loss of lift. In addition to the static lift provided by the gas, pilots could achieve an element of dynamic lift with their flying controls. By trimming the airship to fly at a slightly nose-up angle, the envelope could give lift in the same way as an aircraft's wing amounting to about 10 per cent of the static lift. It was therefore possible for an airship to stall if this lift was lost. It was also possible, if the nose was trimmed into a nose-down attitude, for the airship to stall upwards under some conditions. All gasbags leaked and pilots sometimes had to vent off gas in order to maintain height and so ballast was carried so that it could be dumped in measured amounts to compensate for the loss of static lift. Sand or water were ideal as they could easily be metered but petrol was a viable alternative, giving the potential to extend the radius of action if it wasn't dumped. Airships at low level could dump ballast in large quantities and climb rapidly if necessary. The SS non-rigid airships were considered to be simple to operate and 'capable of being flown by a young midshipman with small-boat training'.[20] Captains were encouraged to recommend junior officers from the Grand Fleet to volunteer for 'special temporary and hazardous service' and one such was Thomas Elmhirst[21] from the battlecruiser *Indomitable*. Civilians who volunteered were also inducted into the RNAS for specialised airship training. The training course lasted about a month and included the theory of aerostatics, aeronautics, navigation, meteorology, engineering, rigging and engine repair. The practical side of the course included balloon flying and mastering the controls of a small airship. They carried out eight flights, six of which were under dual instruction with one of these at night. One trip was flown as second-in-command and the final one solo.

One aspect of airship operations that differed greatly from heavier-than-air aircraft was the need for large handling parties during take-off and landing. They had to be walked out of their hangars by large parties of men holding on to ropes and relying on their combined weight to keep the airship down until the crew were ready to take off. Larger rigid airships used heavy diesel-powered tractors or even tanks later in the war. In calm conditions an airship pilot could 'ballast up' at the end of a flight by venting gas and flying slowly upwind towards the handling party who would attach their lines to the handling guys, take hold of the car and walk the aircraft back into its hangar. Airships were so vulnerable to wind that virtually all had hangars, although in calm conditions some were moored to masts during the day. In rough or windy conditions the airship dropped a long, heavy trail rope which was grabbed by an enlarged handling party who then pulled the still-buoyant airship down. Some of the larger air stations had snatch blocks set in concrete into which the rope could be passed to prevent handlers being pulled off their feet.

Specialised training for tethered or kite balloon pilots was carried out at Roehampton. Although the balloon was tethered to a warship, the pilot still had to have sufficient knowledge of how to keep his balloon at the optimum height by venting gas or dumping ballast as necessary and the training course included several flights in free balloons with an instructor so that the student would know what to do if his balloon broke free from its towing wire. A kite-balloon detachment comprised three officers and eight men and ships carried between twelve and sixty cylinders of hydrogen so that the balloon could be topped up during prolonged periods at sea. It could be winched down with the basket resting on the deck for crew changes and replenishment and then paid out to about 1500ft. One thing the crews did have to get used to was the wallowing movement transmitted up the tethering cable when the parent ship pitched and rolled in rough weather. One huge advantage the kite balloon enjoyed over all other forms of aerial reconnaissance was direct telephone contact with the parent ship's command centre which gave the added benefit that messages were immediate with no need for encryption, transmission and decryption and all the delays they introduced. By 1918 kite balloons were embarked in the Grand Fleet in large numbers but after the war they were soon withdrawn, presumably because embarked aircraft such as the 'Ship' Strutter with their continuous-wave wireless were deemed to have rendered them obsolete.

Observer Training
The training of observers had not at first been taken as seriously as it should have been. The realisation that more aircraft needed to be taken to sea in order to form part of the Grand Fleet's battle plans led to a fundamental reappraisal of the situation by the end of 1915 and in a letter dated 6 January 1916 W A Medrow of the Admiralty Secretariat wrote a minute on the subject for wide circulation. In it he said that expansion of the RNAS

raises the whole question of the status of observers in the Air Service. At present they are all RNVR officers and, therefore, any promotion it may be desired to give them must be made by giving them promotion within that force. This appears to me to be unsatisfactory in view of the fact that these officers will all be demobilized at the end of the war and, therefore, we may find ourselves left without any officers trained to carry out these important duties. I think there is a lot to be said in favour of Wing Captain F H Sykes' proposals to give these officers flight rank and incorporate them in an Intelligence section. On the face of it, it appears to me to be reasonable to expect that observers should receive the same rate of flying pay as pilots receive. Flying pay is presumably a payment made partly for skill and partly for risk. The observer encounters the same risks as the pilot and has skill, though of a different kind to that of the pilot. The establishment of some such intelligence system with permanent officers would guarantee that we should not be left without officers at the end of the war.[22]

The final, handwritten, comment in the docket was by Wing Captain F R Scarlett RNAS and stated that 'observers are now being trained as suggested only more so. Status and pay has [*sic*] been under consideration for some time'.

Bell-Davies described the difficulties observers faced while he was *Campania*'s senior aviation officer during 1917 in *Sailor in the Air*, noting that

in the spring of 1917 the Grand Fleet carried out three large-scale tactical exercises. In each, the first enemy sighting was made by a seaplane, a report being passed by wireless. In none of the exercises did the report reach the C-in-C until after surface contact had been made. The trouble was that we were still using spark wireless sets. For some technical reason the fleet flagship could not keep watch on the seaplane wavelength. A battleship in the flagship's division was, therefore, detailed as aircraft guardship to relay the aircraft's signals to the flagship. There was always a time-lag. Linnel was *Campania*'s signal officer. At that time he was a temporary lieutenant RNVR but he was also a professional electrical engineer who had specialized in wireless. He was developing a continuous-wave set for aircraft; at the same time the Admiralty had also started development and the first continuous-wave sets became available in the winter of 1917.

He then went into more specific detail about the training of observers and explained that

in *Campania* observers were midshipmen RNR selected from boys who at trained in the nautical training establishments *Worcester* or *Conway*. They were excellent material but the trouble was that they had, one and all, volunteered for the job in the hope of becoming pilots and Swann, the commanding officer, felt that it would be most unjust to refuse to recommend a boy for pilot because he was doing well as an observer. The result was that just as they were becoming useful observers they went off to train as pilots. Linnel who did most of the training of observers had realized that it was essential to enter men who would be content to remain observers when trained. The midshipmen's weakest point had been in signal procedure. Linnel therefore suggested that we should draw on the visual signalling branch of the Navy. As a result a number of signal yeomen were entered into the RNAS and trained. They were all volunteers who were entered on the understanding that, if they made good, they would be advanced to warrant officer RNAS. They were trained on board *Campania* during the summer of 1917 and as a result mistakes in signal procedure disappeared.[23]

With the wisdom of hindsight and given that the original aim of aircraft embarked in ships was to extend the visible horizon of the battlefleet, it seems surprising that it took so long for the important role played by the observer to be recognized. The improved status of observers led to the introduction of a flying badge for them, worn over the curl of the left arm sleeve lace. It comprised wings similar to those on the pilots' eagle badge but at its centre it had a prominent 'O'. Shore-based training for observers was established at Eastchurch and at the central training establishment at Cranwell. It included a wide range of disciplines in which pupils had to become proficient before they were appointed to ships. These included practical navigation over the sea, reconnaissance, wireless and visual communications, spotting the fall of shot for surface warships and the skills needed to use Lewis guns on flexible mountings. In addition to observers, other aircrew included the mechanics who flew in flying boats who would also be expected to man the guns and gunlayers, specialist seamen who manned the rear machine gun in two-seater fighters such as the 1½ Strutter.

Mechanics
The first RNAS mechanics were RN carpenters and ERAs who were taught the intricacies of aircraft erection and maintenance at Eastchurch. As the Service expanded large numbers of technical tradesmen were recruited and trained, many of them from civilian engineering specialisations. Men who worked on airframes were known as riggers and those who worked on engines were known as fitters. As the war progressed and aircraft became more complex, specialised electricians and armourers were trained in increasing numbers.

Riggers

The majority of the RNAS' aircraft were constructed of wood although it was recognised that metal construction represented the ideal future as it would withstand age, humidity and temperature better. Just as important, its strength could be more accurately calculated. Whatever the airframe was made of, the riggers' first task was to make sure that it was assembled exactly in accordance with the manufacturer's drawings. Because it was a braced structure, all adjustments had to be made exactly and methodically to ensure that it would fly properly and endure the loads and stresses placed on it in flight. This was usually achieved by supporting the airframe on two or more trestles in such a way that the datum line on the erection drawing was horizontal. This line was often indicated on the fuselage by horizontal marks on the vertical struts. The fuselage would then be measured and adjusted until it was exactly true to the drawing. The wings would then be aligned, commencing with the centre section of the top plane in a biplane. The stagger, dihedral and incidence would then be carefully measured and adjusted if necessary. Lastly the attitude of the tail plane and the fin or rudder with regard to the fuselage and the wings would be checked and the control cables adjusted to give the correct degree of tension with the controls centred. The bracing wires that

RNAS riggers being instructed on an instructional Short seaplane, with its engine removed, in the grounds of the Crystal Palace. Part of the Palace itself can just be made out in the top right-hand corner of the photograph. (Author's collection)

New-entry RNAS pilots undergoing both theoretical and practical rigging instruction from a senior rating inside the Crystal Palace. The aircraft drawn on the chalk-board is a Maurice Farman biplane. (Author's collection)

held the airframe in shape would be checked for the correct amount of tension using a specialised tool. The rigger would be responsible for a number of other tasks including the fitting of equipment, painting or doping the fabric that covered the fuselage and wings when necessary and generally assisting the pilot and tuning the aircraft to his individual specification.

Given that aircraft were largely made of wood, it was important that riggers understood the different types of wood and their uses. The strength of timber was affected by many factors including the season of felling, the method and period of seasoning and the portion of the tree from which it was cut. As the war progressed, artificial seasoning became more common but the process required care and attention, especially in the case of ash. An imperfectly-seasoned strut could warp badly, especially if it was straight-grained on one side and obliquely-grained and wetter on the other during the process.[24] The principal timbers used in aeroplanes were ash and spruce. Ash is tough and very flexible and was considered suitable for structures that required great strength or that were subject to sudden shock. It had to be straight-grained, free from all objectionable defects, felled between the months of September and January, inclusive, in the UK and thoroughly wind-dried. For parts that were bent to shape using steam-heat, ash should not have been felled for less than 18 months. Spruce is light, strong for its weight and can be worked easily. It was obtainable in uniform quality, that from British Columbia being considered the best, and was to be free from cross-shakes, knots, resin pockets and other faults. It should have been rift sawn and have edge-grain. It should have been in stick for at least nine months before shipping. Three-ply woods were used for the manufacture of wing rib webs and fuselages together with other parts that were under stress. Outer layers of the ply could be of ash or birch and the inner ply aspen or American whitewood would suffice. Riggers would have their own tool box, often made by the individuals while under training and they would have been trained to use the machine tools such as lathes and saws found in typical workshops. In an age before the standardised mass-production of components they would often have to make their own replacement for a failed or damaged piece of airframe.

Fitters

Fitters were trained to repair, tune and get the best out of aircraft engines. They had to be capable of stripping them down and re-assembling them as well as making or repairing replacement components using every type of machine and tool available in workshops. Even the austere seaplane carrier conversions had lathes, milling machines, vertical drilling machines, hand shearing machines, emery wheels, coppersmith brazing hearths, benches with vices and an engine washing tank in which components were given a paraffin bath. Some ships also carried portable forges and anvils and these were invariably issued to the larger air stations ashore. When fitting an engine to its airframe it was critically important to ensure that it was not strained in any way and so fitters and riggers had to work closely together. The surfaces on which the engine was to be seated had to be dead true and the fixing bolts carefully tightened on opposite sides in turn. As a rule, aero-engines arrived as a compact unit that had been tested by the manufacturer and should, therefore, be in good order. Once installed the fitter would see that lubrication was in order and the various pipes connected properly. The engine would then be ground-run and tuned to achieve peak performance. Tuning was achieved by setting the closing of the inlet valves and the opening of the exhaust valves as finely as possible by observation and measurement. Tappet clearance also had to be measured and adjusted to the ideal but care had to be taken not to make adjustments unless they were strictly necessary. Valve settings were usually taken with the engine being turned in its normal direction so that any errors due to play in gear wheels could be avoided. Care had to be taken to avoid getting oil or grease on electrical cables After every 12 hours' running time, fitters were instructed to

A Sopwith F.1 Camel packed into its transit crate ready for shipment to an operational air station. (Author's collection)

empty the lubricating system and wash out the crank-case with paraffin to remove all dirt and sediment, the engine then being given about a dozen sharp turns. After every 20 hours running time rotary engines were to be given a very thorough examination and de-carbonising. The engine's compression would be tested at the same time to check that it was as it should be and if low it might be necessary to grind-in the valves, especially the exhaust valve and adjust the tappets accordingly. The cylinders and piston-heads would be carefully cleaned of any sign of carbon deposit and all oil passages carefully cleaned. Every component would need to be tried regularly to make sure that they worked freely as intended. Water-cooled engines were examined every 150 hours and after they had been in service for 300 hours' operation they were removed and sent back to the manufacturer for examination and overhaul.[25] These tasks and many others had to be taught and practised, bearing in mind that the fitter in a single fighter embarked in a cruiser or battleship might be the only man in that ship's company with the skills to do the necessary work. Those embarked in larger units had the advantage of colleagues and senior ratings to help with the work.

Armourers

Armourers were responsible for the stowage, preparation, fuzing and attachment to aircraft of a wide variety of weapons which grew larger as the war progressed. These included bombs, torpedoes, depth charges, rockets and machine guns – the latter both fixed forward-firing through an interrupter mechanism and free-firing from a flexible mount. There was little point in training pilots in the skills needed for accurate weapons delivery if those weapons were not perfectly prepared for the task intended for them. The problems faced by the armament officer of 8 (Naval) Squadron flying Sopwith Camels in support of the Army on the Western Front in 1917 were typical of those which had, as far as possible, to be overcome by training. Training was carried out at the air gunnery school at Eastchurch and the armourers' charges included the care and maintenance of ammunition, bombs and bomb-sights, bomb-release gear, signal flares and the pistols carried by aircrew. Squadrons engaged on other tasks such as strike or anti-submarine warfare could add torpedoes or depth bombs to this list. The course also included instructions on how to carry out a funeral firing party. Within 8 (N) the most pressing need was to ensure that the machine guns fired when the triggers were pressed and kept on firing until they were released but this was not quite as simple as it sounds.

The F.1 Camel used by 8 (N) Squadron had two forward-firing Vickers guns fixed in parallel on the upper deck of the fuselage between the propeller and the cockpit. These guns had originally been designed to be fired from a stationary position on the ground but were now expected to work perfectly at speeds up to 200mph, turning hard through the air with significant forces several times that of normal gravity applied while in combat. To add to that the lubricants used in the gun and its firing mechanism together with the ammunition itself were subjected to extreme changes of temperature. Vickers guns jammed on the ground and so it was inevitable that they would do so to a greater degree in the air:[26] it was the armourer's job through training and experience to minimise the risk. The firing mechanism was the Sopwith-Kauper Interrupter Gear which was intended to ensure that bullets from each gun passed between the blades of the propeller which was revolving at 1400rpm. Consequently a blade passed in front of the guns 2800 times a minute. The interrupter gear was not the original method of firing and put an enormous strain on the gun's firing mechanism because it was taken directly off the propeller shaft. The slightest hang-fire or slackness in the gear, even a tiny delay in the firing operation caused by frozen lubricant might result in a holed propeller. In some cases the propellers were shot away completely.

The armourers in 8 (N) were 'without exception a real willing crowd'[27] and under their officers they developed a system that got the best out of the guns. A log was kept of every gun and its behaviour on every flight. Its faults were recorded together with measures taken to put them right. This was invaluable and the more correctly the log was kept, the greater the efficiency obtainable. Every new gun that arrived was stripped down, various small but necessary alterations made to it, and a thorough trial on the ground was carried out. At the same time the sights

As aircraft were forced to fly at heights above 20,000ft to avoid anti-aircraft fire or make interceptions, aircrew had to provide themselves with warm clothing to provide some protection against sub-zero temperatures. Flight Sub Lieutenant Simms RNAS is seen here demonstrating his goatskin flying jacket and a leather helmet that completely covers his face. After some high flights aircrew were so numb with cold when they landed, despite their protective clothing, that they had to be lifted out of their cockpits and carried somewhere warm to be revived. (Goble Family collection).

were tested and adjusted and the opportunity taken to test any new lots of ammunition that had arrived. Wherever possible the guns were fired on test flights as there often seemed to be further necessary adjustments that did not show up in ground firing. Very careful supervision was given to filling the belts with ammunition and a record was kept of any faults which were reported on subsequent firing. Separated cases, misfires and expanded cases seemed to run in batches and were always reported to the supply base. After every flight when the guns had been fired, they were cleaned, overhauled and oiled, the locks taken off and examined, chutes examined and firing gear cleaned and tested. Reports were sent to the HQ at Dunkirk at regular intervals stating what the general performance of the guns had been and making comments on the behaviour of ammunition. Careful drawings to scale were made of suggested improvements and the reasons explained for recommending them. The results were as good as one could hope for and a tribute to team effort and dedication.

13 Politics

From its earliest days, naval aviation has suffered from the imposition of dogmatic policies by politicians, few if any of whom have had any practical experience of the operation of aircraft or with a fleet at sea. The early days of experiment had not even been allowed to produce a mature policy when the RFC with its Naval and Military Wings was imposed on the Admiralty. It soon became apparent, however, that differing requirements would take the Wings down different developmental paths and the RNAS was formally accepted as a separate entity in 1914. Captain Sueter, who had been appointed Director of the Admiralty's Air Department (DAD) in 1912, was a man of drive and vision whose terms of reference required him to be 'generally responsible to the Board in regard to all matters connected with the Naval Air Service' and 'to keep Their Lordships fully informed of all details in connection with the Air Service which ought to be brought to their notice'.[1] His instructions are worth studying in some detail because he was to advise the First Sea Lord, who had responsibility for all matters of operational policy and war-fighting, 'on all matters affecting the tactical employment of aircraft and all military questions connected therewith'. When required by the Second Sea Lord, he was to 'advise on questions connected with the personnel and training of the Naval Air Service'. He was to advise the Third Sea Lord 'on all questions affecting the design and manufacture of material connected with airships and aeroplanes and bring to his notice all important changes'. A member of the DNC's staff was made available to him to assist in questions of design. It was accepted that Sueter should to able to communicate directly with Air Staff officers at the War Office on matters of detail but on policy and 'important aeronautical questions' the War Office was to notified officially by the Secretary of the Admiralty to the Secretary of the War Office and vice versa. Whenever he desired to be absent on leave, Sueter had to obtain the permission of the Third Sea Lord and his senior assistant had to be available to act for him in his absence.

It is surely an over-simplification, therefore, to say that Sueter was 'subordinate to no particular member of the Board of Admiralty'.[2] Given the limited capability of the RNAS at the time of his appointment and his junior rank, he was actually

Rear Admiral Sir Murray F Sueter CB MP photographed after he had retired from active service with the RN. (Author's collection)

given considerable powers to act through the Board and the Fifth Sea Lord appointed as the focal point on all matters in 1917 had no greater power on paper although the air service had, of course, expanded significantly in both size and capability by then. Prior to the outbreak of war the instructions given to the DAD seem practical and realistic but the rapid increase in technology, the unexpected outbreak of war on a global scale and the outlook of individuals all led to unforeseen problems. Sueter was determined to keep the operational and administrative detail of the air service within his own grasp as far as possible and the general lack of knowledge among senior officers helped him to do so. In February 1914 he wrote that the air service's 'military possibilities will shortly make it practicable for it to render effectual aid to the strategy and tactics of both the Main Fleets and the Coast Defence. The development of its effective value will, therefore, become a matter of close and growing interest to the various naval Commanders-in-Chief of Fleets and Districts and to other Departments connected with the administration of the Navy.' This was all well and good but he also wrote that it was 'essential for the rapid development of this new arm that a steady line of policy, training and internal organisation should be followed and this can only be achieved by the maintenance, for the present, of a central authority which shall remain in close touch with, and in control of, all the details of material and personnel and their work and training'.[3]

A measure of the autonomy that Sueter sought and, for a short while, gained can be gathered from Admiralty Weekly Order Number 166 dated 5 February 1915 in which it was stated that:

> In consequence of the great development which has taken place recently in this branch of the Naval Service, the existing organisation is no longer capable of yielding the best results. The present system, which if the ordinary naval procedure were strictly observed would have necessitated Admiralty orders to air stations being issued through the Commander-in-Chief at the Nore, is especially unsuited for a state of war and has, in fact, already been modified in practice . . . Their Lordships have, accordingly, decided that the whole of the Naval Air Service, including air stations, seaplanes, aeroplanes, airships, balloons, kites and seaplane carriers shall forthwith, subject to any exceptions which may be approved by them hereafter, be placed under the orders of the Director of the Air Department who will be solely responsible to the Board of Admiralty for its proper administration. In the event, therefore, of Commanders-in-Chief and others needing aircraft assistance they must apply, if time permits, to the Admiralty in order that the necessary steps can be taken to detail aircraft for their service without upsetting the general arrangements. In emergency, application is to be made to the air station concerned, the commanding officer of which is to use his utmost endeavours to meet requirements.[4]

This was not an officer subordinate to no particular member of the Board but a Director who had persuaded the entire Board to allow him to follow his own particular line of policy and to announce it through a document that outlined the Admiralty's wartime policy.

Sueter was astute enough to realise that he needed influential support if he was to carry his vision of overall control of the expanding service forward and he was fortunate to gain the backing of the dynamic First Lord. Not only did Churchill allow Sueter to use aircraft for some distinctly non-naval tasks in France and Belgium but he positively encouraged him to broaden the new service's operational and developmental activities into armoured cars, tanks and even armoured trains. Geoffrey Till noted in *Air Power and the Royal Navy* that it was common gossip among junior officers that the Sea Lords gave Churchill a free hand in air matters to divert his attention from the Grand Fleet.[5] There is probably some truth in this assertion and it is undeniably true that the First Lord was less likely to encounter opposition over this novel form of warfare than he would have done over longer-established fleet tactics and strategy. Aviation was new and technically complex so there was inevitably a tendency for it to draw in other new concepts as it evolved.

There was something exciting for the First Lord to promote almost every day and, looking back, one can see the reason for his enthusiasm even if it sometimes fell short of giving the Navy the air arm that it needed. Notwithstanding his support, however, Churchill noted that Sueter 'needed supervision'[6] and at one stage sought to put the Second Sea Lord, Jellicoe at the time, in charge of air matters. The Churchill/Fisher era at the Admiralty ended when both resigned over the failure of the Dardanelles campaign. They were replaced in 1915 by A J Balfour as First Lord and Admiral Sir Henry Jackson as First Sea Lord; Lord Hankey subsequently remarked that 'in place of two men of driving power, initiative and resource, but occasionally lacking in judgement, there were now in charge two men of philosophic temperament and first rate judgement, but less dynamic than their predecessors'.[7] The new regime soon ended Sueter's autonomy; on 29 July 1915 Admiralty Weekly Order Number 1204/15 stated unequivocally that the RNAS 'is to be regarded in all respects as an integral part of the Royal Navy and in future the various air stations will be under the general orders of the Commander-in-Chief or Senior Naval Officer in whose district they are situated'.[8] At the same time a number of officers were appointed to administrative positions within the RNAS who had no specialised air knowledge but who were noted for their power of organisation, strict discipline and untiring energy. The responsibility for the design and procurement of air material was distributed around the existing Admiralty technical departments rather than concentrated within the Air Department. Finally, overall responsibility for the RNAS was removed from Sueter and vested in a flag officer, Admiral C L Vaughan-Lee, who was appointed as Director of the Air Service. Sueter, who by then had been promoted to Commodore 1st Class, was appointed as Superintendent of Aircraft Construction, an important task given the vast expansion of new and exciting aircraft types that was gathering momentum but one which he saw as a demotion.

A number of young pilots resented the changes at first but they were un-doubtedly necessary to align air operations more closely with those of the fleet. Sueter openly challenged Tudor and Vaughan-Lee on several matters and began to declare himself in sympathy with the view expressed by several politicians that there should be a unified Royal Air Service. He was most probably the author of an unsigned minute proposing the establishment of an Air Department that was independent of both the Admiralty and War Office forwarded to the Prime Minister, Asquith, by Churchill in June 1915 shortly after he had left the Admiralty.[9] Asquith's private secretary, Sir Maurice Bonham, forwarded Churchill's copy of the document to Colonel Hankey, the Secretary of the Committee of Imperial Defence, under cover of an incisive letter in which he wrote that it looks to me like a scheme for providing Winston with something to do and though I would gladly see his energies suitably employed, at first sight I cannot say that I like it. The military wing is a success largely because it has been developed and trained as a branch of the Army and with military objects strictly in view. The naval wing is a failure because it has not been designed for naval objects with the result that it has degenerated into a crowd of highly skilled but ill-disciplined privateersmen. What is wanted is to make the naval wing more naval, not more aerial.

His last sentence showed his well-judged appreciation of the situation and Hankey minuted on the back of it 'I agree your remarks'. He attached a typewritten minute for the Prime Minister's eyes which demonstrated the clarity with which he viewed the subject. In it he drew attention to the agreement between the War Office and the Admiralty on 19 November 1913 that

the War Office should be responsible for aerial supremacy in the British isles as well as for any land operations in which the Army was concerned. Owing to its concentration on the needs of the Expeditionary Force the War Office was not in position to fulfil this requirement at the outset of war and, consequently, the Admiralty took over the whole arrangement for the defence of London against aerial attack. The progress of the Naval Wing on the whole has been less definitely naval than that of the Army has been military. The seaplane has not proved a very efficient instrument for work with the fleet, owing to the weight of the floats. The consequence has been that the Admiralty, which has pressed forward its aerial service with the utmost vigour, has been able to devote itself to operations such as the defence of London and to special enterprises such as the attacks on Cuxhaven, Antwerp, on various airship sheds and in the Dardanelles . . . If the two wings had kept in closer touch from the outset, it is possible that there might be something to say in favour of a Ministry of the Air on the lines suggested in the notes under consideration. Colonel Seely was always in favour of this plan but the idea met with strong opposition both in the Admiralty and the War Office. In existing conditions, therefore, when each service has grown up separately and established a certain tradition of which it is not the less proud because of rapid growth, it is difficult to see that any advantage would accrue from the change. I am convinced that it would be most unpopular with both services.

In his last paragraph he noted that 'it is difficult to see why there should be overlapping and counter-bidding . . . between the two services. The Air Committee was set up in order to co-ordinate such matters. As a matter of fact, however, the Air Committee has not received a single word of complaint on this subject from either service since the war began. If it exists now the proper course would be either to refer it to the Air Committee for discussion or else to allow the supply of aeronautical material to become a special branch of the new Ministry of Munitions. The latter course appears desirable as it is understood that the supply of aeroplane engines has been interfered with by other Government work such as the provision of engines for submarines.' Arguments over the command and administration of the RNAS had caused some dissention in 1915. Deeper arguments over the supply of aircraft, equipment and organisation were to follow in 1916 and 1917, begun in large measure by those who, for a variety of personal reasons, favoured the establishment of a single, unified air force.

The RFC had always relied on the Royal Aircraft Factory at Farnborough for its aircraft in the same way that the Army had always relied on the Royal Ordnance Factories for its guns and ammunition.[10] The RNAS, on the other hand, followed its parent service's lead and tended to work with individual manufacturers who were appointed as Admiralty Contractors; the intimacy that existed between Captain Bacon and Vickers over the early submarine and airship contracts is one example and the close co-operation between the pioneers at Eastchurch and the Short Brothers is another. This policy encouraged some of the most enterprising firms in the expanding British aviation industry to experiment and develop new designs, leading to some of the best aircraft of their day. By 1916 this had given the RNAS a distinct advantage and some senior RFC officers began to accuse the Navy of 'deplorable and extensive competition'. The situation came to a head when General Haig called for a huge expansion in the size of the RFC deployed in France. The critical shortage was in aircraft engines because in 1914 there had been no British aero-engine industry to speak of. By 1917 it had expanded enormously but it was still desperately short of materials and skilled men. The three biggest manufacturers were Rolls-Royce, Sunbeam and Beardmore and between them they were producing 600 engines a month. Haig's expansion plans called for 2000 engines that were more powerful and robust than any of their predecessors. Attempts to increase production led to an appalling 90 per cent failure rate in cylinder-block castings, inadequately tested engines going straight into operational aircraft and, worst of all, engines that were known to be faulty being put into airframes regardless of the consequences. The Admiralty's independent policy actually proved to be very much to the nation's benefit when some of the 8000 Hispano-Suiza engines ordered in France became available to make up for the 1719 Sunbeam Arab engines that the company failed to deliver in 1917.

Another, and potentially more serious, challenge to the way in which the naval air service was evolving was raised by Major General Sir David Henderson, the Commander of the RFC and Director General of Military Aeronautics[11] at the War Office. On 28 January 1916 he forwarded a note to the War Committee[12] seeking guidance on the various roles undertaken by the two flying services, in which he criticised the Admiralty's procurement policy for aircraft engines.[13] He accepted that the duties of the RNAS to work with fleets and the RFC to work with the BEF were too obvious to merit discussion but he was concerned about the Admiralty's growing enthusiasm for long-range bomber operations by land-based aircraft operating from French soil. The consequent need for the Navy to procure high-powered engines for the bombers and for the fighters used for the air defence of the UK mainland had led, he claimed, to the military authorities having 'the greatest difficulty in providing engines for the expansion of the Royal Flying Corps, required to meet the requirements [*sic*] of the greatly increased Army. This has been especially the case with regard to the supplies available from France . . . The RFC is now suffering from a lack of suitable engines for its necessary daily work.' At the meeting of the War Committee on 10 February General Henderson was present to expand upon his note and the First Lord, Balfour, and Commodore Sueter were present to put the Admiralty's case before the Prime Minister. He began by making the extraordinary statement that he had 'never known what were the allotted duties of the Naval Air Service and how that Service had been employed'.[14] Despite this, he went on to say that since the outbreak of war the RFC had 'been multiplied six-fold in order to carry out the various requirements of the generals in the field' and had now been instructed to take over the home defence task from the Admiralty. The RFC now needed better aircraft and more powerful engines in large numbers and ought to have a 'fair share' of both. He made no comment on the differing procurement policies or the failure of the RFC to plan ahead for the requirements he now demanded and, viewed in hindsight his argument appears to support the supposition that if you shout loudly enough, someone will listen.

The Prime Minister asked how many aircraft were employed by the Navy and Army respectively. Henderson said that the Army had 296 aeroplanes in France and 24 now employed in Home Defence with new squadrons being formed, a total of some 400 available for war purposes. Sueter stated that the RNAS had 334 seaplanes and 629 aeroplanes, the latter figure including every aircraft that was used for training and non-operational purposes. Henderson conceded that if training machines were to be included, a further 400 machines must be added to his total. An acrimonious discussion followed in the course of which Balfour pointed out that the RNAS had carried out the bulk of the flying tasks in the Dardanelles, Egypt, Dunkirk, East and West Africa and the Persian Gulf.

Reginald McKenna, a former First Lord and now Chancellor of the Exchequer, spoke largely in favour of the Navy and Asquith's interjections appeared to be against it. At one stage Lord Curzon asked if the air work with the BEF was being hampered and Henderson replied that it was 'not being hampered for lack of machines or pilots[15] but for lack of engines'. Curzon said that meanwhile the Navy had been placing huge orders; he could equally have asked why the Army had not been placing huge orders but either this did not occur to him or the question did not suit his purpose. Admiral Tudor informed the meeting that the Navy had placed orders for engines in America but, apparently, the Army had not done so. It seemed that Asquith, Curzon and Henderson were determined to criticise the Navy for doing well in the development and procurement of engines and to turn a blind eye to the RFC's evident failure to predict the requirements that would follow urgent calls for its expansion. Despite its length, the meeting came to no very clear conclusion and it was renewed on 15 February. The Cabinet Secretary Sir Maurice Hankey's solution was to revive the Air Committee which had been in abeyance since the outbreak of war.

From 1916 onwards, the future organisation of the air services came to be linked closely to the question of long-range bombing and the supply of high-powered engines for the aircraft that were to carry it out. Balfour stood firm to his belief that long-range reconnaissance and attacks on enemy naval bases were very much the responsibility of the Navy but the thorny question of who should attack targets further inland was more difficult to resolve. The RNAS had suitable aircraft and trained pilots but any attempt to use them against targets away from the coast would inevitably lead to a clash with Henderson, despite the fact that a large number of engines and aircraft ordered by the Navy had been voluntarily handed over to the Army in order to strengthen its position in France.[16] Vaughan-Lee minuted Vice Admiral H F Oliver, the Chief of the War Staff, on 4 April 1916 about possible ways to counter Zeppelin attacks on the UK and these included retaliatory strikes against targets in Germany from French bases. In a handwritten note on the minute page of the docket, Oliver wrote that he concurred that action should be taken forthwith and that 'it would be very advantageous to pursue an offensive policy from France, at least a dozen large towns are within easy reach of attack'. He added, somewhat disingenuously, that 'possibly the simplest way of doing it would be to say nothing on this side but to make arrangements with the French and then do it. The French might be got to ask for some of the RNAS to be attached to their Southern Army.' The Admiralty acted on this suggestion and in Roskill's words, 'the explosion which resulted in Whitehall was scarcely less violent than that experienced by the bombed enemy towns'. The gap between the Admiralty and the aggrieved RFC hierarchy in the War Office grew wider.

The theory that bombers could easily destroy enemy industrial centres took little account of the contemporary difficulties often encountered finding them. This de Havilland DH 4 of 5(Naval) Squadron is flying a compass course over the kind of extensive cloud cover often found in the maritime climate of Western Europe. If a clear patch cannot be found near its intended target the mission will have to be aborted. (Author's collection)

The constitution and membership of the Joint War Air Committee were agreed by the War Committee on 25 February 1916. Chaired by Lord Derby, the Committee was to collaborate in arranging questions of supplies and design for the material of the Naval and Military Air Services upon such points as would be referred to it by the War Committee, the Admiralty, the War Office or any other Department of State. For those questions upon which a decision was reached by the Committee, that decision was to be final. Where a settlement of the two Departments' claims could not be reconciled, the matter had to be referred back to the War Committee.[17] Under Derby the standing members of the Committee were Rear Admiral Vaughan-Lee, Commodore Sueter CB RN and Squadron Commander W Briggs RNAS for the Admiralty, with Major General Sir David Henderson KCB DSO and Lieutenant Colonel E L Ellington of the General Staff for the War Office. Advisory members could be asked to attend as necessary. In theory the Committee should have been able to sort out the growing problems of supply and interpretation but it proved unable to do so. Derby was a weak chairman who filled a variety of appointments in his political life[18] but in this instance he lacked the drive to carry matters forward and he resigned in April 1916 after only two months because he felt that the differences of outlook and purpose between the two air services appeared irreconcilable and the possibility of achieving a satisfactory compromise too remote. Lord Montagu, who had become an advisory member, also resigned.

Looking back it is interesting to see that while there were undoubtedly instances of overlapping and duplication, little or no credit was given to the Admiralty for balancing these with numerous instances where aircraft and engines were made available to the RFC to strengthen it whenever requests were made and with no question about their intended use.[19] History has not been kind to the Admiralty and even Roskill described the position taken by Balfour as showing 'unreasonable intractability'. Naval opposition to such compromises as were discussed within Lord Derby's committee certainly aroused in a number of politicians feelings of strong hostility. Lord Curzon, who was by then opposed to any aspect of Admiralty policy on aviation, went so far as to claim that the Joint War Air Committee had been 'fatally hampered by the narrowness of its terms of reference and by the complete inadequacy of its powers'. This situation was not alleviated by the attitude adopted at meetings of the Committee by the representatives of the Admiralty who possessed no power to speak for their Department which, moreover, appears to have been opposed in toto to the changes which it sought to introduce.[20] Because of the failure of the previous committee a new Air Board under Lord Curzon's chairmanship was established by the War Committee charged with 'the task of organising and co-ordinating the supply of material and preventing competition between the two Departments'.[21] It was also to 'organise a complete system for the interchange of ideas upon air problems between the two Services and such related bodies as the [Naval] Board of Invention and Research, the Inventions Branch of the Ministry of Munitions, the Advisory Committee on Aeronautics and the National Physical Laboratory etc'. Under Lord Curzon the Board was to comprise Lord Sydenham, Major J L Baird MP, Rear Admiral F C T Tudor, the Third Sea Lord, Rear Admiral C L Vaughan-Lee, the DAS, Lieutenant General Sir David Henderson the Director-General of Military Aeronautics at the War Office and Major General W S Brancker the Director of Air Organisation at the War Office. The Secretary was Sir H Paul Harvey and Assistant Secretary Commander R M Groves RN. The Board's offices were at 19 Carlton House Terrace.

Following the establishment of the new Air Board, Lord Curzon spoke in the House of Lords of the categories into which he anticipated that its work would lead it. First among these, a category upon which he placed the most pressing importance, was the 'supply of machines and pilots to the front and in the various theatres of war, the organisation of a long-range offensive, the defence of this country by aircraft and guns against hostile air raids, the use and development of lighter-than-air craft, the supply of the best types of machines and engines to both Services, the armament of aircraft, the development of new inventions, the provision of training schools and flying grounds'.[22] A less urgent category included questions to be answered after sufficient experience had been gained; these included 'the amalgamation of the contract and designing branches of the two Services and of their inspecting staffs, the desirability of establishing a joint factory and the

The aspect of aviation that Lord Curzon's Air Board failed to comprehend, Short 184s in the hangar of HMS *Riviera* at sea with the fleet providing a third dimension in naval operations. All three aircraft are resting on trolleys upon which they were moved into and out of the hangar. They were hauled aft and forward by wires, one of which can be seen leading to the capstan which provided motive power. The overhead trunking shows that the removal of petrol vapour from the hangar when its doors were closed was a serious concern. Except for the aircraft, this view is not so very different from the interior of a 21st-century RN destroyer or frigate. (Philip Jarrett collection)

possibility of instituting a joint service'. The least urgency was given to the prospect of creating an Air Ministry. Significantly, Curzon made no mention of the operation of aeroplanes from ships at sea, the potential for such aircraft to attack enemy ships at sea and in harbour, the need for high-performance fighters to protect the fleet against air attack and the potential for aircraft to counter U-boats. Sadly Curzon appears to have had little concept of either naval warfare or the roles aircraft might play in it and the Admiralty seems to have made insufficient attempts to educate him. Arguably, it made the situation worse by following a policy of blanket opposition to what it regarded as interference in its own affairs and continued to view the long-range bombing of inland targets from land bases as an important function for naval aircraft.

Curzon's Board had not been existence for very long, therefore, before he clashed with the Admiralty representatives over the degree to which it should have financial control over the design and procurement of naval aircraft. This was something the War Office was prepared to concede but the Admiralty was determined to oppose

An SSZ class airship at RNAS Malahide in Ireland. Note the tented accommodation in the cleared area beyond the airship. By 1917 naval airships provided a vital element of the convoy defences that the nation relied upon yet Lord Curzon failed to value them as highly as his theoretical bombing offensive. (Guy Warner collection)

and arguments continued throughout the summer of 1916. Having strived since 1915 to make the RNAS more naval and integrate it fully within the Naval Service in the same way that the Submarine Branch and the Royal Marines were administered, the Balfour/Jackson administration were in no mood to change their stance. Lord Curzon clearly believed that air operations represented a new form of warfare that would soon replace existing naval and military operations, a view held by an increasing number of politicians after the failure of the battle of Somme to break the deadlock on the Western Front and what they perceived as the lack of an obviously decisive tactical result at the battle of Jutland. Unfortunately, the Admiralty chose to ignore the Air Board rather than face its arguments head on and the result was that there were many in government who thought the Navy out of touch with aviation when in reality it was producing what were arguably the world's best aircraft which had become an important element of sea warfare, now being fought in three dimensions. As far as I have been able to ascertain, Curzon made little attempt to understand the part played by aircraft at sea and cannot have been aware of the necessity for pilots to form part of an operational team with ships' officers. For those with the practical common sense to understand how the war at sea was actually being fought, this was a fatal flaw in Curzon's arguments but the reserved approach adopted by the Admiralty gave him the chance to argue his case without being opposed by factual arguments that would have brought a level of reason and common sense to the Air Board's proceedings.

The controversy continued throughout the summer and autumn of 1916 without any clear conclusion being reached. The issues came to a head on 23 October when Curzon forwarded the first report of the Air Board to the War Committee. In a lengthy document quoted by Roskill[23] he levelled a harsh attack on the Admiralty organisation, the attitude of its representatives towards the Air Board and on its refusal to adopt a system like that of the War Office in which General Henderson controlled all matters concerning the RFC and had a seat on the Army Council. Curzon's diatribe also included criticism of the Admiralty's alleged failure to develop rigid airships which was both ill-informed and unfair but his main thrust was aimed at the naval members of his Board, neither of whom had been able to speak authoritatively on Admiralty policy because neither carried full responsibility for the administration of the RNAS which was now spread throughout several departments and directorates. Roskill commented that 'it is difficult to understand why the Admiralty did not yield gracefully on the comparatively minor issue of appointing a Fifth Sea Lord'[24] to provide the lead on naval air matters. To a certain extent, however, he answered his own question by noting that to do so would have required significant re-organisation throughout the Admiralty, so widespread was the control of air matters. It is probable that Balfour had no wish to do so at the instigation of an outside agency but had he done so it would have eliminated at a stroke one of Curzon's chief complaints and might well have prevented the drive for a unified air service that was to follow in 1917. Arguments between the implacable Curzon and Balfour continued until December 1916 when Asquith's first coalition government fell. It was replaced by a second coalition government led by Lloyd George within which a number of changes were made. Admiral Sir John Jellicoe replaced Jackson as First Sea Lord and Sir Edward Carson replaced Balfour as First Lord. It is to some extent arguable that these changes were influenced by feelings among politicians, including Lloyd George himself, that Balfour's attitude towards the Air Board and its views on the future of air operations had been too intransigent and the Navy was somehow out of step with the aeronautical progress described by Curzon and Henderson. It is also arguable that Henderson regarded himself as the potential head of any unified air service. From his point of view the RNAS took resources from the RFC which was already completely under his control. Given his self-confessed lack of knowledge about naval air operations, his ambition was dangerous and the warning signs of where his arguments were leading ought to have been picked up by the Admiralty and vigorously opposed.

Mechanics of 3 Wing RNAS preparing a Sopwith 1½ Strutter fighter for an escort mission with the Wing's bombers. The fighter version had a second seat aft of the pilot for a gunlayer with a Lewis gun on a flexible mounting. The bomber variant of the type was a single-seater and the bombs were suspended, nose-down, in the space occupied by the second cockpit in the fighter variant. Used by the RNAS as a fighter, bomber and reconnaissance aircraft, the 1½ Strutter has a fair claim to be the world's first multi-role combat aircraft. (Author's collection)

To add to the bitter political arguments in Whitehall, the questions of aircraft procurement, supply and RFC expansion became absorbed into a wider political debate about how new air weapons were to be used tactically and, potentially, strategically.[25] The question of who should bomb inland targets was brought to a head by a letter from General Haig to the War Office in which he protested strongly against the operations of 3 Wing RNAS from the French air base at Luxeuil-les-Bains.[26] He saw this as an intrusion into his own sphere of responsibility, a point of view with which both the War Office and the War Committee were quick to concur. The Admiralty was forced to respond by 'concurring in the gradual withdrawal of the RNAS squadrons operating from Luxeuil'.[27] The political arguments were moving towards their conclusion and on 22 December 1916 the new government's War Cabinet approved the conclusions reached on the reorganisation of the air services recommended to the previous administration by

The officers of 3 Wing RNAS in October 1916. Wing Captain W L Elder RNAS, who commanded the Wing, is seated in the centre with Wing Commander R Bell-Davies VC DSO RNAS, who was in charge of operations, seated to his left. The then Flight Sub Lieutenant R Collishaw RNAS is in the front row standing, second from the left. They are all dressed in field service khaki. (Author's collection)

the War Committee. A Fifth Sea Lord, responsible for air matters, was to be added to the Board of Admiralty and responsibility for the design and supply of all aircraft was to be transferred to the Ministry of Munitions. These measures were accepted by the new Board of Admiralty on 3 January 1917 and implemented with immediate effect. The appointment of a Fifth Sea Lord was a sensible move that should have been accepted earlier but it is interesting to reflect with the benefit of hindsight that the measures regarded as such a victory by Curzon and Henderson included no very real concept of what naval aircraft actually did apart from those small numbers used on inland bombing missions and a only theoretical concept of strategic bombing operations which as yet had no practical basis. It is also interesting to observe that Haig, who had felt moved to criticise the embryonic RNAS bombing campaign against industrial targets, had apparently done little to stimulate a similar effort by the RFC, despite its rapid growth in numbers of men and aircraft during 1916, until prompted to do so for political reasons by Henderson.

Undoubtedly the political arguments of 1916 produced winners and losers and the Admiralty found itself in the latter category because it had not appreciated the dangerous position it was putting itself into. Nor had it taken the steps needed to ward off the ill-informed attack by Lord Curzon and by early 1917 the RNAS was in clear danger of being subsumed into the larger RFC to form a unified air service which would not be focused on naval operations. The political wrangling also produced an unfortunate operational impact. On 20 December 1916 Commodore Sueter wrote a memorandum for the Admiralty Board[28] in which he proposed the use of torpedo-carrying aeroplanes launched from the decks of aircraft carriers to attack the German High Sea Fleet in Wilhelmshaven and the Austrian fleet in the Adriatic. This was a proposal that was becoming a practical proposition with advances in technology but unfortunately he forwarded it just as the political arguments reached their bitter climax when he had spoken out at recent meetings of the Air Board in favour of the amalgamation of the two air services. This had obviously not endeared him to his naval colleagues but he had also failed to appreciate that the very measures proposed by the Air Board which he had supported made torpedo-bombers a more difficult proposition to procure and put into service. They needed to same high-powered engines that Henderson wanted for the RFC and that Curzon had accused the Admiralty of buying in unnecessarily large numbers. In 1917 the Admiralty would not find it easy to get the numbers of aircraft and engines that it needed. It must also be understood that the Air Board's new schemes were not only ill-considered but divisive. Whereas the whole strike force of ships modified with flight decks, lightweight airborne torpedoes and the aircraft to carry them over a reasonable strike radius would have been taken forward within the various departments of the Admiralty, responsibility would now be spread between different government departments. The Admiralty could, ultimately, provide the ships and the necessary weapons but now the aircraft and engines would have to be designed and procured by the Ministry of Munitions to meet its own set of requirements and priorities; these might not accord with those of the Admiralty. General Henderson's bid for increased authority and Lord Curzon's spiteful attack on the Admiralty had operational as well as political fallout and naval aviation, of which neither had a very clear understanding, was the biggest loser.

14 The Report that Forgot about Sea Power

In the early part of 1917 the new coalition government under Lloyd George introduced changes which included the creation of a new Air Board under the chairmanship of Lord Cowdray. It was given considerably greater powers than its predecessor under the New Ministries and Secretaries Act of 1916 and one of its first actions was to secure the transfer of responsibility for the supply and design of aeroplanes and seaplanes with their engines and accessories from the Ministry of Munitions, where it had only lain for a few weeks, to itself. At the same time, RN operational commanders were stressing the need for increased numbers of aircraft on anti-submarine patrols and that the growing requirement for aircraft to operate from warships was being frustrated by a lack of RNAS pilots. In the middle of the year, however, German air raids on London focused the attention of politicians, press and the general public on the defence of the UK itself against air attack. The reaction can fairly be described as panic and led to measures which were to have long-term and unforeseen consequences.

In Germany General Ernst von Hoeppner had formulated plans to use the new force of Gotha G.IV bombers to attack London. The aircraft was advanced for its time with two Mercedes D.IVa engines, each of 260hp, and a crew of three comprising the mission commander/observer, pilot and gunner, and was capable of carrying a bomb load of up to 1100lbs. A special unit was formed to carry out strategic air raids, primarily intended to hit London, known as the 'England' Squadron, and it was commanded by Hauptman Ernst Brandenburg, an observer not a pilot. The plan involved attacking in daylight to ease the problem of navigation and in theory to improve the accuracy of bomb-aiming. The pilots were trained to fly in tight formation so that the concentrated fire from all their gunners could, it was hoped, drive off intercepting fighters and they flew from forward bases in Belgium to limit the time taken to reach their targets. Even then, the flight over the North Sea caused navigational difficulties and mechanical unreliability led at first to the loss of more aircraft than were shot down by the British defences. Hoeppner's first raid was launched on 25 May 1917 when twenty-one Gothas took off to attack London. The formation found the target area to be obscured by thick

Winston Churchill, First Lord of the Admiralty, and Admiral of the Fleet Lord Fisher of Kilverstone GCB OM GCVO, leaving a meeting of the Committee of Imperial Defence before the outbreak of war. Fisher's dynamic enthusiasm for new weapons systems led, among many others, to the *R 1* and SS airship projects. Churchill learnt to fly with the RNAS and came close to taking the qualifying test to become a pilot. Notwithstanding the strong views expressed by his colleagues, he remained the only wartime senior British politician to have taken control of an aircraft. (Author's collection)

haze with towering clouds above it and so they turned south looking for clear air and alternative targets, eventually arriving in clear skies over Folkestone. Some bombs were dropped on a Canadian barracks which might have been considered a legitimate target but the majority missed and fell on the town itself where the streets were crowded because few people had taken shelter and a number were looking up at the aircraft. Casualties included 95 civilians killed and 184 injured. A total of seventy-four defending fighters took off individually after the Gothas were sighted but with no form of aircraft direction, none of them made contact.[1] A second raid was launched two weeks later and this also had to turn away from London because of adverse weather. They eventually bombed an alternate target, the naval base at Sheerness, killing forty-five civilians for the loss of a single Gotha which was shot down by anti-aircraft gunfire.

The third attempt was the first to reach London and it flew over Essex on the forenoon of 13 June 1917 to attack from the north-west where it was expected that the gun defences would be weakest. Twenty-two Gothas had taken off but several were forced to turn back because of mechanical problems and they dropped their bombs ineffectually on targets of opportunity in the Thames estuary. The aircraft flew at a height of about 15,000ft and were clearly visible in their tight formation from the ground, encouraging thousands of Londoners to come out and watch them rather than take shelter.[2] Zeppelin attacks on the British capital had been made largely at night and so the sight of a formation of enemy aircraft was too unusual for most civilians to consider taking shelter.[3] The first bombs fell on the Royal Albert Docks at about 11.30, killing eight civilians and damaging property. The remainder fell on the 'England' squadron's briefed target at Liverpool Street railway station and the area around it. A train full of passengers was about to depart for Cambridge when it received a direct hit and the war poet Siegfried Sassoon had a narrow escape when he was about to board it. He wrote later that 'helpless civilians now had to face the grim prospect of being slaughtered without warning by unseen enemies lurking in the sky'.[4] Thirteen people were killed and many more injured in the station but the most horrific casualties were suffered at Upper North Street School in Poplar where fifteen children were killed and thirty seriously injured when a 110lb bomb fell through the roof and several floors before exploding. The blast collapsed the ground floor into the basement and there were

German drawing of a Gotha bomber produced by the company that designed and built them. (Author's collection)

heart-rending scenes as mothers clawed their way through rubble searching for their children, most of whom were under 5 years old. On this occasion ninety-two defending fighters took off once the raiders were sighted but only one, an RFC Bristol Fighter, managed to close with the enemy and carry out a determined attack. It was driven off by the fire from the Gotha's gunners badly damaged with its gunner dead.

A further raid on 7 July killed 54 civilians in the London streets and injured 190 but on this occasion an RNAS fighter managed to get amongst the bombers as they left the coast and shot one down.[5] Again large numbers of civilians had come out to watch the bombers rather than take shelter, adding to the list of casualties, and the press began to demand action to prevent what was described as the stately procession of enemy aircraft over southern England in broad daylight.[6] The *Daily Mail* compared the raid of 13 June with the national humiliation of 1667 when a Dutch fleet sailed up the Medway unopposed and burnt the English fleet at its moorings.[7] A *Times* editorial after the first attacks declared emphatically that the only means of coping with such attacks was to develop an aggressive British aerial policy since 'in the air, far more than in any other sphere of modern fighting, the overwhelming advantage is always with the attack'.[8] Another leader after the July attack went further and noted that it was the absence of any evidence of the expansion of the air services to meet the increasing menace from the air that was causing public disquiet.[9] The writer wondered whether the government could improve the system of aerial defences in the British mainland without detriment to the 'paramount requirements of the armies'. Ominously, he observed that the air defences had been under the dual control of the Army and Navy and that 'whatever the merits of the case for unified control, past co-operation between the two Services has not been sufficiently close'. The intense interest now being shown by the public, press and politicians was, he felt, due to the 'distinctive recognition that aircraft are rapidly becoming a primary means of gaining ultimate victory'. It must be remembered that Allied hopes that victory might be gained in 1917 had collapsed after the failure of a major French spring offensive on the Aisne.[10] Mutinies had subsequently broken out in the demoralised French Army and on 31 July 1917 the British Army had launched a major offensive intended to break out of the Ypres Salient towards the Belgian coast. Other First World War battles lasted longer and led to higher numbers of casualties but it was this offensive and particularly the efforts, in appalling conditions, to capture the small village of Passchendaele that dispirited British politicians and public alike. The Germans had launched their second unrestricted U-boat offensive and, although the convoy system had been introduced at last, merchant ship losses had been so high that there was a real fear that Britain might run out of both food and the fuel needed for oil-fired warships and aircraft. Talk of a surplus of aircraft engines and a strategic bomber force were of little value if the Navy could not bring the fuel needed to fly them into the UK. The Russian Army was on the verge of collapse and the October Revolution was only weeks away. Given such a period of crisis and low national morale in the second half of 1917, therefore, Lloyd George would have been stung by criticism of Britain's air defences in the press, even if he demonstrably lacked a full understanding of the problem. He did what all politicians do when under stress in such situations; he formed a committee.

Lieutenant General Jan Christian Smuts had distinguished himself in the Boer War fighting for the Transvaal against the British as the leader of a commando force which developed techniques of hit-and-run warfare. He subsequently became a skilled academic, lawyer and a staunch supporter of the British Empire and Commonwealth until his death in 1950. In 1914 he led the South African force that captured German South West Africa[11] and subsequently commanded the British Army in East Africa on operations against German colonial forces. He had been invited to attend an Imperial Conference in London in 1917 and, since he was well known and popular with the British public, he had been asked to stay on in London as an ex-officio member of the War Cabinet. After the press demands for action he was asked to join a new group to be known as the Committee on Air Organisation and Home Defence against Air Raids under the nominal chairmanship of Lloyd George himself.[12] However, faced with the bleak progress of land operations in France and Russia and the need to defeat the U-boats, the Prime Minister's health began to deteriorate and Smuts became the effective, if not the titular, chairman with such advisers as he chose to work with him.[13] Because of his reputation and presumed non-partisan status, he was regarded by politicians as a safe pair of hands who would have a better knowledge than most of unconventional warfare. From an RN perspective, however, he had no knowledge of naval operations and, since he worked alone or in private sessions that were not open to scrutiny by experts or even select committees of MPs, there was no realistic oversight of his thought processes. He had therefore to lean heavily on statements made by advisers who put themselves forward but lacked the specialised knowledge to test the quality of their input. Unfortunately, his own reputation and the fact that he spoke with the authority of the Prime Minister meant that his recommendations seem not to have been questioned with due diligence.

Smuts' first report followed the War Cabinet meeting of 11 July 1917 and dealt solely with the air defence arrangements for London. It described London's vulnerability both geographically and as the focal point of the British Empire's war effort and went on to claim, without any basis in intelligence, experience or scientific analysis, that 'London might through aerial warfare become part of the battlefront' within the next 12 months. There was no comment about the extent to which this would require a massive expansion of German aircraft production, the effect of the British naval blockade which would make it extremely difficult for the enemy to achieve it or the fact that UK air defences could be improved significantly within the same period. One daylight raid by a handful of aircraft had caused panic and Smuts blamed the failure to react effectively on the fact that the defences were structured around countering night raids by Zeppelins using aircraft flown singly and anti-aircraft guns that were not concentrated in batteries near the most obvious targets. The report also mentioned fragmented co-ordination between RFC aircraft over the land, RNAS aircraft over the sea approaches, the Observation Corps and the London anti-aircraft guns and recommended appointing a senior officer of 'first rate ability and practical air experience' to take executive command of the London air defences.[14] The appointment of a dynamic commander was obviously important but what was really needed was an effective system that could give situational awareness of the air battle and which could direct fighters into positions from which they could first see and then intercept the bombers. Brigadier General E B Ashmore was appointed in command of what was now termed the London Air Defence Area in August 1917 and proved to be an ideal choice. A former artillery officer, he had learnt to fly in 1914 and commanded 1 Wing RFC in November 1914. Subsequent commands included both I Brigade and IV Brigade RFC in France before being appointed to command the London air defences. He created an effective system of systems that included the embryonic Royal Observer Corps to track enemy aircraft over the land, the GPO to provide telephone and teleprinter links and sector controlling operations rooms that expanded the area to the coast of Kent and Essex before the war ended and scientists who looked for new ways of locating and tracking aircraft. The system of fighter control used by the RAF in 1940 was actually based largely on Ashmore's work with the added bonus of radar that could track aircraft before they reached the coast but not over the land.

In fact the German capacity to maintain daylight attacks soon began to lose momentum. Some attacks were made on coastal targets but found that the defences had already improved. On 12 August 1917 RNAS fighters drove a formation of Gothas away from Chatham Dockyard but they bombed Southend-on-Sea instead and caused a number of casualties. A single Gotha was shot down over the sea by a Sopwith Pup. By 22 August the Germans had lost nineteen Gothas to all causes, ten of them on 18 August alone. Defences steadily improved and German industry did indeed fail to provide the number of aircraft the 'England' Squadron needed to sustain its operations. Even its supplies of fuel and spare parts were inadequate and difficult to sustain. The German Army High Command concluded that strategic bombing by day had been a failure, that the rate at which aircraft were being lost could not be sustained and that the experiment should be concluded. From then on raids were only made sporadically and at night. Unfortunately, Smuts seemed not to notice and he continued his enquiry into air organisation in private using rooms in the Hotel Cecil in the Strand, London.[15] A number of men were interviewed, among them Sir David Henderson, Director General of Military Aeronautics, William Weir, a Scottish industrialist and member of the Air Board since 1916, Major General Sefton Brancker, Henderson's deputy, Commodore Godfrey Paine, Fifth Sea Lord and Director of Naval Aviation, Rear Admiral Mark Kerr, seconded to the Air Board, Winston Churchill, who was now the Minister of Munitions, Lord Cowdray, the President of the Air Board, his predecessor Lord Curzon, Lord Derby, the Secretary of State for War, and many others. Unfortunately, only three written papers submitted to Smuts seem to have survived; those from Cowdray, Henderson and Kerr.[16]

In the first of these Cowdray told Smuts that he had initially thought that his Board's powers were adequate but had since changed his mind. He now wanted the Board to be established permanently with increased powers. A further memorandum made it clear that he had not recommended an 'independent aerial service' when his existing terms of reference were drawn up because he felt that the current 'administration of the naval and military air services as at present exist, or will exist when their imperative needs are satisfied, should not be changed'.[17] It can be deduced from this that Cowdray's intention in requesting an air staff was to meet wartime expediency and, potentially, facilitate the creation of a unified air service after the war had ended. He was not in favour of a hasty and potentially ill-informed change before the end of the war. Henderson's memorandum advocated a new department 'with full responsibility for war in the air' which he obviously hoped to head. He hedged his bets, however, and added that it should not be created until 'the immediate needs of the Navy and the Army can be supplied' in, he thought, early 1918 when 'a considerable force of bombing machines will be available'. Weir had apparently told the Air Board in September 1917 that British aero-engine production would expand rapidly to the point where production of the major types would reach 15,914 engines by early 1918, a figure that was 3302 engines in excess of the anticipated requirement. Unfortunately, Cowdray took this figure for granted and enquired what ministry should take responsibility for the new fleet of aircraft these engines could equip. This nebulous force became linked with Henderson's 'considerable force of bombing machines' and Smuts was made aware of Weir's forecast when he began his study. In fact, the actual deliveries of aircraft engines fell far short of Weir's prediction; 6571 instead of 15,914. This was a shortfall of 4041 engines below the number needed to meet the existing requirements for aircraft production and there was certainly no question of a surplus to equip Henderson's bombing force.[18] The tragedy here was that Smuts accepted the numbers without question and arrived at the conclusion that there was about to be a force of new aircraft, surplus to the immediate needs of the RNAS and RFC, that could be used on strategic bombing missions independent of naval or military operations. He thus saw a need to rush through an amalgamation of the two air services in order to make use of these 'paper aircraft' in a hypothetical air campaign during the second half of 1918.

The third surviving memorandum was, from a naval perspective, the most damaging and has been referred to as a 'bombshell' by several writers. The son of an admiral, Rear Admiral Mark Kerr had an illustrious career in the RN with a decade of sea commands which included two battlecruisers and two battleships, prior to 1913 when he became naval attaché to Italy and Greece. Whilst on leave in the UK from this appointment, he learnt to fly and became the first flag officer to obtain a pilot's certificate.[19] From 1915 to 1917 he served as the Commander-in-Chief of the British Adriatic Squadron after which, given his air experience, he was appointed as the Admiralty representative on the Air Board.[20]

Besides his qualification as a pilot, Kerr had a keen interest in aviation and had shown an early interest in the development of the flush-deck aircraft carrier. However, by 1917 he seems to have taken at face value intelligence reports he had been shown whilst in his Adriatic command that Germany intended to build a force of large bombers and to use them in raids against the UK. This much was true as we have seen but he believed that there were to be 4000 of these machines intended to destroy large areas of south-eastern England.[21] To counter this offensive he recommended that a force of 2000 bombers, fitted with the illusory surplus engines and under the direction of a new Air Ministry, should be created as quickly as possible to retaliate. It is possible that Cowdray might have persuaded Smuts to put off recommending the amalgamation of the RNAS and RFC until after the war was over but Henderson's view that an independent force was not only easily obtainable but inevitable in the short term and Kerr's dramatic prophecy evidently won him over and elements from both their memoranda can be seen in the final text of Smuts' second report which was submitted to the War Cabinet on 17 August 1917. There was significant criticism of the Admiralty and the report strongly recommended the creation of an Air Ministry with its own 'Air General Staff' and the amalgamation of the RNAS and RFC into a single 'independent' air service. Some of the statements made in this report can only be described as arrogant in their acceptance of unproved theories and visions of the future which could not be justified at the time and hardly so decades later. No attempt seems to have been made to incorporate the wider picture and take into account the everyday activities of aircraft and their crews to bring a third dimension to naval and military operations. Even today, the 'independent' RAF is not capable of effective war-fighting operations that are completely divorced from the activities of the older established services[22] that Smuts predicted for it in 1918. It never has been and Smuts' opinions could not have been more widely misplaced. It is a sign of the strain under which Lloyd George's coalition government was struggling that they accepted Smuts' report without any sort of effective scrutiny.

In detail, the report began with its terms of reference. It was light on substance but contained grand, visionary statements such as the one in paragraph 5 that 'Air Services can be used as an independent means of war operations . . . nobody that witnessed the attack on London in July could have any doubt on that point. As far as can at present be foreseen there is absolutely no limit to scale of its future independent war use'. Smuts' greatest use of hyperbole came in the following sentence '. . . and the day may not be far off when aerial operations with their devastation of enemy lands and destruction of industrial and populous centres on a vast scale may become the principal operations of war, to which the older forms of military and naval operations may become secondary and subordinate'. It is worth pointing out that Smuts used the word 'may' three times in a single sentence, presumably indicating that even he had some doubts about what he was proposing. With hindsight we can note that even in 1942, after several years of re-armament and three years into the Second World War, Bomber Command was nowhere near well enough equipped to achieve the devastation Smuts thought 'may' become a principal operation of war. Did he really think that the engine surplus promised in 1918 and the slow biplanes they would have powered could have created an independent bombing force in 1918 or even 1919 capable of achieving such an effect? Meanwhile anti-submarine warfare, fleet air defence, reconnaissance and strike from the sea were all established and essential parts of the war at sea controlled by the Royal Navy.

The theoretical surplus of engines was clearly one of the biggest drivers behind his recommendations because paragraph 6 begins with the statement that

the urgency for the change will appear from the following facts. Hitherto aircraft production has been insufficient to supply the demands of both Army and Navy and the chief concern of the Air Board has been to satisfy the necessary requirements of those Services. But that phase is rapidly passing. The programme of aircraft production which the War Cabinet has sanctioned for the following 12 months is far in excess of Army and Navy requirements. Next Spring and Summer the position will be that the Army and Navy will have all the air service required in connection with their operations: and over and above that there will be a great surplus available for independent operations. Who is to look

after and direct the activities of this available surplus? . . . the creation of an Air
Staff for planning and directing independent air operations will soon be pressing.
More than that, the surplus of engines and machines now being built should
have regard to the strategical purpose to which they are going to be put. And in
settling in advance the types to be built the operations for which they are
intended apart from naval or military use should be clearly kept in view. This
means that the Air Board has already reached the stage where the settlement of
future war policy in the air has become necessary. The necessity for an Air
Ministry and Air General Staff has therefore become urgent.

This was the reason for the haste Smuts recommended but these were not facts. If
unbiased production experts had been consulted they could have explained that
there was no surplus of engines and thus no expanded bomber formation or attacks
on the enemy on a vast scale. It was a vision incapable of fulfilment. We can all
appreciate visionaries who weigh all the relevant factors and plan a bold way ahead
but Smuts based his vision on a chimera pushed on him by a handful of men who
had their own agendas. Between them they forgot about sea power and the vital
part it played in the British war effort. By August 1917 aircraft had become an
integral part the Royal Navy which had placed their operation in the hands of
senior officers who were responsible for the complete range of three-dimensional
naval activities that Great Britain, its Empire and its allies relied upon to win the
war. In the name of what he considered to be progress and without proper study
and consultation, the Smuts Report demolished this structure at the stroke of a
politician's pen and replaced it with a system that involved a separate service co-
operating with the Navy when its own commanders permitted and its own priorities
allowed. It was a step that was to impact seriously on the ability of both the Royal
Navy and the Army to fight against a sophisticated enemy in the years ahead, but
its full impact was not appreciated at first.

The initial reaction of Sir Eric Geddes, who had only become First Lord on 20
July 1917, was cautious and he sent a copy of the report to Admiral Beatty,
C-in-C of the Grand Fleet, asking for comment. The Board of Admiralty took
some days to consider the report and, to their credit, decided not to support its
recommendations. Their response[23] was compiled by the Naval War Staff under
the direction of Captain T E Crease RN, the Naval Assistant to the First Lord,
and began by outlining the tasks that it was considered essential for naval aircraft
to perform. It was a responsible and pragmatic approach and three paragraphs are
worth quoting to illustrate the Admiralty's view. The Admiralty War Staff observed
that the report had stated that retention of naval control of the RNAS 'would make
the confusion hopeless and render the solution of the air problem impossible'. 'To

the impartial thinker', they felt 'it would rather appear that confusion would be caused by making such a change as that contemplated during the progress of a war'. The response continued that:

> It is also stated that the maintenance of three separate air services is out of the question, but apparently no difficulty is foreseen in having three separate Departments dealing with war operations, one of which has to be entirely created amidst the absorption and turmoil of the daily conduct of the war, and in thus making necessary multifarious operations and co-ordination between three distinct Departments instead of two as at present. It is often said, perhaps with justice, that there is at the present time insufficient and ineffective co-operation between the Navy and Army. The problems of those charged with the conduct of naval operations will not be lessened by the institution of another independent Department to be consulted on these matters.

On the question of the surplus aircraft and the need to define uses for them the War Staff felt that

> the subject of surplus machines over those required for purely Navy and Army work raises important questions of personnel. These machines will be useless without qualified pilots and observers who, from the very nature of the work contemplated must be of the very highest degree of efficiency. At the present moment the great difficulty in the RNAS is the efficient training of sufficient personnel. The limiting factor is personnel and not machines, and many more machines would be requisitioned and used if pilots could be trained to fly them. It is believed that the RFC are in the same position – at all events a considerable number of RNAS pilots and machines have had to be attached on loan to the Army . . .

The response filled several pages and could, perhaps, be criticised for going into too much fine detail and not concentrating on the central issue and its rejection. However, it did conclude that 'a close analysis of the report in detail would enable many dialectical points to be scored if it were desired to do so. But verbal victories here will not enable us to defeat the Germans. There are a host of minor difficulties in making any change such as is proposed. These difficulties could undoubtedly be overcome if the principles of the changes were sound, but the Admiralty are convinced that these proposed changes are fundamentally unsound so far as naval air operations are concerned, and that they should not be made.' Notwithstanding its earlier distrust of the Air Board, the response concluded by expressing its appreciation of the 'valuable assistance' it had given and stating that the Admiralty would be glad to consider any improvements that could now be suggested.[24] But, however well it had been crafted, the Admiralty's response came too late and the recommendations made in Smuts' second report were approved in principle by the War Cabinet on 24 August 1917. Cowdray, Curzon and Churchill had spoken out strongly in favour of Smuts' vision and Lloyd George, who favoured change for its own sake, took no part in the discussion. There was simply too much political momentum to allow rational counter-argument to prevail. Worse still, by the time the War Cabinet had made its decision, Beatty had written to Geddes and surprised both him and the Admiralty War Staff by expressing himself to be in favour of the proposed changes. The views he expressed proved to be as big a 'bombshell' as those expressed by Kerr and his grasp of reality about as far removed since he, too, accepted the projected paper force of aircraft without question. He was to regret his ill-considered response within weeks when it became apparent that the new independent air force was just that, an organisation with its own agenda that did not necessarily match his own. Beatty's letter to the First Lord from his flagship *Queen Elizabeth*, written on 22 August 1917, showed that he neither fully understood the problem nor the proposed solution.[25] After giving it as his opinion that the qualifications required of pilots and observers to work with the fleet were

Admiral Beatty PC GCB OM GCVO DSO was a complex personality who certainly understood by 1918 that aircraft were a critical element of his Grand Fleet's ability to take offensive action against the German High Sea Fleet. Unfortunately his failure to comprehend that the projected independent air force was not just a re-branded RNAS was to have an impact on naval aviation that he was to regret for the rest of his life, especially during his post-war tenure as First Sea Lord. Of interest, his distinctive and unique six-button reefer jacket differed from the standard eight-button RN design and was adopted by the United States Navy as the pattern for the new officers' uniform it introduced after the Great War. (Author's collection)

'not such that they cannot be acquired in a short time' he said that they were 'part of the knowledge required by airmen generally'. He added that 'it would be deplorable if the extension of the use of aircraft were to be confined in any way. I certainly thought that it was recognised by now that we cannot bring the war to a successful conclusion unless we maintain the command of the air.' His most naive comment came in the penultimate paragraph in which he said 'the fears expressed on pages 12 and 13 [of the Admiralty response] that co-operation between the Navy and the new Air Service, and the naval staff and air staff, would be unattainable cannot seriously be considered. Obviously the Admiralty view that the naval staff must control and be responsible for all operations combining naval and air units is the correct one.' Therein lay the problem, because it was not obvious to anyone else in the RN that an independent Air Staff with its own priorities centred on long-range bombing would wish to have any of its resources controlled by the Naval Staff, especially if their need for resources competed directly with the hypothetical bomber force and its supply of high-powered engines. Within weeks Beatty had begun to realise his mistake and was complaining about the lack of air resources being made available to him but by then it was too late.

Outside the circle of politicians within the War Cabinet and those who had thought they had something to gain from the change, several people who thought logically were opposed to Smuts' second report. The First Sea Lord, Admiral Jellicoe, wrote to Geddes[26] on 14 August making several incisive observations. There had been a continual fight between the existing two Services for funding, especially in peacetime, and Jellicoe felt it to be 'obvious that the creation of a third service would add to the difficulties in this respect'. He also made the telling point that 'it is stated in the report under consideration that the Air General Staff will from time to time attach to the Army and the Navy the air units necessary for naval or military operations. It is quite obvious to anyone conversant with the ordinary administration of Government Departments that there is every probability that the Army and the Navy will be starved in their requirements by the Air General Staff in order that the latter may have what they consider sufficient aircraft to carry out their policy. Of course this statement will be denied by those who consider that the proper organisation is that suggested in the report, but it is useless to deny a statement which all experience shows would undeniably be true.' It was true and the situation he described began to happen within days of the absorption of the RNAS into the new Royal Air Force. Jellicoe directly contradicted Beatty by stressing that 'the special training required of a naval air service pilot can only be given by the Navy and that once air officers are trained to carry out naval work they must remain attached to the Navy'. In view of this, he felt that 'even supposing an Imperial Air Service came into being, the naval side of it would necessarily become

Admiral of the Fleet Viscount Jellicoe of Scapa Flow GCB OM GCVO. He had flown in a Zeppelin before the war and always overrated the enemy's ability to use airships for reconnaissance, lying awake at night worrying about the Grand Fleet's shortcomings but not realising that the High Sea Fleet might have similar difficulties. He failed to make the best use of his own aviation assets, especially the seaplane carrier *Campania*, and could have done more to stimulate their practical employment. However, his observations about the creation of an independent air force were shrewd and should have been taken more seriously by the First Lord. (Author's collection)

a specialty immediately and would at once, therefore, become a separate and distinct service. There would thus be nothing gained by embodying the RNAS under a nominal head . . . and there would be a great deal to lose.' Again he had hit the nail accurately on the head. By 1924 naval air operations had evolved into the Fleet Air Arm, albeit under dual control, and in 1937 Lord Inskip the Minister for Defence Co-ordination was to order that full control of naval aviation was to be returned to the Admiralty. The tragedy was that so much experience and knowledge was to be lost in the meantime.

Vice Admiral Sir Henry Oliver, the Second Sea Lord, wrote in September 1921[27] that he had been a member of the Admiralty Board in August 1917 and recalled that 'all the naval members of the Board were opposed to the change as were all the military members of the Army Council. Both bodies agreed to do everything possible to resist the change but the Admiralty Board was informed by the First Lord 'that whatever they did the cabinet intended to make the change'. A Board meeting was held to consider the action to be taken and a memorandum was drawn up giving the considered reasons Board members could use to oppose the change. A second memorandum was drawn up which was only to be used if the War Cabinet forced the change on the Admiralty to attempt to get the best working basis possible if it had to be accepted. At the War Cabinet meeting Geddes was asked to give the Admiralty's view. He read out the first memorandum and then, without a pause, read out the second instead of keeping it for use after the War Cabinet had decided on the main question. This tactic destroyed the Admiralty case and prevented the Army Council representative from properly presenting their own case. Oliver wanted it to be made clear that the naval and military officers on the Admiralty Board and the Army Council were emphatically not, at the time of the War Cabinet decision, in favour of a separate air force.

In France General Foch wrote that the creation of an independent long-range bombing force could not be accepted and that it was impossible to conceive of the development, or even existence, of one of the combatant forces being exempted from the authority of the supreme commander who was responsible for the unified action of all Allied forces.[28] General Haig was also opposed the report's recommendations and wrote that 'I may say at once that some of the views put forward as to future possibilities go far beyond anything that can be justified in my experience . . . apart from the morality . . . of seeking to end the war by devastation of industrial and populace centres on a vast scale, I am unable to agree that there is practically no limit to such methods in this war.'[29] He had no doubt that the views expressed by Smuts required very considerable modification and he desired to point out 'the grave danger of an Air Ministry charged with such powers as the Committee recommends assuming control with a belief in theories which are not in accordance with practical experience'. Even some of those who advised Smuts appeared later to have entertained doubts and Lord Hugh Cecil, when subsequently asked if he was the actual author of Smuts' second report, denied it and said that he had thought the bombing plans rather visionary but had not 'poured cold water' on them as he felt that a change was needed. Arguably, this was the greatest change ever forced on the British armed forces in wartime and, despite all the opposition, Lloyd George clearly felt that if his coalition government was to survive a change had to be made and it had to be one that would be obvious to both press and public. From now on the Admiralty and War Office had little choice but to move swiftly towards and amalgamation of the RNAS and RFC, attempting to minimise the impact on the British war effort.

The date chosen for the implementation of the recommendation to unify the flying arms of the Navy and Army was set as 1 April 1918 which also marked the start of the new British financial year.[30] A transitional Air Council was established on 3 January 1918 and the staff of the new Air Ministry began to assemble at the Hotel Cecil in the Strand where Smuts had done his work, gradually taking over the functions of Lord Cowdray's Air Board. The organisation was to be run at first on the lines of the War Office and discipline was to be enforced under the terms of

The greatly expanded RNAS Eastchurch seen from the air in 1918 gives a very good idea how the whole RNAS had increased in size since its modest beginnings in 1914. (Author's collection)

the Army Act until a new code of RAF discipline could be produced. It was also decided that at first the officers and men of the new air force would adopt Army ranks. Lord Rothermere was the first Secretary of State for the Air Force, appointed on 3 January and on 18 January Major General Sir High Trenchard, commander of the RFC units in France, was appointed as the first Chief of the Air Staff. Rear Admiral Kerr was appointed Deputy Chief of the Air Staff and Commodore Godfrey Paine, who had been appointed Fifth Sea Lord in early 1917, was made the Master General of Air Personnel. From the outset, however, relations between Rothermere and Trenchard were not good and on 19 March 1918 the latter resigned[31] although the fact that he had done so was not announced publicly until 12 April when he assumed command of the Independent Bomber Force based in France. Two days later the Germans launched their massive offensive on the Western Front, the whole Allied position was put in grave danger and Haig issued his famous 'backs to the wall' message. Major General F H Sykes, commander of the RFC, was appointed in place of Trenchard. Within a week Lieutenant General Henderson, the Vice President of the Air Council, resigned after bitter disappointment that he had not been offered the position of Chief of the Air Staff, his likely aim for the past two years. On 25 April Rothermere resigned and was replaced by Sir William Weir, a staunch advocate of independent air operations who, it will be recalled, had originated the fictional aero-engine production numbers that had underpinned Smuts' deliberations.

On 22 May 1918 Geddes wrote to Weir saying that:

> As you know, the Admiralty accepted the transfer of the RNAS to the RAF against its own views and under protest but I am glad to believe that from the date that the cabinet decided against the Admiralty, the RAF has received its heartiest co-operation and assistance in the difficult task with which it is charged. At the same time I feel that I ought to let you know that our fears as to the desirability of the transfer are being confirmed as time goes on. The use of aircraft with the Navy is not developing as it should. Naval representation on the Air Board has been reduced and we do not feel that our particular and rather specialised side of the air problem is receiving the attention that it should.[32]

Eventually, on 14 June 1918, Geddes and Weir signed a memorandum on 'certain lines of policy regulating the conduct of the Air Ministry' which was subsequently accepted by the War Cabinet. It said, inter alia, that

> the decision to constitute an Air Ministry with an Air General Staff was based on the conviction that the possibilities of aerial warfare and their influence on the war might more efficiently be realised by the establishment of a single authority . . . and in particular that a rapid development of aerial forces devoted to the interruption of German industrial effort and kindred objects [note that 'the destruction of industrial and populous centres on a vast scale' prophesied by Smuts had already disappeared from the Air Ministry vocabulary] might be achieved to such an extent as substantially to contribute towards bringing about a definite demand for peace. To attain success in this policy, the Air Ministry must therefore be recognised as the authority on general air policy, except as regards operations forming part of and the closest liaison with the representatives of the Navy and Army as regards the needs of these two forces, and accordingly the Air Staff must command the fullest knowledge of all methods of the utilisation of aircraft and their effectiveness in practice. It is to be recognised that the air forces operated independently by the Air Ministry are, to a certain extent, mobile and their availability is elastic, thus if the Army or Navy has some very important and temporary objective to attack by aircraft, and their own permanent establishment is unable to deal with it, they will be in a position to apply to the Air Ministry, who may detach temporarily sufficient resources to carry out the operation desired, but such forces will be under the control of the Air Ministry for re-allocation. Such specially detached forces will

Like ships, the Admiralty issued RNAS units with bells. A flight lieutenant that I have not been able to identify is seen here smoking a pipe by 5 Wing's bell at RNAS Petite Synthe. (Goble Family collection)

usually be operated under the Admiralty or War Office, but in exceptional circumstances, they may by agreement with the Admiralty or War Office be operated by the Air Ministry.

At least a modus operandi had been agreed that would carry forward the unwanted changes until the end of hostilities with the minimum of disruption but what of the dire predictions about strategic bombing that had so attracted Smuts' attention? Kerr's intelligence sources had predicted a German production run of 4000 giant bombers but such was the impact of the British naval blockade that the German Army only received eighteen Zeppelin-Staaken R-VIs to supplement the Gothas before the Armistice and their use in night raids on London and the southern English counties was a failure. The defences improved and on 19 May 1918 they shot down six Gothas in a single night, inflicting losses that the 'England' Squadron could not sustain. After the German offensive in the West failed the Gothas and R-VIs were only used against tactical targets in France. British bomber plans centred on the enormous Handley Page V/1500 which had a wingspan of 126ft and a maximum all-up weight of 24,700lbs. It could carry up to thirty 250lb bombs depending on its fuel load and the first was ordered by the Air Board on 30 July 1917 but the bulk of the Independent Bomber Force was made up of the earlier and smaller Handley Page 0/400 which had a wingspan of 100ft and a bomb load of up to sixteen 112lb bombs or one 1650lb bomb. They were only used in appreciable numbers in the last three months of the war but prior to August 1918 the most that had taken off on operations at any one time was ten. Independent Force losses were heavy, however, with eighteen aircraft missing over Germany and fifty-one wrecked.[33] The Air Ministry's first provisional expansion programme for the Independent Force was forwarded to the Admiralty and War Office for comment on 20 June 1918. This envisaged a total of 340 RAF squadrons by the end of September and out of that total sixty were to form part of the Independent Bomber Force, forty day bomber squadrons based in France and twenty night bomber squadrons based in England. Two hundred and fifty-five of the big Handley Pages had been ordered but, as with so many predictions of output, only three were available by 11 November. Both the German and British strategic bomber initiatives can thus be seen to have failed both in terms of the limited number of bombers actually produced and their minimal effects on their nations' war efforts, a fact that makes the draconian changes inflicted on naval aviation and the Army's tactical air component in the name of strategic bombing all the more difficult to comprehend.

15 1918: The RNAS' Final Year

Rather than attempt give an overview of every operation carried out by what had grown into a large organisation, I shall describe specific capabilities that show just how far the naval air service had evolved since 1914. At the very time when the RNAS was emphasising its naval focus and demonstrating its ability to operate as part of a task forces at sea, it was swept up into a land-orientated organisation with its own, different, priorities.

Aircraft Embarked in Fighting Ships
The Grand Fleet Aircraft Committee had recommended urgent steps to 'give the Grand Fleet the advantages of scouting by aircraft and at the same time embarrass Zeppelins by imposing limitations upon their movements by the perpetual menace of engagement' by fighters.[1] The first conventional warship to be fitted with a launching platform for wheeled aircraft, as we have seen, was the cruiser *Yarmouth* from which Flight Lieutenant Smart succeeded in destroying a Zeppelin over the North Sea. This had proved the concept to be feasible and a few weeks later the improvised deck was replaced by an improved design that did not limit the forward gun's arc of fire and it was decided to fit similar fixed platforms in the light cruisers *Dublin*, *Cassandra* and *Caledon*. This would allow the light cruiser squadrons attached to the Grand Fleet to have one aircraft-operating ship each for recon- naissance or air-defence duties. The take-off deck on *Cassandra* consisted of an arrangement of troughs fitted over the forecastle, forward of the gun by her builder, Vickers at Barrow-in-Furness, just prior to her completion and the fighter was stowed with its wings folded in a small hangar underneath the bridge. The sheer number of warships already on order left little capacity for the construction of the high-speed, flush-deck aircraft carriers that were now known to be the ideal solution but, with the growing appreciation of the need for aircraft for fleet use, proposals for fitting further cruisers with aeroplane-carrying arrangements followed each other in quick succession. By the autumn of 1918 take-off decks and aircraft arrangements had been fitted to the cruisers *Aurora, Birkenhead, Caledon, Calliope, Carlisle, Caroline, Cassandra, Chatham, Comus, Cordelia, Delhi, Dublin,*

HMS *Caroline*, now part of the National Museum of the Royal Navy's collection and on display in Belfast, is the only vessel left afloat that fought at Jutland. This rare photograph shows her fitted with a fixed take-off platform in 1918 with a Sopwith 2F.1 Camel secured on it. The pilot and his two mechanics are posed in front of it and sailors are working on the forecastle. There are two civilian workers beyond the sailors, indicating that the photograph was taken as the ship emerged from dockyard hands. (Guy Warner collection)

Galatea, Inconstant, Penelope, Phaeton, Royalist, Southampton, Undaunted and *Yarmouth.*

In 1917 the Beardmore WB III was introduced into service as a fleet fighter. It was a folding-wing derivative of the Sopwith Pup, a modification that required the wings to be constructed one above the other without the Pup's stagger and this arrangement caused the machine to lack the Pup's outstanding performance. Despite being easier to stow it was therefore not considered a success and was replaced in operational service by the Sopwith 2F.1 Ship's Camel. This had fixed wings and therefore needed more stowage space and because of this the 1918 cruiser designs included a hangar fitted under the bridge in the 'D' and repeat 'C' classes. This hangar was built in the shape of the letter 'T', the backs of the hangar wings and the back of the middle portion being left open and the whole of the front fitted with roller-blind shutters. A short take-off platform was arranged to project over the gun immediately forward of the hangar. The troughs over the

Another rare photograph of HMS *Caroline*, this time showing her 2F.1 Camel taking off, viewed from the bridge with two officers' heads in the left foreground. The coloured stripes on the elevators show this to be a Beardmore-built aircraft, one of eight that she embarked during her time with the Grand Fleet. (Guy Warner collection)

forecastle in *Cassandra* were found to be difficult to use and they were removed and replaced by take-off platforms like those in other cruisers. Although these had proved effective, the aircraft had to be launched with the wind directly over the bows and very little crosswind could be tolerated; the ships had, therefore, to turn into wind to launch their fighters. By then the success of launching aircraft from a platform fitted on top of a battleship or battlecruiser gun turret which could be rotated to point directly into the relative or felt wind had been demonstrated.

Captain Dumaresq RN, who had temporarily commanded *Repulse* when the turret platform trials were carried out, suggested that his own command, the cruiser *Sydney*, should be fitted with a revolving platform while she was in refit. Other cruisers could be similarly fitted as quickly as possible to achieve the same effect.[2] *Sydney* was modified with a revolving platform over her forward gun at Chatham Dockyard in November 1917. Trial launches of Pups and Camels showed that aircraft could indeed get airborne without the ship having to turn into wind, a big tactical advance over the earlier fixed platforms, and *Melbourne, Birkenhead,*

Beardmore WB-III number N6708. Note that, compared with a Sopwith Pup, the folding wings have no stagger and the interplane struts are broader. The undercarriage struts are noticeably lightweight; this is because this batch of seventy WB-IIIs were designed to jettison their undercarriages after take-off and they did not, therefore, have to bear heavy landing loads. This aircraft was delivered in December 1917 and was embarked several times in HMS *Nairana* before being deleted in August 1918. Most of the others in the batch went straight into storage at Killingholme and were never used operationally. (Author's collection)

Southampton and *Chatham* were subsequently fitted with similar platforms. Their advantages were found to be so great that it was decided to fit revolving platforms where possible in place of the fixed platforms already installed in other light cruisers. *Yarmouth* was modified in June 1918 and *Dublin* in August. In cruisers which had two guns on the centreline forward, one superimposed over the other, the arrangement of this platform on the forecastle was not practicable as it would interfere with gunfire and a modified scheme was prepared for such vessels, the revolving platform being fitted abaft the funnels and arranged to give as much training before and abaft the beam as circumstances would allow. At first there were concerns that ships thus fitted would have to turn out of line in order to get the felt wind along the centreline of the platform but trials with the first ship so fitted proved to be much better than expected, and aircraft were flown off safely with the wind as much as 20 degrees away from the platform centreline. As a result the forward platforms and fixed hangars under bridges were abandoned in all the cruisers still under construction and revolving platforms were substituted further aft. A standard design of revolving platform was prepared that could be manufactured in Dockyards and then fitted in a few hours when the vessel came into port. Platforms of this type were fitted in *Caledon* and *Cassandra* and

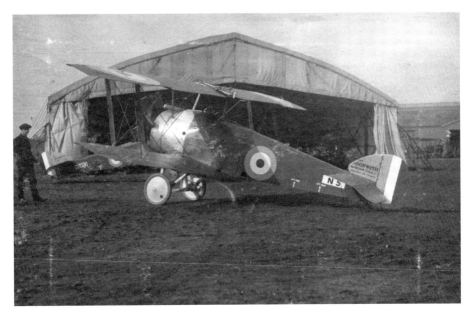

N5, the prototype Sopwith 2F.1 Camel, was delivered to the RNAS in March 1917. Sopwith Triplane N5453, visible in the background, was completed in the same month and the presence of the civilian to the left with a flat cap and cigarette indicates that this picture might have been taken at Sopwith's Brooklands facility. Note the single Vickers gun on the starboard side of the hump forward of the cockpit and the inverted Lewis gun on the upper wing. Inversion was intended to make changing the ammunition tray easier. (Goble Family collection)

constructed ready for fitting in all other cruisers of the *Ceres* and *Caledon* classes but the war ended before they could all be put in place. Similar platforms were fitted in *Delhi* and *Dunedin*.

The great progress in fitting light cruisers to carry aircraft led to a demand that battleships should be able to launch both fighters to intercept and destroy or drive off enemy aircraft and reconnaissance aircraft capable of locating the enemy fleet and spotting for the guns of their own ship when action was joined. Following the successful demonstration of lengthened turret platforms in *Repulse* and *Australia*, platforms were soon fitted in *Repulse*, *Renown*, *Australia*, *New Zealand*, *Inflexible*, *Indomitable*, *Tiger*, *Princess Royal* and *Lion* as well as the light battlecruisers *Courageous* and *Glorious*. Ships usually had two turret platforms so that they were capable of launching a 2F.1 fighter to destroy enemy reconnaissance aircraft as well as the Strutter and experience with these embarked aircraft was so positive that urgent action was undertaken to equip battleships with take-off platforms as well. By November 1918 the Grand Fleet had, in addition to the aircraft carried in the

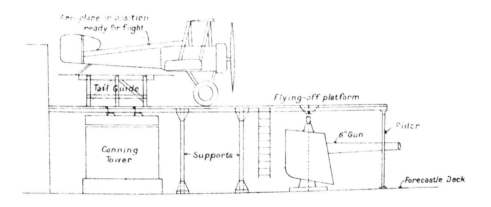

Light Cruisers – Sketch of a fixed flying-off platform as fitted. (Author's collection)

aircraft carriers *Furious* and *Argus* and the seaplane carriers with take-off platforms, the capability to embark over 100 aircraft in battleships, battlecruisers and cruisers. Their distribution was:[3]

Names	Aircraft	Total	Where carried
Repulse, Renown	2 fighters 2 reconnaissance	4	'B' and 'Y' turrets
Tiger	1 fighter	1	'Q' turret
Lion	2 fighters	2	'Q' and 'X' turrets
Princess Royal	2 fighters	2	'Q' and 'X' turrets
Australia, New Zealand	2 fighters 2 reconnaissance	4	'P' and 'Q' turrets
Indomitable, Inflexible	2 fighters 2 reconnaissance	4	'P' and 'Q' turrets

The rotating take-off platform fitted amidships on HMS *Cassandra* with a Sopwith 2F.1 Camel secured on it. (Author's collection)

Names	Aircraft	Total	Where carried
Queen Elizabeth class 5 ships	7 fighters 3 reconnaissance	10	'B' and 'X' turrets
Royal Sovereign class 5 ships	8 fighters 2 reconnaissance	10	'B' and 'X' turrets
Canada	1 fighter 1 reconnaissance	2	'B' and 'X' turrets
Erin	1 fighter	2	'B' and 'X' turrets
Iron Duke class 4 ships	6 fighters 2 reconnaissance	8	'B' and 'X' turrets
Orion class 4 ships	6 fighters 2 reconnaissance	8	'B' and 'X' turrets
Agincourt	2 fighters	2	Number 2 and 3 turrets
Hercules class 3 ships	4 fighters	6	'A' and 'X' turrets
Collingwood class 2 ships	4 fighters	4	'A' and 'Y' turrets
Bellerophon and *St Vincent* classes 4 ships	6 fighters 2 reconnaissance	8	'A' and 'Y' turrets

Pictures of Sopwith 2F.1 Camels in ship's hangars are extremely rare but this photograph of N6602 with its rear fuselage detached for transit in a 32ft cutter shows how small a space the aircraft could be fitted into. N6602 was delivered to the Grand Fleet air park at Donibristle from Brooklands in November 1917. Unusually it was not launched operationally and ditched despite spending periods embarked in *Nairana*, *Lion*, *Furious*, *Glorious*, *Caroline* and *Caledon*. This photograph shows it being brought out to *Furious* in April 1918 and it went on to survive the war, with a spell spent in *Nairana* during 1919. (Philip Jarrett collection)

The light battlecruisers *Courageous* and *Glorious* each carried a fighter on 'Y' turret and a two-seater on 'A' turret, adding a further four aircraft, and the light cruisers attached to the Grand Fleet added a further sixteen aircraft, bringing the total that could be embarked to 103 in addition to those in the specialised aircraft-carrying ships. Including the ships under construction in late 1918 the number of aircraft that could be operated from cruisers was to be:

Carlisle class	5	*Aurora* class	7
'D' class	11	*Cambrian* class	6
'E' class	3	*Caroline* class	6

This gave a further thirty-eight aircraft but they were not all embarked at the same time and the number was actually reduced when it was decided to modify the 'D' class and remove the hangar under the bridge and to remove aircraft from the

Aurora, Cambrian and *Caroline* classes when re-arming these vessels and fitting them with an additional 6in gun amidships. Some monitors and other classes of warship were fitted to operate aircraft, bringing the total to about 150 embarked aircraft; about twenty of these were 'Ship' Strutter reconnaissance aircraft and the balance fighters, mainly 2F.1 Camels. Hoisting aircraft onto the turret roofs presented some difficulties but these were overcome by the application of sound seamanship. Aircraft could be lifted from lighters onto the upper deck using gun barrels as a crane. From the deck they were lifted onto the turret using a jackstay of 4.5in extra-special-flexible steel wire rope fixed between eye-plates at the bow or stern and a convenient mast-head. The aircraft was hoisted close up to this by men hauling on a rope and then hauled into position and lowered onto the platform.

Naval Air Warfare in the North Sea
The 'Spider Web' system of air patrols described in Chapter 10 were flown by flying boats from RNAS Felixstowe. The following sortie details were described by Squadron Commander Theodore Hallam RNAS, who commanded the War Flight at Felixstowe, in his book *The Spider Web*.

Curtiss H.12 Large America flying boat number 8661 on its handling trolley at RNAS Felixstowe. It was one of a batch of fifty built by Curtiss in Toronto and was upgraded from H.8 to H.12 standard by fitting Eagle VI engines. (Author's collection)

Trim, clean, grey and rigged true, just tipping the scales at four and a half tons, 8661[4] stood on her wheeled land trolley just inside the shed. She was a fine machine measuring 96ft from wingtip to wingtip and was, eventually, to have such a long and honourable life, doing 300 hours of patrol work and 368 hours flying in all, that she was affectionately known to all the pilots as Old 61. Her hull was 42ft long, covered with canvas above the water line and flat-bottomed with a hydroplane step to lift her on top of the water when she was getting off and so enabled her to obtain a speed at which the wings had sufficient lift to pick her up into the air. She carried six and a half hours' fuel at a cruising speed of 60 knots, her top speed in level flight being 80. The working party of 20 men gathered around Old 61 and rolled her out of the shed to the concrete area.[5]

Here they chocked her up under the bow and tail with trestles in order to prevent her standing on her nose when the engines were tested. Two engineers then climbed up to each engine and started them. After they had been run slowly for about 15 minutes in order to warm up their oil, they were opened out until they were giving their full revolutions, the tremendous power shaking the whole structure of the boat.

In the meantime the armourer's party had fitted the four Lewis machine guns and loaded four 100lb bombs, two on each side tucked up under the wing roots. Each bomb was fitted with a delayed-action fuze which detonated them about two seconds after it hit the water or a submarine. In water they would therefore explode between 60 and 80ft below the surface. Bombs that detonated near a submarine might merely shake it, blow circuit-breakers and extinguish electric lights but even this was bad for the crew's morale and lowered their efficiency. Better, a near-miss might cause a leak, perhaps by buckling a hatch which pumps might not be able to contain; it might also puncture an external oil tank leading to a loss of fuel, reducing endurance and giving away the boat's position. Periscopes might be shaken or damaged, reducing the captain's ability to see when dived or hydroplanes might be damaged making the boat difficult to control. All of these things might not destroy the boat but would limit its ability to carry out its mission and might force the captain to return to base for repairs, keeping him out of the front line for the time being and reducing the threat to merchant shipping. Direct hits, when achieved, usually destroyed the submarine, with wreckage and a patch of oil giving silent witness on the surface over where it sank.

When the boat was ready the crew climbed on board. In the specific sortie described, Hallam flew as second pilot with Canadian Flight Sub Lieutenant B D 'Billiken' Hobbs RNAS as first pilot.[6] The four-man crew comprised first and second pilots, a wireless operator and engineer.

Master of 700 roaring horsepower, responsible for all things connected with the
operation of the boat and having to make instant and correct decisions as to the
nationality of submarines seen at strange angles and oddly foreshortened, the
first pilot had to be a very fine fellow indeed. He was the captain and took the
boat off the harbour and brought her in again, flew her on the hunting ground
and in an air fight and saw to it that the remainder of the crew knew and
practised their duties. From the repairing of the flying boats and their handling
on shore to the dropping of a bomb on a submarine it was a seamanlike business
that had to be learned and this took time. Good first pilots were few and when
found they were usually worked hard because the stress of steering careful
compass courses for hours was considerable and the effort of keeping a constant,
efficient lookout was tiring. To add to this the H-12 Large America boats were
usually either nose or tail heavy in normal flight, adding further to the strain on
the pilot as the control loads were far from light.

Canadians made excellent flying boat pilots and a large number served at
Felixstowe, including both Hallam and Hobbs. Hobbs took his seat in a little
padded armchair on the right-hand side of the control cockpit which ran across the
full width of the fuselage some distance aft from the nose. The cockpit had a
transparent perspex cover, referred to as the wheelhouse, so that the pilot did not
need to wear goggles to protect his eyes from the slipstream, an important
consideration when carrying out a visual surface search. Before him on the
instrument panel was a compass, an airspeed indicator, an altimeter, a bubble cross
level which indicated whether the boat was correctly balanced laterally, an
inclinometer which gave the fore-and-aft angle at which the boat was flying, the oil
pressure gauges and the engine revolution counters. Close to hand were the engine
switches and the throttle control levers. Immediately in front of him was an 18in
wheel, like those found in motor cars but carried vertically upright on a wooden
yoke, with which he controlled the boat in flight. He worked the rudder bar with
his feet. As second pilot on this occasion, Hallam stood beside Hobbs. If a U-boat
was sighted he ducked forward into the cockpit at the very nose of the boat where
the forward Lewis gun, bombsight and the bomb-release levers were situated. The
second pilot's duties were important and to help them learn, a handbook was
produced at Felixstowe.

In this it was stated that watch-keeping was to begin at once, reporting to the
first pilot all buoys, lightships, wrecks or other objects that would help him to fix
his position accurately. Second, pilots were advised not to assume that the first pilot
had seen anything they had seen until it had been pointed out and acknowledged.
Observing everything above, below, around, in front and behind their aircraft was

emphasised. Furthermore, the second pilot must be prepared to give the aircraft's position without hesitation to the first pilot or wireless operator at any time throughout the patrol. To achieve this they made small pencil marks on the chart every 15 minutes and at every alteration in course, writing the times against these marks. Other points to note were that bombs only worked when dropped if they had been properly fuzed and that if a crash had become inevitable and anything could be saved, four items were to take priority. In order these were the pigeons, emergency rations, Verey pistol with its cartridges and the Red Cross outfit. Second pilots must learn how to tie a bowline since this was considered to be 'the simplest, quickest and most reliable knot for making fast your machine to a tow-line'; other useful knots should also be mastered. They should also 'study the methods of handling machines on the slipway, both going out and coming in. You may be in charge of this operation some day and the responsibility will be yours.'[7] The handbook ended by stating 'know the boat and all that therein and thereon is thoroughly, and its capabilities and efficiencies, if you wish to become not only a good pilot but capable of command. This information is acquired from time spent in the shed and not from time spent reclining on wardroom settees.'

After the pilots, the wireless operator climbed into his place and sat facing forward on the right-hand side of the boat immediately behind the first pilot. He had a wireless cabinet containing his instruments before him and could send or receive for a distance of about 80 to 100 miles, He coded and decoded all signals and his codebook had weighted covers so that if the boat was likely to be captured by the enemy it would sink immediately when thrown over the side. He also had an Aldis signalling-lamp for communicating with ships, airships and other flying boats. He looked after the Red Cross box which contained a tourniquet and a first aid kit and also took charge of the sandwich box and Thermos flask for in-flight meals, the emergency rations which were expected to last for five days and, not the least important, the carrier pigeons. The engineer's cockpit was in the middle of the boat, surrounded by petrol tanks, a maze of piping and innumerable gadgets. His duties were principally to keep an eye on the two engines, see that the water in the radiators did not boil and to take care of the petrol system. Two wind-driven pumps forced the petrol up from the main tanks to a small tank in the top wing from which the engines were fed by gravity and any surplus petrol that had been pumped up ran back down into the main tanks again. The engineer had to regulate the flow so that fuel drawn up that overflowed back down did so in such a way that the fore-and-aft balance of the aircraft was maintained. If anything went wrong with an engine he had to climb out on the wing, with any tools he needed, and if possible make a repair. On one patrol a flying boat attacked a U-boat at low level; its bombs missed but enemy machine-gun fire drilled a hole in one of its radiators.

The engineer climbed out onto the wing and put a plug into the hole before the water ran out but had to hold it in place while the pilot carried out a second attack which hit the U-boat. He then had to stay holding the plug in place all the way back to Felixstowe. The second pilot, wireless operator and engineer all manned machine guns to give defensive fire if the flying boat was attacked by enemy aircraft.

Once the four crew members were in place the working party attached a line to the rear of the trolley, knocked away the chocks and rolled the boat out on the slipway to where it began to slope down into the water. Here six waders took charge and steered the boat down into the water as the working party eased it down by carefully paying out the line. Waders wore waterproof breeches which reached up to their armpits with weighted boots to give them a secure foothold when the tide was running. They did not have an easy job and at some air stations where there was a strong tide some of them had been washed off the slipway and drowned. As the flying boat entered the water, it floated off the trolley and the thrust of the engines moved it forward. In the typical flight being described, Hobbs taxied out into the harbour, turned into wind and opened the engines full out. Driven by the full 700hp, the boat moved forward with increasing speed with spray under the bow. As speed increased the hull lifted onto the hydroplane step until it seemed to skip lightly over the surface with the airspeed indicator (ASI) reading 35 knots. Then Hobbs pulled back the control wheel, the boat climbed into the air and the ASI jumped to 60 knots. The aircraft was then climbed in a straight line until it reached 1000ft before turning out to sea.

The 'Pigeoners' at Felixstowe are also worthy of mention. They occupied a small 'caboosh' or hut near the hangars and, besides caring for the pigeons, undertook a number of other tasks. One had to be on duty before dawn when the first patrols went out and another was still there when the last patrol was hoisted in after dark. If you mislaid your life-jacket he provided a replacement from his store. They comprised airbags, worn like a waistcoat over flying clothing, and were inflated by pulling a handle which punctured the cap in a small compressed-air bottle. All aircrew wore them in flight. He kept a store of leather jackets and trousers for rating aircrew (officers were expected to purchase their own), and engineers drew their tool kits from them. He also dispensed Red Cross boxes, sea-anchors, jerseys for the ratings provided by the RNAS Comforts Fund and cameras, all of which were routinely carried in the aircraft. His primary task, however, was the care and provision of pigeons. Large wicker baskets of them were brought down from the military loft in Felixstowe town each morning. While at the air station they were watered but not fed and before a flying boat took off, either two or four of them, depending on the mission, were put into a basket, each with its own lidded compartment, which was stowed in the aircraft. They had to be placed well up from the deck as petrol fumes tended to gather there and made them stupid.[8] Each pigeon had a tiny aluminium receptacle clipped to its leg to hold a message and a ring with its number so that it could easily be identified if it came back without a signal. Pigeons could not fly in mist or at night and had to be specially trained to fly over the sea. Two 'squeakers', as the young birds were called, were taken out in each boat for training. Sometimes pigeons even refused to fly off in daylight, perching when released on part of the machine. When these 'wash-outs' were eventually recovered they were generally killed and eaten but these were exceptions and the majority did heroic service. This was how the flying boat crews operated. There were usually no more than eight serviceable boats at Felixstowe at any one time and the following examples will give readers some idea of how they were used in action.

Shortly after 03.00 on 14 June 1917 the duty captain at the Admiralty rang the First Lieutenant at Felixstowe to deliver a coded message that 'the little woman at Borkum said Anna was at the Dogger Bank going south'. In turn he telephoned Squadron Commander Hallam, the commanding officer of the War Flight, to inform him that first contact had been made by a patrolling warship with an airship which, 20 minutes earlier, had been above the centre of XYB on a squared chart of the North Sea. Hallam looked at the recording barometer in the mess and stepped out onto the quarterdeck to check the weather, which he decided was fine, with stars shining and very little wind. He set in train the call-out system and within minutes the duty pilots, wireless operator, flying engineer, working parties, engineers and armourers had made their way to the hangar[9] where the flying boat at readiness, 8677 which was specially fitted with long-range fuel tanks, was on its trolley just inside the doorway. It was pushed out sideways, jacked up and pointed towards the water. The engineers started the engines while the armourers fitted on the Lewis guns and provided 97-round trays loaded with ball, tracer, Brock and Pomeroy ammunition. While the engines were warming up a working party loaded a packet of sandwiches, a bottle of water, five days' emergency rations, the Red Cross box and the pigeon basket into the fuselage and, when the engine oil temperatures were within limits, the engines were opened up to full power one at a time and tested.

The crew on this occasion comprised Flight Sub Lieutenant B D Hobbs DSC RNAS, Flight Sub Lieutenant R F L Dickey RNAS, Air Mechanic 2nd Class H M Davis and Air Mechanic 1st Class A W Goody, and they took off as the first light of dawn appeared in the east at about 05.00. Hobbs flew over the Shipwash Light Vessel at 500ft and then flew towards the Dutch coast in misty conditions by dead reckoning navigation flying an accurate compass heading. The mist got thicker and the glare of the low sun made it difficult to read the instruments for a while but after

2 hours 15 minutes they made an accurate landfall off the island of Vlieland and began to patrol off the coast. By 08.30 they were off Vlieland again when Dickey saw a Zeppelin on the starboard beam at about 1500ft. Hobbs pointed straight at it, opened the engines to full power and climbed towards the airship to close with it as quickly as possible. Dickey manned the bow gun, Davis manned the midships gun and Goody manned the stern guns; all noted that the Zeppelin appeared to be moving very slowly with its propellers merely ticking over. 8677 was not seen by the enemy until it had reached 2000ft, slightly above its prey and about 1000 yards from it. The airship was seen to accelerate and turn away but Hobbs dived towards it at 140 knots and passed diagonally across it from starboard to port. Dickey opened fire with two bursts from about 100ft above and 200ft away from the airship but his gun jammed after only fifteen rounds and while he attempted to clear the stoppage, Hobbs turned hard to the right and got into a position where he was slightly below the enemy but closing with it again. Its immense size in close proximity surprised him and he made out its number, *L 43*. As he closed he suddenly noticed little spurts of flame emerging where the explosive bullets had torn through the fabric and he pulled back on the control wheel to pass clear above the airship. The whole crew then saw the enemy erupt with a tremendous burst of flame as the gasbags full of hydrogen ignited. Within seconds the airship broke in half and each part fell towards the sea continuing to burn fiercely. They saw *L 43's* top gunner fall from his gun and three of its crew fall from the control cars to hit

A Felixstowe F.2A flying boat carrying out a 'Spider Web' patrol over the North Sea. From 1917 onwards aircraft from Felixstowe and Yarmouth were each painted in unique, colourful paint schemes so that aircrew could identify other machines in flight. The scheme had the secondary merit that the aircraft were conspicuous if forced to come down in the sea after a technical malfunction. (Author's collection)

394 THE ROYAL NAVY'S AIR SERVICE

the water before the wreckage. Then he turned for home, leaving a dense pillar of smoke above the point where the wrecked Zeppelin had hit the water.

In July 1917 the German U-boat *UC 1* sailed from Zeebrugge to lay mines off Harwich. Having done so he surfaced to the west of the North Hinder Light Vessel and headed for home without realising that he was crossing the area covered by the 'Spider Web' patrols. Unfortunately for him his passage coincided with the largest patrol yet to be carried out in the area, led by Wing Commander J C Porte RNAS himself in a Felixstowe F2. Five flying boats took part in the patrol; they took off together and flew over the Shipwash Light Vessel in formation. After passing over the North Hinder Light Vessel they saw *UC 1* on the surface and three flying boats attacked at once while the enemy dived; the other two aircraft stood by in case a second attack was necessary. Porte and Cooper in N-65 dropped two 230lb bombs onto the spot where the U-boat had just disappeared below the surface; so too did Flight Sub Lieutenants T H Newton and T C Trumble in 8689 and Flight Sub Lieutenants E J Cuckney and C J Clayton in 8676 dropped a single bomb. Immediately after their detonations a large patch of oil spread on the surface and a continuous stream of bubbles were seen. The enemy had been destroyed.

The end of July also saw the destruction of *UB 20* as it passed through the 'Spider Web'. Two flying boats, Flight Sub Lieutenants E J Cuckney and C J Clayton RNAS with Air Mechanic J A Mortimer and Wireless Telegraphist Barrett in 8676 with Flight Sub Lieutenants C L Young and A T Barker RNAS with Air Mechanic W J Priest and Leading Telegraphist H T Wilks in 8662, were patrolling the Web when they saw *UB 20* on the surface 10 miles west of the North Hinder Light Vessel. The enemy probably never even saw them and made no attempt to evade or submerge as they dived on it and dropped two 230lb and two 100lb bombs from 800ft. All hit or detonated close to the U-boat which was observed to dive but come up to the surface again while turning erratically. After seven minutes *UB 20* began to sink by the stern and further bombs were dropped, one of which was seen to hit just forward of the conning tower. After that the stern went down rapidly and she slid backwards in a froth of white water and oil.

Towed Lighters

As RNAS flying boats carried their offensive patrols further to the eastern shores of the North Sea, a number of schemes were introduced to extend their radius of action. One of the more imaginative was proposed as early as September 1916 by Wing Commander Porte at Felixstowe. It involved the design and construction of lighters, each capable of carrying a Large America flying boat, which could be towed by destroyers at high speed. Representatives of DNC visited Felixstowe to discuss the design and it was quickly finalised. The lighters were 58ft long with a chine to allow them to be towed at high speed.[10] The bottom was very flat aft but sufficiently V-shaped forward to enable them to surmount high seas without pounding severely. Model tests at the Admiralty Experiment Works at Haslar revealed that the original hull design would throw up a solid sheet of water which would have smothered and damaged the wings of the flying boat. A revised design was produced immediately in which the chine was lowered and the sections below it made concave to give more lift and throw down the water. The result proved very successful and reduced resistance as well as curing the trouble with the bow wave. At first it was thought that the lighter should submerge bodily for the flying boat to be hauled onto it but practical experiment showed that it would be better to have a large trimming tank aft which could be flooded to submerge the after end; the aircraft was then hauled into position by a winch fitted on the fore deck. The lighters had five transverse watertight bulkheads which divided them into compartments. The foremost acted as a store and provided bench seating for the five-man lighter crew to shelter in during passage, albeit in fairly cramped conditions but they were at least dry and it was fitted with small scuttles to provide some light. The aftermost compartment contained fixed ballast weights and the compartment forward of it, between frames

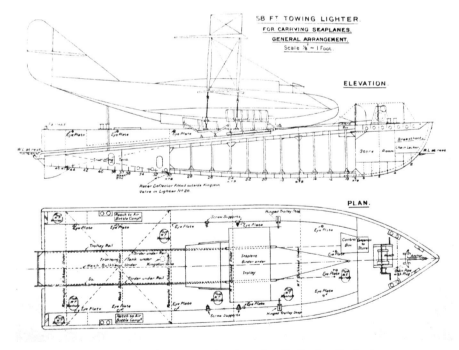

58ft Towing Lighter with a seaplane secured on its trolley. (Author's collection)

30 and 45, was the trimming tank which could be flooded by means of a 10in Kingston valve at its forward end. When full, this lowered the after part of the lighter sufficiently to enable the flying boat to be floated in while the side decks provided working gangway above the water surface on each side of the aircraft fuselage. Four air bottles were fitted under the side decks aft; these contained 10.8ft^3 of air at 2500psi, a quantity sufficient to blow the trimming tank dry twice. The admission of air into the tank was controlled by a valve at a control position forward at which the Kingston valve was also operated. The towing hawser was attached to a bridle fixed to the lighter's sides above the chine and about 12ft abaft the stem and, in order the keep it on a straight course, three plate skegs were fitted under the bottom aft, there being no rudders.

Once Wing Commander Porte had inspected a prototype and the Board had approved the design, orders were placed with Thorneycroft at Southampton for four lighters. The first of these was completed in June 1917 and tested at RNAS Calshot where a flying boat was successfully hauled in and subsequently re-launched. Towing trials behind a destroyer also proved very successful. Further trials were carried out in the North Sea which Commodore Tyrwhitt considered to be successful and orders were placed for fifty more lighters at the new government shipyard at Richboro' where the works was carried out by Royal Engineers. Modifications were made in successive lighters to enable them to carry Felixstowe F2 and F3 flying boats in addition to the Large Americas. Thirty-one were delivered by November 1918, the first twenty-five of which had their steelwork galvanised as a protective measure against salt spray. Five more were completed after the Armistice and the remaining fourteen were cancelled. In operation, the lighter was towed by a cutter to a position close to one of the slipways at Felixstowe and the trimming tank was flooded by opening the Kingston valve. The cradle that supported the aircraft was pulled to its aftermost position on its running rails and the flying boat was floated onto it. When the handling party were satisfied that it was positioned correctly it was pulled forward on its cradle by a winch. As the aircraft moved forward, air was admitted into the tank, expelling the water and allowing the stern of the lighter to rise, reducing the angle and making it easier to winch the cradle forward. Once in position, supports from the side decks were fitted to the strongest parts of the lower wings to hold the aircraft in position and support it in a seaway. A portable, padded prop was used to support its after fuselage. To launch the aircraft the reverse process was carried out with the lighter stationary. In *The Spider Web*, Hallam describes a typical lighter sortie by three flying boats which took place on 19 March 1918.[11]

The three flying boats, Large America 8677, Felixstowe F3 N4282 and Felixstowe F2A N4513, had all been carefully weighed and checked to make sure that they were capable of taking off from the open sea and, as light was fading, they were rolled out of their hangar onto the concrete. An electric heater to keep the oil warm was clipped under each engine and thick padded covers fitted over the engines to keep the heat in so that they would start easily. Once they were pushed down into the water, motor boats took charge of them and towed them to the lighters which had already been flooded down by their crews. The boats were quickly floated onto their cradles, winched forward and secured. With a hiss of compressed air the trim tanks were blown dry and the lighters brought to towing trim. By then the aircrew carrying their flying gear had assembled on the slipway and were taken out to the lighters by the motor boats which removed them from their mooring and pulled them close to their respective destroyers. By then USN pilots were being appointed to the War Flight at Felixstowe to gain combat experience before the USN was able to deploy flying boat squadrons of its own and the six pilots included two Americans. Crews included Flight Lieutenant N A Magor RNAS and Ensign S Potter USN, Flight Sub Lieutenant Webster RNAS and Ensign F Fallon USN and Flight Sub Lieutenants C J Clayton and A T Barker RNAS. Hallam was going aboard the leading destroyer to observe the operation and as they drew close the ship switched on a yardarm group to illuminate the flying boat in its lighter and her own stern with its waiting men. A wire hawser was made fast to towing bollards and a waterproof electric cable was passed to provide current for the electric heaters fitted to the aircraft's engines and the lighter's cramped crew compartment. The lighter swung with the tide and a wing came close to the destroyer's side but was fended off successfully by a sailor with a 'pudding bag' at the end of a boathook specially prepared for just such an eventuality. When all was secure the motor boat came alongside the destroyer and both Hallam and the flying boat crew clambered on board. The latter would transfer to the lighter when it was stopped ready to launch the flying boat. As soon as they were on board the destroyer gave a short blast on its siren, the yardarm group was extinguished and she moved ahead. Astern the other two destroyers could just be seen following in station. Less than five minutes had elapsed since Hallam left the slipway.

Outside the British defensive minefields they were joined by the Harwich Force of cruisers and destroyers and together they crossed the North Sea at high speed. After spending some hours on the bridge, Hallam slept for a few hours on the First Lieutenant's bunk but was woken just before dawn when a signal was received that the aircraft were to stand by. It was a perfect morning for flying with a clear sky and a 10-knot wind ruffling the surface of the water. The Haaks Light Vessel was visible to the east and, having accurately fixed its position, the whole flotilla turned south for 10 miles until at 06.00 the signal for action was received. The lighter crews stripped the heaters and covers from the engines, the tow was shortened and the aircrew transferred by boat. The aircraft engines were all started and tested; when they were ready they were throttled back until they were just ticking over. When all was ready, the flying boat engines were stopped, the destroyers were slowed to 3 knots, the lighters flooded down and the aircraft slid backwards into the water. The destroyers then made a right-hand turn and drew away to join the flotilla which circled the flying boats at four miles, travelling at speed to deter any potential attack by U-boats. The flying boats re-started their engines and ran along the water in loose formation, bucketing a bit in the swells created by the ships, but soon became airborne. This was a reconnaissance mission intended to photograph German activity in the Heligoland Bight and they closed Terschelling at first. After photographing minesweepers and surface craft they noted their positions on their charts but at Borkum they were intercepted by two German two-seater seaplanes. Magor turned into a firing position astern of the first enemy allowing Potter to engage it with short burst from his Lewis gun and they saw it burst into flames and nosedive into the water, leaving a column of black smoke. Clayton turned towards the second enemy aircraft but his gunners failed to obtain hits. He did, however, chase the aircraft to the island of Borkum where it alighted close to a gunboat, ceasing to be a threat. However, Magor found that his opponent had scored a number of hits before being shot down; some of these had drilled holes in the aircraft's petrol tanks but fortunately these were all above the level of the liquid inside them and made little immediate difference to the aircraft's ability to fly. More seriously, a bullet had pierced the water pipe connecting the port engine to its radiator, forcing Magor to shut down that engine before it overheated. He managed to stay in formation with the other two aircraft, however, and they continued on the briefed reconnaissance mission. Taking the opportunity while the aircraft was in straight and level flight, Magor's engineer, Anderson, stripped off his leather flying coat and climbed out onto the wing with his tool bag to see if he could repair the damaged pipe. The aircraft was flying at 60 knots which caused his clothing to whip against his arms and legs, making them difficult to move. In his subsequent report Magor described how Anderson had to 'maintain his vigilance to prevent himself from being blown overboard' and had to keep this up for an hour while he completed the repair. Magor re-started the port engine, completed the recon-naissance and turned towards Felixstowe which was 200 miles away.

As 1918 progressed a further use for these lighters was recognised. Destroyers were too small to be fitted with aircraft take-off platforms and on sweeps in the eastern part of the North Sea they were sometimes too far detached from cruisers that were so fitted to be covered by quick-reaction fighters. It was therefore considered to be worth modifying lighters with wooden flying-off platforms from which a 2F.1 Ship's Camel could be launched when towed at speed.[12] Twelve lighters

Lighter *H3* being towed by a destroyer at high speed with a Sopwith 2F.1 Camel secured to its deck. The aircraft has no guns fitted and has no covers so both it and the large handling party are being soaked by spray. The proximity to land and the generally casual attitude indicate that this is a trial run not an operation. (Author's collection)

were modified and trials were carried out in the summer of 1918; this was after the RNAS had been subsumed into the RAF but the work had begun as a naval initiative and is therefore worthy of mention. The decks were of 2in pine stoutly supported and securely braced in all directions, the main uprights being fastened to the inner sides of the lighters. The platform extended from the fore deck to right aft with wing decks forward for the mechanics to work on the aircraft's engine; these overhung the lighters' sides by 4ft and were hinged to fold back to prevent damage when coming alongside a destroyer. The beams supporting these side wings were made to slide inwards. A collapsible derrick was also provided which, when fitted, enabled the aircraft to be recovered if possible after it had ditched. The redoubtable Commander Samson, by then a Colonel RAF, carried out the first trial take-off but the deck had been installed level with the lighter's upper deck and at 30 knots the lighter had a pronounced bow-up attitude which meant that the aircraft had to climb a steep slope when it was released. This caused Samson to stall, ditch just ahead of the lighter and he was lucky to survive when it ran over him. Both pilot and Camel were subsequently fished out of the water. As a result of this experience, the deck and the structure under it were modified to make it level when the lighter was moving forward at high speed under tow.

Flight Sub Lieutenant S D Culley RNAS
photographed before he shot down
Zeppelin *L 53*. (Author's collection)

Zeppelin *L 53* had monitored a number of lighter operations by the Harwich Force and it was decided to have a go at it with a towed fighter. There was an unsuccessful attempt on 5 August 1918 but on the evening of 10 August the destroyer *Redoubt* sailed with the Harwich Force towing lighter *H3* with Sopwith 2F.1 Camel N6812 secured to its deck. The pilot was Flight Lieutenant S D Culley RNAS, one of many Canadians who had joined the Service, now a Lieutenant RAF. Three other destroyers towed lighters with flying boats and three cruisers each carried two high-speed coastal motor boats (CMBs), on deck. These were to be launched off Terschelling Island from where they were to pass over the minefields and penetrate the Heligoland Bight with the intention of torpedoing minesweepers and any other surface craft they encountered. At dawn on 11 August all was ready and at 06.10 the destroyers slowed and shortened their towing hawsers so that the flying boat crews and Culley could man their aircraft.[13] Unfortunately there was little or no wind and a long swell which effectively prevented the heavy flying boats from getting airborne and they had to be floated back onto their lighters. Having dispatched the CMBs, the Harwich Force cruised off Terschelling without air cover; four German seaplanes were seen in the distance but, while they kept watch, they didn't close. Three other flying boats were airborne from

Yarmouth and they arrived over the Force at 07.10 when Tyrwhitt ordered them to close with the enemy seaplanes and drive them off. Their participation in the operation was planned but they would obviously have less time on task than the boats launched from the lighters.

The enemy aircraft were visible from the ships and there was some surprise therefore when the flying boats headed off in a different direction to search for them. The problem was that although the surface visibility was good, it was patchy in the air and a combination of mist and the low sun made the enemy seaplanes invisible to the Yarmouth boats, a situation Tyrwhitt had not foreseen. After an hour's fruitless search the flying boats returned to the Harwich Force to request further instructions.[14] They were told to locate the CMBs which, it was calculated, should be on their way back. They found no trace of the CMBs but did sight Zeppelin *L 53* so they broke off their search and, rather than break radio silence, they returned to the force to give a warning by visual signal. In fact, Tyrwhitt had already been advised by the Admiralty that a Zeppelin was in his vicinity and had turned west at 08.30 to entice it further out to sea after his force. Obligingly *L 53* followed and at 08.41 Culley was flown off his lighter to intercept it. He climbed hard and the same patchy visibility worked against the Germans this time and the Zeppelin's crew failed to see him. Shortly before this operation N6812 had been modified with a non-standard armament layout; it had two Lewis guns with 97-round trays of ammunition fitted to the upper wing instead of the normal one and the Vickers gun forward of the cockpit was deleted.[15] This meant that both guns could fire explosive Brock and Pomeroy ammunition clear of the propeller arc. He had intended to attack the airship from above but he reached his aircraft's effective ceiling at 19,000ft and could climb no higher. Having carefully kept *L 53* in sight he turned towards it and opened fire head-on at 09.41. His fire was immediately effective and watchers in the Harwich Force below saw a sudden burst of flame in the sky followed by a column of smoke and falling debris. Smoke was made to guide Culley back but again the visibility proved fickle and it took Culley two hours to locate the Harwich Force. Shortly before his fuel ran out he saw a destroyer less than two miles from him; the burning Zeppelin had been 50 miles away from the flagship when its destruction was observed. This was the occasion on which Tyrwhitt sent his famous signal to the Harwich Force, 'Flag – General – Your attention is called to Hymn 224 Verse 7'. As his commanding officers consulted their hymn books they found that this verse read 'Oh happy band of pilgrims, look upward to the skies, where such a light affliction shall win so great a prize'. The prize in this instance was the destruction of *L 53*, proof if it were needed that Zeppelins could no longer expect to operate safely in close proximity to British warships.

By the time Culley and his aircraft were recovered, however, the CMBs were considerably overdue. After leaving their cruisers they had followed the Dutch coastline towards German waters, about a mile outside territorial waters. Six seaplanes were seen flying towards them and the CMBs closed up to give the maximum covering fire with their Lewis guns. A firefight had ensued without decisive results for about 30 minutes after which the CMB leader decided to turn back towards the Harwich Force. Unfortunately this put the low sun behind the attacking aircraft which could see the CMBs in clear detail. Another four enemy seaplanes joined in and they all maintained accurate long-range fire from the east while the British gunners had great difficulty in marking their targets. Despite this they shot down a single seaplane which was seen to crash into the sea. The CMB crews fought with great gallantry but ran out of ammunition and none returned to their parent ships. One boat with faltering engines reached shore, another caught fire but was navigated to within half a mile of the Dutch coast before being blown up; two more with engines and guns useless were sunk by their crews who spent three hours in the water before being picked up by a Dutch torpedo boat. Two more, badly damaged, drifted into territorial waters where they were salvaged by the Dutch. None of their ships' companies were killed but four officers and two of their men were wounded.

The Appointment of the Admiral Commanding Aircraft, Grand Fleet

By late 1917 the extent to which air operations had permeated throughout the Grand Fleet led its Aircraft Committee to recommend to Admiral Beatty that a flag officer should be appointed to command the activities of all seaplane and aircraft carriers. Beatty agreed and Admiralty approval for the appointment was given on 19 November 1917.[16] The first Admiral Commanding Aircraft (ACA), was Rear Admiral R F Phillimore who flew his flag in *Furious*. He was an ideal choice having previously served as the Flag Officer 1st Battlecruiser Squadron and taken a keen interest in the development of naval aviation including the turret platforms tested in *Repulse*. His terms of reference described him as being 'responsible to the Commander-in-Chief Grand Fleet for the efficient training of personnel and the upkeep of material as well as superintending all experiments, trials and practices of aircraft'. Orders for operations in which seaplane carriers were to take part were to be sent through him and he would be in charge of such operations when present. His status in this respect was seen as being analogous to that of the Flag Officer Flotillas who commanded the work of destroyer flotillas within the Grand Fleet. ACA was empowered to correspond directly with the DAS in the Admiralty on all matters of detail but must submit for the consideration of the C-in-C all proposals or remarks which involved questions of principle or policy. Phillimore's appointment was dated 6 January 1918 and in the letter informing Beatty of his selection,[17] the Admiralty took the opportunity to inform him that following the demise of the RNAS agreed by the War Cabinet on 24 August 1917, the air units of his fleet were become known as 'Air Force Contingents' in HM Ships. The appointment of ACA was not terminated or transferred on the formation of the RAF and Phillimore continued to hold the post until after the Armistice. Even then he continued to be closely involved in aviation as President of the Post-War Questions Committee set up by the Admiralty.[18]

The Influence of Captain J S Dumaresq CB CVO RN on Fleet Aviation

Advocates of naval aviation were not all pilots and nor did they all serve in the RNAS. John Saumarez Dumaresq was an excellent example of a career naval officer who was quick to see the advantages of having aircraft operating as an integral part of the fleet. He was born in Sydney, New South Wales in 1873 into a family which had a long tradition of service in the RN and which moved back to the UK when he was 2. He entered the Britannia Royal Naval College in 1886 and eventually specialised as a torpedo officer with a genius for invention that came to the Admiralty's notice in 1904 when he designed and produced a trigonometric slide-rule calculator which improved gunnery accuracy. When set with the courses of the firing ship, the target ship and its bearing, it indicated both the rates at which

Commodore (1st Class) J S Dumaresq CB CVO RN in 1919. The chevrons over his right sleeve lace indicate sea service in every year of the Great War and he was widely regarded as a man of exceptional ability with a gift for technical and tactical development. (Sea Power Centre – Australia via John Perryman).

range and deflection changed, essentially the basis of computation for all subsequent mechanical fire-control computers. By 1914 it was a standard item of equipment throughout the Grand Fleet.[19] A man of unrelenting principles, Dumaresq held a patent on the device but sought no profit from its production, receiving only a one-off payment of £1500 from the Admiralty. He assumed command of the armoured cruiser *Shannon* in 1913 and was with her at Jutland. After that he became chairman of the Grand Fleet Cruiser Committee and then, wishing to gain light cruiser experience, he requested an appointment to HMAS *Sydney* which he went on to command for two years, regularly taking command of the 2nd Light Cruiser squadron during his flag officer's absence.[20]

On 4 May 1917 Dumaresq, in HMAS *Sydney,* was leading a high-speed sweep through the cleared channels near the Dogger Bank with *Dublin* and four destroyers fitted with high-speed minesweeping gear.[21] No seaplane carrier was included in the force because at the time none had the speed to maintain formation with it. On that day three Zeppelins, *L 23*, *L 42* and *L 43*, were patrolling in the Heligoland Bight from north to south. *L 43* was one of the first Zeppelins designed to reach heights in excess of 20,000ft and, finding good visibility off Terschelling Island, its commander decided to extend his patrol to the west. At 10.15 he saw the British force manoeuvring at high speed near a sailing ship, made an enemy contact report by wireless and began to climb above 10,000ft where he hoped to be above effective anti-aircraft fire while getting the airship into a position from which it could bomb the ships below. *L 43* came under constant but ineffective fire from the force and dropped three 50kg bombs at 12.14 on a ship he identified as a light cruiser, believing that at least one of them hit. The force turned to the north-west and *L 43* dropped its remaining bombs without observing hits due, the commander reported, to the 'extraordinarily skilful manoeuvring of the enemy who steers a constant, unpredictable zig-zag and circling course'. *L 42* came up in response to *L 43*'s signals at 13.20 but lost sight of the ships and, *L 43* having expended all its bombs, both airships withdrew to the east.

From *Sydney*'s bridge the action appeared more complicated and convinced Dumaresq that his cruisers must have weapons capable of fighting aircraft on a regular basis as well as surface ships and submarines. The first airship had been seen low on the horizon to the south-east as the destroyer *Obdurate* stopped to lower a boat which was to examine a Dutch trawler. The cruisers both turned to close the Zeppelin and opened fire with their 6in main armament as well as their single 3in anti-aircraft guns; the destroyers were ordered to cut their sweep wires and follow. It was at first thought that *L 43* had turned to keep out of effective range but several ships reported sighting periscopes and Dumaresq thought that it might be attempting to lure him into a submarine trap. At 11.20 he reversed *Sydney*

HMAS *Sydney*'s Sopwith 2F.1 Camel on its rotating take-off platform photographed from the ship's spotting top with the bridge in the foreground. Of interest, the bridge is not manned so this picture was probably taken while she was at anchor in the Firth of Forth. The Camel does not have its Lewis gun fitted. Note the white rectangles at the corners of the deck's forward edge; these were intended to show the pilot, as he ran past them, that he had run out of deck. (Sea Power Centre – Australia via David Stevens).

and *Dublin*'s course, ordered one destroyer to support *Obdurate* and the other two to work their way beyond the airship. By 12.15 Dumaresq's force had encircled *L 43* and the two cruisers turned towards it using their 3in guns as it climbed. The destroyers added the fire of their 2pdr pom-poms. The airship's first bombs had actually been aimed at *Obdurate* rather than a light cruiser and the explosion that had caused the smoke and flash that its commander had taken to be a hit had actually been a near miss that showered the vessel in splinters but caused no damage. As *L 43* manoeuvred to drop bombs, Dumaresq positioned himself with his back against the bridge screen and his feet on the base of the compass from where he could keep the airship in sight and anticipate its every manoeuvre; he made constant course changes which kept the Zeppelin on or before *Sydney*'s beam, thus keeping the arc of fire for his 3in gun open and forcing *L 43* to have to aim at a rapidly crossing target with little realistic chance of obtaining a hit. The ship's executive officer, Commander Henry Cayley RN, 'enjoyed himself immensely' and

Sopwith 2F.1 Camel N6822 taking off from HMAS *Sydney* with the platform rotated to starboard into the relative wind. It has its Lewis gun in place but this aircraft was only delivered in June 1918 and was not, therefore, the one flown by Sharwood. It spent some time embarked in *Sydney* during July and August but otherwise alternated between Smoogroo and the Grand Fleet air parks at Turnhouse and Donibristle before being deleted in 1919. (Sea Power Centre – Australia via David Stevens).

described how bombs fell with 'a long drawn out sort of wail and then a terrific roar and a big column of dirty looking smoke and water rose up'. On this occasion neither side inflicted damage on the other but readers will recall that *L 43* met its end a month later when it was intercepted and destroyed by a flying boat from Felixstowe.

In August 1917 *Sydney* was taken in hand by Chatham Dockyard for an extensive refit intended to cure boiler defects and bring her up the latest standards. Dumaresq left Commander Cayley in charge of her and went to fill a temporary vacancy in command of the battlecruiser *Repulse*, flying the flag of Rear Admiral Phillimore, BCS 1. He was therefore in command when Rutland carried out his turret platform take-off demonstrations in October 1917 and would have seen first-hand the advantages of a take-off deck that could be turned into wind. While he was in *Repulse*, Dumaresq had insisted on a number of improvements being fitted to *Sydney* during her refit; among these were more powerful searchlights for night fighting and, more significantly from an aviation perspective, she was the first British cruiser to be fitted with a rotating aircraft platform that could launch a fighter into the relative wind without the ship itself having to alter course. It was completed to Dumaresq's own design and fitted forward of the bridge over the armoured conning tower and the forward 6in gun mounting without inhibiting its arc of fire. It was successfully demonstrated for the first time on 8 December 1917 when Flight Sub Lieutenant Harold Brearley RNAS flew a Sopwith Pup off the deck while the ship was steaming at 20 knots with the platform trained forward. A further demonstration was made on 17 December, this time with the platform trained 40 degrees to port into the felt wind and again the launch was successful. In fact it was so successful that Admiral Beatty directed that every cruiser not fitted with a kite balloon was to be fitted with a flying deck of similar design. The Grand Fleet's instructional manual on air matters, entitled 'Use and Maintenance of Planes Embarked'[22] was written by Dumaresq and remained the only document on the subject in use until the Grand Fleet dispersed.

Operation 'F 3'

This operation took place after the RNAS had ceased to exist but I have included it because it illustrates the culmination of the Service's efforts over the previous four years to defend the fleet against enemy air activity and in practical terms it was an RNAS 'show' in all but name. Operation 'F 3' was intended to provide Battlecruiser Fleet support for a reconnaissance of the Heligoland Bight by the Harwich Force which was in turn briefed to engage any enemy minesweepers, light forces and aircraft it encountered. A secondary objective was to cause the enemy to carry out the maximum amount of signalling around midday when their daily codes were changing so that signal intelligence could be gathered that would help to break the new codes. To achieve this three flying boats from Felixstowe were towed into the operational area on lighters and a fourth flew direct from Yarmouth tasked with co-relating enemy signal traffic with observed ship movements. Two other forces were at sea further north engaged on minelaying and patrol work; overall the Grand Fleet had nearly seventy ships at sea on this day.

The commander of the Battlecruiser Fleet, Admiral Pakenham, flew his flag in *Lion* accompanied by 1 BCS comprising *Princess Royal*, *Tiger*, *Repulse* and *Renown*; 1 CS with *Courageous* and *Glorious* and 2 LCS with *Birmingham*, *Sydney*, *Dublin* and *Melbourne*. The whole force sailed from the Firth of Forth at 14.00 on 31 May 1918 for this large-scale operation but it is *Sydney*'s part that now concerns us. In early 1918 the Sopwith 2F.1 Camel had replaced the Pup as the Grand Fleet's principal fighter; its significant engine torque made it a difficult and potentially dangerous aircraft to fly, even for experienced pilots, but it was especially so for

Flight Lieutenant A C Sharwood RNAS.
(Australian War Memorial – Image
Reference Number A02873).

pilots converting onto it from the Pup. Brearley was killed on 30 January 1918 during a practice flight when he lost control and span into the ground. *Sydney's* new pilot was the 19-year-old Flight Sub Lieutenant Albert 'Cyril' Sharwood RNAS who flew his 2F.1 off the deck for the first time on 27 February.[23] On that occasion he was able to land ashore but under operational conditions in the eastern North Sea he would have had to ditch. The 2F.1 Camel had airbags fitted in its rear fuselage that experiments had shown would keep the aircraft afloat for about 30 minutes. The weight of the engine would drag the nose down though, leaving the rear fuselage floating vertically about 6ft out of the water. Some pilots had their mechanics fit rope handles onto the fuselage to give something to grab hold of while they waited for rescue. In 1971 Sharwood wrote to the Royal Australian Navy describing how the Camel was ditched.

> The Camel was brought down to about 4 or 5ft above the wave tops and held off until it stalled, then the fun began. The safety belt was released when the wheels and fixed undercarriage struck the water at perhaps 40 or 45 knots; the tail went up like greased lightning and the nose of the machine plunged down into the sea. Just before the cockpit submerged the pilot was flicked out as the tail went

up. If he had done all this nicely he went over the top wing through a semi-circular cutaway and went into the ditch head first with life-vest inflated and leather coat on about 20 yards ahead of the Camel.[24]

Sharwood did not mention that the airbags had a bung which was removed in flight so that the bags did not expand and burst as the aircraft climbed to high altitude; pre-ditching checks included the essential measure of re-inserting the bung before the aircraft hit the water. If a pilot misjudged his impact with the water his survival was by no means certain and even a successful ditching might cause him to hit the top wing and suffer facial abrasions. Sharwood's detachment included Australian-born engine fitter Lewis Birch and a joiner, air mechanic Jacob Graffy and, having lost some skin off his face when he ditched during a trial flight, he instructed Graffy to enlarge the cut-out portion of his upper wing by several inches.

For Operation 'F 3' *Sydney* embarked 2F.1 Camel N6783 from the fleet air park at Donibristle a few days before she sailed. It was one of a batch built by Beardmore and had only been delivered to the fleet in May; this was its first operational deployment. Admiral Packenham's orders required all aeroplanes to be ready to launch at daybreak and so Sharwood and *Sydney*'s mechanics would have removed the aircraft covers in the dark, started and warmed up the engine, checked fuel and oil levels, checked ammunition and test-fired the guns. N6783 was a standard 2F.1 with one Vickers gun under the starboard side of the Camel's 'hump' forward of the cockpit and a Lewis gun with a 97-round ammunition tray loaded with ball, tracer, Brock and Pomeroy fitted to the top wing. By 07.00 on 1 June 1918 1 CS and 2 LCS were forming a north-south line five miles east of the battlecruisers with the cruisers three miles apart. Intermittently they saw some Dutch fishing smacks and ships of the Harwich Force but no enemy was seen until 09.40 when two German seaplanes emerged from the low clouds and dropped bombs near *Tiger* which straddled one of her escorting destroyers. They then closed *Courageous* and dropped further bombs which missed. Both *Sydney* and *Melbourne* launched their fighters but other ships were unable to react in time. Sharwood recalled getting airborne at 09.55 as the enemy passed overhead and were engaged by the 3in gun. *Melbourne*'s Flight Lieutenant Leslie Gibson RNAS in Camel N6785 got airborne three minutes later but failed to see either Sharwood or the enemy so he circled overhead until 11.20 when his low fuel state forced him to ditch. The fleet's aircraft recognition left much to be desired and *Lion* opened fire on him but fortunately missed and he came down safely alongside the destroyer *Osiris* which rescued him. Unaware that Gibson had been launched. Sharwood climbed through 2000ft and turned south-east as he had been ordered by Dumaresq. In his own words he subsequently sighted ahead of me two two-seater enemy seaplanes steering approximately south-east at an altitude of about 8,000ft. After about 20 minutes during which time the seaplanes had dived to gain speed, I caught up the rearmost two-seater who was by then at about 5,000ft. I dived and opened fire but suddenly found myself under fire from an enemy single-seater seaplane scout who had dived on my tail from behind. Previously this machine had been above me unnoticed. By 'cart wheeling' and climbing to the left[25] I found myself able to open fire on his tail. I repeated this manoeuvre twice successfully. In the third dive I noticed my tracer bullets to be entering the scout's fuselage. Soon after this he began to side-slip and then fell into a spinning nose dive. Not knowing whether he was hit or merely attempting to escape I dived after him. As he disappeared into the haze and cloud below, which were at about 2,500ft, I came under fire from the two two-seater seaplanes which were at about 4,000ft or slightly higher. Getting under the tail of one of them I fired one burst when my Vickers' gun jammed with about 100 rounds unfired. As the Lewis gun pan had been emptied during the fight with the scout I had to break off the engagement.[26]

Another of Dumaresq's innovations was to ensure that N6783 was fitted with wireless so that it could be used for gunnery spotting but the aerial had been shot away during the fight so that Sharwood could not report the direction of the Germans' retreat for other aircraft. When he turned towards *Sydney*'s estimated position he encountered a strong westerly wind which slowed his progress. He saw nothing for 20 minutes and then turned onto north feeling exhausted and badly wanting a drink but was eventually rewarded by sighting the Harwich Force below him. He identified the ships as friendly but their own recognition was less impressive and several ships opened fire on him but he held on and ditched in textbook style a few hundred yards ahead of the destroyer *Sharpshooter*. There was a thump as the undercarriage dug in and he sailed clear over the top wing through the enlarged cut-out before swimming back to the Camel's tail where he grabbed the hand-holds until a boat came to collect him. He found *Sharpshooter*'s officers to be 'more than hospitable' as they plied him with alcohol and enthusiasm and the light cruiser *Canterbury* recovered the Camel. Of interest, N6783 was returned to Donibristle where it was stripped of re-usable spare parts and then written off charge in July. It only ever flew this one mission in its six-week service life, illustrating how very short the life of an embarked aircraft was in this era of one-shot launches.

Captain Dumaresq was quick to emphasise the tactical lessons that had been learned and stressed the need for aircraft to be launched quickly so that they could join up and act decisively in time to counter enemy air attacks. Captain Rushton of *Melbourne* foresaw the need to have 'a constant high patrol' of fighters to avoid the otherwise inevitable delay in engagement, effectively predicting the combat air patrols that were to play such an important part in the Second World War. Sharwood lobbied for better aircraft-recognition training in the Grand Fleet[27] and for the re-organisation of all the Camels embarked in 2 LCS as a cohesive flight. With Dumaresq's full support this happened and he was placed in command of it as the Senior Naval Flying Officer 2 LCS. To his credit, Sharwood was not certain in his own mind that he had shot down the enemy single-seater and never claimed it as a kill but other fleet pilots gave him credit and so did Admiral Phillimore who wanted to capitalise on what was undoubtedly a successful action in order to encourage RAF pilots to volunteer for service with the Grand Fleet. He suggested that the Admiralty publish details of the action in its next periodical summary of air operations. Beatty vetoed the idea, however, describing himself as being against the proposal because it was 'opposed to the traditions of the Naval Service, in which the feeling of duty well performed and its recognition by superior authority is considered sufficient reward'. He dismissed the fact that Sharwood was actually a member of the RAF by adding that 'officers of the Royal Air Force when serving with the Royal Navy have the privilege of being governed by these same traditions to which advertisement in the public press is entirely foreign'.[28] Unfortunately, therefore, no official communiqué describing this action was ever issued although Sharwood was eventually awarded a mention in despatches for 'valuable service rendered'. Its significance was, thus, not fully appreciated outside the Grand Fleet and, I suspect, only by a thoughtful few within it. However, for the first time in history a ship-launched fighter had taken off to carry out an airborne inter-ception of enemy heavier-than-air aircraft that were attacking the fleet. A method of warfare that was to become fundamental to the success of fleets in action after 1939 had been demonstrated for the first time on 1 June 1918. By their diligence and careful planning, not to mention courage in the face of a difficult situation, Dumaresq and Sharwood had ushered in a new era of naval warfare.

Kite Balloons

By 1918 the Grand Fleet had a number of warships capable of operating kite balloons and the technique had expanded significantly from its modest beginnings during the Gallipoli campaign. A number of difficulties had been overcome, among them the need to develop a towing cable capable of taking the strain as ships manoeuvred at high speeds in high winds and the need to stabilise the balloons more efficiently to prevent unsteady motion which had induced airsickness in many observers. The wear and tear on the balloons as they swayed also had to be taken into account, as did the need to overcome oscillations as the balloons were winched

HMS *Cardiff* with its kite balloon aloft as it leads the German High Sea Fleet to surrender in the Firth of Forth on 21 November 1918. The kite balloon is riding at about 1500ft at the top centre of the picture. Lower and to the left is the semi-rigid airship *SR 1*. A number of British aircraft took part in this historic event. (Author's collection)

down close to the ship because this tended to make the landing of the basket on deck to change crews a difficult and dangerous operation.[29] As if these problem were not enough, there was at first no available cable that provided the necessary qualities of flexibility, small diameter and great strength in combination with an insulated electric core for telephone communication.

These difficulties had been steadily overcome by the Admiralty's Kite Balloon Department and by mid-1916 it was possible to put kite balloons up in almost any weather and tow them safely in relative wind speeds of up to 80 knots with observers remaining at their post for what were described as 'very prolonged periods'. The utility of kite balloons was demonstrated by towing trials using *Campania* and *Engadine* and the best method of installing kite balloons in fighting ships was given careful consideration. It was decided that they should not be inflated on board because of the danger arising from stowing large numbers of hydrogen gas cylinders; a shell hit among them would have had devastating consequences. It was also clear that warships had insufficient space to keep the balloons lashed down fully inflated on deck. It was decided, therefore, to inflate the balloons ashore, pass them onto lighters without observers in the basket and then tow the lighters, with balloons, to their intended warships. They were then secured to the towline running from the ship's balloon winch and held at any convenient height while the ship proceeded to sea. When the balloon was to be manned, it was winched down to the deck, the observer got in and then the towline was paid out until the desired height, usually about 1500ft, was reached. Kite balloons had the big advantage over aircraft that the observer was connected by telephone directly to the ship's bridge and had, therefore, no need to encode messages as they were not being transmitted. His observations were therefore immediate and in clear voice. There were some concerns that the sight of balloons appearing above the horizon would betray the fleet's position to the enemy but with many battleships still burning coal they were hardly likely to be more visible than the pall of smoke that rose from the ships and the extended range at which observers could see the enemy was felt to outweigh any disadvantages.

Further trials were carried out in the summer of 1916 using the battleship *Hercules* in Scapa Flow and its adjacent training areas. The value of the high-flying observer for spotting the ship's fall of shot during firing practice was immediately obvious and in July Jellicoe asked for all his battleships and cruisers to be fitted with winches to operate kite balloons. In the autumn the cruiser *Chester* was fitted out and conducted a further series of trials in the Firth of Forth. Their success led immediately to an extensive programme for the supply of kite balloons for other vessels of the Grand Fleet. The work was supervised from *King George V* in which an electrically-driven winch had been installed in January 1917. In May a kite-balloon base was opened at North Queensferry, just east of Rosyth. Another was set up at the RN air station at Houton on the north shore of Scapa Flow. As well as big ships, destroyers engaged on anti-submarine work were fitted with balloon winches and their perseverance with the new techniques were rewarded in July 1917 when a U-boat was destroyed with the aid of a kite balloon towed by *Patriot*. By 1918 the use of balloons for observation and photographic work in connection with torpedo exercises was widespread and resulted not only in a great saving in torpedoes but in a great improvement in torpedo practice because they allowed a better understanding, backed up by photographic records, of the actual courses of the torpedoes and their behaviour once fired. Experience also showed the great value of observation from balloons when enemy vessels attempted to hide behind a smokescreen and for this reason all ships fitted with kite-balloon installations were ordered to take balloons to sea on all possible occasions. By mid-1918 there installations in every type of warship from battleships to armed trawlers and corresponding progress was made by the Admiralty in fitting out the battleships and destroyers of the US Navy as they arrived in UK waters.

Anti-Submarine Warfare

By 1918 aeroplanes were regarded as having significant advantages over seaplanes in that they were able to take off and land again when a rough sea would have

SSZ class airship *SSZ 59* landing on HMS *Furious'* after deck in 1918 during trials intended to prove that an airship's time on patrol could be greatly extended if it could land on a deployed aircraft carrier to change crews, refuel and re-arm. Note that the first line has been passed from the airship and so, like a warship, it has broken out a Union Jack forward as well as a White Ensign aft. The trial was successful but the war ended before the scheme could be widely implemented. (Author's collection)

precluded seaplanes from going on patrol. Also, since they were not burdened with floats, they were able to carry a greater load of weapons. On the other hand, there were still concerns about the unreliability of aircraft engines which caused an increased risk to aircrew flying long patrols over water in aircraft without flotation gear. Although inflatable flotation bags had been developed and tested at the Isle of Grain, their bulk created considerable drag and lowered the performance of aircraft to which they were fitted.[30] In summary there was still a lack of confidence in aircraft that lacked a boat hull or floats on long missions over water despite the fact that the latter were known to be fragile and often break up in rough sea states. The Admiralty felt that the solution 'may be found in a seaplane which is capable of rising from and alighting on land as well as water, thus avoiding the disadvantages from which seaplanes at present suffer'.

By the beginning of 1918 SS airships had largely been replaced by the superior SSZ type and the overall number of airships had increased. A number of mooring-out sites had been established around the coast between the permanent airship

Airship crews needed to have a head for heights; this view looking aft from the car of a North Sea class airship shows three of its crew members. One is crouching on the catwalk between the engine and the engineers' cabin; a second is standing on the engine maintenance platform next to the starboard engine which is stopped and a third is manning a Lewis gun. (Author's collection)

stations and these had led to a notable increase in efficiency by the time of the Armistice. During 1918 there were a number of days on which it was too windy for airships to fly but heavier-than-air craft had been able to do so. However, the Admiralty noted that there were also days when airships were able to operate despite mist or rough sea surface conditions when seaplanes were unable get airborne. By the end of the war successful trials had been carried out with an SSZ airship lowering a hydrophone into the water and towing it at low speed. While successful, the range was somewhat limited but further trials were abandoned with the end of hostilities. In another trial a non-rigid airship was towed by a destroyer fitted with a kite-balloon winch, again with successful results. The idea was the airship could be towed out to sea beyond the range of other aircraft patrolling from shore bases. It could be hauled down onto the warship's deck to be refuelled, re-armed and to change crews then re-launched for a further patrol, giving considerably extended endurance as well as range. The Admiralty had hoped to replace kite balloons with airships from 1919 but further work in this direction ended with the Armistice.[31]

Admiralty analysis of the use of aircraft against enemy submarines led to a number of conclusions. First it was found that barrage patrols by aircraft of narrow waters such as the Fair Island Channel might seem, in theory, to take the offensive against U-boats but they actually had little practical value. They required a considerable number of aircraft during daylight and even then U-boats could cross the area by night, in low visibility or submerged. On the other hand, patrolling an area where submarines would want to operate in order to do their work proved to be of great value because it prevented them from coming to the surface to take bearings to fix their position, to charge batteries or to examine an approaching target and get into a firing position. When escorting convoys it was considered essential for aircraft to remain close to them, paying particular attention to the side from which attack was most likely to occur, for instance a U-boat would be likely to attack down sun. An airship, however, took a long time to get over a position up-wind and would, therefore, be better positioned to windward, ready to move quickly downwind to bomb a submarine as soon as it was sighted. During 1918 the Director of Naval Intelligence (DNI), classified 192 sightings of U-boats by aircraft, leading to 130 attacks of which four were regarded as successful, six as probably seriously damaging the target U-boat and twenty less seriously. A statistical comparison between the work of airships and that of seaplanes and aeroplanes showed some advantages for the former because a larger proportion were ready for service, their average patrols were of longer duration and they suffered less engine trouble. On the other hand airships were not launched in doubtful weather whereas heavier-than-air aircraft were. Persistent attacks were

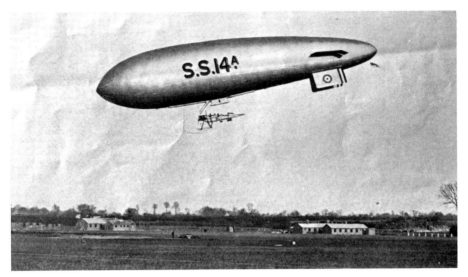

Originally built as *SS 13* and delivered to Folkestone in 1915, this airship had an interesting service life. It was used for night-flying tests at Capel in 1916 followed by a further test in which Sir Brian Leighton jumped from it with a parachute to prove that they worked satisfactorily. On 29 April 1917 it force-landed in the sea off Eastbourne but was subsequently salvaged and repaired at Wormwood Scrubs by September. In October 1917 it was re-numbered as *SS 14A*, as seen here, before being deployed to Luce Bay. Arguably the longest-serving airship in the RNAS, it took part in a number of further experiments at Pulham before being deleted in 1919. (Author's collection)

carried out during 1918 against U-boat bases in Flanders at Ostend, Zeebrugge and Bruges both by day and night. What material damage was done and how far it interfered with enemy operations was at the time largely a matter for conjecture. One thing, however, was clear and that was the enemy felt it necessary to build most elaborate and expensive shelters for the boats at these bases. For some time before their evacuation in 1918 submarine activity from these bases had practically ceased but how far this was due to bombing and how far to blocking operations and the perfecting of British minefields cannot be determined precisely.[32]

In addition to specific attacks on U-boats at sea and in their bases, DNI drew the Admiralty's attention to the fact that there must have been a large number of occassions when submarines were prevented from getting into a position to attack shipping by the presence of aircraft or, having got into position, failed to carry through the attack because of their presence. Evidence was cited which pointed to the sapping of the moral of U-boat crews by persistent bomb attacks and captured logbooks contained statements such as 'aircraft alarm – dived'. Compelling U-boats to remain dived was in itself an achievement of great value but was one

C*1 was built at Kingsnorth in January 1918. It was first of ten airships of the Coastal* class and had a gas capacity of 210,000ft³. It was allocated to East Fortune in February and flew for 868 hours before being deleted in 1919. This class was to have been armed with circling torpedoes with depth settings intended to hit U-boats at periscope depth. The idea was good but ahead of its time and was not fully implemented by the time the war ended. (Author's collection)

that was not considered at the time to be capable of numerical analysis. A whole book could be devoted to the work of anti-submarine patrols by aircraft but the following examples give some idea of what they were like. The Coastal airship crews needed great reserves of concentration and tenacity to be effective. Most flew in open cars next to the roaring engine on patrols that lasted up to 20 hours and to sustain them they were issued with in-flight rations like the flying boat crews from Felixstowe.

Crews from RNAS Mullion in Cornwall were given sandwiches filled with either salt bacon or marmalade,[33] milk tablets, chocolate and a Thermos flask of tea.[34] Take-off for a dawn patrol was carried out in the dark and night landings were commonplace, aided by a few lanterns carefully placed on the ground. Thick flying clothes were essential including long leather coats, heavy boots and gauntlets. Concentration during the patrol had to be intense if the crew were to have any chance of sighting a periscope as it appeared on the surface or the blurred image of a U-boat at periscope depth. Most crews were utterly exhausted, both mentally and physically, when they returned to base and had to be helped from their cockpits by the ground crew. Usually a surfaced submarine would see the airship first and dive before it could get into an attacking position but, notwithstanding their potential to attack a contact, by 1918 it had come to be appreciated that the

North Sea class airships had a disposable lift of 10.85 tons and could carry six 230lb bombs and up to five Lewis guns on patrol. Gas capacity was 360,000ft³ and *NS 6*, seen here, was delivered to Longside in January 1918. It flew for 397 hours before being deflated for the last time in October 1919. (Author's collection)

fundamental strength of air patrols lay in their deterrent value. Their principal contribution to the campaign, which was easier to recognise with hindsight, was that what mattered most to ensure an uninterrupted flow of merchant shipping in convoy was not necessarily the destruction of U-boats but preventing them from getting into an attacking position. Fear of being detected by patrolling aircraft if they surfaced to recharge batteries or gain a firing position on a target made U-boat commanders less effective and severely limited their options. While on patrol airships transmitted their call-sign every hour by wireless and when these were received by direction-finding stations such as those at Mullion, Prawle Point and Devonport the airships' positions could be accurately plotted. The enemy could of course read these transmissions but by 1918 was not in a position to do anything about them. Wireless was also used to alert the relevant SNO when a U-boat was sighted and airships, aeroplanes and destroyers all operated on a common wavelength to simplify the prosecution of contacts.

During January 1918 it was estimated that some 60 per cent of shipping losses to U-boats happened within 10 miles of the British coast because the enemy had been frustrated by the introduction of the convoy system in the open ocean. Consequently the Admiralty reacted by instituting regular inshore patrols around the British Isles by fixed-wing aircraft. RNAS Padstow was a typical example of the type of base from which these sorties were flown and in the last weeks of the RNAS a number of types were pressed into service for this work including de Havilland DH 6s and even some training types such as Avro 504Ks and Curtiss JN-4s.[35] Patrols were typically of about two hours' duration covering an area close to the coast at low-level in order to stand the best chance of seeing a U-boat. Here again the aircraft were more valuable for their deterrent value than the direct threat they posed to an enemy submarine.

Strike Operations by Shore-Based Aircraft of the RNAS

By 1918 several of the naval air squadrons in the Dover/Dunkirk command had been using Sopwith 1½ Strutters and later de Havilland DH 4s to attack enemy docks and shipping in Ostend, Zeebrugge and Bruges for nearly two years. 5 (Naval) Squadron at Petite Synthe was a typical example and Squadron Commander Charles Bartlett DSC RNAS gave a vivid description of sorties in *Bomber Pilot*.[36] 5(N) was re-equipped with DH 4s in May 1917 and found the aircraft to be an effective day bomber. It had a crew of two, pilot and gunlayer, the latter armed with twin Lewis guns on a Scarff mounting. The pilot had two fixed synchronised Vickers guns firing forward through the propeller arc and the aircraft could carry a 450lb bomb load. The early DH 4s were powered by the reliable 250hp Rolls-Royce Eagle VI engine which gave a top speed of 110 knots and a ceiling of 15,000ft. By 1918 later versions had the 375hp Eagle VIII which gave 130 knots and up to 22,000ft with a bomb load but was somewhat less reliable. An effective bomb sight was fitted that enabled precision bombing to be carried out by the gunlayer who steered the pilot over the target by means of string 'reins', the only means of communication between the rear cockpit and the pilot.

On 17 June 1917 Bartlett took off at 08.40 leading three other aircraft for an attack on Bruges docks. He led the formation along the coast to a point near the Dutch frontier before turning inland and Burdett, his gunlayer, gave him a good course, using the string reins, over the target where he dropped one 65lb and twelve 16lb bombs. They observed many explosions among the shipping in the western basin and on the quayside where a stack of wood was set on fire. Anti-aircraft fire was very heavy but not particularly accurate and Bartlett assessed that the gunners were probably put off by the haze. He passed within 500 yards of two enemy two-seaters heading in the opposite direction but, although he was alone at the time, they took no notice and since bombers were briefed to return without looking for trouble, Bartlett left them alone.

By 1918 bombing missions had become much larger affairs, with attacks on multiple targets escorted by fighter sweeps with other RNAS and RFC aircraft

The officers of 5 (Naval) Squadron at RNAS Petite Synthe. The commanding officer, Squadron Commander S J Goble DSO DSC RNAS, is seated at the centre with a cane. (Goble Family collection)

taking part. 5(N) came to specialise in attacks on enemy airfields, a tactic that would be known to a later generation of naval pilots as a 'ramrod', intended to allow other bombers to attack briefed targets without interference from enemy aircraft. On 30 January 1918 Bartlett took off from Petite Synthe at 11.50 as part of a force which included seven bombers and three fighters for an attack on the enemy airfield at Oostcamp which was five miles south of Bruges. The force gained height over Calais and crossed the lines in good formation at 16,000ft; the objective was visible from a considerable distance and Bartlett got a good line over it from south-west to north-east, gaining a direct hit on a large hangar in the southern corner which went up in flames. Several other bombs burst among sheds in the north corner but as soon as the bombing run was over they were engaged by some fifteen to twenty enemy aircraft which 'seemed to appear suddenly from nowhere, diving down out of the sun and choosing their attack when our formation was split up after dropping and had not time to reform'. Bartlett found three of them on his tail and a fourth coming head on and firing; he zoomed to avoid him, never had time to use his front guns and the enemy aircraft passed under him and joined the three on his tail. At this point Bartlett's engine cut out on three cylinders, revolutions dropped to 1300 and he saw the water temperature gauge rise rapidly to boiling point and then drop back to zero; his radiator had obviously been hit and the water in it lost. Naylor, his gunlayer, was dealing with the four aircraft on their tail and when he shot one down in flames the other three hung back and fired from a distance with their tracer going wide. With his badly-missing engine 'vibrating like hell' he turned towards base, diving to gain speed and attempting to cool the engine as much as possible while Flight Lieutenant Lupton RNAS led the remainder, now back in tight formation, as slowly as possible to keep him in sight and cover him against further attacks.

Despite missing, banging and vibrating badly, Bartlett's engine continued to give about 1300rpm and he flew over Ghistelles ahead of the formation and about 4000ft below it expecting the engine to stop at any moment. He saw another three enemy aircraft about 800ft below him but, to his relief, they made no attempt to attack him and he realised afterwards that with the rest of the squadron visible above him, the enemy must have thought he was a decoy trying to lead them into a trap. He finally made the lines and even landed safely at Petite Synthe where the radiator was found to be empty and the engine so hot that the mechanics could not get near it. They could not imagine why it had not seized. A bullet had severed the induction port feeding the front three starboard cylinders and another one had made a mess of the radiator and Bartlett felt that the fact that the engine had got him home spoke volumes for the Rolls-Royce Eagle.

The Big Handley Page Bombers

The big Handley Page O/100 bombers, Sueter's 'bloody paralysers', proved to be more complicated and difficult to develop than had at first been anticipated. One of the first four delivered to France on 1 January 1917, piloted by Flight Lieutenant Vereker RNAS, flew for some time in and over unbroken cloud cover and he eventually landed at the first airfield he saw after descending through it and seeing the ground at 500ft. By bad luck he was 12 miles behind enemy lines and an example of the RN's new bomber was delivered undamaged to the Germans. In April four more O/100s were delivered to Dunkirk to form the nucleus of 7 (Naval) Squadron and a fifth went to 3 Wing at Luxeuil-les-Bains. 7(N) was used at first to carry out daylight patrols off the Belgian coast and on 23 April three aircraft, each armed with fourteen 65lb bombs, attacked five German destroyers off Ostend, scoring several direct hits and leaving one vessel damaged and listing. Three days later, however, an O/100 was shot down on a similar operation and the type was confined to night bombing, a role pioneered on 16 March by the aircraft in 3 Wing which had attacked a railway station at Moulin-les-Metz. 5 Wing O/100s were used to attack enemy destroyer and U-boat bases at Bruges, Zeebrugge and Ostend.[37]

During the German offensive in March 1918 O/100s of 7 and 14 (Naval) Squadrons were used in interdiction operations behind the German lines with the aim of disrupting communications. On the night of 26/27 March five aircraft from each unit set out to bomb the crowded railway junction at Valenciennes. Seven reached the target and dropped a total of four 250lb and seventy-six 112lb bombs which caused significant disruption and damage. Naval 'A' Squadron flew its O/100s to Ochey on 17 October 1917 to become the first British heavy bomber squadron in the organisation that later became the Independent Force of the RAF. In fact it was the only such unit in operation until August 1918 when 97 Squadron RAF joined it, equipped with Handley Page O/400s. Despite the enthusiasm of politicians in 1917 and Smuts' prediction that bombing might introduce a new form of warfare, heavy bombers made a negligible impact before the Armistice. Up to the end of August the greatest number used in a single night raid was ten. These attacked Mannheim, Saarbrucken and airfields at Buhl and Boulay on the night of 15/16 August; one turned back because of engine trouble and another because of poor visibility so only eight actually dropped bombs. By September strikes by up to forty aircraft were being launched but that on 14/15 September had nine aircraft turn back with engine problems, one made a forced landing on the Allied side of the front line and three were shot down over their targets. Such losses would have got worse as enemy defences reacted to the threat and would have been difficult to sustain.

Fighter Operations over Dunkirk and the Western Front

The RNAS maintained fighters in the Dover/Dunkirk command throughout the conflict to prevent the Germans from gaining air superiority over the narrow seas and fighter squadrons from this command were placed under RFC command when requested by Trenchard to make up for the RFC's heavy losses in action. It is these units that seem to have caught the public's imagination more than any other despite the fact that they represented only a small part of RNAS activity. Fighter operations in the vicinity of the Western Front grew dramatically in intensity during 1917 as both sides realised the importance of air reconnaissance and interdiction and tried to deny these capabilities to the enemy. Many of the most successful pilots came from Canada and Australia to join the RNAS, among them Flight Commander R A Little DSO DSC* RNAS who scored forty-seven aerial victories in Sopwith Pups, Triplanes and Camels, making him the top-scoring

Despite the fact that wheeled fighters operating from ships' take-off platforms had demonstrated much better performance for fleet operations, some seaplane fighters remained in use until 1918. This Sopwith Baby, N1437, was one of a batch of forty aircraft built by the Blackburn Aeroplane & Motor Company under licence in Leeds. It was delivered to Calshot in September 1917 and then served at South Shields until late 1918. It was not finally deleted until 1919. Note the Blackburn company badge on the tailplane and port float. (Author's collection)

Australian 'ace' in history.[38] A fellow pilot in 8 (Naval) Squadron, Flight Commander Robert Compston RNAS described Little as 'not so much a leader as a brilliant lone hand'.[39] He said that there could be few better shots than Little, who could hit bottles thrown into the air while they were still travelling upwards with a shot from his pistol. He always took the fight to the enemy and never gave up. His bravery was summed up in the citations for the two DSCs he was awarded.[40] The citation published in the *London Gazette* on 16 February 1917 stated that the then Flight Sub Lieutenant Robert Alexander Little RNAS had acted with

conspicuous bravery in successfully attacking and bringing down hostile machines on several occassions. On 11 November 1916 he attacked and brought down a hostile machine in flames. On 12 November 1916 he attacked a German machine at a range of 50 yards, this machine was brought down in a nosedive. On 20 November 1916 he dived at a hostile machine and opened fire at 25 yards range, the observer was seen to fall down inside the machine which went down in a spinning nose dive. On 1 January 1917 he attacked an enemy scout which turned over on its back and came down completely out of control.

In the *London Gazette* published on 22 June 1917 the then Flight Lieutenant Little received a bar to his DSC for 'exceptional daring and skill in aerial fighting on many occassions'. They were too many to enumerate but the following examples were given 'on 28 April 1917 he destroyed an Aviatik; on 29 April he shot down a hostile scout which crashed. On 30 April with 3 other machines he went up after hostile machines and saw a big fight going on between fighter escorts and hostile aircraft. Little attacked one at 50 yards range and brought it down out of control. A few minutes later he attacked a red scout which was larger than the rest. This machine was handled with great skill but by clever manoeuvring Little got into a good position and shot it down out of control.' Unfortunately, Little was killed in action on 27 May 1918 while in acting command of his squadron during the commanding officer's absence on leave. His friend Flight Commander L H Rochford DSC* RNAS later described that the pilots of what had just become 203 Squadron, the former 3 (Naval), had gone to their mess at Ezil Le Hamel for drinks shortly after nightfall when a German bomber was heard to fly over. Little left the mess and shortly afterwards his colleagues heard him take off in his Camel. Later Lieutenant 'Kiwi' Beamish came in and told them that Little had gone after the bomber since it was clear night with good visibility. As the hours passed and he had not returned, they realised that he must be out of fuel and the next morning they learned that his body had been found in his crashed aircraft. Squadron Commander Collishaw, the commanding officer, returned from leave the next day to discover that Little had been hit in the groin, crashed and bled to death. The great Little, he found, 'had fallen to a random bullet fired by an unknown assailant'. Collishaw described his fighting career as 'an inspiration to his contemporaries'. Rochford described Little as the bravest man he had known who loved air fighting and was completely without fear. I find it moving that his mechanics carved a wooden cross to mark his grave and still described him as a Flight Commander RNAS and his unit as 3 (Naval) Squadron. When it was replaced by a standard Commonwealth War Graves Commission headstone after the war, the original wooden cross was given to his widow. It is now on display in the Australian War Memorial in Canberra.

Squadron Commander Raymond Collishaw DSO DSC RNAS was a Canadian who became the top-scoring fighter pilot in the RNAS with a total of sixty aerial victories in Sopwith 1½ Strutters, Pups, Triplanes and Camels. The citation for his own DSC, published in the *London Gazette* on 20 July 1917, recognised his services on various occassions, especially the following. 'On 1 June 1917 this officer shot down an Albatross scout in flames. On 3 June 1917 he shot down a further Albatross scout in flames. On 5 June 1917 he shot down a two-seater Albatross in flames. On 6 June 1917 he shot down 2 Albatross scouts in flames and killed the pilot in a third. He has displayed great gallantry and skill in all his combats.' In Collishaw's autobiography *Air Command*[1] he describes sorties which were typical at the time he commanded the Seaplane Defence Squadron at Dunkirk. Fleet protective patrols involved flying out as far as 50 miles from the coast and locating the ships they were detailed to cover. They were invariably greeted by a barrage of anti-aircraft fire even when the ships knew exactly when they were due to arrive, the number of aircraft and their type. Unceasing complaints failed to improve the situation but they were otherwise dull affairs that led to few encounters with enemy aircraft but required precise navigation with no room for error. Offensive patrols over enemy bases usually produced more action and that of 14 January 1918 produced more than most when a formation of enemy seaplanes and fighters was encountered near Zeebrugge. Collishaw shot down one and other members of the squadron two more.

The extent to which air combat had developed over the Western Front is illustrated by Collishaw's description of an offensive patrol over Ypres in July 1918 leading what was now 203 Squadron. After taking off they encountered and attacked a flight of six Fokker D-VIIs; Collishaw closed to within 30 yards of one and opened fire, seeing his tracer rounds going right into the cockpit. The aircraft went into a dive but still seemed to be under control. Three other Fokkers then attacked him, forcing him down to 2000ft before he could disengage. Thirty minutes later over Dixmunde he saw two DFW two-seaters slightly above his squadron's altitude and climbed to get in position above them. Once in position he attacked one which was flying a little above the other and got in a number of good bursts, estimating about 150 rounds in all with the tracers going right into the enemy's cockpit. The pilot must have been hit because his machine nosed down and crashed onto the top of the other, both being locked together as they fell.

16 HMS *Argus* – The World's First True Aircraft Carrier

The crowning achievement of the RNAS was the design, commissioning and the preparation for operational service of HMS *Argus*, the world's first true flush-deck aircraft carrier capable of launching and recovering aircraft and the progenitor of every subsequent carrier design in the world including those of the United States Navy. To put this achievement into full perspective it must be remembered that the first tentative steps to evaluate the operational usefulness of aircraft launched from a ship's deck in the open sea had taken place in *Hermes* during 1913 and *Argus* joined the Grand Fleet only five years later with the majority of the features we take for granted in modern carriers.[1]

Prior to the battle of Jutland in May 1916, Admiral Jellicoe had called for aircraft that were more effective than the seaplanes in service at the time and which could be operated from the decks of ships. He also asked for a new ship to be laid down to augment or replace the collection of converted merchant ships that provided his fleet with its only aviation capability. This request began the chain of decisions that led to the completion of *Argus* a little more than two years later. In December 1916 Murray Sueter endorsed a Paper written by Lieutenant Hyde-Thomson RN, supported by sketches, that proposed an attack on the enemy fleet in its harbours by torpedo-carrying aircraft. The Admiralty supported the idea and the Sopwith Company was instructed to begin design work on the aircraft, a task made more difficult at the time by the lack of a suitable engine. By 1917 higher-powered engines were becoming available and the design evolved into the Sopwith T.1 Cuckoo. Work on the projected torpedo attack continued within both the Admiralty and the Grand Fleet during 1917 but Sueter's advocacy for an independent air force isolated him and the driving force for the attack shifted to the Grand Fleet's aviation committee. A developed plan was approved and put forward by Admiral Beatty in September 1917 based on a force of the new Sopwith T.1s operating from eight large fast liners converted with full-length flight decks. Such ships had other important uses, however, not least as troopships and as auxiliary cruisers on the Northern Patrol enforcing the blockade against Germany. They could not be made available for conversion but the importance of such a strike was

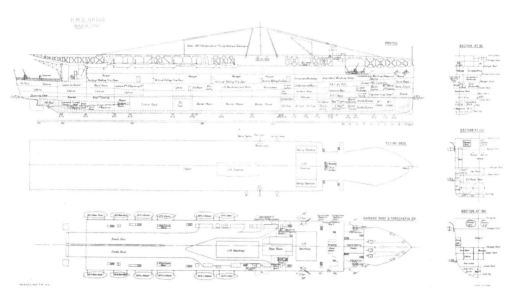

HMS *Argus* (Author's collection)

appreciated within the Admiralty and other means of providing aircraft carriers were studied. As a first step it was decided to build four carriers with speeds of 24 to 25 knots[2] which would allow them to operate with the Battlecruiser Fleet. Two were to have full-length flight decks and be capable of operating fourteen aircraft while the other two would only have flying-off decks and operate eight aircraft. Frequent changes were made but the line of development that led to the completion of *Hermes* and *Eagle* after the war can be traced from the requirement for the first two ships. The requirement for the simpler ships was met by the later seaplane carrier conversions.[3]

In 1915 two officers had forwarded sketch proposals for aircraft-carrying ships to the Admiralty. The first was Lieutenant R A Holmes RNVR, a naval architect working for the Cunard Shipping Line, who had served in *Riviera* before moving to the Air Department in the Admiralty. His proposal was for a seaplane carrier with a ramp aft for the recovery of seaplanes and a flush deck for the operation of aeroplanes. Funnel smoke was to be discharged aft through long horizontal ducts under the flight deck. The second officer was Flight Lieutenant H A Williamson RNAS who had flown seaplanes from *Ark Royal* during the Gallipoli campaign and become convinced that the operation of wheeled aeroplanes from an unobstructed flight deck was the best solution. In 1916 Constructor J H Narbeth, the Assistant DNC, was asked to design an aircraft carrier, making use of an

A view of *Argus'* hangar looking forward from the after lift which is in the down position allowing a fair amount of light onto the aircraft. Four Sopwith T.1s of 185 Squadron are visible, all with their wings folded. N6982 and N6977 can be identified. N6982 was completed in September 1918 and was part of 185 Squadron during its embarkation in *Argus* during November 1918. It was subsequently damaged and written off in December 1918. N6977 was delivered to the same squadron at East Fortune in September 1918 and embarked in *Argus* during November. It too was damaged and written off in the following December. (Author's collection)

incomplete liner hull to save time. The hull in question was that of the *Conte Rosso* ordered for the Italian Lloyd Sabaudo Line and laid down by Beardmore on the Clyde in June 1914. Work was suspended after the outbreak of war and she was still on the stocks in frame during 1916. She was purchased by the Admiralty in August 1916 when her modification and completion were described as urgent.

Narbeth studied both the earlier proposals and incorporated some of their features but the basic design evolved from his own ideas and the experience he had gained with the 1914 *Ark Royal*. At first his brief was to produce an improved *Campania* but the design went through several rapid evolutions before the ship was eventually completed. The central feature was an aircraft hangar 330ft long with a clear width of 48ft and a clear height of 20ft. For much of its length it was up to 68ft wide. Unlike any subsequent British aircraft carrier, *Argus* was fitted with an overhead gantry system which allowed serviceable aircraft at the rear of the hangar to be lifted over any unserviceable aircraft forward of them that obstructed their movement and then set down near the lifts from where they could be ranged to the flight deck. This was an ingenious solution to a problem that still exists but it soon became impractical as new aircraft grew in both height and weight. While he was working on the design, the seaplane carrier *Ben-my-Chree* was hit by shore batteries while she was anchored off Castelorizo Island on the southern coast of Turkey on 9 January 1917. Subsequent fires and explosions, ascribed to petrol vapour in empty aircraft refuelling cans, became uncontrollable and she sank in shallow water,[4] the only aviation vessel to be sunk in action during the Great War. This led Narbeth to design exceptionally thorough measures to prevent the spread of fire in the new ship which were to be repeated in every subsequent British aircraft carrier. The hangar was isolated from the rest of the ship by airlocks and it was divided into four sections by fire-resistant roller screens. At the rear a steel roller-door could be opened to give access to the quarterdeck from which seaplanes could be lowered onto the water and recovered by two cranes. It was believed that this would give the ship the capacity to operate aircraft fitted with floats even when she was in harbour or at anchor but in practice it was little used. Ventilation was installed throughout the hangar to disperse petrol fumes and the deck was given steel non-skid strips rather than wooden planking because of fears that the latter would become a fire hazard when soaked in oil and petrol. Each section was well-equipped with sand boxes and Pyrene fire-extinguishers to suppress flames before they could take a hold.

Following the experience gained with the seaplane carrier conversions, Narbeth decided not to fit a bulk fuel stowage system because he felt that it would be impossible to ensure that pipe joints would not leak and thus build up pockets of explosive petrol vapour. Instead petrol was embarked in 4000 two-gallon cans of the type used in the motor industry and seaplane carriers. They were stowed in a separate hold space forward which had its own ventilation system and was isolated from the rest of the ship by void spaces which could be filled with water. The cans were taken to the flight deck, where aircraft were refuelled, in a two-stage lift with a fire barrier at the half-way point. When aircraft were refuelled petrol was poured from the cans by hand, through fine gauze to remove particulate impurities, into the aircraft tanks. A Sopwith T.1 took 50 gallons requiring twenty-five cans; a Sopwith 2F.1 Camel took 37 gallons requiring nineteen cans and so it will be seen that refuelling and re-arming aircraft after a twenty-aircraft strike operation would have been a complicated business, requiring hundreds of petrol cans in addition to torpedoes, machine-gun ammunition, flares and smoke bombs. The RN preoccupation with preventing fuel-vapour fires was to lead, on the one hand, to very safe aircraft operation in the decades ahead but, on the other, to more limited stowage of fuel than in American or Japanese aircraft carriers.

The original hull sides of the liner design were continued up to the hangar roof which became the strength deck. The flight deck was supported 14ft 6in above this

Argus in September 1918 showing how funnel smoke was exhausted right aft. The aircraft approach path would have been above it but this was clearly not an ideal arrangement. (Author's collection)

by a light lattice structure and can be considered as superstructure with expansion joints to ensure that it did not carry any longitudinal bending loads. The flight deck surface was formed of light steel plates flush-welded to give a smooth, unpainted surface and she was completed with no arrester or retaining wires in place. Narbeth seems to have hoped that airflow through the space under the deck might prevent the formation of eddies at the stern but the clutter between the hangar roof and the flight deck left no space, negating any hope of a smooth airflow. Unfortunately, Narbeth followed Holmes' suggestion in this area and the boiler exhaust was carried away in two large oval ducts, each 14ft 3in wide by 8ft high internally, running between the hangar roof and the underside of the flight deck. Annular casings, also of oval section, each 15ft 9in wide by 9ft 6in high, surrounded the ducts, along which cooling air was blown by fans and the funnel gases exhausted just under the after end of the flight deck. There were concerns that a strong following wind could blow into the ducts and cause a backdraught in the boilers and so to prevent this happening, electric fans were fitted in the ducts to maintain a positive exhaust pressure. Overall, it was not a very successful scheme and has never been repeated. Even with lagging and the cooled outer casings the ducts got very hot and aircraft had to pass over the hot gases, although they did not fly through them, just as they were approaching the deck to land. The original liner design had included five double-ended and four single-ended coal-fired boilers intended to produce a maximum speed of 19.5 knots. Experience had shown that coal dust had caused wear in the engines of aircraft embarked in *Campania* and the Admiralty wanted a higher speed so the boiler design was modified to six boilers of each type, all of which were oil-fired. The new arrangement developed 21,376 shp on trials giving a speed of 20.5 knots; the best that could be hoped for but slightly slower than the maximum speed of the contemporary battle-line.

This wooden wind-tunnel model shows the original design intended for HMS *Argus* with two islands, port and starboard, connected by a bridge and navigating position. The latticework structures visible against the forward island bulkheads are cranes for lifting seaplanes onto and off the water. Note how narrow the take-off deck was to be, leaving clear arcs of fire for the single 4in HA guns. The LA 4in guns are visible aft at quarterdeck level. In 1917 it was thought that aircraft would be launched from a trestle as they would have been from a seaplane carrier deck so a wider deck was not thought to be needed. The wind-tunnel tests did show that the islands would cause turbulence over the after deck that would have made landing difficult but the actual degree of difficulty was not fully realised until the *Furious* trials confirmed the fact. The gap between the islands was intended to allow aircraft to be handled from one deck to the other, they were not expected to take-off or land-on through it. (Author's collection)

The first evolution of the design featured two flight deck areas, a tapered take-off area forward which was 200ft long and a landing area aft which was to be 300ft by 68ft. They were connected to the hangar deck by two lifts, both of which had to be sited forward of the funnel ducts, another disadvantage of that feature. The after one proved to be of little use and was eventually welded shut. A narrow passage-way connected the forward and after decks which passed between two small superstructures, or 'islands', set to port and starboard which were connected by an overhead bridge. An accurate model of the design was made and tested in the National Physical Laboratory (NPL) wind tunnel at Teddington during November 1916, one of the earliest experiments ever carried out on a structure other than an aircraft. These showed that the islands would cause severe turbulence aft that would have made landing dangerous, if not impossible, but in the absence of real-world evidence the design was not altered and the ship was launched with the name *Argus* on 2 December 1917. In March 1918 landing trials were carried out on the after

HMS *Argus* under construction at Beardmore's shipyard in early 1918. The port island is already in place with two of the beams that would have connected it to the starboard structure. The completed starboard island can be seen on the jetty waiting for the giant crane to lift it into place. Both were discarded when the design was re-cast with a flush deck. (Author's collection)

deck just fitted to *Furious* and these provided the necessary evidence that turbulence aft of block superstructures was severe enough to make landing dangerous. By that time the islands were actually being fitted to *Argus* but they were quickly removed and the design re-cast to provide a fully flush flight deck covering the full length of the hull. It came to a point at the forward end which was to give *Argus* the nickname she retained throughout her life, the 'floating flat-iron'.

In place of the islands, *Argus* was fitted with a hydraulically-raised compass platform and charthouse from which she was controlled when flying was not taking place. When it was lowered for flying operations the ship was navigated from bridge wings either side of the flight deck,[5] about a quarter of the ship's length from the bow. A flat, or corridor, connected the two bridge wings with the compass platform, off which compartments were modified to provide space for the bridge wireless office and sea cabins that were originally to have been situated in the islands. The arrangement gave some unique problems for captains, navigators, officers of the watch and their assistants. Firstly, the compass platform was not initially fitted with a physical lock with the result that if hydraulic pressure was lost it sank gracefully out of sight taking the captain and his team with it. As soon as it was low enough to open the door they had to run along the flat to the most suitable bridge wing to resume safe navigation. Secondly, neither bridge gave all-round vision and if multiple bearings had to be taken the relevant readings had to be passed between bridge wings by voice pipe.

Even in the early phases of the design it had been clear that an aircraft carrier might have to stop to recover seaplanes or turn away from the main body of the fleet into wind to launch or recover aircraft and might become isolated whilst doing so. It was therefore clear that she would need sufficient gun armament to defend herself against an attack by enemy destroyers or torpedo boats. As the number of actions between ships of the Grand Fleet and enemy aircraft grew in 1917 it also became clear that she would need a reasonable battery of guns to defend herself against air attack or at least join in a barrage of anti-aircraft fire from the task force she would operate with. The original sketch design included two 4in low-angle guns and two 4in high-angle guns for anti-aircraft work. During build two further 4in high-angle guns were added. All were mounted at hangar deck level along the ship's side; the two anti-aircraft guns forward needed large cut-outs into the flight deck to give what were considered to be adequate arcs of fire at high elevation.

Deck-Landing Trials

In September 1918 Admiral Phillimore, RAA Grand Fleet, was flying his flag in *Furious* and the Admiralty instructed him to organise *Argus'* flying trials with a view to getting her into service as quickly as possible. The ship's senior flying officer was Commander R Bell-Davies VC DSO RN who had, since 1 April, held a temporary commission as a Lieutenant Colonel RAF and who had previously been the senior aviation officer in *Campania*. Apart from being one of the most senior pilots in the RNAS, Bell-Davies was the officer who had the most experience with embarked operations in large warships. Phillimore ordered him to take charge of the trials and gave instructions to Rosyth Dockyard that it was to do anything he asked.[6] *Argus* was commissioned in Beardmore's yard at Dalmuir on 14 September 1918 and subsequently arrived in the Firth of Forth just as the Grand Fleet was about to sail for a North Sea sweep and a series of tactical exercises so Bell-Davies had to hand over *Furious'* aircraft to Wilfred Acland, his second-in-command, and move across to the new ship. His team of experienced Camel and 1½ Strutter pilots were obviously needed in *Furious* but he found an experienced Strutter pilot named Cocky at Turnhouse and 'roped him in' to help with the initial deck-landing trials. After the failure of *Furious'* after landing deck caused by turbulence from the centrally-mounted superstructure, it was important to prove as quickly as possible that *Argus'* flush deck would really work. A series of planning meetings with RAA

Not of the best quality but a unique photograph of a Sopwith 2F.1 Camel landing on *Argus* in 1918. For four years after this photograph was taken, she was the only aircraft carrier in the world. (Author's collection)

and other interested parties had been held in *Furious* and Bell-Davies wasted no time in discussing the initial landings with Captain H H Smith RN, *Argus*' captain who had until recently commanded *Campania*, and Clark, his navigating officer. Between them they agreed that on the next day the ship would proceed to a point at the mouth of the Forth near May Island but inside the anti-submarine defences. Once in position she was to turn into the prevailing westerly wind and manoeuvre to give a relative wind of about 20 knots straight down the deck. A 'negative' flag would be displayed prominently until Captain Smith was satisfied that all was ready; it would then be replaced by an 'affirmative' flag. Bell-Davies and Cocky, both in 1½ Strutters, took off from Turnhouse and joined the ship in formation to orbit as it got ready. The plan was that they should carry out six landings each in turn. They would not attempt to stop after each one but after their wheels touched the deck they would roll forward and then fly off again. Two sailors were equipped with paint pots and brushes and told to wait in the nettings alongside the deck. After each landing one was to run onto the deck and put a blob of paint at the exact point where the aircraft had touched down; Bell-Davies' blobs were white and Cocky's were red. The Strutter had no brakes and to come to a full stop the pilot would have to switch off the ignition and rely on friction and a small handling party to stop his aircraft. Bell-Davies' plan was the quickest way of determining whether deck landing on *Argus* was a viable proposition or not and showed the urgency that was placed by both the Admiralty and the Grand Fleet that the new carrier should be made ready as quickly as possible.

A view looking aft from the forward part of *Argus'* forward hangar with the after lift in the down position. At least four Sopwith T.1s are visible with their wings folded and some have their engine cowlings removed to give fitters better access to their engines. (Author's collection)

On 24 September 1918 Bell-Davies made history by making the first world's landing on a flush-deck aircraft carrier. As he made his final approach off a left-hand visual circuit he was rather daunted at first by the big, square appearance of the after end of the flight deck and hangar since *Argus* was built without a round-down aft and the dark structure had the appearance of a cliff.[7] He kept well above it and landed about half-way down the deck. Once he got used to the deck, however, he gradually crossed the after end lower and his blobs of white paint moved further aft. To his 'intense annoyance', when Cocky's turn came he put all his red blobs well aft alongside the best of his white ones. After this first series of landings, both pilots returned to Turnhouse, the Grand Fleet aircraft depot, where they landed. Further landings were carried out on the next day and over the two days a total of twenty-one deck landings were carried out without incident.[8] Their series of successful landings on a bare steel deck had demonstrated that *Argus'* flush deck design was viable; the next step was to prepare her for the routine operation of Sopwith 2F.1 Camels and T.1 Cuckoos in the open sea as quickly as possible.

In *Sailor in the Air* Bell-Davies mentions the 'extraordinary number of ideas' about the safe recovery of wheeled aircraft onto a carrier 'put forward by people in the fleet as well as by the Admiralty'. He remembered one officer who had said that

A Sopwith 2F.1 Camel on *Argus'* forward lift during flying trials in 1918. (Author's collection)

he had noticed that aeroplanes stopped quickly in ploughed fields and suggested therefore that the flight deck should be covered with a good, sticky layer of soil. Captain Nicholson of *Furious* had watched Dunning's landings as well as all the early attempts to land on her after deck and was convinced that the essential thing was to hold the aircraft securely after landing to prevent it being blown overboard like Dunning. Aware of the development work at the Isle of Grain he proposed that a line of hooks, like broad arrowheads, should be fitted to the bottom of the wooden fairing on the axle between the main wheels. These would engage in retaining wires fitted fore and aft over part of the flight deck. Bell-Davies agreed in general with this idea but added a few practical refinements of his own. It was decided that once the practicality of landing on a bare deck had been demonstrated, *Argus* should be fitted as quickly as possible with retaining wires before any further landings were carried out. The agreed scheme was to build two wooden ramps about 30ft apart, the first of which was to be about half way up the deck. Both were to slope upwards from aft to forward, their tops being about 2ft above the deck. The retaining wires were stretched fore and aft between them and the idea was that pilots would land on the clear area of deck aft, maintain the aircraft's forward speed and taxi up the after ramp. From there it would drop off the ramp into the 'trap' and the hooks would engage the wires. As the aircraft ran up the forward ramp the hooks would pull on the taut wires and the resultant friction would bring it to rest. Given the landing speeds involved there was no great need for arresting wires rigged athwartships to

Commander Bell-Davies taking off in a Sopwith 'Ship' Strutter from *Argus* in October 1918.
There is no observer or passenger and the hooks intended to engage the retaining wires are
clearly visible under the axle between the wheels. The steam jet to starboard shows that the
wind is blowing straight down the flight deck. (Author's collection)

stop the aircraft but the retaining wires did prove slow to use as it was a time-
consuming evolution to extricate the aircraft from them after it came to a stop. With
the wisdom of hindsight we can deduce that trials with a system of arresting wires
would have provided a better solution because they would have allowed higher
landing speeds and held the aircraft until a handling party took charge of it when
the engine was stopped. However, the retaining wires solved the perceived problem
of retaining lightweight aircraft on deck after landing and they could be fitted
quickly. Extended trials and the installation of arrester wires would have taken time
which was not available if the planned strike on the High Sea Fleet was to be carried
out as soon as the first squadron of torpedo aircraft was ready.

Immediately after the first deck-landing demonstration *Argus* was taken into
Rosyth Dockyard where 'an army of shipwrights started work on the ramps'. They
were ready in early October 1918 but Cocky came down with influenza and all the
subsequent deck-landing trials were carried out by Bell-Davies alone. RAA shifted

his flag from *Furious* to *Argus* for the next set of trials and experts embarked from the Admiralty and Air Ministry. They included Groves and other constructors from DNC's Department and Busteed from the Isle of Grain experimental establishment. A 1½ Strutter had been fitted with axle hooks at Turnhouse for these trials and this was embarked before the ship left Rosyth and all subsequent trials were carried out by this aircraft operating from the ship. Its stowage in the hangar, refuelling, ranging onto the flight deck and striking down into the hangar played an important part in setting the ship's aviation systems to work and preparing her for operational service. Modern first-of-class flying trials are very similar and differ only in detail as aircraft of increasingly complex technology have been absorbed into service. Aircraft torpedoes, bombs and belted 0.303in ammunition were embarked while she was in Rosyth so that the torpedo body rooms and magazines could be tested and set to work. *Argus*' first-of-class flying trials took advantage of the experience gained recently with *Campania* and *Furious* but getting such a novel ship ready for operational service in a little over six weeks was a remarkable achievement.

The second series of deck-landing trials began in early October and were also carried out in the secure waters at the eastern extremity of the Firth of Forth. Once the ship was steady at 10 knots into a natural wind of 10 knots, these combined to give 20 knots relative wind down the deck, Bell-Davies took off and flew a left-hand pattern to land in exactly the right place on the after part of the flight deck. The Strutter continued to move forward as planned, climbed the after ramp, dropped into the 'trap' and easily came to rest. By definition, this had to be a full-stop landing and it took some time to extricate the aircraft and set it in position for a further take-off. Bell-Davies went over to the bridge, an easy thing to do in this ship since it was at the deck edge and he could simply lean across and talk to the captain. For his second landing, a higher wind over the deck was required and the ship worked up to its full speed giving a relative wind speed of about 30 knots. He found landing to be even easier in this condition since the aircraft's speed of approach relative to the deck was slower. Again the landing was successful and while the Strutter was prepared for a further launch Groves asked Bell-Davies to land next into a low wind over the deck. The natural wind was dropping and by the time he took off it was estimated to be about 4 knots; *Argus* had reduced to 4 knots, giving a relative speed of about 8 knots, but after he took off the natural wind dropped still further and the third landing was actually made with less than 8 knots down the deck. His speed relative to the deck was much greater and to cope with this, shot mats had been placed on the slope of the forward ramp to increase friction as the aircraft moved up it. The landing was in exactly the right place again and the aircraft fell into the 'trap' but this time

Bell-Davies' 'Ship' Strutter at the top of *Argus*' after ramp about to engage the retaining wires as it drops onto them during deck-landing trials in the Firth of Forth during October 1918. As soon as the aircraft stops, he will turn off the engine ignition and a handling party will set about extricating the aircraft from the wires. (Author's collection)

its greater forward momentum took it all the way along it and right up the forward ramp before it came to rest. This day's trials had proved that the system of retaining wires worked and that *Argus* was capable of launching and recovering aircraft in a wide range of wind conditions over the deck. By modern standards a greater number of landings with different weapon loads and with the wind at an angle to the ship's centreline would be deemed essential but Bell-Davies had proved that the ship's basic design was right and more experience would be gained by the operational T.1 Cuckoos, 2F.1 Camels and 'Ship' Strutters when they embarked to work up to operational efficiency.

We can get a very good idea of how the second phase of deck-landing trials were carried out because they were filmed and the footage is now in the archive of the Imperial War Museum at Lambeth. Techniques included such tried-and-trusted methods as were already in place but others obviously had to be tried for the first time after careful thought and practice ashore at Turnhouse. For the first take-off the aircraft was ranged forward of the forward lift with its tail-skid on a trestle, exactly as if it were to be launched from the forward deck of *Furious* or another seaplane carrier. It was held fast by rope lashings attached to ring bolts let into the deck for the purpose arranged to fall forwards and lie flush with the deck when not in use.[9] The lashings were not removed until the ship was steady into wind and when they were two men held each wingtip firmly and four others held the tailplane onto the trestle. Even then the aircraft rocked noticeably. In order to make sure that the ship was absolutely into wind a steam jet was let into the forward part of the flight deck and a portable version, with steam passing through a flexible hose, could be moved around the deck in front of the aircraft to ensure that all was well before launch. An officer with a hand-held anemometer checked the actual wind over the deck near the aircraft at frequent intervals. Rotary engines tended to overheat if run for any length of time on deck as they relied on airflow over the cylinders to cool them. Thus Bell-Davies' 'Ship' Strutter was not started until all was ready with the ship steady into the briefed wind over the deck, lashings removed and the hold-back manned. When a green flag signal from the bridge was given, the engine was started by a mechanic who swung the propeller. It would have been warmed through by another mechanic earlier so that all was ready and as soon as the pilot was happy with his engine temperature, oil pressure, fuel mixture setting and revolutions he waved his arm, the hold-back was released and the aircraft moved forward in a flying attitude, ponderously at first, to lift off the deck and fly away. The trestle was moved away to a safe stowage by the deck edge when not needed. Paint marks on the deck were made to show where it was to be re-positioned for the next launch.

To carrier pilots of later generations like me, the final approach to the deck seemed to begin very low over the water. The cameraman stood on the flight deck well forward of the retaining wires and the aircraft occasionally disappeared below flight deck level as Bell-Davies made his approach. Throughout the recovery an officer stood forward of the retaining wires holding up a green flag to show the pilot that the deck was ready for him and give an idea of the wind speed and direction down the deck. If there was a problem, he would raise a red flag and Bell-Davies would have aborted the landing and climbed to fly another circuit to land. The footage shows several approaches where he was not entirely happy with things and flew over the deck to go round again. His technique was obviously to make a long, slow, flat final approach to pass about 5 or 6ft above the after end of the flight deck at slow speed, cut the engine to drop onto the clear area and then roll forward into the retaining wires. Once the aircraft had stopped moving the handling party waited until the propeller had stopped turning after the pilot had switched the ignition off before running in to take charge of the aircraft. They would push the wires down to extricate the axle hooks and then manhandle the aircraft up the forward ramp and forward to where it could either be positioned for another launch with its tailplane on the trestle or struck down on the forward lift into the hangar. This low approach explains why Bell-Davies was concerned by the lack of a round-down and the cliff-like appearance of the after end of the ship as it loomed towards him on finals.[10] From the moment when the wheels first touched the deck until the aircraft came to rest in the retaining wires took about 18 to 20 seconds depending on the aircraft's speed relative to the deck on entry. Once the handling parties gained experience, extricating the aircraft took about 30 seconds. One interesting feature of every launch and recovery on *Argus'* deck was that Admiral Phillimore, distinguishable by his frock coat and the chin-strap on his hat worn down, was right there among the handling parties talking to them, studying their every move and finding out for himself exactly what they were doing, how they were doing it and mentally seeking ways to streamline deck operating technique.

The problem with the retaining wires was immediately obvious. Aircraft could not taxi over them and could not therefore use the whole deck for take-off. Aircraft would have to be ranged and take off from the area forward of the 'trap'. The arrangement fitted to *Argus* for the landing trials in October 1918 was, of course, a purely temporary structure to prove the concept and something more permanent and operationally-acceptable would be needed to operate large numbers of aircraft efficiently on a regular basis. Bell-Davies suggested an arrangement of hinged steel plates which could be pushed up electrically or by hydraulic ram to form the ramps and which, when not in use, could lie flush with the deck. This would allow the whole deck to be used for ranging and launching aircraft and would make the space between the retaining wires more easily accessible for handling parties since they were difficult to pick their way through when raised. Captain Smith agreed with these proposals and Rosyth Dockyard was instructed to design and construct such a system with urgency but it was not completed and installed until December 1918 by which time the war was over.[11]

Bell-Davies was in a slightly difficult position as he was a temporary lieutenant colonel in the RAF, a new and different service, so he was not 'borne on the books' of *Argus* but was only attached to it for the trials period. He still thought of himself as a naval officer, however, and fortunately for the RN he was one of the few officers who refused to transfer permanently to the RAF after the war and he reverted to his naval rank of commander. I am not sure that he ever wore RAF uniform as, like many others, he continued to wear his RNAS uniform after 1 April 1918. Despite the problems induced by politicians his relationship with Captain Smith was good, helped by the fact that they had known and trusted each other in *Campania*. In *Sailor in the Air* he said that he 'could not have had a better person with whom to collaborate' and described Smith as 'enthusiastic but always ready to see both sides of a question and never lost his temper'. Their relationship of mutual respect is well summarised in a story told by Bell-Davies about *Argus'* First Lieutenant who was very keen to be the first man ever to land on an aircraft carrier as a passenger.

Argus fitted with a wood-and-canvas island mock-up on the starboard side of the flight deck amidships in October 1918 while she carried out flying trials in the Firth of Forth. Far from finding it a problem, Commander Bell-Davies liked the island because it helped him to judge his height over the deck and the ideal landing point. Note that in this photograph, *Argus* has her hydraulic bridge in the raised position; the island was purely an aerodynamic shape that could not be used for practical navigation. (Author's collection)

The Strutter had a second seat so it was possible to take him up but even after the first series of deck landings there was still an element of risk and Bell-Davies felt he ought to seek the captain's permission before doing so. Captain Smith's response was apparently to say 'What do you ask me for? It's your aeroplane isn't it?' Bell-Davies replied 'Yes, but your First Lieutenant' 'Pooh' said Captain Smith 'there are plenty more First Lieutenants'.

In October 1918 *Argus* had a high priority but so too did the carriers *Eagle* and *Hermes* which were still under construction. *Argus* had proved that a flush deck was viable but DNC wanted to simplify the funnel, bridge, signalling and communications arrangements by completing the later ships with an island structure on the starboard side. If the idea was to prove unworkable time would be lost converting the ships into a flush-deck design and so, notwithstanding the urgent need to get *Argus* into service, time was taken to use her for an experiment to see if an island was acceptable from a flying viewpoint. The shipwrights at Rosyth were instructed to make a dummy island out of wood and canvas and this was fitted on the starboard side amidships on 4 October. It was rectangular in shape with a dummy bridge at the forward end and a large funnel shape but no mast. Smoke generators at the after end were activated before any aircraft landed and showed that the wind-tunnel tests at the NPL were closely replicated in the real world and there was no dangerous turbulence to contend with. The only potential problem was that her deck was fairly narrow with a maximum width of only 68ft and the island structure obtruded into this by about 15ft. The Strutter had a wingspan of 33ft 6in and Bell-Davies was concerned that he might easily foul it with a wingtip so he had a Sopwith Pup modified at Turnhouse with hooks under its axle. This had

The island mock-up in closer detail with the forward lift in the foreground. Note the cameraman with his tripod and movie camera on the far side of the lift showing that this photograph was probably taken during the second series of deck-landing trials that were filmed from several angles. (Author's collection)

a wingspan of 26ft 6in and no problems were encountered passing the island. Other landings were carried out by a 2F.1 Camel which had a wingspan of 26ft 11in. Experience showed that his fears were unfounded and, with the landing area offset to port of the ship's centreline, there was ample space for Pups, Camels and Strutters. With a wingspan of 46ft 9in, however, the T.1 Cuckoo would have been tight with the dummy island in place and the urgent requirement to get these aircraft on board led to the rapid removal of the wood and canvas structure once it had served its purpose. Before any landings were carried out with the dummy island in place a Camel and a Pup from Turnhouse flew around and over the ship and through the wake from a variety of directions to ensure that there was no turbulence.[12] Bell-Davies landed successfully in the Pup soon after the island was installed and commented that far from inhibiting deck landing, the island actually improved the pilot's ability to judge height and position relative to the deck accurately and represented a significant improvement over the flush deck. About thirty landings were made by 2F.1 Camels and Pups with the dummy island in place, all of them successful and, based on this experience, the Controller took the decision to complete *Eagle* and *Hermes* with islands.[13]

After this third phase of deck-landing trials the dummy island was removed and between 10 and 19 October 1918 she embarked the Sopwith T.1 Cuckoos of 185 Squadron, the first squadron in any navy to be equipped with carrier-borne torpedo-attack aircraft. Both ship and squadron were to gain experience and work up to operational efficiency as quickly as possible. The squadron had been working up ashore at what was now the RAF airfield at East Fortune. Preparations for the planned attack on the High Sea Fleet in its harbour were taken forward as quickly as possible given the fact that 185 Squadron had new and untested aircraft, the ship had been built to a radical new design and was only a month out of builders' hands and the techniques both were to use had never been tried before and literally had to be evolved on a day-to-day basis. The planned torpedo attack would have

A Sopwith 'Ship' Strutter being hoisted onto HMAS *Australia*'s 'Q' turret having been ferried out to the ship at her anchorage in the Firth of Forth by lighter from the Grand Fleet air park at Donibristle in March 1918. This particular aircraft was first delivered to the RNAS in May 1917 and converted to a 'Ship' Strutter at East Fortune after being involved in a crash at Cranwell. It was subsequently embarked in *Furious* and a number of other warships between spells back at Donibristle. (Sea Power Centre – Australia via David Stevens)

Argus as completed in September 1918 with a disruptive-pattern paint scheme intended to break up the ship's outline when seen through an optical rangefinder. She is at anchor in the Firth of Forth and the aircraft on deck are Sopwith T.1s. *Furious* is visible at anchor beyond her bow and a kite balloon is visible beyond her stern. (Author's collection)

pre-dated the Battle of Taranto by 22 years and will be described in the next chapter.

The Sopwith 1½ 'Ship' Strutter

Strutters had been used as both bombers and escort fighters by the RNAS in France and the Aegean but the recommendation made by the Grand Fleet Aircraft Committee in 1917 that spotter and reconnaissance aircraft flown off ships should be fitted with short-range wireless sets brought a new role for the type.[14] Take-offs from turret platforms in *Australia* and *Repulse* described earlier had demonstrated that launching 'Ship' Strutters from capital ships was a practical proposition but the RNAS did not have enough of them to meet the requirement. Earlier Strutters had been built in two versions, a single-seat bomber with a bomb-bay aft of the cockpit and a two-seater fighter version with a second cockpit for a gunlayer with a Lewis gun mounted on a Scarff ring. Both versions had also been used by the RFC and built under licence in France[15] but by 1918 newer types such as the de Havilland DH 4 were replacing them. Batches of ex-RFC and French Strutters were procured for conversion into 'Ship' Strutters to meet the requirement but there was a further problem that made the conversion of a large number of machines a necessity. The 'Ship' Strutter was a 'one-shot' system like the fleet-defence fighters if it was launched out of range of an airfield ashore and since most would be launched in the eastern North Sea, they were lost after their first operational sorties. If there was time and no immediate U-boat threat the destroyer that rescued the aircrew might salvage the aircraft from which some items, such as the engine and machine guns, could be re-used but the airframe and wireless would usually have to be written-off. A continuous stream of 'Ship' Strutters was required, therefore, to meet the need.

The first 'Ship' Strutter conversions used two-seater airframes which were fitted with slinging points to hoist the aircraft onto its turret platform, internal flotation bags to keep it afloat after ditching and a wireless-telegraphy set which was powered by a wind-turbine driven generator. The supply of two-seater airframes began to run out in 1918 and single-seaters had to be re-built into two-seater configuration, work that involved changes to the fuselage structure, fuel tanks and plumbing. The work was carried out at the RAF's Number 2 Aircraft Repair Depot at Coal Aston. The first 'Ship' Strutters went to sea in *Furious* in December 1917 and more followed as capital ships were fitted with their turret platforms. A number of Strutters were used for ditching trials at the Isle of Grain including N5245 which was used for flotation bag experiments. The aircraft intended for use in *Argus* were fitted with propeller guards extended from the undercarriage so that the retaining wires would not shatter the propeller if the aircraft nosed forward as it dropped off the after ramp. The strutter flown by Bell-Davies lacked the W/T installation, generator and guns to save weight and no doubt to preserve valuable equipment if the aircraft went over the side.

The 1½ Strutter was developed for the Admiralty by the Sopwith Company and the first prototype, number 3686, had been completed in 1915. It was a handsome two-seat biplane and the name is said to have stemmed from the outer struts of the central wing bracing which were thought by pilots to look like half-sized interplane struts. The outer, full-size, struts joined the upper and lower wings in the conventional way.[16] It was the first aeroplane to have Sopwith's iconic fin and rudder shape and was fitted with a wheeled undercarriage in which each wheel was mounted on a half axle with its inner end pivoted at the mid-point of the spreader bar. Shock absorption was by means of the rubber cord which bound each half axle to the apex of the corresponding vee-strut. Its structure was conventional and comprised wire-braced wooden members covered with clear-doped Irish linen; there was plywood decking on the top surfaces in the vicinity of the cockpits. The pilot sat directly under the upper wing and the observer/gunlayer's cockpit was further aft, the space between the cockpits being filled by the fuel tank which

Argus' handling party taking charge of a Sopwith 'Ship' Strutter to move it clear of the retaining wires. The difficulty of moving across the landing area with the wires raised is shown by the officer treading carefully to the right of the propeller. (Author's collection)

contain 40 gallons of petrol. The 'Ship' Strutter was 25ft 3in long and had a wingspan of 33ft 6in. Several different engines were used but the most powerful was the Clerget 9Ba rated at 135hp. It could be armed with a single fixed forward-firing Vickers gun mounted centrally on top of the fuselage forward of the cockpit, firing through the propeller arc with an synchronising mechanism. The after cockpit had a free Lewis gun on a Scarff mounting. The maximum permissible take-off weight was 2205lb sand the maximum speed that could be achieved was 100 knots at 6500ft. A climb to 10,000ft would take 17 minutes 50 seconds but operationally 'Ship' Strutters would have operated lower than that, the ideal height depending on cloud cover and sea state.

17 Tondern and the Planned Attack on the High Sea Fleet in Harbour

The 'Ship' Strutter described in the last chapter was one element of a trio of aircraft types that could be embarked in *Argus* to form the world's first carrier air group capable of carrying out a range of tasks at short notice from a floating base. The other types that joined the Strutter in 1918 were the Sopwith 2F.1 Camel, sometimes referred to as the 'Ship' Camel, and the Sopwith T.1 Cuckoo.

Sopwith 2F.1 Camel
By mid-1917 the Sopwith Pup and its derivative Beardmore WB III were outclassed by the latest generation of German fighters which they might have to fight when covering fleet operations in the eastern North Sea. The Sopwith F.1 Camel was designed as a replacement for land operations and another variant was designed specifically for operation from ships; it differed sufficiently to be given a separate Sopwith type number, the 2F.1.[1] The first prototype, N5, was tested in March 1917 powered by a 130hp Clerget rotary engine but most production aircraft were fitted with the more powerful Bentley BR.1 which developed 150hp. The biggest difference between the 2F.1 and the F.1 was the former's detachable rear fuselage, intended to reduce the space needed to stow it in a ship's hangar. When assembled the rear fuselage was locked onto the front section by four turnbuckles, a design feature that had been pioneered on later versions of the Sopwith Baby for the same purpose. There were horizontal and vertical spacers on each side of the fuselage break point which provided rigidity. A joint box sleeved each of the four front longerons and each of these incorporated a tongue which mated into a corresponding space in the four after longerons when the fuselage sections were fitted together. To lock the two sections together there were four turnbuckles, one hinged on each of the four front fuselage joint boxes. The 'T' shaped end of the turnbuckle was placed in the lug on the rear joint box and it was then tightened 'finger-tight' with a marlinspike or screwdriver shaft and wire-locked in position to mate the two sections firmly together.[2] The rear fuselage was lifted into position and subsequently removed by a party of sailors and the whole process could be completed in a few minutes. The rear fuselage was filled with a flotation bag which

meant that the control runs to the elevators had to be run from rocking levers sited immediately behind the break point outside the fuselage and similar external arrangements were made for the rudder. The control runs had to be disconnected when the fuselage was split, then re-connected and tested during re-assembly.

The 2F.1 had a number of other distinguishing features including a shorter wing centre section which reduced the overall wingspan by a little over one foot. The centre-section was supported on steel-tube struts which, in front elevation, were splayed less sharply than the spruce struts of the F.1 and were noticeably more slender. One of the 2F.1's most important tasks was the interception and destruction of Zeppelins searching for the Grand Fleet and to facilitate this they were to be armed with tracer, Brock and Pomeroy explosive ammunition. To avoid the danger of an exploding round hitting the propeller, it was decided to fit a Lewis gun with a 97-round ammunition tray on the top wing centreline, which would fire clear of the propeller arc. A single fixed Vickers gun was mounted on top of the fuselage, forward of the cockpit to port of the centreline to fire conventional belted ball and tracer ammunition through the propeller arc by means of a synchroniser system. Some 2F.1s operated by the Felixstowe War Flight on anti-Zeppelin patrols dispensed with the Vickers gun altogether and substituted a second Lewis gun on the top wing to double the weight of explosive and incendiary fire, a modification which might have been fitted to more aircraft if the war had continued into 1919. The second Vickers gun mounted to starboard of the first in the F.1 was deleted in this version. The Lewis gun was fitted on a Bowen and Williams, Admiralty Pattern top-plane mounting which enabled the pilot to engage a lever in the cockpit which would swing the gun from horizontal to the vertical. This allowed the pilot to fire upwards into an airship that he was unable to climb above or to replace the tray of ammunition with a full one after the first had fired out without having to un-strap and stand up to reach the weapon. It also allowed him to re-cock the weapon in the event of a jam or misfire. As in all fighters of this generation it was important to count the number of rounds fired as accurately as possible in order to have an idea of how much ammunition remained for a fresh attack. 2F.1s could, optionally, be fitted with racks under the lower wings, each of which could carry a 50lb bomb which made the Camel into an effective strike fighter.

One interesting aspect of 2F.1 development was the decision taken in early 1918 to evaluate the carriage of fighters under rigid airships so that they could be released to defend them against attack by enemy fighters. The first experiments were carried out with *R 23* from the naval air station at Pulham.[3] A special horizontal surface was attached to the keel of *R 23* and the upper wing of a 2F.1 was secured tightly against it. A quick-release hook was passed through the cut-out in the central section of the Camel's upper wing, to be actuated by the pilot when he had climbed down into the cockpit, strapped in and was happy. Two 2F.1s, N6622 and N6814, were modified with components made at Great Yarmouth and the first was dropped in June 1918 with the controls locked and a dummy pilot. This was obviously deemed to have been successful[4] and a live drop was carried out by Lieutenant R E Keys DFC RAF. He was able to start the Camel's engine by diving to get the propeller turning and switching on the ignition. After that he flew round the airship and then returned safely to Pulham. The Armistice ended the requirement for airship flights and development ceased although the US Navy continued to show practical interest in the concept.

At least 230 2F.1 Camels were delivered before the Armistice and in addition to Sopwith, batches were made by Clayton and Shuttleworth, Hooper & Co and Beardmore. The latter used Arrol-Johnston as a sub-contractor. Aircraft intended for operation from *Argus* were fitted with hooks under the undercarriage axle to engage the retaining wires on deck and a propeller guard was fitted to prevent it hitting the wires and shattering as the aircraft reached the forward ramp. The 2F.1 had a wingspan of 26ft 11in, a height of 9ft 1in and a length of 18ft 8in. The maximum permissible take-off weight was 1530lbs and it had two fuel tanks; a main pressure tank with 30 gallons and a gravity tank with 7 gallons giving a total of 37 gallons. The oil tank had a capacity of 6.5 gallons. The 2F.1 could climb to 15,000ft in 25 minutes and the top speed at 10,000ft was 122mph. Endurance was approximately three hours.

The Tondern Strike

2F.1 Camels attacked the German naval airship sheds at Tondern in July 1918, the first strike operation in history to have been carried out by aircraft that took off from the deck of a carrier.[5] *Campania* had been used for sweeps into the eastern North Sea during the summer of 1917 in the hope that her Sopwith Baby seaplane fighters could intercept Zeppelins that were searching for British convoys to and from Norway. Both her commanding officer, Captain Swann, and her senior aviation officer, Wing Commander Bell-Davies, considered this a poor use of resources and recommended a strike against the bases known to be at Tondern and Ahlhorn as the best option but the Grand Fleet command had been so disappointed by the earlier failures of attempts to use seaplanes in this way that Admiral Brock, the Chief of Staff, refused to consider anything but a sweep looking for patrolling Zeppelins. Bell-Davies was well aware that the Baby was unsuited to this sort of work and even if a Zeppelin was sighted from the fleet it would only have to ditch ballast and climb in order to evade the slow-climbing seaplane fighter. By 1917 it had also to be conceded that the lumbering Short 184 seaplane was of little use for attacking targets inland even if it could get airborne in the prevailing sea conditions off the enemy coast. In the event no Zeppelins were seen during this sweep.

Bell-Davies discussed the need for better aircraft when Wing Commander Longmore, who was serving in the Admiralty Air Department, visited *Campania* shortly after the abortive sweep. Bell-Davies had experience of the 1½ Strutter while he was serving with 3 Wing in France and believed that it would make a much better strike aircraft than the Short; the only problem was that its wings did not fold and it would thus be difficult to stow in a ship. However, knowing the aircraft as he did, he believed that it would be perfectly straightforward to make the wings detachable and asked for an aircraft to be made available to test his theory.[6] A two-seater fighter variant was promptly sent to the naval air station at Smoogroo on the north shore of Scapa Flow near *Campania*'s anchorage. Bell-Davies took a team of mechanics ashore who made some small modifications and then devised a drill that would allow the aircraft to have its wings removed and re-fitted as quickly as possible on board. He took the modified aircraft up for a trial and as far as he could see the modification made no difference to the machine's handling qualities and performance. With practice, the mechanics proved able to take the wings off in a little over a minute and rig them back in place ready for flight in 45 seconds; an astonishing achievement which leaves a modern pilot wondering what safety checks were carried out before the aircraft was deemed to be ready for flight. By the end of 1917 when Bell-Davies was re-appointed from *Campania* to *Furious,* she could operate wheeled 2F.1s and Strutters from her deck. Work to modify a further batch of Strutters for carrier use was carried out at Turnhouse. Unfortunately, both were still one-shot systems in this ship since they could not land back on board after a sortie. That would have to wait until *Argus* was completed in 1918. The modified Strutter had played its part, however, and it was now accepted in the Admiralty and the Grand Fleet that wheeled aircraft operating from a flight deck represented the way ahead and that seaplanes lowered onto the water had represented a blind alley.

By the summer of 1918 Bell-Davies' air group offered considerably greater potential than the earlier seaplanes. The exact number of each aircraft type to be embarked depended on the type of mission in prospect. Given the potential of the new aircraft, he was disappointed to learn that the Grand Fleet staff were planning another sweep just like the early ones carried out by *Campania* with her seaplanes. There was a difference this time, however, in that air operations were now co-ordinated by RAA Admiral Phillimore and Clark-Hall his air staff officer who was now a Lieutenant Colonel RAF. With Captain Nicholson's full support Bell-Davies urged that a strike against the Zeppelin bases would be far more likely to achieve decisive results than a sweep looking for airships that might or might not happen

Rear Admiral Phillimore, RAA Grand Fleet, on the flight deck of HMS *Furious* during flying trials. Characteristically, he has his chin-stay down so that his hat will not be blown off by the wind and his enthusiasm to learn all about what is going on is evident. From left to right the people in this photograph are Flight Lieutenant Jackson RNAS, Captain Wilmot Nicholson RN, captain of *Furious,* Captain Clark Hall RN, chief-of-staff to RAA, Rear Admiral Phillimore and Squadron Commander H Busteed RNAS. (Author's collection)

to be airborne.[7] Clark-Hall agreed but when the two of them discussed the practical implications of planning such a strike they decided that before RAA could put the plan before Beatty they must have a plan that could be implemented quickly. *Furious* would have to carry a full complement of fighters to defend the fleet against air attack and, although the 'Ship' Strutters had been modified with this very purpose in mind, they were now regarded primarily as reconnaissance and spotter aircraft with an important role to play in a fleet action. In any case, they were only available in small numbers and their use for a strike operation might not therefore be acceptable to the C-in-C. Asking for more Strutters to be modified would lead to delay and so the two officers decided that they would have to use the assets they had, the 2F.1 Camels. These could be modified with bomb racks but their range was not great; they could not reach Ahlhorn but Tondern was only within their radius of action if they took off from a position near the Danish coast. They did have the distinct advantage, however, that if they were spotted and intercepted by enemy aircraft some at least would be able to fight their way to the target and attack it. Having decided on the basic outline of a plan, Clark-Hall briefed Admiral Phillimore, stressing the offensive nature of the proposal. Phillimore went straight to Beatty's flagship *Queen Elizabeth* and briefed the C-in-C. He came back with the good news that the sweep was cancelled and that the attack on Tondern was to be carried out as soon as possible.

Bell-Davies gave instructions that seven of *Furious'* Camels were to be fitted with bomb racks capable of carrying 20lb bombs and selected some of his more experienced pilots to begin training ashore at Turnhouse for the attack. The strike required precise navigation and flying to and from the target was to be carried out at low level. Fuel was only just sufficient and since the aircraft could not be recovered because of the turbulence over *Furious'* after flight deck, the mission would end with a ditching in the cold North Sea even if the pilots were able to locate the task force. Training to use the Camel as a glide-bomber had to be completed in the shortest possible time but the six most experienced pilots soon became proficient. Youlet, the last to join and least experienced, needed longer to reach the standard required and so, since there could be no delay, Bell-Davies had the unpleasant task of telling him that he would not form part of the strike team. The seventh Camel would be used as a spare to replace any one of the other six that failed to start. Early in July 1918 *Furious* sailed from the Firth of Forth with an escort of destroyers and made for the briefed position off the Danish coast. After midnight the weather began to deteriorate, coming on to rain and blow hard. By the planned take-off time just before dawn it was worse and the operation had to be aborted. The task force returned to the Firth of Forth and the aircraft disembarked to Turnhouse to resume the pilots' intensive training for the operation. This gave Youlet some more time to practice and after he demonstrated that he had reached the required standard, Bell-Davies decided to allow him to fly on the strike.

On 18 July 1918 *Furious* sailed with her destroyer escort for a second attempt, the mission being designated as Operation 'F7' by the Grand Fleet staff. Again the weather deteriorated during the middle watch and Bell-Davies began to worry that the operation might have to be abandoned again. He went up to the bridge and spoke to RAA. His words quoted in his autobiographical *Sailor in the Air*[8] show just what a ridiculous position the politicians had put naval aviators into. He was

Looking forward from the bridge of HMS *Furious* in July 1918 over the seven Sopwith 2F.1 Camels ranged ready for the Tondern strike. The aircraft are protected from the wind by the raised Yorkshire breaks which have been painted to blend with the ship's disruptive pattern paint scheme. It can be seen that the take-off deck has been widened since Dunning's landing nearly a year earlier. Note how the aircrafts' national markings have been toned down with grey paint to make them less conspicuous. (Author's collection)

now a lieutenant colonel in charge of an RAF contingent although his RNAS background made him feel part of the ship. Sensing his unease about whether to go ahead despite the adverse weather or abort for a second time, Admiral Phillimore said 'It's for you to decide and I shan't influence you but I expect you know what I hope'. Bell-Davies replied that the decision would be taken at 04.00

and went down to the ship's intelligence office. The strong westerly wind persisted and it seemed doubtful if the Camels would be able to get back to the task force after their strike. However, it had not got any worse and the Camel pilots would certainly have enough fuel to make the Danish border where they could land and give themselves up to the neutral authorities. At 04.00, therefore, he informed RAA that the mission could go ahead as planned. The ship turned into wind and the Camels took off in two flights into the early twilight. Those on board *Furious* watched them fly away and then settled down anxiously to await their return.

At last, after two hours three of the Camels were seen returning and they ditched neatly in rapid succession near the destroyers. Their pilots, Dickson, Smart and Jackson, reported complete success. *Furious* waited off the coast until Bell-Davies was quite sure that the remaining aircraft must have come down somewhere at the end of their endurance, everyone hoping that the 'somewhere' was in neutral Denmark. When nothing more was seen of them, the task force turned west and headed back to its anchorage in the Firth of Forth. They learnt that two Zeppelins, *L 54* and *L 60*, had been destroyed and that both large sheds had been burnt out and the gas plant damaged. Although they did not yet know it, Tondern was to play no further part in the war. News of three more pilots was received but to Bell-Davies' great regret there was no news of Youlet. The Germans made no claim to have shot down any of the attacking aircraft and the other members of his flight lost sight of him shortly after take-off. He must, therefore, have suffered an engine failure over the sea and ditched out of sight of either land or the task force and was never seen or heard of again.

One of the pilots who came down inside Denmark was Williams. Realising that he was nearly out of fuel he elected not to try and locate *Furious* but landed near a Danish village on the coast. The villagers gathered round and he asked them where he could obtain petrol. They appeared willing to help but before they could do so the village policeman arrived. He explained that it was against his orders to allow a British aircraft to be refuelled in Denmark and asked Williams to accompany him to the police station. Once there they were joined by an official in plain clothes who said that he would have to take Williams to Copenhagen. They arrived at a hotel in the city where, on entering, the official hung up his raincoat and bowler hat on a peg in the hall. He then conducted Williams to a room in which the other two pilots who had also landed in Denmark had already been installed. Soon afterwards the official left the room and they began to discuss their chances of escape. Believing that his best chance was right there and then, Williams walked out of the room and back to the hall. He put on the official's hat and coat and went out into the street where he asked the first well-dressed passer-by for directions to the British Embassy. He was answered in fluent English and made his way there promptly. The embassy staff immediately put him in a car and drove to the docks where a Norwegian ship was about to sail for Aberdeen. Williams' passage was booked, he went on board and the ship sailed. On arriving in Aberdeen he found that he was just in time to catch the Edinburgh Express. This was not scheduled to stop at Turnhouse but it slowed to a walking pace as it passed through the station and he jumped out, made his way to the naval pier and found one of *Furious'* boats alongside. Minutes later he was back on board, only 48 hours after the ship itself had returned from the operation.

The Tondern strike did more than eliminate two Zeppelins and damage their base. It finally overcame the belief, fostered by the unsuccessful attempts made by seaplanes and their carriers, that strikes on land targets by aircraft operating from ships at sea were not a good idea. The immediate result was that the C-in-C wanted Ahlhorn to be attacked but it was too distant for any of *Furious'* aircraft and *Argus* was not yet ready. There was, of course, no longer an Air Department at the Admiralty but Groves, now a brigadier RAF, had an office where he acted as liaison officer. He visited *Furious* and discussed the possibility of using a force of embarked de Havilland DH 4s for such an attack. Some could, he said, be sent to Turnhouse and modified for the task with extra fuel tanks and removable wings. His concept was that the aircraft could be launched off the Danish coast like the Camels, attack Ahlhorn and then fly on to cross the Western Front and land behind the Allied lines in France. Groves managed to organise the despatch of several DH 4s to Turnhouse but the war ended before they were ready.

The Sopwith T.1 Cuckoo
Commodore Sueter's enthusiasm for a torpedo attack by aircraft on the High Sea Fleet in its harbours led him to invite Thomas Sopwith to the Admiralty to discuss the idea.[9] This was a logical step because Sopwith Aviation had the status of being an Admiralty contractor and had produced some outstanding aircraft designs. The result of the discussion was a memorandum from Sueter dated 9 October 1916 tasking Sopwith to investigate the possibility of manufacturing torpedo-carrying aircraft capable of carrying one or, unrealistically, two 1000lb torpedoes with fuel for an endurance of four hours. As if that were not a big enough specification, the memorandum also called for the probable use of a catapult to launch the aircraft despite the fact that, at the time, no British catapult existed or was even being developed. Sueter probably had in mind that the aircraft would take off from the foredeck platforms of *Campania* and other seaplane carriers and then either ditch on return to the fleet or land in neutral Holland or Denmark if they failed to find it. He does not seem to have envisaged the aircraft landing back on their parent carriers. It is also worth noting that although he seems to have had the initial bright

idea, he had little grasp of the practical engineering development and time-scale needed to achieve it; the prospect of a single-engined aircraft carrying two torpedoes in 1917 was a fantasy. Sopwith thought that the requirement would not be easy to meet but his team produced a draught design for a single-engined, single-seat biplane capable of carrying a single 1000lb torpedo with an endurance of four hours. It was designated the Sopwith T.1 and work on the construction of a prototype, N74, began at once but after Sueter's departure from the Admiralty interest faded temporarily and the incomplete prototype was apparently slung from the beams of one of the erection shops as production concentrated on fighters.

However, in February 1917 Wing Commander Longmore RNAS, recently appointed to the technical staff of the new Air Board based at the Hotel Cecil in the Strand, saw the aircraft on his first visit to the factory and, on finding out its purpose, gave instructions that it was to be finished as quickly as possible. N74 was eventually flown and passed by the Sopwith Experimental Department on 6 June 1917. The T.1 emerged as a three-bay, equal-span biplane powered by a 200hp Hispano-Suiza engine with wings that folded backwards to facilitate stowage in a carrier and increase the number of aircraft that could be embarked. The fold was at the innermost interplane struts which were fitted at the outer extremities of the

A Sopwith T.1 with its torpedo loaded. Part of the fuselage fabric covering, the engine cowlings and the exhaust pipe have been removed to show the internal arrangements. (Author's collection)

centre-section structure. The vee undercarriage struts were also in line with the inner interplane struts and there was no axle between them so that the torpedo could be suspended beneath the fuselage. Construction was conventional with a wooden structure cross-braced internally by steel wire and covered in fabric except for the top decking around the cockpit which was covered by plywood. Official trials of the prototype were carried out at the Isle of Grain in July and the official performance report was signed on 20 July 1917. The Admiralty wanted the type put into production as quickly as possible but Sopwith lacked the capacity to add T.1s to its large orders for fighters. A contract for 100 machines was therefore placed with the Fairfield Shipbuilding and Engineering Company of Govan in Glasgow. Additional orders for T.1s were placed in late 1917 and early 1918 with both Fairfield and Pegler and Company in Doncaster. These brought the total on order to 300 following pressure from Admiral Beatty to provide the resources for an air attack on the enemy fleet. The type was given the name Cuckoo after the Armistice; the apocryphal story behind this choice is sometimes held to be the fact that these aircraft had been intended to attack the enemy in his bases, in other words 'putting an egg in his nest'. An alternative, and more believable, theory is that the T.1 was a Sopwith design built by others as eggs in their nests. The latter seems more plausible but neither may have any foundation in fact and it is certainly the case that aircraft of the period were given some odd names by later standards.[10]

A number of factors combined to slow production and they illustrate the sometimes large gap between a theory and its realistic application. Among these was the decision by the Air Board that priority for Hispano-Suiza engines should be given to SE 5a fighter production for the RFC and the consequent need to redesign the T.1 to take the Sunbeam Arab engine. The Arab suffered a number of developmental problems which delayed its certification for service use and even when it was accepted it suffered a number of failures. Worse, neither Fairfield nor Pegler were experienced in aircraft construction and the change of engine required a considerable number of modifications and the production of large numbers of new drawings, some of which caused problems when they were found to have been incorrectly copied. It became obvious that deliveries from these sources could not be expected for some considerable time and so fifty machines were ordered with high a priority from the Blackburn Aeroplane and Motor Company which was sufficiently experienced to implement the changes quickly. This order was placed in February 1918 and the first production machine from this batch delivered in May. By the time of the Armistice a total of ninety T.1s from all sources had been delivered. Fairfield handed over its first aircraft in September and Pegler its first in October. The first Blackburn-built Cuckoo was sent for evaluation tests at the Isle of Grain and the second, after certification, was sent to Number 201 Torpedo

Blackburn-built Sopwith T.1 N6954 dropping a practice torpedo in the Firth of Forth. This aircraft was delivered in June 1918 and issued to 201 Training Squadron at East Fortune. It only had a short life and was deleted in October 1918. (Author's collection)

Training Squadron at East Fortune on 3 July 1918 for torpedo-dropping tests in the Firth of Forth. As further aircraft where delivered to East Fortune the training of torpedo-attack pilots began.

The first operational squadron equipped with T.1 Cuckoos was designated as 185 Squadron RAF; it formed on 7 October 1918 at East Fortune and embarked in *Argus* shortly afterwards to work up to operational efficiency. They were ready and waiting for suitable weather when the Armistice ended hostilities on 11 November. The Cuckoo was popular with pilots and was regarded as being both strong and agile, good attributes for an aircraft that was intended to attack targets at low level. The type remained in service after the war and was eventually fitted with stub axles inboard and outboard of the wheel hubs on which there were hooks that could engage the retaining wires. They left sufficient space under the fuselage for the torpedo to be loaded and dropped but were not always fitted since, with a maximum take-off weight of 3883lbs, the T.1 was heavy enough not to be affected

A practice torpedo loaded under a Sopwith T.1 on *Argus'* flight deck showing the ducted exhaust pipes running along the weapon to warm it in flight. The warhead was designed to float above the surface when the weapon finished its run and was brightly painted with a ring fitted to help the torpedo-recovery vessel hook it and hoist it inboard when it was located. (Author's collection)

by the gusty conditions on deck that affected lightweight fighters. It had a wingspan of 46ft 9in, a length of 28ft 6in and a height of 10ft 8in. The Sunbeam Arab developed 200hp like the Hispano-Suiza that it replaced and tankage for 50 gallons of fuel gave an endurance of four hours. Maximum speed was 103mph at 2000ft and the aircraft could climb to 10,000ft with a torpedo in 31 minutes. Of interest the British Naval Aviation Mission to Japan in 1921 took with it six Wolseley Viper-engined Cuckoo Mark IIs to teach the Imperial Japanese Navy how to carry out airborne torpedo attacks on ships. They also revealed the plan for the attack on the High Sea Fleet and it is from these origins that the Japanese operational doctrine that led to the attack on Pearl Harbour in 1941 can be said to have originated.

The Planned Attack on the High Sea Fleet in its Harbours
The concept of an airborne torpedo attack on an enemy fleet in harbour can be traced back to at least 1911 when officers connected with the project to build the

RN's first rigid airship at Barrow-in-Furness had discussed the possibility at great length but at the time there was no engine powerful enough to allow a fixed-wing aeroplane to carry a half-ton torpedo over a meaningful distance and the idea could not be taken forward.[11] In 1912 Lieutenant Hyde-Thomson RN, who was a torpedo specialist rather than an aviator at the time, wrote a service paper on the subject in which he outlined the potential importance of airborne torpedoes.[12] He was subsequently appointed to the Torpedo School, HMS *Vernon*, at Portsmouth to develop his theory and progress was made with a prototype 14in torpedo weighing 900lbs dropped by Squadron Commander Longmore from a Short 160 Gnome-powered seaplane based at the naval air station at Calshot in the Solent on 28 July 1914.[13] Churchill took a keen interest in the development and asked for work to be carried out as quickly as possible; the prototype made use of work carried out to develop small torpedoes for use by capital ships' picket boats against enemy vessels in harbour. Despite the success of the demonstration, the aircraft was at the extreme limit of its performance envelope simply getting airborne with the torpedo and could not yet be considered a viable weapon system. The next step came in 1915 when the seaplane carrier *Ben-my-Chree* took three early-production tor-pedoes to the Dardanelles and they were used with some success by seaplanes against Turkish shipping. While these attacks had shown encouraging potential, they were not yet of a high enough standard to be considered a viable strike method against warships moored in a defended harbour.

By 1917 a more advanced 18in torpedo weighing 1000lbs had been developed for use by aircraft and a growing number of officers saw it as the weapon most likely to be effective against the German High Sea Fleet which remained, for most of the time, in its harbours behind minefields and coast defences. Admiral Beatty adopted the concept enthusiastically when he was made aware of it and wrote to the Admiralty on 11 September 1917 that such an attack method still had many difficulties to overcome but he believed strongly that they were not insuperable and the results would be worth the effort. The Imperial Japanese Navy was to prove him absolutely right 24 years later at Pearl Harbor.

There were many reasons why such an attack appealed to the Grand Fleet staff at this time but the most immediate was the need to prevent U-boats sailing from their bases into the open sea for their unrestricted campaign against Allied merchant shipping. Mines, blockships and constant patrols by cruisers and light forces could achieve this on a temporary basis but they would only be fully effective if the enemy was unable to counter or remove them. As long as the enemy retained an intact fleet in being in the German Bight that was likely to be superior to anything the British could permanently maintain in these waters, the enemy could sweep the mines and U-boat movements could not be limited. It was therefore the opinion of Beatty and his staff that if the High Sea Fleet would not come out and fight in the open North Sea, it must be neutralised in its harbours and tactical aircraft operating from specialised aircraft carriers and armed with torpedoes were recognised as the best way of achieving this aim.

The scale of attack projected in 1917
As the detailed arrangements for such an attack evolved, the staff at first favoured a single knock-out blow and decided that it must be carried out by as many aircraft as possible, not less than 121, to be launched from 'specially fitted carrier ships' about an hours' flying time from the target. The launch position was to be reached at or before dawn and the strike aircraft were to be flown off each of the eight projected carriers in flights of five, making a total of forty in each attacking wave. A soon as the first flights were clear, second and third flights would be ranged and launched, each again totalling forty aircraft, to maintain the weight of attack on the enemy fleet. That explains a total of 120 aircraft but the extra one is interesting. The staff saw this as being a flight co-ordinator who was to fly a brightly-coloured aircraft that would be obvious to all the others. He would not be armed with a torpedo but would carry extra fuel to remain over the target while the three waves carried out their attacks. The size of the individual five aircraft flights were also carefully worked out. Five was a good number to handle into position and launch quickly from a deck; there was at the time no experience of launching larger numbers in sequence. Furthermore, engines tended to overheat if kept running on deck and so they were started just before take-off; again five seemed to be a practical number to start and get airborne in a single batch. It was also deemed to be the minimum number of torpedo aircraft necessary to cripple a single capital ship at anchor with multiple hits, bearing in mind that the 170lb warhead of a single weapon would be unlikely to cause fatal damage unless it hit at a particularly vulnerable spot.

The pilots were to be briefed to attack individual battlecruisers and battleships first, giving the highest priority to the newer vessels. Once these were all seen to be well hit and sinking, later flights could be instructed by the strike co-ordinator to attack dock caissons and floating docks, light cruisers, torpedo boats and submarines in that order of priority.[14] Two interesting features emerge from this plan; first the carefully-described role of the strike co-ordinator was the first mention of such a role to my knowledge. The British Pacific Fleet subsequently appointed just such an officer in 1944 for its set-piece attacks on Japanese targets, Major R C Hay DSO DSC* RM, who excelled in the role. The second point of note is the high priority given to dockyard installations rather than smaller warships. It is at least arguable that if the Japanese had targeted dockyard facilities and fuel storage facilities rather than 'Battleship Row' at Pearl Harbor they would have more effectively neutralised the US Pacific Fleet. The staff hoped that like the 1½ Strutter, the T.1 could be fitted with a fixed Vickers machine gun mounted forward of the cockpit, firing through the propeller arc with a synchronising mechanism. This would have added considerably more weight to the aircraft but once they had dropped their torpedoes it would have allowed the first wave to defend the subsequent waves against interference by enemy fighters and to strafe and suppress anti-aircraft fire from ships and shore batteries. The staff also hoped that their fire could hamper repair parties and tugs as they attempted to salvage stricken ships. When the strike co-ordinator decided that the operation had been satisfactorily completed he would drop smoke and flares to order aircraft to proceed to a rendezvous with the carriers off the Dutch coast. The waters off Vlieland to the west of Terschelling were suggested as being suitable, being further west and thus nearer the UK than the launch position but sufficiently close to it for the task force to get into position while the strike aircraft were airborne.

In addition to the carrier-borne torpedo aircraft, the 1917 plan also called for H-12 flying boats from Felixstowe to take part in the operation using 230lb bombs against floating docks, dockyard engine houses, magazines and submarines in the basin where they were known to be moored alongside each other, thus presenting a larger target that would be easier to hit. The flying boats were to attack at the same time as the T.1s, helping to saturate the defences, and it was decided to give them navigational assistance to the target area to ensure an accurate landfall; this was to be provided by destroyers spaced out across the North Sea shining lights upwards. The flying boats would have insufficient fuel to return to Felixstowe from the target area and so they were to be briefed to alight alongside destroyers off the Dutch coast and refuel from them. Any that were damaged would have their crews taken off before being sunk; those that were unable to reach the rendezvous were to make for Dutch waters and give themselves up to the neutral authorities.

With accurate foresight the Grand Fleet planning staff believed that merchant ship hulls could easily be modified to operate T.1s by erecting flight decks onto them above the existing superstructure. It was calculated that such ships could embark seventeen T.1s and two 2F.1 Camels and so eight ships would be needed to carry the full strike force. The fighters were intended to destroy any Zeppelin scouts or seaplanes that might attempt to locate the task force and attack it. In his letters to the Admiralty Beatty stressed the need to carry out the attack as soon as the aircraft, the carriers and their crews were ready. He also noted that such an operation would be dependent on weather and might be delayed by a succession of gales. He felt, therefore, that the forces needed to carry out the strike should be increased by at least 25 per cent to allow the larger scale of attack to balance, as far

An image from the 1918 edition of the torpedo pilot training manual showing how the attack on the High Sea Fleet was to be executed using smoke to confuse the enemy anti-aircraft defences. (Author's collection)

as possible, the chance that over an extended timescale the enemy might learn that it was being prepared. This is an interesting point and it might explain why the Admiralty made no comment about such an attack in its arguments with Smuts and his advisors.

Each aircraft carrier was to be capable of flying off its five-aircraft flights in quick succession to form up into attacking waves of forty, with the first led by the strike co-ordinator. Had the attack gone ahead in the numbers projected this is an area that would have required considerable practice since the pre-dawn form-up of large numbers of aircraft from multiple carriers was a technique that had still not been perfected in the British Pacific Fleet in January 1945. On the other hand, opposition would not have been as intense and provided the individual flights stayed close, the overall formation could have been loose provided they could all see the co-ordinator and his flare signals. The two subsequent waves of forty would have had their launching sequences controlled by visual signals from the flagship and would have had the benefit of greater light as the sun rose higher. A key element of their attacks would have been the need to pick out the strike co-ordinator as he orbited over the target area. This is why his aircraft was to be brightly coloured and the same need would have applied to the flying boats as they arrived in the crowded battle-space. The need for the whole force to complete the strike in the shortest possible time meant that the converted carriers had to be capable of ranging all seventeen aircraft on deck so that the flights could be started and flown off with the minimum delay, any non-starters being pushed to one side or even ditched to clear the deck. A deck big enough to meet this requirement meant that there was no need for hangars under the deck or lifts to range aircraft from them. Aircraft would be loaded onto the deck just before the mission sailed. The conversion could therefore be quite simple with wood being used extensively for decking. Ships taken up for conversion were to be the fastest available and in addition to their arrangements for operating aircraft, Beatty wanted them fitted with side blisters and paravanes for protection against U-boats' torpedoes and mines. The Grand Fleet staff suggested that armed merchant cruisers attached to the Northern Patrol's 10th Cruiser Squadron would be suitable for this purpose and asked for them to be made available. Timing was a critical factor and the Admiralty was urged to identify which ships could be used as quickly as possible. The longer it took to convert the chosen ships the more likely, it was felt, that the enemy would learn about their intended purpose and so the Grand Fleet staff displayed considerable imagination in proposing methods that would conceal the ships' true purpose. Their intended role as aircraft carriers could hardly be disguised but their destination could be obscured by installing fittings such as fans, ventilation and awnings which would suggest employment in the Persian Gulf, Egyptian waters or the Red Sea. No deceptive measure was felt too trivial to be put forward and the detailed plans produced for this enterprise even suggested delaying and censoring the ships' company mail to make it appear that it was being despatched to and from the Middle East. The presence of a squadron of seaplane carriers in the Eastern Mediterranean at this time lent credence to this scheme.

It was anticipated that a large number of aircraft might be lost during the attack and Beatty stressed the need for continued large-scale production of the T.1. Even if the first attack achieved only limited success, it was felt that 'there would still be much work for aircraft of this type in attacking enemy merchant shipping in the Elbe, at Emden and Bremerhaven. No limit should, therefore, be put on [T.1] construction but a minimum of 60% spare should be immediately aimed at.' This represented an ideal but, as mentioned above, production figures for both aircraft and engines were far below those anticipated and the higher numbers were unlikely to be achieved. The focus of Smuts and Weir on independent long-range bomber operations with their potentially huge requirement for both airframes and engines made Beatty's plan for T.1s to be built in large numbers exceedingly difficult, if not impossible, to achieve and it is difficult to comprehend why he did not see this.

The weapon that would equip the T.1 was a specially-designed lightweight torpedo. Like other torpedoes designed for the RN it had a diameter of 18in and

Torpedoes were complicated weapons that needed to be kept warm before and during flight so that their engines would start instantly when they were released. This photograph shows a torpedo loaded onto a Sopwith T.1 on the flight deck of HMS *Argus* in November 1918 with a steam-heating trough placed under the weapon to warm it through. Also visible above the rough are the extensions to the aircraft's engine exhausts which ran along the sides of the torpedo to keep it warm in flight. (Author's collection)

was the product of a design team which had accumulated a great deal of war experience. The warhead contained 170lb of a specialised torpedo explosive known as Torpex which was detonated by a contact pistol on hitting the target. This was about half the size of the warhead fitted in torpedoes used by submarines and destroyers, hence the stated need for five-aircraft flights to attack each individual capital ship to achieve multiple hits. It was envisaged that the torpedoes would impact below the waterline, under the armoured belt where they would open up the hull to cause extensive flooding and damage. Had the projected attack achieved surprise, as the attacks that evolved from it at Taranto and Pearl Harbor did, the enemy ships would probably not have been prepared for action, many watertight doors might well have been open and little of their machinery would have been running, thus reducing the number of pumps immediately available to limit the ingress of water and allow counter-flooding to keep ships level.

In addition to specifying the ships, aircraft and weapons required to execute it, the 1917 plan contained specific details of how the task force was to execute the projected strike operation. The carrier task force was to work up to operational efficiency based in Scapa Flow; as soon as it was considered ready it was to proceed to its point of departure. The Wash was suggested for this purpose as it offered a considerable expanse of water which was out of immediate contact with large centres of population or shipping. Flying practice could be carried out at nearby airfields ashore until the order to prepare was signalled when the forecast conditions were just right; the aircraft could then be taken out to the ships by lighter, in the way that they were taken to Grand Fleet ships, to avoid the risk of accidental losses. The similarity between the Wash and the Imperial Japanese Navy's choice of Hittokapu Wan, Eroforu, in 1941 prior to the attack on Pearl Harbor is interesting as both met the same purpose. The chosen launch position was to be off the island of Ameland which was close enough to the Wash to enable the carrier task force to make the passage from the Wash in the hours of darkness at a speed of only 12 knots during the autumn months. A force of cruisers and destroyers was to provide close escort for the carriers and German light forces from

An illustration from the 1918 manual showing how pilots were to use the speed indicators on the torpedo attack sight to estimate the correct amount of aim-off to hit a moving target. The Fairey Swordfish used the same kind of sight and technique two decades later and well into the Second World War. (Author's collection)

Emden were to be blocked in by mines laid in the hours of darkness preceding the attack. A second group of light cruisers was to prevent these mines being swept and intercept any enemy forces that managed to get past them into the open sea. These cruisers carried their own aircraft which were to be used to give warning of any enemy movements in the Ems River. The whole Grand Fleet was to be at sea to provide distant cover. It will thus be seen that this was not just an air operation but an early example of a new form of three-dimensional naval warfare in which elements on, above and below the surface all had mutually dependant parts to play.

The actual disposition of the enemy ships in harbour was, if at all possible, to be made known to the strike co-ordinator but direct air reconnaissance was not to be used to achieve it because constant over-flights might heighten German suspicions that such an attack was imminent. Tactically it was stressed that flights were to make every effort to make their attacks as decisive as possible and that if they did so, twenty-four of the enemy's capital ships would be neutralised. One point that the plan failed to take into account, however, was that ships would be sunk in shallow water, thus allowing salvage teams to recover and ultimately repair them as proved to be the case at Taranto and Pearl Harbor. Damage on the scale projected in 1917 would, however, have been beyond the capacity of the German salvage organisation to cope with fully, another advantage of an attack on a large scale. The staff made detailed examinations of tidal conditions together with the number and position of ships' anti-aircraft guns when making their plans. Thus, if the guns were mounted aft, a low-flying attack from seaward on a flood tide would provide advantages for the attackers as the targets would initially present their bows to the strike aircraft. A low tide would assist attacks on dock gates and allow them to be destroyed more effectively. We now know that a front gun would have added too much weight to the T.1 and, in fact, none was ever fitted to one and so plans for their use would not have been practical. Once the first wave departed, the strike co-ordinator was to remain over the target area and give directions to the succeeding two waves of aircraft, his increased fuel tankage allowing him to do so. Apart from the distinctive colour of his aircraft which would enable pilots to see and follow him, he was to use a pre-arranged code of signals to communicate his intentions to the second and third waves as they arrived in the target area. He was also to be in tactical command of the flying boats and their pilots needed to be fully conversant with his signals which might be by hand motions or coloured flares from a Verey pistol.

Admiralty reaction to the 1917 Plan
Admiral Beatty's plan was forwarded to the Admiralty in September 1917. The response from Jellicoe, 1SL, came a fortnight later and was, in outline, both positive

and warm to the idea. It must be remembered, however, that he was under intense personal strain at this time and his delay in introducing convoys as a defence against U-boat attack had caused Lloyd George and other politicians to call for his dismissal. He pointed out to Beatty that the number of aircraft that could be operated by the Grand Fleet was steadily increasing with the arrival of *Furious* being particularly noteworthy. Dunning had landed on her only six weeks earlier and he told Beatty that a landing deck aft was to be fitted to *Furious* as quickly as possible. Given this most significant step forward the Admiralty agreed to complete *Argus* as a flush-deck aircraft carrier to operate T.1s and expected her to be available in mid-1918. She would be able to carry twice the number of T.1s projected for a single merchant ship conversion and with *Furious, Vindictive* and, perhaps, *Campania* a considerable strike force could be embarked by the autumn of 1918 although not all the aircraft could be landed on after the attack. Furthermore, orders for a number of T.1s had been placed and 200 torpedoes were on order.

This was all positive but Jellicoe felt unable to offer Beatty the merchant-ship carrier conversions that he had asked for. Other hulls were earmarked for construction as carriers with high priority but the attack could not be made on the scale the Grand Fleet has wanted. The core of the Admiralty's argument not to convert eight merchant ships into carriers was that these ships could not be spared from their existing duties. Those already converted into armed merchant cruisers were needed for defensive patrol work and others were needed to carry vital war material to Britain. A similar argument was to be used two decades later to oppose the construction of escort carriers in the early years of the Second World War. Beatty countered these objections in a letter dated 7 October 1917 in which he put forward arguments that were both cogent and well-considered; they still have resonance today. In it he stated that:

I have given much consideration to the question of air attacks from the sea, on a large scale, against enemy naval bases. Besides being one of the few ways in which offensive action against the German Fleet is possible, it is one of the few ways in which our command of the sea can be turned to active account against the enemy. It is fully realised that the requirements in aircraft carriers can only be at the expense of other important services, but it is urged that the claims of the offensive should take precedence. Successful operations of the nature indicated would almost certainly curtail enemy activity against trade, and so reduce the calls for protection. Every effort should be made to have the ships ready for service by April 1918. A sustained air offensive on the scale proposed would impose upon the enemy the necessity for active measures of defence.

Attempts to attack the carriers and their covering forces might well lead to actions of increasing magnitude involving their heavy ships, thus affording opportunities that have, hitherto, been denied to us.

The Admiralty's reply stated that

. . . with reference to your remarks on the general question of an offensive by air from the sea, it is accepted by Their Lordships that, under existing circumstances, the air presents the greatest facilities for conducting an offensive against the enemy's vessels and bases and the possibilities of developing such an offensive in the future are being fully considered. My Lords are fully alive to the importance of air attacks against the enemy's North Sea bases and are determined that the possibilities of such attacks from seaward shall be given full consideration and be correlated into the general scheme of operations.

The projected 1918 attack

An attack on the scale proposed by the Grand Fleet in 1917 was, therefore, not to be. Fewer than 121 Sopwith T.1s had been delivered by the autumn of 1918 and the conversion of eight ships into austere carriers would have taxed the dockyards. However, by the second half of 1918 the Grand Fleet had a Flying Squadron under Rear Admiral Phillimore, *Furious* was a known quantity and *Vindictive*, a cruiser completed to a similar standard, had joined the Grand Fleet in September 1918, the same month as *Argus*. Between them these ships offered a viable striking force but given the limited number of T.1s available in October 1918 the first attack on the enemy fleet in harbour was to be launched by a single squadron of twenty aircraft

Would that we two had met.

Our Weapon

Our Objective—BUT THE HUNS SURRENDERED.

185 Squadron at East Fortune produced this Christmas card in 1918. The captions speak for themselves. (Author's collection)

operating from *Argus*. Given her extensive hangarage, workshop facilities and endurance she could have remained at sea for days waiting for the ideal weather to attack and it would not have been necessary to pre-position her in the Wash or any other isolated base. The first T.1 squadron worked up ashore in the torpedo-attack role during October and then spent a week in *Argus* preparing for the attack on the High Sea Fleet. The squadron's role required both skill and practice to perfect the technique since torpedoes had to be dropped at very low level with no yaw or drift. Aim had to be exact while the pilot set the weapon's running depth with a small hand-wheel to the left of his wicker-work seat, all the while keeping formation with the rest of the flight, watching the strike co-ordinator for signals and looking out for enemy aircraft and gunfire.

By early November 1918 both the squadron and *Argus* were ready but the Armistice agreement which came into effect on 11 November prevented the attack from being carried out. The 1918 East Fortune Christmas Card perfectly illustrated their frustration and under the heading 'Would that we two had met' there was a photograph on the left of a T.1 dropping its torpedo with the caption 'Our Weapon'. On the right there was a photograph of the line of German battleships steaming into captivity with a caption which read 'Our Objective – BUT THE HUNS SURRENDERED'. Despite the pilots' frustration, the idea had been born and it was to be revived by the RN for potential use against the Italian Fleet during the Abyssinian Crisis and, of course, for the famous attack on the same fleet in its main base at Taranto in November 1940.

A post-war demonstration

The long-awaited attack on the High Sea Fleet had been frustrated by the Armistice in November 1918 but 185 Squadron was given the chance to demonstrate the potential of air-launched torpedoes in 1919. By then the Grand Fleet had dispersed but on Saturday, 6 September 1919 the 2nd Battle Squadron was moored in Portland Harbour ready, at a pre-arranged time, to be attacked by eleven Sopwith T.1 Cuckoos of 185 Squadron. Eight aircraft carried torpedoes with inert warheads[15] and the remaining three carried smoke bombs intended to cover the attackers' approach and confuse the defenders. Since it was primarily a demonstration of the new form of attack the aircraft attacked in clear daylight rather than at dawn or dusk but they did divide tactically into two groups. The larger of these comprised five aircraft with torpedoes and two smoke bombers, all of which flew low over the land to the north in order mask their approach. The smaller group comprised three torpedo-armed aircraft and a single smoke bomber and they attacked from the south slightly later than the northern group. The shallow water in Portland Harbour presented a technical problem since

A practice torpedo drop in the Solent off Fort Grange at Gosport in 1919. Note how low the aircraft is and that the splash from the weapon's water entry has actually hit the Sopwith T.1's rear fuselage. (Author's collection)

torpedoes that dived below their set running depth on release ran the risk of hitting the seabed.

Admiral Madden, the C-in-C Atlantic Fleet, commented in his subsequent Report of Proceedings (ROP) that the demonstration attack was well executed. Furthermore, he had little doubt that even under the clear conditions that prevailed and with the exact hour of the attack known beforehand, anti-aircraft gunnery could not have stopped more than a small proportion of the attacking aircraft. The attack from the south, when all attention was focused on the aircraft to the north, would have succeeded unopposed. Some of the smoke bombs failed to ignite but those that did formed an effective screen against aimed fire from the target ship at the most critical moments. The demonstration convinced Admiral Madden that this method of attack was extremely effective, simple and easily adapted to awkward conditions such as the shallow water. The results were impressive by any standard; the five northern torpedo aircraft scored one hit each on *Barham* and *Malaya* and two on *Implacable*. The fifth torpedo dived into the seabed. The three southern torpedo aircraft scored two hits on the flagship *Queen Elizabeth* and the third weapon dived into the seabed. The flagship was not meant to be attacked but

The demonstration attack on the Atlantic Fleet anchored in Portland Harbour in 1919. The aircraft are flying in formation and attacking through smoke. (Author's collection)

the pilots subsequently claimed to have mistaken her for *Barham* and dropped their torpedoes against her in error. Admiral Madden further noted in his ROP that the Cuckoo must be considered an operationally effective aircraft and that the technical difficulty of dropping torpedoes in shallow water had been sufficiently overcome since only two had been lost in water of a depth that was known to be about the minimum in which a battleship could be expected to anchor. He considered that, even at their present state of development, aircraft were the most effective platform for launching torpedo attacks on capital ships. Torpedoes were clearly more lethal and accurate than bombs had yet proved to be and several new lines of development were proposed. Clearly the means of communication between the fleet, reconnaissance and strike aircraft needed to be improved to derive the best results from the new weapons and this would need to be matched with intelligence about enemy forces both at sea and in harbour. The Fleet view about airborne torpedoes was that a larger warhead was desirable but not at the expense of making the aircraft carrying it less manoeuvrable. An increase in speed was also desirable but not at the expense of a heavier warhead. An ideal torpedo would be a modified Mark VIII capable of running at 35 knots out to 3000 yards with a 400lb warhead.

The Fleet's gunnery officers recognised that the demonstration must lead them to consider their options for defending a fleet in harbour. They felt that the best defence would be by fighter aircraft with accurate situational information fed to them from picket ships or lookouts on land. In the absence of defensive fighters, gunfire could mount a defence in clear daylight given some warning of an attack. It was suggested that battleships' secondary armament could be used to create a 'splash barrage'[16] to disconcert the attackers with continuous fire using whatever ammunition was available at the guns over the widest possible arc. Inside 3000 yards high-angle guns could keep up a continuous aimed fire at individual aircraft using fixed sights. No correction or control would be required against aircraft flying straight at a ship at anchor. The shells used should be high effect with 'graze' or 'time mechanical' fuses. Inside 2000 yards 2pdr 'pom-poms' could maintain continuous aimed fire over open sights against individual aircraft and Lewis guns mounted on open superstructures could fire explosive bullets and tracer on an opportunity basis. Significantly, the gunnery officers noted that gun defence was capable of inflicting casualties on attacking aircraft only in clear daylight and could

Aircraft of the northern attacking force clearing Portland Harbour after the demonstration attack on the Atlantic Fleet. (Author's collection)

not be expected to stop an attack; especially one carried out by a large number of skilfully-handled aircraft. Worse, attacks at dawn or during darkness could not be prevented at all by existing gun defences and capital ships might no longer be able to use harbours that were not protected by aircraft and some form of net defence to limit the attackers' options. Light cruisers and smaller warships were considered less vulnerable because they could anchor in water considered too shallow, at the time, for torpedoes to run effectively. The restriction on an enemy's use of harbours in wartime was almost universal since the RN now posed a threat from carrier-borne strike aircraft able to move across the oceans of the world to get at them.

A Postscript

It is clear from their letters that Admirals Beatty and Madden both believed that in the carrier-borne torpedo aircraft the RN had evolved its most devastating weapon. Even Jellicoe's more conservative approach to deploying them recognised the importance of these aircraft. In a mere six years the air-dropped locomotive torpedo had evolved from a bright idea beyond the capability of current technology into a practical weapons system capable of deployment at sea. The problem lay with the creation on 1 April 1918 of the independent air force as the airborne element of system which, unfortunately, regarded all naval and military operations as obsolescent. A contemporary view of the situation may be gathered from the text of an undated letter written by the then Air Commodore Oliver Swann RAF to a friend. After his distinguished service in the RNAS he had been one of many who had transferred to the RAF on 1 April 1918. On hearing about the success of torpedo aircraft while he was serving at the headquarters of the RAF in the Mediterranean he wrote 'I wish I could bring myself to make the plunge of returning to the RN. I feel sure, under the latest developments, that the RAF will become purely a supply depot for the Navy – we shall never keep hold of the show [torpedo aircraft] now that the Navy realise it is a good show.'[17]

18 Retrospection

At one minute after midnight on 1 April 1918 all the Royal Navy's aircraft, air stations, aircrew and maintenance personnel were handed over to a new Service at the stroke of a politician's pen and without any period of transition. Military ranks were imposed and the proud achievements and traditions built up by the RNAS swept away, literally overnight. Overall there was a feeling of sadness and loss with some writing that the Admiralty had let them down by not arguing its case strongly enough. Others continued to think of themselves with pride as former RNAS men.

Flight Sub Lieutenant Willis RNAS was well liked and respected by his colleagues in 5 (Naval) Squadron. Sadly he was blinded and badly burned when his de Havilland DH 4 crashed into a railway yard after he lost control taking off in a strong crosswind on 13 January 1918. His gunlayer sustained a broken leg but Willis died of his injuries at 17.10 on 15 January. He was buried in Dunkirk Cemetery on 18 January 1918. (Goble Family Collection).

Among them was Squadron Commander R L G Marix DSO RNAS, who had had a leg amputated after crashing in a Nieuport fighter shortly after take-off in October 1918. The story is told that he attended a dinner intended to celebrate the amalgamation of the RNAS and RFC shortly after 1 April 1919 at which Trenchard was guest of honour. After having consumed a number of glasses of champagne and despite having an artificial leg, he climbed onto the table at the height of the festivities, lifted his glass high and called out the toast 'Long live the Royal Naval Air Service'.[1] Trenchard apparently took a dim view and his subsequent career in the RAF suffered for several years although he eventually achieved high rank. Undoubtedly there were some who relished the challenge of the new service but everyone with a regular commission on that day had the right to opt to return to their old service. One of the few to exercise that right was Bell-Davies who was still serving in *Furious* in early 1919.[2] Not wishing to leave the Navy, he applied to revert to general sea service but heard nothing for several weeks. One morning he found two letters on his desk, one from the Admiralty and one from the Air Ministry. Opening the former he found an appointment to *Lion*, so he put on his naval uniform and placed the Air Ministry letter into his pocket. After turning over the air department of *Furious* to Lieutenant Colonel Acland RAF he moved across to *Lion* where he opened the second letter and found it to contain an appointment to the Air Ministry. To this, he replied stating that he was unable to comply as he had already taken up a naval appointment and 'a few days later poor Acland received a rude letter from some official at the Air Ministry protesting that the whole procedure was irregular. He sent it over to me so I put a minute on it: "This must not occur again", and sent it back to him.'

   The vast majority of pilots did not have regular commissions, however, and did not have the option to return to the Navy. Many would have been content to be demobilised at the end of hostilities but, to those who hoped to obtain regular commissions, the RAF must have seemed the only option since they would have had to re-train for non-aviation duties in the RN and would then have been at a disadvantage compared with officers who had specialised from the outset in general service. At a time of likely large-scale disarmament they felt it was probably best to stick with what they knew. For me the saddest aspect of the new air force's political implementation was that, whilst making no positive impact on the conduct and outcome of the war, it partially erased the RNAS from history. Overnight, pilots had to adopt military ranks and squadrons were re-numbered[3] in the remaining weeks of the war before the Armistice on 11 November and Air Ministry insistence that there should be a separate air history removed the development of the RNAS from the naval history where it rightfully belonged. Had the RAF not been created with such haste a more rational debate after 1919 might have looked

Alec Little's loss on 27 May 1918 was keenly felt by the men who had served with him in 3 (Naval) Squadron. Some of his fellow pilots are seen here pausing for thought as they stand at his graveside. From left to right they are Flight Lieutenant L Bawlf RNAS, Flight Lieutenant A T Whealy DSC* RNAS, Flight Lieutenant H F Beamish DSC RNAS, Squadron Commander R A Collishaw DSO DSC RNAS and Flight Commander L H Rochford DSC* RNAS. At this time they had achieved, between them, more than seventy aerial victories. Collishaw is in blue uniform, the others are in RNAS field service khaki and all have retained their RNAS insignia. Squadron mechanics have inscribed the wooden Celtic cross with the words 'No 3 NAVAL SQUADRON - IN MEMORY OF FLT CDR R A LITTLE DSO DSC RN - KILLED IN AERIAL COMBAT MAY 27th 1918 - AGED 23 YEARS'. Their loyalty clearly still lay with the RNAS and they respected Little as part of its achievements. A Commonwealth War Graves Commission headstone replaced it when the formal cemetery was laid out after the war and Alec's widow, Vera, took the wooden original to Australia. In 1978 the family donated it to the Australian War Memorial where it has been displayed prominently, together with his medals. When compared with this photograph the cross is a moving link with the RNAS. (Author's collection)

at things more logically. This might still have decided to create an air force although more war experience counted against the idea than for it but the case for the RNAS should have prevailed and, with any logic, it should have survived as part of the naval service, albeit in smaller numbers after the inevitable post-war run-down.

One of the arguments levelled against the Admiralty by the proponents of an independent air service in 1917 had been the fact that the Royal Navy lacked senior officers with air experience. Those who advanced this idea had failed to take into account the fact that the rapid advance of aviation technology in 1916/17 meant that no senior officer could have first-hand experience of combat flying. Certainly Trenchard and Henderson showed no knowledge of the skills and tactics needed by long-range bombers crews. It is one of the interesting features of aviation that the men who lead units at squadron level are the best exponents of this form of warfare and it is the role of senior officers to understand and administer them to best advantage. It could equally be argued that few senior RN officers had commanded a submarine but this did not stop them from making good use of this new form of warfare as it evolved. Dynamic technological advances after 1906 also meant that no senior officer before 1914 had ever commanded a British fleet that

In 2017 there is sadly no national memorial dedicated solely to the RNAS and its achievements. However the Air Forces Memorial on the western Thames embankment in London does have the following inscription. 'IN MEMORY OF ALL RANKS OF THE ROYAL NAVAL AIR SERVICE, THE ROYAL FLYING CORPS, THE ROYAL AIR FORCE AND THOSE AIR FORCES FROM EVERY PART OF THE BRITISH EMPIRE WHO GAVE THEIR LIVES IN WINNING VICTORY FOR THEIR KING AND COUNTRY 1914 – 1918.' (Andrew Hobbs collection)

could not be seen completely from his bridge and which moved at such continuously high speeds. No admiral had ever commanded a task force involved in a high-speed gunnery engagement at ranges over 20,000 yards whilst having to take into account the possibility of U-boat traps and recently-laid minefields. Novelty was not just something that affected aviation; all new technologies take experience and practice to assimilate and the Great War Royal Navy contained so many new technologies that it inevitably took time to absorb them. As the war progressed Admiralty technical departments made considerable progress with ship design and construction, submarines, aircraft including airships, gunnery, mines, torpedoes, anti-submarine sensors and weapons, task force command and control, communications, operational technique and tactics together with, certainly not least, the use of the SIGINT information available to a shore headquarters to assist fleets at sea. Many of these developments were world leaders at the time and for some years after the war. The sheer breadth of equipment to be perfected and the interlocking parts they all had to play in naval warfare were an unstated reason for the Admiralty's reluctance in the 1917 arguments to have just one element, aviation, removed from its control for no very good reason. Those who criticised the Admiralty for its early solutions to technological change run the risk themselves of being criticised for failing to understand the problems.

One of the most important aspects of tactical command was what would now be called situational awareness. It affected every form of warfare but especially operations at sea and in the air; the latter both as the third dimension of naval operations and as part of the defence of the UK against attack from the air. Prior to 1914 naval exercises had not been carried out at high speed in the eastern North Sea, open sea where ships could not fix their positions by taking bearings of conspicuous land features. It was not at first appreciated, therefore, that it would be difficult to know exactly where every element of the Grand Fleet was, let alone the enemy. The operations plot was an ingenious idea but it was only as good as the information fed into it and the constant practice of those tasked with keeping it up to date. Accurate navigation on or over the featureless sea on the scale required was not yet a practical proposition in 1914 and if the sky was overcast enough to prevent sun or star sights, ships might not fix their positions accurately between sailing and returning to the coast. Variable wind, tides and currents could make differences to heading and distance covered that could not be accurately estimated and the indicated speeds of both aircraft and ships could not be calibrated with precision. It was also difficult to evaluate what type of weapon enemy tactics might be favouring. Jellicoe was convinced that the enemy might try to lead him over a U-boat or mine trap without thinking through the difficulty of trying to do so and his assumption that the High Sea Fleet was well served by Zeppelin reconnaissance shows that he had not fully realised the difficulties of navigation, command and identification-friend-or-foe that needed to be overcome. Getting reliable information from an airship that was unlikely to know its own position accurately and passing it in code to a flagship that could not see it and might have significant navigational errors of its own was never going to be easy and Zeppelins never achieved the capability Jellicoe ascribed to them in 1914. The Grand Fleet did not begin to solve the problem of tactical reconnaissance with its own aircraft until 1917. After that effective steps were taken at once and large numbers of Sopwith 'Ship' Strutters were embarked in a variety of fighting ships, all of which could link with some success into a tactical grid which would feed information to the fleet command and its plot. They could also assist by spotting the results of gunfire at extreme range to correct shells onto the target at or beyond the firing ship's visible horizon. This should, of course, have been recognised by Smuts and the Air Board as a vital naval activity, not an independent function that was divorced from all the activity going on around it. The Air Board should have recognised that Henderson was not a credible expert when he admitted having no knowledge of what the RNAS actually did.

Lack of situational awareness was central to the problem with air defence at first. Exactly where were the enemy aircraft? How could fighters find them visually in the night sky after taking off and spending up to 30 minutes climbing to height? What were the most appropriate fighter weapons? These were all questions that were not easy to answer in 1915 but the solutions were eventually found by the RFC through experience, good administration, the development of technology, training and constant practice. The sector operations rooms which fused incoming information and fed it to the weapons systems are normally associated by the public with RAF Fighter Command in 1940 but were actually evolved by the RFC in 1917. Navigation and situational awareness also proved to be key elements of the anti-submarine campaign and it should be remembered that unlike the later Fleet Air Arm, the RNAS controlled all naval aircraft including flying boats and airships so that their operations could be closely integrated with those of the fleet and with convoy escorts. The ability to co-ordinate the activities of flying boats in the 'Spider Web' and airships making their hourly transmissions on coastal patrol work enabled shore plots to fuse SIGINT, intelligence data and enemy sighting reports and pass them to aircraft for effective action. These were lessons that had to be re-learned after 1939.

Captain G W Steele USN, the observer sent in 1918 to study aviation in the Grand Fleet and to report his findings to the General Board, commented that so many ideas had been gained from the British 'that any discussion of the subject must consider their methods'.[4] Despite this recognition of its importance, however, aviation was not a 'silver bullet' weapon that could win the war unaided by other technologies. Rather, it was an increasingly important element within a system of systems that delivered reconnaissance, intelligence and growing capabilities in the fields of air-to-air combat and strike missions. Had the war continued into 1919 torpedo attacks on warships at sea and in harbour would undoubtedly have achieved major importance but it was the reconnaissance role that stands out in any study of RNAS achievements. Locating the *Königsberg*, spotting enemy troop movements in Gallipoli and the Middle East, France and Belgium, and correcting ships' gunfire off Belgium and in the Middle East are but a few of the RNAS' successes. Integration within the Grand Fleet took time and, at first, the technology went down some blind alleys but by any yardstick progress was rapid after Dunning showed the way forward. The successful completion, trial and operational work up of the world's first aircraft carrier were major achievements and although *Argus* finally emerged some 20 weeks after the creation of the embryonic RAF, the achievement was in all but name completely the work of the work of the Navy and its air service.

Throughout its existence, the RNAS was successful and innovative but that very success brought its own problems. In 1914 it represented, with the submarine service, some of the RN's most innovative technology and the path that development would follow was by no means obvious. This caused some of the early pioneers to lose their focus and the situation was made worse by Churchill's enthusiasm for novel ideas while he was First Lord of the Admiralty. It also exposed the service to the petty jealousy of outsiders who had not inspired such advances themselves but wanted control of them when their value became evident. Of course, technologies did not always work out as they were expected to. For instance, seaplanes which had seemed such ideal aircraft for naval use in 1913 proved to have severe limitations when attempts were made to use them in the open sea from 1914 onwards. Sometimes the solutions to problems stared people in the face but had not been recognised as such. One thinks of Jellicoe's comment '. . . unless it be by the use of wheeled aircraft taking off from the deck of a ship . . .' but it took Dunning, a man of singular character and initiative, to make it happen. Individuals could obviously make a difference but this was not always for the good, as Beatty proved in 1917. Why on earth he imagined that signing away the effective ownership and control of the Grand Fleet's aviation assets to a new force created with the aim of advancing strategic bombing as a means of waging war is difficult to imagine, especially given his evident enthusiasm for using air operations as a means of bringing the High Sea Fleet to action on terms he could dictate.

We look back now with the full knowledge of what was possible, what was difficult to achieve and what actually happened. Other than the immediate erasure

Other than the individual graves beautifully maintained by the CWGC and the names on the RN War Memorials for those with no known grave but the sea, few tangible links with the RNAS survive today but occasionally some emerge unexpectedly. A few years ago this Gladstone bag was found in a rubbish tip in southern Queensland, Australia. Fortunately it was examined and found to contain relics of Alec Little including clothing and his flying helmet and goggles. They now form a valued part of the collections held by the Australian Fleet Air Arm Museum at Nowra, New South Wales. (Australian Fleet Air Arm Museum via Terence Hetherington)

of naval ranks and unit identities, the Union Flag replaced the White Ensign at naval air stations ashore on 1 April 1918 but for the remaining weeks of 1918 the spirit of the RNAS was not entirely eradicated; that happened after 1919 when the full impact of the RAF's land-centric outlook became evident. As Captain Steele told the USN General Board, the RNAS had done remarkably well and was the first to introduce many ideas than have subsequently been taken for granted by the world's air arms, not just those of the British Commonwealth.

Above all the Royal Naval Air Service was a sea service that proved itself, like the Royal Marines and the Royal Naval Division between 1914 and 1918, to be adaptable enough to project sea power over the land when called upon to do so. That it could do this as well as creating an effective ship-borne fleet air arm with aircraft embarked in a number of fighting ships, seaplane carriers and the world's first aircraft carrier is greatly to its credit. Its history should be included with that of the Navy of which it formed a significant part and not portrayed as some sort of early prototype for an independent air force. As important, it must be realised that it deserved to survive as a part of the naval service in 1918, not subsumed into an organisation that cared little for the sea power on which Great Britain and its Empire depended.

Appendix A   Maps showing Significant Airfield Sites used by the RNAS during the Great War

The sites varied from temporary bases with little more than an area of flat land with canvas hangars for aircraft storage and workshops with tented accommodation to large permanent establishments that lasted for many years after the war. The largest concentrations were in the UK and around Dunkirk on the Western Front but there were others in the Mediterranean and Egypt which have not been shown.

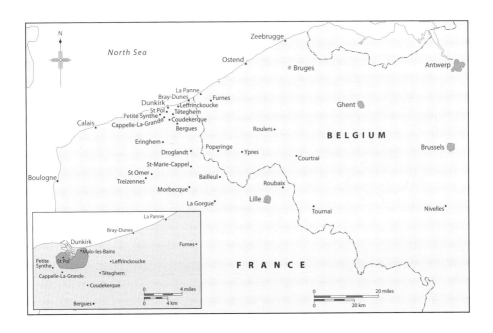

Fixed-wing Air Stations

N

SCOTLAND

Smoogroo

Leuchars Junction

Donibristle
Turnhouse

New Haggerston • Seahouses

Machrihanish

Ashington
Tynemouth

*NORTH
SEA*

Seaton Carew • Redcar

West Ayton •

Atwick
Owthorne

Greenland Top • North Coates Fillies

IRELAND

*IRISH
SEA*

Dublin

Bangor

Cranwell

Holt • Bacton

Burgh Castle •

ENGLAND

Aldeburgh Covehithe
Butley

WALES

Chingford

Isle of Grain
Eastchurch
Dover (land) • Walmer
Telscombe
Cliffs

Westward Ho!

Gosport

Padstow

Chickerell

Bembridge Foreland

Prawle Point

English Channel

Airship, Balloon and
Seaplane Air Stations

Steness
Caldale
Houton Bay

Catfirth

Strathbeg
Longside

SCOTLAND

Auldbar

Dundee

Rosyth
Hawkcraig Point
North
Queensferry
East Fortune

Chathill

NORTH
SEA

N

Ballyliffin
Rathmullan
Larne
Luce
Bay

Seaton Carew II
Kirkleatham

Ramsey

Lowthorpe
Hornsea Mere
Howden
Killingholme
Immingham

IRELAND

IRISH
SEA

Malahide

Anglesey

ENGLAND

Hinkling Broad
Yarmouth
Pulham
Lowestoft

Fishguard

WALES

Shotley
Felixstowe

Killeagh

Milford Haven
Pembroke

Richmond Park
Sheerness
Westgate
Kingsnorth
Godmersham Park
Lee-on-Solent   Tipnor   West Mersham
Slindon   Dover (marine)

Bude
Bridport
Upton   Calshot
Capel
Polegate
Bembridge   Newhaven
Merifield   Laira
Torquay
Portland   Harbour

Cattewater
Tresco   Newlyn   Mullion

English Channel

Appendix B – RNAS Uniform

The RN adopted khaki uniform for men deployed on land operations at about the same time as the British Army. Military training had formed a substantial part of sailors' training prior to 1914 and companies of sailors, as well as Royal Marines, had been landed to fight in a number of colonial campaigns. In 1914 the RNAS, RND and the men who manned the armoured trains wore their standard blue uniforms but from 1915 these were replaced by khaki uniform drawn from Army stocks although ratings wore their naval rate badges. The men also wore Admiralty-pattern leather webbing until it was replaced by Army canvas webbing from 1916 onwards. Specialist RNAS Armoured Car badges were produced and worn on jacket lapels by personnel serving in armoured car squadrons. There was also an armoured train badge and an RNAS AAC badge woven in red cotton for wear on the right-hand jacket sleeve of men serving in these units. Of interest, in 1914 the

Flight Commanders R Jope-Slade RNAS (left) and T F Le Mesurier (right) of 5 (Naval) Squadron show the two uniforms most commonly worn by RNAS officers after 1916, khaki working dress ashore and the more formal blue uniform worn at sea. (Goble Family Collection).

RN used the long Lee-Enfield rifle which had a number of detailed differences from the Army's standard weapon, the Short Magazine Lee-Enfield (SMLE), and so the latter weapon replaced the former in the RND and RNAS from 1916.

Some of the men used in handling parties were seamen and wore the standard working dress of blue or white bell-bottom trousers, jumper, blue-jean collar and round hat, known as 'square rig'. White was worn in hotter climates but was also commonly used as working rig in ships of the Grand Fleet as its white duck material was more easily washed than blue serge. All RNAS mechanics, however, were deemed to be men 'not dressed as seamen' and they were dressed in what was known as Class III or 'fore and aft rig'. The same rig was worn by artificers, members of the supply and secretariat branch, sick berth attendants and locally-entered personnel. It comprised a blue serge jacket most commonly single-breasted with four buttons but could be double-breasted with six buttons, waistcoat and trousers worn with a white shirt, detachable collar and black tie. Headwear comprised a peaked cap like that worn by junior officers with a red cotton cap badge comprising, at first, a crown over a foul anchor. From 1914 a woven RNAS eagle replaced the foul anchor. When working on aircraft overalls could replace the jacket and trousers or be worn over them depending on temperature. From 1915 'fore and aft rig' was replaced as a working rig for men drafted ashore in both

An RNAS mechanic in blue uniform.
(Author's collection)

the UK and abroad by khaki jacket and trousers. In most ships of the Grand Fleet there were no formalised laundry arrangements and sailors did what they had done for hundreds of years, they washed or 'dhobeyed' their own clothes in a bucket when they washed themselves, using a block of hard soap and a scrubbing brush. The expression 'bath and dhobey' was still common at the end of the twentieth century despite significant improvement in accommodation standards. RN ratings were generally expected to 'make and mend' their own uniforms after their initial issue so there were no large scale stocks of blue uniforms in 1914; this is one reason why the use of stock khaki uniform became widespread and popular.

In 1916 khaki service dress was ordered for all officers serving in the RNAS and RND ashore outside the UK. Rank lace was worn on the sleeves exactly as in blue service dress but dark material was substituted for gold braid. Those in the UK and at sea continued to wear their blue uniform with its eight-button double-breasted reefer jacket. Officers were given cash grants on promotion but were subsequently expected to purchase their own uniforms, blue, khaki and even warm flying clothing from naval outfitters although they were given some tax relief that was expected to cover normal wear and tear. Pilots' wings comprised a gilt eagle in flight facing aft worn over the left sleeve lace of the reefer jacket or over the left breast pocket of the khaki tunic. In June 1917 one or two gilt stars were introduced over the flight lieutenant's gold sleeve lace to indicate their promotion to flight commander (one) or squadron commander (two). A week later a winged 'O' badge was introduced for observers and this was worn in the same place as the eagle device. Swords had ceased to be considered as fighting weapons on conclusion of the Boer War but were retained for ceremonial dress purposes. Some were produced for direct-entry RNAS officers in which the foul anchor device on the hand-guard was replaced by an RNAS eagle.

Appendix C RN Ships Fitted to Operate Aircraft during the Great War

Specialised Aircraft and Seaplane Carriers

Anne
Argus
Ark Royal
Ben-my-Chree
Campania
Empress
Engadine
Furious
Manxman
Nairana
Pegasus
Raven II
Riviera
Vindex
Vindictive

Battleships and Battlecruisers

Ajax
Australia
Barham
Bellerophon
Benbow
Canada
Centurion
Collingwood
Conqueror
Courageous
Emperor of India

Erin
Glorious
Indomitable
Inflexible
Iron Duke
King George V
Lion
Malaya
Marlborough
Monarch
Neptune
New Zealand
Orion
Princess Royal
Queen Elizabeth
Ramillies
Renown
Repulse
Resolution
Revenge
Royal Oak
Royal Sovereign
Tiger
Valiant
Warspite

Cruisers

Aurora
Birkenhead
Brisbane

Caledon

Calliope

Carlisle

Caroline

Cassandra

Chatham

Comus

Constance

Cordelia

Coventry

Dauntless

Delhi

Diana

Doris

Dragon

Dublin

Dunedin

Endymion

Euryalus

Galatea

Hermes

Inconstant

Melbourne

Minerva

Penelope

Phaeton

Royalist

Southampton

Sydney

Undaunted

Weymouth

Yarmouth

Other Types of Ship

Albion III

Angora

Beryl

Brocklesby

Cantatrice

Christopher

City of Oxford

Cleethorpes

Dryad

Dufferin

E22

Eridge

General Crauford

Geranium

Golden Eagle

Halcyon

Hardinge

Himalaya

Jerico

Killingholme

Kinfauns Castle

Kingfisher

Laconia

Laurentic

Lordship

Manica

Mantua

Melton

Minerva

Northbrook

Orotava

Peony

Princess Margaret

Princess Victoria

Raglan

Roberts

St Germain

Severn

Sir John French

Sir Thomas Picton

Slinger

Tarlair

Notes

Chapter 1: Origins

1. Richard Hough, *First Sea Lord, an Authorised Biography of Admiral of the Fleet Lord Fisher of Kilverstone* (London: George Allen & Unwin, 1969), pp 169, 210–11, 238.
2. Norman Friedman, *The British Battleship 1906–1946* (Barnsley: Seaforth Publishing, 2015), p 76.
3. Hugh Popham, *Into Wind – a History of British Naval Flying* (London: Hamish Hamilton Ltd, 1969), p 1.
4. It was the first to have a lightweight cylinder block, cast from an alloy comprising 92 per cent aluminium and 8 per cent copper. The Wright Brothers' mechanic Charlie Taylor made it, without drawings, in their bicycle workshop.
5. Walter Raleigh, *The War in the Air* (Uckfield: The Naval & Military Press, a reprint of a work first published in 1922), Vol 1, pp 65 et seq.
6. Ibid, p 116.
7. J David Brown. 'The Genesis of Naval Aviation' in *Les Marines de Guerre du Dreadnought au Nucleaire* (Paris: Service Historique de la Marine, 1988), p 97.
8. David Hobbs, *A Century of Carrier Aviation* (Barnsley: Seaforth Publishing, 2009), p 13.
9. Captain S W Roskill, *Documents Relating to the Naval Air Service Volume 1, 1908–1918* (Bromley: The Navy Records Society, 1969), p 6.
10. Lieutenant Commander P K Kemp, *Fleet Air Arm* (London: Herbert Jenkins, 1954), p 15.
11. Len Deighton and Arnold Schwartzman, *Airshipwreck* (London: Jonathan Cape, 1978), p 9.
12. Reginald Baliol Brett, second Viscount Esher after 1899, was Chairman of the War Office Reconstruction Committee from 1903 and had recommended a number of Army reforms from 1904 that had resulted in the creation of the Imperial General Staff. He was a member of the CID from 1904 and was known for his enthusiastic support for innovation and reform.
13. Roskill, *Documents Relating to the Naval Air Service Volume 1*, p 6.
14. CID. 106B. Cab. 38/15/3 dated 28 January 1909 quoted in ibid, p 7.
15. *The Oxford English Dictionary* defines a dirigible airship as one that is able to be steered.
16. No doubt with the strategically-significant Kiel Canal in mind.
17. David Hobbs, 'His Majesty's Rigid Airship Number 1', *Dirigible, The Journal of the Airship Heritage Trust* 58 (Autumn 2009), pp 8 et seq.
18. Admiralty, *Handbook for HM Rigid Airship Number 1* (London: Admiralty, 1913), part 1, p 3.
19. Ibid, p 1.
20. Filling the post of 'naval air assistant' in the staff recommended by Bacon in his 21 July 1908 letter.
21. The Wolseley motor car and engine company was owned by Vickers.
22. Order-in-Council 112 dated 28 November 1910, a copy of which is held in the archive of the Naval Historical Branch in Portsmouth.
23. Later to earn distinction as the designer of a series of flying boats for the RNAS.
24. 'British Aviators and Aeronauts', *Flight* (21 June 1910), p 490.
25. Ibid.
26. Later to become RNAS Gosport and, later still, HMS *Sultan*, the RN Engineering School.
27. Jack Bruce. 'John Porte and his Felixstowe Flying Boats', *Papers from 'Cross & Cockade' 25th Anniversary Seminar held at Wyboston Lakes*, 23–25 June 1995, pp 34 et seq
28. He changed his name to Swan in 1917.
29. *Flight* (7 October 1911).
30. Which is in the Archive of the National Museum of the Royal Navy, Fleet Air Arm Museum, at RNAS Yeovilton. I have a photocopy of this document in my own archive.

31. Philip Jarrett, *Frank McClean – Godfather to British Naval Aviation* (Barnsley: Seaforth Publishing, 2011), pp 59 et seq.
32. Formerly owned by G C Colmore.
33. Jarrett, *Frank McClean*, p 61.
34. 'The Foremost Four', *Air Enthusiast* No 46 (July 1992), pp 62 et seq.
35. *1912 Navy List* (London: Admiralty, February 1912).

Chapter 2: Practical Progress
1. Hobbs, *A Century of Carrier Aviation*, pp 12 et seq.
 2. Ibid, p 21.
 3. Popham, *Into Wind*, pp 7 et seq.
 4. Hobbs, *A Century of Carrier Aviation*, p 22.
 5. Air Chief Marshal Sir Arthur Longmore, *From Sea to Sky – Memoirs 1910–1945* (London: Geoffrey Bles, 1946), p 14.
 6. An interesting comparison with the £4000 the Wright Brothers had wanted to charge for each aircraft in 1907.
 7. Jarrett, *Frank McClean*, p 177.
 8. Ray Sturtivant and Gordon Page, *Royal Navy Aircraft Serials and Units 1911–1919* (Tonbridge: Air Britain (Historians), 1992), p 19.
 9. Secretary of State for War 1905–12; he had a reputation as a reformer and was responsible for introducing the Army's General Staff. He became a Viscount in 1911 and moved from the Liberal to the Labour Party in 1924.
10. Captain Donald Macintyre, *Wings of Neptune – The Story of Naval Aviation* (London: Peter Davies, 1963), pp 4 et seq.
11. Among others, he taught Major Trenchard DSO Royal Scots Fusiliers, later to command the RFC in France, to fly.
12. Longmore, *From Sea to Sky*, pp 32 et seq.
13. Ibid, p 33.
14. Who later commanded the RFC in France and, as the post-war Chief of the Air Staff, became the proponent of strategic bombing as a means of waging war.
15. Longmore, *From Sea to Sky*, p 26.
16. Hobbs, *A Century of Carrier Aviation*, pp 27 et seq.
17. David Hobbs, 'The Royal Naval Air Service', a paper read at the 2013 King-Hall Naval History Conference in Canberra organised by the Sea Power Centre – Australia, p 3.
18. Raleigh, *The War in the Air*, Vol 1, pp 266 et seq.
19. Longmore, *From Sea to Sky*, p 34.
20. Raleigh, *The War in the Air*, Vol 1, pp 268 et seq.
21. Ibid, p 265.
22. Flight Sub Lieutenant R A J Warneford RNAS was to use a similar bomb-dropping technique to destroy Zeppelin *LZ 37* on 7 June 1915.
23. J David Brown, 'The Genesis of Naval Aviation'.
24. Raleigh, *The War in the Air*, Vol 1, p 269.
25. The expression 'give it the full 9 yards' is said to originate from the weapon's land application when the gunner told his number 2 how many rounds he intended to fire at a given target. It may or may not be true.
26. Macintyre, *Wings of Neptune*, p 7.
27. Longmore, *From Sea to Sky*, p 36.
28. Sturtivant and Page, *RN Aircraft Serials and Units 1911–1919*, p 36.
29. Roskill, *Documents Relating to the Naval Air Service Volume 1*, p 45.
30. Admiralty, *Handbook on HM Rigid Airship Number 9* (London: Admiralty, 1918), p 5.
31. Ces Mowthorpe, *Battlebags – British Airships of the First World War* (Stroud: Alan Sutton Publishing, 1995), p xxii.
32. Longmore, *From Sea to Sky*, pp 28 et seq.
33. Hobbs, *A Century of Carrier Aviation*, p 32 et seq.
34. A 'tramp' steamer was a cargo ship that followed no set trade route or timetable but, rather, went wherever a cargo was contracted by its owners. The alternative was a 'liner' that did follow set routes and timetables.

35. David Hobbs, *British Aircraft Carriers – Design, Development and Service Histories* (Barnsley: Seaforth Publishing, 2013), pp 19 and 20.
36. Contained in ADM 1/8378 at the National Archive at Kew and quoted in Roskill, *Documents Relating to the Naval Air Service Volume 1*, pp 156 et seq.
37. Vice Admiral Richard Bell-Davies, *Sailor in the Air – the Memoirs of the World's First Carrier Pilot* (Barnsley: Seaforth Publishing, 2008), p 87.

Chapter 3: The Outbreak of War

1. While working on a project in the Naval Historical Branch (NHB), in 1997, I was shown an uncatalogued history of air operations in the Great War which had been prepared by the Admiralty in 1919 for inclusion in a more general work. A note attached to the manuscript said that other copies had been destroyed but this single copy had been retained for potential use by historians. Fortunately, David Brown, the head of the NHB, encouraged me to make a copy which I have retained. Some passages from this manuscript clearly found their way into the official *War in the Air*, by Walter Raleigh and H A Jones, others did not. Where I make reference to this manuscript I have called it the NHB Air History. In this, first, instance the reference is to the NHB Air History p 37.
2. Raleigh, *The War in the Air*, Vol 1, p 271.
3. Ibid, p 274.
4. Sir Julian S Corbett, *Naval Operations – History of the Great War at Sea* (Reprinted by the Naval & Military press and Imperial War Museum from an original work published in 1920), p 39.
5. Described in detail in my earlier book *British Aircraft Carriers*, pp 20 et seq.
6. Ibid, pp 22 et seq.
7. The first time in history that a warship at sea had been sunk by torpedoes fired from a submarine.
8. NHB Air History, p 40.
9. Roskill, *Documents Relating to the Naval Air Service Volume 1*, pp 168 et seq.
10. The battleship *Iron Duke*, completed at Portsmouth Dockyard in March 1914, is believed to be the first British warship to be fitted with anti-aircraft guns; two 3in Mark 1 on HA mountings.
11. Admiralty, *Notes and Orders for Officers – Anti-Aircraft Corps of the Royal Naval Air Service* (London: Admiralty, 31 December 1914), pp 7 et seq.
12. Rear Admiral Murray F Sueter, *Airmen or Noahs – Fair Play for our Airmen* (London: Sir Isaac Pitman & Sons, 1928), pp 166 et seq.
13. Air Commodore Charles Rumney Samson, *Fights and Flights* (London: Ernest Benn Limited, 1930), pp 3 et seq.
14. The Webley automatic was prone to jam if it got mud or grit into its mechanism and so the Army continued to use the Mark 6 revolver throughout the Great War and beyond as it was robust and relatively foolproof.
15. My underlining to emphasise the point being made.
16. C F Snowden Gamble, *The Story of a North Sea Air Station* (London: Oxford University Press, 1928), pp 100 et seq.

Chapter 4: The First Strikes by Aircraft

1. Christopher Page, *Command in the Royal Naval Division – A Military Biography of Brigadier General A M Asquith DSO* (Staplehurst: Spellmount, 1999), pp 24 et seq.
2. Leonard Sellers, *The Hood Battalion* (London: Leo Cooper, 1995), pp 13 et seq.
3. Samson, *Fights and Flights*, p 96.
4. John Lea, *Reggie – The Life of Air Vice Marshal R L G Marix CBE DSO* (Edinburgh: Pentland Press, 1994), pp 22 et seq.
5. J M Bruce, *British Aeroplanes 1914-1918* (London: Putnam, 1957), pp 521, 522.
6. Sturtivant and Page, *Royal Navy Aircraft Serials and Units 1911–1919*, p 42.
7. Reading contemporary accounts of operations in 1914 it is interesting to note that regular officers such as Gerrard continued to use their non-RNAS ranks, in his case Major RMLI. The new RNAS ranks were mainly used by direct-entry officers but their use spread to the regular officers as they gained promotion in air ranks.
8. NHB Air History, p 41.
9. Referred to in the early days of aviation as 'volplaning'.
10. Raleigh, *The War in the Air*, Vol 1, p 389.

11. Lea, *Reggie*, p 27.
12. Unlike later aircraft which used ailerons, these early Tabloids used wing-warping to apply bank. A normal turn would involve the pilot applying both rudder and wing-warp.
13. Sueter, *Airmen or Noahs*, pp 12 et seq.
14. Two of his designs, the Pemberton-Billing PB-9 and the PB-25, were subsequently bought by the Admiralty in small numbers but neither saw operational service.
15. Bruce, *British Aeroplanes 1914–1918*, p 52.
16. Sturtivant and Page, *Royal Navy Aircraft Serials and Units 1911–1919*, pp 42 and 49.
17. Raleigh, *The War in the Air*, Vol 1, pp 396 et seq.
18. Sueter subsequently tried to claim sole credit for the concept of the strike in *Airmen or Noahs*, p 9, where he wrote 'I obtained from Mr Churchill permission to send some seaplanes into the Heligoland Bight to ascertain the whereabouts of the German fleet and also to drop bombs on points of military importance'. In doing so he contradicted his own orders for the strike which gave priority to the airship sheds, believed to be at Cuxhaven. These are preserved in Air 1/2099 at the National Archive, Kew.
19. R D Layman, *The Cuxhaven Raid – The World's First Carrier Air Strike* (London: Conway Maritime Press, 1985), pp 36 et seq.
20. A Temple Patterson, *Tyrwhitt of the Harwich Force* (London: Macdonald, 1973), p 82.
21. Admiral Viscount Jellicoe of Scapa, *The Grand Fleet 1914 – 1916. Its Creation, Development and Work* (London: Cassell & Co, 1919), p 165.
22. Winston S Churchill, *The World Crisis* (New York: Scribner 1951), Vol 1, p 490.
23. NHB Air History, p 47.
24. Layman, *The Cuxhaven Raid*, p 46.
25. Bowhill had earned a master's certificate under sail before joining the RN and went on to have a long and distinguished career in the RAF after 1918.
26. A cable is 200 yards or 10 per cent of a nautical mile.
27. From the easternmost island, Wangeroog, the islands would have been passed in the order Spiekeroog, Langeoog, Baltrum and then Norderney.

Chapter 5: Technology and Technique

1. J M Bruce, *The BE.2, 2a and 2b* (Leatherhead: Profile Publications, 1966).
2. Sturtivant and Page, *Royal Navy Aircraft, Serials and Units 1911–1919*, p 29.
3. Bill Gunston, *World Encyclopaedia of Aero Engines* (Cambridge: Patrick Stephens Ltd, 2003), p 135.
4. Alec Lumsden, *British Piston Engines and their Aircraft* (Marlborough: Airlife Publishing, 2003), p 225.
5. Bruce, *British Aeroplanes 1914–1918*, p 481.
6. Ibid, pp 269 et seq.
7. Lumsden, *British Piston Engines and their Aircraft*, p 183.
8. Following the Admiralty practice of giving aircraft a Type number based on the airframe number of an early production example.
9. Patrick Abbot, *The British Airship at War* (Lavenham: Terence Dalton Ltd, 1989), pp 22 et seq.
10. The nose was strengthened by stiff canes positioned radially and the internal pressure of the envelope was increased.
11. Guy Warner, *Lighter than Air, the Life and Times of Wing Commander N F Usborne RN* (Barnsley: Pen & Sword Aviation, 2016), pp 216 et seq.
12. Owen Thetford, *British Naval Aircraft since 1912* (London: Putnam, 1962), p 182.
13. Bruce, *British Aeroplanes 1914–1918*, p 236.
14. Letter from the C-in-C Grand Fleet to the Admiralty in July 1915, a photocopy of which is in the author's archive.
15. Report by Wing Captain O Schwann, commanding officer of HMS *Campania* to the Director of the Admiralty Air Department dated 8 August 1915, contained in ADM 1/8430 at the National Archive, Kew and quoted in Captain Roskill's, *Documents Relating to the Naval Air Service Volume 1*, pp 218 et seq.
16. Hobbs, *A Century of Carrier Aviation*, p 48.
17. H A Jones in Raleigh and Jones, *War in the Air* gives the pilot's name as Towler but in his Report of Proceedings the commanding officer of HMS *Vindex* refers to him as Fowler. Since the captain would have known the officer personally I have used the name stated in his report.

Chapter 6: A Widening War

1. This chapter is based on material from the unpublished NHB Air History, augmented where necessary by a number of further sources.
2. Ibid, p 76.
3. Harold Rosher, *In the Royal Naval Air Service – War Letters of Harold Rosher* (London: Chatto & Windus, 1916), pp 76 et seq. Rosher was killed test-flying an aeroplane at the naval air station at Dover on 27 February 1916.
4. Jones, *The War in the Air*, Vol 2, p 345.
5. Ibid, p 79.
6. Details of these and all British seaplane and aircraft carriers can be found in my earlier book *British Aircraft Carriers*.
7. The vessel was requisitioned from the Isle of Man Steam Packet Company on 1 January 1915 and her name translates into English from Manx as 'Woman of my Heart'. The firm is still in business in 2016 and operates a ship named *Ben-my-Chree VI*.
8. The 80hp Le Rhône rotary engine had no throttle, only a mixture control to maintain smooth running at differing altitudes; it was either switched 'on' or 'off' and pilots usually switched their engine off in a dive to prevent over-speeding and consequent damage.
9. Deighton and Schwartzman, *Airshipwreck*, p 30.
10. Mary Gibson, *Warneford VC* (Yeovilton: Friends of the Fleet Air Arm Museum, 1979), p 99.
11. Ibid, pp 112 et seq.
12. Jones, *The War in the Air*, Vol 2, p 360.
13. Unpublished NHB Air History, p 86.
14. Jones, *The War in the Air*, Vol 2, p 355.
15. Raleigh, *The War in the Air*, Vol 1, pp 486 et seq.
16. *The Distinguished Service Cross 1901–1938* (London: The London Stamp Exchange Ltd, 1991), p 11.
17. Unpublished NHB Air History, pp 92 et seq.
18. While there he wrote a service paper on the features of an ideal aircraft carrier. He was only too well aware of the shortcomings of seaplanes since his crash was probably caused by the propeller being damaged by spray on take-off. He was believed to have carved a wooden model carrier, complete with an island/bridge structure on the starboard side to illustrate his argument. Both paper and model were forwarded to the Admiralty but have not survived.
19. Bell-Davies, *Sailor in the Air*, p 119.
20. A former British tramp steamer detained on the outbreak of war.
21. Frederick Sykes, *Many Angles – An Autobiography* (London: Harrap, 1942).
22. Samson, *Fights and Flights*, p 265.
23. Liman von Sanders, *Five Years in Turkey* (Annapolis: Naval Institute Press, 1927), p 73.
24. Bell-Davies, *Sailor in the Air*, pp 134 and 135.
25. Ibid, p 135.
26. Given Cutler's non-naval background and the urgency of finding the enemy cruiser's exact location, it is surprising that naval officers were not included in the first sorties.

Chapter 7: Armoured Cars, Trains, Tanks and Aircraft Procurement

1. Samson, *Fights and Flights*, pp 9 et seq.
2. Ibid, pp 15 and 16.
3. Ibid, p 34.
4. Ibid, pp 47 et seq.
5. Ibid, p 91 et seq.
6. Major General N W Duncan, *Early Armoured Cars* (Windsor: Profile Publications, undated), p 3.
7. Ibid, p 5.
8. Ibid, p 9.
9. When stationary, a Union Jack was hoisted on the forward part of the train and battle ensigns were flown when engaging the enemy.
10. "L F R', *Naval Guns in Flanders 1914–1915* (Uckfield: Naval & Military Press, 2004 reproduced from an original in the Library of the Royal Military Academy, Sandhurst of a volume first published in 1915), pp 26, 27.
11. Sueter, *Airmen or Noahs*, p 190.
12. Ibid, p 191.

13. Ibid, p 195.
14. Ibid, p 196.
15. Ibid, p 199.
16. Sueter subsequently went into politics, becoming an independent MP sponsored by the Anti-Waste League and a Conservative MP from 1923 to 1945. He was knighted for his services to politics in 1934. He died in 1960 at the age of 87.
17. Snowden Gamble, *The Story of a North Sea Air Station*, pp 152 et seq.
18. Ibid, pp 110 et seq.
19. Bruce, *British Aeroplanes 1914–1918*, pp 497, 498.
20. Ibid, p 543.
21. Ibid, p 565.
22. Those involved with the F-35 Lightning II project in 2016 may find these words familiar. Although their problems appear larger in scale, they are, in many ways, similar to the problems faced by the RNAS and RFC from 1916 onwards.

Chapter 8: The RNAS at Sea and Ashore

1. NHB Air History, pp 154 et seq.
2. In July 1919 the second of these airships, *R 34*, built by Beardmore flew from the UK to the USA and back.
3. Hobbs, *A Century of Carrier Aviation*, pp 48 and 49.
4. It was preserved by the Imperial War Museum after the Great War but damaged in a German air raid during the Second World War. The remains, including the intact cockpit section and engine, are preserved and on display in 2017 at the Fleet Air Arm element of the National Museum of the Royal Navy at RNAS Yeovilton.
5. Admiralty, *Naval Staff History – The Battle of Jutland*, Admiralty Library, pp 65 and 66.
6. Observers at the time were not always regular aircrew and were selected for their light weight and ability to transmit Morse code with reasonable proficiency. They could be members of the RN, RNR or RNVR but were not necessarily members of the RNAS; many were midshipmen. A flying grade of Observer, complete with a winged 'O' flying badge, was belatedly introduced in 1917.
7. Quoted in H W Fawcett and G W W Hooper, *The Fighting at Jutland* (London: Chatham Publishing, 2001), pp 25 et seq.
8. NHB Air History, pp 161 et seq.
9. CMBs achieved their greatest success in the Baltic during operations against the Bolsheviks in 1919. A force of boats attacked an enemy fleet in Kronstadt and sank the battleships *Petropavlosk* and *Andrei Pervosvanni*, together with a submarine depot ship.
10. Having been briefed that there were no British submarines in the area.
11. NHB Air History, pp 167 et seq.
12. Although not with the French, German and subsequently US structures. They continued to base air formations on Wings (*Geschwader*) comprising a number of Squadrons (*Staffeln*).
13. The official Admiralty designation for the new fighter was the Sopwith Type 9901 following the usual policy of naming types after an early production example. To the aircrew who flew it, however, it seemed to resemble a scaled-down version of the 1½ Strutter and was nicknamed its 'Pup'. The name suited it perfectly and, despite official opposition at first, it has remained in use.
14. NHB Air History, p 170.
15. It had nothing to do with the 'A' Flight based at Furnes.
16. Both were former German merchant ships captured in Port Said on the outbreak of war, modified into basic seaplane carriers by the British and commissioned into the RN. For details see my *British Aircraft Carriers*, pp 25 and 27.
17. NHB Air History, pp 180 et seq.
18. Ibid, p 181.
19. A tactic that would be referred to by the American commander of Coalition forces during a later conflict in the region as using 'shock and awe' to defeat the enemy.

Chapter 9: The Use of Aircraft in Fleet Operations

1. Snowden Gamble, *The Story of a North Sea Air Station*, p 299.
2. R D Layman, *Naval Aviation in the First World War – Its Impact and Influence* (London: Chatham Publishing, 1996), p 22.

3. James Goldrick, *Before Jutland – The Naval War in Northern European Waters, August 1914 – February 1915* (Annapolis: Naval Institute Press, 2015), p 47.

4. There were, in fact, two War Rooms; Number 1 covered home waters and Number 2 the rest of the world.

5. If the Grand Fleet and High Sea Fleet steamed towards each other at 21 knots, they would be closing a combined 42 knots or 48 statute miles per hour.

6. Norman Friedman, *Fighting the Great War at Sea – Strategy, Tactics and Technology* (Barnsley: Seaforth Publishing, 2014), p 77.

7. Goldrick, *Before Jutland*, p 49.

8. Leading to the creation of the Radar Plot (RP) Branch in the Second World War.

9. Layman, *Naval Aviation in the First World War*, pp 157 et seq.

10. The Review itself was an economy measure and had been organised to take the place of the annual naval manoeuvres as an impressive but much less costly alternative. As cover the Admiralty explained that the lessons from the 1913 manoeuvres were still being analysed.

11. These comments on machine-gun ammunition used by the RNAS have been researched using the website British Military Small Arms Ammunition.

12. Having said that it took a long time to get fighters to sea, it is worth mentioning that the UK government decided to build a new class of aircraft carriers in its 1998 Strategic Defence Review. The first ship is not expected to be operational at sea until 2021, an interval of 23 years. The gap between Samson taking off from *Africa* in May 1912 to Bell-Davies landing on *Argus*, the world's first true aircraft carrier, in September 1918 was a mere 6 years and 4 months. Perhaps the original delay getting aircraft to sea was not as long as it might have been.

13. Dick Cronin, *Royal Navy Shipboard Aircraft Developments 1912–1931* (Tonbridge: Air-Britain (Historians), 1990), p 14.

14. Bell Davies, *Sailor in the Air*, p 168.

15. J M Bruce, Gordon Page and Ray Sturtivant, *The Sopwith Pup* (Tonbridge: Air-Britain (Historians), 2002), pp 104 et seq.

16. Desmond Young, *Rutland of Jutland* (London: Cassell, 1963), pp 25 et seq.

17. Ibid, p 27.

18. Ibid, p 34.

19. Hobbs, *A Century of Carrier Aviation*, pp 51 et seq.

20. David Hobbs. 'Fighters Over the Grand Fleet', *FlyPast* (September 2008), pp 88 et seq.

21. An RN expression for time off duty dating back to the time when sailors literally made and repaired their own clothing.

22. Now Edinburgh International Airport.

23. Hobbs, *A Century of Carrier Aviation*, pp 53 et seq.

24. He was lent to the ship while his own command, HMAS *Sydney* was refitting in Chatham. See Chapter 15.

25. 'Aircraft Carriers' Part IV, 'Aeroplanes carried in Fighting Ships', DNC Department (London: Admiralty, March 1921).

26. David Stevens, *In All Respects Ready – Australia's Navy in World War One* (Melbourne: Oxford University Press, 2014), p 259 et seq.

27. Admiral Commanding Aircraft to C-in-C Grand Fleet, 7 March 1918', contained in ADM/137/2133 at the National Archive, Kew.

Chapter 10: Expansion and Reorganisation

1. NHB Air History, pp 246 et seq.

2. Ibid, p 248.

3. Sturtivant and Page, *Royal Navy Aircraft Serials and Units 1911–1919*, p 141.

4. Lieutenant Commander Lawrie Phillips, *The Royal Navy Day by Day* (Stroud: Spellmount, 2011), p 290.

5. Ibid, p 421.

6. NHB Air History, p 251.

7. Sturtivant and Page, *Royal Navy Aircraft Serials and Units 1911–1919*, p 142.

8. NHB Air History, p 252.

9. Sturtivant and Page, *Royal Navy Aircraft Serials and Units 1911–1919*, p 141.

10. NHB Air History, p 253.

11. Sturtivant and Page, *Royal Navy Aircraft Serials and Units 1911–1919*, p 141.
12. Ibid, p 141.
13. Phillips, *The Royal Navy Day by Day*, p 341.
14. Snowden Gamble, *The Story of a North Sea Air Station*, pp 259 et seq.
15. Regrettably the airframe number of the DH 4 does not seem to have survived.
16. Snowden Gamble, *The Story of a North Sea Air Station*, p 269.
17. Stuffed bird, glass case and brass plate are now in the collections of the RAF Museum at Hendon.
18. NHB Air History, p 261.
19. Thetford, *British Naval Aircraft since 1912*, p 413.
20. NHB Air History, p 263.
21. Ibid, pp 267 et seq.
22. Ibid, p 272.
23. Ibid, p 274.
24. At the time it was thought that demolition of the building would destroy the machinery inside it. Subsequent post-war analysis of the effect of bomb detonation showed that this was not necessarily the case and machinery often survived.
25. The range at which these bombers operated and the limited fuel supply they had to achieve it prevented them from varying their return route from targets in the UK to any very great extent. Once the attack had given away the fact that they were airborne they became vulnerable to interception on their way back.
26. NHB Air History, p 279.

Chapter 11: Deck Landing

1. To be fair, it should be pointed out that in 1909 the French engineer Clement Ader had described an aircraft-carrying ship with a continuous wide flight deck, a hangar beneath it for the stowage for aircraft and lifts to move them to and from the deck in his book *L'Aviation Militaire*. However, Williamson took the concept several practical steps further based on his experience flying from the seaplane carrier *Ark Royal* in the Gallipoli campaign.
2. Bruce, Page and Sturtivant, *The Sopwith Pup*, p 111.
3. Flight Lieutenant C T Freeman RNAS is logged as having flown an air-defence sortie in N9497 on 13 June 1917.
4. This same system of control wires continued in use, in improved forms, until the widespread introduction of 'fly-by-wire' and 'fly-by-light' systems from the 1970s onwards.
5. L F E Coombs, 'Front Office Evolution', *Air Enthusiast Magazine*, Vol 2 No 2 (February 1972), pp 63 et seq.
6. Every engine start-up routine differed slightly in detail but the basic technique involved a mechanic turning the propeller by hand while the pilot sat in the cockpit with the ignition switched off in order to charge the cylinders with petrol and move lubricating oil through the system. Once the engine was primed the pilot would switch on the ignition and the mechanic would swing the propeller sharply; if the procedure had been followed correctly the engine should fire and warm up quickly. If it failed to do so, the propeller might have to be turned a few more times with the ignition off to clear excess petrol as flooded cylinders would be unlikely to start up properly.
7. Coombs, 'Front Office Evolution', p 66.
8. Bruce, *British Aeroplanes 1914–1918*, pp 552 et seq.
9. J D Brown. Documents relating to early naval aviation collected when he was Head of the Naval Historical Branch, copies of which are now in the author's archive.
10. Hobbs, *A Century of Carrier Aviation*, pp 65 et seq.
11. Contained within ADM/196/54 at The National Archive, Kew, p 135.
12. His service record in The National Archive is quite emphatic about the number of days' leave he was granted during his short initial career.
13. ADM/273/4/69, p 69 in The National Archive at Kew.
14. Sturtivant and Page, *Royal Navy Aircraft Serials and Units 1911–1919*, p 45.
15. Handwritten insert in p 69 of ADM/273/4/69.
16. This is when wind hits the slab-sided hull of a ship it is deflected upwards, tending to lift any aircraft that flies through it.
17. Like all RN ships' logs, those for *Furious* in 1917 are in The National Archive at Kew.
18. Now the West End Hotel at which I have stayed on a number of occasions when giving talks in the Orkney Islands.

19. W G Moore, *Early Bird* (London: Putnam, 1963), p 101.
20. In The National Archive at Kew, entries for 7 August 1917.
21. Copied document in the author's collection.
22. Young, *Rutland of Jutland*, p 62.
23. Hobbs, *A Century of Carrier Aviation*, p 70.
24. Group Captain H R Busteed RAF. Letter to the Air Historical Section dated 11 March 1930.
25. Moore, *Early Bird*, p 115.
26. Hobbs, *A Century of Carrier Aviation*, pp 74 et seq.
27. Contained in ADM 137/1956, 'Report of the Advisory Committee on Naval Aeronautics' in The National Archive at Kew.
28. Hobbs, *British Aircraft Carriers*, p 43.

Chapter 12: Training and Experience
1. David Hobbs, 'The Royal Naval Air Service', in Andrew Forbes (ed), *The War at Sea 1914-18, Proceedings of the King-Hall Naval History Conference 2013* (Canberra: Sea Power Centre – Australia, 2015), pp 213 et seq.
 2. Bell-Davies, *Sailor in the Air*, pp 48 et seq.
 3. At the time, *Flight* was the journal of the Royal Aeronautical Society.
 4. Bell-Davies, *Sailor in the Air*, pp 70 et seq.
 5. Rosher, *In the Royal Naval Air Service*, pp 4 et seq.
 6. Raymond Collishaw with R V Dodds, *Air Command, A Fighter Pilot's Story* (London: William Kimber, 1973), pp 4 et seq.
 7. Ibid, p 18.
 8. Mike Rosel, *Unknown Warrior – The Search for Australia's Greatest Ace* (Melbourne: Australian Scholarly Publishing Pty, 2012), pp 20 et seq.
 9. Leonard H Rochford, *I Chose the Sky* (London: William Kimber, 1977), pp 19 et seq.
10. Rosel, *Unknown Warrior*, p 33.
11. Guy Warner, *World War One Aircraft Carrier Pioneer – The Story & Diaries of Jack McCleery RNAS* (Barnsley: Pen & Sword Aviation, 2011), p 9.
12. His father was a dedicated member of the Irish Temperance League from 1890 to 1927 and its president from 1911.
13. R Borlase Matthews, *The Aviation Pocket Book for 1918 – A Compendium of Modern Practice and a Collection of Useful notes, Formulae, Rules, Tables and Data relating to Aeronautics* (6th edition, London: Crosby Lockwood & Son, 1918), p cvi.
14. Warner, *World War One Aircraft Carrier Pioneer*, pp 18 et seq.
15. Ben Warlow, *Shore Establishments of the Royal Navy* (Liskeard: Maritime Books, 2000), p 44. The nominal depot ship from which the air station took its name was an iron screw battery ship built at Poplar in 1856. In 1873 she became a floating pier head at Chatham and it bore the name *Daedalus* from 1916 to 1918 as the nominal depot ship for the RNAS. She was rammed by a tug and sunk in 1948 but raised in 1949 and scrapped on a river bank. Data from J J Colledge and Ben Warlow, *Ships of the Royal Navy* (London: Chatham Publishing, 2006), p 351.
16. *Piloteer*, the magazine of RNAS Cranwell, an early edition.
17. Temporary Flight Sub Lieutenant G R G Daglish RNAS was killed on that day at Cranwell flying BE 2C number 8620.
18. Abbot, *The British Airship at War 1914–1918*, p 11.
19. Ibid, pp 7 et seq.
20. Guy Warner, *Airships Over the North Channel* (Ulster Aviation Society, 2005), pp 17 et seq.
21. Later to achieve high rank in the RAF.
22. Quoted from Air 1/668 in the National Archive at Kew in Roskill, *Documents Relating to the Naval Air Service Volume 1*, pp 277 et seq.
23. Bell-Davies, *Sailor in the Air*, pp 163 et seq.
24. Borlase Matthews, *The Aviation Pocket Book for 1918*, pp 65 et seq.
25. Ibid, pp 111 et seq.
26. E G Johnstone (ed), *Naval Eight – A Classic Memoir of a World War 1 Fighter Squadron* (London: Arms and Armour Press, Lionel Leventhal Ltd, 1972), pp 128 et seq.
27. Ibid, p 142.

Chapter 13: Politics
 1. Instructions for the Director of the Air Department dated September 1912 contained in Air 1/361
    at the National Archive, Kew, and quoted in Roskill, *Documents Relating to the Naval Air Service
    Volume 1 1908–1918*, p 60.
 2. Geoffrey Till, *Air Power and the Royal Navy 1914–1945 – A Historical Survey* (London: Jane's
    Publishing Company, 1979), p 111.
 3. ADM 1/8378. Draft Proposals by Captain Murray F Sueter, Director of the Air Department,
    Admiralty, for the Reorganisation of the Naval Air Service, quoted in Roskill, *Documents Relating
    to the Naval Air Service Volume 1*, p 145.
 4. ADM 1/8408 quoted in Roskill, *Documents Relating to the Naval Air Service Volume 1*, p 193.
 5. Till, *Air Power and the Royal Navy*, p 111.
 6. Ibid, p 112.
 7. Lord Hankey, *The Supreme Command 1914–1918* (London, Allen & Unwin, 1961), Vol 1, p 335.
 8. ADM 1/8408 quoted in Roskill, *Documents Relating to the Naval Air Service Volume 1*, p 212.
 9. ADM 1/8621. Unsigned Memorandum dated 10 June 1915 quoted in Roskill, *Documents Relating
    to the Naval Air Service Volume 1*, p 207.
10. Popham, *Into Wind*, p 68.
11. Roskill, *Documents Relating to the Naval Air Service Volume 1*, pp 269 et seq.
12. He actually referred to it as the War Council which had ceased to exist in May 1915 but presumably
    meant to refer to the War Committee.
13. CID G.55 Cab 42/8 quoted in Roskill, *Documents Relating to the Naval Air Service Volume 1*, p 285.
14. Extracts from the Proceedings of the 69th Meeting of the War Committee on 10 February 1916
    quoted in Roskill, *Documents Relating to the Naval Air Service Volume 1*, p 286.
15. At the time the RFC had about 440 trained pilots and the RNAS 250.
16. Memorandum by Rear Admiral C L Vaughan-Lee (DAS), on Defence against Zeppelin Raids
    dated 4 April 1916, ADM 1/8449, quoted in Roskill, *Documents Relating to the Naval Air Service
    Volume 1*, pp 342 et seq.
17. Roskill, *Documents Relating to the Naval Air Service Volume 1*, p 308.
18. Junior Lord of the Treasury 1895–1900, Financial Secretary 1900–03, Postmaster General 1903–
    05, Director of Recruiting 1915–16, Under Secretary of State for War 1916, Secretary of State for
    War 1916–18, British Ambassador in Paris 1918–20.
19. The reader is recommended to study Bruce, *British Aeroplanes 1914–1918* for specific details of
    aircraft production and allocation during the Great War.
20. Extracts from the First Report of the Air Board to the War Committee dated 23 October 1916, Air
    1/2311 and CAB 22/75 quoted in Roskill, *Documents Relating to the Naval Air Service Volume 1*,
    pp 389 et seq.
21. Roskill, *Documents Relating to the Naval Air Service Volume 1*, p 362.
22. Ibid, p 391.
23. Ibid, pp 389 et seq.
24. Ibid, p 273.
25. Popham, *Into Wind*, p 69.
26. Letter OB 1837 from General Sir Douglas Haig, C-in-C British Armies in France, to the War Office
    dated 1 November 1916 quoted in Roskill, *Documents Relating to the Naval Air Service Volume 1*,
    p 405.
27. Admiralty Letter M.02380 of 4 March 1917 to the War Office, contained within ADM 1/8449 at
    The National Archive, Kew and quoted in Roskill, *Documents Relating to the Naval Air Service
    Volume 1*, p 411.
28. 'Policy to be Followed as Regards Development and Use of Torpedo-carrying Seaplanes' dated 20
    December 1916 contained in ADM 1/8477 in The National Archive at Kew and quoted in Roskill,
    Documents Relating to the Naval Air Service Volume 1, p 434.

Chapter 14: The Report that Forgot about Sea Power
 1. Wing Commander H R Allen, *The Legacy of Lord Trenchard* (London: Cassell, 1972), p 16.
 2. Anthony J Cumming, *The Battle for Britain – Inter-service rivalry between the Royal Air Force and
    Royal Navy 1909–1940* (Annapolis: Naval Institute Press, 2015), p 20.
 3. Warnings to take cover could only be given once enemy aircraft were seen to cross the coast. They
    comprised policemen on bicycles with placards on string around their necks which said 'Take
    Cover'. They attracted attention by ringing hand bells or blowing whistles.

4. S Sassoon, *Memoirs of an Infantry Officer* (London: Faber and Faber, 1930), p 208.
5. H G Castle, *Fire over England – The German Air Raids in World War 1* (London: Leo Cooper, 1982), p 185.
6. Cumming, *Battle for Britain*, pp 21 et seq.
7. N Longmate, *Island Fortress – The Defence of Great Britain 1603–1945* (London: Pimlico, 2001), pp 449 et seq.
8. 'Lessons of the Air Attack', *Times* editorial/leader dated 28 May 1917, p 7.
9. 'The Bombing of London', *Times* editorial/leader dated 9 July 1917, p 7.
10. H P Willmott, *World War 1* (London: Dorling Kindersley, 2012), pp 203 et seq.
11. Now Namibia.
12. Cumming, *Battle for Britain*, p 23.
13. Roskill, *Documents Relating to the Naval Air Service Volume 1*, p 453.
14. War Cabinet Committee on Air Organisation and Home Defence Against Air Raids, First Report, GT 1451, CAB 24/22, The National Archive, Kew, London.
15. Where a blue plaque now informs passers-by that the RAF was created in the building.
16. Cumming, *Battle for Britain*, p 24.
17. Ibid, p 25.
18. Allen, *The Legacy of Lord Trenchard*, p 24.
19. Number 842 dated 16 July 1914.
20. During 1918 he served briefly on the nascent Air Staff. He was Deputy Chief of the Air Staff before the RAF came into being but disagreed over strategy with Trenchard and left to become the General Officer Commanding Number 2 Area, RAF, based at Salisbury in Wiltshire on 1 April 1918. In May he became GOC of the restructured RAF South Western Area and but retired in October 1918.
21. M Kerr, *Land, Sea and Air: Reminiscences* (London: Longman, 1927), pp 290–1 quoted in N Hanson, *First Blitz – The Secret German Plan to Raze London to the Ground in 1918* (New York: Doubleday, 2008), p 322.
22. Even at the height of its campaign in the Second World War Bomber Command still relied on the Merchant Navy and its escorting warships to bring sufficient fuel into the UK to allow its aircraft to fly. It never had the luxury of operating in isolation even if its protagonists did not realise the fact.
23. ADM 116/1606 at the National Archive, Kew, London.
24. The Admiralty response is quoted in Roskill, *Documents Relating to the Naval Air Service Volume 1*, pp 501 et seq.
25. Contained in ADM 116/1606 at the National Archive, Kew and quoted in Roskill, *Documents Relating to the Naval Air Service Volume 1*, pp 520 et seq.
26. 'Remarks on a scheme of an Imperial Air Policy', dated 14 August 1917 contained in ADM 116/1606 in the National Archive, Kew, and quoted in Roskill, *Documents Relating to the Naval Air Service Volume 1*, p 498.
27. Contained in ADM 1/8611 at the National Archive, Kew, quoted in Roskill, *Documents Relating to the Naval Air Service Volume 1*, p 517.
28. Allen, *The Legacy of Lord Trenchard*, p 20.
29. Ibid, pp 20 and 21.
30. A date which is also known throughout the English-speaking world as 'All Fools' Day'.
31. Andrew Boyle, *Trenchard – Man of Vision* (London: Collins, 1962), pp 264 et seq.
32. Contained in ADM 116/1805 at the National Archive, Kew, and quoted in Roskill, *Documents Relating to the Naval Air Service Volume 1*, p 670.
33. Bruce, *British Aeroplanes 1914–1918*, p 275.

Chapter 15: 1918: The RNAS' Final Year
1. Admiralty, *Aircraft Carriers Part IV, Aeroplanes Carried in Fighting Ships* (London: Admiralty, 1921), p 3.
2. Dumaresq was an Australian serving in the RN. He had been selected to command the Australian Fleet on promotion to rear admiral and was re-appointed from HMS *Repulse* to HMAS *Sydney* to gain experience of an RAN warship in operational service before being promoted.
3. Tables based on those in *Aircraft Carriers Part IV*, p 6.
4. A Curtiss H-12 Large America.
5. T D Hallam (P.I.X.), *The Spider Web – Royal Naval Air Service Flying Boat Operations During the*

     First World War by a Flight Commander (Driffield: Leonaur, an imprint of Oakpast Ltd, 2009), pp 36 et seq.

6. As far as I am aware we are not related.

7. Very similar instructions were given to me in my first squadron 50 years later. A professional outlook remains constant.

8. Hallam, *The Spider Web*, p 88. Hallam does not say what the fumes might do to the human aircrew.

9. Ibid, pp 78 et seq.

10. Admiralty, *Aircraft Carriers Part III, Towing and Docking Lighters for Carrying Aircraft 1916-1918* (London: Admiralty, 1921), p 3.

11. Hallam, *The Spider Web*, pp 147 et seq.

12. Admiralty, *Aircraft Carriers Part III*, p 4.

13. Hallam, *The Spider Web*, p 153 et seq.

14. Jones, *The War In The Air*, Vol 6, pp 372 et seq.

15. N6812 was recovered after this famous action and subsequently presented to the Imperial War Museum. In 2017 it is on display at the Museum's building in Lambeth.

16. Roskill, *Documents Relating to the Naval Air Service Volume 1*, p 586.

17. Admiralty letter of 19 November 1917 contained within ADM 1/8504 in the National Archive at Kew and quoted in Roskill, *Documents Relating to the Naval Air Service Volume 1*, pp 586 and 587.

18. After a spell commanding the Reserve Fleet he was C-in-C Plymouth between 1923 and 1926 by when he had become Admiral Sir Richard Phillimore. He retired in 1929 and died in 1940.

19. Stevens, *In All Respects Ready*, pp 250 et seq.

20. After the Great War Dumaresq was promoted to Rear Admiral and succeeded Rear Admiral Sir Lionel Halsey as Rear Admiral Commanding Australian Fleet, leading it home in 1919. He remained a staunch advocate of naval aviation and was bitterly disappointed that government economies prevented the formation of an Australian Naval Air Service. He was appointed back to the RN in April 1922 but it transpired that he had been suffering from tuberculosis for a number of years and had refused to consult a doctor. During his return voyage to the UK illness forced him to break his journey in the Philippine Islands where he was taken to the American Military Hospital. After eight weeks he died of pneumonia and was buried with full naval honours in a local cemetery. A stern disciplinarian and hard taskmaster, he was popular with his subordinates who admired his drive and energy. He contributed much to the fields of gunnery and aviation and deserves greater recognition for his outstanding achievements.

21. Stevens, *In All Respects Ready*, pp 242 et seq.

22. BCF 733/10A dated 26 December 1917, preserved in ADM/137/2135 at the National Archive, Kew and quoted in Stevens, *In All Respects Ready*, p 258.

23. Stevens, *In All Respects Ready*, pp 260 et seq.

24. Sharwood's letter dated January 1971 is preserved in the Archive of the Sea Power Centre – Australia where I was able to obtain a copy.

25. Because of its engine torque the Camel could turn 270 degrees to the left faster than it could turn 90 degrees to the right.

26. Flight Lieutenant Sharwood combat report to Captain Dumaresq dated 4 June 1918 contained within ADM/137/877 at The National Archive, Kew.

27. Of interest, visual aircraft recognition by RN warships in the Second World war and even a century later is little better!

28. Letter from Admiral Beatty to Admiral Commanding Aircraft Grand Fleet dated 24 June 1918 contained in ADM/137/877 at The National Archive, Kew.

29. Admiralty, *Aircraft Carriers Part II, Kite Balloon Ships and Installations* (London: Admiralty, 1921), p 8.

30. *The Technical History and Index, A Serial History of Technical problems Dealt with by Admiralty Departments Volume 1 Part 4. Aircraft versus Submarine – Submarine Campaign 1918*, Technical History Section (London: Admiralty, 1919), pp 6 et seq.

31. It seems surprising in retrospect that the idea was not resurrected after 1939 to provide air cover for convoys in mid-Atlantic.

32. *The Technical History and Index, A Serial History of Technical problems Dealt with by Admiralty Departments Volume 1 Part 4. Aircraft versus Submarine – Submarine Campaign 1918*, Technical History Section (London: Admiralty, 1919), p 19.

33. Although these might seem unusual in-flight rations to a modern reader, both sandwich fillings

were safe to eat over a prolonged period without being kept in cold storage and therefore their use was logical.

34. Peter London, *U-Boat Hunters – Cornwall's Air War 1916–1919* (Truro: Dyllansow Truran Croft Prince, 1999), p 21.
35. Ibid, p 59.
36. C P O Bartlett, *Bomber Pilot 1916–1918* (Shepperton: Ian Allen, 1974), p 73.
37. Bruce, *British Aeroplanes 1914–1918*, p 275.
38. Since the Great War an 'ace' has been deemed to be a fighter pilot who has shot down five or more enemy aircraft. The term was first used by the French and then taken up by the Americans. It was used unofficially in Britain but was frowned on by the authorities and was never adopted officially.
39. Rosel, *Unknown Warrior*, p 47.
40. F H Feyver, *The Distinguished Service Cross 1901–1938* (London: Naval & Military Press reprint of the original London Stamp Exchange edition, 1991), pp 20 and 29.
41. Collishaw, *Air Command*, p 143.

Chapter 16: HMS *Argus* – The World's First True Aircraft Carrier

1. To put that achievement into proper perspective, it must be remembered that the British government announced in 1998 that it intended to build a new generation of aircraft carriers. Notwithstanding the RN's 90 years of experience with such ships, poor project management by the Ministry of Defence which had taken over the responsibility for warship procurement from the Admiralty's Directorate of Naval Construction, the analysis of too many unsuitable designs and political argument all combined to cause delay. The first ship, *Queen Elizabeth*, is not expected to enter operational service until 2021, nearly a quarter of a century after the project started.
2. D K Brown, *The Grand Fleet – Warship Design and Development 1906–1922* (London: Chatham Publishing, 1999), pp 115 et seq.
3. Described in my earlier book *British Aircraft Carriers*, pp 26–34.
4. Ibid, p 33.
5. J D Brown, *Aircraft Carriers* (London: Macdonald and Jane's Publishers, 1977), p 34.
6. Bell-Davies, *Sailor in the Air*, pp 180 et seq.
7. The ship's stern was already stained black by funnel smoke as it emerged from the ducting.
8. D K Brown, *The Grand Fleet*, p 117.
9. Arranged this way round an aircraft wheel would knock the ring bolt down flush with the deck if it had not been lowered properly. The other way round it would stay erect if a wheel hit it, would not be knocked flat and might burst a tyre.
10. Modern carrier aircraft approach the ship on finals down a 5-degree glide slope which, when the forward motion of the ship is taken into account, equates to a 3-degree glide slope onto the landing point. Bell-Davies' approach was almost level, certainly averaging less than 1 degree.
11. Hoobs, *British Aircraft Carriers*, p 47.
12. Norman Friedman, *British Carrier Aviation – The Ships and their Aircraft* (London: Conway Maritime Press, 1988), p 67.
13. There was only one more British-built flush deck carrier without an island, *Furious* in her first post Great-War reconstruction. This was only a partial success and her half-sisters *Courageous* and *Glorious*, together with every subsequent British carrier, were completed with islands.
14. Mick Davis, *Sopwith Aircraft* (Marlborough: The Crowood Press, 1999), pp 118 et seq.
15. The Sopwith 1½ Strutter was, arguably, the world's first joint strike fighter design.
16. Bruce, *British Aeroplanes 1914–1918*, p 541.

Chapter 17: Tondern and the Planned Attack on the High Sea Fleet in Harbour

1. Bruce, *British Aeroplanes 1914–1918*, pp 583 et seq.
2. Davis, *Sopwith Aircraft*, pp 113 et seq.
3. Bruce, *British Aeroplanes 1914–1918*, p 588.
4. Both aircraft were still in existence some months later so the dummy drop obviously did not lead to them being written off.
5. Earlier attacks on airship bases were carried out by seaplanes that were lowered onto the water for take-off.
6. Bell-Davies, *Sailor in the Air*, pp 167 et seq.
7. Ibid, pp 177 et seq.
8. Ibid, p 178.

9. Bruce, *British Aeroplanes 1914–1918*, pp 596 et seq.
10. The post-war Gloster Gnatsnapper is probably the most bizarre.
11. Arguably, the concept could also be said to owe something to the RN's historic use of fireships to attack an enemy fleet in harbour. The aims are the same, only the methods are different.
12. David Hobbs, 'The First Pearl Harbor – The Attack by British Torpedo Planes on the German High Sea Fleet planned for 1918', *Warship 2007* (London: Conway, 2007), pp 29 et seq.
13. Longmore, *From Sea to Sky*, p 36.
14. The bulk of this section is taken from correspondence by Admirals Beatty and Madden in the Naval Historical Branch, copies of which are in the author's archive, and papers on the development of airborne torpedoes in the archive of the Fleet Air Arm Section of the National Museum of the Royal Navy at RNAS Yeovilton in Somerset.
15. Made of copper which were designed to crush on impact with the target to cause little or no damage.
16. This was done in the Second World War by German and Italian battleships attacked by RN torpedo aircraft.
17. Original in the Archive of the Fleet Air Arm Section of the National Museum of the Royal Navy at RNAS Yeovilton and a copy is in the Author's archive.

Chapter 18: Retrospection

1. Lea, *Reggie*, p 66.
2. Bell-Davies, *Sailor in the Air*, p 184.
3. RFC squadrons retained their original numbers, and histories, thus 1 Squadron RFC became 1 Squadron RAF but RNAS units had 200 added to their squadron numbers, thus 1 (Naval) Squadron became 201 Squadron RAF and its earlier history was eclipsed.
4. Hobbs, 'The Royal Naval Air Service', in Forbes (ed), *The War at Sea 1914-18*, p 201.
5. Although, sadly, the system of numbering naval air squadrons used at present in the RN and RAN dates from 1933 with the result that no naval air squadron can trace its ancestry back to the pioneering units of the RNAS.

Bibliography

Primary Sources

Admiralty, *Handbook for HM Rigid Airship Number 1* (London: Admiralty, 1913).

_____, *Handbook on HM Rigid Airship Number 9* (London: Admiralty, 1918).

_____, *A Serial History of Technical Problems dealt with by Admiralty Departments. Aircraft v Submarine – Submarine Campaign 1918* (London: Admiralty Technical History Section, 1918).

_____, *The Development of British Naval Aviation 1919-1945 Volume 1* (London: Admiralty, 1954).

_____, *Aircraft Carriers Part I, 1914–1918, Seaplane and Aircraft Carriers* (London: DNC Department, Admiralty, 1918).

_____, *Aircraft Carriers Part II, Kite Balloon Ships and Installations 1915–1918* (London: DNC Department, Admiralty, 1918).

_____, *Aircraft Carriers Part III, Towing and Docking Lighters for Carrying Aircraft 1916–1918* (London: DNC Department, Admiralty, 1918).

_____, *Aircraft Carriers Part IV, Aeroplanes Carried in Fighting Ships* (London: DNC Department, Admiralty, 1918).

_____, *Naval Historical Branch – unpublished History of Great War Air Operations* (London: NHB, Admiralty, 1919).

Ministry of Defence, *The Hobbs Report – Part 1 – An Historical Analysis of RN Clothing* (London: Ministry of Defence, 1995).

ADM 1/8378	*Draft Proposals by Captain Murray F Sueter for the Reorganisation of the Naval Air Service.*
ADM 1/8408	*Admiralty Weekly Order Number 166 dated 5 February 1915.*
ADM 1/8611	*Comment by Vice admiral Sir Henry Oliver on the Smuts Report.*
ADM 1/8621	*Proposal for an Independent Royal Air Service.*
ADM 116/ 1606	*Admiralty Response to the Recommendations in the Smuts Report.*
ADM 137/877	*Grand Fleet Reports of Proceedings 1918.*
ADM 137/877	*Combat Report by Flight Lieutenant A C Sharwood RNAS to Captain J S Dumaresq CB CVO RN.*
ADM 137/1956	*Report of the Advisory Committee on Naval Aeronautics.*
ADM 273/4/69	*Service History of Squadron Commander E H Dunning DSC RNAS.*

Published Secondary Sources

Abbott. Patrick, *The British Airship at War, 1914-1918* (Lavenham: Terence Dalton Ltd, 1989).

_____, and Walmsley, Nick, *British Airships in Pictures – An Illustrated History 1784-1998* (Isle of Colonsay: House of Lochar, 1998).

Admiralty, *Anti-Aircraft Corps of the Royal Naval Air Service – Notes and Orders* (Uckfield: Naval & Military Press in association with the Royal Armouries, reprint of a volume first published by the admiralty in December 1914).

Allen, Wing Commander H R, *The Legacy of Lord Trenchard* (London: Cassell, 1972).

Apps, Lieutenant Commander Michael, *The Four Ark Royals* (London: William Kimber, 1976).

Bacon, Admiral Sir R H, *The Life of John Rushworth Earl Jellicoe* (London: Cassell and Company, 1936).

Bartlett, C P O, *Bomber Pilot 1916–1918* (Shepperton: Ian Allen, 1974).

Bell-Davies, Vice Admiral Richard, *Sailor in the Air – the Memoirs of the World's First Carrier Pilot* (London: Peter Davies, 1967).

Benbow, Tim (ed), *British Naval Aviation – The First 100 Years* (Farnham: Ashgate Publishing, 2011).

Brown, J David, *Carrier Fighters* (London: Macdonald and Jane's, 1975).

_____, 'The Genesis of Naval Aviation', in *Les Marines de Guerre du Dreadnought au Nucleaire* (Paris, Service Historique de la Marine, 1988).

Borlase Matthews, R, *The Aviation Pocket Book for 1918 – A Compendium of Modern Practice and a Collection of Useful notes, Formulae, Rules, Tables and Data relating to Aeronautics* (6th edition, London: Crosby Lockwood & Son, 1918),

Brown, D K, *The Grand Fleet – Warship Design and Development 1906–1922* (London: Chatham Publishing, 1999).

Bruce, J M, *British Aeroplanes 1914–1918* (London: Putnam, 1957).

_____, *The BE.2, 2a and 2b* (Leatherhead: Profile Publications, 1966).

_____, *The Sopwith 1½ Strutter* (Leatherhead: Profile Publications, undated).

_____, *The Sopwith Pup* (Leatherhead: Profile Publications, 1965).

_____, *The Sopwith Triplane* (Leatherhead: Profile Publications, 1966).

_____, *The Sopwith Camel F.1* (Leatherhead: Profile Publications, undated).

_____, *The Short 184* (Leatherhead: Profile Publications, undated).

_____, *Sopwith B.1 & T.1 Cuckoo* (Berkhamsted: Albatross Productions, Windsock Data File No 90, 2001).

_____, Page, Gordon, and Sturtivant, Ray, *The Sopwith Pup* (Tunbridge Wells: Air-Britain Historians Ltd, 2002).

Burns, Ian M, *Ben-my-Chree – Isle of Man Packet Steamer and Seaplane Carrier* (Leicester: Colin Huston, 2008).

Burt, R A, *British Battleships of World War One* (Barnsley: Seaforth Publishing, 2012).

Carlyon, Les, *Gallipoli* (Sydney: Pan Macmillan Australia, 2002).

Chesneau, Roger, *Aircraft Carriers of the World 1914 to the Present* (London: Arms & Armour Press, Lionel Leventhal Ltd, 1984).

Churchill, Winston, *The World Crisis 1911-1918* (London: Penguin Books, 2007).

Collishaw, Air Vice Marshal Raymond, with R V Dodds, *Air Command – A Fighter Pilot's Story* (London, William Kimber, 1973).

Coombs, L F E, 'Front Office Evolution', *Air Enthusiast Magazine*, Vol 2 No 2 (February 1972).

Corbett, Sir Julian S, *Naval Operations* (Volumes 1 to 5) (London: Longmans, Green & Co, 1920 onwards).

Cormack, A J R, *Webley and Scott Automatic Pistols* (Windsor: Profile Publications, 1971).

Cronin, Dick, *Royal Navy Shipboard Aircraft Developments 1912–1931* (Tonbridge: Air-Britain Historians Ltd, 1990).

Crouther Gordon, Rev Dr T, *Early Flying in Orkney* (Kirkwall: BBC Radio Orkney, 1985).

Cumming, Anthony J, *The Battle for Britain – Inter-service rivalry between the Royal Air Force and Royal Navy 1909–1940* (Annapolis: Naval Institute Press, 2015).

Davis, Mick, *Sopwith Aircraft* (Marlborough: The Crowood Press, 1999).

Duncan, Major General N W, *Early Armoured Cars* (Windsor: Profile Publications, undated).

Ellis, Paul, *Aircraft of the Royal Navy* (London: Jane's Publishing, 1982).

Fevyer, W H, *The Distinguished Service Cross 1901–1938* (London: The London Stamp Exchange, 1991).

Forbes, Andrew, *The War at Sea 1914–18*, *Proceedings of the King-Hall Naval History Conference 2013* (Canberra, Sea Power Centre-Australia, 2015).

Friedman, Norman, *British Carrier Aviation, The Evolution of the Ships and their Aircraft* (London: Conway Maritime Press, 1988).
_____, *Fighting the Great War at Sea, Strategy, Tactics and Technology* (Barnsley: Seaforth Publishing, 2014).
Gibson, Mary, *Warneford VC* (Yeovilton: Friends of the Fleet Air Arm Museum, 1979).
Goldrick, James, *The King's Ships Were at Sea* (Annapolis, Maryland: Naval Institute Press, 1984).
_____, *Before Jutland* (Annapolis, Maryland: Naval Institute Press, 2015).
Gordon, Andrew, *The Rules of the Game* (London: Penguin Books, 2015).
Grey, C G, *Sea-Flyers* (London: Faber and Faber, 1942).
Guttman, Jon, *Naval Aces of World War 1* (Oxford: Osprey Publishing, 2011).
Hallam, Theodore Douglas, *The Spider Web – RNAS Flying Boat Operations During the First World War by a Flight Commander* (Driffield: Leonaur, an imprint of Oakpast Ltd, 2009).
Hewison, W S, *This Great Harbour Scapa Flow* (Stromness: The Orkney Press, 1985).
Hezlet, Vice Admiral Sir Arthur, *Aircraft & Sea Power* (London: Peter Davies, 1970).
_____, *The Electron & Sea Power* (London: Peter Davies, 1975).
Hobbs, David, *Aircraft Carriers of the Royal and Commonwealth Navies* (London: Greenhill Books, Lionel Leventhal Ltd, 1996).
_____, *A Century of Carrier Aviation* (Barnsley: Seaforth Publishing, 2009).
_____, *British Aircraft Carriers – Design, Development and Service Histories* (Barnsley: Seaforth Publishing, 2013).
Jackson, Robert, *Strike from the Sea – A History of British Naval Air Power* (London: Arthur Barker Ltd, 1970).
Jarrett, Philip, *Frank McClean – Godfather to British Naval Aviation* (Barnsley: Seaforth Publishing, 2011).
_____, *The Royal Naval Air Service in the First World War* (Barnsley: Pen & Sword Aviation, 2015).
Jellicoe of Scapa, Admiral Viscount, *The Grand Fleet 1914–16 Its Creation, Development and Work* (London: Cassel and Company, 1919).
Jenkins, Commander C A, *HMS FURIOUS Parts 1 and 2*, Warship Profiles 23 and 24 (Windsor: Profile Publications, 1972).
Jerrold, Douglas, *The Royal Naval Division* (Uckfield: Naval & Military Press reprint of a volume first published in 1923).
Johnstone, E G (ed), *Naval Eight – A Classic Memoir of a World War 1 Fighter Squadron* (London: Arms and Armour Press, Lionel Leventhal Ltd, 1972).
Jones, Ray, *Seagulls Cruisers and Catapults* (Hobart: Pelorus Publications, 1989).
Jose, A W, *The Royal Australian Navy, The Official History of Australia in the War of 1914-1918* Volume IX (St Lucia: University of Queensland Press, 1928).
Kealy, J D F, and Russell, E C, *A History of Canadian Naval Aviation* (Ottawa: Naval Historical Section, Department of National Defence, 1965).
Kemp, Lieutenant Commander P K, *Fleet Air Arm* (London: Herbert Jenkins, 1954).
King, Brad, *Royal Naval Air Service 1912–1918* (Aldershot: Hikoki Publications, 1997).
Kinsey, Gordon, *Pulham Pigs* (Lavenham: Terence Dalton Ltd, 1988).
Layman, R D, *The Cuxhaven Raid – The World's First Carrier Air Strike* (London: Conway Maritime Press, 1985).
_____, *Before the Aircraft Carrier – The Development of Aviation Vessels 1849–1922* (London: Conway Maritime Press, 1989).
_____, *Naval Aviation in the First World War – Its Impact and Influence* (London: Chatham Publishing, 1996).
Lea, John, *Reggie – The Life of Air Vice Marshal R L G Marix CBE DSO* (Bishop Auckland: The Pentland Press, 1994).
Lind, Lew, *Historic Naval Events of Australia Day-by-Day* (Frenchs Forest NSW: AH & AW Reed Pty Ltd, 1982).

'L F R', *Naval Guns in Flanders 1914–1915* (Uckfield: Naval & Military Press, 2004 reproduced from an original in the Library of the Royal Military Academy, Sandhurst of a volume first published in 1915).

London, Peter, *U-Boat Hunters – Cornwall's Air War 1916–19* (Truro: Dyllansow Truran, 1999).

Longmore, Air Chief Marshal Sir Arthur, *From Sea to Sky – Memoirs 1910–1945* (London: Geoffrey Bles, 1946).

Lumsden, Alec, *British Piston Engines and their Aircraft* (Marlborough: Airlife Publishing, 2003).

Macintyre, Captain Donald, *Jutland* (London: Evans Brothers, 1957).

_____, *Wings of Neptune – The Story of Naval Aviation* (London: Peter Davies, 1963).

Malmassari, Paul, *Armoured Trains: An Illustrated Encyclopaedia 1825–2016* (Barnsley, Seaforth Publishing, 2016).

Moore, Major W G, *Early Bird* (London: Putnam, 1963).

Mowthorpe, Ces, *Battlebags – British Airships of the First World War* (Stroud, Alan Sutton Publishing, 1995).

Page, Christopher, *Command in the Royal Naval Division – A Military Biography of Brigadier General A M Asquith DSO* (Staplehurst: Spellmount, 1999).

Phillips, Lieutenant Commander Lawrie, *The Royal Navy Day by Day* (Stroud: Spellmount, 2011).

Popham, Hugh, *Into Wind – A History of British Naval Flying* (London: Hamish Hamilton, 1969).

Raleigh, Walter, and Jones, H A, *The War in the Air, Volumes 1 to 6 plus Appendices* (Uckfield: Naval & Military Press reprint of a work originally published from 1922 onwards).

Reece, Colonel Michael, *Flying Royal Marines* (Eastney: Royal Marines Historical Society, 2012).

Roberts, Chris, *The Landing at ANZAC 1915* (Sydney: Big Sky Publishing for the Australian Army History Unit, 2015).

Robertson, Bruce, *British Military Aircraft Serials 1878–1987* (Earl Shilton: Midland Counties Publications, 1979).

Rochford, Leonard, *I Chose the Sky* (London: William Kimber, 1977).

Rosel, Mike, *Unknown Warrior – The Search for Australia's Greatest Ace* (Melbourne: Australian Scholarly Publishing Pty, 2012).

Rosher, Harold, *In the Royal Naval Air Service – War Letters of Harold Rosher* (London: Chatto & Windus, 1916).

Roskill, Stephen, *Documents Relating to the Naval Air Service Volume 1 1908 – 1918* (Bromley: Navy Records Society, 1969).

_____, *Admiral of the Fleet Earl Beatty – The Last Naval Hero: An Intimate Biography* (London: William Collins & Sons, 1980).

Samson, Air Commodore Charles Rumney, *Fights and Flights* (London: Ernest Benn Ltd, 1930).

Snowden Gamble, C F, *The Story of a North Sea Air Station* (London: Oxford University Press, 1928).

Sparrow, Geoffrey, and Macbean-Ross, J N, *On Four Fronts with the Royal Naval Division* (London: Hodder & Stoughton, 1918).

Stevens, David, *In All Respects Ready – Australia's Navy in World War 1* (Melbourne: Oxford University Press, 2014).

Sturtivant, Ray, and Page, Gordon *Royal Navy Aircraft Serials and Units 1911–1919* (Tonbridge: Air-Britain Historians Ltd, 1992).

Sueter, Rear Admiral Murray, *Airmen or Noahs – Fair Play for our Airmen* (London: Sir Isaac Pitman & Sons, 1928).

Thetford, Owen, *British Naval Aircraft since 1912* (London: Putnam, 1962).

Till, Geoffrey, *Air Power and the Royal Navy 1914–1945* (London: Jane's Publishing Company, 1979).

Vicary, Adrian, *Naval Wings – Royal Naval Carrier-Borne Aircraft since 1916* (Cambridge: Patrick Stephens Limited, 1984).

Warner, Guy, *World War 1 Aircraft Carrier Pioneer – The Story & Diaries of Jack McCleery RNAS RAF* (Barnsley: Pen & Sword Aviation, 2011).

_____, *Lighter than Air – The Life and Times of Wing Commander N F Usborne RN Pioneer of Naval Aviation* (Barnsley: Pen & Sword Aviation, 2016).

Warship, Volumes I to XXXVIII (London: Conway, 1977 to 2016).

Westrop, Mike, *A History of No 6 Squadron Royal Naval Air Service in World War 1* (Atglen PA: Schiffer Military History, 2006).

Young, Desmond, *Rutland of Jutland* (London: Cassell, 1963).

Index